W9-BCJ-684

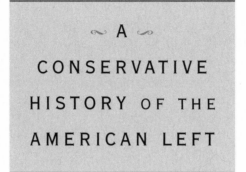

~ A ~
CONSERVATIVE
HISTORY OF THE
AMERICAN LEFT

A CONSERVATIVE HISTORY OF THE AMERICAN LEFT

DANIEL J. FLYNN

CROWN
FORUM
NEW YORK

CROWN FORUM with Design is a registered trademark of Random House, Inc.

Library of Congress Cataloging-in-Publication Data
Flynn, Daniel J.
   A conservative history of the American Left / Daniel J. Flynn.—1st ed.
     p.   cm.
   Includes bibliographical references and index.
   1. Socialism—United States—History.   2. Radicalism—United States—History.   I. Title.
   HX83.F59 2008
   335.3—dc22   2007045664

ISBN 978-0-307-33946-1

Printed in the United States of America

Design by Philip Mazzone

10 9 8 7 6 5 4 3 2 1

First Edition

CONTENTS

BOOK THREE: THE OLD LEFT

BOOK FOUR: THE NEW LEFT

BOOK FIVE: THE 9/12 LEFT

A
CONSERVATIVE
HISTORY OF THE
AMERICAN LEFT

INTRODUCTION

Shall man be justified in comparison of God; or shall a man be more pure than his maker?

—JOB 4:17

WHERE DID HILLARY Clinton get the idea to compare marriage and the family with "slavery" and the "Indian reservation system"?[1] Why does Thomas Frank write in *What's the Matter with Kansas?* of "the borderline criminality of capitalism"?[2] Who put it into Michael Moore's head that religion is a device to manipulate "gullible" and "easily misled" Americans?[3]

Robert Owen, a rags-to-riches Welsh industrialist who brought a new gospel to America, identified private property, religion, and marriage as "the most monstrous evils"—*almost two centuries ago.*[4] The bugbears Owen railed against in 1826, leftists still attack today.

Rather than the bearers of a cutting-edge philosophy, American leftists are the inheritors of a long tradition that predated Robert Owen and outlived him, too. Self-mythologizing portrays the Left always and everywhere as challenging stale pieties with new and fresh ideas. But the knowledge that people two centuries ago preached identical theories tends to undermine claims to modern, original, forward-looking ideas. Hillary Clinton, Thomas Frank, and Michael Moore, aware or not, mouth the platitudes passed on from generations preceding their grandparents' grandparents.

The Left is not a monolithic entity. Even in labels—leftist, radical, progressive, socialist, communist, liberal—there are preferential differences and disagreements in definition. But there is continuity. Certain gripes and hopes recur. Rather than a laundry list of complaints and wishes, an attitude better captures the Left.

It is, in its simplest form, scorn for what is and hopes for what could be. The ideology's appeal exists in neither the experienced past nor the concrete present, but in the imagined future. In the world dreamt, a universal human family replaces parochial nuclear families, benevolent men share burdens and bounty equally, conflict disappears, man becomes superman, and earth becomes heaven. With promises so magnificent, is it any wonder the Left is so resilient?

"THE STUDY OF American socialism begins in Europe," Princeton University history professor E. Harris Harrison wrote at the midpoint of the twentieth century. "Any understanding of socialistic thinking and practice in American life must rest upon knowledge of the part played by socialism in European history."5 In fact, the first three chapters of the book where Professor Harrison's article appears—1952's landmark *Socialism and American Life*—focus on Europe specifically and Western civilization generally, not America. A Europhilia among American progressives often finds the creation of all that is great and good across the Atlantic. After all, has not all of Europe abolished the death penalty, instituted universal health care, and shown a greater willingness to defer to international institutions? History, too, provides cover for a European creation story. The French Revolution and the publication of *The Communist Manifesto* happened in Europe. What of comparative importance in the history of the Left happened here? Conservatives, meanwhile, are only too happy to second the contention that the Left is the product of an alien soil.

Nonetheless, much of the American Left is firmly rooted in the American tradition. Even when European leftists devised theories for saving society, America more often than not provided the laboratory for their theories.

Radicals left the Old World for the freedom awarded by the New World, even when they wished to make the New World less free. Religious persecution in their homelands prompted Mother Ann Lee and Father George Rapp to migrate to America in the late eighteenth century and early nineteenth century, respectively; political hostility in Europe exiled communist Joseph Weydemeyer and anarchist Johann Most to the United States later in the nineteenth century; and ethnic discrimination sent Herbert Marcuse and Theodor Adorno west in the twentieth century. They all came to America to do what they could not in Europe. Only in America could they test their experiments or air their unconventional views without risking state harassment, jail, and death.

Imported ideas, thus, sometimes acquired a homegrown flavor in America. The absence of a feudal tradition made class consciousness more difficult to evoke than in Europe. Capitalism fostered a salesman attitude, with socialists occasionally hawking socialism the way merchants hawk laundry soap. Freedoms—of movement, speech, and religion—fostered experimentation undreamt of by the subjects of kings, czars, and strongmen. Open space provided theorists with ample testing grounds. Immigration repeatedly altered the dynamic of the American Left by infusing European ideas into American politics. This led to the Americanization of European ideas, or, alternatively, the Europeanization of American leftists.

Radicals possessed no automatic immunity from the patriotic fervor that surrounded them. Communists adopted the slogan "Communism Is Twentieth-Century Americanism" in the 1930s, for instance, and Abbie Hoffman testified to Congress in the 1960s dressed as a Minuteman. The American Left is at its most effective when it accepts that it is an *American* Left. When it forgets where it comes from, the American Left plays to an internal audience eager for purity but unconcerned with persuasion.

Friends and foes alike mistake the Left for Marxism and Marxism for the Left. For the Right, this means hackneyed denunciations of ideas they dislike as "Marxist." For the Left, this means dating the history of their movement to when Marxism arrived on America's shores. The history of the American Left is deeper and more dynamic than that simplification suggests. Not only is Marxism just one among many variants within the greater Left, it is just one of many variants of communism. The followers of Robert Owen, Charles Fourier, and John Humphrey Noyes came before Marx, and in fact they fit the definition of "communist"—one who lives communally—better. Marx derided his predecessors as "utopians," but it is hard to adhere to such a pejorative when its author worked his ideas out in the library of the British Museum and its targets worked them out in actual communes.

When it is not Marx blamed or credited with launching the American Left, the genesis typically offered begins and ends with the 1960s. This sixties creation story serves both Left and Right by crediting still-living radicals with undue influence and by relieving conservatives (ever protective of the myth of a pre-sixties Eden) of the need to research a difficult and occasionally obscure topic.

Apart from misconceptions regarding from where, when, and whom the American Left came, present leftists unimaginatively imagine past leftists as earlier versions of themselves. Current crusaders against racism (of a kind both real and imagined) conveniently overlook Robert Owen's ban on African Americans from New Harmony, union attacks on Asian immigrants, the most influential publication in the history of the American Left supporting segregation, icon John Reed referring to blacks as "niggers" and "coons," Planned Parenthood founder Margaret Sanger speaking at a Ku Klux Klan rally, and the American Communist Party kicking out Japanese Americans following Pearl Harbor.[6] It just doesn't fit the narrative.

Like race, religion abounds in misconceptions. Before the religious Right, there was a religious Left. The twentieth-century American Left got ideas from Karl Marx; the nineteenth-century American Left, from Jesus Christ.

"Religious Left" strikes contemporary ears as an oxymoron. Could Michael Moore, Bill Maher, or Susan Sarandon venture inside a church without melting? There are the reverends Jesse Jackson, Al Sharpton, and Barry Lynn, but they preach politics. The hostility to religion often associated with the Left was not always so pronounced. Indeed, Christianity once served as the primary influence upon American leftists. Its influence on early American leftists was so profound that it put its stamp on their decidedly irreligious offspring. Secular reformers admired the sacrifice and the communal unity of the early religious fanatics but not, generally, the religious beliefs. Religion and politics mixed in the Social Gospel, whose enthusiasts ultimately reached for more social, less gospel. What emerged was a political religion, or, perhaps more accurately, a religious politics. The secular kept the forms without the function. They promised salvation, exalted saints, pursued heretics, revered holy books, enforced dogma, viewed history teleologically, and acted with a self-righteousness generally confined to the elect and an ends-justifies-the-means mentality characteristic of millennial deliverers. They lost faith in God, but not faith itself.

THE LEFT IS about events and ideas. But people drive events and produce ideas. The story of the Left is the story of people—progressives and populists, radicals and reformers, socialists and single-taxers, and leftists of every other stripe. So this book is about people: Bible-thumping wife swappers, pacifist bombers, flag-waving traitors, and other arresting characters. Through names and dates, one knows boredom. Through leftists, one knows the Left.

The story contains heroes: Eugene Debs running for president from an Atlanta jail; William Jennings Bryan dramatically sermonizing easterners not to crucify their countrymen on a cross of gold; Martin Luther King Jr. laying down his life for the better world possible. It contains goats: the

McNamara brothers, who let socialists champion their innocence only to admit killing twenty-one *Los Angeles Times* workers in a 1910 bombing; New Dealer Alger Hiss, who betrayed his nation to the Soviet Union; Peoples Temple leader Jim Jones, who claimed the lives of more than nine hundred followers through "revolutionary suicide."

There are fanatics, such as Daniel De Leon, who purged his own son from his socialist party, and Mike Gold, who browbeat writers as Joseph Stalin's literary commissar in America. There are free spirits, such as Bronson Alcott's "consociate family" at Fruitlands and Ken Kesey's Day-Glo-bus-traveling Merry Pranksters. And there are combinations of the two, puritanical perverts John Humphrey Noyes, Alfred Kinsey, Wilhelm Reich, and Timothy Leary—those overbearing personalities whose zeal for sex, drugs, or whatever other pleasure made them paternalistic libertines.

There are entrepreneurial leftists, such as pioneering female presidential candidate Victoria Woodhull, "Prince of Cranks" Ignatius Donnelly, the People's Party's "Sockless Jerry" Simpson, socialist evangelist J. A. Wayland, and the "Kingfish," Huey Long, all colorful characters who sold radicalism to millions and profited handsomely. There are altruists, such as Hull House's Jane Addams and the Catholic Worker movement's Dorothy Day, who eschewed wealth to better serve those without.

There are adventurers, including Weatherman Mark Rudd and playboy Communist John Reed. There are brakemen urging caution, including the Knights of Labor's Terence Powderly and anti-poverty campaigner Michael Harrington.

There are splitters. In one generation, dueling schismatics claim to be the true representatives of the International Workingman's Association in America; in the next the Socialists endure a pope/anti-pope feud; and two decades later two Communist parties claim the same name and issue identically named newspapers, exactly as the socialists of the preceding era had done.

There are martyrs. John Brown reincarnates as Joe Hill, Joe Hill as Tom Mooney, Tom Mooney as the Rosenbergs, the Rosenbergs as Mumia Abu-Jamal, and so on.

Heaven on earth is always imminent yet never experienced.

THERE IS NO accurate single-bullet theory of history. The past doesn't fit in boxes or conform neatly to stages introduced at a later date. Nevertheless, a few themes emerge:

- The Left has a rich, vibrant, exciting history, but because of the suspicions of tradition inherent within radicalism, it largely ignores that past. Part of the amnesia is convenient. Panaceas radicals have touted include Graham bread, the water cure, phrenology, spiritualism, bimetallism, eugenics, orgone energy, and LSD. But the amnesia has a deeper source: one preoccupied with the triumphal future cannot pause to learn from the mistakes of the past. The Left is about making history, not studying it. Its failure to study history enhances the odds that it does not make history but relives it.

· The relationship between radicals and reformers is here symbiotic, there antagonistic. Radicals push the boundaries of debate. Public policy and cultural norms may never go so far as they hope, but they reach as far as they do because radicals give reformers political cover. In return, reformers give radicals legislation, albeit watered-down legislation, that pushes society leftward. Radicals play bad cop; reformers, good cop. But the sides do not always appreciate that they serve each other's interests. Frustrated with the pace of change, radicals lash out at reformers. As the internecine feud rages, reactionaries take advantage. Alternatively, reformers, tasting power and outraged by the slings and arrows hurled their way, silence, jail, deport, or otherwise suppress their erstwhile allies in ways not dreamt of by reactionaries. Radicals are reformers' worst critics and reformers are radicals' worst persecutors. In better times, each group is the other's best friend.

· A Force Left and a Freedom Left employ opposing means for the same ends. So committed to its aims is a Force Left that it condones coercion, violence, and revolution. So confident in its ideas is a Freedom Left that it trusts persuasion, reason, and demonstration. Robert Owen's communists versus Karl Marx's Communists, Yankee do-your-own-thing anarchists versus foreign do-our-thing anarchists, and hippies versus New Leftists all exhibit this tension between force and freedom. It is the ongoing fight between those two great American icons, the Cowboy and the Puritan. A Force Left forever mouths the language of a Freedom Left, and a Freedom Left, dejected at the failure of private choice to produce the desired ends, forever defects to the Force Left.

· A desire for doctrinal purity clashes with a desire to speak convincingly to the American experience. Class consciousness, for instance, is at the heart of Marxism but peripheral to a nation with no aristocratic tradition and a relative fluidity of wealth. Fidelity to Marxoid, class-warfare jargon outside the time and place in which it was written alienates many a leftist from countrymen he wishes to persuade. The most successful leftists are those who defer to American institutions—religion, patriotism, and even entrepreneurialism. The purist, not without merit, counters that such leftists are not leftists at all. This dilemma—crafting a radicalism unique to the American experience while risking doctrinal purity, or adhering to a radicalism true to foreign theory but alien to the American experience—perpetually confronts radical activists.

The Left's adversaries take heart in such self-inflicted handicaps. The Left, it appears, is doomed. But as a 1960s activist down and out in the 1970s observed, "The Left bobs up and down in American history, a battered and leaky craft which often disappears beneath the tide but somehow never sinks."[7]

From persuasion to politics, politics to revolution, and revolution to a long march through the institutions, the Left's methods for transforming society have evolved. The ends, though, have remained more or less the same. A brotherhood of man, human perfection, complete equality, needs provided without cost, wants pursued without consequence, heaven on earth—ideas too impractical to live in practice, ideas too beautiful to die as ideas.

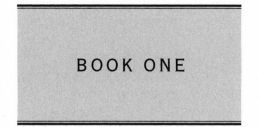

BOOK ONE

BACKWOODS
MILLENNIALISTS

⟡ 1 ⟡

THE RELIGIOUS LEFT

Thy kingdom come. Thy will be done on earth as it is in heaven.

—MATTHEW 6:10

UTOPIAN AND COLLECTIVIST ideas are as American as Plymouth Rock.

The Pilgrims, like America's secular communists of the nineteenth century, hoped to build a city upon a hill. And like other sectarian groups that later found refuge in America, the Pilgrims attempted to build their utopia upon communist principles. In contrast to nineteenth-century American communists, sectarian and secular, and akin to most twentieth-century Europeans living under communists, the Pilgrims' system was imposed on them from without. The edict to abolish private property and pool resources came from an unlikely source: Plymouth colony's capitalist investors, who unwisely, and ironically, feared that the colonists' private greed would eat away at investment profits. Under communism, which reigned in Plymouth colony from 1620 to 1623, Pilgrim bellies and investor wallets starved.

Historians look back and ascribe myriad causes for these lean years. But the man whom the Plymouth colonists elected as their governor more than thirty times emphasized the role communism played in the colony's early woes. In *Of Plymouth Plantation*, William Bradford wrote:

For the young men, that were most able and fit for labour and service, did repine that they should spend their time and strength to work for other men's wives and children without any recompense. The strong, or man of parts, had no more in division of victuals and clothes than he that was weak and not able to do a quarter the other could; this was thought injustice. The aged and graver men to be ranked and equalized in labours and victuals, clothes, etc., with the meaner and younger sort, thought it some indignity and disrespect unto them. And for men's wives to be commended to do service for other men, as dressing their meat, washing their clothes, etc., they deemed it a kind of slavery, neither could many husbands well brook it.[1]

Rather than "languish in misery," Bradford parceled land to families for private use, which "made all hands very industrious." An abundance of corn replaced an abundance of hunger pangs. "The women now went willingly in the field, and took their little ones with them to set corn; which before would allege weakness and inability; whom to have compelled would have been thought great tyranny and oppression."[2]

Bradford concluded: "The experience that was had in this common course and condition, tried sundry years and that amongst godly and sober men, may well evince the vanity of that conceit of Plato's and other ancients applauded by some of later times; that the taking away of property and bringing in community into a commonwealth would make them happy and flourishing; as if they were wiser than God."[3]

OTHER RELIGIOUS EXILES followed the Pilgrims to America. Many didn't learn from Plymouth colony's mistakes.

A recurring theme of socialists centered on schemes to play God. For Christian socialists, this involved charismatic figures claiming to be God, or at least God's chosen earthly representative. For atheist socialists, this involved deposing God and putting man in his place. For who else but God could be so all-knowing as to plan from afar distribution of goods and jobs to all men?

Men submitted to intrusive schemes based on the loftiest of promises: heaven on earth. Sectarian communists undertook such endeavors to prepare for the end of the world; secular communists undertook such endeavors to embark upon the beginning of the world. With rhetoric that invoked both Genesis and Revelation, the religious and non-religious utopian dreamers displayed the intellectual debt owed to the Bible. Man, again and again, fell victim to the conceit of believing himself "wiser than God."

The Dutch followers of Jean de Labadie awaited the eschaton in mid-Atlantic America in the 1680s. Escaping Holland as their founder escaped France, the Labadists lived communally and shared possessions. There existed a "check on all individuals so detailed that a record was kept of how many slices of bread and butter were consumed by each person at each meal," Mark Holloway writes.[4] The intrusions proved too burdensome to both the collective economy and the individual. By 1698, the Labadists had begun to divide their common land into private tracts.

Johann Jacob Zimmermann surmised that the world would end in 1694. To prepare for the union of heaven and earth, his followers left Rotterdam a day after Zimmermann's death and made off to the forests of Pennsylvania. In the tradition of spiritual orders, the members of the "Woman in the Wilderness"—a name that alluded to the true church as a woman and to the book of Revelation's prophecy of Armageddon arriving in the wilderness—were single-sex (all men), celibate, and uniformed. They also lived communally. Judgment Day failed to appear for humanity but came unexpectedly for Zimmermann's immortal successor, Johannes Kelpius. Sect members then reexamined their ideas and slowly rejoined the world.

Conrad Beissel came to America in hopes of joining Woman in the Wilderness. Finding it gone, he secluded himself in a cave and eventually launched his own sectarian community, the Ephrata Society. Launched in 1732, Ephrata became the most enduring communist enterprise in American history, lasting in one form or another into the twentieth century. The Ephratans lived as destitute monks, forgoing possessions, sex, and individuality.

In most ways, the early sectarian communities bore no resemblance to the fantasies of leftists, past or present. In several crucial ways, however, Ephratans, Labadists, and other religious communists embodied the radical's dream: they eschewed private property for collectivism, rejected traditional Western civilization, and envisioned earth becoming heaven.

These communities were not demonstrations to prove the tenets of socialism, but spiritual fortresses to protect inhabitants from the sinful world surrounding them. Their inhabitants were monastic rather than evangelistic. More concerned with their own salvation than humanity's, sectarian communists built cities beyond rather than upon hills. Sectarian communists did not intend for their communities to serve as models for replication. Secular communists nevertheless saw them as such.

Such communities flourished in America thanks to the unique qualities of the new republic. In Europe, peculiar religious sects were unwelcome where there was unity of church and state, while centralized governments, rigid class structures, and a paucity of land made separation from society possible only by the drastic act of emigration. In contrast, America's federalism allowed for a diversity of governments and a plethora of competing experiments. The unsettled frontier provided plenty of land to conduct experiments in communal living. Religious freedom promised that sects could go about their business unmolested by government. And the open-door policy invited those whose beliefs conflicted with the beliefs that governed their homelands.

Disaffected Europeans came through that open door. The Shakers came from England, the Harmonists and Zoarites from the German states, and the Jansonites from Sweden. A wave of secular communists followed the wave of sectarian communists—Icarians from France, the Modjeskans from Poland, Owenites from Great Britain. Ideas, unaccompanied by masses of people, immigrated, too. Fourierism was a system made in France but tested in America.

America's first aliens were aliens twice over. Outsiders in their own countries for economic, religious, political, or myriad other reasons, misfits in Europe often came to America, where they found that they were misfits once again.

JESUS CHRIST CAME to America in 1774, and her name was Ann Lee. Like Jesus of Nazareth, Ann of Manchester came of humble (earthly) parentage. Neither fisherman nor carpenter, Lee did work in a cotton factory and as a cook in an infirmary (in which she was later committed). Lee never learned to read or write, so her life's works were chronicled by her followers. She faced persecution—by the state in Britain, by the mob in America.

In jail, where many find Christ, Ann Lee found herself. Confined to a Manchester cell for two weeks, Lee discovered that she was the second coming of Jesus Christ. Lee additionally discovered that she did not like jail. So, at God's request, she left England for America. Her followers, numbering eight, naturally followed. They settled in upstate New York, performing odd jobs, until a revival swept through the area in 1780. Lee preached. Mother Ann's charisma, despite her strange doctrines, made converts. Inspired, she traveled and made more converts. A religious cult bloomed.

Ann Lee was the leader, but not the founder, of the Shakers. The Shakers were originally Quakers who took to ritualistic shaking, hence the redundancy "Shaking Quakers" or the amalgam "Shakers." Their dancing and screaming disturbed the peace of cramped Manchester and later frightened the inhabitants of sparse New England towns into thinking that Indians were afoot. Ann, and other Shakers, spoke in tongues. Ann recalled how several ministers interrogating her "said that I spoke in seventy two different tongues, and that I spoke them more perfect than any in their knowledge were able to do." These British men of the cloth evidently possessed good senses of humor, as they tried to goad Ann into teaching them the languages she spoke.5 In America, Ann took to randomly making accusations against strangers—"whore" being a favorite taunt. She accused one man of mating with beasts and charged one young woman with living "in whoredom with married men, young men, black men and boys."6

There was a message amidst the madness. Lee waged war on marriage, demanding celibacy from her followers and cleaving wife from husband upon conversion. She condemned competing religions, going so far in Manchester as to disrupt a Church of England service. She and her flock lived communally, if nomadically, and shared all. If all of this wasn't controversial enough to invite persecution from the riffraff, Ann preached pacifism in rural, Revolutionary-era America. The Shakers made no secret of their English origins, and Ann, a *woman*, claimed to be Christ. Mobs frequently beat the Shakers, with one pack of night riders absconding with Ann in a horse-drawn sleigh to engage upon her "acts of inhumanity and indecency which even savages would be ashamed of."7

Jailed, beaten, committed, ridiculed, and nearly thrown overboard upon passage to America, Ann Lee died just sixteen years after recognizing herself as the second incarnation. Lee's followers, like Christ's, lived on after their messiah's 1784 death. From New York and New England, they spread to Ohio, Kentucky, and points beyond. For Shakers, communism was an aspect of Christianity, not something larger. Hadn't the apostles lived communally? It was in imitation of the early church that the Shakers wished to live after their messiah's death. "The five most prominent practical principles of the Pentecost Church were," according to the Shakers, "first, common property; second, a life of celibacy; third, non-resistance; fourth, a separate and distinct government; and, fifth, power over physical disease."8 "If [converts] brought children into the community," Mark Holloway informs, "they were separated from them, and might only see them privately once a year, in the presence of an elder, for a very brief interview."9 The lifestyle and religion proved especially attractive to women, who greatly outnumbered men at Shaker communities.10 Mothers escaped child-rearing burdens. Old maids found shelter from a world that offered little in the way of opportunities for self-support and much in the way of stigma. And in contrast to nearly every other religion, a woman played a central role in the Shaker faith.

And that woman, after her death, occasionally reappeared at nightly gatherings to deliver food and drink to believing Shakers, who also caught ghostly visions of Beelzebub, Indian tribes, and Arabs far from home. But such visions grew foggier as death, celibacy, and insulation subtracted from their ranks, which had peaked at about five thousand. While the first coming of Christ now claims more than two billion adherents, the second coming claims less than a dozen people in two New England states.

THOUGH THE SHAKER religion failed to inspire waves of converts, the Shaker way of life inspired waves of imitators. The Shaker embrace of a proto-feminism, pacifism, and egalitarianism; the group's rebellion against marriage, the family, and all post-first-century Christianity; and, especially, its communities serving as proof that communism wasn't mere theory—all generated interest in Ann Lee's religion far beyond what a small cult normally warrants.

In 1804, the Harmonists (as they called themselves) or the Rappites (as others called them) followed George Rapp to America. Father Rapp's six-hundred-plus flock settled outside of Pittsburgh the next year. In 1814, Rapp sought sunnier skies and greener pastures for the group's vineyards, so they packed up and moved to the banks of the Wabash in southwestern Indiana. Finding scorching summers, freezing winters, and malaria, the Harmonists departed the misnamed Harmony, Indiana, but not before their leader could play a crucial role in the founding of the state.[11] They returned to the Pittsburgh area in 1825 and established the town of Economy.

After siring four children, Rapp forbade his followers from engaging in sex. The Harmonists grew tobacco but their leader forbade its use. Amidst this puritan atmosphere, an English visitor noted, "during the whole time I was at Harmonie I never saw one of them laugh."[12] The Rappites lived humbly, save Father Rapp, who dwelled in a large and ornate home. Rapp's "word was law on every subject," wrote William Hinds, a historian of and participant in communist communities.[13] Rapp's followers held the same godly view of Rapp as Rapp held of himself. Appearing as if he had stepped out of the pages of the Old Testament, the leader had a ZZ Top—like beard (sans mustache), solemn countenance, and simple dress that reminded followers that there walked the genuine article. So worshipful were the Harmonists of Father Rapp that in 1805 they deeded all of their earthly possessions to him.[14] In return, Father Rapp agreed to supply "all the necessaries of life, as clothing, meat, drink, lodging," and should any Harmonists "become sick, infirm, or otherwise unfit for labor," Harmony's patriarch would provide security, "medicine, care, attendance, and consolation."[15]

The Harmonists prepared for the end of the world. It didn't come. But the end came for Father Rapp in 1847, and nearly six decades later for the community he started.

The Germans of the Society of Separatists of Zoar emigrated from the same area as Father Rapp's Harmonists. Like the Shakers and Rappites, their migration had as much to do with conditions in Europe as with conditions in America. In Württemberg, the Separatists played Martin Luther to the established Lutheran Church. They were Protestant Protestants. "[W]e reject all intervention of priests or preachers," they proclaimed to local authorities. "We cannot send our children into the schools of Babylon. . . . We cannot serve the state as soldiers, because a Christian cannot murder his enemy, much less his friend."[16] They found Europe's intolerance intolerable, and they migrated en masse to the open spaces of the American heartland.

The Zoarites settled in eastern Ohio with no intent to live communally. The uncertainty of life on the newly settled frontier, and the number of elderly Zoarites, dictated a change in plans. They came to America to worship freely, but quickly decided to live under group coercion. "All inequalities and distinctions of rank and fortune shall be abolished from amongst us," their 1833 constitution declared, "that we may live as brethren and sisters of one common family."[17]

Entered into pragmatically, communism soon took on religious connotations. As one Zoarite explained, "In heaven there is only Communism; and why should it not be our aim to prepare ourselves in this world for the society we are sure to enter there? If we can get rid of our wilfulness and selfishness here there is so much done for heaven."[18]

But what were the earthly advantages of collective living? "All distinctions of rich and poor are abolished," Zoarites told Hinds in 1876. "The members have no care except for their own spiritual culture. Communism provides for the sick, the weak, the unfortunate, all alike, which makes their life comparatively easy and pleasant. In case of great loss by fire or flood or other cause, the burden which would be ruinous to one is easily borne by the many. Charity and genuine love to one another, which are the foundations of true Christianity, can be more readily cultivated and practiced in Communism than in common, isolated society. Finally, a Community is the best place in which to get rid of selfishness, wilfulness, and bad habits and vices generally; for we are subject to the constant surveillance and reproof of others, which, rightly taken, will go far toward preparing us for the large Community above."[19]

Whatever wonders communism did for the community above, it did little for the Zoarite community here on earth. "The little town of Zoar, though founded fifty-six years ago, has yet no foot pavements," Charles Nordhoff wrote upon visiting the community in 1874; "it remains without regularity of design; the houses are for the most part in need of paint; and there is about the place a general air of neglect and lack of order, a shabbiness."[20] Twenty-four years later, the communists decided to no longer be communists. The 222 Zoarites went their separate ways. William Hinds returned to Zoar in 1900 and found, to his obvious dismay, that "individualism was rampant."[21] "Yes," Zoar's former schoolteacher told Hinds, "every one can do as he pleases, like all the world."[22]

WE SEE FLASHES of twentieth-century Bolshevik communism in nineteenth-century Christian communism. We see charismatic dictators and communities of Big Brothers. We see centrally planned economies, the belief in man's perfectibility, and the imminence of heaven on earth. But we also see elements missing from twentieth-century Bolshevism. We see, most conspicuously, Bibles, churches, and references to Jesus Christ instead of Karl Marx, or Vladimir Lenin, or Joseph Stalin. Less obvious, but not less important, we see breakaways. Christian communism was voluntary. Communists could and did secede from the communes. Thousands of Americans used their freedom to associate for the purpose of rejecting freedom. If life under communism didn't suit them, no Checkpoint Charlie stopped them, no Siberia awaited them. They just left.

The relationship between today's irreligious Left and yesterday's religious Left is lineal. Christian communitarians attacked the established churches, the institution of marriage, and private property. They embraced proto-feminism, pacifism, it-takes-a-village child rearing, and numerous objectives that subordinated the individual to the group. That they did so in the name of Christianity is less important than the fact that they did so.

Still more direct is the line from America's sectarian communists to America's secular communists. The intellectuals who established utopias in America's heartland during the nineteenth century gained inspiration from the religious communitarians who preceded them. The transition from sectarian to secular was immediate in the case of the Rappites and the Owenites. In 1824, British socialist Robert Owen—whose followers coined the term "socialism"—purchased Harmony, Indiana, from Father George Rapp.[23] He renamed it New Harmony and embarked upon the most famous experiment in communal living in American history.

"George Rapp founded New Harmony, Indiana, with the intention of awaiting the millennium there," Indiana University professor William Wilson observed. "Robert Owen came to town believing he brought the millennium with him."[24]

~ 2 ~

NEW HARMONY

And they said: Come, let us make a city and a tower, the top whereof may reach to heaven: and let us make our name famous, before we be scattered abroad into all lands.

—GENESIS 11:4

ROBERT OWEN DELIVERED his "Declaration of Mental Independence" at New Harmony, Indiana, on July 4, 1826: "I now declare to you and to the world, that man up to this hour has been in all parts of the earth a slave to a trinity of the most monstrous evils that could be combined to inflict mental and physical evil upon the whole race. I refer to private property, absurd and irrational systems of religion and marriage founded upon individual property, combined with some of these irrational systems of religion."[1]

Robert Owen would feel more at home in a world with gay marriage and easy divorce, which excludes nativity scenes and the Ten Commandments from the public square, and where courts grant governments the "right" to redistribute property from rightful owners to covetous developers. This is because that is the world Robert Owen helped make.

For Owen, timing was everything. He arrived in a nation ripe to challenge the status quo. Over the previous fifty years, Americans had withstood two wars with the world's greatest power, fought Indians on the frontier, and ejected the Spanish from Florida. With potential enemies amassed on the continent, first-generation Americans were in no mood to criticize their own institutions. But by 1824 many of the dangers had passed. Americans now felt confident that their nation would not be reabsorbed into the British Empire, destroyed by roaming tribes of Indians, or victimized by some other European power on the North American continent. With threats evaporating, Americans looked inward, criticized institutions, and dreamed of a better way. America was the blank slate upon which every man could project his ideal. As time passed, it became apparent that reality didn't match ideals. The idealists clamored for something better. Enter Robert Owen.

BORN TO A saddler in Wales in 1771, Robert Owen became a manager of a cotton mill at nineteen and within a few years a part owner of another cotton mill. After marrying the daughter of the owner of the mill at New Lanark, Scotland, Owen purchased it with several partners. He gradually removed small children from factory work. He shortened the workday for older children from fourteen hours to less than eleven. He transformed New Lanark into a self-contained entity featuring stores, clinics, housing, transportation, and other utilities. Fans saw in New Lanark a forerunner of a future world of cooperation and community. Critics called New Lanark a glorified company town.

Owen's radical business practices coincided not with New Lanark's ruin but with its prosperity. In Owen's estimation, his reforms made him, "perhaps, the most popular man in the world."[2]

Emboldened by success at his factory, Owen set out to reform Great Britain, America, and then the world. In 1815, he embarked on a campaign to decrease children's time in factories and increase their time in schools. What he established at New Lanark a few years earlier he wanted Parliament to establish in all of Great Britain. Specifically, Owen wanted children under ten out of the factories; he wanted limitations on work hours and prohibition of night work for minors; and he wanted government inspectors to ensure the law's enforcement.[3] Convinced of the rectitude of his ideas, the political novice Owen was aghast that his proposed legislation actually encountered opposition. In 1819, Parliament passed a watered-down version of his proposals. This partial victory was no victory at all for Owen, who was unused to compromise. The "defeat" signaled a change of direction: society, not just a few laws, needed to be overturned. Owen the reformer became Owen the revolutionary, albeit the peaceful revolutionary, the revolutionary armed with reason rather than a rifle.

Owen decided to transform society from a basis of competition to cooperation, from the individual to the group, from private profits to public sharing. This transformation would come about by way of associations, which Owen planned in intricate detail. Owen commissioned scale models of his ideal commune, laid out as a parallelogram—not a circle, not a trapezoid, *a parallelogram*. Residents would live along the four sides of the quadrangle, with a meeting house and stores in the middle. The ideal number of communists would lie somewhere between 500 and 2,500.[4] Why not 250, 4,147, or 12,879? Owen did not explain.

Other aspects of the plan seemed less arbitrary. Group kitchens would liberate women from the drudgery of cooking and cleaning, double the workforce, and increase production. Middlemen and other aspects of capitalism deemed parasitic would be eliminated by the public distribution of necessities. Surpluses, instead of languishing in a farmer's silo or a banker's safe, would be put at the disposal of the community. Despite its quirks, Owen dubbed his plan "universal and applicable to all times, persons, and circumstances."[5] He set about proving this.

The self-made industrialist transitioned from politics to propaganda. Owen cajoled the British government into sending his writings to continental officials and universities. He crashed a conference of European heads of state in 1818 to distribute his pamphlets. All politely accepted literature save the Russian czar, who offered the excuse that he had no pockets in which to keep it. He once cornered John Quincy Adams, then U.S. minister to Great Britain, and dumped copies of his *A New View of Society* on him to disseminate among American political leaders.[6]

"To the end of his days Owen believed that these ventures into high diplomacy had been master strokes of propaganda," historian Arthur Bestor observed, "and he gave unhesitating credence to a tale that his writings had converted the defeated Napoleon from the ways of war to peace. What wonder then that he believed that the volumes sent to America had prepared the nation for his later coming?"[7] In fact, Owen's writings preceded his arrival in America in but small doses. Ironically, his failures as a propagandist benefited him. The amorphous knowledge of a self-made philanthropist created a favorable impression of Robert Owen as a down-to-earth humanitarian. The specific knowledge of Owen's proposals—to eliminate personal responsibility, the nuclear family, private property, religion, and marriage—would have prejudiced minds into dismissing him as a crank.

IN 1824, WELL over a century before a Beatle-led British invasion, and more than a decade after a Sir Isaac Brock–led British invasion, Robert Owen took America by storm. His whirlwind tour of the United States spurred Owenite clubs, press attention, and interest at the highest levels of government. He was the flavor of the month. With entourage in tow, he toured Father Rapp's New Economy community outside Pittsburgh and visited a Shaker village in New York. He approved of what he saw, save for the matter of religion. He didn't seem to understand that religion served as the main purpose of the Shaker and Rappite communities rather than as some curiosity to be overlooked.

The dual purpose, propaganda and action, of Robert Owen's trip intersected at the Rappite community. Owen had been corresponding with George Rapp since 1820. Father Rapp's success as a communist suggested to Owen that his dream could be realized. With Rapp looking to sell and Owen looking to buy, the Welshman and the German struck a deal. During a visit to southwestern Indiana in the winter of 1824–25, Owen paid more than $100,000 for twenty thousand acres, Harmony, Indiana, and the hundred-plus buildings on the site. Owen renamed Father Rapp's Harmony "New Harmony" and ratcheted up his publicity campaign to solicit participants in his great experiment.[8]

His wealth opened the corridors of power. His ideas exerted a pull over other dreamers. For a young America in the throes of an inferiority complex, the vague notion that Europeans held Owen in great esteem proved enough to bowl over citizens of the geographically isolated nation. This meshed with Owen's conceptions. He saw himself as the teacher and Americans, even presidents, generals, and professors, as his students. He said as much in his triumphant address to inaugurate New Harmony: "I am come to this country, to introduce an entire new state of society; to change it from the ignorant, selfish system, to an enlightened, social system, which shall gradually unite all interests into one, and remove all cause for contest between individuals."[9] *I'm here. All of your problems are solved.*

A mix of Ross Perot, Harold Hill, Karl Marx, and Jimmy Swaggart, Owen managed to preach his socialist gospel to many of America's most important leaders. He outlined his ideas to New York governor-elect DeWitt Clinton, secretary of war and vice-president-elect John C. Calhoun, treasury secretary William Crawford, General Andrew Jackson, and even a number of Indian chiefs. He secured audiences with outgoing president James Monroe and incoming president John Quincy Adams. He met with Adams's father in Boston, Thomas Jefferson at Monticello, and James Madison at Montpelier. Within just a few months, Owen held court with seven of the first eight presidents of the United States.* Somehow he convinced America's leaders to allow him to address a joint session of Congress—twice. He postponed the second installment without

---

* So addicted to conversing with czars and presidents did Owen become that in his final years, when existing leaders would no longer entertain him, he communicated through spiritualism with the likes of Benjamin Franklin and Thomas Jefferson, despite his earlier, lifelong hostility toward religion.

informing President Adams, who walked in the cold from the White House to the Capitol only to be stood up. Still, Owen managed to reschedule, and addressed an audience that included both houses of Congress, Supreme Court justices, and presidents Monroe and Adams.

Of course, many other Americans began to question Owen's credibility once he opened his mouth. He deemed marriage "the sole cause of all the prostitution" and declared that "every child born within any state is the child of the state."[10] Religion, he professed, "is one of the most common causes of insanity" and "has made the world . . . one great lunatic asylum."[11] He called paid employees "white slaves" and employers "mere slave-drivers."[12]

The foreigner's dark assessment of current customs seemed, well, foreign. His rosy conception of a future world after the elimination of property, marriage, religion, and other would-be anachronisms struck many Americans as even more peculiar. Employing biblical rhetoric, Robert of New Lanark promised an "earthly paradise," "salvation from ignorance, poverty, sin, and misery," a "New Jerusalem," and a "millennium state of existence."[13] He informed the faithful, years later, that "the mission of my life appears to be to prepare the population of the world to understand the vast importance of the second creation of humanity."[14] The first creator, apparently, was not up to the task.

As Marxist communists would later rail in frustration about the working class's "false consciousness," Owenite communists, when confronted with mass opposition, lamented man's failure to follow his "true interests"—for example, "the new system makes man familiar with his true interests."[15] The prevailing, false interests Owen lambasted were individual interests. These included the profit motive, competition, and familial betterment. The true interests that Owen's "new system" promised to inaugurate were group interests, to be ushered in by replacing the nuclear family with the human family, pooling profits rather than hoarding profits, and establishing communal living arrangements in place of individual homes.

Owenites needn't debate or even consider the arguments of opponents. Anyone failing to see the rectitude of communism had obviously been indoctrinated by the old system. They were to be pitied. They were to be enlightened. They were not to be engaged. If the ideas skeptics spouted weren't their own, why should a communist waste his time debating what amounted to programmed robots?

"For men, as they have been hitherto educated, are incompetent to form a correct or sound judgment on any subjects except those which are connected with the certain sciences, in which they have been instructed," Owen explained in the *New Harmony Gazette*. "On all others, in consequence of being compelled from infancy to receive the absurd doctrine of free-will and responsibility, they have necessarily been rendered irrational."[16]

In his second address to Congress—a speech that moved an again annoyed John Quincy Adams to note that at times it seemed as if the speaker merely read from a book[17]—Owen explained: "The old system of the world, by which I mean all the past and present proceedings of mankind, presupposes, that human nature is originally corrupt—that man forms his own belief and his own character—that, if these shall be formed in a particular manner, the individual will deserve an artificial reward, both here and hereafter; but if this belief, and this character shall not be so formed, the individual will deserve an artificial punishment both here and hereafter. The theory of the old system is therefore founded on notions directly opposed to our nature, and its practice is individual rewards and punishments."[18] More concisely put, man was for Owen free from original sin and not responsible for his own actions.

Owen often expounded on this idea. The core principle of socialism, as understood by the Owenites who coined the term, was the transferal of responsibility from the individual to the social. Since society, not its individual components, is responsible, it is society that should be punished or rewarded, blamed or credited. Today, socialists generally apply this idea to economics. The original socialists went further. Robert Owen sought to remove incentives and disincentives from the criminal justice system, education, and personal relationships, in addition to economics.

"Every fact which comes within the cognizance of our senses, proves beyond the possibility of doubt that man does not—that he cannot possess any, even the smallest conceivable power of his own, and that of himself he cannot do anything whatever," Owen contended. "All his thoughts, feelings, propensities, words and actions are preordained for him."[19] It was fortuitous for Owen that he found success as an industrialist in New Lanark. For Scotland was a land steeped in Calvinism. In denying free will and accepting preordination, Owen, whether consciously or not, was pushing a secularized Calvinism that meshed with the existing religious beliefs of the locals. "Man does not form his own character; it is formed for him by the circumstances that surround him."[20] If external factors, and not the man himself, determined the outcome of a man's life, it followed, as Owen preached, "that none can rationally, or justly, be made responsible for that of which he is not the willing author."[21]

But America was not Scotland, and a competing Calvinist ethic reigned. America extolled hard work, thrift, and rugged individualism tinged with noblesse oblige, and often looked upon wealth as a sign of God's blessing. The principles of socialism and Americanism, then, clashed. Birth did not determine an American's destiny.

The European in Owen did not understand this aspect of Americanism. The respect and politeness shown to him in his travels led him to believe America ripe for socialism. He wrote, giddily: "In fact the whole of this country is ready to commence a new empire upon the principle of public property & to discard private property & the uncharitable notion that man can form his own character as the foundation & root of all evil."[22] Nothing, save Owen's hopes, indicated anything like this.

Had Owen been more of a listener and less of a talker he might have gleaned a realistic picture. He confused the patience, indulgence, and silence of the people he trapped in conversations for agreement. Supreme Court justice Joseph Story found the Welshman "so visionary an enthusiast that he talks like an inhabitant of Utopia."[23] Ashbel Green, the retired president of Princeton University, wrote in reaction to a Philadelphia talk that the lecturer "appeared not only exceedingly visionary, but in some particulars dangerous."[24]

But not everyone was a skeptic. When the propaganda campaign turned to action, thousands of Americans joined the cause. Owen used his Capitol Hill speeches as a gigantic megaphone to issue an open invitation for Americans to join him at New Harmony. When he arrived there in April 1825, Owen discovered that many who had heard the call made it there first.

Never had a utopian community benefited from so many advantages from the start. The New Harmonists arrived not in the wilderness but at a village. They did not face the hardship of constructing a community from scratch. Houses, churches, mills, workshops, dorms, roads, tilled fields, vineyards, and even a textile factory awaited them. The *New Harmony Gazette* described thirty thousand acres of "beautiful" land, where the "timber is generally heavy." The trees offer "an abundant supply of fruit" and the "river abounds with fish."[25]

Robert Owen saved the communists from having to pool financial resources to purchase land. Unlike previous sectarian endeavors, communists needn't transfer their savings to their leader. Unlike future secular endeavors, communists needn't purchase subscriptions to gain admittance. Through his own fortune, Owen bought the completed Rappite village and its thousands of acres of land. No one, save Owen and a few lesser partners, invested money to conduct the experiment. Enthusiasts need only travel to southwestern Indiana, which many did, not only from

Philadelphia and Cincinnati but also from Wales, Scotland, and France. Most, though, came from west of the Appalachians.

New Harmony's location, too, proved ideal. Although New Harmony offered eastern conveniences, its distance from population centers made it immune from the lures of the big city and external corruptions of socialist purity. When the going got tough, it would be tough to get going. New Harmony's isolation at the frontier crossroads of Indiana, Illinois, and Kentucky, perhaps as much as the continuing illusion that heaven on earth was just around the corner, kept communists in the commune.

Despite these advantages, New Harmony lasted as a communal enterprise for slightly more than two years. A proper obituary might have read, "Killed by bad ideas."

CAPITALISM WORKS FOR men who do. Socialism works for men who don't.

At New Harmony, it didn't pay to work. What was good for the commune was not necessarily good for the communist. When you don't profit from your own labor, why labor? Why not paint pictures or write poetry? Or why not get drunk every day? These thoughts occurred. Many acted on them. Work time took on the characteristics of leisure time. Thomas Pears, initially a fervent believer in Owen's theories, painfully observed of them in practice that "the men generally do not work as well as they would for themselves."[26] Men played cards. They put on puppet shows. They debated issues. They didn't work, at least not hard.

The communists faced a catch-22. Removing shirkers would be an admission of flaws in the system, since it promised to transform selfishness into altruism. But clearly, the system hadn't sparked individuals to abandon self-interests in favor of group interests. Harboring shirkers, too, stood to damage the system. Shirkers drained resources, bred resentment, and spread their disease to others. Kicking out shirkers and instituting a stricter admissions policy would have abated the laziness problem, but since such actions would have invalidated the promises of the system, they weren't entertained until it was too late. But even had the communists worked harder, they would still have had the problem of not working smarter.

Strangely, Owen, who had made his success in manufacturing, was determined to make agriculture the center of his communal experiment. Not only did Owen possess no experience as a farmer, his followers largely did not, either. "We are now, as we have been, without vegetables except what we buy," Thomas Pears noted in September 1825.[27] Fewer than forty agricultural workers appeared on October's community roster. New Harmony's population at the time exceeded eight hundred. The community,

Pears noted, neglected to work the fields during the spring's growing season. They paid for it that fall. New Harmony's leaders had essentially given
up on the idea of farming in Owen's absence. They ignored planting
save for winter barley, which was needed for a product in great demand
at New Harmony: beer. Despite ready-made factories and cleared fields,
New Harmonists counted soap, candles, and glue as the only products they
possessed in surplus for external sale.[28] Acquiring anything else necessitated dipping into Robert Owen's piggy bank.

The situation, given the manufacturing background of Owen and several other community leaders, dictated industry. The ideology predeter-
mined farming as the preferred occupation. Ideology won. People lost.

Repeatedly, ideology trumped practical concerns. The burdensome
process of obtaining available necessities, instituted to alleviate the evils
of the free market, created greater evils. But sticking to the plan, hatched
from one man's mind rather than the trial and error of others, meant
more to the Owenites than succeeding. To ensure a fair allotment of goods,
an onerous system of distribution was put in place. Clerks monitored pa-
perwork to guarantee that no one got more than his share. Lines ensued.
So did shortages.[29] With central planners, and not the market, determining production, basic food staples became unavailable.

Visitors reported rotting animal carcasses littering the village and
gangs of pigs roaming the streets. Humans had less freedom of movement.
Overcrowded accommodations pushed family upon family. Cramped
rooms became more cramped with strangers. But since everybody was
part of the same family, the human family, this wasn't a bother. Right?
Eventually, about a thousand people settled at New Harmony. One person
who left almost immediately was Robert Owen. His absence lasted from
June 1825 until January 1826. If an Owenite had Owen's money, he might
have left, too. But since all of the Owenites had Owen's money, they stayed.

Because inhabitants weren't owners, property decayed. New Harmony
was a giant housing project, albeit a housing project on the dime of a rich
guy instead of the taxpayers. But the inhabitants acted as though they lived
in a housing project nonetheless. They may not have urinated in the hall-
ways, spray-painted on their residences, or mugged neighbors, but they
treated the community they lived in rather shabbily. It wasn't theirs. Why
should they care for it as if they owned it? Roads, particularly during
the harsh winters, fell into disrepair. Journeys from the wilderness
outpost to the civilized world, which became ever more necessary as
the community failed to sustain itself, proved treacherous. Nearly everything a contemporary visitor to New Harmony sees was built by George
Rapp's Harmonists, not by Robert Owen's New Harmonists. The secular

communists added little to the physical plant that lasted. They did destroy a few buildings they had inherited, dismantling log cabins to provide much-needed firewood.[30]

NEW HARMONY ACTED as a magnet to the eccentric. Ideas mocked elsewhere were shown great respect at New Harmony. The village oddball was no oddball in this village of oddballs.

Owen's architect, Stedman Whitwell, found the frequency of such city names as "Concord," "Springfield," and "Watertown" troubling. At New Harmony, he launched a plan to rename cities and towns in a more ordered, scientific, and rational manner. Just based on a town's name, such as the New Harmony subcommunity designated "Feiba Pevili," one would, in theory, be able to determine under Whitwell's system its location. Whitwell assigned each number from 0 to 9 a consonant and a vowel and then determined new names based on the letters that corresponded to a location's longitude and latitude grid. Thus, Boston becomes "Odda Natvu," Indianapolis "Fieky Pyvat," and Chicago "Einin Kalovu."[31] It didn't catch on.

Following Owen's "Declaration of Mental Independence," in which Owen declared war on marriage, private property, and the family, his followers, like French Jacobins three decades earlier, scrapped the anno Domini calendar. Inspired by their leader's Fourth of July speech, the New Harmonists declared year one of Mental Independence. The failure of the New Harmony community to survive through year two of Mental Independence doomed M.I.'s chances of replacing A.D.

To avoid repeating the capitalist's sin of exploiting another's labor for his own gain, and to establish a better system of trading between the sections of New Harmony, Owenites established a currency of labor notes. The residents received goods or services by handing over a promissory note for future labor at a value equivalent to the value of the goods or services received. This ensured fair exchanges and prevented inequitable ones. Instead of gold, the notes were backed by another's work. Josiah Warren, father of American anarchism and resident of New Harmony, would later apply the idea of a straight exchange of labor in his Time Stores, early examples of cooperative markets. But at New Harmony, the labor notes established a currency between the main community of New Harmony, and Feiba Pevili, Macluria, and the other breakaway communities within greater New Harmony. The notes eliminated skimming off the top of the laborer's product by middlemen, investors, employers, and bankers.

Like currency, the calendar, and geographic names, schooling became an opportunity for experimentation. For socialists who believed that society had corrupted man, education represented the chance to perfect imperfect man. Thus, the New Harmonists separated children from their parents at an early age to prevent impurities from corrupting the socialist education. "I saw my father and mother twice in two years," recalled one student.[32] Because Robert Owen disliked books, he deemed them improper for children and their use was scant. Because Owen liked talking, he encouraged the lecture method. Owen put into practice in 1826 his vision for social education, which called for "no distinction of teacher and pupil."[33] This edict affected the entire community, child and adult alike. At the Hall of New Harmony, communists met several times a week at Owen's direction for their educational betterment. This lasted for a few weeks, and then the plan, like so many others at New Harmony, fell apart.

New Harmonists counted among themselves quite a few utopians who, for hobby, drew up constitutions for nations they had never set foot in. New Harmonists devised seven actual constitutions to govern themselves. Each one failed more conspicuously than its predecessor. Their failure to perfect a governing system for a community so close did nothing to temper their enthusiasm for drawing up governing documents for nations so far away.

People were always talking. People were rarely doing.

Adding to this salon-on-the-frontier atmosphere was the derisively named "Boatload of Knowledge." Arriving by way of a keelboat called *The Philanthropist* in January 1826, this "troop of brilliant, eccentric, and lighthearted people" was the last thing New Harmonists needed, wanted, or expected.[34] The community needed farmers, mechanics, and laborers. It got educational theorists, botanists, and amateur scientists.

Owen's return on the Boatload of Knowledge was a reality check. In their leader's absence, New Harmonists had deluded themselves into believing that their problems would disappear, or at least dissipate, upon his return. They didn't. The overcrowded community didn't need any more people, and it certainly didn't need any more people allergic to work. But that's what it got.

"Mr. Owen says we have been speaking falsehoods all our lives, and that here only we shall be enabled to speak the truth. I am sure that I cannot in sincerity look upon these as my equals, and that if I must appear to do it, I cannot either act or speak the truth," departing and disillusioned communist Sarah Pears confessed. "I think that the person who wrote that this is a terrestrial paradise must have very odd ideas of paradise, or it must be meant as a joke."[35]

New Harmony stumbled on. Whatever morale boost Owen injected upon his return, its effects dissipated shortly thereafter. Communists, despite free rent and a free ride, chose, like Sarah Pears, secession. Others, disappointed in the results of New Harmony, formed competing sister communities nearby. But all the communities relied on the same sugar daddy, and believed in his basic ideas, and so they failed, too.

SHOULD NEW HARMONY collapse, there were always the dozen or so imitation communities that had sprung up around the United States in the wake of Robert Owen's 1824–25 publicity campaign.

"Everything appears to be going on prosperously and harmoniously," noted a sympathetic newspaper account of Kendal, Ohio's, Friendly Association for Mutual Interests. In December 1826, the reporter found the community of 150 "bustling," "rapidly on the increase," and containing "not a sick person on the premises."[36] But less than two years later, the community began to disintegrate. "There was no dramatic crisis to account for this: apparently the members came to the conclusion that communitarian life did not benefit them substantially more than individual society," historian John F. C. Harrison noted.[37] With fever claiming the lives of several communitarians, and debt weighing down on them, the Friendly Association for Mutual Interests opted out of their mutual interests and returned to individual interests. Outlasting New Harmony by two years, Kendal disappeared into history in 1829. One member looked back at the experiment with fondness: "The failure never for a moment weakened my faith in the value of Communism."[38]

For Frances Wright, communism was a means and not an end. At Nashoba, Tennessee, the Scottish radical bought hundreds of acres in the fall of 1825. She also bought slaves. She set about emancipating blacks by becoming their mistress. The multi-racial commune would prepare slaves for liberty through education and social interaction. But the social interaction that occurred at Nashoba proved more damaging from a public relations standpoint than anything, including repeated failures, which befell the communists. Like Owen, Wright fled her venture shortly after launching it. In her absence, rumors spread of miscegenation and free love. Some of the rumors proved true. James Richardson, a trustee of Nashoba, took Josephine, a free "quadroon," as his consort. A slave named Isabel charged a white man named Redrick "for coming during the night . . . to her bedroom, uninvited, and endeavoring, without her consent, to take liberties with her person."[39]

In a damage-control effort, Wright did more damage. Upon her return to the United States, Wright publicly endorsed "the amalgamation of the races" and lambasted the "tyranny" of marriage and the "ignorant code of morals."[40] Wright's southern neighbors weren't ready for her vision. From that point forward, communes became associated with free love. Ironically, the venture that brought the greatest contemporary shame upon communism brought it the greatest historical credit. Wright, upon the dissolution of Nashoba, arranged for the emancipation of the slaves there. Wright's goals weren't to transform America into one giant commune but to free slaves. She did that.

So motivated by Robert Owen's visit to Cincinnati were several hundred Swedenborgians that they launched the Yellow Springs community before Owen launched New Harmony. "Men who seldom or never before labored with their hands devoted themselves to agriculture and the mechanical arts with a zeal which was at least commendable, although not always according to knowledge," recalled a young member of the community.[41] But zeal yielded to recriminations when zeal alone failed to yield fruitful harvests and surplus products. "The industrious, the skillful, and the strong saw the products of their labor enjoyed by the indolent, the unskilled, and the improvident, and self-love rose against benevolence," observed fellow communist John Humphrey Noyes. "A band of musicians insisted that their brassy harmony was as necessary to the common happiness as bread and meat, and declined to enter the harvest-field or the work-shop. A lecturer upon natural science insisted upon talking only while others worked. Mechanics, whose single day's labor brought two dollars into the common stock, insisted that they should in justice work only half as long as the agriculturalist, whose day's work brought but one."[42]

Yellow Springs as an Owenite community lasted three months. But its imprint upon present-day Yellow Springs, the offbeat home to artists and activists, survives to this day.

ALL OF THE Owenite communities that dotted the American landscape in the 1820s expired before the 1820s did. None lasted more than four years. This included the mother ship, New Harmony, which ceased to exist as a cooperative exercise in June 1827.

The verbose Mr. Owen delivered his farewell addresses at the Hall of New Harmony over two nights. As New Harmony disintegrated, he told his dejected followers: "The social system is now firmly established."[43] Almost immediately Owen set about establishing a new colony based on socialist principles in Mexico. It never got off the ground. He lost the better part of his fortune on New Harmony. He still believed his system flawless. The vision's light blinds socialists to reality's darkness.

Not everyone's illusions survived. William Maclure, who, next to

Owen, sank the most money into New Harmony, wrote in the dying days of the experiment: "My experience at Harmony has given me such horror for the reformation of grown persons that I shudder when I reflect having so many of my friends so near such a desperate undertaking."[44] Maclure didn't give up hope on instilling socialist principles in growing persons. Following the New Harmony debacle, he turned exclusively to his passion of education.

A. J. Macdonald, a Scottish admirer of Owen and participant in several communes, visited New Harmony fifteen years after its demise and found that disdain for socialism ran heavy. "I was cautioned not to speak of Socialism, as the subject was unpopular," this chronicler of American socialism wrote. "The advice was good; Socialism was unpopular, and with good reason. The people had been wearied and disappointed by it; had been filled full with theories, until they were nauseated, and had made such miserable attempts at practice, that they seemed ashamed of what they had been doing. An enthusiastic socialist would soon be cooled down at New Harmony."[45] That these words were written by an "enthusiastic socialist" makes them doubly powerful.

John Humphrey Noyes, who relied on Macdonald's notes to pen the first history of American socialism, concluded about Owen: "The Professor appeared on the stage with a splendid reputation for previous thaumaturgy, with all the crucibles and chemicals around him that money could buy, with an audience before him that was gaping to see the last wonder of science: but on applying the flame that was to set ablaze with happiness and glory, behold! the material prepared would not burn, but only sputtered and smoked; and the curtain had come down upon a scene of confusion and disappointment!"[46]

But Robert Owen gloried in the scale models, the elaborate blueprints, and the publicity campaigns. The execution bored him so much that he went home two months into it. During the turmoil at New Harmony, Owen confided in his diary: "The enjoyment of a reformer, I should say, is much more in contemplation, than in reality."[47] Unfortunately for his followers, they experienced the pain of reality and not the euphoria of contemplation. If Owen had only stuck to his preference for theory and abandoned his penchant for action, he would have helped avert trouble for so many.

The official name for the grand experiment was the New Harmony Community of Equality. But this title conveyed about as accurate a picture of Owen's communism as the name "People's Republic of China" did for Mao's communism. The preliminary constitution awarded all power to Owen, who retained the right to appoint the governing committee. Appointed committees, Owen maintained, circumvented "the numberless evils of elections and electioneering."[48] Owen, while campaigning in Great Britain, noted that he did not want "the opinions of the ill-trained and uninformed on measures intended for their relief and amelioration. No! On Such subjects, until they shall be instructed in better habits, and made rationally intelligent, their advice can be of no value."[49]

Owen's paternalism stemmed from the paternalistic ideology he promoted. To go from dictating by remote where in the parallelogram people should live or what crops should be planted to disregarding as irrelevant an individual's ideas about his self-interests is no long journey. It's not that socialism inevitably leads to oppression. Socialism is oppression.

3

YANKEE UTOPIANS

My doctrine is not mine, but his that sent me.

—JOHN 7:16

FROM NEW HARMONY, Robert Owen told his followers: "I am come to this country, to introduce an entire new state of society; to change it from the ignorant, selfish system, to an enlightened, social system, which shall gradually unite all interests into one, and remove all cause for contest between individuals."[1]

From Paris, Charles Fourier told his followers: "I come as the possessor of the book of Destiny to banish political and moral darkness and to erect the theory of universal harmony upon the ruins of the uncertain sciences."[2]

Unlike Owen, Charles Fourier never made it to America. His philosophy, however, did. Central to that philosophy were the twelve passions: the five senses, plus friendship, love, and ambition, and what Fourier called "parentalism," "analysism," "alternatism," and "synthesism." Fourier added a thirteenth passion, "unityism"—man's passion to work together with other men—which combined the existing twelve passions and served as the basis of his system to organize humanity. For in united communities, with individuals pursuing the passions they are drawn to, humanity would finally realize social harmony.

Fourier contended that he was no theorist, but a discoverer. He didn't invent the thirteen "passions." God did. Fourier merely recognized God's plan through his own reason and revealed it to his fellow man. Marriage laws, commerce, the moral code, schools, and a host of other institutions had suppressed man's passions. Association, the organization of mankind into millions of communal living arrangements, would reorient men toward their interests, their attractions, their passions. If it feels good, do it. God wouldn't have made you passionately drawn to something, Fourier reasoned, if He didn't want you to act on those passions. Pursuing the passions would hasten the arrival of social harmony. Passions complemented other passions. Since some men harbored passions that other men did not, combining humans into groups would fit all the pieces of men's passions together. It would make a perfect whole.

Fourier saw a disordered, unplanned, anarchic world. Order, design, and science would cure all that. The phalanstery, the architectural center-piece of Fourier's self-sustaining villages, achieved symmetry through its two wings. The phalanxes needed to have just the right number of people, corresponding to Fourier's calculations of 810 passional combinations. Multiply that by the number of sexes and you had 1,620—the precise number needed for harmonious equilibrium. This number would make a phalanx, two million of which would spring up on earth. Within each phalanx, bureaucratic subgroups, or series, divided the labor by channeling individual passions in a manner useful to the community—for example, into animal husbandry, mechanical pursuits, teaching, or cooking. The phalanx placed individuals in numerous series to balance their many passions. Working in their various series and exhibiting all of the passional combinations, the 1,620 members of the phalanx would perform all of the necessary work. Thus, the individual and the community would be satisfied. Once established, the phalanx conformed to history's plan, which conformed to neat stages of eighty-thousand-year durations.

But would a better life result from solving a mathematical equation, achieving geometric symmetry, or organizing future ages based on imagined stages?

Fourier's ideas, along with his ego, resembled Owen's. Both men lambasted marriage, free enterprise, and traditional religion. Both promoted communal living as a panacea. Each saw himself as the catalyst for a new age. Each compared himself to the most important figures in history.[3] Owen lived to see the trial (and failure) of his ideas. Fourier died, in 1837 at age sixty-five, before ever witnessing his ideas in action (not that seeing them fail would have changed his mind).

Like all utopians, Fourier exaggerated the grimness of the present and the glory of the future. The Frenchman described the world as "oppressive," having "lost all hope," full of "irremediable misery," and trapped in a "night of moral and political ignorance."[4] In contrast, his system would "lead to the establishment of universal Unity on the globe," "banish from our midst not only wars and revolutions, but all poverty and injustice," and achieve "two thousand years of social progress in a single leap."[5] "Every year during this grand metamorphosis will be worth whole ages of previous existence," Fourier promised.[6]

Owen spent his manufacturing fortune on his ideas. Fourier, his family's wealth expropriated in the aftermath of the French Revolution, lived on a modest trust fund. It could barely support him, let alone his grandiose vision. During his final decade, Fourier waited daily for the postman to deliver a promissory note from some idealistic millionaire so that he could put his ideas into action.[7] The money never came. Albert Brisbane did.

THE SON OF a wealthy New York merchant, Brisbane traveled to Europe in 1828 to imbibe the heady theories served by Continental sophists. "I fully accept this world of new ideas which is emerging in France, and the grand and glorious future it promises," Brisbane exuberantly declared in a letter to his family. "We must do away with present society in all its aspects. I renounce liberalism, and republicanism."[8] After sipping St. Simonianism, Hegelianism, and other doctrines, Brisbane settled on Fourierism as his potion of choice.[9]

Brisbane encountered the master himself in 1831—"I never saw him smile"—and for a small fee the traveler hired Fourier to teach him his theories.[10] Brisbane was a better propagandist than his teacher. He returned to America intent on evangelizing Fourier's world-saving message. "Our object has been to vindicate Human Nature, to show the fitness of Man for Social Harmony and for fulfilling a noble Destiny on Earth," Brisbane said of his master and his master's acolytes. "If we have proved this point, our faith in the Future, our hope in the Elevation of Man and his social Redemption from the Evils which scourge and degrade his terrestrial existence, are based on a sure and solid foundation."[11] For a $500 fee, Brisbane secured in 1842 a front-page column that extolled Fourier's ideas in Horace Greeley's fledgling *New York Tribune*. Brisbane quickly converted Greeley and many of his readers.

The American followers mimicked the French leader's hell on earth/heaven on earth dichotomy of present and future in the pages of the *Phalanx* and the *Harbinger*, the movement's leading periodicals. American Fourierists described themselves as "the ministers of that faith which alone can rescue mankind from this horrible depravity and wretchedness."[12] They spoke of America as a "Social Hell."[13] Associationism, on the other hand, would usher in "the perfected earth" and bring to man his "introduction into the Kingdom of God on earth."[14] They boasted, "[O]ur moral aim is the grandest that ever elevated human thought."[15]

The followers also obscured, ignored, and excused portions of the master's instruction. "Instead of simply translating Fourier's works," historian Carl Guarneri points out, "French and American disciples wrote their own tracts which in the guise of summarizing his ideas limited them to his philosophy of history, theory of the passions, and plan for model communities."[16] For instance, Fourier described a highly regulated free-love society, where a Court of Love would coordinate the varied sexual passions of phalanx members. A guaranteed minimum of sexual experiences leveled the erotic playing field for the ugly, shy, and awkward. Tolerance would allow previously anathematic practices to flourish. Fourier confessed to the orientation of "sapphianism," a love of lesbians, which he thought present in just thirty-three of every million.[17] The phalanx had room for Fourier's allegedly uncommon tastes, as well as homosexuality, polygamy, incest, and just about every interest one can imagine. Thus, Albert Brisbane, a keeper of mistresses and the father of three illegitimate children, saw the appeal of Fourier's sexually free lifestyle but understood that knowledge of it in America would prove fatal. On this and so many other peculiarities of the master's teaching, Brisbane, St. Paul to Fourier's Christ, stayed quiet. Never bothering to tell American followers just what they were signing up for, Brisbane and other leaders started a movement.

The allure of Fourierism erased memory of Owenite failures. The American Left welcomed another wave of communism.

THE MOST FAMOUS of the Associationist experiments did not start on Fourierist principles. Brook Farm was a commune established by Transcendentalist renegades within the Unitarian Church. The Transcendentalists split from the Unitarians, who split from the Puritans, who split from the Anglicans, who split from the Catholics. Tellingly, the Transcendentalists also split over Brook Farm, their great reform project.

Transcendentalists believed that knowledge often transcended the grasp of the senses. They saw God in men, trees, and rocks, but were quick to deny pantheism. This impulse led to a proto-environmentalism; Brook Farm was itself the manifestation of a back-to-the-land movement. Like existentialism, postmodernism, and other intellectual fads, Transcendentalism is easy to describe but difficult to define. "I was given to understand," Charles Dickens noted after a trip to New England, "that whatever was unintelligible would be certainly transcendental."[18]

From their Puritan forbears, Transcendentalists retained moral righteousness and the desire to unite the here with the hereafter. Unitarian

minister William Henry Channing, a key supporter of Brook Farm, proclaimed that "a new era in Humanity is opening, and sounds forth more
fully than ever before the venerable yet new gospel, that the kingdom of
HEAVEN IS AT HAND."[19] Transcendentalists also retained the Puritan conviction that they were the elect. From above, they sniped at their country.
"Proto-feminist" Margaret Fuller told Europeans that America was
"spoiled by prosperity" and "stupid with the lust of gain," while Transcendentalist par excellence Ralph Waldo Emerson sniffed, "America is a vast
know-nothing party."[20] The Transcendentalist looked at the world his
Puritan ancestors had bequeathed, and thought: *I could do better.*

This notion animated Brook Farm's founder, George Ripley, a Unitarian minister and the host of the Transcendentalist Club's first meeting.
Ripley boasted to his friend Emerson that he hoped to build the "city
of God."[21]

In 1840, Ripley, as Emerson had done eight years earlier, stepped
down from the pulpit. Anticipating the proponents of the Social Gospel,
Ripley wanted Christianity "to redeem society as well as the individual
from all sin."[22] Social projects replaced Christ as man's redeemer.

Emerson noted the transformation of Puritan New England into liberal
New England: "[T]he Church, or religious party, is falling from the church
nominal, and is appearing in temperance and non-resistance societies, in
movements of abolitionists and of socialists, and in very significant as-
semblies, called Sabbath and Bible Conventions,—composed of ultraists,
or seekers, of all the soul of soldiery of dissent, and meeting to call in
question the authority of the Sabbath, of the priesthood, and of the
church."[23] Emerson might as well have been talking about himself, or
George Ripley. Emerson declined the invitation to join Ripley's Brook
Farm, however. "I think that all I shall solidly do," the Concord sage
concluded, "I must do alone."[24] Henry David Thoreau, too, remained
skeptical. Ridiculing the millennial pretensions of the Brook Farmers,
Emerson's protégé explained, "As for these communities, I think I had
rather keep bachelor's hall in hell than go to board in heaven."[25]

Ripley formed a joint-stock company in 1841 that purchased a 160-
acre dairy farm in West Roxbury, Massachusetts, to "insure a more natural
union between intellectual and manual labor" and "to combine the
thinker and the worker."[26] Novelist Nathaniel Hawthorne, whom Ripley
succeeded in recruiting to Brook Farm, captured the high hopes of the
communitarians in *The Blithedale Romance.* "We had left the rusty iron
frame-work of society behind us," Miles Coverdale narrates in the novel.
"We had broken through many hindrances that are powerful enough to
keep most people on the weary tread-mill of the established system, even

while they feel its irksomeness almost as intolerable as we did. We had stept down from the pulpit; we had flung aside the pen; we had shut up the ledger; we had thrown off that sweet, bewitching, enervating indolence, which is better, after all, than most of the enjoyments within mortal grasp. It was our purpose—a generous one, certainly, and absurd, no doubt, in full proportion with its generosity—to give up whatever we had heretofore attained, for the sake of showing mankind the example of a life governed by other than the false and cruel principles, on which human society has all along been based."[27] Alas, communism dashed the hopes of the characters in *The Blithedale Romance* just as it did those of its author at Brook Farm.

Problems were present from the beginning. For all Ripley's lofty aims, he did not understand how to provide for his community's most basic needs. As historian Sterling Delano notes, "Ripley should certainly have recognized that the reason Charles and Maria Ellis's West Roxbury property was, and had been, a dairy farm was because the relative sterility of the soil made it unsuitable for any other kind of farming."[28] But Reverend Ripley, like nearly 90 percent of his Brook Farm flock, was not a farmer.[29] He attempted to compensate for this handicap by reading books. Delano writes:

> Ripley went to the Boston Athenaeum and charged out *Lowe's Elements of Agriculture*, the first of many titles having to do with farming that he borrowed there. In the months before heading to the Ellis Farm in West Roxbury, where, it had been decided, the community would be located, he immersed himself in the pages of the *Farmer's Magazine*, *Laudon's Encyclopedia of Gardening*, and, the paper that he found most useful, the *New England Farmer and Horticultural Register*. He borrowed the weekly *New England Farmer* more often than any other paper.[30]

All the books in the world cannot help the best farmer yield a bountiful harvest from sandy, rocky soil.

Despite Ripley's enthusiasm, whether behind a book or behind a plow, he and his followers endured a standard of living at Brook Farm well below what they were accustomed to in the outside world. They worked harder for less. Worse still, their labor produced no spiritual or intellectual growth. It just made the laborers tired.

In *The Blithedale Romance*, Hawthorne depicts neighbors spreading tall tales of cows kicking over milking pails as the bovine jesters laughed at the Brook Farmers, members cutting off their own fingers through dilettante use of hay cutters, and communitarians cultivating weeds they thought cabbages.[31] Reality never got so bad, but it's worth noting that the Brook Farmers, who lived on a dairy farm, depended on the outside world for milk.[32] The situation was desperate. So when Ripley proposed a structural overhaul in the community's second year, members were receptive.

Leaders of communities want their communities to be part of communities. By 1844, Fourierist clubs, Fourierist articles, and full-fledged Fourierist experiments, thanks to the Johnny Appleseed propaganda of Albert Brisbane, began popping up. Ripley was won over, and so were the Brook Farmers. The farm transitioned from a Transcendentalist society into a Fourierist association in 1844, making it official the following year.

"The point that must be emphasized from the outset is that the farm was a well-grounded institution which lasted nearly six years, a respectable time for a utopian community," contends Richard Francis in *Transcendental Utopias*.[33] But the community was never well grounded.

In the fall of 1844, one of Brook Farm's many committees withdrew such basic items as meat, coffee, and butter from meals. An uproar, concentrated among boarders more concerned with getting their breakfast tea today than with ensuring Brook Farm's existence tomorrow, ensued. The community restored the vanished staples to a separate dinner table, but members required the permission of their fellow Associationists to have the meat and other supposed luxuries.[34] The situation worsened. Despite selling a pair of oxen in November 1845 for $100, the community found that their dire circumstances did not permit Thanksgiving dinner. Two generous neighbors supplied turkeys for the hapless communitarians.[35]

As the internal situation worsened, Brook Farm's leaders looked for an external savior in the form of designation by the national Fourierists as America's model phalanx.[36] But that good news, and the donations that would have arrived with it, never came. Bad news did. On March 3, 1846, a fire consumed the three-story, 175-foot-long phalanstery the community had been constructing for almost two years. The fire, likely the result of a faulty chimney, "spread with almost incredible rapidity . . . and in about an hour and a half the whole edifice was burned to the ground," the *Harbinger* reported. Brook Farm's leaders put on a brave face: "It leaves no family destitute a home; it disturbs no domestic arrangements; it puts us to no immediate inconvenience. The morning after the disaster, if a stranger had not seen the smoking pile of ruins, he would not have suspected that anything extraordinary had taken place." In fact, the blaze demoralized Brook Farmers. The community witnessed years of work, and $7,000 in material and labor, turn to ash and rubble.[37]

Six months after the fire and twelve months before the formal abandonment of the endeavor, mounting debts compelled Ripley to auction off much of his massive book collection, which had served as the basis of Brook Farm's library. "I can now understand how a man would feel if he could attend his own funeral," he lamented.[38]

Here were Boston Brahmins, Harvard graduates, descendants of the Pilgrims failing at subsistence farming, auctioning off their most prized possessions, and eating Thanksgiving dinner by the grace of charity. Could it have been any other way? No one would doubt the foolishness of a mob of illiterate farmers demanding to run Harvard College. Why did Harvard College think that it could run a farm?

THE 1840S WERE an age of homeopathic medicines, Graham bread, mesmerism, vegetarianism, abolitionism, free love, séances, phrenology, women's rights, water cures, and temperance. Following the societal democratization of the age of Jackson, in the face of slavery and other injustices, and in the midst of economic depression, antebellum America was understandably a time of causes, movements, and experiments—some fleeting, others not. "What a fertility of projects for the salvation of the world!" Emerson observed. "One apostle thought all men should go to farming; and another, that no man should buy or sell: that the use of money was the cardinal evil; another that the mischief was in our diet, that we eat and drink damnation. . . . Even the insect was to be defended—that had been too long neglected, and a society for the protection of groundworms, slugs, and mosquitoes was to be incorporated without delay."[39] It was from this milieu that Fourierism grabbed hold.

"I would rather be president of the North American Phalanx," Horace Greeley quipped, "than of the United States!"[40] The New York Tribune editor got to be neither, serving as vice president of the North American Phalanx and falling short of the U.S. presidency to U. S. Grant in 1872. The North American Phalanx endured the longest life span of any Fourierist community of the period.[41] In 1842, readers of Greeley's Tribune called for a phalanx that existed in substance rather than the phalanx that existed only in the ink of Albert Brisbane's column. Brisbane responded by calling for two hundred enthusiasts to invest $1,000 each in a North American Phalanx (NAP). The next year, a dozen investors fronted a total of about $8,000 to establish the 673-acre endeavor in Red Bank, New Jersey.

Several hundred people passed through the North American Phalanx between 1843 and 1855. At its peak, membership hit around 150. Charles Sears, a participant and chronicler of the commune, remembered that "it would scarcely be an exaggeration to say that our days were spent in labor and our nights in legislation for the first five years of our associative life."[42] The *first* five years? Of the twenty-nine Fourierist communities that dotted the American landscape in the mid-nineteenth century, twenty-seven never made it to their fifth year.[43] The NAP made it past twelve. Why?

The NAP attracted men and women accustomed to hard work. Unlike New Harmony and Brook Farm, dreamers and philosophizers generally stayed away. The communitarians learned the merits of exclusivity from failed experiments that hadn't practiced any. Between 1847 and 1850, which coincided with the collapse of numerous communist experiments, the NAP rejected 70 percent of applicants (many of whom were residents of those failed experiments in search of a new place to subsist).[44] Red Bank's proximity to the commercial capital of the Western Hemisphere, and to various waterways that they navigated with steamships they partly owned, made NAP more economically viable. Community business efforts, such as the production of America's first boxed cereal, were aided immensely by these advantages of geography. In contrast to New Harmony, where members got the run of a rich man's savings, and Brook Farm, "where bookkeeping seemed less a skill than an exercise in wishful-thinking," the NAP followed strict accounting rules.[45] These factors combined to allow the community to pay $4,000 in dividends over its first four years.[46]

Despite the publicity and noteworthy names associated with Brook Farm, the NAP clearly was in a better financial state than its sister community. With its proximity to the American Fourierist epicenter in New York, the North American Phalanx, not Brook Farm, was poised to serve as the model phalanx. This brought the NAP the financial support that Brook Farmers had sought in vain. Red Bank's phalanx benefited from thousands of dollars in loans and donations.

But if association was superior to competition, why did it need charity to keep it afloat?

Despite its aspirations as an agricultural community, the NAP, like Brook Farm, attracted just over 10 percent of its membership from the farming professions.[47] A correspondent from the sympathetic *New York Tribune* unsympathetically noted, "They find it necessary to employ hired laborers to develop the resources of the land."[48] The NAP found it difficult to retain its most skilled members. The wages they paid simply couldn't compete with the wages paid by external enterprises. In the words of Edward K. Spann's *Brotherly Tomorrows*, "Even their maximum wage of $1.13 per day was little more than half that paid to housepainters in nearby New York City."[49] William Hinds noted, "A skillful teacher, who received at the phalanx nine cents an hour, on going into the outside world was paid five dollars for two hours' labor."[50] Adding to these payment problems were planning problems. A Fourierist bureaucracy stifled enterprise and limited consumer choice. Wrote a former Fourierist, "There was what was called the Council of Industry, which discussed and decided all plans and varieties of work. With them originated every new enterprise. If a man wanted an order for goods at a store, they granted or refused it."[51]

The permanent systemic flaws that plagued the phalanx were joined by two immediate disasters that resulted in the dissolution of the NAP. In 1852, a religious schism resulted in the offshoot Raritan Bay Union, which seduced about a quarter of the North American Phalanx's members into defecting. This jolt to the community was followed in 1854 by a fire that destroyed the phalanx's new mill and $3,000 worth of purchased grain. The fire needn't have been catastrophic. Unlike Brook Farm's phalanstery, the NAP's mill was insured. The community was prepared to move on and rebuild. But a dispute over where to construct the replacement mill resulted in frank discussions about whether the communitarians were better off becoming individuals again. Rather than live under a heavy debt, they dissolved the North American Phalanx.

True believers still believed. "But all of this talk about wage-troubles, to my mind, only proves that the great objects which originally drew the members together had lost their first power over them, and that lower and more material considerations were becoming dominant in their hearts and minds," eulogized William Hinds.[52] In other words, the fault wasn't in the noble system but in the ignoble people.

Even a reporter for the *New York Tribune* was prepared to write the community's obituary a year before its actual 1854 passing: "The Phalanx people, having deferred improving the higher faculties of themselves and children until their lower wants are supplied, which can never be, are heavily in debt; and so far as any effect on the outer world is concerned, the North American Phalanx is a total failure. No movement based on a mere gratification of the animal appetites can succeed in extending itself."[53]

LEAVING ASIDE THE cold *Tribune* depiction of the NAP's dire straits, Horace Greeley's *New York Tribune* gained notoriety for serving as a "booster" paper encouraging Fourierist communities. It also famously advised Americans to go west. The organizers of the Wisconsin Phalanx followed the *Tribune*'s counsel on both counts.

In 1844, eighty enthusiastic settlers formed the Wisconsin Phalanx, which they dubbed "Ceresco." Within a few months, the hearty group had planted 120 acres of crops, completed three buildings to serve as wings for a future phalanx, and constructed a sawmill. The site, outside of Ripon, Wisconsin, ultimately attracted as many as 180 residents.

The religious differences, laziness, fires, debt, and financial disputes that struck the death knell for so many other communes spared the Wisconsin Phalanx. The lack of misfortune may have had something to do with the community's loose interpretation of Fourier's principles. Community members found that Fourier's elaborate work series schemes were "complicated, and could never be satisfactorily arranged."[54] Thus, they scrapped the master's direction. "There was a faithful attempt to carry out the complicated plan of Fourier in personal credits and the equalization of labor by reducing all to what was called the class of usefulness; and under this arrangement some of the most skilful workmen were able to score as many as 25 hours' labor in one day," noted a bemused observer.[55] They eventually proved flexible rather than dogmatic on that point, too. Soon most of the Wisconsin Phalanx shunned the community dining touted, but not decreed, by Fourier. A Fourierist principle that they stayed true to, unitary dwelling—which, according to one member, "induced many of the best members to leave"—harmed the community greatly.[56]

By 1846, Warren Chase, leader of the Wisconsin Phalanx, proclaimed to the Fourierist readers of the *Harbinger:* "Success with us is no longer a matter of doubt."[57] But four years later, Chase and his associates disbanded.

"It was a social failure, largely because we could not at the time make the home attractive and pleasant," admitted Chase. "Many thought they could do better with their means outside. We could not induce others with means to join us and purchase the stock of the discontented, as their desire to get out discouraged others from coming in, and finally the discontented obtained a majority and voted to dissolve."[58] Chase, a New Hampshire transplant who had gone west with so many of his countrymen, hoped to make Ceresco "a new heaven and new earth."[59] He didn't. But he did close his venture without debt (in great part because of rising land values). It is noteworthy that the Fourierist enterprise that followed the Frenchman's program most loosely was the only one that left its accounts in the black.

IN KEEPING WITH antebellum America's diversity of causes, not all of the period's communal experiments followed the Fourierist model.

In 1842, the followers of William Lloyd Garrison launched the Northampton Association of Education and Industry on principles of abolitionism and non-resistance. The Massachusetts joint-stock venture allowed members to retain private property, and initially paid wages to its workers. Equality, between the sexes and the races, stood as a major goal of the community.[60] To these ends, former slaves David Ruggles, who helped Frederick Douglass and hundreds more to freedom along the Underground Railroad, and Sojourner Truth, the powerful abolitionist and women's rights preacher, found a home in the Northampton Association. The association achieved income equality between the sexes, but by lowering the hourly wages of men rather than by boosting the hourly wages of women.[61]

The Northampton Association's economic situation became so dismal that the community transformed its school, which educated two of Garrison's children and served as an important industry for the association, into a repository of child labor. "In the silk growing department we find occupation for about twenty small girls and boys, who, in ordinary state of society, would be of no service whatever to their parents or themselves—but here they can at least earn their subsistence, and acquire industrious habits without being oppressed."[62] These "students" learned by working in the communally run silk mill. "By mid-1844 the community's descriptions of its schooling sought to make a virtue out of necessity by arguing that pupils learned from working, but this was a thin disguise for the increasing use of child labor," asserts historian Christopher Clark.[63] After four years, the Northampton Association, which had attracted as many as 120 people at one time, dissolved. One of the community's founders later reflected, "The millennium we thought so near seems a good way off now."[64]

In 1848, two years after the Northampton Association folded, Etienne Cabet dispatched sixty-nine followers from France to Texas to establish a new communal colony. Cabet characterized the send-off as "one of the grandest acts in the history of the human race."[65] History is not kind to judgments made in its name about the future from the past. Unlike the characters and events in Cabet's movement-launching novel *Voyage to Icaria*, the people and circumstances outside of his book rarely conformed to the author's intentions.

In Texas, the entire "Icarian" advance party fell to malaria. Things went from bad to worse when the party's only doctor lost his mind. Back in the mother country, three weeks after the advance guard set sail, the French established the Second Republic. This severely depressed interest in the Icarian colony scheme. An expected second wave of more than one thousand Icarians turned out to be a relief party of nineteen. They removed the sickly Icarians from their arid Texas habitat to connect with four hundred Icarian recruits from France. Four died on the trek from Texas to New Orleans, where several hundred skittish Icarians opted to withdraw.[66]

Cabet's vision ("The earth would be a fairy-land; the habitations palaces; the labors of the people mere pastimes; and their whole lives pleasant dreams")[67] acted as a powerful glue to hold the remaining Icarians together. In 1849, 280 Cabetian communists again moved, this time to Nauvoo, Illinois, which the Mormons had recently abandoned in great haste. After the Icarians approved of Cabet as their dictator for life, the great man abdicated. But democracy suited Cabet at Nauvoo as much as it had suited Owen at New Harmony. When a majority unfavorable to Cabet won office, the great man tried to reassume his throne. His coup failed. Cabet and his minority of followers simply refused to work, and then demanded that the state legislature repeal the community's act of incorporation. They were, as socialist Morris Hillquit noted of his political ancestors, "seemingly determined to ruin if they could not rule." Cabet, who two decades earlier had been forcibly exiled from his native France for his strident attacks on the government, found himself in 1856 expelled from the utopian community he had founded. A month later he was dead.[68]

The Icarians persevered. They founded seven colonies in all, the last of which, hounded by old age and failing principles, gave up the ghost in 1895. By the end, the group's former president recalled, "There were so few of us left it was not much different from the selfish world surrounding us."[69] From that selfish world they came. To that selfish world they returned.

BROOK FARM WAS too compromised, too worldly, and not idealistic enough for Concord mystic Bronson Alcott and Englishman Charles Lane. But so was private ownership of land and labor for financial gain, which posed problems for their alternative to Brook Farm. How to launch a commune without owning land? How to survive while avoiding work?

So not to violate scruples against private property, Alcott recruited his friend, Ralph Waldo Emerson, not to join their venture, Fruitlands, but to put the deed for the hundred acres of breathtakingly scenic Massachusetts land in his name. The land was technically deeded to Emerson but, at least in the minds of the Fruitlanders, now belonged to no one. The arrangement, the communists gleefully reported, "liberates this tract from human ownership."[70]

Work was a trickier matter. "Mr. Alcott cannot bring himself to work for gain," beleaguered wife Abigail confided to her diary, "but we have not yet learned to live without money or means."[71] This inability for the principle to mesh with the practical plagued the whimsical venture.

In Fruitlands, the Transcendentalist duo of Alcott and Lane established a "consociate family" (largely peopled by their own families) based on animal rights and other radical principles. Meat, wool, leather, silk, milk, manure, and even the use of animals to plow fields were strictly off-limits. "The greater part of man's duty consists in leaving alone much that he does now," Louisa May Alcott has her father announce in *Transcendental Wild Oats*, a fictionalized account of Fruitlands that she wrote five years after *Little Women*. "Shall I stimulate with tea, coffee, or wine? No. Shall I consume flesh? Not if I value health. Shall I subjugate cattle? Shall I claim property in any created thing? Shall I trade? Shall I adopt a form of religion? Shall I interest myself in politics? To how many of these questions—could we ask them deeply enough and could they be heard as having relation to our eternal welfare—would the response be 'Abstain'?"[72] To this series of prohibitions, Alcott's partner Lane might have further counseled listeners, in contradistinction to the Alcott patriarch's beliefs, to ditch their families for the human family.

The strange men who founded the Harvard, Massachusetts, commune attracted stranger followers: a man named Abram Wood, who, to be different, changed his name to Wood Abram; Samuel Larned, a vegetarian who dined exclusively on apples one year and crackers the next; Isaac Hecker, a celibate who heard voices and refused to eat leavened bread; Joseph Palmer, a bearded free spirit once jailed for his grooming enthusiasms (or lack thereof); and Samuel Bower, a nudist despite New England's climate.[73] "One youth, believing that language was of little consequence if the spirit was only right, startled new comers by blandly greeting them with 'good-morning, damn you,'" *Transcendental Wild Oats* reports. "A second irrepressible being held that all emotions of the soul should be freely expressed, and illustrated his theory by antics that would have sent him to a lunatic asylum, if, as an unregenerate wag said, he had not already been in one. When his spirit soared, he climbed trees and shouted; when doubt assailed him, he lay upon the floor and groaned lamentably."[74] While the Fruitlanders tolerated these and other eccentricities, they expelled Anna Page for eating a piece of fish.[75]

The high-minded eschewal of animals to till the land and of manure to fertilize the soil jeopardized the Fruitlanders' yield. Lane and Alcott jeopardized the crops further when, during harvest season, they walked to Boston, visited with radicals in New York, meandered through New Haven, and journeyed to rural New Hampshire. As Louisa May Alcott mockingly put it, "About the same time the grain was ready to house, some

call of the Oversoul wafted all the men away."[76] A historian congenially inclined toward the Fruitland patriarchs concludes, "Perhaps this tendency
to wander off just when there was important farming work to be done was
an attempt to avoid fixation in space and frozen representativeness."[77] A
less convoluted explanation suffices: laziness.

"The place has very little fruit upon it, which it was and is their desire
should be the principal part of their diet," observed Isaac Hecker, the celibate afflicted with auditory hallucinations.[78] Historian Sterling Delano
found the very name "Fruitlands" ironic "because not a single fruit tree
ever provided even an ounce of nourishment for the small group who
gathered there."[79] Starvation neared, and America's most peculiar communal experiment, filled with the most peculiar communal experi-
menters, was gone six months after it appeared. The world became more
interesting with these people in it again.

TWO YEARS BEFORE his 1837 death, Charles Fourier sent one of his detailed blueprints for the organization of humanity to the American embassy in Paris. The consul reported to a friend that the material was
"either a genuine curiosity or the emanation of a disturbed brain."[80]

Fourier offered this assessment of his own philosophy: "I, alone and
unaided, shall have confounded twenty centuries of political imbecility; it
is to me that present and future generations will owe the initiative of their
immense happiness."[81]

Fourier was neither genius nor insane genius. He was just insane. His
"scientific" explanation of the northern lights contended that "the Earth
is violently agitated by the need of creating; we see this by the frequency of
the aurora-borealis, which is a symptom of the rut of the planet—a useless
effusion of prolific fluid which can not combine with the fluid of the other
planets till the human race shall have accomplished the preparatory
works."[82] Once humanity achieved social harmony through Fourier's prescriptions, the northern lights would form an electrical crown, a ring
around the earth like Saturn's, which would alter the earth's climate, de-
salinize the oceans, and usher in new, pacific creatures. "The maritime
coasts of Siberia, now impracticable, will possess the mild temperature of
Nice and Naples," he calculated.[83] The "decomposition of sea-water by the
boreal fluid is one of the necessary preliminaries to the new marine creations," Fourier pointed out. "These creations will consist of a host of am-
phibious servants for drawing vessels, and for the service of the fisheries,
in place of the legion of monsters now infesting the sea, which will all be
exterminated by the effect of the boreal fluid and its purification of
the seas. An instant extermination will purge the ocean of these horrible

creatures which in their implacable wars serve only to symbolize the fury of our passions."[84] In addition to the new ring, the earth would receive five new moons.[85]

Giant men living for eight hundred centuries in four hundred bodies, friendly sharks and lions, oceans resembling lemonade, beings residing inside the sun—this was the Charles Fourier the American Fourierists ignored, obscured, or never saw.[86] But what they did see wasn't on the right side of sanity either, was it?

Yet somehow thousands of Americans prostrated themselves to the delusional schemes of this muddleheaded lunatic. Among those suckered were the best and brightest of the American Left: Horace Greeley, the *New York Tribune* editor who was the Democratic Party's presidential nominee in 1872; Brook Farmer Charles Dana, who served as the assistant secretary of defense during the Lincoln administration and later as editor of the *New York Sun*; James G. Birney, the two-time presidential candidate on the fringe Liberty Party ticket, who purchased a parcel of land at the Raritan Bay Union; Robert Gould Shaw, the leader of the famous Massachusetts Fifty-fourth Infantry Regiment, who spent his boyhood at Brook Farm only to return there to train when Brook Farm became a Union camp during the Civil War; Theodore Weld, the abolitionist who spent several years running Raritan Bay's school; Weld's wife, abolitionist/suffragette Angelina Grimké, who joined her husband at Raritan Bay, and Grimké's famous abolitionist/suffragette sister, Sarah, who joined them both; and William Henry Channing, a familiar face at Brook Farm who became the chaplain of Congress during the Civil War.

The control pathology displayed by socialists of all types displayed itself in exaggerated form in Charles Fourier. Like Hegel before and Marx after, Fourier saw history conforming to teleological stages. There was a purpose, a structure, to it all. Inside Fourier's head, people were not independent, unpredictable individuals, but pieces of a larger puzzle significant only when they fit themselves with the other 1,619 puzzle pieces to form the perfect whole (the phalanx). One system explained the past unhappiness, and contained the key to the future happiness, of mankind. Fourier, like so many socialists, was a political neat freak. It is comforting to impose artificial order on a disordered history, to see symmetry, patterns, and categories where none exist, to allow a single idea to explain everything, to immanentize the eschaton. It is not realistic.

Fourier's utopian promise reminded American Protestants of God's promise. But it has never been on earth as it is in heaven. Tired of waiting on God, Christians took up the millennium themselves. Christians transitioned from saving souls to saving the world. Thus, Christians transitioned from Christianity to humanism, from the New Testament gospel to the Social Gospel. How did Massachusetts Bay Colony Puritans become Massachusetts liberals? Thusly.

"There is absolute unity of opinion on . . . the sphericity of the Earth and its rotation round the sun" and that "two and two make four," Albert Brisbane pointed out. "When Human Reason more advanced, shall have discovered a Positive Theology, based like the Positive Sciences on the laws of Universal Order, the Human Race will accept it unanimously as they now accept the fundamental principles of Mathematics and Astronomy; it will then establish on the Earth ONE RELIGION, and with the reign of Religious Unity, as, by the discovery of a Positive Social Science, it will establish One Social System with the reign of Social Unity."[87]

In the name of reason, Brisbane propagated a most unreasonable course for humanity. Reason never serves unreason's ends more than when it puts complete trust in itself. Men, relying on their own reason, arrive at different, even opposing conclusions. Reasoning with the unreasonable, too, is itself unreasonable. Reason promises enlightenment, but some answers are beyond reason's reach. The diversity among the creatures employing reason, and that they are creatures and not creator, dooms the prospects of reason eliminating conflict, establishing social harmony, and solving all problems. But some faiths are unshakable, and so it was with the post-Enlightenment congregants of the Church of Reason.

Reason unaided by experience can lead one astray, as it did Albert Brisbane. Reason employed by one devoid of it will lead one astray, as it did Charles Fourier. Reason failed Horace Greeley, George Ripley, Charles Dana, and so many other distinguished Americans during the 1840s.

For Brisbane, whose unwillingness to actually join a Fourierist experiment made him especially immune to experiential contradictions to the master's theory, the delusion persevered. Fourierism had never really been tried, his lame postmortem went, so it had never really failed.[88] But twenty-nine phalanxes, by historian Carl Guarneri's count, had been launched in the United States. And twenty-nine phalanxes expired, most quickly. Few met Brisbane's threshold of 400 members, and none met Fourier's threshold of 1,620 members. "When I asked them what would have been the result if they had had this number," a New York Tribune reporter wrote in 1866 of his conversations with members of the defunct North American Phalanx, "they said they would have broken up in less than two years."[89] The most successful phalanxes were the ones that steered furthest from Fourier's instruction. The most successful Fourierists were the ones who, like Brisbane, never bothered to put their ideas to trial at all.

"I am weary of this place," Nathaniel Hawthorne's Zenobia notes of Blithedale, "and sick to death of playing at philanthropy and progress. Of all varieties of mock-life, we have surely blundered into the very emptiest mockery, in our effort to establish the one true system."[90] Hawthorne lost but a few months of his life, and $524.05, to Brook Farm.[91] His fictional character, Zenobia, loses something more precious. Before meeting her fate, Zenobia laments: "It was, indeed, a foolish dream! Yet it gave us some pleasant summer days, and bright hopes, while they lasted. It can do no more; nor will it avail us to shed tears over a broken bubble."[92]

～ 4 ～

BIBLE COMMUNISTS

Be you therefore perfect, as also your heavenly Father is perfect.

—MATTHEW 5:48

PRESENT-DAY RADICALS may find a religious fanatic who nominated Jesus Christ for president an unlikely ancestor.[1] Evangelicals may find a wife-swapping communist an unlikely fellow Bible-thumper. But Perfectionist John Humphrey Noyes, founder of the Oneida Community, was the latter *and* the former, Christian revivalist and American communist.

Born into establishment respectability, Noyes proudly pointed out in his epic *History of American Socialisms* that most Perfectionists, believers that we live on a post-millennial earth where Christ has long since redeemed fallen man, "are descendants of New England Puritans."[2] Noyes's father served in the U.S. House of Representatives, as did his wife's grandfather. His father-in-law was the lieutenant governor of Vermont. Noyes's first cousin was Rutherford B. Hayes, nineteenth president of the United States. Noyes's connection to Hayes's successor was more ignominious. A troubled former follower would murder President James Garfield.[3]

Noyes, along with his classmates at the Andover Theological Seminary and the Yale Divinity School, imbibed heavily at the fount of America's Christian revivals of the 1830s. The political upheaval of the age of Jackson permeated religious life. The common man was determined to rule not just in both houses of Congress but in houses of worship as well. The zeitgeist clearly influenced the patrician Noyes—certainly an uncommon

"common" man—who declared that "professors of orthodox religion in this day fill the front rank of the army of hell."[4] Whereas the Protestant Reformation sought to cut out the middleman of the clergy, America's revivalists sought to cut out the middleman favored by fellow Protestants: the Bible. "Under the old covenant God said: 'Do according to all I command you, and ye shall live,' " Noyes reported. "Under the new covenant, where its powers are fully developed, he may safely say: 'Do as you please; for I promise that your pleasure shall be mine. I will write my law upon your hearts.' "[5]

Noyes surmised that the second coming had already occurred, around seventy years after Christ's first coming. The world was thus already divided between sinners and saved. So on February 20, 1834, a day Perfectionists thereafter commemorated, Noyes declared: "He that committeth sin is of the devil."[6] Did Noyes mean to imply that he was without sin? He was stating it, plainly, firmly. Noyes continued to proselytize, in one instance causing an audience member to faint.[7] His overseers at Yale had had enough. They banned him from the campus and revoked his license to preach just a year after he had received it in 1833. No matter, thought Noyes: "I have taken away their license to sin, and they keep on sinning. So, though they have taken away my license to preach, I shall keep on preaching."[8]

Wandering throughout New England, the twentysomething John Noyes was a preacher without a pulpit. He also was without money, job, roof, or ride. "He is doing nothing here but talking with people as he has opportunity," Noyes's sister wrote about him to their father. "He is not earning anything, and has no funds but what I have furnished."[9] Noyes trudged from snowy village to snowy village, packing little except the word of God. Farmers gave the traveler food and shelter. Other travelers provided transportation. A few admirers sent money. Noyes had little to show for his hardships. Outside of family members and hometown acquaintances, Noyes had made few converts and many enemies. Life's head start had already been erased. The appeal of communal life for a religious theorist unwilling to earn his daily bread is not so hard to figure out.

Though Noyes appeared as a vagabond to the unconverted, he appeared as something more glorious to the converted: "If Jesus Christ has *ever* come in the flesh of his saints, I believe he is in *John*."[10] Noyes saw himself in these terms as well. He pointed to his own life as "a perfect example for imitation."[11] He referred to his own mother as "daughter" and demanded that she refer to him as "father."[12] His sanctimoniousness struck some relatives as saintly. It struck others as sanctimonious. "He is so much afraid of being influenced by *man's* wisdom and of being under bondage, as he calls it, that he will not listen to advice or reproof, especially from any of his relatives," his sister warned. "So beware!"[13]

In 1837, John Humphrey Noyes "renounced active co-operation with the oppressor on whose territories I live" and assumed "the title Jesus Christ to the throne of the World."[14] If his hatred of the government and love of himself weren't unconventional enough, Noyes developed the idea of Complex Marriage, which he soon put into practice.

Noyes's inspiration for Complex Marriage came not from the heavens but from his groin. When God widowed an old crush, Noyes sent an emissary to recruit her into his nascent love cult. Finding him and his doctrines weird, she declined, and Noyes was stuck with but one wife. But his good friend George Cragin had a wife. And in May 1846, Noyes engaged in "some personal liberties" with Mrs. Cragin. Following their dalliance, the couple sought the permission of Mr. Cragin (Mrs. Noyes had already assented to the general concept of Complex Marriage). Met with vituperation, Noyes ultimately persuaded George Cragin.[15] Mr. and Mrs. Noyes and Mr. and Mrs. Cragin were now declared man and wife and man and wife.

Ultimately, Complex Marriage wedded hundreds of people together. But New England proved inhospitable to free love. Within a year of the consummation of Complex Marriage, Noyes faced an adultery trial (another husband found Noyes's swinging proposal unpersuasive). Removed from the ranks of licensed reverends, banned from Yale University's campus, and indicted in Vermont, the preacher pariah absconded to a former Indian reservation in upstate New York. There, in Oneida, he started a commune for his followers.

WORK, ASSIGNED; MONEY, non-existent; possessions, shared: the Perfectionists lived in a world apart from *the* world. "God the Creator has the first and firmest title to all property" and "the right of distribution," the Perfectionist manifesto, *Bible Communism*, held. When humanity adopts Bible Communism, "the reign of covetousness, competition and violence, will come to an end."[16]

To this end, the citizens of the Oneida Community deeded their property to a quartet headed by God's earthly representative, releasing "all the right, title, claim and demand whatsoever that we, the undersigned, ever had, or now have, or which we or our heirs, executors, administrators or assigns hereafter can have, by reason of any matter, cause or thing whatever."[17] Oneida was so pure in its communism, author Spencer Klaw noted, "that for a time even watches were owned by the Community rather than by the men who carried them in their pockets."[18]

By the birth of the Oneida Community in 1848, the two trends that had given it life had largely faded from American life. The fires of the Christian revivals that had "burnt over" much of the Empire State during the 1820s and 1830s had long been extinguished. All but a handful of the Fourierist Phalanxes of the 1840s, too, had expired. But time stands still for the group that secludes itself on a vacated Indian reservation.

"Those of us who wish to be happy in communism will have to get rid of the idea that communism can be carried on without interfering with individual liberty," Noyes's son Theodore relayed to disgruntled Perfectionists.[19] And for most of the thirty-two years at Oneida, its residents were "happy in communism." Unlike the rundown Zoar or the malarial campsite Icaria, Oneida did fulfill the lofty dreams of many of its joiners. The gigantic mansion the communists built contains a five-hundred-seat theater, a stunningly beautiful library, a dining room to accommodate hundreds, and high-ceilinged living quarters. Green fields and trees surrounded the commune. It was a perfect setting for people who sought perfection.

But the upstate Eden came at a price. Communists exchanged personal autonomy for material comforts. "I shall watch and admonish all with whom I am associated until they are without fault," Father Noyes ominously promised.[20] He kept his word by instituting among the communists a practice called "mutual criticism." This formal, public procedure involved a single community member facing a gauntlet of criticism. Everything from reading novels excessively to spending too much time on artistic pursuits to wearing hair beyond acceptable lengths was fair game.[21] The words of friends stung. The exposure of faults embarrassed. Noyes, who undoubtedly found in mutual criticism an effective control mechanism, exempted himself from the barbs and charges of others. What god is fit for human criticism?

All of this was too much for some to take. More than 125 people, according to Oneida Community records, "seceded."[22] In this sense, nineteenth-century communists possessed a crucial freedom unknown to their twentieth-century counterparts: they could leave.

But hundreds chose to stay. During the 1860s, the community boasted 250-plus members. Prior to its dissolution, it reached a peak of about 300 members.[23] Communists desiring a break from Oneida needn't reenter the world. They could relax at the community's lakefront vacation home or move to a satellite commune in Brooklyn or Connecticut. Life at Oneida suited many just fine. The communists staged plays, performed concerts, and put on giant strawberry-and-cream parties. By day, they toiled not in monotonous fashion but at a variety of jobs: catering to silkworms, manufacturing animal traps, printing tracts, farming. By night, they met as a group and discussed religion, current events, business, and other topics of interest and concern. Though life on a commune isolated the Perfectionists from the world, it connected them, even if too closely for some tastes, with their fellow man. The stresses of putting food on the table, a roof over one's head, and money away became group stresses rather than individual ones. All shared in triumph and in tragedy.

THE BIBLE COMMUNISTS' sharing of property, work, and a mansion struck others as peculiar. That they shared wives struck others as criminal. "The fashion of the world forbids a man and woman who are otherwise appropriated, to love one another burningly," Noyes reported. "But if they obey Christ they must do this."[24] So Noyes's followers obeyed.

Noyes may have coined the term "free love," but love at Oneida was obligatory, directed, monitored—everything but free. A committee, which reported to Noyes, reviewed all proposals for sex. If the petitioner had questioned or in some way annoyed Father Noyes, the petition might be denied. In the more likely event that the committee approved the proposal, a set of "Rules for Sexual Intercourse" governed the passionate encounter. The sex committee, and the tight quarters the communists lived in, enabled Noyes to know the innermost details of his followers' sex lives. Any partners forming too tight a bond would soon be divided. Coupling or intentionally reproducing without Noyes's permission was grounds for expulsion. Prior to the advent of Complex Marriage, one couple married without first seeking the blessing of Father Noyes. He expelled the newlyweds for their "act of gross and deliberate insubordination."[25] There is, then, more than a grain of truth in Noyes's admission that "there has been far less freedom in sexual intercourse among us than there is in ordinary society."[26]

Noyes liked sex but not its consequences. He watched his wife suffer through several miscarriages, and noted the economic drag that children had on his community. Noyes thus "discovered" a method to cheat sex of its gift. Noyes called his method "male continence." Male continence is the sexual act sans male climax. Misunderstanding human nature, or at least male human nature, Noyes held that "men are entirely competent to choose in sexual intercourse whether they will stop at any point in the voluntary stages of it."[27]

Noyes believed that in formulating this technique he had made "a valuable addition to science," and that "the true story of the discovery should be put on record."[28] He did so in his pamphlet *Male Continence*. He directed his followers to put into practice his methods—lest they become impoverished by hordes of babies leeching off the community's bottom line. Noyes directed men who failed to withhold ejaculation to hone their skills on post-menopausal women—or sent them into sexual exile. Accidental pregnancies occurred, but there were, surprisingly, few. However silly male continence appeared in theory, Noyes's idea worked near to as advertised in practice.

The children the community did bring into the world were raised less on biblical guidelines than on ones found in Plato's *Republic*. Mothers nursed their children, but they didn't mother them. With one gigantic family—everyone married to everyone, every woman a sister, every man a brother—children had numerous parents rather than two. The community removed children from their birth mothers shortly after their first birthday and sent them to the Children's House. There they lived with other children. Designated community members oversaw their development. Noyes believed this scientific method of raising children, as opposed to the anarchic method of automatically granting biological parents the right to rear their offspring, had eradicated "sickly maternal tenderness." The accounts of former inhabitants of the Children's House suggest otherwise. "What she felt during these periods I can only guess," Corinna Ackley Noyes explains of the mother who had been separated from her as a small child,

> but I can remember my own feelings well when, during one two-week period of separation, I caught a glimpse of her passing through a hallway near the Children's House and rushed after her, screaming. She knew— what I was too young to know—that if she stopped to talk with me another week might be added to our sentence. There was no time to explain. Hoping, I suppose, to escape, she stepped quickly into a nearby room. But I was as quick as she. I rushed after her, flung myself upon her, clutching her around the knees, crying and begging for her not to leave me, until some Children's House mother, hearing the commotion, came and carried me away.[29]

Although Noyes condemned abortion, his rhetoric justifying male continence would be echoed a century hence by the promoters of the "terrible deed." Noyes held that "good sense and benevolence will *very* soon sanction and enforce the rule that women shall bear children only when they choose. They have the principal burdens of breeding to bear, and they rather than men should have their choice of time and circumstances, at least till science takes charge of the business."[30]

Science, or something calling itself science, soon took charge at Oneida. Desirous of numbers—Perfectionists weren't celibate Shakers, after all—Noyes carefully selected subordinates to partake in a reproductive experiment in 1869. The experiment "deserves a distinct name," Noyes wrote, "and we will take the liberty to call it *Stirpiculture*."[31] Later socialists would call it eugenics.

The community kept detailed records, as a "service for race-culture," that noted head size, weight, and other characteristics of the stirpicultural babies. The record book they printed sought "to preserve the characteristics, physical and mental, of the future parents of the Community, for comparison with their offspring, and to serve as a guide to improvement in propagative combinations."[32] Let down by God's failure to unite heaven and earth, the Oneidans now aimed to perfect humanity in a genetic rather than strictly spiritual manner. The generational time line of this scientific endeavor contrasted with the believed imminence of God's Kingdom reigning over the temporal world. Having waited, and waited, for the millennium, the eugenics enthusiasts could never hope to live long enough to see the perfection of humanity under their experiment.

The community's offspring, like the community itself, needed to be planned to perfection. Complex Marriage was ideally suited for this. "Undoubtedly the institution of marriage is an absolute bar to scientific propagation," Noyes opined. "It distributes the business of procreation in a manner similar to that of animals which pair in a wild state; that is, it leaves mating to be determined by a general scramble, without attempt at scientific direction."[33] John Humphrey Noyes himself provided that "scientific direction" at Oneida. He concluded, whether through science or a more primitive impulse, that he was ideally suited for mating with Oneida's most eligible ladies. He so decreed it. The women under his influence complied. In all, stirpiculture produced nearly sixty children between 1869 and 1880. Noyes fathered nine of these children and Noyes's blood flowed through nineteen of them.[34]

The mother of one of Noyes's stirpicultural children was also his niece. By partaking of incest, Noyes practiced what he preached. "A male animal may sometimes be paired with his daughter, granddaughter, and so on, even for several generations, without any manifest bad results," Noyes reported.[35] Unlike a future enthusiast of eugenics, Noyes identified his master race as the Jews of the Bible, a "superior variety of the human race" made so by the "practice of breeding in and in."[36] Noyes found both science and religion approving of incest.

There is no evidence that Noyes's attempts at "breeding in and in" included his own daughters. But much evidence is gone. To avoid further embarrassment, descendants incinerated thousands of pages of documents in the 1940s that detailed the community's history.37 What could be worse than what is already known? The answer is lost to history.

More problematic for Noyes than his familial relations was his decision to introduce teenagers to sex. Twelve to fourteen, Noyes judged, was the ripe age for a girl's deflowering. But if a boy of proximate age shared the pleasures of the girl's bed, the experience might be underwhelming and foster a negative sexual attitude within the girl. Someone older, more experienced, would have to initiate the teen virgins, someone like . . . John Humphrey Noyes. By devising a concept called "ascending fellowship" that paired the inexperience of youth with the wisdom of elders, Noyes secured himself first dibs on the fit girls of the community. Father Noyes's benevolence was interpreted as predacious by the community's other fathers. But why? Weren't such taboos contrary to the progressive spirit that ruled Oneida? Hadn't the specialized love of a father for a daughter been done away with by community child rearing? Wasn't John Humphrey Noyes in direct communication with the invisible world?

Nothing will shatter illusions so thoroughly as a creepy senior citizen desiring to know your pre-teen daughter.

For these and other reasons, the Oneida Community came apart. Outside, ministers and moralists sought prosecution for imagined transgressions that paled next to transgressions unimagined. Inside, Noyes's poor health and poor judgment cultivated factionalism. His decision to anoint his son as his successor, despite Noyes's professed opposition to "specialized love" and *his son's disbelief in God*, caused Bible Communists to wonder if they were really dealing with God's earthly agent. Would these unhappy subordinates dare snitch to the authorities about Noyes's affairs with pre-teen girls and his own relatives? Such questions most certainly went through Noyes's mind when confronted with a Syracuse newspaper story that reported his imminent arrest. In the face of danger, John Noyes did what he had done thirty-two years earlier in Vermont. He fled. In the middle of the night in June 1879, without announcement, Noyes made off to Niagara Falls, Ontario. He never returned to Oneida.

A DRESS REHEARSAL for the twentieth century was played out in rural New York from 1848 to 1880. In the name of heaven on earth, a strongman directed his followers to give him everything so that he could allocate material goods based on fairness and equality. In pursuit of human perfection, a strongman dictated who must procreate and who mustn't procreate. The utopian delusions of Russia and Germany were first the utopian delusions of Oneida.

Like all socialists, John Humphrey Noyes sought control. He gained it over the religious beliefs, property, travel, sexual lives, and children of his followers. When faced with losing control, he abandoned his life's project. "I was the president from the beginning, called not by vote of the members but by the will of God, and as such I formed the Community," he reminded rebellious communists. "That relation between me and the Community has remained through its entire history. There has never been a time when I did not claim the prerogative of criticism and final decision over the whole Community and over every member of it: and there has never been a time when the Community as a whole did not concede me that prerogative. We have had free discussions, but these discussions on the one hand have been proposed and granted by me, and on the other hand have been brought to a close by me, and the final decision has been referred to me as judge after the debate."[38] People who want control over others seldom accept the control of others over themselves.

Thirty-eight years before Indiana put forth the modern world's first eugenics law, Bible Communists initiated a eugenics experiment that brought nearly five dozen children into the world—and kept many more out. Seven decades before Bolsheviks united heaven with earth in Mother Russia, the Perfectionists did so in Oneida, New York. A century before the pill, John Noyes sold the bargain of more-sex-less-children through male continence. And before hippie gurus counseled followers to "make love, not war" in the turbulent 1960s, John Humphrey Noyes did the same in the more turbulent 1860s by instructing his followers to buck the draft. Oneida's Perfectionists anticipated future Lefts. Economic collectivism, free love, hostility to the nuclear family, pacifism, anti-Americanism, and eugenics—forever "new," "fresh," and "cutting-edge" ideas—characterized the outlook of the inhabitants of Oneida's Mansion House. The world did not begin in the 1960s.

Bible Communism favored direction over freedom, a design over the organic, the communal over the private, conformity over individuality, the centralized over the divided, flawless man over fallen man, and autocracy over democracy. It professed man's perfectibility and then blamed man's imperfections for the system's collapse.

The socialist distrusts man and resents God. Man is subjective, autonomous, and non-conforming. Without coercion, man won't do what other men *know* he should do for the good of all. God is all-powerful and all-knowing. This is an affront to the socialist, whose system—not some deity—explains all of human history and can direct the affairs of all present humanity. The socialist either links himself to God, as John Noyes did, or denies His existence, as Karl Marx did. When man dethrones

God, man's penchant for ungodliness is unlimited. Child rapist John Noyes proved this in the nineteenth century. Mass murderer Joseph Stalin proved this in the twentieth century.

John Humphrey Noyes suffered an unhappy ending. Convinced of the rectitude of his ideas but confronted by their failure, Noyes lashed out: "Communism is not for swine, but only for the sons and daughters of God."39 His Complex Marriage ended in one big divorce. The stirpicultural children who were to usher in a race of supermen were now called bastards by lowly children without such a scientifically determined pedigree. Seven years after sneaking off, John Humphrey Noyes died in self-imposed exile on April 13, 1886.

The Oneida Community's end, on the other hand, was a new beginning. As their leader's grip on the community loosened in the late 1870s, Oneidans lunged for freedoms unknown to them. One scandalized spinster noted "a strong effort to get long hair and long dresses going."40 Harriet Skinner complained of communist youth "amenable to no authority and under no moral instruction."41 Theodore Noyes, onetime atheist dauphin of the Oneida Community, recalled "some of the younger generation" leaning toward "Agnosticism or Scientific Materialism."42 Frank Wayland-Smith, a trusted advisor to Noyes, bluntly wrote to the community's leader in exile: "There is among the young women a powerful sentiment in favor of marriage, pure and simple."43 The dam was about to burst.

On August 28, 1879, the Oneida Community abandoned Complex Marriage. Three days later, Oneida's governing committee took up a petition brought by F. A. Marks: "Martha J. Hawley and I wish to get married, and desire to learn what steps are necessary to enable us to."44 Another couple, living by the never-give-a-bureaucrat-a-chance-to-say-no rule, infuriated the committee by informing its members of their decision rather than asking permission. By the close of the year, more than thirty other Bible Communists had married.45

On New Year's Day 1881, Bible Communists ceased to be. The community embraced the free market. "A good many have gone to work today that haven't done but precious little for months and months," Julia Ackley noted on January 3, 1881, two days after the transformation of the Oneida Community into Oneida Community, Limited.46 A new day had dawned. The scene at the Mansion House previewed Eastern Europe at the end of the next century. The older generation mourned times gone by; the young celebrated a wide-open future.

And wide open the future was. Oneida Community, Limited marketed their canned fruit, animal traps, silk, and eating utensils. Ultimately, they focused on flatware. They sent former communists to South America, Australia, and Europe to open up markets. Their factories employed workers in Toronto, Canada; Sheffield, England; and Oneida, New York. They reinvested profits in advertising in 1910—"the first 'pretty girl' advertising in America"—and the company took off.[47] The community that forbade its sons to fight the Civil War paid "full factory wages to employees who had enlisted in the Spanish American War"; manufactured knives, cartridge cases, periscopes, and gun parts during World War I; and earned four "E" awards from the military during World War II as 742 of its American workers left for wartime service.[48]

The Bible Communists became everything Marxist communists hated: wage employers, global capitalists, and rich. Oneida became the world's leading manufacturer of flatware. Alas, a century and a quarter after the Oneida Community's dissolution, Oneida Community, Limited declared bankruptcy.[49] As the company lays off workers, relocates factories, and defaults on pensions, John Humphrey Noyes wonders from the grave why no one questions the system in which it rose and fell.

~ 5 ~

ANTEBELLUM REFORMERS

For God doth know that in what day soever you shall eat thereof, your eyes
shall be opened: and you shall be as Gods, knowing good and evil.

—GENESIS 3:5

"SHE IS, I think, a Mesmerist, a Swedenborgian, a phrenologist, a homeopathist, and a disciple of [hydropathy founder] Priessnitz—what more I am not prepared to say," Edgar Allan Poe noted of his friend Mary Gove Nichols.[1] Her biography, and that of her second husband, Thomas Low Nichols, for that matter, tells the story of the antebellum Left in microcosm. The couple was who the radicals called "radical."

Mary Gove Nichols was the "Where's Waldo?" of the antebellum Left, appearing *somewhere* in the scene of virtually every reform movement. She ran a boarding house based on the dietary and health principles of Sylvester Graham—vegetarianism, no tobacco, no alcohol, no coffee, and most importantly, lots of Graham bread. She authored a pamphlet, *Solitary Vice*, warning of the dangers of masturbation ("Almost every form of disease may be produced by it.")[2] She took her wedding vows in a Swedenborgian ceremony. Along with her new husband, she opened in 1851 the American Hydropathic Institute, the nation's first medical school based on the principles of the water cure—for the uninitiated, the act of bathing in cold water, drinking vast amounts of water, purging oneself with water. An interest in hydropathy resulted in several businesses—she reported making $99 (more than $2,000 in 2007 money) in a single week in 1849, and the same monthly about a decade later—based on the ideas of cold-water enemas, vaginal syringes, cold-water baths, full-body douches, and damp-towel wraps.[3] She advocated free love. She launched communal endeavors. In 1855 at Modern Times, a community of individualists on Long Island started by Josiah Warren, the father of American anarchism who learned to despise centralism, conformity, and direction while living under it at New Harmony, the Nicholses launched the short-lived School of Life, a free-love community within a community. She communicated with spirits. Spirits communicated with her. She showed up, in the background or in the foreground, of the myriad reformist crusades that predated the Civil War.

Reform the body, Mary Gove Nichols believed, and society will follow. "Believing all sickness to be the ultimation of sin in the individual, or the inherited consequence of the sins of our progenitors, I am of necessity a religious teacher," Nichols maintained. "If there were no sin, there would be no sickness."[4] Reformers like Nichols sought to cure what ailed America by purifying it of sin.

Antebellum America is a time of forgotten causes. The communes were the foci of these causes. Christianity was the inspiration.

The religious Left saw in political activism a way for men to live according to biblical precepts, to prepare for the millennium, to redeem sinners, to do on earth as it is in heaven. They, not Christ, would redeem mankind. "That is the only true church organization, where heads and hearts unite in working for the welfare of the human race," reflected one abolitionist.[5] The focus of religion shifted from worshipping God to serving men. But what of the dangers of mixing religion with politics? "Mix them, and mix them, and mix them," one abolitionist counseled, "and keep mixing, until they ceased to be mixed, and politics became religion and religion, politics."[6] Thus did politics become a religion. Thus did Christians become atheists.

The emergence of race-, sex-, and, to a lesser extent, class-based political agitation coincided with the communal period. Communitarians involved themselves in the age's multitudinous causes. Some communitarians found the peripheral causes distracting to communism, the sun around which so many political creeds orbited. Others, such as Mary Gove Nichols, fervently served the political creeds by using the communes as platforms to showcase their panacea of choice. Most saw in the communes the clearinghouse, the proving grounds, and the nerve center of reform.

THE UGLIEST BLIGHT that radicals sought to eliminate, slavery, colors the way that twenty-first-century observers view nineteenth-century politics. History forgets that abolition and the commune competed for the allegiance of nineteenth-century activists.

The Garrisonian Northampton Association, Frances Wright's Nashoba, and the Raritan Bay Union of Theodore Weld and the Grimké sisters demonstrate the attraction communism had for abolitionists. Before the South seceded from America, the communists did. If the surrounding society was inherently sinful and tainted by slavery, abolitionists could create a separate society that rejected the evils of the surrounding culture. But as not all abolitionists were communists, not all communists were abolitionists. The abolitionism of the residents of Northampton, Nashoba, and Raritan Bay stood in contrast to the racism, and indifference to it, exhibited at many other communes.

New Harmony's Constitution expressly forbade the membership of blacks. "Persons of color may be received as helpers to the Society, if necessary; or if it be found useful, to prepare and enable them to become associates in Communities in Africa; or in some other country, or in some other part of this country," the document explained.[7] The North American Phalanx promptly evicted the ex-slaves who had for decades inhabited the land on which the Fourierists hoped to inaugurate utopia.[8]

On the crucial issue of the antebellum era, most communists punted, or worse, fanatically counseled abolitionists to abandon their anti-slavery activism in favor of the One True Reform, communism.

In a fit of hyperbole, Robert Owen favorably compared the life of black slaves to white wage earners:

> Those whom you employ are now the slaves of the non-producing classes in society; and you are no better, under this system, than mere slave-drivers; with this difference upon the part of your slaves, compared with those I have seen in the West Indies, and in the Southern States of North America, that your slaves have no legal claim upon you, when you do not require their services, for houses, food, clothes, medicine, and medical advice, when necessary; all of which coloured slaves have, and are, therefore, free from the excess of anxiety and corroding care with which your white slaves are overwhelmed.[9]

The followers of Charles Fourier sang from the same sheet of music. The lead article in the *Phalanx*'s inaugural number attacked abolitionists as fanatics, called for gradual emancipation through reason, and warned against prematurely ending slavery before a better arrangement could be found. Slavery "should not . . . be attacked first, and above all not separately. There are other social evils growing out of the same original falseness in the present system, which are equally unjust and oppressive as slavery, and which first demand our consideration." The Fourierist journal obtusely dubbed chattel slavery as one of "nine different kinds of slavery," which included "Hireling Dependence," "Domestic Service," "Perpetual Monastic Vows," and "Poverty." "There are upon the earth over two hundred millions of human beings condemned to absolute slavery, and to limit our efforts to the enfranchisement of three millions of slaves in our own country, and to contemplate giving them only corporeal liberty, seems to us to be taking a very narrow and insufficient view of the grand question of a reform of Slavery. The talent, energy and means which are now devoted to abolition agitations, should be directed to the discovery and application of means for effecting the abolition of universal servitude upon earth."[10] That meant discarding abolitionism and adopting the principles of Charles Fourier, for them the Rosetta Stone of all reform.

Baby steps were backward steps. The fanatic could conceive only one giant leap for mankind.

Mary Gove Nichols seconded the Fourierist resentment at the attention paid to black slaves. "The Northern wife is worse off than the Southern slave," she recalled boldly telling Garrison. While she later backed off from that claim, she still maintained that wives endured oppression similar to slaves'.[11] In 1853, the year Harriet Tubman launched her line of the Underground Railroad, Nichols designated numerous crimes as more menacing than chattel slavery: "Modern finance is a scheme of oppression and slavery."[12] She even penned what she hoped would be the *Uncle Tom's Cabin* of marriage: *Mary Lyndon*, a hardly fictionalized autobiography featuring a woman who becomes a Quaker and gets trapped in matrimony with a husband who withholds her income, burns her mail, and forbids her from writing poetry. The material came straight from Mary Gove Nichols's horrible first marriage. "Reader," the novel lectured, "have you any clue of principle to guide you through the chaos of false social relations? Do you believe that God intended women and negroes for freedom?"[13]

Abolitionists, understandably, came to resent the rhetoric comparing paid workers and married women to chattel slaves. In time, abolitionists viewed the communist fixation on northern capitalists as fodder for the propagandists of the South's peculiar institution. "As early as 1846," historian Carl Guarneri writes, "the Garrisonians had decided that *The Harbinger* and its critique of free labor were essentially proslavery, and now the southerners' use of the socialist critique seemed to realize their fears of a sinister alliance between hypocritical slaveholders and northerners more interested in economic reform than in moral purity. Had not the Fourierists sparred with [Wendell] Phillips over 'wage slavery' in 1847 just as [George] Fitzhugh was doing in 1855? Even abolitionists sympathetic to communitarianism, such as Adin Ballou and Theodore Weld, backed away in the 1850s."[14]

But others backed away from abolitionism. Like antebellum communism, abolitionism was a religiously inspired movement. God had sent the abolitionists on a righteous mission, and any means of doing God's work was moral. The abolitionists' own extremism alienated those otherwise sympathetic.

One part of the anti-slavery movement appealed to the lofty rhetoric of the Declaration of Independence and the brash actions on behalf of freedom by the Minutemen at Concord and Lexington. These opponents of slavery saw themselves as the conservators of the American tradition. It was slavery, they reasoned, that contradicted American values. Others lashed out at America for slavery, ignoring world history and arguing that something uniquely sinister within America fostered slavery. William Lloyd Garrison, for instance, advocated secession, hoped for a Mexican victory in the Mexican-American War, and burned a copy of the Constitution on the Fourth of July in 1854.[15] Still other abolitionists, such as Frederick Douglass and Wendell Phillips, vacillated between cloaking abolitionism in patriotic garb and fiercely assailing America.[16]

The War Between the States proved problematic for the Left. Leftist historians have depicted the conflict as a rude interruption of impending radical progress, rather than an agent of progress itself. The Depression-era history *Rebel America* laments that "the radical philosophies then attracting so much attention in Europe would undoubtedly have gained a foothold in the United States had it not been for the increasing tension over slavery."[17] "The psychology of patriotism, the lure of adventure, the aura of moral crusade created by political leaders, worked effectively to dim class resentments against the rich and powerful, and turn much of the anger against 'the enemy,' " Howard Zinn notes in 1980's *A People's History of the United States*.[18] "Northern wage earners who rallied to the Union cause became allied with their employers."[19]

The war presented non-resistant abolitionists with moral dilemmas. War was bad. Slavery was bad. But what about a war to end slavery? Among the war's many victims was non-resistance, the Garrisonian ideal that had eschewed political participation and any form of coercion. When the war for union transitioned into a war to end slavery, most non-resistants, if they hadn't already, abandoned pacifism and picked up the gun. They still, curiously, considered themselves pacifists.

"Christ says, 'If a *man* smites thee on the one cheek, turn to him the other also,' " explained Charles Stearns, a correspondent in "bleeding Kansas" for Garrison's *Liberator*. "These Missourians are not men. I have always considered that, bad as they were, they had an infinitessimal [*sic*] spark of divinity in them; but . . . our invaders were wild beasts, and it was my duty to aid in killing them off. When I live with men made in God's image, I will never shoot them; but these pro-slavery Missourians are demons from the bottomless pit and may be shot with impunity."[20] "We must put them down, utterly down, as wicked rebels against God," opined Samuel May, who had earlier condemned Elijah Lovejoy for defending his press and person.[21] "Every slaveholder," Garrison expressed after John Brown's ill-fated Harpers Ferry raid, "has forfeited his right to live, if his destruction be necessary to enable his victims to break the yoke of bondage."[22]

As Yankees and Confederates commenced slaughtering one another, one Garrisonian noted: "Events have so changed the position of affairs that our old-time policies are no longer applicable."[23] Indeed they had.

WOMEN PLAYED A major role in anti-slavery movements. More than half of the four hundred thousand signatures the American Anti-Slavery Society (AASS) collected in its 1837–38 petition drive came from women.[24] Probably a still greater percentage of women collected those signatures. The issue of slavery was controversial enough. Now women's rights confronted the abolitionists from within their own house. Feminists charged that they, like the southern slave owners, were oppressors.

In 1838, many men boycotted the New England Anti-Slavery Convention, outraged that women were permitted to attend. They believed that linking abolition, already an unpopular cause, with alien causes would only drive abolitionism further from the mainstream.[25] In 1839, single-issue abolitionists seceded from the Massachusetts Anti-Slavery Society (MASS) to form the Massachusetts Abolition Society. "The [Massachusetts Anti-Slavery] Society is no longer an *Anti-Slavery* Society *simply*, but in its principles and modes of action, has become a *women's-rights*, *non-government Anti-Slavery Society*," lamented the reverend Amos Phelps, who had resigned his MASS leadership position in protest.[26]

The regional spat over women's rights went national. In 1839, women finally gained election as AASS delegates. Abbey Kelley won a position on the AASS committee the following year, and that proved the final straw for abolitionists repulsed by the organization's creeping feminist direction. They walked out, never to return.[27]

Women speaking at abolitionist churches and at abolitionist meetings generated controversy among the listeners, and often radicalized the speakers. The abolitionist Liberty Party became the first U.S. political party to support female suffrage; women within the party received votes for president and vice president at conventions in 1847 and 1848.[28] The logic of anti-slavery, the mere involvement of women in politics, and the internal disputes over women's roles in the movement all pointed activists toward women's rights.

The women's rights movement found some of its most articulate exponents within abolitionism and on the commune: women's rights pioneers Sojourner Truth, Angelina and Sarah Grimké, and Frances Wright all involved themselves heavily in abolition and communal projects. Crossover abounded within the reform efforts.

For women frustrated with the limitations of nineteenth-century America, the commune presented an ideal to project fantasies upon. It also presented real opportunities not generally found outside. Communes offered women easier situations to rear children, cook, and wash clothes, broader employment opportunities, and a less restrictive social life. Widows, often dependent on charity on the outside, could lead dignified lives in group settings. But what was the norm in society—males running things, women excluded from governance, a gender gap in wages—was the norm in the communes, too. Communities generally deferred to male leadership, barred women from internal votes, and codified wage disparities between the sexes.[29]

The upper-class women involved in volunteerism—to save the drunk, to save the slave, to save the child from labor—grew frustrated at their inability to institute reforms. Amidst work for so many causes, the women found a new cause: themselves.

The Seneca Falls Declaration of Sentiments had very little impact on the America of 1848. But it is a significant document because so many of the demands it articulated would eventually be granted.

The Seneca Falls Declaration, adopted by a conference of anti-slavery activists concerned also with women's rights, was at once radical and reformist, revolutionary and conservative—much like the anti-slavery movement that gave birth to it. On the one hand, the document called on women to "refuse allegiance" to the government, which it described as a "tyranny" and a "despotism." On the other hand, it appealed to the American tradition by modeling itself on the Declaration of Independence. It also reflected the religious obsessions of its time, referring to God or religion more than a dozen times.[30]

The document called for participation in the society it denounced. Women wanted the right to speak in public meetings, to divorce equitably, to preach the gospel, to work in whatever profession, to attend whatever college, to vote.³¹ This last point sparked controversy at Seneca Falls, but for peculiar reasons: the Garrisonian non-resistants who peopled the convention opposed voting, no matter which sex cast the ballots.³²

Mary Gove Nichols found the ballot mania peculiar, too, but for different reasons. "It would be a gross injustice to allow married women, slaves, or children under the control of their parents, the right of suffrage," Nichols and her husband wrote. Woman suffrage really awarded woman's oppressor—her husband—two votes, the Nicholses reasoned, because of the marital rite's stress on uxorial obedience.³³

A week after the Seneca Falls Declaration was adopted, with the room "filled with the perfume of flowers," Mary Gove Nichols met her second husband at the altar. "It was a truly happy day—the happiest of my life," Mrs. Nichols contended.³⁴ But the timing in proximity to the Seneca Falls convention proved no ironic contrast between women's liberation and marital submission. Mary vowed fidelity to her own desires. "I enter into no compact to be faithful to you," she told Thomas Low Nichols. "I only promise to be faithful to the deepest love of my heart."³⁵ The groom had no problem with any of this, and likewise pledged allegiance to himself.

Six years after their wedding, the couple—who claimed "as blessed a union, probably, as now exists, or ever existed, upon this earth"— ironically authored a book denouncing marriage as an evil worse than prostitution and slavery.³⁶ They directly blamed marriage for business fraud, poverty, disease, crime, stinginess, and masturbation.³⁷ The happily married couple styled themselves as marriage abolitionists and offered complete sexual freedom as the replacement to connubial binds: "Would the loving union of one man with seven women, and of one woman with seven men, provided no health law were violated, and no harm in any way done to society—would this love be a curse to you, or to others?"³⁸ The Nicholses weren't oblivious to the radical nature of their message. "In God's name, let us destroy society," they wildly exclaimed.³⁹

"What a folly, then, to talk of Woman's Rights," the Nicholses scolded the Seneca Falls activists, "while upholding an institution which comprehends all of Woman's Wrongs!"⁴⁰ To the Nicholses, the Declaration of Sentiments—so radical to so many in its time—called for milquetoast reforms. Marriage needed to be abolished before women's suffrage could make a difference. As Mary later remarked of feminist contemporaries, "These women know not what they ask."⁴¹

Nevertheless, the women kept asking—nay, demanding. Two decades after the Seneca Falls meeting, feminists surmised that they finally had their opportunity, in the reconstruction following the Civil War, to attain their voting rights alongside the newly freed slaves. As congressmen debated the Fourteenth Amendment, women's rights activists schemed to extend the amendment's verbiage to include women as well as blacks. But the feminists failed. "Some of them, including [Susan B.] Anthony and [Elizabeth Cady] Stanton, thought it would be better if the amendment were defeated, while others, including [Lucy] Stone, argued that if women could not win their political freedom, it was well that Negro men could win theirs," observed historian Aileen Kraditor.[42]

This split foreshadowed a schism in the women's rights movement that lasted decades. "In 1869," Kraditor wrote, "two separate organizations came into being: the National Woman Suffrage Association (led by Mrs. Stanton and Miss Anthony) and the American Woman Suffrage Association (led by Henry Ward Beecher and Mrs. Stone). The split lasted until 1890 when the two factions merged into the National American Woman Suffrage Association (NAWSA), and a new era in woman suffrage history began."[43] Divided, the suffragists accomplished little. United, in a later age, the suffragists would, like the abolitionists whence they came, accomplish their goal.

TEMPERANCE PROVED A far more popular crusade for antebellum women than suffrage. The crusade to put down the bottle predated the United States.

Medical doctor and founding father Benjamin Rush attempted to persuade his fellow countrymen of the health benefits of temperance by authoring several tracts against alcohol. In the mid-nineteenth century, clergymen such as Lyman Beecher led campaigns to elicit pledges forswearing alcohol. Voluntary conversions, however, failed to satiate the intemperate drive for temperance. Starting with Maine's prohibition law of 1851, the temperance crusaders began to impose their beliefs on entire states, à la the anti-tobacco crusade of today. All of New England, New York, and eight other states followed Maine's example.[44] The Civil War, which had made numerous reform efforts irrelevant, broke up that initial prohibition crusade. As with woman suffrage, the seeds of prohibition were sown by antebellum reformers but reaped by progressive era do-gooders.

To hasten Christ's second coming, many Christians increasingly came to believe that man had to achieve spiritual *and* physical perfection. As the American Physiological Society (APS) explained, "The millennium can never reasonably be expected to arrive, until those laws which God has implanted in the physical nature of man are, equally with his moral laws, universally known and obeyed."[45] For the APS, this meant eating Graham bread, abstaining from alcohol, and becoming vegetarian. For others, especially Mary Gove Nichols, it meant partaking of hydropathy, the water cure. Perhaps in a moment of excitement, perhaps as an attempt to convince herself, Louisa May Alcott, in her diary at the short-lived Fruitlands, exclaimed: "I love cold water!"[46] There the water cure's popularity reigned. But there winter came and with it the end of Fruitlands and enthusiasm for cold-water baths.

Still others, the enthusiasts of phrenology, sought physical perfection through examining the size and characteristics of the human skull. The Bible Communists, for instance, dutifully measured the skulls of newborns, noting the phrenological characteristics for their experiment in eugenics.[47] If men could determine character and intelligence through the circumference of, and bumps on, one's head, then they could scientifically breed a better race—a perfect race. One man's quackery is his great-grandfather's science.

And so much of what Mary Gove Nichols thought science we think quackery. She followed Sylvester Graham and his dietary proscriptions. She forgave the abuse of her first husband because the phrenological pattern of his head indicated to her that he couldn't help his beastly nature. She swore off traditional medicine as "one of the greatest evils that now rests on the civilized world." She employed magnets and spirits to cure sickness.[48]

A direct line extends back from the current Left to Mary Nichols. She advocated free love. She declared war on traditional religions, though she claimed that her ideas followed the divine path. She established communal living arrangements to replace individual families. She preached the curative power of alternative medicines.

Her most radical act proved too radical for radicals. She converted to Catholicism.

AS THE NICHOLSES dabbled with their latest reform, spiritualism, Francis Xavier and Ignatius Loyola contacted the couple and implored them to become Catholics. In 1857, to the horror of their activist friends, they converted. After a lifetime of searching for the solution, of floating from one cause to the next, Mary Gove Nichols and Thomas Low Nichols found permanence in that most permanent of institutions: the Catholic Church.

"We have just come to life," Mary informed a poet friend of her baptism. "[A]ll our 'Reforms' are changed to us now. We move only with the approbation of the Church. We condemn what the Church condemns, & strive to live fully to its discipline." America's most notorious proponent of free love acknowledged, "This may seem strange to you: indeed it was to us, but we are now humble believers in the Emmanuel . . . and the Church that He established. We are unspeakably happy in this faith, and ask only to be allowed to live and die humble Catholic Christians."[49] To the amazement of skeptical Catholics and stunned reformers, they did just that.

If that radical act of conversion didn't put the coda on this age of radicalism, the event that inspired the couple's next act would. Disgusted by the Civil War and the government crackdown on dissidents, the Nicholses surreptitiously boarded a boat and sailed to England. They never returned.

HAD THE NICHOLSES come back, to America and the Left, it would have been to a country and a movement greatly altered from the ones that they had departed. Perhaps they would have recognized the postbellum Left as a mutation from their Left, but they never would have conceded it as their Left. Responding to a straw man's contentions that the masses must dictate right and wrong to the individual, including fashion tastes—"we are to work to a true idea"—Mary Gove Nichols's fictional mouthpiece in *Mary Lyndon* declares, "The sentence, '*We* are to work,' contains the chit and the very germ of despotism. You take it for granted that two or more men can live the same life. No two ever did or ever could. No two spires of grass, no two leaves, are exactly similar. Each must grow according to its own life-law. So must you and I. I have wants of appetite, of taste, of Being, generally, that are not yours."[50] Because Nichols did her own thing and not the masses' thing, she belonged to the antebellum and not the postbellum Left. "I am called to serve God, and not the world," she further wrote in *Mary Lyndon.*[51] But God, like mere persuasion, played less and less of a role in future Lefts.

The Civil War is the demarcation point between an agrarian America and an industrial America, between the United States plural and the United States singular, between a mind-your-own-business, laid-back country and a mind-your-neighbor's-business, crusader state. This bloody event had massive ramifications for the American Left.

Communal experiments persisted after the Civil War, but the "communitarian moment" had clearly passed. For all their bombast, Robert Owen and Albert Brisbane focused on small communities rather than an entire nation. If the nation were to become one massive commune, and they certainly believed that it would, it would do so voluntarily, by the inspiration of example, and not by force. The economic activity to usher in utopia would be growing food rather than manufacturing goods.

Local instead of national, persuasion instead of compulsion, agriculture instead of industry—all of this seemed passé after the example of the Civil War. Karl Marx's violent, one-size-fits-all, industry-centered ideology meshed better with the post—Civil War American Left than did the gradualist, experimental, agrarian-centered projects of the antebellum years. Compounding these changes to America was the influx of immigrant masses, who brought Old World ideas such as Marxism.

"There was a common conviction shared by antislavery men and women, woman's rights advocates, and pacifists (especially nonresistants) as their causes evolved in the antebellum period, propelled in part by events and in part by the logic of abolitionism itself," historian Ronald Waters writes in *American Reformers*. "They all expressed a belief that the world should be ruled by God's law, not force, and that people could act morally and of their own free will."[52] All that would change when Jefferson Davis ordered the siege of Fort Sumter. Like the two world wars, and perhaps 9/11, the Civil War marked the end of one Left and the beginning of another. All causes seemed minor next to the cause of uniting the states and freeing the slaves. The Left viewed communism as the One Big Cause, but history vindicates the fight against slavery as the One Big Cause of the era. With the example of a righteous path blazed through violence, completed by the industrial North in the face of resistance from the agrarian South, and forged through the entire nation, the coming Left took note.

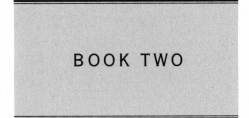

BOOK TWO

REFORMERS AND RADICALS

~ 6 ~

THE AMERIKAN
INTERNATIONAL

And I saw a new heaven and a new earth.

—APOCALYPSE 21:1

THE GERMAN KARL Marx was one in a long line of communist prophets. His predecessors included the Welshman Robert Owen and the
Frenchman Charles Fourier.

Marx coined neither "socialism" nor "communism." He expropriated
them, just as he urged his followers to expropriate the bourgeoisie's property. In particular, he latched on to "communism" because "socialism"
had been so closely associated with Robert Owen. Like so many leftists
who came after him, Marx refused to acknowledge his debt to the leftists who came before him. Gods can't have ancestors.

In terms of ends, little distinguished Marx from Owen, Fourier, or
Cabet. Like his forerunners, Marx noted that "the theory of the Communists may be summed up in the single sentence: Abolition of private property."[1] He targeted the family for extinction. "Do you charge us with
wanting to stop the exploitation of children by their parents?" Marx and
collaborator Friedrich Engels asked in *The Communist Manifesto*. "To this
crime we plead guilty."[2] "Communism abolishes eternal truths, it abolishes all religion, and all morality, instead of continuing them on a new
basis; it therefore acts in contradiction to all past historical experience."[3]

What, precisely, did Marx say there that Owen hadn't in his Declaration of Mental Independence? Private property, the family, and religion

had been the bogeymen of leftist rhetoric long before *The Communist Manifesto*'s 1848 appearance. So why did Marx, rather than one of his predecessors, become *the* leftist prophet? It was no accident of history.

In terms of means, Marx differed from those he mocked as "utopian socialists." Owen, Fourier, Cabet, and others put the onus for socialism's ultimate success on non-socialists. They tasked socialists with proving the merits of their program by example. It was up to non-socialists to decide to adopt the program. To Marx, this was laughable: "Hence, they reject all political, and especially all revolutionary, action; they wish to attain their ends by peaceful means, and endeavour, by small experiments, necessarily doomed to failure, and by the force of example, to pave the way for the new social Gospel."[4]

Marx put the means to attain socialism in the hands of his followers. They would institute by violence what previous prophets of the Left had hoped to institute by persuasion.

THE EARLY MARXIST parties in America were an extension of European Marxist parties. After the doomed revolutions of 1848 in France and Germany, political émigrés brought Old World ideas to the New World, especially the notions of two German expatriates, Karl Marx and Friedrich Engels.

Joseph Weydemeyer was one such immigrant bringing Marxism across the Atlantic. Like many socialists, Weydemeyer, who would soon fight for the Union in the Civil War, found the commercial nature of the republic offensive. "I did not go to America of my own volition," he wrote Marx and Engels shortly after his 1851 arrival, "but I must confess that so far I have seen nothing which can awaken within me the slightest affection for America. I don't think there is another place where one encounters the shopkeeper's mentality in more revolting nakedness. Any other aim in life besides making money is considered an absurdity here, and you can see it on every face, on every brick."[5] Instead of adjusting to his new surroundings, Weydemeyer went about adjusting his new surroundings. He helped establish the Proletarian Club, the Workers' League of America, and other groups in the 1850s that laid the groundwork for bringing socialism from Europe to America. He wrote and edited the German-language Marxist publications *Die Revolution* and *Die Reform*. He shopped the writings of Marx and Engels to American publications, finding them a home in Horace Greeley's reform-minded *New York Tribune*, which had played so crucial a role in propagandizing for that earlier socialist prophet Charles Fourier.[6]

The seeds Weydemeyer left sprouted. His associates launched a

communist club that ultimately found affiliation with the First International. Tellingly, this, America's first branch of the International, did not
affiliate until several years after the International's 1864 founding conference. Though the organization touted itself as a worldwide force, the International Workingman's Association initially took little interest in the world
beyond Europe and the world beyond Europe took little interest in it.

Karl Marx hijacked the First International in London from workingmen, and strangely hoped that workingmen would flock to an organization
that had just been stolen from them. They didn't. Other intellectuals, with
competing theories, did.

In America, reformers of the previous age, including Horace Greeley
and Wendell Phillips, rushed to support the First International.[7] The
dream of millions of men of hundreds of nations uniting under the One
True Cause appealed to leftists in the 1860s and 1870s just as it had appealed to them in the 1820s when Owen came to America and in the 1840s
when Albert Brisbane imported the ideas of Fourier. Briefly, in the early
1870s, an alliance between established American leftists and Continental
Marxists seemed possible. But, as the Yankee reformers discovered, Marx
did not accept allies, only followers.

The Yankee Internationalists saw Communism as one reform within a
cornucopia of reforms. The Marxist Internationalists saw Communism
as the only reform.

Woodhull & Claflin's Weekly, the first U.S. publication to print *The Communist Manifesto* in English, briefly served as the International's American mouthpiece.[8] The women behind the weekly were the loud and
colorful sisters Victoria Woodhull and Tennessee Claflin. Star attractions
in the family's traveling scams, the young Victoria practiced medical clair-
voyance on Ulysses Grant's near-deaf father and sister Tennie fled a
manslaughter indictment and a ward of terminal patients after her
cancer-curing elixir cured only gullibility.[9] They took their hustle to more
fertile grounds: Wall Street. Woodhull biographer Lois Beachy Underhill
notes, "The sisters projected good breeding and sexual availability, gentil-
ity and sensuality: 'ladies' in the drawing room, lovers in the bedroom."[10]
Victoria ingratiated herself with the reformist community by bedding
the powerhouse Reverend Henry Ward Beecher and his forever-linked
parishioner Theodore Tilton; Massachusetts congressman Benjamin
Butler; Benjamin Tucker, last of the Yankee anarchists; and doubtless
other unchronicled conquests. Tennie tagged the biggest prize in
Cornelius Vanderbilt, who subsequently underwrote many of the sisters'
ventures.[11] It was a match. The commodore liked sex and dripped money.
Tennie liked money and dripped sex.

Politics became a racket like fortune-telling, magnet healing, and marital gold-digging. Tennessee volunteered herself to command a state militia regiment in New York while Victoria ran for president of the United States. The duo fell short of their ostensible aims but generated much publicity. A female president? Women soldiers? The publicity stunts made some people laugh and others think.

Though Woodhull did not get sworn in as president in 1872, the National Association of Spiritualists made her their president the year previous. From that perch, she announced that the spirit world encouraged the reform of the material world through woman suffrage, free love, communism, and other causes popular among leftists present and the ghosts of leftists past.

Woodhull rejected the separation of religion and politics as a "delusion." "Instead of having nothing to do with politics, religion should be the rule governing all political action." She combined politics and religion in what she called "the religion of humanity."[12] In doing so, she reversed the traditional roles of faith and reason in relation to religion and politics. With table rappings, the appearance of apparitions, and communication from the dead through mediums, Spiritualism offered "a religion based not on conjecture but fact."[13] Politics, on the other hand, required faith in any number of untried schemes.

On what commandments did Woodhull's "religion of humanity" rest?

First, faith in reason to solve conflict: "[T]he apparent clashing arises from the fact that when people express themselves they do not properly formulate their own thoughts." In other words, disagreements stem from misunderstandings rather than fundamental differences. Second, eschewal of absolutes in favor of relatives: "To the cannibal the taste of human flesh is very good; while to us the mere thought is horrible, is revolting. And yet, the cannibal, equally with us, is the offspring of the Great Creative Power, and as rightfully and legitimately possessed of his taste for human flesh, as we are of a predisposition against it." Third, social responsibility instead of personal responsibility: "Scarcely a single act of any person can be traced, wholly, to circumstances within his control; in fact, almost all acts are largely the result of causes over which the actor can have no possible power." Fourth, cooperation supplanting competition: "The profit making system together with the theory of demand and supply as the regulators of price, are the relics of the semi-barbarous ages, which the new theory of industrial equity—of equal rights, equal opportunities and equal compensation will soon relegate to the limbo of the past, and forever settle the present vexatious and irritating questions between labor and capital." Fifth, acceptance of a single cause by every human being: "This unitary idea of humanity is no idle nor wild Utopian dream."

Though the religion of humanity abolished heaven and hell, it promised beautiful rewards for faith and dire consequences for disbelief. "Believe it or not," Woodhull preached, "unless a salvation, now seemingly hopeless, come to this generation, a destruction such as has never yet overwhelmed the world must surely come. In the far-reaching, all-embracing principles of Spiritualism as the Religion of humanity, does this hope, this salvation reside, since they are as potent as they are comprehensive."[14]

Woodhull & Claflin's Weekly acted as a bridge from the antebellum Left to the grimy, industrial Left. Even while it served as the International's official publication in America, it consistently printed the articles of familiar reform personalities from the antebellum era. New Harmony communist-turned-anarchist Josiah Warren, Fourier's evangelist Albert Brisbane, and Mary Gove Nichols's free-love disciple Mary Chilton were among the voices of the age gone by who found a place in the newspaper. At the same time, the sisters' weekly regularly attacked Horace Greeley and his *New York Tribune*. The leftover Left didn't receive automatic deference from the upstart Left. The antebellum reformers who stayed relevant adapted to the changing times, which generally meant putting justice for workingmen closer to the forefront of reforms and acknowledging Karl Marx as a visionary. The various ingredients in the postbellum Left made for a strange concoction.

The six-year history of *Woodhull & Claflin's Weekly* features a vast array of causes. Stephen Pearl Andrews contributed a regular column on the "Pantarchy"—the world government. Andrews highlighted the New Catholic Church, which he imagined as the future humanitarian religion of earth, and provided instruction in Alwato, an invented language that Andrews imagined would subsume the cacophony of tongues.[15] *Woodhull & Claflin's Weekly* touted the virtues of stirpiculture and euthanasia, and condemned marriage and the death penalty.[16] Amidst leftist reforms that strike moderns as, well, modern, the publication also discussed communication with spirits, predicted the date for the likely end of the world (which passed without event), noted extraterrestrial life on Saturn, and prominently featured advertisements from magnet healers, mediums, clairvoyants, and other assorted shamans.[17]

What was the dogmatic Marx to think seeing his ideas in print aside articles on reincarnation?[18] His shoddy treatment of the Yankees—1870s versions of the utopians he had castigated in 1848's *Communist Manifesto*—provides the answer.

As Marx purged the International of European rivals, cleansing the American sections of "bogus reformers, middle class quacks, and trading politicians" fell to Marx's deputy in Hoboken, the German immigrant Friedrich A. Sorge.[19]

At 1871's close, the mandate of the German-dominated central council of the American branch of the International neared its end. A new election would certainly shift power from German immigrants to native Yankees. Sorge, described as "more Marxist than Marx," secretly convened a meeting of the delegates of the immigrant-dominated sections one hour prior to the meeting advertised to all the delegates.[20] At the covert gathering, the immigrants named themselves the new Provisional Federal Council and established rules barring the native Yankee sections from participating in the International. The Yankee sections arrived at New York's Tenth Ward Hotel at the scheduled time only to find the immigrants well into their meeting. An angry shouting match broke out. The betrayal necessitated a schism, and henceforth both a Yankee International and a Sorge International claimed to represent the International Workingmen's Association in America.[21] This would be the first split for Marxists in America, but not the last.

The Yankees naively believed that as soon as the General Council of the International in London discovered this usurpation it would side with right. They sent William West to England to plead their cause. Unbeknownst to the Yankees, Marx's henchmen had hidden from the General Council the prior correspondence detailing the Sorge clique's abuses, and shared only the information that strengthened Sorge's case.[22] Thus, when West arrived in January 1873, the council refused to seat him as a delegate and expelled him from the premises. His section, after all, had been suspended by Sorge's council in America. When West knocked upon Marx's door, the theoretician refused to see him.[23]

The old man persevered. He traveled to The Hague, where the International was holding its first multinational gathering in two years. West managed to gain the floor and detail the slimy tactics Sorge had employed to expel the native American sections. But by then, even West, who had arrived with high hopes, knew that his rhetorical broadside was an act of mere catharsis.

To Marx, the Yankees were bourgeois reformers interested in frivolous issues such as woman suffrage, spiritualism, and global brotherhood. To the Yankees, Marx was an Old World autocrat. "The days of the International under the despotism of Marx, Sorgee [sic], & Co. are numbered," boasted *Woodhull & Claflin's Weekly* after coming to terms with the perfidy, "a sovereign section of what pretends to be the most democratic society in existence is summarily ejected from affiliation by a more high-handed outrage than any monarch of modern time would dare perpetrate."[24]

The despotism Sorge had introduced in America was a microcosm of the despotism Marx imposed on the entire International. Rather than leave outcomes to the uncertainty of ballots, Marx usurped the decision-making power of elected delegates in a largely unelected council. That centralized council, rather than the delegates representing the sections in Europe and North America, suspended groups, including America's Section 12, that proved recalcitrant in accepting Marx's dogma to the letter.[25] When the outcome of the International's Hague Congress seemed uncertain, Marx's acolytes forged credentials for those without them. "This man, Sorge," West wrote with disgust, "seemed abundantly supplied with blank credentials, to be filled up with the names of any persons he could find willing to enter the service of Marx & Co."[26] Engels spread his wealth around to fund the travel of delegates supporting Marx.[27]

West could see that he was pleading his case not to the International but to Marx's cronies. Heartsick and cash-poor, he managed to travel from The Hague back to London. There, the former tinsmith and policeman was reduced to begging the U.S. embassy for the few pounds necessary for return passage to America, a situation that, the industrialist Engels cruelly gossiped to the boardinghouse landlord Sorge, "amused us greatly."[28]

WEST'S CASH CRISIS resulted from Victoria Woodhull's legal crisis. Shortly before West harangued the closed-minded delegates, Woodhull, in an act of political blackmail, boldly outed America's most beloved preacher as an adulterer. Henry Ward Beecher, brother of Harriet Beecher Stowe and rector of Brooklyn's Plymouth Church, refused to endorse free love from the pulpit, so *Woodhull & Claflin's Weekly* exposed him as a practitioner of free love in the bedroom. Woodhull had bedded both Beecher and Theodore Tilton, the Christian newspaperman whose wife received Beecher's affections. Woodhull's peccadilloes escaped inclusion in the hit piece. The mudslinger soiled her target, but muddied herself, too. Charged with obscenity, the first female presidential candidate spent Election Day incarcerated. Unleashing the most notorious sex scandal of the age brought the sisters heightened newspaper sales but diminished fortunes and reputations. Woodhull's second husband, Colonel James Blood, who had promised West funds for passage home, withheld the subsidy because of the unforeseen legal and financial troubles.

William West left London penniless. Victoria Woodhull and Tennessee Claflin arrived there four years later with visions of the mother lode. With scams dried up in America, the sisters fixed their aim on the English aristocracy. Victoria denied that she had ever promoted free love and even changed the spelling of her last name to escape her past. The sisters concocted noble lineages. Tennie bagged a baronet, granting her the ironic title "lady." Victoria, purchasing her own engagement ring when a rich suitor vacillated, tacitly threatened her paramour with a lawsuit should he refuse marriage. He acquiesced, and Victoria eventually inherited one of the greatest fortunes in England.[29] In love, in health, in money, in politics, the artful sisters knew the ease with which hopes lent themselves to exploitation. They also knew, exemplifying the history of the American Left writ small, the value of disavowal and reinvention.

THE DALLIANCE WITH Marxists disgusted Americans schooled in republican virtues and unschooled in the strongman ways of Europe. After the purge of sections dominated by native-born Americans, the International's remaining immigrant-dominated American sections descended into internecine bickering—in German.[30] They quickly disappeared. The International itself, which ironically moved from London to New York at the congress that gave its imprimatur to the expulsion of the native American sections, similarly evaporated.

Marx chose to rule and then his rule ruined. *Woodhull & Claflin's Weekly* concluded that "it cannot be expected that Americans, with American ideas, either can or will submit to any foreign systems of arbitrary control."[31]

The Marxists never came around to the American way. In time, some Americans came around to the Marxist way.

7

KNIGHTS OF LABOR, IMMIGRANT ANARCHISTS, AND WHITE-COLLAR REDS

The labourer is worthy of his reward.
—TIMOTHY 5:18

BEFORE KARL MARX fingered the workers as the means for making real his idealized world, Robert Owen had. Before Marx and Engels released their manifesto, Charles Fourier's disciples in America had injected themselves into the workingman's movement with an eye toward using "wage slaves" as the transformative agent. Marx copied. He then had the gall to project his own lack of credentials as a workingman upon the Fourierists and Owenites, whom he dismissed as "bourgeois" reformers. In truth, Marx, like Fourier and Owen, and much of the Yankee International for that matter, was himself a bourgeois reformer. The radical prophets of the day shared many traits, but one common denominator stood out: they didn't partake of physical labor.

For much of the nineteenth century, secular millennialists courted the workingman. Had they dispensed with the visions of a heavenly future, they might have made more headway. Blue-collar workers wanted higher pay, shorter hours, and better working conditions. They didn't want free love, phalansteries, Alwato, revolution, Graham bread, or whatever other panacea the secular millennialists happened to be offering. But the secular millennialists kept offering.

The American labor movement developed with the constant interference of millennialist schemers. The worker became another's object, but he had his own objectives. Rather than remain pawns in another's chess match, unions eventually moved to their own chessboard. But not before a long seduction of the workingman by Owenites, Fourierists, Marxists, and other schemers resulted in numerous false starts and aborted endeavors.

ROBERT OWEN'S DREAM of communal utopia didn't die with New Harmony. The former company-town industrialist reinvented himself as an organizer of workers in 1830s Great Britain. At the same time, his son, Robert Dale Owen, immersed himself in the nascent labor movement in New York.

The modern American labor movement was started in Philadelphia by a group of mechanics in the late 1820s. They organized the Mechanics Union, which ultimately won the ten-hour day within the city, and then the Workingmen's Party, which put the laborers' interests up for a vote. Laws keeping adolescents in schools and out of the factory and limiting workdays to ten hours spread beyond Philadelphia.

Robert Dale Owen and his close friend Frances Wright, of Nashoba commune free-love infamy, targeted the workers in New York state. Whereas aristocrats Owen and Wright, along with mechanic and labor editor George Henry Evans, stressed compulsory education that removed children from families at an early age, machinist Thomas Skidmore fixated upon property distribution schemes (which later so enamored Evans). The workers tired of Skidmore's panacea, then tired of Owen, Wright, and Evans. By 1831, New York's Workingmen's Party, which had started just two years prior, was dead.[1]

Maintaining the unions that gave life to the Workingmen's parties proved difficult once hard times arrived in the 1830s. As depression set in, laborers took the wages they could get and unions lost leverage. Their issues absorbed by the major parties, the economy playing havoc with their politics, and outside agitators dividing the ranks, the Workingmen's parties died and so did many of the unions that gave rise to them. But what started in Philadelphia provided lessons for future organizers: to beware of aristocrat agitators, that workingmen can force political change, and that a union's ties loosen once jobs become scarce.

The post-Owen communitarians who surfaced in 1840s America concerned themselves with diverting the workers' movements to communitarian ends. For the members of the Oneida Community and the North American Phalanx, this meant becoming communist capitalists— employing large numbers of outside workers in profit-making schemes as they advocated the joys of cooperation.[2] The presence of laborers at Brook Farm enhanced the community's bottom line but made life uncomfortable for old-money Yankee intellectuals unaccustomed to such vulgar company. "Soon after this Fourierist agitation began" among the workers, Brook Farmer Arthur Sumner remembered, "some very unpleasant people appeared on the scene. They seemed to us boys to be discontented mechanics. They soon fell into a group by themselves. After dinner, they would collect together in the great barn, and grumble; and when others passed through, the malcontents eyed them with suspicion, and muttered 'Aristocrats!' "3

The "Fourierist agitation" Sumner referred to also involved commune leaders inserting themselves in the fledgling labor movement. As well-to-do Christians embarked upon their agrarian experiments, industrial workers agitated for better conditions and better pay. The communists took notice. They took their message to industrial laborers.

The *Harbinger* and the *Phalanx* frequently reported on the burgeoning workingman's movement. The Fourierist journals opined that "competition is directly and positively hurtful and ruinous to all and at all times," complained that self-interest is "the guide in all business matters," and maintained that "[l]abor is the origin of all wealth."4

If one gleans a proto-Marxist vibe from the small-"c" communists and the workingmen they admired, it is only by reducing all leftist thought to its relationship with Marxism and by ignoring the workingmen's decidedly anti-Marxist sentiments. While they embraced Marx's theory of surplus value—simplified, the notion that profits amounted to ripped-off, unpaid labor—they displayed no enthusiasm for economic determinism and rejected outright Marx's call for class warfare. For example, an 1844 meeting of the mechanics and workingmen of Boston, which caught the notice of the *Phalanx*, resolved: "That while we contend for the *rights of labor*, we show no hostility to *capital*; seeking merely the peaceable possession of the one, and determined only to resist *the aggressions* of the other, and conceding willingly to ALL the rights we would claim for our-selves."5 The following year, the New England Convention of Mechanics and Working Men met at Lowell, Massachusetts, and labeled as "one of the great primary evils . . . [t]he divorce and separation between capital and labor, which arrays the capitalist against the laborer, and the laborer against the capitalist and produces reciprocal hostility, aggression, injustice and hatred, widens the distinction and division of classes, and leads to the subjection and oppression of the one by the superior management and advantages of the other."6

The small-"c" communists, like the later capital-"C" Communists, took a paternalistic view of workers. Brook Farmer Charles Dana, who fantasized of a workingman's movement "in our hands," remarked to *New York Tribune* writer Parke Godwin in the fall of 1844, "We are in fact the only men who can really point out their course for them & they can hardly help looking to us for their advisors." Goodwin responded to Dana: "The working classes are ready for us—and absolutely ask for instruction and guidance."[7] The public condescension was nearly as brazen. The *Phalanx* noted of a workingman's publication, "To our brothers, then, engaged in the *Labourer*, who have caught a partial glimpse of the coming Light, we extend our warmest sympathy, in the hope that they may soon be led to see that all for which they are sighing and struggling is provided for in the Social Science discovered by Fourier."[8]

At the opening convention of the New England Working Men's Association in 1844, the delegates recommended a campaign for a ten-hour workday. "Almost immediately, however, the campaign was submerged," Joseph Rayback reports in *A History of American Labor.* "The convention had not only attracted workingmen but Fourierites and land reformers, and the persuasive eloquence of these delegates shifted the attention of the convention from the ten-hour day to utopianism and homesteads."[9] The problems faced by the Workingmen's parties of a decade earlier were repeating themselves. The patrician reformers thought they knew the interests of the workingmen better than the workers themselves did.

But as the communists suffered their own problems, they gradually ceased trying to solve the problems of workers. Relieved of the distractions of the utopians, the Bay State workers resumed their campaign for a ten-hour day. The effort succeeded. By the 1860s, a Grand Eight Hour League of Massachusetts coaxed the state's Republican Party to build its issue into its platform. Labor convinced the Bay State to establish the nation's first state bureau of labor statistics.[10] The relatively modest goals of the workers had been achieved. The Fourierist goal, heaven on earth, never came.

And those very different goals, more than anything, highlight the unbridgeable gulf between the workers and the utopians. It was the hereafter versus the here and now, spiritual as opposed to material, saving the world against saving some extra money. Workingmen and Yankee reformers favored different parties, spoke with different accents, and came from different pedigrees. But the most important distinction involved the contrast between the practical, attainable desires of the worker and the impractical, unattainable hopes of the utopian. The worker wasn't going to forgo putting food on his family's table to usher in the millennium, and the utopian wasn't going to delay the millennium to feed a hungry child. There would never be a rapprochement between these very different groups with very different aims. There would be repeated attempts.

·   ·   ·

ONE SUCH ATTEMPT came in 1866, when the coachmakers and iron mold-
ers united to form the National Labor Union (NLU). The venture expanded
to numerous trades, making it America's first bona fide national trade
union. The NLU discouraged strikes and friction between labor and management, and advocated the eight-hour day and cooperative enterprises.
Northwestern historian Gerald Grob noted that "the National Labor
Union was more a reform movement than a modern job- and wage-
conscious phalanx, and drew more from the humanitarian heritage of the
ante-bellum period than it contributed to the development of a modern
labor ideology."[11] Strangely, the monetary program of Edward Kellogg and
the land-reform ideas of George Henry Evans, both by this time decades
old, came to dominate internal NLU discussion. The actual laborers
within the ranks ballooned to several hundred thousand at the union's
1869 peak and questioned what any of the holdover reforms of the previous era had to do with bettering their conditions in the present.[12]

Old allies became adversaries within the new framework of labor
unions and industrialism. The NLU expelled Susan B. Anthony, who had
earlier struggled for credentials within the union, when she found employment for a group of women as strikebreakers. Reformers, who had
championed abolition in the earlier age, butted heads with workers, who
viewed blacks as capitalist tools whose willingness to work for lower wages
resulted in weakened unions and broken strikes.[13]

By 1870, the Cigar Makers' Union decided to leave the NLU "for the
reason of it being an entirely political institution, and no benefits deriving
therefrom."[14] An 1872 NLU-sponsored foray into presidential politics
ended in disaster, and that same year, a mere seven delegates attended the
NLU's convention. A familiar obituary was written for the union: death by
immersion in politics, meddlesome upper-class reformers, and a changing economy. The NLU's quick collapse taught future unions a lesson
against embracing politics to the exclusion of bettering workplace conditions and pay.

Around the time of the NLU's demise, workers made a second, more
successful attempt at a national labor union. Caught up in the national
mania for secret societies (and the reality of jurists finding in labor organizations conspiracies against trade), Uriah Stephens and fellow Philadelphia garment workers formed on Thanksgiving Day 1869 the Noble Order
of Knights of Labor of America, cryptically known as "*****," with each
star designating a word of the order's name. Passwords, secret handshakes, and cryptic signs soon followed. The Knights eventually dropped
much of the secrecy and the quasi-religious rituals, but the mystique
remained.

Unlike previous efforts at organizing workers, the Knights of Labor stayed firmly in the grip of labor. Though the union ventured inside the political arena—Terence Powderly, Grand Master Workman of the Knights during its heyday, served as the mayor of Scranton, Pennsylvania, for six years—it focused on bettering the conditions of workers by pressing employers as well as the state. Instead of Owenites and Fourierist meddlers, the Knights of Labor faced Marxists and anarcho-communist agitators infiltrating their ranks. The interlopers viewed Grand Master Workman Powderly with disdain. Powderly reciprocated. "I have noticed that most of the spouters and mouthers of bolshevism could not be guilty of having ever soiled their hands with honest labor," Powderly later reflected in his posthumously published autobiography.[15]

The Knights' Declaration of Principles warned, "The alarming development and aggressiveness of great capitalists and corporations, unless checked, will inevitably lead to the pauperization and hopeless degradation of the toiling masses." To check *great* capitalists and corporations required a *great* union. Of the government, the Knights demanded a bureau of labor statistics; restrictions on transfers of public land into the hands of private industrialists; safeguards and measures for occupational safety and health; the recognition of trade unions by incorporation; a graduated income tax; postal savings banks; state seizure of telegraph, telephone, and railroad service; and restrictions on child, convict, and foreign labor. For themselves, the Knights preferred arbitration to strikes, pooled resources for emergencies, required three-fourths of locals to be composed of wage earners or farmers, and banned lawyers, bankers, stockbrokers, and those involved in the alcohol trade from membership.[16]

Long before the federal government became a welfare state, Powderly demanded that it do so. "It seems to me that something should be done by the national Legislature to relieve the distress of the people who cannot find employment. There are improvements to be made in all parts of the country where men could be set to work if Congress will only enact the proper legislation."[17] Conveniently, such legislation would help eliminate low-wage competition to union workers, just as legislation eliminating child and prison labor, "protecting" women from night work and dangerous industrial work, and barring immigrant labor eliminated competition. Labor unions almost universally favored such restrictive legislation. Union leaders recognized labor as a commodity, and worked to keep the price of their commodity as high as possible. This meant banning the competition. Violence worked to do this. The law worked to do this better.

Like the NLU, the Knights united diverse trades under its protection—not just the garment cutters in one factory, but the garment cutters in competing factories; and not just the garment cutters, but the bricklayers, carpet weavers, the brewers, the machinists, and so forth. Workers needed something greater than a mere guild for leverage against absentee industrialists employing thousands in diverse fields across state, and sometimes national, lines. Workers consolidated as the industrialists had.

Terence Powderly bragged that he never ordered a strike. He preferred negotiation, and only if that failed would he consider a strike, and then he would only agree provided that the proposed strike met four conditions: justice, the exhaustion of all other honorable options, an even chance of victory, and the possession of enough cash reserves to fund the strike and the temporarily unemployed strikers.[18] Powderly acted conservatively in pursuit of radical ends. Why so cautious? "Precious lives were lost in strikes; homes were wrecked and children deprived of education through strikes, millions of dollars were lost to labor through them, and in the main this great waste and loss could have been avoided."[19] Contra Marx, Powderly did not see workers as a means to an end; he saw them as ends in themselves. He saw them as people. Powderly came to his ideas not in the British Museum but on the shop floor. In the days when a strike meant a *strike* and not just a mere work stoppage, Powderly knew that employers would not turn the other cheek when struck.

Ironically, the Knights' sharp rise in prestige in the mid-1880s resulted from a threatened strike against Jay Gould's railroad interests. Gould caved to the Knights before they even wielded their might. "The Gould strikes made the Knights the undisputed leaders of the labor movement," historian Joseph Rayback writes. "While their membership and influence had been growing steadily through those years, occasioned largely by the assistance the Knights had given the unorganized, the growth had been slow. The Gould strikes completely changed the pace. Labor at last had found an organization capable of wringing concessions from employers. All the bitterness and resentment which had accumulated among workingmen during two years of depression, all the frustration produced by wage cuts, all the fury created by employer use of Pinkertons, black lists, and yellow-dog contracts suddenly burst forth to create a wild rush to join the ranks of the Knights of Labor."[20] From 7 members in 1869 the Knights expanded to 69 after a year, to 50,000 after a decade, and to more than 500,000 by 1886's end.[21]

AS TERENCE POWDERLY edged the trade union movement into the American mainstream, anarchism endured a reverse "Yankeefication." Thoreau retreating to Walden and withholding his coin from the tax man, Lysander Spooner undercutting the post office with a private mail service, and Josiah Warren launching Modern Times as a disunited nation of free spirits upon Long Island yielded to Johann Most touting dynamite over ballots, Leon Czolgosz murdering the president, and August Spies cajoling a labor union to declare, "Death to the foes of the human race."[22] A do-as-you-will anarchism became a do-as-I-will-it anarchism. Anarchism became its opposite but retained its name. The black flag from Europe smothered the star-spangled anarchism that predated the migrant hordes.

Anarchism's transformation highlighted two competing strains on the wider Left. One face of the Left says: *Smoke whatever, bed down with whomever, and live however.* Another face says: *We will tell you how to run your business, we will spend your money better than you do, and we will uplift private behavior to conform to our public ideal.* This tension is on display most obviously in anarchism, where extreme libertarianism gave way to extreme compulsion. This Jekyll and Hyde phenomenon, juxtaposing a Freedom Left with a Force Left, endures. And many who start out for freedom drift to force when freedom fails to bring forth the results, behaviors, and beliefs that they had expected it to unleash.

"Anarchists," chronicler Corinne Jacker noted, "believe in the perfectibility of mankind and that, left to himself and properly educated, man would voluntarily act in an ethical and socially beneficial way."[23] The antebellum anarchist who saw anarchism as a means to this perfect end might have found it easy to defect in frustration from individualist anarchism to anarcho-communism. For anarchists who saw anarchism—government by the person as opposed to government by the people—as the end, no frustration with the results of anarchism could be so great as to change their minds.

But, in the soot-saturated age following the Civil War, imported anarchism didn't so much change minds as it alarmed and upset them.

Marxism, anarcho-communism, and organized labor all faced the same problem: the American public saw them as foreign movements based on alien principles pushed by strangers speaking strange tongues. The causes that did not "Yankeefy" faced great hurdles. Though the workers occupied center stage in the scene envisioned by Marxists and anarcho-communists, they, in large part, refused the starring role offered them.

Only more radical elements embraced the violent methods of confrontation advocated by anarcho-communists and Marxists but heretofore generally discouraged by labor unions. In the anthracite region of Pennsylvania, Irish immigrants who mined the coal brought with them such alienating customs as drinking, fighting, ethnic insularism, and faith in the ancient Roman church. The Molly Maguires combined booze, brawling, nationalism, and Catholicism in a terrorist organization whose maleficent deeds calcified native hostility to the newcomers. During the 1860s and 1870s, the Mollies lethally settled scores against those who collaborated with the government to enforce the draft, against ethnic rivals, against mine bosses, against lawmen, and against one mine owner.[24]

The Molly Maguires, through intimidation, ethnic solidarity, and sympathy of aims, evaded prosecution until a detective from the Pinkerton agency, James McParlan, bravely infiltrated the ranks of the murderous secret society and brought it down. Ten Mollies ultimately turned against their brethren, and the secrets of the secret society began to spill out. By 1877, the state hung its last Molly and the group's last victim had felt its brutalities. Upon eradication, Molly Maguires stood convicted of murdering sixteen men.

THE COAL EXTRACTED from the earth in eastern Pennsylvania fueled the trains crisscrossing the expanding nation. The steel smelted in western Pennsylvania built the trains and the tracks upon which they ran. A mobile nation granted little sympathy to those impeding the trains from running on time.

On July 6, 1892, Henry Clay Frick attempted to get his boss Andrew Carnegie's Pittsburgh Bessemer Steel Works running again. The Homestead, Pennsylvania, steel factory had been closed on the orders of the Amalgamated Association of Iron and Steelworkers (AAISW), who posted an army of union men around the steelworks to prevent the steelworks from reopening with non-AAISW workers.

To secure the factory from the union mob, Frick hired a small army of Pinkertons. Since they had risen to fame disbanding the Molly Maguires, the Pinkertons had sunk to infamy as enemies of workingmen. General Master Workman Powderly did not overstate the opinion of many in the labor movement when he deemed them "hired assassins," "thugs," and "creatures who are outcasts from decent society" and who are "gathered from the brothels and gambling dens of our large cities."[25] When Frick's boatload of Pinkertons floated down the Monongahela, the union men fired rifles, shot cannonballs, pushed rafts of burning lumber, hurled sticks of dynamite, and even attempted to flood the river with oil to incinerate the barges. A battle left ten dead. The strikers claimed the day, keeping the steelworks idle and force-marching the defeated Pinkertons through a gauntlet of angry townspeople. Struck with bullwhips, parasols, and poles, made to salute the American flag, spat upon, kicked, and punched by men, women, and children, the Pinkertons were driven like cattle to a makeshift jail in the town's Opera House. An investigation by the House of Representatives called the abuse "too indecent and brutal to describe."[26]

Two of the strikers who fell that day did so from friendly fire. Friendly fire helped kill the cause they served as well.

Unwittingly helping management's cause was Alexander Berkman, the bespectacled anarchist who shot and stabbed Henry Clay Frick multiple times during the strike. The coward's blows were of the type anarcho-communist Johann Most, Berkman's hero, had earlier called "propaganda by deed." Johann Most might have been the guy Emma Lazarus had in mind when she wrote of the Statue of Liberty taking in the world's "wretched refuse." Bearded, bushy-haired, deformed, and a real bastard, Most got expelled from Austria in 1870. In 1878, he fled Germany, where he had briefly served in the Reichstag, after running afoul of the authorities for advocating violence. The Crown expelled him from Great Britain for glorifying the assassination of the Russian czar. In America, Most spectacularly published a pamphlet entitled *Science of Revolutionary Warfare: A Manual of Instruction in the Use and Preparation of Nitroglycerine, Dynamite, Gun-Cotton, Fulminating Mercury, Bombs, Fuses, Poisons, Etc., Etc.* But when Berkman attempted to murder Andrew Carnegie's second in command, Most washed his hands of his acolyte, whom he alternatively dubbed a crank and an agent provocateur. The betrayal incensed Berkman's squat and homely lover, Emma Goldman, whose first date with Berkman had occurred at a Most lecture. The fiery Lithuanian Jew horse-whipped Most at a public meeting.[27]

Ironically, Goldman played Most to Leon Czolgosz's Berkman less than a decade later, when her follower assassinated President William McKinley in 1901 after attending one of *her* lectures. Like Most, she began to question the wisdom of earlier, brash proclamations. Like Most, she denied that her words had inspired the anarcho-communist Czolgosz and denounced him as a crank. Goldman went into hiding before a partisan of Czolgosz, assuming one existed, could horsewhip *her*.[28]

Berkman, a resident of New York City who had no connection to the striking workers at the Homestead, marred the cause. Instead of patriotic, small-town Americans repelling hired guns, the story of the Homestead strikers became entangled with wild-eyed, foreign fanatics. The workers' own acts of barbarism fueled this impression. Berkman's sneak attack on Frick solidified it. Frick's heroic role in apprehending his own assailant, as well as his stoic response to the stab and gunshot wounds (he returned to his desk to finish his work after a doctor had removed bullets without the benefit of anesthesia) impressed the public and shifted perspectives.[29]

Just as the unionists had reneged on their pledge to give the surrendering

Pinkertons safe passage out of the town, the law reneged on its pledge to charge the captured Pinkertons with murder. Reinforced with 8,500 troops, the law finally established order in Homestead and returned the factory to its owner. More than four months after the bloody clash with the Pinkertons, the workers voted to go back to the factory on the company's terms. No injury inflicted upon the workers by Andrew Carnegie, Henry Clay Frick, or the Pinkertons damaged their cause as much as Berkman's inhumane and impetuous act.

Two years after the Homestead strike, American Railway Union leader Eugene V. Debs led a strike against the Pullman Car Company, which had cut wages in the midst of company losses in the severe economic downturn of the mid-1890s.

George Pullman decided to remove his company from Chicago proper to the outlying areas largely in response to the labor violence that plagued the Windy City, most horribly exemplified by the Haymarket Square bombing. On May 1, 1886, thereafter celebrated by the Left across the globe as "May Day," workers in Chicago rallied for an eight-hour workday, a cause that Chicago's sizable contingent of anarchists had recently ridiculed.[30] But the professional activists knew when to make a cause their own. The anarchists co-opted the drive for eight-hour workdays just as they inserted themselves into strikes. During an assault on replacement workers at the McCormick Harvester Works on May 3, a Chicago policeman shot and killed an assailing striker. August Spies, a local anarchist leader, demanded revenge. The following day, despite having no stake in the dispute at McCormick Harvester, Spies drummed up a gathering of more than a thousand people in Haymarket Square, addressing the throngs in German. As expected, police congregated in case of disorder. As Spies and his cohorts finished speaking, someone hurled a bomb at the police. The blast, and the ensuing small-arms exchanges, left eight policemen dead.

With prescience, Terence Powderly had distanced America's premier labor organization from the eight-hour cause and from the anarchists. Eight months before that tragic day in Chicago, Powderly had told his flock:

Up to the present time we have been somewhat indifferent to the statements made from the public platform by men who professed to speak for the Knights of Labor. Some of the most impracticable and visionary schemes have been ventilated as the plans of this Order. Some speakers have advocated the use of firearms, dynamite, and in fact every known method of destruction. None of these things have ever been recommended in any of the sessions of the General Assembly, and the time has arrived to put a stop to such false and pernicious teachings. It will not do to say that we do not advocate such things, and that such persons as talk in that way are in error; we must go a step further and declare that such conduct shall be a sufficient cause for expulsion from the Order.[31]

Alas, Powderly's desire to distance the Knights from revolutionaries was matched by a desire among revolutionaries to get closer to the Knights. Albert Parsons, an Alabama-born leader of the mostly foreign anarchists tried for the Haymarket Square bombing, was a Knight.

The ensuing trial, and the public outrage, left four anarchists to swing on the gallows. A fifth, Louis Lingg, an amateur bomb maker thought to have made the deadly device unleashed at the rally, escaped the hangman by chomping on an explosive smuggled into his cell. The four condemned men went to their deaths preaching anarchy and extolling the virtues of dynamite.[32] A Chicago socialist wryly eulogized, "They worshipped at the shrine of force; wrote it and preached it; until they were overpowered by their own Gods and slain in their own temple."[33]

It was this chaotic milieu, where wild-eyed radicals crashed labor disputes to propagandize extraneous ideas, from which George Pullman wished to escape. The manufacturer of passenger train cars thus manufactured a town, Pullman, Illinois, and set about making it immune from industrial strife.

George Pullman resembled Robert Owen not only in his rags-to-riches life story but also in his attempt to elevate the condition of his workers through a model company town. Though the workers in Pullman, Illinois, lived in better houses, walked on cleaner streets, and enjoyed better parks, libraries, and theaters than workers elsewhere, they were also denied the freedom to drink alcohol, own homes, and open businesses. With company and landlord one, paychecks shrank to pay back rent. Termination meant eviction. Many Pullman residents feared a spy network within the town snitching private conversations to the bosses.[34]

In the summer of 1894, the Pullman workers lashed out. The strike received welcome aid from their fellow rail men and unwelcome aid from anarcho-communists and other ne'er-do-wells. The rails crossed the entire nation. The death and destruction unleashed by the strike did as well.

In the late hours of July 5, saboteurs struck the Illinois Central Railroad. "During the night forty-eight of their cars had been burned, and a passenger train had been boarded, the engine detached and permitted to run wild down the track," historian Almont Lindsey recounts. The following night "an epidemic of fires destroyed at least seven hundred cars at the Panhandle yards in South Chicago." On a Sacramento–San Francisco line, "[s]ome fish bars and spikes had been expertly removed, causing the rails to spread. The engineer and three soldiers were killed outright, while several soldiers were wounded, one mortally." In the Oklahoma territory on the evening of "July 12 the piling was sawed from under a bridge and dynamite planted therein, and when the train crossed there was an explosion, wrecking thirteen cars of freight and severely injuring several members of the crew."[35] George Pullman had wanted to get as far away from Haymarket Square as possible. Haymarket Square came to him.

A judge invoked the Sherman Antitrust Act, a law passed to prevent business monopolies, to jail the union leaders behind the strike, including Eugene Debs. When allies posted bail, Debs refused to be moved: "The poor striker who is arrested would be thrown in jail. We are no better than he."[36] Socialists found a hero in Woodstock Prison. In Woodstock Prison Eugene Debs found socialism.

THE KNIGHTS OF Labor could not thrive amidst strikes, bombings, and murder.

As the Knights reached their height in 1886, the agent of its demise, the American Federation of Labor (AFL), emerged. Founded that year in substantial part by the cigar workers whose defection from the NLU had led to that union's downfall, the AFL challenged the Knights of Labor over their cautious stand on strikes and eight-hour-workday legislation, as well as their geographic, rather than profession-based, organization of workers. These were differences of means, not of ends. The dispute centered on power and degenerated into a personal quarrel between Powderly and Samuel Gompers, the cigar maker turned AFL head. "If the official organ of the American Federation of Labor editorially stated that that organization would gobble up the whole Order of the Knights of Labor in five years, or five months," Powderly boasted in 1890, "I would not mind it, for it could not be done."[37] It was done. The AFL replaced the Knights of Labor as the One Big Union during the 1890s. The One Big Union it remained.

Powderly, who became a player in Republican presidential administrations after the Knights deposed him in 1893, eulogized the Knights of Labor with no sense of failure. "Turn to the statutes of the United States and of the various states and stamped there—indelibly it may be—you'll find plank after plank of the platform of the Knights of Labor. We did not live or speak or work in vain."[38]

. . .

THE BRIGANDS WHO terrorized the Pennsylvania mine country and the anarchists who hurled bombs at the Chicago police started life in Europe. If one faced foreign occupiers in Ireland or the Kaiser's iron hand, violence might be a legitimate option. But in America, where labor, speech, and the ballot were free, the violence of the Molly Maguires and the Haymarket bombers seemed wildly out of place. In addition to the nation making Americans out of Europeans, immigrants were making America more like Europe.

This alienated old-stock Americans not only from the newcomers but from organized labor as well. Anarchists convicted of the Haymarket Square bombing had been members of the Knights of Labor and the National Labor Union and at least one of the Molly Maguire murderers operated as an aboveground labor leader.[39] Strikes by legal labor organizations, such as those against the interests of George Pullman and Andrew Carnegie, often resulted in violence as well.

Just as Frances Wright, Mary Gove Nichols, and John Humphrey Noyes synthesized socialism and free love in the public's mind, the Molly Maguire assassinations, Haymarket Square bombing, Homestead battle, and Pullman sabotage married labor unions with violence. Labor leaders fought hard to divorce the two in the public's perception. The fight would be long and hard but successful. The workers who played so great a role in the fantasies of Karl Marx rejected Marx in reality.

∾ 8 ∾

SINGLE-TAXERS

A prophet is not without honour, but in his own country and in his own house and among his own kindred.

—MARK 6:4

THREE OVERLAPPING WAVES—populism, progressivism, and socialism—crashed upon America between the Civil War and the Great War. Intellectual agitation prefaced each movement. Henry George's "single tax" movement, launched after the 1879 release of his book *Progress and Poverty*, foreshadowed the grievances of the populists, if not the solutions.

George grew up in the Philadelphia home of an Episcopalian vestryman who earned his daily bread as the printer of religious books. After sailing the seas, dabbling in gold mining, and working as a scribe for start-up newspapers, Henry George took what he had learned from his father and typeset his own book, which was to inspire a religious following. *Progress and Poverty* wouldn't outsell the Bible, but for a time it came close. Translated into most European tongues, the book eventually sold more than three million copies. "With the exception of the Bible it was probably the most popular nonfiction book published in the English language before the twentieth century," historian Edward Spann contends.[1] Henry George became the high priest of the Church of the Single Tax. "It is the culmination of Christianity—the City of God on earth, with its walls of jasper and its gates of pearl!" George proclaimed of his idea. "It is the reign of the Prince of Peace!"[2]

George was a product of his times. The book he wrote, and the movement he led, spoke to those times.

. . .

LIKE SO MANY other men during the 1850s, Henry George went to California to get rich. The mother lode eluded him. He retreated to the family profession of printing, but that, too, paid little. "I came near starving to death," George confessed.3 He incurred debts, worked as a "scab," and became so desperate that, on at least one occasion, he begged.4 "I stopped a man—a stranger—and told him I wanted $5," he explained in later, better times. "He asked what I wanted it for. I told him that my wife was confined and that I had nothing to give her to eat. He gave me the money. If he had not, I think I was desperate enough to have killed him."5

In contrast to his family's miserable state, George saw great wealth all around him in San Francisco, and after a journey back east, in New York. George himself experienced the closing of the frontier, the appreciation of money that made debts more burdensome, and the growing conflict between labor and capital as anonymous, distant employers replaced friends, family members, or oneself as the boss. The juxtaposition of great wealth with great poverty ceased to strike him as ironic. The two went together like hand in glove.

"The association of poverty with progress is the great enigma of our times," George wrote in 1879.6 He purported to solve this enigma in *Progress and Poverty*.

George's single tax idea promised to solve a multitude of problems. He sought onerous land taxes that, in effect, would have forced property holders to rent land from the state. The American people would become the collective landlord. "To extirpate poverty, to make wages what justice commands they should be, the full earnings of the laborer, we must therefore substitute for the individual ownership of land a common ownership," he wrote. "Nothing else will go to the cause of the evil—in nothing else is there the slightest hope."7

Land ownership, George contended, was "usurpation," "robbery," and "slavery."8 In fact, chattel slavery stood "small" and "trivial" next to the slavery due to private land ownership.9 He professed: "We did not abolish slavery when we ratified the Fourteenth Amendment; to abolish slavery we must abolish private property in land!"10 Once the land was nationalized, George warned, the claimants should not be reimbursed.11 After all, if private land ownership truly was slavery or robbery, then it would not be justice to benefit the slavers a second time around or reward the thieves.

George's solution, a tax on land equivalent to its annual worth, would compel land use and would therefore democratize it.

Many ingredients came together to make *Progress and Poverty* a runaway best seller. Years in journalism and hard-luck experiences as a workingman afforded George the ability to write, in a popular style, a book with authority and feeling on the widening gulf between rich and poor. Henry George—shipmate, prospector, failed investor, typesetter, and not a university professor—was the perfect person to write the book. *Progress and Poverty* articulated the revolt against the "gilded age." It spoke to those enraged by land giveaways and welfare to the railroads, caught up in Western land booms and busts, and seeing everywhere great wealth but experiencing only great poverty. George offered a radical solution, but he did so only after critiquing other radical ideas, and painstakingly laying out the problem. Thus, he established credibility. George softened up readers with body blows before attempting the knockout punch. One reads *Progress and Poverty* for hundreds of pages before coming upon George's call for land expropriation. Had he proposed such a radical solution on page one, most readers would have stopped before page two. Because he gradually prepared readers for the startling remedy, they were more ready to accept it.

And accept it many did.

HENRY GEORGE, NOT Karl Marx, was the American Left's intellectual leader during the 1880s. The war on private property that Robert Owen introduced in the 1820s, Henry George continued in the 1880s. And like Owen, George advanced some decidedly non-Marxist notions. George professed that "it is not capital which employs labor, but labor which employs capital." And, in fact, since capital stemmed from labor, the two were not at war at all. The "real parties pitted against each other" were "not labor and capital. It is laborers on the one side and the owners of land on the other."[12] Labeling strikes a "destructive contest" that harmed both labor and capital, George united capitalist and workingman against landowner.[13] Marx's enemy, the capitalist, was a friend; the villain, at least in George's script, was played by the landlord.

This put George at odds with Marxists. A year prior to the publication of *Progress and Poverty*, both the Democratic and Workingmen's parties nominated George as a delegate to a constitutional convention in California. When George confessed that he did not subscribe to every tenet of the Marxist-oriented Workingmen's Party platform, his nomination was revoked. He lost the general election.[14] In 1881, Marx, forever jealous of rival prophets, dubbed George "utterly backward."[15]

George remembered the intolerance of the Marxists. In 1887, members of the Socialist Labor Party attempted to hijack George's United Labor Party. Why, George wondered, would members of one political party seek to gain control of another? Didn't they already have their political vehicle? As his party's convention approached, George held firm. "Either they must go out," he explained, "or the majority must go out, for it is certain that the majority of the men who constitute the United Labour Party do not propose to nationalise capital and are not in favour of the abolition of all private property in the 'instruments of production.'"[16] The socialists didn't succeed in their takeover efforts. But they would try, try again with other movements and parties.

As George alienated the rising Marxist Left, he gained converts from the departed, agrarian, communal Left. After finding Marxism unpalatable, the holdover reformers anxiously sought a new elixir. Francis Gould Shaw, Brook Farmer and father of the fallen Colonel Robert Gould Shaw, purchased one thousand copies of *Progress and Poverty*.[17] Charles Nordhoff, the chronicler of the communistic societies of the previous Left, pushed George to run for Congress.[18] Between 1895 and 1932, at least ten single-tax-inspired colonies sprouted up throughout America.[19] But the American Left had moved on. It had attempted to persuade by microcosmic example. At New Harmony, at Brook Farm, at Fruitlands, it didn't work. Now the Left sought to impose by national legislation and other governmental mechanisms.

George, who made several unsuccessful attempts for office in California prior to *Progress and Poverty*, found his political prospects rising in the East following the publication of his book. In 1886, the United Labor Party nominated him for mayor of New York. George made a valiant effort, speaking sometimes more than a dozen times a day.[20] He lost. Despite heading a third-party ticket, he came in second place to the Tammany Hall candidate. He did beat out an upstart Republican named Theodore Roosevelt.

A symbiotic relationship between his book and his political ambition resulted. Book sales fueled George's political profile, which fueled his book sales. A congressman actually attempted to pass George's single tax but received the support of just five of his colleagues.[21] Again, George's supporters coaxed him to run for mayor. The results of his 1897 run were much worse than the results of his 1886 race.

In the dramatic account of Henry George's son, a doctor warned Henry George Sr. that proceeding with his second New York City mayoral race would likely prove "fatal." "You mean it may kill me?" "Most probably, yes," the doctor responded. According to his son's biography, Henry George Sr. decided to run, willing to give his life for the single-tax cause. "How can I die better than serving humanity? Besides, so dying will do more for the cause than anything I am likely to be able to do in the rest of my life."[22] A few days before the 1897 election, the exhausted candidate fell into eternal rest. All that was missing from his son's depiction was the cross and crown of thorns.

Despite his loyal namesake's best efforts, Henry George is not imagined as a Christ-like figure by contemporary leftists. This is because, overwhelmed by Marxism, few contemporary leftists remember their non-Marxist forebears. But George's contemporaries certainly did. He flashed, burned white hot, and was gone. In a fit of overly generous praise, which ages poorly, philosopher John Dewey held: "It would require less than the fingers of the two hands to enumerate those who, from Plato down, rank with Henry George among the world's social philosophers."[23] Though very few leftists today concur with Dewey's assessment, it's worth noting that quite a few leftists yesterday heartily agreed.

~ 9 ~

NATIONALISTS

Speak not in the ears of fools: because they will despise the instruction of thy speech.

—PROVERBS 23:9

UTOPIAS FAILED MISERABLY in the 1820s and 1840s. They succeeded marvelously in the 1880s and 1890s. The change in fortune resulted from a change in venue. What stumbled across the ground of the American heartland took flight in the pages of novels. Utopia evaded humanity's grasp at New Harmony, Brook Farm, and Oneida. In *The Crystal Button*, *A Traveler from Altruria*, *Freeland*, and other late-nineteenth-century novels, utopia eluded man no longer.

No utopian novel had as great an impact on the progressive era as Massachusetts newspaperman Edward Bellamy's *Looking Backward*, published in 1888. "As surely as *Progress and Poverty* is the Old Testament of our American social Bible, so surely is *Looking Backward* the New," opined the reverend John Haynes Holmes, a prominent preacher of the social gospel. "The two books fit together perfectly as the two parts of a completed whole."[1] Bellamy, Mark Twain proffered, "made the accepted heaven paltry by inventing a better one on earth." Twain dubbed *Looking Backward* "the latest and best of all Bibles."[2]

Six months after its initial appearance in Great Britain, the book had gone through an additional seventeen printings. It went through six Hungarian printings by 1920. *Looking Backward* inspired a Bellamy Congress in Java nearly a half century after its publication. Bellamy's views "became formative influences in establishing the Australian Labour Party," according to Sylvia E. Bowman in *Edward Bellamy Abroad*, and a leading Australian trade-union journalist, seeing in *Looking Backward* "the Christ-spirit breathing," led an expedition of enthusiasts to Paraguay to start a colony based on Bellamyite principles. Translations appeared in Russian, Chinese, Hebrew, German, and, perhaps most appropriately, Esperanto.[3]

The U.S. run approached a half million copies within ten years of publication. By then, it had outsold all nineteenth-century works of fiction save *Uncle Tom's Cabin*, and like that earlier novel it had a profound impact on public affairs. By 1891, the rage over *Looking Backward* spurred political scientist Franklin Giddings to comment, "[T]here has been no more curious phenomenon in recent times than the wholesale hypnotizing of clever literary people by Mr. Bellamy's dazzling vision."[4]

IN LOOKING BACKWARD, Julian West, a wealthy nineteenth-century Bostonian, falls into a trance-induced sleep only to be awakened 113 years, 3 months, and 11 days later—in the year 2000. The nation, West's host, Dr. Leete, informs him, has become "the sole capitalist and land-owner."[5] Americans have conscripted themselves into a giant industrial army, containing such components as a "musical service," a "corps of domestic servants," an "invalid corps," and a "women's army."[6] The state is the grocery store. The state is the publisher. The state is the factory. The state is the farm. The state is everything. And this is for the good. As Dr. Leete's daughter, Edith, tells West: "[T]he world is now heaven compared to what it was in your day."[7] There is full employment. All Americans have all of their needs supplied all of the time. There is no war. Crime is virtually non-existent.

Julian West seems more astounded by these dramatic societal changes than by the fact that he slept for more than a century. In a typical exchange, Dr. Leete informs West: "There is neither selling nor buying nowadays; the distribution of goods is effected in another way. As to the bankers, having no money we have no use for those gentry." West responds by telling Edith Leete that her father is "making sport of me." "Father has no idea of jesting," Edith says.[8]

The manner in which the Leetes bring West up to speed on current events becomes formulaic. Dr. Leete matter-of-factly reveals some drastic change—collective kitchens, collective laundries, even giant collective umbrellas. The ignorant visitor expresses disbelief. The indulgent hosts gently laugh at West's ignorance. They assure him that what they say is true. West questions ("Such stupendous change" must have been effected by "great violence"). Leete answers his concern ("On the contrary . . .").⁹ West then realizes how backward he and his contemporaries truly were.

Bellamy's utopian America does away with state governments, juries, jails, judicial appeals, labor unions, political parties, the military, tax collectors, and democracy itself. The anarchic, unplanned society of Julian West's 1880s gives way to Dr. Leete's scientific, centrally planned America of 2000. As Dr. Leete informs West, the economic system of 1887 was "as absurd economically as it was morally abominable."¹⁰ With all of society regimented as an army, society operates more efficiently and, strangely, more compassionately.

JULIAN WEST WASN'T the only one impressed by a visit to year-2000 Boston. So successful was *Looking Backward* that it inspired dozens of pro and con copycat books, many of which, such as *Looking Within*, *Looking Forward*, *Looking Further Backward*, *Looking Further Forward*, and *Mr. East's Experiences in Mr. Bellamy's World*, advertised the similarities in their titles.

In William Dean Howells's *A Traveler from Altruria*, Mr. Homos's description of his homeland leaves one minister to gush, "The kingdom of God upon earth."¹¹ "Jealousy, envy, hate, malice, anger, lust, had become obsolete" in Godfrey Sweven's Limanora.¹² Theodor Hertzka dubs Freeland a "Paradise," "a miracle," and an "Eden."¹³ Bellamy himself was no less chiliastic. "With a tear for the dark past," he proclaims in *Looking Backward*, "turn we then to the dazzling future, and, veiling our eyes, press forward. The long and weary winter of the race is ended. Its summer has begun. Humanity has burst the chrysalis. The heavens are before it."¹⁴

The past and present didn't fare as well in utopian fiction as the future did. Awakened and enlightened, Julian West looks upon Bostonians of 1887 as a "festering mass of human wretchedness," "all quite dead," and "living sepulchers."¹⁵ Gabriel Tarde's *Underground Man* details "that fortunate disaster which compelled the overflowing flood of civilisation to disappear for the benefit of mankind."¹⁶ Ignatius Donnelly creates in *Caesar's Column* a macabre monument "*composed of the bodies of a quarter million human beings, who were once the rulers, or the instruments of the rulers*," to warn future generations to "*restrain selfishness and live righteously.*"¹⁷

A misanthropic tone permeates the genre. The imagined man of the future was a god. The real man of the present wasn't even a man. Utopian authors generally held living, breathing men in disdain. In their place, they created men without self-interest, men without physical blemishes, men without envy. In other words, they created something other than man, a creature they thoroughly detested. The fiction writers eagerly sacrificed humans for an abstraction known as humanity. Life would imitate art in the next century.

THE PROGRESSIVE ERA novelists' ideas of utopia were as peculiar as their directions showing readers how to get there.

Socioland "abandoned the jury system as too expensive and cumbrous, and abolished the right of appeal to higher courts."[18] "Can't a man do what he pleases with his own in Altruria?" "No," answers the Altrurian Mr. Homos, "he can only do right with his own."[19] H. G. Wells imagined utopia as a land without meat.[20] John Macnie's America of 9600 outlawed the First Amendment: "It was strictly prohibited to print any reading of a kind unsuitable for unripe minds. Short of this, there was complete liberty of printing."[21]

One man's *Altruria* is another man's *1984*. Generally, the people who invent utopias, intellectuals, find them a dream world. The people intellectuals create them for, the masses, find them a nightmare. The intellectual's utopia is the common man's hell.

On no issue is this more apparent than eugenics. That declared "science," "the wave of the future," and "progress" in fiction's 2000 had become anathema by history's 1945.

Looking Backward details how "untrammeled sexual selection" brings about "race purification." Dr. Leete boasts that "for the first time in human history the principle of sexual selection, with its tendency to preserve and transmit the better types of the race, and let the inferior types drop out, has unhindered operation."[22] Bellamy was not alone in his enthusiasm for state-directed biological experiments. Utopian novelists engaged in a group fantasy that saw future ages creating a race of supermen.

In the forty-ninth-century Boston of Chauncey Thomas, "[n]o diseased or deformed person who is liable to communicate serious imperfection of any kind to offspring is ever allowed to marry."[23] "By the aid of the physiological and biological experts," Godfrey Sweven's Limanorans "were able to fix the two out of which the individual parents would have to be chosen; and from their knowledge of the character and history of every member, the elders of these two families along with the medical elders were able to indicate the man and the woman who would exactly fulfil the purpose of the state."[24] In Gabriel Tarde's utopia, "[t]he right to have children is the monopoly and supreme recompense of genius. It is besides a powerful lever for the uplifting and exaltation of the race. Furthermore a man can only exercise it exactly the same number of times as he produces works worthy of a master." Thus, in year 596 of the era of Salvation, humanity had become "a race of Titans."[25] H. G. Wells wrote that "idiots," "drunkards," "perverse and incompetent persons"—"these people spoil the world for others." "You must resort to a kind of social surgery" in utopia, he wrote, to extricate the undesirables.[26]

LOOKING BACKWARD INSPIRED men to put their dreams to paper. It also inspired them to make their dreams reality. In 1888, a group of Civil War veterans, impressed by Bellamy's vision of a militarized society, formed the Boston Bellamy Club. The veterans were joined by journalists, Boston Brahmins, and Theosophists, and soon became the Boston Nationalist Club. This was no book-discussion club.

The Nationalists, as their name implied, sought to nationalize. They called for a government takeover of the railroads, telegraphs, telephones, and coal mining. They demanded that municipalities replace private companies in providing the public with heat, light, and transportation.[27] And this was just the beginning. Ultimately, the Nationalists wanted the America Bellamy wrote about to replace the America in which they lived.

Bellamy, boasting a lineage of ministers and a brother who authored the Pledge of Allegiance, ensconced Nationalism firmly within the American tradition. Aware of the Communists' reputation for co-option and fanaticism, he worked to expel them from Nationalist clubs. Keenly aware of the public's association of socialism with atheism, free love, and other unpopular causes, he wisely avoided the "s"-word in marketing his ideology and movement.[28] The term "nationalism" implied patriotism, a notion that socialists had generally scoffed at (to their detriment). Christianity, traditional morals, patriotism, elitism, and the martial spirit combined to make a leftist doctrine at odds with leftist doctrines.

Whereas the socialists appealed to the working class, the Nationalists appealed to the moneyed class. "Our movement," founding member Stansbury Norse pronounced, "is not that *of* the proletariat, but *for* the proletariat."[29] For other socialists, "revolution" was the watchword. For Nationalist socialists, a more appropriate watchword might have been "evolution." "We propose no revolution," Bellamy explained, "but that the people shall resist a revolution. We oppose those who are overthrowing the republic. Let no mistake be made here. We are not revolutionists, but counter-revolutionists."[30] Such calming words put at ease an upper class uneasy with strikes, anarchist violence, and wild talk of overthrowing the government. So, too, did the Nationalist appeal to patriotism and military values. The Nationalists positioned themselves as conservatives saving the republic, rather than radicals overthrowing it. Just as Bellamy's patrician lineage and literary reputation appealed to elites, the centrality of military order, discipline, and efficiency attracted respectable former army officers.

Bellamy had spent his youth in the shadow of the Civil War. He admired the mechanized efficiency of a well-disciplined battalion of troops. He recognized the strength in numbers. He marveled at how the army transformed mere individuals into "a single organism." Of the "imposing mass" of the army, Bellamy wrote: "One forgets to look for the individuals in it, forgets that there are individuals." He longed to sacrifice himself for a great objective. "Life seems of value only as it gives the poorest something to sacrifice. It is dying that makes the glory of the world, and all other employments seem but idle while the regiment passes."[31]

The young Bellamy dreamed only of becoming a cadet at West Point and leading men on some great cause. Shortly after the cessation of armed hostilities between North and South, West Point dashed his hopes by rejecting the sickly teen. His martial obsessions remained, and ran deep through *Looking Backward*. In an age of anarchists and industrial strife, it is easy to see how those who had experienced the precision, strength, unity of purpose, and sacrifice of the army during the war flocked to a movement applying the techniques of the armed forces upon the entire society. The military defeated the South and helped free the slaves. Just think of what society could accomplish if it were organized along military lines.

THE NATIONALISTS AND the Socialists shared the ends of turning over the instruments of production to the state. They diverged on means. The Nationalist appeal to the establishment—the military, the aristocracy, the intellectuals—contrasted with the socialist fetishization of the worker. Ironically, the exclusivity of the Nationalist movement provided universality to the Nationalist message. Nationalists weren't the people trying to sabotage the local factory or kill your mayor. A Nationalist was more likely to run your local factory or be your mayor. Cyrus Field Willard, a member of the Boston club, commented on the strategy of appealing to society's elites:

We have been unjustly criticized on the ground that we were too exclusive or felt too good to mix with the common people, were "rose-water revolutionists" and so on, simply because we desired to pick the best material for effective work and not admit any and every person who came along with a burning desire to reform the world or join a club for the sake of joining. As has been said by Henry A. Ford of Detroit, "The Nationalist Club is not a cave of Adullam for the debtor and the 'malcontent.'" Some of the men who founded the first club had had experience in trying to change social forms before *Looking Backward* was written and they had often been told that it was the unsuccessful man, the ignorant and the violent, who desired a change. Therefore, it was made an unwritten law that this new club should be composed as much as possible of men who had been successful in the present fierce competitive struggle. They were not the weak, crying for mercy; they were the strong, demanding justice.[32]

This spin proved effective. More than 150 Nationalist clubs, in addition to the original club in Boston, dotted the American landscape in the late 1880s and early 1890s. Prominent members included Unitarian minister Edward Everett Hale in Boston, attorney Clarence Darrow in Chicago, and Columbia University law instructor Daniel De Leon in New York, who later led one of America's socialist parties and helped found the Industrial Workers of the World.

In an earlier age, such people might have chaired their church's abolitionist group, collected temperance pledges, or perhaps even joined a commune. In the steel-and-soot era of the 1880s and 1890s, they swore by Henry George's *Progress and Poverty* or joined up with the Nationalists. Bellamy's movement stood out, a contemporary critic noted, because "it signifies an inclination to question the prevailing social order in a large class of people not to be ranked as working men or women."[33] Amidst movements geared toward foreigners, workers, and extremists, elitists with an interest in reform carved out a movement for themselves.

Nationalism grew from an idea in a novel to an actual propaganda movement to political activism. "As a literary man I fear I am 'a goner' and past praying for," Bellamy wrote a solicitous fiction editor following *Looking Backward*'s success. "There is one life which I should like to lead, and another which I must lead."[34] The life Bellamy felt he *must* lead was that of movement leader. Bellamy managed to pen another book, *Equality*, in his remaining years, but devoted his efforts primarily to building the Nationalist movement. The Bellamy publication *New Nation* reminded readers itching for direct political action "that nationalism is a movement and not a party."[35] But the movement would soon hitch itself to a political party.

Nationalists played key roles in launching the People's Party in the early 1890s. Eight of the twenty-seven People's Party national committeemen were Nationalists.[36] Consistent with Nationalism's veneration of all things military, the party nominated Civil War general James B. Weaver for president in 1892. Ignatius Donnelly, author of *Caesar's Column*, penned the preamble to the party's platform. The actual platform

endorsed the nationalization of railroads, telegraphs, and telephones—
just as *Looking Backward* did.[37]

As the People's Party rose, however, the Nationalist movement collapsed. One problem for the Nationalists was that the People's Party into
which they were subsumed represented an unnatural union of farmers
and intellectuals. This oil-and-water mixture displayed itself most conspicuously in the 1892 People's Party platform. To assuage debt-ridden
farmers anxious about losing ownership of their farms, the platform
called for the coinage of inflationary silver. To assuage intellectuals desiring collective ownership of land, the party called for the expropriation of
land from corporations "in excess of their actual needs." Thus the farmers' needs—individual ownership—were in opposition to the intellectuals'
demands for collective ownership. The groups had nothing in common,
save alienation.

Another cause of the Nationalist movement's collapse was the economic depression in 1893. Edward Bellamy's *New Nation* suffered from
declining subscriptions and ultimately folded. The terrible economy had
another, less direct influence on Nationalism: intellectuals pursued more
radical solutions to the radical problems that beset the United States. Evolution, after all, was not as quick as revolution.

Hindered by the tuberculosis that would claim his life in 1898, Bellamy
was in no condition during the 1890s to lead a cause as large as the Nationalist movement. The decline in Bellamy's health coincided with the decline in the movement's health.

Perhaps the greatest impediment to the longevity of Nationalism was
that the movement comprised political vagrants who drifted from one
cause to the next. Nationalism today; prohibition, woman's suffrage, and
socialism tomorrow. Nationalism initially benefited from this brief mob
popularity typical of political manias. Ultimately, when attention spans
waned, the joiners moved on and Nationalism perished.

But *Looking Backward* lived on in high school English classes. The principles have endured, too. In subsequent decades, the U.S. government experimented with Bellamyite ideas. It nationalized the railroads. It sent
young men to militarized work camps. It put a general in charge of organizing industry. It dictated prices and wages. It administered a universal
pension plan. A majority of the United States instituted eugenic laws. But
none of this worked as well in fact as it had in fiction.

❧ 10 ❧

THE PATERNALIST DYNASTY I: PRAIRIE POPULISTS

And thou shalt sanctify the fiftieth year, and shalt proclaim remission to all the inhabitants of thy land: for it is the year of the jubilee. Every man shall return to his possession, and every one shall go back to his former family.

—LEVITICUS 25:10

CHANGE CAME SWIFTLY to postbellum America. Factory workers experienced that change and organized to alleviate its new burdens. Farmers did, too.

"The United States was born in the country and has moved to the city," observed historian Richard Hofstadter.[1] The transition from a rural, agrarian society to an urban, industrial society was but one adjustment farmers faced. The currency, which the Congress had tied strictly to gold in 1873, proved inelastic. When it did fluctuate, it tended toward deflation instead of inflation. Many entrepreneurial farmers, particularly out West, had purchased their land at boom prices and struggled to repay the money they had borrowed when the bust inevitably came. In the South, farmers increasingly worked via the lien system on estates of wealthy landowners. Declining crop prices compounded problems. For instance, in 1885 the price of wheat was at its lowest point in forty years.[2] The increased distance to population centers meant that the days of carting crops to farmers' markets were over, at least for farmers interested in keeping their daily bread. The railroad, hungry for profits, transported crops to consumers hungry for food back East. But this came at a price that occasionally gave the railroad a greater profit from the crop than the farmer.

On top of all that, America's West became farther west—so far west that there was now no more West to flee to when prospects dimmed. Frederick

Jackson Turner merely articulated in 1893 what the People's Party, and Henry George before it, had expressed through their programs: "the frontier has gone." "American social development has been continually beginning over again on the frontier," Turner advanced in his famous frontier thesis. "This perennial rebirth, this fluidity of American life, this expansion westward with its new opportunities, its continuous touch with the simplicity of primitive society, furnish the forces dominating American character."3 All of that, many a common man feared, had vanished with the frontier.

The workers and farmers who organized themselves to cope with this rapidly changing America formed a new movement that became known as "populism." Though the populists prescribed radical cures, they offered a reactionary diagnosis. Whereas the progressives who succeeded them looked to the future, the populists' golden age lay in the past. They proved unlikely leftists, and when the dust cleared, many populists realized that they were not leftists at all. But in their sojourn on the Left, they left a blueprint of government involvement for future Lefts to follow. The populists launched a wave of reform born again in the progressive era, the New Deal, and the Great Society.

FARMERS HAD IT rough during the 1870s and 1880s. That railroad directors, bankers, and politicians had it so easy made the farmers' travails even harder to bear. Farmers' crops yielded less money and cost more to transport. The farm depreciated as the loan to pay for the farm appreciated. This is to say nothing of such perennial enemies of agriculture as bad weather and bugs.

The financial difficulties might have been easier to endure had not the social standing of the farmers fallen to such depths after the Civil War. The antebellum ideal of the gentleman farmer gradually gave way to a post-war stereotype of the backcountry rube. The rural life was no longer idealized; it was pitied.

As workers formed unions, farmers organized themselves, first into the Patrons of Husbandry, more commonly known as the Grange, and then into the Farmers' Alliance. Like the Knights of Labor, the Patrons of Husbandry formed amidst a national fad of secret societies in the late 1860s. Unlike the Knights of Labor, the Patrons of Husbandry was the creation of men outside the professions the organization purported to represent. As one writer dismissively but accurately observed, the Grange was the creation of "one fruit-grower and six government clerks."4 The Grange offered desolate farmers a multitude of services. It was part social mixer, part peddler of wholesale goods, part insurance provider, part lobbying group, and part religious revival. It was this quasi-religious function of the Grange that drew many participants to its successor, the Farmers' Alliance. Members proclaimed that "the Alliance was born in heaven," ranked "the Alliance next in importance to the church of the living God," and even ventured that "the Alliance is in a great measure taking the place of churches."5

The fact that the first of the farmers' organizations started in the nation's capital rather than its breadbasket foreshadowed future developments. Eventually, the farmers ceased looking to one another and began looking to the federal government for assistance. But before they looked to the federal government, the federal government—or at least six government clerks turned political entrepreneurs—looked to the farmers. Who needed whom more: the patrons or the patronized?

UNLIKE THE ANTEBELLUM communists, populists turned to government to solve problems. They sought political solutions not only to political problems but also to grievances involving banks, insurance, railroads, and even the effects of the weather. "Government should be more than a neutral observer, a policeman collecting taxes and seeing to it that business goes on as usual," averred historian Norman Pollack in summarizing the populist outlook. "Government, instead, must be a dynamic force in bringing about equality. It was created to serve man, and not simply to protect property or prevent individuals from cutting each other's throats. Thus, populists contended, government must be a responsive tool, one which can actively intervene in the economy to regulate matters affecting the public interest, and when necessary own outright monopolies of this character, and can just as actively aid the underprivileged and work for a more equitable distribution of wealth."6 From the populists comes the modern American state.

"I have a dream of the future," Kansas's People's Party governor Lorenzo Lewelling announced at his 1893 inauguration. "I have the evolution of an abiding faith in human government, and in the beautiful vision of a coming time I behold the abolition of poverty."7 "We have to expand the powers of government to solve the enigma of the world," Ignatius Donnelly wrote in his propagandistic novel *Caesar's Column*.8 "The corporation has absorbed the community," editorialized the *Farmers' Alliance* newspaper of Lincoln, Nebraska. "The community must now absorb the corporation—must merge itself into it. Society must enlarge itself to the breadth of humanity. A stage must be reached in which each will be for all and all for each."9

The government had freed the slaves and preserved the union of states.

Certainly it could take over the railroads, provide low-interest loans, and maintain cheap, communal grain elevators. If the federal government refused to intervene, would not the United States disintegrate just as it would have had the federal government not intervened in 1861?

This was the heart of the populist paradox. The populists appealed to the public's desire for peace as they threatened violence. They decried business monopolies as they called for government monopolies. They played the role of conservators of the republic as they radically altered it.

"That the revolution is to come in one form or another is as certain as that God's eternal justice must eventually prevail among men," foretold the *Topeka Advocate*.[10] "There is no wiping out the fact that this is a revolution," claimed one of Georgia's many populist newspapers, the *Farmers' Light*, "and it depends upon the enemy whether it shall be a peaceful or a bloody one. To be candid about the matter we believe it will be the latter."[11] "Six million people in this land of plenty are today suffering for bread," Kansas governor Lewelling pointed out. "Is it any wonder that there are anarchists"?[12] W. Scott Morgan, populist chronicler of the Farmers' Alliance, depicted America as free "only in name. Free, only in the fact that we still have a glimmering hope of crushing this monstrous system of robbery by an intelligent use of the ballot; that failing, all hope is lost, except that last fearful resort—revolution. May the God of our fathers prevent it."[13] In other words, do what we want or you will be made to do as we want. The anarchists played "bad cop" to the populist "good cop."

NOT SATIATED BY free land, a Department of Agriculture, or the various state-sponsored agricultural colleges that sprouted up during the 1860s, farmers wanted more, more, more. When the two major parties refused their entreaties, they launched their own parties.

The Grangers convened in Toledo, Ohio, in 1877, and established the Greenback Party. In 1891, the Farmers' Alliance organizations, the heir to the Grange movement, met in Cincinnati, Ohio, and formed the People's Party. Both parties boasted similar platforms, attracted the same activists, and even nominated the same man for president, James B. Weaver. The general initially opposed launching the People's Party, but Ignatius Donnelly convinced him of the need for it by asking if he truly thought "5000 people had traveled thousands of miles to get there [Cincinnati], at their own expense, simply to pass a few resolutions and go home."[14] The People's Party—whose members, because of the difficulty in describing them en masse as "Peoples," were called "Populists"—was born. Immediately, rural America channeled its frustrations into activism for the upstart party.

On the Fourth of July, 1892, Populists gathered in St. Louis and advanced a program that paid homage to America's glorious past while warning of a dark future. "[W]e seek to restore the government of the Republic to the hands of the 'plain people,' with which class it originated," the Populists declared. Their platform called for state ownership of the railroads, telegraphs, and telephones; an income tax; a bimetal currency (that is, tied to both silver and gold); and a ban on foreign ownership of land. An expression of sentiments, outside of the official platform, endorsed the Australian ballot, abolition of the electoral college, the direct election of senators, national referendum and initiative, presidential term limits, and various genuflections to organized labor, including a ban on Pinkerton detectives, immigration restrictions, and strict observance of the eight-hour workday.[15]

That was the substance of the Populist creed. The symbolism, offered up in the Donnelly-penned preamble, proved more interesting. The colorful preamble reads like a parody of a demagogue's rant, with crude references to the "vast conspiracy against mankind," "usurers," "land concentrating in the hands of capitalists," "grievous wrongs . . . inflicted upon the suffering people," and "a nation brought to the verge of moral, political, and material ruin." "They propose to sacrifice our homes, lives, and children on the altar of mammon," Donnelly thundered.[16] Very little of what Donnelly said can be taken literally. But it was that red-meat rhetoric that Populists devoured.

What Populists said was rarely as important as how Populists said it. Part revivalist preacher, part snake-oil salesman, part conspiracy theorist, the Populist orator aimed to get the heart pumping rather than the head thinking. He, or she, was a sheriff delivering a motivational speech to the posse. To bring down the criminals—the plutocrats, the politicians, the professors—the sheriff occasionally had to whip the posse into a frenzy. It was them versus us, city versus country, rich versus poor, East versus West and South. The enemy was never a tangible person—a neighbor, a businessman in town—but a distant villain who lent himself to caricature. More than a century later, one can almost see the torches and pitchforks, smell the dust blowing through the air, and hear the cries of "Amen!"

In Populist rhetoric, there was no limit to the good that Populist principles would unleash if enacted. Populism "means work for the thousands who now tramp the streets . . . means food and clothes for the thousands of hungry and ill-clad women and children . . . means the reopening of closed factories, the relighting of fires in darkened furnaces; it means hope instead of despair; comfort in place of suffering; life instead of death."[17] Similarly, there was no bottom to the evils of the Populists' enemies, a "pampered aristocracy," "men without conscience" who "prey upon the people" and "fatten on the failures of other men."[18] Populists spoke in Technicolor. Other politicians spoke in black and white.

If the Populists employed colorful rhetoric, it was because they were colorful people. In more than two centuries of political characters, America has never before or since seen the likes of Ignatius Loyola Donnelly. Donnelly migrated from Philadelphia to Minnesota, from Catholicism to an amorphous Christianity suitable to midwestern Protestant voters, and from the Democracy to the fledgling Republican Party. That initial political migration was the first of many. Donnelly was an Anti-Monopolist before a Populist, a Farmer-Laborer before an Anti-Monopolist, a Greenbacker before a Farmer-Laborer, a Liberal Republican before a Greenbacker, a People's Independent before a Liberal Republican, a Republican before a People's Independent, and a Democrat before a Republican. In October 1888 alone, Donnelly ran for governor on the Farmer-Laborer ticket, dropped out, and then campaigned for the Republican ticket as he ran for state representative as a Democrat.[19] His political wanderings were all the more remarkable because he gave up a rewarding career in Republican politics to pursue them: he had served as Minnesota's lieutenant governor from 1859 through 1862 and as a U.S. congressman from 1863 through 1868.

Dubbed the "Sage of Nininger" by friends and the "Prince of Cranks" by foes, Ignatius Donnelly had a literary career even stranger than his political career. He wrote a book, *Atlantis*, purporting to show the existence of the lost city referred to by Plato, and within a decade of its release it had gone through twenty-three editions in America and twenty-six in England.[20] Donnelly claimed to have discovered, and cracked, a code within Shakespeare's plays that proved Francis Bacon their true author. The world remained unconvinced. "I stand astounded before the stupidity of mankind," he told his diary.[21] Mankind reciprocated, but in a more public way. Later, Donnelly went further, claiming that Bacon had not only penned Shakespeare's plays but written works credited to Cervantes and Marlowe as well.[22] The conspiratorial rhetoric that drew listeners to his oratory drew readers to his books. In literature, a small but committed group of followers can earn riches for an author. In politics, it just earns a politician a small but committed group of followers.

Donnelly's Populist colleagues also brimmed with personality.

"Queen Mary" to friends, "Mary Yellin' " to foes, Kansan Mary Lease famously instructed farmers to "raise less corn and more *Hell.*"[23]

The electrifying Georgia congressman Tom Watson challenged the one-party South, and the white supremacy upon which it was based, by spearheading People's Party efforts in Dixie and sharing the podium with blacks, nominating blacks for party offices, and even saving a black preacher from a lynch mob.[24] "I love the Bible. I love Jesus Christ. I love the People's Party, and I love Tommie Watson," spoke an enthusiastic supporter of the red-haired congressman.[25]

"Sockless Jerry" Simpson, thrice elected to represent Kansas's Seventh District in Congress, passed through the Greenback and Union-Labor parties before finding fame as the "Sockless Socrates" of the People's Party. Despite his reputation as a rube, Simpson's friends privately referred to him as "a farmer by consent for political purposes," one reporter discovered. Another writer denied Simpson's reputation as "a sockless clown." "The real Jerry Simpson profited by the fame of his own effigy."[26]

Populist leaders played their aw-shucks roles perfectly, but they were generally not *of* but *above* "the people." Tom Watson was one of the most prodigious landowners in Georgia, biographer C. Vann Woodward informs, "with more tenants on his land than his grandfather had slaves."[27] Congressman Donnelly abused his office to transmit inside information to an investor.[28] Out of office, he lobbied for Jay Cooke, James J. Hill, and other moneyed interests.[29] He vigorously pursued patronage for himself and associates.[30] "Sockless Jerry" likely colluded with another bidder on a government construction project to inflate the price paid by a Kansas town. He railed against low-wage, high-work jobs, but caused a minor scandal by paying his workers skimpy wages while working them long hours.[31] After a career of damning the railroads, Simpson took a job as a land agent with the Santa Fe line, for which he promptly sold overpriced lands.[32]

Just as slaves didn't abolish slavery and peasants didn't overthrow the king of France, dirt farmers didn't lead the Populist movement.[33] When Populist leaders crusaded against corruption, the aristocracy, or railroad scams, chances were they knew more of what they spoke than they allowed.

THE PEOPLE'S PARTY was the most successful third-party venture since Abraham Lincoln's 1860 Republican Party. The Populists garnered 8.5 percent of the popular vote in the 1892 presidential election, winning the electoral votes of Kansas, Colorado, North Dakota, Idaho, and Nevada, and taking one of Oregon's electoral votes as well. In the midterm elections of 1894, the party won seven seats in the U.S. House of Representatives and six in the U.S. Senate.

But the People's Party died soon thereafter. The killing blows would have been familiar to activists within earlier Lefts and would become familiar to activists of future Lefts. Co-option, prosperity, and war killed Populism.

The ballot-box success of the People's Party in 1892 and 1894 put a scare into the established parties. Nothing forces politicians to alter existing prejudices as does the threat of expulsion from office. Endangered Republicans in the West and Democrats in the South began to give deference to populist ideas, which in turn removed the raison d'être of the People's Party.

In 1896, the Democrats nominated for president a corn-belt bimetallist who spoke the language of populism. "Burn down your cities and leave our farms and your cities will spring up again as if by magic, but destroy our farms and the grass will grow in the streets of every city in the country," William Jennings Bryan told Democrats gathered in Chicago in 1896.[34] The "Cross of Gold" speech divided America by region and interest. As alienating as it was to easterners and capitalists, it was electrifying to farmers of the South and West, so much so that the People's Party seconded the Democratic Party's nomination. In doing so, the party effectively signed its own death warrant.

When the Populists nominated Tom Watson as Bryan's running mate, Bryan treated the former congressman from Georgia as a pariah. The Populists couldn't stomach Bryan's running mate on the Democratic ticket, Arthur Sewell, an eastern banker, railroad magnate, and trust operator. So they nominated Watson for vice president and hoped that Bryan would see the light. He didn't. "It is doubtful whether any candidate ever to appear on a presidential ticket found himself in quite the humiliating position that Tom Watson occupied in 1896," C. Vann Woodward notes. "Not only were he and his party publicly insulted by his running-mate's representative, but Bryan himself studiously ignored his Populist running-mate throughout the campaign."[35] Soon, everyone would be ignoring the Populists. As Watson himself put it, "They have taken our doctrine, but they don't like our doctors."[36]

BRYAN DIDN'T WIN in 1896. Worse still for the Populists, the return of prosperity in the late 1890s quieted their complaints regarding railroads, politicians, bankers, and other alleged conspirators against the farmer. Populist issues were no longer salient. "Sockless Jerry" Simpson, defying every stereotype of him, had adeptly grasped this concept amidst deep economic depression, and high Populist hopes, in 1894. At his party's apex, he maturely explained: "[W]hen times improve, when idle men find employment and better industrial conditions prevail, then the populist party will cease to be. It will have no excuse for living, and it will go out of existence."[37] Thus it did.

America waged war against Spain over Cuba in 1898. War's demands for undivided national attention made the domestic crusades of reformers seem distracting, minor, and selfish. "The Spanish War finished us," Tom Watson lamented. "The blare of the bugle drowned the voice of the Reformer."[38]

In the days not long after the rowdies and rubes established the People's Party, one Kansas editor resigned himself to the present reality that his party was a magnet for cranks while taking solace in the past, which suggested to him that "the cranks always win." Thus, despite contemporaneous ridicule, he looked with optimism upon the future:

> The cranks are those who do not accept the existing order of things, and propose to change them. The existing order of things is always accepted by the majority, therefore the cranks are always in the minority. They are always progressive thinkers and always in advance of their time, and they always win. Called fanatics and fools at first, they are sometimes persecuted and abused. But their reforms are generally righteous, and time, reason and argument bring men to their side. Abused and ridiculed, then tolerated, then respectfully given a hearing, then supported. This has been the gauntlet that all great reforms and reformers have run, from Galileo to John Brown.[39]

After the demise of the People's Party, populist ideas became governing ideas. America became more democratic, and less republican, during the progressive era that followed. The state dictated rail rates through the Interstate Commerce Commission. The U.S. government pursued a more inflationary currency through the adoption of the Federal Reserve, and dropped gold entirely during the New Deal.

No longer content to referee, government became a participant in the economy. Capital-"P" Populism lost. Lowercase-"p" populism won.

~ 11 ~

PREACHERS OF THE
SOCIAL GOSPEL

*And in those days, the number of disciples increasing, there arose a mur-
muring of the Greeks against the Hebrews, for that their widows were neglected in the daily ministration. Then the twelve, calling together the
multitude of the disciples, said: It is not reason that we should leave the
word of God and serve tables.*

—ACTS 6:1–2

"WHAT JESUS WAS, humanity is becoming," prophesied Lyman Abbott
in 1897.[1] Wrapped in the short statement were numerous Social Gospel
assumptions: evolutionary progress, faith in humanity, the perfectibility
of man. Abbott served as pastor of Brooklyn's Plymouth Church, a post he
inherited following the 1887 death of Henry Ward Beecher. In the antebellum era, Plymouth Church served as a stop on the Underground Railroad
and the point of supply for "Beecher's Bibles"—firearms—sent to free-
soil settlers migrating to Kansas. In the progressive era, Plymouth Church
became a fount of the interdenominational creed known as the Social
Gospel. One religious Left handed the baton to another religious Left at
Plymouth Church.

The leading figures of the Social Gospel found inspiration in the
gospels according to George, Bellamy, Marx, and Engels. As with the actual
gospel, which also inspired their outlook, the Social Gospel inspired differing interpretations.

"I owe my own first awakening to the world of social problems to the
agitation of Henry George in 1886," admitted Baptist preacher and professor Walter Rauschenbusch, who acknowledged his "lifelong debt to this
single-minded apostle of a great truth."[2] George's *Progress and Poverty* had
a profound influence on Congregationalist pastor Washington Gladden's
social thought, though Gladden never fully endorsed George's single tax.[3]

Lyman Abbott, who thought the single tax on solid ground, nevertheless found that the alacrity with which George sought to implement it might do more harm than good.4

Similarly, Rauschenbusch defended Bellamy's *Looking Backward*, while Gladden found the changes wrought in Edward Bellamy's one-hundred-years-in-the-future novel too fast for his gradualist tastes.5 Though Rauschenbusch was a socialist in all but party registration, even he rejected the violent path of Marx and Engels.

The Social Gospel was very much at home within the larger progressive movement. Abbott's weekly *Outlook*, the circulation of which ultimately reached 125,000, ran the work of proto-muckraker Henry Demarest Lloyd, urban reformer Jacob Riis, Unitarian clergyman/novelist Edward Everett Hale, and, in its greatest coup, former president Theodore Roosevelt, who served as an editor of the magazine after his failed Progressive Party bid to recapture the White House.6 Washington Gladden similarly opened up his Columbus church to such nationally renowned speakers as Lloyd, Abbott, Hale, and William Dean Howells.7

If the Social Gospel allowed for a devil, it was the capitalist. Rauschenbusch proclaimed that "competition has proved itself suicidal to economic welfare" and that evolution was taking "society from the present temporary stage of individualism to a higher form of communism."8 If the government wouldn't seize the railroads outright, Washington Gladden called on it to bring them under federal control.9 Congregationalist pastor Josiah Strong playfully called for "a society whose members would refuse to buy certain articles or to trade with certain men, because their prices are *too low*."10 The Social Gospel movement worked to transform society from a basis of selfish individualism to altruistic cooperation.

Social Gospel preachers were men of radical ends but of conservative means. Washington Gladden represented progressive Protestants in denouncing the violence of labor strikes, rejecting the cheap money of the Populists, criticizing the 1894 march on Washington by Jacob Coxey's "army," and damning the anarchists who bombed policemen in Haymarket Square in 1886 and murdered the president of the United States in 1901.11 A middle ground lent itself to naïveté just as easily as to common sense. Gladden sermonized in 1910, for example, "How easy it would be to settle all the trouble, if all these men on both sides would only say, 'Come! Let us be friends.' Is that, brother men, a hard thing to say?"12 The power of reason to settle disputes was very much a part of the Social Gospel faith. That some individuals' self-interests conflicted with those of others—for example, the factory owner's interest in higher profits versus the factory worker's interest in higher wages—didn't seem to register with liberal ministers delving into politics.

Progressive Protestants were haves speaking for have-nots. The have-nots did not always relate to the language of the haves, just as the language of the haves did not always relate to the situation of the have-nots. Larger gulfs than railroad tracks separated money and poverty in American cities.

"PROGRESS" WAS THE watchword of the era. Josiah Strong, contemplating the achievements of the age, wrote: "The question, then, arises whether this great advance along physical and intellectual lines is to be followed by a new advance along spiritual lines."[13] The adherents of the Social Gospel answered in the affirmative. If industry, government, and science moved forward, then religion must, too.

The evolved church was to bring perfected man. "The swiftness of evolution in our own country proves the immense latent perfectibility in human nature," Walter Rauschenbusch wrote in *Christianity and the Social Crisis*.[14] But before man could be made superman, society must be reformed to allow for the engineering of such spiritually, morally, physically, and intellectually perfect beings. This would serve as the catalyst for the perfection of man, which would in turn serve as the catalyst for the millennium.

During the progressive era, big businesses subsumed small businesses, the national government absorbed the functions of state and local governments, and individual rights yielded to individual duties to the state. Religious trends followed suit. Rauschenbusch, perhaps the leading exponent of the Social Gospel, spoke of "national sin and salvation" and claimed that "no man is saved to himself alone."[15] Whole societies, rather than lone individuals, would achieve salvation. "We have seen that the prophets demanded right moral conduct as the sole test and fruit of religion, and that the morality which they had in mind was not the private morality of detached pious souls but the social morality of the nation."[16] The Social Gospel meshed so well with progressivism in part because its exponents were political progressives recasting their religions upon their political ideas—progress, the perfectibility of man, a paternalistic state, collectivism. (Or were these religious ideas injected into politics that found their way back to religion?) Perhaps in greater part the Social Gospel resembled progressivism because it was an integral part of, and influence on, progressivism.

Under the Social Gospel, Christianity transformed from a religion that worshipped God into one that worshipped man. Man, usually an urban,

Yankee, Protestant minister, would redeem fallen man. Man, not God, would be the catalyst for the millennium, or, as progressive Christians termed it, "the Kingdom"—the union of heaven and earth as foretold in the book of Revelation. They mistakenly believed in the nearness of the eschaton, and that it would arrive through human agency. "The kingdom of God is Utopia made rational and destined to be made actual," Josiah Strong proclaimed in *The Next Great Awakening.* "It is the new social ideal perfected. It is the New Jerusalem, come down from God out of heaven and resplendent with his glory."[17] Like so many other radicals, religious progressives sought to establish heaven on earth, the Kingdom, the millennium. They pursued religious ends by political means, and thus injected a fanaticism, self-righteousness, and dogmatism into politics. Who dares oppose the will of God?

But what was God's will? Neither priests nor the Bible held the key. The answer came from God himself, who instructed each individual personally. The Social Gospel efficiently eliminated the middleman. "Each Christian," Rauschenbusch contended, "has his own inner Bible."[18] As Rauschenbusch's theology recalled John Humphrey Noyes's, Lyman Abbott's recalled the Transcendentalists': "I believe in a God who is in and through and of everything—not an absentee God, whom we have to reach through a Bible, or a priest, or some other outside aid, but a God who is close to us."[19] When the Bible conformed to the Social Gospel, such as with the Sermon on the Mount, progressive Protestants quoted the Bible. When the Bible clashed with the Social Gospel, such as passages outlining judgment and damnation, progressive Protestants rejected the Bible in favor of God's personal instruction. Every man became his own priest; every heart, its owner's Bible.

Washington Gladden, elected moderator of the Congregationalist church and author of the lyrics of "O Master, Let Me Walk with Thee," proclaimed that "several of the best books of the Old Testament are works of fiction."[20] The declaration rubbed fundamentalists raw. Lyman Abbott, a proponent, like so many advocates of the Social Gospel, of prohibition, found the wine of Christ's day devoid of intoxicating alcohol.[21] Abbott professed doubts about the Virgin Birth and Christ feeding the multitudes with loaves and fishes.[22] "What interests me in this incident is not the multiplication of the loaves, but the spirit of consideration and helpfulness which is manifested."[23] "An infallible book is an impossible conception, and to-day no one really believes that our present Bible is such a book," Abbott held.[24]

The saving of souls gave way to the saving of people. The Social Gospel would minister to the material, rather than the spiritual, needs of the flock.

ACHIEVING AN EARTH worthy of heaven would require transformations on a massive scale, transformations that seemed even more divine in scope now that the wretched refuse of Europe had landed on America's shores. A great transformation occurred within American cities between the Civil War and the Great War. The Yankee clergymen who ministered to urban communities endured an influx of newcomers not only of a different ethnic stock, but of alien religions—or of no religion at all. The newcomers drank excessively and bred irresponsibly; brought gambling, prostitution, and prizefights to once staid neighborhoods; lived in squalid, overstuffed tenement houses and worked long hours for low wages in ghastly conditions; and polluted the streets, the gene pool, and the political process. At least that is how the Protestant reformer saw things. The newcomers couldn't help themselves; Protestant ministers could. And if it was beyond their capabilities to help those who needed it, Social Gospel ministers directed the government how to direct the less fortunate.

The most successful, and most celebrated, of all do-gooder projects of this era of do-gooder projects was launched by a pair of domestic missionaries.

Hull House was school, church, art gallery, lecture hall, nursery, library, almshouse, and youth center rolled into one Chicago mansion. A mere mansion wasn't large enough to house the venture's many programs, and so the complex expanded to include an entire city block worth of buildings. Nestled on immigrant-rich Halsted Street, Hull House was the brainchild of Jane Addams and Ellen Gates Starr, who, upon a trip to London, gained inspiration from the East End's Toynbee Hall. As their peers traveled to Asia, Africa, and points beyond to perform missionary work, Addams and Starr awaited the foreigners who came to Chicago. They established a "settlement" in their home state's largest city to service the needy. The times were ripe for the project. The ongoing domestic migration from the country to the city, and the ongoing international migration from Europe to America, transformed cities seemingly overnight. People got left behind.

"We have in America a fast-growing number of cultivated young people who have no recognized outlet for their active faculties," Addams lamented. "They hear constantly of the great social maladjustment, but no way is provided for them to change it, and their uselessness hangs about them heavily."[25] Was it Hull House's purpose to satiate the do-gooder impulses of young intellectuals or to improve the lives of the urban poor? The answer never became clear, although the project succeeded in both of these aims.

Appropriately, Hull House's self-described "first resident" had also been a resident at Brook Farm. She regaled Addams and Starr with readings from Nathaniel Hawthorne's works and tales of her interactions with the famous author. Addams recounted that the elderly woman came to Hull House because "she wished to live once more in an atmosphere where 'idealism ran high.'"[26] Like the ministers George Ripley and William Henry Channing of Brook Farm, seminary graduates Jane Addams and Ellen Gates Starr of Hull House wished to put Christ's words into action. In doing so, the actual gospel became the Social Gospel. Addams observed:

> [M]any young men and women . . . resent the assumption that Christianity is a set of ideas which belong to the religious consciousness, whatever that may be. They insist that it cannot be proclaimed and instituted apart from the social life of the community and that it must seek a simple and natural expression in the social organism itself. The Settlement movement is only one manifestation of that wider humanitarian movement which throughout Christendom, but preeminently in England, is endeavoring to embody itself, not in a sect, but in society itself.[27]

The Social Gospel became more social than gospel, and soon its advocates had little interest in the actual gospel. Apart from secularizing Christianity, Hull House encapsulated another development on the Left during the age: the transition from voluntary activism for the amelioration of social ills to agitation for the state to take on that activism. Hull House cleaned the neighborhood, opened up a park, taught adults to read, sheltered battered women, offered day care, and provided instruction in arts and crafts. Soon they wanted the city to assume these tasks. "One of the first lessons we learned at Hull-House was that private beneficence is totally inadequate to deal with the vast numbers of the city's disinherited," Addams wrote.[28] In other words, government should become one giant Hull House. In fact, many of the private organization's leaders abandoned volunteer work at Hull House for jobs on the city payroll as factory inspectors, as child welfare agents, and in other areas of social work.

The broader Social Gospel movement concurred with Addams's preference for public welfare supplanting private charity. "The Church by the voluntary gifts and labors of a few here tries to furnish what the entire

cooperative community ought to furnish," Walter Rauschenbusch complained.[29] To that end, Rauschenbusch, while a minister in Hell's Kitchen,
successfully lobbied New York's city government for the installation of
sand piles in parks for the children of the concrete jungle to play in safely.
As a minister and a college professor in Rochester, Rauschenbusch demanded city-financed swimming pools for the public.[30] From the pulpit,
Rauschenbusch, like Washington Gladden in Columbus, Ohio, didn't hesitate to direct his parishioners where to mark their ballots.[31] Gladden went
so far in combining religion with politics that he won a seat on the Columbus city council from 1900 to 1902. If the state were to take on the church's
traditional role, salvation must come through the ballot box.

Against the current of the turn-of-the-nineteenth-century Left, the
Social Gospelers sought God's government. They were throwbacks to
an earlier Left, though it was not yet clear that a Christian Left was an
anachronism. Josiah Strong called for the spiritualizing of the temporal
world by way of "every act" done for the "glory of God," noting, "there is
no room for the so-called 'secular,' and that whatever cannot be done to
God's glory and the upbuilding of the kingdom is forbidden and unholy."[32]
"Whoever uncouples the religious and the social life has not understood
Jesus," Rauschenbusch proclaimed. "Whoever sets any bounds for the re-
constructive power of the religious life over the social relations and institutions of men, to that extent denies the faith of the Master."[33] The Baptist
preacher envisioned Christ's church "nudging the reluctant State along
like an enlightened pedagogue."[34]

IT WAS NOT merely on domestic affairs that the Social Gospel could be of
service to the state. The liberal principles progressive Protestants sought
to inject into the governance of American cities must also be injected into
the governance of foreign lands. It was bad enough that a Spanish
monarch reigned over Cuba, an island ninety miles from the land of the
free. That the monarch was a papist, as were his distant subjects, further
violated Social Gospel sensibilities. In 1898, when America launched a
war with Spain over its colonial outpost of Cuba, liberal Protestant ministers provided William McKinley's administration with religious sanction
and its most vocal support.

As was the case four decades before, a righteous cause converted pacifists into warriors. As a young preacher, Lyman Abbott used the pulpit to
reconcile the Civil War with Christianity.[35] During the Spanish-American
War, Abbott rehashed his arguments. "I am not arguing for war," Abbott
told his flock on Sunday, March 13, 1898, "nor for national aggrandize-
ment, but I am for this: that we as a nation share in the responsibility,

not only for our own national affairs but for the order and peace of the whole world."[36] He supported violent means when they served righteous ends, such as the Civil War and the Spanish-American War. Abbott cited scripture, and Christ's example in the temple, to rationalize his advocacy of war for God's purposes. "Christ used force to defend others," he explained years later, "but never to defend himself. The fundamental principle in Christ's teaching is this: Love may use force; selfishness may not."[37]

Abbott lived long enough to again recycle his righteous-war arguments for World War I. Other preachers, inspired by the Social Gospel, contemporaneously recycled his arguments during the Spanish-American War.

"America is being used to carry on the work of God in this war, which no politician could create, control, or gainsay," declared William Rainsford, rector of St. George's Episcopal Church of New York.[38]

"I do not believe that there ever was a war more righteous than that which we have undertaken, nor one closer to the law of the self-sacrificing Christ that we bear one another's burdens," Wayland Hoyt, pastor of New York's Brick Presbyterian Church, maintained of the Spanish-American War. "If there ever was a war simply for the sake of humanity with no desire or purpose of national greed of any sort, it is the one that now is upon us, calling our soldiers and the navy to arms."[39]

Washington Gladden justified not only the invasion of Cuba but also the subsequent occupation: "To help them overthrow the Government of Spain, and then go away and let them set up savagery in the place of tyranny would be a disreputable proceeding."[40] Gladden foresaw the day when America would provide deliverance to the oppressed of all humanity.[41] The Spanish-American War would be the first of many such conquests for liberation. Foreign wars, marketed as redemptive crusades, followed each of the four great attempts at redemptive reform in American history—populism, progressivism, the New Deal, and the Great Society. That the foreign wars effectively ended the domestic crusades is widely understood. That they were extensions of those crusades is not.

The Social Gospel took up the white man's burden to seek another's profit and work another's gain. But Filipinos, Hawaiians, Puerto Ricans, and Cubans didn't necessarily see things that way. They didn't want the type of help the U.S. government offered. The beneficent intentions behind the war policy didn't matter to them. The ghastly results did. Idealists didn't have to live with the grim reality their lofty ideals created. This protected their ideals from reevaluation. Such are the dangers of reform from above. Though paternalism revealed its deficiencies most obviously in violent crusades for redemption, the pattern of results wildly escaping intentions and of beneficiaries becoming victims repeated itself in future progressive reform attempts.

THE CLOSING OF the frontier inspired Henry George to offer his single tax to solve the problem of rising land costs. It compelled conservative farmers to become radical populists. It sparked adherents of the Social Gospel to revive Manifest Destiny. The impulse that had once coveted northern Mexico and the British Canadian southwest now desired lands far away. Other voices from the American past, notably Washington and his "disinterested warnings of a parting friend" not to "quit our own to stand upon foreign ground," were echoed in warnings from former president Grover Cleveland, steel tycoon Andrew Carnegie, and industrialist-turned-political-maestro Mark Hanna.[42] Wasn't America founded in rebellion against imperialism? That was the past, and progress meant moving forward, moving away from the past.

Just as the Social Gospel's theological quirks caused rifts within Protestantism, sparking the birth of modern fundamentalism, the Social Gospel's stand on the Spanish-American War caused fissures among progressives that never healed.

Reverend William H. P. Faunce, soon to be president of Brown University, quipped that "the Kingdom of Heaven is to come as a grain of mustard seed, not as a thirteen-inch shell."[43] "Every congressman and senator who votes for war should be obliged to join a regiment and go to the front," maintained Herbert Casson, pastor of the Labor Church in Lynn, Massachusetts. "Let them go to Cuba, and if they never come back there will be no valuable lives lost."[44] "One hardly knows what to say of the earnestness with which in certain Christian journals and Christian pulpits expansion is put forth as a means of extending the Kingdom of Christ," confessed Presbyterian minister and Anti-Imperialist League vice president Charles H. Parkhurst. "It is a novel idea that the reign of Jesus is to be widened in the world under protection of shells and dynamite."[45]

One side of the debate saw war as justified when used as a tool for progressive purposes. The other side of the debate saw no justification for war. Particularly pronounced within religious circles, the debate largely characterized the argument over war within the larger Left. The disagreement on the Left between pacifists and crusaders started well before the Spanish-American War, and continued long after its cessation.

THE SOCIAL GOSPEL failed to convert socialists, labor activists, and progressives to its brand of Christianity. It did convert many Christians to socialism, progressivism, or some other leftist variant. A religion obsessed with the material has little attention for the spiritual. It ceases to be a religion and becomes an ideology.

Soon, leftism—a set of ideas first advanced on these shores by Christian fanatics—became increasingly inhospitable to Christians. Jesus Christ yielded to Karl Marx.

∽ 12 ∽

THE PATERNALIST DYNASTY II: PATRIOTIC PROGRESSIVES

Look up to heaven and see, and behold the sky, that it is higher than thee.

—JOB 35:5

As THE NINETEENTH century transitioned into the twentieth century—the American century—Americans had cause to think that they lived in an age of progress.

Man no longer depended on the sun for light, but instead looked to Thomas Edison. Man relied less on the horse for transportation and more on Henry Ford. And man turned to the Wright brothers to break the oppressive chains of gravity. The sky, it seemed, wasn't the limit.

The progressive era was a time of unbounded optimism. Businessmen and inventors relied, with great success, on scientific principles. Wasn't it time for government officials to do the same? Surely this was the road to progress.

On this premise, the state grew, and grew, and grew. So did many of the problems the progressive state promised to abolish. Even an army of experts, culled from the best universities and corporations, couldn't manage an entire society. But they thought that they could. Afflicted with the arrogance that led contemporaries to declare the *Titanic* an unsinkable ship, progressives believed that poverty, war, disease—all that ailed man—could be eradicated through the power of the state. Like the *Titanic*, the managers, planners, and experts of the progressive era crashed into reality.

·   ·   ·

PROGRESS IMPLIES MOVEMENT toward a designated end. Progressives, thus, differed from radicals in means. Progressives were gradualists, not immediatists. Progressives sought to reform, not to overthrow. Their antecedents included Bellamy and George, not Marx.

Progress also implied a difference in ends with radicals. To opt for reform over revolution is to concede that something about the existing system is worth saving. Radicals conceded no such thing.

This deference to the existing system likely had something to do with the status of progressives within it. Whereas labor radicals, anarchists, and socialists often had no major stake in the United States of America, progressives did. They were generally middle-class people committed to the rehabilitation, the perfection even, of fallen man. They looked down and tried to reorient the leisure activities of the lower class. They looked up and tried to reorient the financial priorities of the upper class. Were poor people visiting brothels, staging prizefights, idling, spending time in barrooms? Were rich people throwing extravagant parties, flaunting their wealth, not donating enough to charity, paying their workers less than they should? Yes, and when the rich and poor transgressed progressive values, progressives were there to set them right. Progressives were very much about telling other people what to do.

Working within the democratic system, progressives had a far greater impact on American governance than earlier Lefts generally had. Through their reforms, the state began telling people what to do also. The state told men to join its army. The state confiscated the incomes of wealthy Americans because it believed that it could spend that money in a more enlightened manner. The state forbade certain Americans from breeding to protect the purity of the gene pool. The state manipulated the value of the currency. The state dictated what prices corporations could sell certain goods at. The state told the citizens what they couldn't drink and what the charge for certain foods would be. The state even dictated to foreigners what type of government would serve them best.

THE RAPID WEALTH creation during America's industrial age, which had widened the gap between rich and poor and attracted the dispossessed and radical of Europe to America's shores, also had served as a third catalyst for the Left's surge. The money spawned a rather large leisure class with the time, and the alienation, to criticize, and at times despise, the surrounding culture.

Thorstein Veblen's *Theory of the Leisure Class*, published in 1899, was a broadside against servants, fineries, fraternities, sports, cap-and-gown graduations, classic languages, duels, religion, walking sticks, property rights, hunting, manners, and other extravagances, traditions, and pastimes of the wealthy. The sins of the "leisure class," according to Veblen, included engaging in non-productive work, setting a fashion of the antiquated way of life, and blocking reform in order to conserve the status quo.[1] By using the terms "conservative" and "wealthy" interchangeably— "The leisure class is the conservative class"—Veblen, himself a member of the leisure class he castigated, made the enduring mistake of all ideologues by conveniently relegating enemies (conservatives) to a numerically insignificant group (the wealthy) distinct from the surrounding society.[2] He complained that "the wealthier class comes to exert a retarding influence upon social development far in excess of that which the simple numerical strength of the class would assign it. Its prescriptive example acts to greatly stiffen the resistance of all other classes against any innovation, and to fix men's affections upon the good institutions handed down from an earlier generation."[3] Tradition and wealth were hindrances to progress, or at least what Thorstein Veblen saw as progress. Class warfare had rarely been dressed up in such urbane, sesquipedalian words, and never had it been generaled, at least on the proletarian side, by an academic named Thorstein.

The pragmatism of William James contained what *could have* become an antidote to the age's many dogmas and isms. Instead, it added to them. Pragmatism asked that we judge ideas not based upon tradition's or ideology's demands but by the way ideas work in present practice. Corrupting this commonsense wisdom was the confusion of practicality with truth. Pragmatism's "only test of probable truth is what works best in the way of leading us, what fits every part of life best and combines with the collectivity of experience's demands, nothing being omitted," James wrote. "If theological ideas should do this, if the notion of God, in particular, should prove to do it, how could pragmatism possibly deny God's existence?"[4] Taking a bit from the utilitarians who preceded them, leaving a bit to the relativists who followed them, the pragmatists—John Dewey, F. C. S. Schiller, George Herbert Mead—found their ideas popularized in James's 1907 offering, *Pragmatism: A New Name for Some Old Ways of Thinking.* "Ought we ever not to believe what it is *better for* us to believe?" *Pragmatism* asked. "And can we then keep the notion of what is better for us, and what is true for us, permanently apart?"[5] Pragmatism answered no.

Charles Beard's 1913 indictment of the Founding Fathers, *An Economic Interpretation of the Constitution of the United States*, mirrored contemporary charges against politicians and captains of industry. It also resembled Karl Marx's economic interpretation of history. Beard proposed that the Framers knew they would financially benefit from a more centralized government, which abolished internal trade restrictions, and, perhaps most importantly, which paid its debt to the wealthy noteholders. "The members of the Philadelphia Convention which drafted the Constitution were, with a few exceptions, immediately, directly, and personally interested in, and derived economic advantages from, the establishment of the new system," Beard concluded. "The Constitution was essentially an economic document based upon the concept that the fundamental private rights of property are anterior to government and morally beyond the reach of popular majorities."[6]

To remake America anew, it is helpful to discredit the past. Progressives, who would both ignore and amend the founding document with great frequency, discovered valuable ammunition in *An Economic Interpretation of the Constitution.*

Charles Beard's academic investigation into the financial interests of the Founding Fathers paralleled the journalistic investigations into contemporary political and industrial leaders. Beard was called "historian." His media colleagues were called "muckrakers."

"I DID NOT want to preserve, I wanted to destroy the facts," investigative journalist Lincoln Steffens admitted. "My purpose was no more scientific than the spirit of my investigation and reports; it was, as I said above, to see if the shameful facts, spread out in all their shame, would not burn through our civic shamelessness and set fire to American pride."[7] To that end, Steffens investigated the municipal governments of St. Louis, Chicago, New York, Minneapolis, Philadelphia, and Pittsburgh for *McClure's Magazine.* He ultimately housed the sensationalistic articles he produced under the roof of the 1904 book, *The Shame of the Cities.* In St. Louis, Steffens told of "great furniture vans" bringing repeat voters from precinct to precinct.[8] Pittsburgh, Steffens contended, "was turned over by the State to an individual to do with as he pleased."[9] The mayor of Minneapolis handed "the city over to outlaws who were to work under police direction for the profit of his administration."[10] If the "shameful facts" showed that officeholders abused power, why did Steffens, like so many progressives, strangely offer the antidote of even more power for public officials?

Steffens was probably foremost in the mind of President Theodore Roosevelt when, recalling John Bunyan's *Pilgrim's Progress*, he chastised "the Man with the Muck-Rake, the man who could look no way but downward, with a muck-rake in his hand; who was offered a celestial crown for his muck-rake, but who would neither look up nor regard the crown he was offered, but continued to rake to himself the filth of the floor."[11] Such negative, sensationalistic, advocacy journalism cut both ways for Roosevelt. So much of his domestic program passed because of it. But as a progressive posing as a conservative (or was he a conservative posing as a progressive?), Roosevelt, as he did on most issues throughout his political career, equivocated on the muckrakers. He was a politician, after all, and a superb one at that. He played all sides. On the one hand, he said that the man who "consistently refuses to see aught that is lofty . . . speedily becomes, not a help to society, not an incitement to good, but one of the most potent forces for evil." On the other hand, Roosevelt conceded that the "men with the muck-rakes are often indispensable to the well-being of society."¹² Roosevelt saw himself as a responsible man tasked with channeling the irresponsible catcalls of would-be revolutionists into healthy reform that would preserve, not overthrow, the American system.

One of those hoping to overthrow, and not preserve, the system was Upton Sinclair, who wrote the muckraking novel *The Jungle* with revolutionary intentions.¹³ The public's reading of it begot reformist results.

The Jungle depicts the American dream as the American nightmare. Jurgis Rudkus emigrates from Lithuania to Chicago, where a series of misfortunes, all linked to capitalism, befall him and his extended family. Dangerous workplace chemicals eat the flesh off Jurgis's father's body and kill him. Layoffs and job-related maimings plague the family. Jurgis turns to drink. His wife, Ona, gets molested by her boss. Jurgis seeks revenge on the politically connected man, which results in jail and the blacklist. His house gets repossessed. Second-rate medical treatment takes the life of Jurgis's newborn and his wife, who gets buried in a pine box in a potter's field. Jurgis's son Antanas drowns in the street when it floods after municipal neglect.

Jurgis can't beat the rotten system, so he joins it. Jurgis sells his vote, begs, robs, involves himself in vice, and becomes a "scab." His life improves. The lesson? The system rewards evil and punishes good. Alas, Jurgis falls out with capitalism's criminal in-crowd—the police, the politicians, the bosses—but, in a moment of absolute despair, he becomes reborn in socialism. He finds in socialism a "message of salvation," "deliverance," and "the new religion of humanity—or you might say it was the fulfillment of the old religion, since it implied but the literal application of all the teachings of Christ."¹⁴

The Jungle, despite being a work of fiction, pays homage within its pages to Eugene Debs, Henry Demarest Lloyd's book *Wealth Against Commonwealth*, and J. A. Wayland's paper *Appeal to Reason*, where the novel was initially serialized. Sinclair's socialism is homegrown. But among foreign socialist prophets, Robert Owen exerts greater influence on the book than Karl Marx does. Indeed, one passage seems a regurgitation of Owen's "Declaration of Mental Independence," in which he lambasted capitalism, marriage, and religion. "The purpose of government," Sinclair writes, "was the guarding of property rights, the perpetuation of ancient force and modern fraud. Or was it marriage? Marriage and prostitution were two sides of one shield, the predatory man's exploitation of the sex pleasure. The difference between them was a difference of class. If a woman had money she might dictate her own terms: equality, a life contract, and the legitimacy—that is, the property rights—of her children. If she had no money, she was a proletarian, and sold herself for an existence. And then the subject became Religion, which was the Archfiend's deadliest weapon. Government oppressed the body of the wage slave, but Religion oppressed his mind, and poisoned the stream of progress at its source."[15]

Sinclair's socialism of 1906 hardly differed from Owen's socialism of 1826.

Despite its over-the-top proselytizing for socialism, *The Jungle* primarily enlisted converts for a different crusade. Jurgis's bad experiences with capitalism primarily occur in Chicago's Packingtown, where "rats, bread, and meat would go into the hoppers together" along with the "dirt and rust and old nails and stale water" of emptied "waste barrels." It all wound up on the kitchen table.[16] The novel's most arresting passage describes a man falling into a lard vat only to eventually make his way to some unwitting cannibal's frying pan.[17] Despite being a peddler of fiction, Sinclair declared this and other fantastic passages factual. "Naturally this was a hard matter to prove," Sinclair would later maintain, "since in each case the families had been paid off and shipped to other parts of the world."[18] To Sinclair's dismay, the reading public seized on the issue of unsanitary food, not capitalism. "I aimed at the public's heart and by accident I hit it in the stomach."[19]

An outraged public demanded action. President Theodore Roosevelt read *The Jungle* and summoned Sinclair. Roosevelt castigated Congress for its passivity. The federal government investigated the novel's charges. Foreigners seized on the book to support restrictions on meat imports from America.[20] And Congress, partly based on the controversy generated by *The Jungle*, passed the Pure Food and Drug Act of 1906, which empowered the federal government to inspect food, directed truthful labeling, and outlined sentencing guidelines for offenders.[21]

The Jungle played an important role in molding public opinion and advancing legislation. The days of the Left retreating to woodland communes or urban debating societies were over. No longer on the fringe, the

Left was a force. Theodore Roosevelt, Woodrow Wilson, and other politicians of import took notice. They catered to the ideas and visions of this constituency.

The Jungle was one of many books that directly impacted public policy. Henry Demarest Lloyd's *Wealth Against Commonwealth* and Ida Tarbell's *History of the Standard Oil Company* focused attacks on John D. Rockefeller's behemoth Standard Oil. Because such muckrakers aimed at influencing public policy, they often bent the truth to serve their political ends. Sinclair, for instance, later wrote a book rallying the Left to Sacco and Vanzetti's defense as he privately conceded the anarchist pair's guilt.[22] Ida Tarbell, who penned her exposé of Standard Oil after it put her oilman father out of business, grew weary of the politicized genre. "I soon found that most of them wanted attacks," Tarbell complained of the audience she had cultivated. "They had little interest in balanced findings."[23]

But muckraking journalism, balanced or not, led to law.

AMID ECSTATIC CONVENTIONEERS singing "Onward Christian Soldiers," former president Theodore Roosevelt accepted the Progressive Party's nomination for president in 1912. In his "Confession of Faith" acceptance speech, the party's nominee informed: "We stand at Armageddon, and we battle for the Lord."[24] Chief among the demons the Progressives itched to cast out from their envisioned crusader state was the greedy businessman. "Whenever in any business the prosperity of the business man is obtained by lowering the wages of his workmen and charging an excessive price to the consumers, we wish to interfere and stop such practices," Roosevelt explained. "We will not submit to that kind of prosperity any more than we will submit to prosperity obtained by swindling investors or getting unfair advantages over business rivals."[25] Such was the attitude that breathed life into the nascent regulatory state.

Populist agitation gave birth to 1887's Interstate Commerce Act. Progressive courts, congresses, and presidents gave the act teeth. The legislation established the Interstate Commerce Commission (ICC), gave it power to investigate railroads and publish its findings, outlawed rebates and other forms of price discrimination (excepting, tellingly, discounts for the government), mandated that railroads compile data for the government, and forbade "unjust and unreasonable" pricing, whatever that meant.[26] The legislation was the first instance of bureaucratic regulation of private business at the federal level. What began as government tinkering during the administration of Grover Cleveland ended up as a complete government takeover during the administration of Woodrow Wilson. In between, the ICC gradually became a fourth branch of government that usurped powers from the three constitutional branches. Federal involvement in the railroads prefaced federal involvement in all sorts of business activities.

The Sherman Antitrust Act of 1890 further expanded government's power in private business. It made cutthroat competition a felony. It prohibited business "in restraint of trade or commerce," creating maximum penalties of three years in prison or, in the case of corporations, $10 million fines.[27] The alleged victims of cutthroat competition, the consumers, were victimized twice over with the passage of this bill. Sour-grapes companies, whose competitors enlarged their market shares by *lowering* prices, no longer needed to compete in the market. By crying "no fair" to the government, they could now hamstring business adversaries. The Supreme Court initially derailed the legislation, but then reinvigorated it with 1904's *Minnesota v. Northern Securities.* President William Howard Taft then used the law to break up Standard Oil and American Tobacco.

The Hepburn Act of 1906 enhanced the power of the ICC, established rules making corporations charged by the ICC guilty until proven innocent, and empowered government to set maximum railroad shipping rates to not exceed what it considered just and reasonable prices.[28] A revolutionary transformation of commerce ensued. The government, and not the parties involved (railroads and customers), determined prices. The market, planners explained, was too anarchic, too irrational, and too inefficient to set prices for an ordered, rational, and efficient age. The ICC commissioners, unable by law to have any connection to the railroad business, would now determine prices for the railroad business.

The Clayton Antitrust Act of 1914 forbade companies from offering the same goods or services for different prices, and empowered a governmental commission with judicial powers that placed "the burden of rebutting the prima-facie case . . . upon the person charged with a violation of this section."[29] At the same time, Woodrow Wilson's legislative program instituted the Federal Trade Commission (FTC) to enforce the Clayton Antitrust Act. But like so many government programs, it quickly engaged in activities beyond its initial mandate. In addition to acting as a quasi-judiciary, the FTC acted as a quasi-legislature by making rules and investigating alleged infractions, and as a quasi-executive by enforcing the rules it created. Aside from the obvious conflict in acting as accuser and judge, how, in a republic, did an unelected body get to make law? What the ICC was to the railroads, the FTC became to other industries.

The domino effect of the Interstate Commerce Act was to permanently establish a government beyond the control of the governed, a pseudo-government that governed matters beyond even the real government's

constitutional purview. The U.S. government became less the government of the voters, despite superficial moves in that direction during the
progressive era, and more the government of technocrats, lawyers, and
managers.

Businessmen, defeated in the open market, now vanquished foes
with the aid of the state. The referee became a participant. Losers became
winners.

But the complaints of the businessmen now on the outs rang hollow.
Hadn't railroad magnates accepted subsidies from the federal government? Hadn't railroads gotten their land for free? Hadn't they constructed
deliberately circuitous routes after charging the government by mile of
track laid? The railroads had played the government for a sucker. The government now exacted its awful revenge.

The ICC had five times as many employees in 1909 as it had in 1890.
After the Hepburn Act's passage, complaints grew exponentially as well.[30]
Bureaucratic regulations at the federal level, nonexistent prior to the Interstate Commerce Act, naturally expanded. All of this took its toll. Railroad prices had decreased as railroad profits increased prior to the
Interstate Commerce Act. Railroad prices increased and railroad profits
decreased after the ICC became empowered during Theodore Roosevelt's
administration.[31]

The federal government dictated to the railroads their prices, confiscated excess profits, and forced them to operate unprofitable lines. Private railroads could not long survive under such "progressive" conditions.

Grover Cleveland had signed the legislation creating the ICC.
Theodore Roosevelt had, through the Hepburn Act's expansion of the
ICC, directed private industry by government "experts." Woodrow Wilson
dropped the pretense of a "private" railroad industry operating amidst the
progressive state.

In 1917, the federal government took over operation of the formerly
private railroads. A year later, Walter Weyl of the *New Republic* cheered
going from the "organized chaos" and "forced dissociation" of 2,905 railroad companies to "the advantage of unity" in one railroad company run by
the U.S. government.[32] In reality, there was little to cheer. After the government took over the railroads, the ICC raised freight rates by 28 percent and
passenger rates by 18 percent. Contrary to Weyl's claims, too, the nationalization of America's railroards did not lead to vast savings. Within two years
of operation the Railroad Administration was $1.2 billion in the red.[33]

Edward Bellamy's dream had become America's nightmare. Wilson's
folly lasted until 1920. The ICC folly lasted seventy-five years more.

. . .

IF THE PROGRESSIVES fulfilled the hopes of populists with the ICC, they dashed them with Western land set-asides.

In 1892, John Muir founded the Sierra Club. Whereas populists lamented the closing of the frontier because of its deleterious effects on the availability of cheap land, progressives lamented the closing of the frontier because it represented the dwindling domain of Mother Nature. To preserve what remained, Muir and his followers urged the federal government to close off acreage to development. One conservationist, having absorbed the progressive vibe, explained that "what we want is the best for the people, not the individual."[34]

America's transformation from a rural to an urban nation transformed American values. In 1900, six in ten Americans lived in towns of fewer than 2,500 people. By 1920, most Americans lived in communities with more than 2,500 people.[35] The individual nature of country life yielded to the social nature of urban life. As the power shifted, along with the people, to the cities, the cities imposed their values—collective over individual—upon the country. This proved especially true with conservation. As the view from America's window increasingly contained tenements, automobiles, and piled garbage, and not mountains, trees, and grazing animals, Americans attached a mythical quality to the distant West. Nature was gone from where they lived, but city dwellers hoped to save it where others lived. Westerners, who in turn coveted aspects of eastern living—wealth, convenience, concrete footpaths—resented easterners who sought to deny to them what they wanted. Why, Coloradans, Wyomingites, and Montanans must have wondered, should a New Yorker dictate how their states' lands should be used?

In 1903, President Roosevelt and John Muir went camping in Yosemite. Muir caught his ear. Yosemite caught his eye. Already an outdoorsman, and attracted to conservation's rhetoric of collectivism and statist methods, Roosevelt acted. He declared spacious areas national parks and national monuments and set aside tens of millions of acres of land, therefore rendering a substantial portion of the West off-limits to construction, mining, logging, and farming. Outraged at Roosevelt's heavy-handedness, Congress curtailed the president's ability to withdraw lands from use. But Roosevelt set a precedent of exerting federal power for environmentalist ends. Rather than trust private owners not to destroy the value of their property, environmentalists put faith in bureaucrats to steward the land. Environmentalism, from the progressive era onward, saw the state as the means through which it would achieve its ends.

. . .

THE CONSTITUTION TASKED Congress with coining money. Congress abdicated that responsibility by passing the Federal Reserve Act of 1913. No longer did the elected representatives of the people determine the money supply. A cast of banking experts, led by a chairman appointed by the president, did.

Under the Constitution, the original dollar inflated less than 10 percent in the 125 years leading to the establishment of the Federal Reserve. Since 1914, the currency has been inflated more than 2,000 percent.[36] The same year that Congress inaugurated the backdoor tax of inflation through the Federal Reserve it legalized a more blunt method of confiscation: the income tax.

The winner of the presidential election was uncertain in the summer of 1912. One outcome of the election, the income tax, was not. All four candidates—Democrat Woodrow Wilson, Republican William Howard Taft, Progressive Theodore Roosevelt, and Socialist Eugene Debs— supported an income tax.

To impose one, a constitutional amendment was needed. Though an income tax had been established during the Civil War without court interference, its return in 1894 received a quick rebuke from the Supreme Court, which deemed the direct tax a violation of the Constitution's rule of uniformity in *Pollock v. Farmers' Loan & Trust*.

The Sixteenth Amendment was ratified in 1913, providing more evidence that an age of persuasion had been replaced by an age of compulsion. The resulting income tax confiscated for the federal government a relatively modest 7 percent of the wealthiest earners' incomes. Most Americans paid nothing. Within four years, the government's take from the highest earners had become eleven times its initial rate and many who didn't pay under the initial rates suffered greatly.

A 77 percent tax rate, however, was too low for some of President Wilson's staunchest supporters. In a piece entitled "The Conscription of Income," a war-crazy *New Republic* suggested that *all* income above $100,000 should go to the federal government. Such taxation would "check positively indecent extravagance," result in a "nearly complete cessation of civilian purchases of clothes" (leaving all for the soldiers), and cripple charity, which, the writer opined, would be a positive development because that "which is now left to private benevolence is properly a government function and could be far more effectively handled through its agency."[37]

President Warren Harding's postwar return to "normalcy, not nostrums," so welcome in the face of such "abnormalcy," included a drastic reduction in tax rates. The top marginal rate sank from a wartime high of 77 percent in 1918 to 25 percent under Harding's successor, Calvin Coolidge. Alas, federal income taxes never dropped to their initial 7 percent rate—let alone reverted to non-existence, the status quo for most of U.S. history.

THE CONSTITUTION HAD been amended just three times in the 109 years preceding the Sixteenth Amendment. The Constitution would be amended four times during the seven years that followed Woodrow Wilson's election to the presidency. Two of these alterations on the founding document involved the process of elections.

America became more of a democracy and less of a republic during the progressive era. The populists had planted the seeds. The progressives harvested the crop.

"The first essential in the Progressive programme is the right of the people to rule," Theodore Roosevelt told the Progressive Party's convention in 1912.[38] Like much of Roosevelt's rhetoric, it reflected rather than shaped the age. Roosevelt was the ultimate populist, one who identified the public's desire and capitalized. The public desired a more direct role in governance. Sometimes they got it. Sometimes they did not.

First came the secret, or Australian, ballot. This allowed, as the former name implies, privacy in the act of voting. This arrived, as the latter name implies, in America after its use in other nations. Before the Australian ballot became universal, ballots cast were often marked, or colored, or produced by the parties themselves, which indicated to bystanders the choice of the voter. Purchasing votes or intimidating voters, it was argued, would be more difficult with ballots cast in private. Massachusetts inaugurated the ballot's use in 1888, and by 1910 every state had followed.[39]

Primaries replaced parties as the main method of candidate selection. Increasingly, Democrats and Republicans no longer had the prerogative of nominating the candidates who would represent their parties. The people now did. In some instances, the people choosing a party's nominee were not even members of that party. In 1910, Oregon inaugurated the practice of binding delegates to represent the primary voters. Most states—some immediately, others over time—followed suit.

More than a dozen states adopted the recall, the means to eject politicians from office between elections, but they infrequently employed the measure. Voters have recalled just two governors, both on the political Left, which places the recall in the category of law passed by progressives but used by their enemies.[40]

Progressives deemed it insufficiently democratic to elect lawmakers to make laws. Rejecting the American tradition of amendments, the veto, and other republican measures designed to check temporary passions, they looked to Switzerland, which had, for many years, relied on popular legislation. In 1898, South Dakota instituted the initiative to empower the people to initiate legislation, and the referendum to refer passed laws to the people for their rejection or affirmation. Utah, Oregon, and then the rest of the West (save New Mexico) followed suit. By the time America had entered Woodrow Wilson's war for democracy, nineteen states had joined South Dakota in moving from representative democracy to a mixture of representative democracy and direct democracy.[41]

"The political reformer in a representative government who seeks through the referendum to find a short cut to political purity and ideal lawmaking seems doomed to disappointment," political scientist W. Rodman Peabody wisely noted in 1905. "Like many other short cuts it apparently leads into a forest of new complications."[42] The complications, and disappointments, for the advocates of the direct legislation included so many examples of reactionary ends achieved through progressive means.[43] Historian Richard Hofstadter noted that "the more ardent reformers who expected that the public will, once expressed directly, would bring a radical transformation of the old order were surprised to find voters exercising their prerogative in the most conservative way, rejecting, for instance, proposals for municipal ownership, the single tax, and pensions for city employees."[44]

With the passage of the Seventeenth Amendment in 1913, progressives forever altered the design of the Founding Fathers for the upper chamber of Congress to represent the states and the lower chamber to represent the people. By abolishing the election of senators by state legislatures and instituting direct elections by the people, the amendment left the state governments with no representation under the ostensibly federal system.

Progressives failed to abolish the electoral college, establish elections for federal judges, or institute nationwide initiatives, referenda, and recalls. For better and worse, they did significantly alter the way that all American voters cast ballots. The impact was especially pronounced for American women, who could vote in just a handful of states prior to ratification of the Nineteenth Amendment.

"The woman suffrage movement had no official ideology," Aileen Kraditor writes in *The Ideas of the Woman Suffrage Movement, 1890–1920*.[45] The suffragists were predominantly wealthy, college-educated, Protestant, white women with self-interests in mind.[46] "Few suffragists were radicals; the vast majority of them simply wanted the right to participate more fully in the affairs of a government the basic structure of which they accepted."[47]

For the anti-suffragists, the family stood as the political unit of society, with the patriarch—the ruler of that unit—representing it in the political process. Each family's ruler, the argument went, collectively determined who ruled the local family, the state family, the national family. Even though the suffragists weren't necessarily radicals, the attainment of their goals radically altered society. Voting now meant something different. Individual representation replaced family representation.

Supporters of woman suffrage surely included reformers who fantasized that if women had the vote, then alcohol, child labor, prizefighting, and other evils would be eradicated. At the same time, racists—in the North, alarmed at the immigrant invasion of the cities; in the South, in perpetual fear of rule by the black man—envisioned female suffrage as doubling the white vote and protecting the political supremacy of the white race.

Suffragists astutely exploited the sometimes contradictory desires of their supporters.

"The National [Association] has always recognized the usefulness of woman suffrage as a counterbalance to the foreign vote, and as a means of legally preserving white supremacy in the South," wrote one leader of the National American Woman Suffrage Association (NAWSA) to a colleague.[48] Elizabeth Cady Stanton offered a number of arguments for an education requirement for suffrage, including that it would exclude the "violent, unreasoning, ignorant" strikers and "limit the foreign vote."[49] Carrie Chapman Catt blamed "the inertia in the growth of Democracy" on "aggressive movements that, with possibly ill-advised haste, enfranchised the foreigner, the negro, and the Indian. Perilous conditions, seeming to follow from the introduction into the body politic of vast numbers of irresponsible citizens, have made the nation timid."[50]

The female suffragists were just that: *female suffragists*. By the turn of the century, Kraditor observes, "The woman suffrage movement had ceased to be a campaign to *extend the franchise to* all adult Americans. Instead, one important part of its rationale had become the proposal to *take the vote away from* some Americans—Negroes in the South, and naturalized citizens in the North."[51] In 1893, NAWSA passed a resolution pointing out that literate white women outnumbered negro and foreign voters.[52] In 1913, NAWSA leaders requested that Ida Wells-Barnett not march with the Illinois delegation in the massive Washington, D.C., inauguration-eve suffragist march. She was black, and southern suffragists objected to marching with a black woman. She marched anyway, but only by sneaking into the parade after it had started.53 Six years later, NAWSA, again afraid to rock the boat, discouraged an application for affiliation from an organization of black women suffragists.54

If racial insensitivity and outright bigotry were needed to amend the Constitution to allow women the vote, then so be it. And anyhow, hadn't women been thrown under the bus when they were excluded from the Fifteenth Amendment? Partly reacting to the realities of their time, partly reflecting the realities of their time, the leading female suffragists clearly looked away from the racism in their own movement when they weren't drumming it up.

The women's rights movement had hitched its star to anti-racist movements prior to the Civil War with no reward. When it remained indifferent, or hostile, to the grievances of racial minorities in the progressive era, it attained its goal of a constitutional amendment forcing all states to grant women the vote.

It is flattering, but rarely accurate, to cast one's favored group as history's heroes. While many progressives, some socialists, and a few populists supported woman suffrage, a few progressives, some socialists, and many populists opposed it. To be a leftist in the early years of the twentieth century did not mean to be a suffragist. And to be a suffragist did not mean to be a leftist. To project our ideological needs upon the past makes the past more the present than the past.

UNLIKE THE DIVORCE of woman suffrage from anti-racist movements, the movements to attain women's suffrage and to prohibit alcohol stayed married. As feminist and prohibitionist Alice Stone Blackwell put it, "In the main suffrage and prohibition have the same friends and the same enemies."55 This symbiosis endured through the three waves of prohibition that hit America. Just as Susan B. Anthony, Lucretia Mott, and Elizabeth Cady Stanton had joined feminism and temperance in America's first wave of prohibition in the 1840s and 1850s, suffragists and prohibitionists allied the causes in the culminating, early-twentieth-century wave.

The temperance crusade interrupted by the Civil War began anew in the decades that followed. In 1880, Kansas codified prohibition. The Sunflower State's famous daughter, Carry A. Nation, eschewed agitation for "hatchetation." She smashed up bars and saloons with an ax. "Sometimes a rock; sometimes a hatchet; God told me to use these to smash that which has smashed and will smash hearts and souls."56 With God on her side, Carry knew best: "I have often taken cigars and cigarettes out of men's and boy's mouths. I wished to show them the wrong and that I was a friend."57

Nation, whose providentially assigned name and initials served alongside her hatchet as a key marketing gimmick, represented a growing number of radicals who sought to dictate what their fellow citizens could and could not drink. The ax, after all, could not be mistaken for the voluntary temperance pledges distributed at churches in the 1830s.

The third wave of prohibition began with the 1893 formation of the Anti-Saloon League and culminated in the passage of the Eighteenth Amendment to the Constitution in 1919.

Anti-alcohol reformers tried holding individuals to temperance pledges, giving cities and towns the "local option" to ban alcohol, and banning alcohol at the state level. Their successes didn't beget the desired results. If their experiments were to work, they would have to convert the entire nation—some hoped the entire world. Although Russia, Finland, Iceland, Norway, and parts of Canada passed through a prohibitionist phase, American temperance activists failed to convert humanity, or, as it turned out, even all of their fellow countrymen. But for fourteen years they forced their vision of morality on America.

Historian William O'Neill maintains that "among middle-class people in the progressive era no cause was more respectable or ardently fought for."[58] Prohibition was a progressive cause that admirers of the progressives disown after the fact. "Prohibition was a pseudo-reform," Richard Hofstadter contends. "To hold the Progressives responsible for Prohibition would be to do them an injustice."[59] But the same paternalistic impulse that moves contemporary liberals to ban cigarettes moved their forbears to ban alcohol. "Prohibition was typically progressive in that it was based on scientific premises, advanced in an organized and efficient manner, shrouded in moral hyperbole, and expected to produce fantastic benefits," O'Neill writes. It didn't, O'Neill concedes, but "there is no reason for mocking those who attempted it."[60]

Progressive warriors set on making the world safe for democracy set out to make it unsafe for Pabst, Schlitz, Budweiser, and other German-sounding beers. Prohibition was an intersection upon which the Left convened. Anti-business, muckraking journals such as *McClure's* and *Collier's* featured exposés on Big Liquor. William Jennings Bryan and his populist followers were among prohibition's greatest proponents, as were Jane Addams and the urban missionaries of the Social Gospel. The Federal Council of Churches, forerunner to the National Council of Churches, endorsed prohibition.[61] The *Masses*, the supposedly gay and lighthearted Greenwich Village monthly, spoke favorably of prohibition. Its imitator, the Communist *New Masses*, in the repressive law's death throes, continued to peddle muckraker Upton Sinclair's prohibitionist novel, *The Wet Pa-*

rade.[62] Progressive Party lawmakers, in state capitals and in Washington, supported prohibition by overwhelming numbers.[63] "The Progressive party," boasted its Ohio affiliate in 1914, "is the only political party this year that stands for State and Nation-wide Prohibition."[64]

Why did progressives find prohibition attractive? In the words of historian James H. Timberlake, "The moral idealism of Wilsonian progressivism, the growing cult of efficiency and the intense absorption in material progress, the widening knowledge of the scientific case against moderate drinking, and the increasing public hostility to the liquor interests, all gave prohibition added momentum."[65] Alcohol, progressives maintained, restrained the efficiency of industry and the war effort, polluted the gene pool and damaged health, and corrupted the morals of immigrants, the poor, and racial minorities. Differing rationales led progressives to come to the same conclusion: alcohol must go. And go it did.

Thus, the War Prohibition Act, the Eighteenth Amendment, and the Volstead Act all passed over the objections of Woodrow Wilson. The president, like most labor unions, some socialists, and various other elements on the Left, found himself in discord with fellow progressives over prohibition. Despite not being in a war any longer, the nation went dry under the War Prohibition Act three days before the Fourth of July in 1919.

Commenting on governmental excess during prohibition, specifically the practice of deliberately poisoning industrial-use alcohol, historian Andrew Sinclair points to the "nasty truth that the very same reformers who had supported the Hepburn Pure Food and Drug Bill twenty years before now wanted to put poison into alcohol which they knew would be drunk by human beings."[66]

An unmitigated disaster, the Eighteenth Amendment was nullified by the Twenty-first Amendment. The progressives of the 1930s undid this painful error of the progressives of the 1910s.

FROM ITS ORIGINS, the temperance movement united religion and science. Doctors such as Benjamin Rush would be succeeded as movement leaders by ministers such as Lyman Beecher. Eugenics developed along similar lines. Bible Communist John Humphrey Noyes's stirpiculture experiment, which produced dozens of children and prevented dozens more, utilized scientific ideas to produce a perfect race of men to usher in the millennium. Human perfection, and the millennium, proved elusive. But imperfect men dreamt. Edward Bellamy fantasized of "race purification" in *Looking Backward*, a fantasy shared by a horde of copycat utopian novelists. Human engineering appealed to people more powerful and mainstream than cult leaders and visionary scribblers.

In 1907, Indiana's government became the first in the modern world to codify eugenic principles. More than two dozen U.S. states, including California, Virginia, and Kansas, followed suit. The states didn't dictate positive eugenics—that is, the coupling of ideal mates—as Noyes had. They embraced aspects of negative eugenics—specifically, sterilization (a word that reflected the progressive era's obsession with all things hygienic) of those harboring unclean and impure genes, as Bellamy had advocated.

Eugenics was the latest in a long line of leftist health crusades that included Graham bread, the water cure, vegetarianism, and prohibition. It meshed with the racial obsessions of the age, as well as with the progressive era's faith in science, the future, efficiency, the state, and human perfectibility. The piggybanks of the Left, the Rockefeller Foundation and the Carnegie Institution, donated copious sums to organizations furthering eugenics. The movement's flagship publications, the *Nation* and the *New Republic*, wrote in eugenics' favor. A belief in sterilization brought together diverse strains of leftists, including Emma Goldman, the anarcho-communist deported on the "Soviet Ark"; W. E. B. Du Bois, author of *The Souls of Black Folk* and a founder of the NAACP; and Margaret Sanger, the founder of Planned Parenthood.[67]

The enemies of the progressive initiative in human breeding were familiar enemies for the Left: limited-government advocates and the Church. "Are we to accept that modern scientific fatalism known as laissez faire, which enjoins the folding of the arms?" Brown University sociologist Lester Ward rhetorically asked in 1913. "Are we to preach a gospel of inaction? I for one certainly am not content to do so, and I believe that nothing I have thus far said is inconsistent with the most vigorous action, and that in the direction of the betterment of the human race. The end and aim of the eugenicists cannot be reproached. The race is far from perfect. Its condition is deplorable. Its improvement is entirely feasible, and in the highest degree desirable."[68]

The Church's position, that no matter how unequal people's minds and bodies were, their souls were equal in the eyes of God, came under attack, too. "My own position is that the Catholic doctrine is illogical, not in accord with science, and definitely against the social welfare and race improvement," Margaret Sanger held. "Assuming that God does want an increasing number of worshipers of the Catholic faith, does he also want an increasing number of feeble-minded, insane, criminal, and diseased worshipers?"[69]

Progressive America's embrace of eugenics made waves that reached the other side of the Atlantic. Great Britain, where Charles Darwin's cousin Francis Galton coined the term "eugenics," never adopted compulsory sterilization but was home to some of the Left's leading propagandists for eugenics, including H. G. Wells, Harold Laski, Sidney and Beatrice Webb, Edward Aveling, and George Bernard Shaw, whose eugenic visions went beyond mere sterilization to include human euthanasia.[70] Canada, Switzerland, and Scandinavia imitated U.S. sterilization laws. One nation went beyond them.

New Jersey's state eugenicist under Governor Woodrow Wilson, Edwin Katzen-Ellenbogen, more directly influenced eugenics in Europe. After finding himself a prisoner of the National Socialists, Katzen-Ellenbogen, a former professor at Harvard University's medical school, made himself valuable to his German captors by applying his expertise in eugenics. At the Buchenwald concentration camp, he had life-and-death power over his fellow prisoners, and in fact was accused of murdering one thousand prisoners by lethal injection. Following the fall of the Third Reich, a war crimes tribunal sentenced him to life in prison for his collaboration with the Nazis.[71] His collaboration with Woodrow Wilson went unpunished.

Madison Grant's influence was less direct but more pernicious. A friend of Theodore Roosevelt, Grant affected another world leader more profoundly. Adolf Hitler told Grant that *The Passing of the Great Race* was his Bible. Grant's book, published in 1916, proclaimed the superiority of "Nordic" Europeans.[72] Devoting much of his life to saving endangered animals, Grant is better remembered today as the idea man for exterminating large numbers of humans.

The depth of American progressives' impact on eugenic policies within Europe is debatable. Within America, the question, though seldom asked, has a clearer answer.

By 1927, the U.S. Supreme Court had thoroughly imbibed many of the shibboleths of the progressive age, including that it was the state's prerogative to determine who should and who should not reproduce. Proper Bostonian Oliver Wendell Holmes, the court's great liberal, wrote for the majority in the infamous *Buck v. Bell* decision:

> We have seen more than once that the public welfare may call upon the best citizens for their lives. It would be strange if it could not call upon those who already sap the strength of the State for these lesser sacrifices, often not felt to be such by those concerned in order to prevent our being swamped with incompetence. It is better for all the world if, instead of waiting to execute degenerate offspring for the crime or to

let them starve for their imbecility, society can prevent those who are manifestly unfit from continuing their kind. . . . Three generations of imbeciles are enough.[73]

States eventually sterilized more than sixty thousand Americans, including the plaintiff, Carrie Buck, based on this logic.[74]

It can't happen here? It did.

THIS AGE OF crusades culminated in the ultimate crusade: the Great War.

The war in Europe hit progressives like a sucker punch. "It can't be so," an academic reportedly responded. "They aren't telling the truth. Why, there's a treaty between Belgium and Germany that would prevent it!"[75] But it was true.

Initially, many progressives sought neutrality. Former president Theodore Roosevelt was an exception. His war drums inspired more drummers when German submarines sank the British passenger ship *Lusitania*, killing 128 Americans aboard. Roosevelt charged that "the murder of the thousand men, women and children on the Lusitania is due, solely, to Wilson's abject cowardice and weakness."[76] Just as Roosevelt had relied on a mix of progressivism and jingoism to counsel Wilson to invade Mexico, he also demanded war with Germany. Wilson ultimately found war's pull too strong. Roosevelt's fellow progressives did, too.

Though Germany's U-boat campaign resulted in the deaths of hundreds of Americans, and its machinations fomented thoughts of reconquest among Mexicans, the president of the United States and his progressive lackeys couldn't stomach a war of retaliation, of defense, of national interest. Something loftier, nobler, more idealistic was in order. The progressives, after all, thought of themselves, and their motives, in those pure terms.

"The world must be made safe for democracy," Woodrow Wilson told Congress on April 2, 1917. The president explained that America's was a fight to liberate the people of the world. "We have no selfish ends to serve. . . . we shall fight for the things which we have always carried nearest our hearts—for democracy, for the right of those who submit to authority to have a voice in their own governments, for the rights and liberties of small nations, for a universal dominion of right by such a concert of free peoples as shall bring peace and safety to all nations and make the world itself at last free."[77] The United States thus enlisted alongside the French and British empires.

Wilson's rhetoric appealed particularly to Protestant clergymen and followers of the Social Gospel, who imagined America as a Christ-nation, sacrificing itself for humanity's redemption. Christ, as he had done on the eve of the Civil War and the Spanish-American War, revealed himself in the rhetoric of his earthly agents as less the Prince of Peace and more the Driver of Moneychangers from the Temple. That the U.S. declaration of war arrived on Good Friday further encouraged portrayals of America as the Messiah nation.

Liberal Protestant ministers rationalized war with their pacific principles.

"If we used language with accuracy, we should not talk of a war in Europe," Lyman Abbott opined. "There is no war in Europe. There is a posse comitatus summoned from the various civilized nations of the world to protect the peaceable nations of Europe from the worst and most efficient brigandage the civilized world has seen."[78]

Brooklyn's Plymouth Church, where Abbott had told parishioners in 1898 that God wanted war with Spain and Henry Ward Beecher had sent rifles in the 1850s to free-soilers in Kansas on the eve of the Civil War, forwarded Woodrow Wilson its own declaration of war on Germany just a few days before Congress declared war. Its pastor, Newell Dwight Hillis, announced that he would grant Germans forgiveness once they had all been shot.[79]

Washington Gladden went from making speeches for the Anti-Preparedness Committee to suggesting that the war might turn out to be "the greatest blessing that has ever befallen this land." "The central army is fighting to make war perpetual," Gladden claimed, "while the western army is fighting to make war impossible."[80]

"If any country would be great it must become the servant of all. That is what our Republic is just now trying to be—the servant of all," preached Charles Jefferson of Manhattan's Broadway Tabernacle Church. The reverend sermonized that the "work of destruction is only preparing the way for building up a world federation by which a recurrence of the present heart-breaking catastrophe may be forever avoided, and all the nations may live in peace and mutual helpfulness forevermore."[81]

From the mouth of Woodrow Wilson, from the pages of the *New Republic*, from the pulpits of the Social Gospel preachers, the Great War became, as historian Richard M. Gamble writes in *The War for Righteousness*, "an abstract war emptied of its historical content and infused with a transcendent significance, as a total war between absolutes: democracy against autocracy, Christian civilization against pagan barbarism, Good against Evil."[82]

The Great War became the progressive war, the war to end all wars, the war for democracy, the war to save civilization, and the war to make it anew, the war for peace. Just as the progressive state demanded that individual interests bow to social interests, so did the progressive war demand that America forgo its national interests in favor of world interests. Like the progressive state, the war was big and impersonal. It harbored pretensions of science, efficiency, and modernity. It encompassed the entire globe, and thus was an international rather than a parochial conflict. It promised a rational system of adjudicating disputes, a League of Nations, which would end war forever. It was a war fought for others, devoid of selfishness, and full of altruism.

World War I was all of those things in the rhetoric of progressives. It was none of those things on the battlefields of Europe. The war directly led to the Bolshevik power grab in Russia and indirectly led to the Nazi ascension in Germany. The war did remake the world order, just not as its Social Gospel backers had prophesied. Poison gas, indiscriminate aerial bombardment, and unconditional surrender became a part of the "total war" that left more than ten million dead, including more than a hundred thousand Americans.

One of the war dead was Quentin Roosevelt. Theodore Roosevelt's youngest, Quentin quit Harvard and postponed a marriage to fight in the Great War. The martial spirit that Theodore Roosevelt had caught marching up San Juan Hill in 1898, he passed on to his five children. The whole brood, including daughter Ethel, made off for Europe to do their part for the Allied war effort. With courage surpassing judgment, the fighting Roosevelts took risks—none greater than Quentin, who, in aviation's infancy, volunteered to fly behind enemy lines. Quentin, Teddy's favorite, the boy who had grown up in the White House, the most promising of the Roosevelt children, died over France on July 14, 1918, by the mounted gun of a German ace. He was identified by the love letters from his fiancée in his pocket. Brokenhearted, the father died less than six months after the son. Not all progressives were immune from the repercussions of their policy prescriptions.

As WOODROW WILSON'S army ventured forth to redeem Europe, Wilson's bureaucratic army embarked upon its wartime crusade to redeem America. The federal government nationalized the railroads, forced men into its army, forbade speech against it, and dictated the price of basic foodstuffs, such as wheat. The total war pushed America to the closest it ever came to the total state.

One of Wilson's industrial-policy lieutenants fondly recalled the power his government brought to bear against an automaker who had unwisely insulted war planner Bernard Baruch and imprudently announced his refusal to abide by the government's command to reduce automobile production: "No retort was made, but when his coal pile was ordered to be commandeered and the Railroad Administration refused him cars for any purpose, even for his Government business, and it came to his ears that he would soon be taking orders from a smooth-faced lieutenant, if permitted to remain in his own plant at all, he saw a great light. He saw not only his folly, but also his selfishness. His submission was characteristically picturesque, and not wholly printable, but it was submission."[83] The anecdote exemplifies the progressives' yen for exerting power over others, an impulse that, once acted upon, diminished freedom.

WOODROW WILSON FAILED to establish democracy abroad and helped destroy it at home. "In the name of democracy," a disgusted Warren Harding observed in 1920, "we established autocracy."[84] America agreed, and elected Harding president. To move America forward, Americans opted to relegate progressivism, at least for a few years, to the past.

～ 13 ～

STAR-SPANGLED
SOCIALISTS

*Dost thou know the order of heaven? And canst thou set down the reason
thereof on the earth?*

—JOB 39:33

"SOCIALISM IS COMING," *Appeal to Reason* editor Julius Augustus
Wayland prophesied in 1902. "It's coming like a prairie fire and nothing
can stop it."[1]

This mind-set of socialists in turn-of-the-century America was one of
irrational hope. Despite scant party membership, rejection by the working people they claimed to represent, and few electoral victories, socialists
purported that America would soon be the first socialist nation.

"If my reading of history is correct," Socialist Labor Party leader
Daniel De Leon asserted, "the prophecy of Marx will be fulfilled and
America will ring the downfall of capitalism the world over."[2]

The talk of prophecy, preordination, and imminence had a millennial
ring. For a movement styled as "scientific," socialism certainly borrowed
much of its language from the superstitions it sought to replace. Great expectations naturally led to great disappointments. Just like the movement
they joined, socialists themselves burned white hot and then burned out.

J. A. WAYLAND discovered this the hard way. The writings of Edward
Bellamy, Lawrence Gronlund, and John Ruskin transformed this successful businessman into an evangelical socialist.[3] Wayland, with a convert's
zeal, moved quickly, and without knowledge of failed communal experiments of the recent past, to set up a socialist community based on the vi-

sions of such writers. To this end, and by similarly blind means, Wayland bought a thousand acres in Tennessee sight unseen to launch his "Ruskin" colony. The land proved as infertile to crops as the experiment was to prosperity.

Had Wayland been familiar with Robert Owen's New Harmony, he might have hesitated to forward money to Ruskin's advance party, which gave new meaning to the phrase by living it up in a hotel instead of preparing the actual colony. Had he been familiar with Brook Farm's troubles with rocky soil, he might have taken greater care in buying land. Had he been familiar with the revolt against dictatorship at Oneida Community, he might have remained truer to his rhetoric of equality and democracy.[4] But had Wayland been familiar with the history of American socialism, he might never have tried. The zealot has no time for the past when there's a future to be made.

Wayland left the Ruskin commune in July 1895, less than a year after he had founded it. One month later, he promptly launched *Appeal to Reason*, the publication that consumed the remaining seventeen years of his life. The commune struggled, moved a few times, died. Wayland lost a year of his life, thousands of dollars, and, temporarily, his newspaper, the *Coming Nation*, to the mob at Ruskin, Tennessee. But he claimed to have profited in wisdom. "The Ruskin failure shocked him into the realization of the fact that before men can dwell together on terms pictured by the Utopians, capitalism must be abolished entirely," one of his colleagues later wrote in *Appeal to Reason*.[5]

Ruskin's failure disproved, to Wayland at least, not socialism, but colonies as an effective tool in establishing socialism. "We receive hundreds of letters at this office enquiring how to organize co-operative stores and colonies," *Appeal to Reason* informed its readers seven years after Wayland left Ruskin. "To all those we return one answer: Save your money and organize a Socialist local, and then buy literature, and circulate Socialist papers." The publication, which had printed nearly one million copies of its 1900 election issue, made but "one immediate demand . . . an invincible and uncompromising Socialist party."[6] The commune yielded to the ballot box as the means by which socialism would triumph.

A CIRCUITOUS BUT uninterrupted line reaches from Karl Marx and Friedrich Engels to Joseph Weydemeyer and his proto-communist groups, to the Friedrich Sorge—aligned sections of the First International, to the Workingmen's parties of the 1870s, to the Socialist parties that followed.

Until the end of the nineteenth century, these American socialist groups were operated by Europeans who spoke a language both figuratively and literally foreign to American ears. At the 1876 founding convention of the national Workingmen's Party, the gathering ordered five thousand copies of a pamphlet outlining the new group's principles and constitution—a majority of which were to be printed in German.[7] The lingua franca of American socialism did not change when the Workingmen's Party morphed into the Socialist Labor Party the following year. Socialist leader and chronicler Morris Hillquit reported that of at least twenty-four socialist newspapers founded in America between 1876 and 1877 just eight were printed in English, with German newspapers outnumbering newspapers printed in the native tongue. Those few English-language periodicals had all expired by 1879.[8] No more than 10 percent of the Socialist Labor Party's members in this era were native-born.[9] Even in the early 1890s, as the party's membership ballooned, about a third of new sections added consisted of native-born Americans.[10]

This began to change. In 1897, the advent of what became the Socialist Party, led by the Hoosier Eugene Debs of the American Railway Union, who found Marx during his stint in prison following the bloody Pullman strike of 1894, facilitated native interest in socialism. So, too, did the Intercollegiate Socialist Society and the Christian Socialist Fellowship, which brought socialism into the universities and churches, respectively.

More than any other force, it was the Girard, Kansas-based *Appeal to Reason* that reached Americans with the message that had been heretofore explained in a German, Yiddish, or Russian accent, but never with a Bible-belt twang. The *Appeal* was folksy, laden with homespun anecdotes, and peppered with cartoons, ALL CAPS for stressed phrases, and screaming headlines that reached the common man's ears but irritated the intellectual's. It was the socialism of Bellamy and Debs more than the socialism of Karl Marx. Yet in it Marxism finally found its American voice. It was big-picture socialism, unmolested by obscure phraseology and the minutiae of theoretical disputes. *Appeal to Reason* was unapologetically American.

Wayland enlisted readers in the "Appeal Army," which counted tens of thousands within its ranks. The army distributed the paper to new recruits and signed up additional subscribers. Wayland printed the names of Appeal Army "comrades" with distinguished records in signing up additional subscribers ("Comrade Claffin of Manchester, N.H. lands a shell on our breastworks that contains ten new names").[11] He delivered an official "certificate of membership in the Appeal Army" to members who met subscription goals.[12] He offered substantial prizes, such as a complete brass-band set of instruments or eighty acres of land in the Ozarks, to the comrades who outperformed the rest of the Appeal Army.[13] Wayland was that most peculiar of socialists who could have taught the capitalists he railed against a thing or two about salesmanship.

Girard, Kansas, became the unlikely capital of the American Left. A delegate to 1908's Socialist Party convention, who had wandered from Chicago to Girard, deemed the latter miniopolis "the Mecca of Socialism, the center of the revolutionary universe, the place from which emanates the flashes of light and the glory that shall finally illuminate the world!"[14] Kate Richards, the famous socialist who would be imprisoned during the Great War, married Frank O'Hare at Wayland's Girard home. Mother Jones spent the winter of 1897–98 holed up at Wayland's house. The paper's most famous paid staffer, Eugene Debs, made regular pilgrimages to the *Appeal*'s headquarters, the "Temple of the Revolution" in downtown Girard.[15] The place to be for American socialists was not Harvard Square, Telegraph Avenue, or Greenwich Village. It was Girard, Kansas.

From the heartland, echoes of populism could be heard in the rhetoric of Wayland and his publishing empire. Indeed, Wayland had cut his teeth in politics electing a Populist governor in Colorado in 1892.[16] The populist spirit never quite departed. The *Appeal* mocked "diamond bosomed college professors who talk about Socialism destroying 'incentive.'"[17] The *Appeal* appropriated the Bible and the Founding Fathers for Socialist ends. It was not yet another socialist rag about workers and farmers read by professors and professional agitators. It was a socialist weekly for workers and farmers read by farmers and workers.

By 1908, the Socialist Party could report that born-and-bred Americans outnumbered immigrants seven to three on their membership rolls.[18] In these years, the Socialist Party's presidential ticket found its support greatest not in the immigrant-rich Northeast or rust-belt states, but in Oklahoma, Nevada, and Montana.[19] In its early years, socialism failed to connect with Americans because it failed to speak to Americans in the language most Americans spoke. J. A. Wayland changed that.

"THE SYSTEM UNDER which society is now organized is imperfect," the organizing platform of the Socialist Labor Party (SLP) declared in 1877. Its platform, borrowed heavily from the platform of the Workingmen's Party, included several points—the repeal of anti-union conspiracy laws, prohibition of pre-teen industrial labor, compulsory education, the prohibition of prison labor for private companies—that are now commonplace in American law. But much more of it, such as the common ownership of the means of production, a ban on women working in certain professions, a government takeover of banking and insurance, and making national laws the subject of popular vote, never took flight.[20]

Daniel De Leon, a sectarian theorist of Marxism, joined the Socialist Labor Party in 1890. The onetime Bellamyite and former single-taxer soon became the SLP's "undisputed leader" and "the dominating figure in the American socialist movement for more than fifteen years," as biographer Carl Reeve put it.[21] Tellingly, Lenin expressed greater admiration for the doctrinaire De Leon than any other American contemporary.[22] A serial joiner of causes, the Curaçao-born professor never let go once he latched on to Marxism. He attacked labor unions, condemned fellow socialists as fakers and frauds, and purged members, including his own son, by the hundreds for disagreeing with him.[23] Minor disputes over process became occasions to brand opponents traitors. Daniel De Leon was Friedrich Sorge reincarnated.

In 1899, when De Leon's faction of the Socialist Labor Party lost an internal party election, he split off and set up an alternative SLP. "Each side styled itself the Socialist Labor Party, each had its own national committee, its own secretary and headquarters, and each published a paper called *The People.*"[24] In a final indignity, the schism compelled De Leon to appeal to the capitalist courts to settle the dispute. They did so in his favor.

Along with the schisms, De Leon's ill-advised assault on labor unions contributed to the SLP's decline. Prior to De Leon, socialists generally sought to capture labor unions by "boring from within." This tactic failed to inspire workingmen to abandon their immediate goals, such as wage increases and shorter workweeks, for long-term (and impractical) socialist goals, such as the abolition of the wage system and worker ownership of the means of production. Increasingly, then, socialists preached the tactic of "dual unionism," which involved setting up competing unions.

The Socialist Trade and Labor Alliance, launched in 1895, was De Leon's first experiment in dual unionism. He had been stung by the dying Knights of Labor's failure to live up to an alleged backroom deal to place De Leon in charge of the union's newspaper, and by the group's subsequent dismissal of the non-laboring De Leon from its labor union. The man American Federation of Labor head Samuel Gompers ridiculed as the "professor without a professorship" failed to siphon off union members.[25] But De Leon did succeed in dividing socialists and turning organized labor further against socialism.

Both "boring from within" and "dual unionism" necessarily led to embarrassing questions about socialism. If socialism really was the political arm of industrial unionism, why did socialists have to establish phony, alternative unions, or clandestinely infiltrate existing unions, to influence workers? Shouldn't socialism, if it truly were the party of the proletariat, have already won the workers over without subterfuge?

The dirty little secret of socialism is that it was a movement *about* workers but not *of* workers. The socialists hoping to fight the class war were a foreign legion. The affluent mercenaries waging the workingman's battles included Lincoln Steffens, who grew up in the home that became the California governor's mansion; Daniel De Leon, Columbia University law instructor; John Reed, onetime Harvard University cheerleader; and Gaylord Wilshire, the socialist capitalist who was nearly as rich as the boulevard that today bears his name. Real workers resented the imposition into their affairs by people richer than their bosses.

Samuel Gompers, the immigrant cigar maker who led the American Federation of Labor in its formative years, vividly remembered socialists transforming peaceful labor protests into violent outbursts against the police: "I saw the danger of entangling alliances with intellectuals who did not understand that to experiment with the labor movement was to experiment with human life."[26] Gompers did not forget. "You must not allow the socialists to get control of your assembly," Uriah Stephens, first Grand Master Workman of the Knights of Labor, cautioned. "They are simply disturbers and only gain entrance to labor societies that they may be in better position to break them up."[27] The major labor unions saw socialists as enemies, not friends. Daniel De Leon saw the major labor unions the same way that they saw him.

MOST SOCIALISTS FOUND much to be desired in a socialist party that expended its resources attacking unions and fellow socialists. Thus, in 1897, Eugene Debs, Ella Reeve "Mother" Bloor, Victor Berger, and other like-minded activists formed the Social Democratic Party. In 1900, Debs made his first of five runs for the presidency, each effort gaining more votes than the last. The Social Democratic Party (SDP) doubled the votes of the Socialist Labor Party in the 1900 presidential contest, elbowing the SLP into permanent fringe status within a fringe movement. The following year, the SDP became the Socialist Party of America, thereafter generally referred to as *the* Socialist Party (SP).

The SLP persisted in the style of Friedrich Sorge and the SP represented Victoria Woodhull's dream of a socialist party with an American accent. What they had in common was that both the SLP and the SP were Marxist parties. The SLP, under its Workingmen's Party name, was founded out of the ashes of the First International; the SP had been a part of the Second International. Rank-and-file members may have been influenced more by Henry George, Edward Bellamy, or Henry Demarest Lloyd than by Karl Marx, but the parties themselves were organized along Marxist lines.

Socialists, whether under the SLP umbrella or inside the SP, believed in the expropriation of land, state ownership of the means of production and natural resources, full employment ensured by the government, the abolition of the wage system, and social equality through leveling. Turn-of-the-century American socialists also absorbed various causes from their time and place that weren't intrinsically socialistic. These causes included a preference for direct democracy (federal ballot initiatives, direct elections of senators and the president, abolition of judicial review) over checks and balances (the electoral college, the executive veto, the burden-some constitutional amendment process); for international arbitration over unilateral exercises of national sovereignty; and, in theory at least, for no war but the class war.

Socialist leaders believed that once attained these policy goals would unleash miracles. J. A. Wayland's *Appeal to Reason* promised "there will be no taxes under Socialism."[28] "There will be almost no crime, for the cause of crime is injustice."[29] Socialist schools "would develop millions of Ruskins, Carlyles, Spencers, Shakespeares."[30] "Under Socialism there will be no WAR, for the cause of war is foreign markets."[31] "Socialism will solve the race question."[32] "There will be no tramps, no beggars, no un-employed."[33] The readers of *Appeal to Reason* were bombarded with irre-sponsible promises made by crude, capitalist advertisers: "Cancer Cured," "Free Gold Watch," "Deafness Can Be Cured," "Make Money Easy."[34] How different were these get-rich-easy schemes and snake-oil cure-alls from the promises of socialism found in the surrounding arti-cles? The fairyland resultant from socialism, rather than the directions (nationalized industry, expropriated land, free medicine, etc.) to it, pri-marily motivated Wayland and his faithful readers.

Because historians sympathetic to socialism project personal political sympathies upon socialists, it is often more difficult to understand what socialists did *not* believe. Socialists were wrought with divisions mirroring the divisions in the surrounding society on questions regarding suffrage, race, labor unions, immigration, and war.

With its scientific pretensions, socialism attracted many who also bought into eugenics, phrenology, and other pseudoscientific fads. What appears to the present as ugly relics of the past appeared to the past as the wave of the future. Most socialists, like most Americans, remained indif-ferent to institutionalized racial discrimination. Some were anything but indifferent. Those interested in race questions included William English

Walling, who helped found the National Association for the Advancement of Colored People (NAACP). But others interested in race questions took a decidedly different approach.

Victor Berger, the Socialist Party's first representative in Congress, represented many in his party in his outspoken white-supremacist views. Berger contended, "There can be no doubt that the negroes and mulattoes constitute a lower race—that the Caucasian and indeed even the Mongolian have the start on them in civilization by many thousand years—so that negroes will find it difficult ever to overtake them. The many cases of rape which occur wherever negroes are settled in large numbers prove, moreover, that the free contact with the whites has led to the further degeneration of the negroes, as well as all other inferior races."[35]

According to the dust jacket of his biography, Daniel De Leon "championed the cause of the Black people."[36] But as the same biography points out, De Leon dismissed anti-lynching and voting-rights laws.[37] "The disfranchisement of the negro," De Leon wrote, "does not hurt the revolutionary party in the least. The negro vote in the Socialist Labor Party is unimportant, and the negro is so tightly stuck to the Republican party, and so completely befooled by the fakirs of his own race in the pulpit and press that he is not likely to play an important part in the revolution."[38]

Socialist groups in the Deep South, just as most clubs in the Deep South, organized along segregationist lines.[39] "Any man who knows the negro knows that it is the all-absorbing, overpowering desire of every negro to possess a white woman," a southern socialist wrote in *The Call*, objecting to equalitarian calls within the publication.[40] The Socialist Party's national committee-man from Texas observed: "You know that capitalism never examines the color of the skin when it buys labor power and I have seen white men walking the streets of the city of Dallas side by side with negroes when the heat of summer was such that if the negro could ever be offensive to a white man he must have been then. Moreover I have seen WHITE and BLACK working thus under A NEGRO FOREMAN."[41]

J. A. Wayland and his *Appeal to Reason* loudly led the chorus proclaiming that while socialism meant segregation, capitalism meant integration. The *Appeal* bragged in 1899 that socialism would settle racial problems without reference to race. "It will be done in just the way the government or society now employs colored soldiers or provides schools for them separate from the whites." Whereas "private ownership of industries mixes up the races, *reducing* blacks, whites, and yellows to a common level . . . socialism would separate the races and *lift* them all to the highest level each were capable."[42]

A few years later, the *Appeal* refuted myths that socialism had anything to do with racial equality. "The white worker in the shop, mine and factory is told that Socialism means race equality," *Appeal to Reason* complained. But the reality was that "capitalism has forced him to work side by side with the negro, and for about the same wage. . . . in the SIGHT OF THE CAPITALIST ALL WORKERS LOOK ALIKE." For the black man, socialism would mean "separate territory in the United States to live in, where he can work out his own destiny, undisturbed by the presence of the white man."[43]

A socialism that incorporated the realities of America into its philosophy didn't just incorporate the pleasant realities. Race, which hardly involved itself in socialist debates in Europe, lay stitched into the fabric of the American story and thus into the story of the American Left.

As believers in an ideology that provided an economic explanation for everything, socialists often refused to recognize struggles against racial discrimination independent from the class struggle. It is not merely that socialists viewed fighting racial injustice as subordinate to fighting economic inequality, but that socialists viewed it as a diversion from socialism. If socialism solves all problems, then focusing on anything else is a waste of time. Many held the more extreme attitude that anyone not part of the class-struggle solution was part of the problem.

The race prejudice of socialists targeted not just native-born blacks but immigrant Asians as well. "Workers of the World Unite" became "Workers of the World Keep Out." The movement peculiarly sought the exclusion of the very people who had made that movement possible. The ideological transformation indicated the demographic transformation. As natives peopled the Socialist Party, the Socialist Party became less tolerant of foreigners.

Appeal to Reason accused capitalists of enticing "the lowest scum of Europe" to our shores, wrote hysterically of "Mongolian hordes," and termed Asian immigration the "yellow peril."[44] The dehumanizing tone emanating from Girard, Kansas, is perhaps unsurprising in that few of the "Mongolian hordes" or "lowest scum of Europe" ever came within a hundred miles of Wayland's rural outpost. Immigrants became caricatures rather than people because Wayland and his staff encountered few living, breathing immigrants.

But many of the most passionate and best organized socialists remained immigrants. The party's two congressmen, Meyer London and Victor Berger, emigrated from the Russian and Austro-Hungarian empires, respectively, and even by 1916, the English language claimed just two of the fifteen daily socialist newspapers printed in the United States.[45] If socialism still struck Americans as foreign in spite of the inroads of

Hoosiers Wayland and Debs, it was largely because many socialists were still foreigners.

As they did with the struggle for racial equality, socialists generally stood on the sidelines of the women's suffrage movement. Though many individual socialists sympathized with extending the vote to women, collectively the movement viewed women's rights as a distraction from the real campaign. As inaction placated socialist opponents of women's suffrage, it also satisfied proponents by deluding them into believing the class struggle would ultimately solve all problems.

On women's rights issues, the socialists bequeathed, at best, a mixed legacy. The Socialist Labor Party's inaugural platform dismissively referred to "the so-called women's rights question."[46] At the 1910 Socialist Party convention, delegates voted down a resolution to support the women's suffrage movement.[47] In 1912, a Socialist New York assemblyman wrote, "Equal suffrage advocates of middle class or plutocratic affiliation do not fail to accuse Socialists of apathy and indifference to their cause. They do not appreciate that economic justice is infinitely more important than the mere political enfranchisement of their sex."[48]

Socialists did not support all workingmen, just the workingmen who supported them. "A man that will not fight the employers and their stool pigeons," the socialist labor publication *Industrial Worker* held, "is a moral eunuch, and the sooner the boss works him to death the better for humanity."[49] Eugene Debs likened a worker who didn't vote for the Socialist Party to a "scab," describing such a workingman as "a betrayer of his class and an enemy of his fellow-man."[50] The *New York Worker* melodramatically asked, "Why don't they see that there is no need for them to do all the work while their masters live filled with beauty? Why don't they see that all men and all women and all little children might be living that life? Oh, we have shown them so many times. Why don't they see? If they won't see, they deserve to be slaves!"[51] For many Socialists, even ones such as Debs who spent years toiling in hard jobs, workers weren't real workers, or even human, when they rebelled against the ideas Socialists presented. They degenerated into "scabs," "apes," and "cattle."[52]

"I can conceive of no greater traitor to the working class than the man who refuses to be guided by the collective will of the party whose cause he has espoused," noted Fred Warren, Wayland's able protégé.[53] Frustrated, the *Appeal*'s writers began uncharacteristically referring to workers as "slaves," "fools," and "stupid."[54] The tone grew patronizing and condescending: "The laboring class of Colorado have only themselves to blame for the ills that they are suffering." "In time, however, the workers will be forced to open their eyes." "I don't blame the masters so much; they are working for their interests, but that the working class can be so easily duped."[55]

Historians influenced by recent race-, sex-, and class-based movements look upon the socialists of a century past and see a mirror's reflection. Though these modern academics share the socialists' dedication to financial equality and economic interventionism, the socialists did not share the historians' interest in sexual and racial equality, and in a number of cases they proved hostile to such ideas. Individual socialists occasionally rose above the prejudices of their age, but socialists as a whole were *of* and not *ahead* of their time.

THE CONDESCENSION THAT socialists displayed toward movements for women's suffrage and racial equality extended to the labor movement as well. Indeed, socialists imagined labor unions as their political playthings. When union members resisted their advances, socialists started their own unions. But with so many chiefs and so few Indians, socialist labor unions could not credibly challenge the dominance of traditional labor unions.

In 1905, members of both Socialist parties came together to form the Industrial Workers of the World (IWW), reviving the dual-unionism policy of the Socialist Trade and Labor Alliance. By then, Socialist Party leaders had become as frustrated with labor unions as SLP strongman Daniel De Leon. "The working class and the employing class have nothing in common," the IWW's founding document proclaimed. From that premise, the IWW condemned existing unions as collaborators for reaching agreements with employers. "[T]he trade unions aid the employing class to mislead the workers into the belief that the working class have interests in common with their employers."[56]

Socialists saw workers as a means to an end. Workers saw socialists as arrogant, paternalistic, and cut loose from reality by being fused to theory. Non-worker socialists haughtily spoke for non-socialist workers. Workers didn't know what they wanted. Socialists did. At least that is how socialists saw things. "The Socialist party is the political expression of the economic interests of the workers," the 1912 platform claimed. "Its defeats have been their defeats and its victories their victories."[57]

Just as socialists called on blacks and women to subordinate their interests to socialist goals, they called on laborers to subordinate worker goals to socialist goals. But textile workers, miners, and cigar makers had individual interests, a concept that socialists never wrapped their minds around. Socialists, in fact, looked upon workers as an imaginary,

dehumanized mass of uniformity, as mere cogs that would fulfill the
Marxist prophecy.

"What intelligent workingman can hold out against the irresistible
claim the Socialist movement has upon him?" Eugene Debs asked. "What
reason has he to give? What excuse can he offer?" Debs answered himself
emphatically: "None! Not one!"[58] Unlike De Leon and other socialist leaders, Debs came from working-class origins and took his lumps organizing
laborers. But workers found even his admonitions tiresome. Debs contended "that no workingman can clearly understand what Socialism
means without becoming and remaining a Socialist. It is simply impossible for him to be anything else and the only reason that all workingmen are
not Socialists is that they do not know what it means."[59] In other words,
workers whose political beliefs differed from Eugene Debs's were, according to Eugene Debs, either ignorant or not true workers.

The IWW's insistence on society-transforming demands rather than
workplace-transforming demands immediately crashed into reality.

First, why would workingmen wish to organize under an outfit that rejected raises and improvements in working conditions as legitimate objects of a labor union? When the IWW lived up to its principles by
expelling locals that entered into agreements with employers, critics
found them impractical. When they won concessions, critics found them
hypocrites.

Second, why would an employer wish to negotiate with a union that
stated openly it had no obligation to live up to its agreements with employers? "The question of 'right' and 'wrong' does not concern us," admitted
IWW general secretary Vincent St. John. "No terms made with an employer are final. All peace, so long as the wage system lasts, is but an armed
truce."[60] The organization itself held: "The contract between an employer
and a workman is no more binding than the title deed to a negro slave
is just."[61]

Skilled professions generally stuck with their unions. The Western
Federation of Miners defected to the IWW, but, for the most part, the
Wobblies, the nickname for IWW members, were stuck with attempting to
organize unskilled laborers. This may have added to their allure among
socialists.

The socialist fetishization of the worker manifested itself in an exalted
status for the actual workers within the movement's ranks. "Jimmy
Higgins," the mythical union laborer who in his off hours toiled for the
party by hawking literature on street corners, manning socialist rallies,
and faithfully attending party meetings, became the most sought-after

socialist. The IWW out–Jimmy Higgensed the other labor organizations by seeking out the bluest of blue-collar workers. Thus the Wobbly gained a reputation as a free-living, street-fighting man. He put into practice the thoughts of the socialist intellectual, and for that, the socialist intellectual was grateful. But the type of action the Wobblies engaged in divided socialists yet again.

The IWW differed from ordinary unions in that it cared little for employer concessions to employees. It also differed in that it was a "syndicalist" organization, meaning it favored direct action—sabotage, strikes, violence—over political action. The ultimate purpose of direct action was the seizure of industry for the workers.

Daniel De Leon, eager for the IWW to become a recruiting ground for his Socialist Labor Party, opposed the group's focus on action to the exclusion of politics. Just as the rule-or-ruin mentality spurred the establishment of the IWW, the rule-or-ruin mentality inspired De Leon's defection from the IWW to form an alternative IWW. Just as there had been two SLPs in 1899 when De Leon's faction lost power, in 1908 there were two IWWs—the main IWW, and De Leon's Detroit-based IWW. A group of splitters became the victim of splitters.

The IWW—De Leon's fake one—led a nominal existence. The IWW—the real one—expanded its influence. The Wobblies gained clout through their role in strikes at McKees Rocks, Pennsylvania, in 1909; Lawrence, Massachusetts, in 1912; and Paterson, New Jersey, in 1913. But the group's strength lay in the western half of the United States due to the Western Federation of Miners' brief affiliation. The IWW's reach, as its name suggested, extended into Canada, Australia, and beyond. But its roster, if it ever entered into the six digits, flirted with that number briefly. Its importance as a historical subject resides in its violent radicalism, not in its influence as a labor union, which was small and fleeting.

The IWW strikes often involved a great deal of violence, much of it instigated by the Wobblies. The McKees Rocks strike, for instance, left seven dead, including three policemen, and more than six dozen wounded. Since the Wobbly violence occurred within an atmosphere of anonymous violence, the IWW became the symbol of assassination, bombings, and sabotage—even when its fingerprints were nowhere near the actual crime scene. When its fingerprints were all over the crime scene, conversely, the IWW's backers alleged setup, agent provocateurs, or some other conspiracy theory. The IWW, which openly supported violence in its publications, never actually engaged in violence—at least according to the naive accounts of courtier journalists and camp-follower historians. For their enemies, Wobblies acted as updated Molly Maguires.

The IWW did engage in violence, as did other turn-of-the-century leftists. The times were politicized and violent. Anarcho-communist Leon Czolgosz, a follower of Emma Goldman, assassinated President William McKinley in 1901. In 1905, former Idaho governor Frank Steunenberg, a longtime foe of the Western Federation of Miners, was assassinated by a bomb planted in his front yard. The confessed murderer implicated "Big Bill" Haywood and other socialist activists in the killing, but his charge did not stand up in court. IWW member Joe Hill murdered a former policeman and his son in 1914. Czolgosz's fellow anarchists abandoned him. Haywood's time in the dock elevated him to a status among socialists that briefly rivaled that of Debs. Joe Hill became the stuff of song and campfire stories.

One cause célèbre, *the* cause célèbre of the age, failed to pass into leftist historiography. The government accused James McNamara, a member of the Typographical Union, and his brother Joseph, a leader of the International Union of Bridge and Structural Workers, of the 1910 bombing of the *Los Angeles Times. Appeal to Reason*, in turn, accused the *Times*, and its anti-union allies, of acting as agent provocateurs. Wayland's paper sent a reporter, George Shoaf, to Los Angeles to exonerate the McNamaras. The evidence he found, apparently, convinced him otherwise. Instead of correcting his earlier reports that had declared the McNamaras the victims of a frame-up, Shoaf faked his own disappearance. The *Appeal* played up the disappearance, suggesting that Shoaf had found proof of the defendants' innocence and had been abducted—or worse—for his journalistic efforts. Alas, Shoaf was discovered to have staged his disappearance so he could pursue an adulterous escapade with the teenage daughter of veteran socialist Ernest Untermann.[62] There seemed to be no escape from scandal for *Appeal to Reason*, until a larger embarrassment engulfed the entire Left.

The *Los Angeles Times* bombing killed twenty-one people, but it was the McNamaras' subsequent admission of guilt that had the greatest effect on the Left. "Perhaps nothing has ever so stunned the labor and radical world as the McNamara confession just a few days before the [Los Angeles mayoral] election. Even among some of those few very close to the case who knew the brothers to be guilty, the idea of a confession, after the tremendous campaign of propaganda that had been waged in their behalf, seemed incredible. The announcement was followed by several suicides and cases of mental collapse among their followers. In Los Angeles, men broke into sobs in the courtroom or wandered dazed about the streets."[63]

Violence became a cause of growing embarrassment within the Socialist Party. In 1912, the Socialist Party resolved: "Any member of the party who opposes political action or advocates crime, sabotage, or other

methods of violence as a weapon of the working class to aid in its emancipation shall be expelled from membership in the party." Through his one
good eye Big Bill Haywood clearly saw what was going on: "That looks like
it was aimed at me."[64] The specific effect was Haywood's expulsion. The
general effect was to distance the Socialist Party from more radical elements, such as the anarchists and the IWW.

THE BAN ON violence made the Socialist Party appear more mainstream.
In truth, however, 1912 marked the apex of the Socialist Party rather than
the beginning of its move to the mainstream. The reality is that the party
never effectively appealed to the mainstream.

Histories of American socialism are wont to point out in laundry list
fashion that by 1912 the Socialists boasted a U.S. congressman; the mayors
of Schenectady, Milwaukee, and more than four dozen other municipalities; thirteen daily newspapers, including five published in English; more
than 125,000 party members; and a presidential ticket that 6 percent of
the voting public awarded ballots to.[65]

Yet the Socialist Party had less influence than other third-party movements in America. New York's Conservative Party elected more senators.
The short-lived Populist Party elected more members of the House of
Representatives. The Reform Party elected more governors. The Know-
Nothings, Populists, Progressives, Dixiecrats, Libertarians, American Independence Party, and National Unity Party all received a greater number
of electoral votes for president. But Socialists generate the greatest interest from historians. This is because a great number of historians happen
to be socialists, not because socialism was one of the more important
third-party movements.

Part of the blame for socialism's failure to gain traction lay with socialists themselves. The party's resolution banning violence, for instance, did
not push socialists closer to the mainstream because the outsiders who actually peopled the party's ranks had little interest in achieving such political success if it meant sacrificing ideological purity.

As the early Socialist parties solicited the public's votes, they ridiculed
the act of voting. "The ballot-box has in this country long ceased to be
the expression of the popular will, but has rather become an instrument
for its subversion in the hands of the professional politicians," declared
the initial platform of the proto-SLP Workingman's Party.[66] That early
disconnect from reality—a political party boycotting the political
process—foreshadowed future disconnects from reality. As other parties
chased votes, Socialists chased them away.

In 1888, the Socialist Labor Party presented a slate of presidential electors, but since the party sought to abolish the presidency, they instructed their slate to vote "no president" in the unlikely event of an SLP presidential victory.[67] Four years later, they offered a presidential slate at the same time their platform promised to abolish that office.[68] If voters had heard of the SLP and knew of its platform, they might have been confused. But since they hadn't, no one picked up on the curiosity of a presidential candidate seeking to abolish the office he sought.

The Socialist Party's 1908 platform called for abolishing the Senate and amending the Constitution by majority vote.[69] A Socialist state legislator in Pennsylvania campaigned to abolish the state police.[70] In 1915, party members voted by a fourteen-to-one ratio to expel Socialist officeholders who appropriated public money for the military, no matter how small the amount.[71]

Socialist leaders prepared for members who bucked party discipline. The party regularly compelled its candidates to sign undated letters of resignation from the offices they sought.[72] The party kept the letters on file. If the Socialist, once in office, allowed his conscience to guide him, instead of the collective party conscience, then theoretically the party could force him from his elected post. This mere threat became an effective weapon to ensure conformity, as did party expulsions.

"By 1913 the Socialist party had expelled a dozen of its representatives serving in public office," recount authors Seymour Martin Lipset and Gary Marks. "In the state of Washington, for example, the left-wing state party refused to allow a Socialist state legislator to cooperate with labor and farmer representatives and censured him when he voted for a Progressive for speaker on the grounds that he should have nominated and voted for himself. In Los Angeles in 1915 a lone Socialist councilman was forced to resign from the party because he voted for a Democrat for council president."[73] In Canton, Ohio, the Socialist candidate for mayor mounted a judicial challenge to contest his defeat, "but the Canton local refused to support him on the grounds that to do so would be an inexcusable surrender of the party's revolutionary principles to political opportunism. When the candidate insisted upon a contest, the local expelled him. Subsequently, the courts held he had been elected, and he took office as an ex-Socialist."[74]

Socialist attitudes, whether toward electoral politics or the labor movement, consistently trespassed into the fantastical. Little wonder, then, that socialism never played a significant role in American governance.

THE GREATEST FACTOR that contributed to socialism's decline after its 1912 peak was World War I. The Great War divided socialists. Was it a war for democracy? Was it an imperialist war? Was it the war to end all wars? Was it a war that could be exploited for socialist ends? Was it a war to grease the pockets of industry with the blood of the workingman?

How a socialist answered such questions usually determined how he viewed the war. Lowercase-"s" socialists held no party-line position on World War I. Capital-"S" Socialists did. The divergence of views came to a head when the United States entered the war in April 1917. At an emergency meeting convened in St. Louis one day after Congress declared war, Socialists, by an overwhelming majority, resolved: "We brand the declaration of war by our government as a crime against the people of the United States and against the nations of the world."[75]

It's hard to exaggerate how much this stance harmed the Socialist Party. The government cracked down and jailed anti-war Socialist leaders. Anti-war Socialists cracked down and purged pro-war Socialists. Novelist Upton Sinclair, muckraker John Spargo, and even the party's 1916 presidential candidate, Allan Benson, were among those who parted ways because they supported the war and their party did not. One writer's clever resignation from the party displayed the bitterness the war wrought. Sent to the man most responsible for the St. Louis anti-war declaration, Morris Hillquit, the letter of resignation signed off:

> You are my enemy and I am,
> Yours,
> W. J. Ghent[76]

Pro-war Socialists attacked the patriotism of anti-war Socialists. Anti-war Socialists purged pro-war Socialists for bucking the party line. Both extremes attacked the ambiguity of Victor Berger and Meyer London, the party's two congressmen. No one emerged unscathed. But emerge they did, as the war stripped Socialists of votes and members. After a last hurrah, the courageous presidential run by Eugene Debs from Atlanta's federal penitentiary in 1920, Socialists rode off into obscurity.

WHY DID SOCIALISM fail to attract Americans in the way that it attracted Germans, Frenchmen, Swedes, Chinese, Ghanaians, Mexicans, and Egyptians?

First, America had no rigid class structure, no titled aristocracy, no real history of rich versus poor. European socialists projected the history of their continent upon the United States, but class warfare's place in American history is slim. Ethnic and racial strife overshadow it. It is not just that the words "bourgeois" and "proletariat" struck American ears as foreign; the concepts behind them did as well. Farmers didn't want to eliminate land ownership. They dreamed of it. Factory workers didn't want to kill the foreman. They wanted to be the foreman.

Second, America's winner-take-all system of representative democracy encouraged two parties and two parties alone. This blame-the-system-rather-than-the-socialists approach appealed to party stalwarts. "I have sometimes told English friends," Norman Thomas, Debs's successor as party leader, reflected in 1963, "that had we had a centralized parliamentary government rather than a federal presidential government, we should have had, under some name or another, a moderately strong socialist party."[77] Even the most committed socialists were compelled to migrate to one of the two main parties to bring their ideas to the table of government. By 1960, long after Americans had forgotten that there even was such a thing as the Socialist Party, Michael Harrington and other socialists belatedly concluded that "there was no sense in running a campaign every four years which only revealed the weakness of the movement and took a few votes away from liberal candidates to boot."[78]

Third, government suppression of socialists during Woodrow Wilson's administration put the party into disarray. The federal government revoked the mailing privileges of such socialist publications as Margaret Sanger's *Woman Rebel*; the party's scholarly organ, the *International Socialist Review*; the party's official weekly, the *American Socialist*; the *Jewish Daily Forward*; and the *New York Call*. The government deported Emma Goldman and Alexander Berkman on the "Soviet Ark" and jailed Kate Richards O'Hare, Bill Haywood, Rose Pastor Stokes, and Eugene Debs. When the vindictive Wilson declined to pardon Debs, the imprisoned socialist leader properly noted, "It is he, not I, who needs a pardon."[79]

Fourth, capitalism's success doomed socialism's failure. America, the most free-market nation in the world, was also the richest nation in the world. American workers enjoyed a standard of living that exceeded upper-middle-class standards of living in most European nations. Poverty, not affluence, is the breeding ground for socialism. As German philosopher Werner Sombart put it, "All Socialist utopias came to nothing on roast beef and apple pie."[80]

Fifth, those Americans for whom capitalism did not result in the American dream could migrate within the United States—move to open land in the West—just as newcomers had opted to immigrate to the United States to better their economic prospects. The frontier may have been closed by the dawn of the twentieth century, but open land and open opportunities still existed. It didn't elsewhere, which is why so many foreigners either turned to socialism in their homelands, or came to

America, or turned to socialism and came to America. The American response to hard times was not to overthrow the government, but to go west and start anew.

Sixth, socialists spent time and resources purging fellow members, fighting labor unions, expelling socialists fortunate enough to win elective office, and splitting into offshoot parties instead of putting forth a unified, positive agenda. The drive for purity and the internecine battles took their toll. "One of the most serious errors of the Socialist Party was its failure to behave the way political parties in the United States must in order to be successful," historian David A. Shannon concluded. "The Socialist Party never fully decided whether it was a political party, a political pressure group, a revolutionary sect, or a political forum."[81] Socialists organized within what they called "parties," but behaved as members of revolutionary sects. They split, and split, and split. Socialists learned the hard way: it is difficult to multiply when you are constantly dividing.

Seventh, the unimpeded flow of Europeans that characterized the period between the Civil War and World War I ended shortly after the Treaty of Versailles. The party's core constituency, whose influence within American Socialism was already waning, was kept out of the country through immigration restrictions. The foreigners already here integrated more seamlessly into American life, which necessarily meant a separation from the fringe Socialist Party.

Eighth, the Communist parties that sprung up in the wake of the Russian Revolution replaced the Socialist parties as the political vehicle for the far Left. Socialism offered a dream. Communism offered reality in the form of the Soviet Union.

The final consideration is most significant.

"Suppose," historian Aileen Kraditor writes in *The Radical Persuasion*, "a movement has for the past century preached that it was inevitable that the great mass of people would come to see the truth of numerology and that some historians have written the history of the United States in terms of the question, 'Why have the mass of Americans not come to believe in numerology?' The reader would see at once that something is wrong with the question."[82] Put another way, however many external reasons one might find to explain the non-rise and fall of socialism, the plainest reason socialism failed in America was socialism itself. Instead of asking, as Werner Sombart famously did, "Why is there no socialism in the United States?" a better question might be the one counterposed by Princeton University's Wilbert Moore: "Why are there *any* socialists in the United States?"[83]

. . .

"INDICATIONS ARE THAT Truly 'This Is Our Year,'" *Appeal to Reason*'s banner headline shouted a few days before the 1912 election.[84] But, like earlier predictions of Socialist victory, it was not to be. J. A. Wayland's high hopes were dashed by low realities, as they had been at the failed Ruskin colony that predated the *Appeal*. The Socialist Party garnered 6 percent of the presidential vote.

On the Sunday following the election, a beleaguered Wayland made a tired climb up the stairs of his stately Victorian home to his second-floor bedroom. Shortly after midnight, Wayland wrapped a muffling bedsheet around a gun, which he stuck in his mouth. *Appeal to Reason*'s perennially optimistic founder had lost all hope.[85] In 1902 he had posited the imminence of a Socialist America, comparing socialism to an unstoppable prairie fire. Now, a decade later, he saw things differently. "The struggle under the competitive system is not worth the effort," his suicide note counseled. "Let it pass."[86]

Letting it pass seemed the furthest thing from the minds of Socialists enthused by the party's relatively strong 1912 showing. But pass it did. Despite continued success in such localities as Milwaukee and Berkeley, and garnering still-noticeable vote totals in the presidential races of 1920 and 1932, the Socialist movement declined rapidly in the years following Wayland's suicide. The socialist prairie fire that Wayland had alluded to in 1902 had been extinguished in Girard, Kansas, and beyond.

Another fire, ignited in St. Petersburg, had taken its place.

BOOK THREE

THE OLD LEFT

∾ 14 ∾

RED-WHITE-AND-
BLUE REDS

*The fool hath said in his heart: There is no God. They are corrupt, and are
become abominable in their ways: there is none that doth good, no, not one.
The Lord hath looked down from heaven upon the children of men, to see if
there be any that understand and seek God. They are all gone aside, they
are become unprofitable together: there is none that doth good, no, not one.*

—PSALMS 14:1–3

JOHN WINTHROP SAW in Plymouth colony a city upon a hill. Three centuries later, a jaded Left no longer held out hope for America. But a new
city upon a hill rose on the steppes of the old continent. In Moscow, hopes
had been transformed into reality. Disillusioned Americans imagined a
better life in old Europe. It was the American Dream in reverse.

"I suddenly realized that the devout Russian people no longer needed
priests to pray them into heaven," John Reed, observing a mass Bolshevik
funeral, noted in *Ten Days That Shook the World*. "On earth they were building a kingdom more bright than any heaven had to offer, and for which it
was a glory to die."[1]

Soon, because of Jack Reed, the pilgrimage to Soviet Russia became as
obligatory for leftists as the pilgrimage to Mecca is for Muslims. When
others echoed the religious language of Reed, it was because for the Left
the Russian Revolution served as a religious event comparable to the rap-
ture. Jack Reed no longer worshipped the God of his ancestors, but he still
worshipped. Within the forms of the old religion, a new one emerged.
Popes, excommunications, saints, martyrs, holy books, and schisms characterized the development of "scientific" socialism.

Reed's mentor Lincoln Steffens rushed, on the younger man's advice,
to Petrograd to witness the dawn of the new Russia. Writing under the
nom de plume "Christian" in the *Nation*, the magazine of William Lloyd

Garrison's grandson Oswald Garrison Villard, Steffens prophesied: "The revolution in Russia is to establish the Kingdom of Heaven here on earth, now; in order that Christ may come soon; and, coming, reign forever. Forever and ever, everywhere. Not over Russia alone. The revolution in Russia is not the Russian revolution. It is 'The Revolution.' "[2]

"I stand in astonishment and wonder at the revelation of Russia that has come to me," evangelized W. E. B. Du Bois on his visit to "Holy Moscow" in 1926. "I may be partially deceived and half-informed. But if what I have seen with my eyes and heard with my ears in Russia is Bolshevism, I am a Bolshevik."[3]

"Our visit," University of Chicago professor Paul Douglas said of his 1927 pilgrimage, "strengthened my faith in socialism." Douglas, who became a U.S. senator from Illinois, gushed that "the spiritual fact behind all this material evidence, is that there is a real community of belief, a national ideal and moral unity, which is the solid basis of the new Russia—they have really a new religion—the building up of a People's Society."[4]

Russian reality did not match up to the dreams of Americans.

Within a year of 1917's October Revolution, the Bolsheviks had executed more political prisoners than their czarist predecessors had *sentenced* to death in the previous ninety-two years.[5] They set up a press court to try opposition journalists.[6] From May through June 1918, they quickly shut down more than two hundred newspapers.[7] State journalism replaced a free press. "The best place for strikers, those noxious yellow parasites," announced *Pravda*, the most notorious of the state-run newspapers, "is the concentration camp!"[8] A better place, thought Lenin, was at the bottom of a river or at the end of a rope. When the state is the sole employer, unions and strikes amount to treason. In fact, the Bolsheviks launched their secret police by using them as a strikebreaking force in St. Petersburg.[9] A few months later, in Astrakhan in March 1918, they tied stones to the necks of hundreds of strikers and their soldier allies and threw the offending parties into the Volga River.[10] The Communists executed 8,100 priests, nuns, and monks in 1922 alone.[11] They inflicted cultural genocide upon the Cossacks.[12]

But the American Left did not see this reality. The Left's leading journals presented a very different Russia to their readers back in the United States.

In the aftermath of the Bolshevik takeover, the *New Republic* maintained that "the Soviet government has abolished capital punishment"; that "Soviet power is an extreme instance of decentralization"; and that "the most democratic franchise yet devised in our world, providing for absolute universal suffrage and proportional representation" existed in

Russia.[13] Readers of the *Nation* learned that "there was so little killing, looting, burning, in Petrograd, Moscow, Vladivostok—wherever and so long as the mob reigned supreme"; that "[t]he day is apparently approaching when they [Russian intellectuals] will realize that their opportunities are greater than have ever been the opportunities of intellectuals anywhere"; and that "even with the property-owners excluded the franchise is more democratic in Russia than in England or the United States."[14]

The blinding light of heaven on earth obscured terror, repression, and murder. Organized chaos reigned in Russia. Amidst the ruins of once rock-hard principles survived one principle: the ends justify the means. Flattered into believing that their ideas reigned in Soviet Russia, many liberals rushed to declare the results of those ideas an unmitigated success. Economist Rexford Guy Tugwell, philosopher John Dewey, social worker Jane Addams, and labor leader Sidney Hillman were among the many non-Communist leftists and liberals who praised Lenin's fledgling enterprise while downplaying reports of savagery.[15] As Berkeley professor Lewis Feuer would note several decades later, "American liberalism at this time did not believe in Acton's metaphysical law that evil means necessarily corrupt the end."[16]

Violence was present at the creation. Violence did not end when the revolution did. Instead, state-initiated violence was the normal condition during Lenin's reign, and during the reign of his successor, Stalin, and to a lesser extent, during the reigns of every successor thereafter. Moreover, a similar pattern occurred in every nation that followed in the path of Russia. In some countries, such as China and Cambodia, the violence was more intense. Elsewhere, such as Eastern Europe and Central America, it was weaker. But wherever Marx's Communism traveled, in whatever variation, its servant violence followed.

All that history had yet to occur when an American adventurer in St. Petersburg scribbled the notes that became *Ten Days That Shook the World*. But the blood and violence of the Russian Revolution, and the terror in its aftermath, had happened. Americans dreamt that it hadn't.

John Reed was the American most responsible for launching those dreams.

JOHN REED GREW up a weak, sickly rich kid in Portland, Oregon. When he wasn't taking a circuitous route to school to avoid bullies, he was paying them to leave him alone. His money, or more accurately his father's money, bought him the popularity he craved later in life, as it had bought him respite during boyhood.[17] Cut from the freshman football team and crew, Reed found a place at Harvard as a cheerleader, a member of Hasty

Pudding, the editor of two publications, and the manager of a drama club, among numerous other pursuits.[18] The on-campus extracurricular activities didn't satiate. He extended a spring break by making off to Bermuda with a classmate. Harvard answered the affront by reviving an ancient punishment, rustication, which exiled Reed to rural Concord, where he finished the term in solitude.[19]

Described as "a self-centered young man" by biographer Robert Rosenstone, Reed escaped after graduation to Europe, where he relied "heavily on his father's account."[20] He flashed bill rolls, dropped gaudy tips, and even made a show of his wealth by ordering a second dinner at a restaurant in Spain to feed the dogs.[21] He ate well, drank much, and frequented the most available prostitutes. John Reed made a philosophy out of spending other people's money.

He did so with the "Queen of Greenwich Village," Mabel Dodge. The heiress—"a pioneer in the cult of the orgasm"—spoiled Reed with sex and money. When he ditched his older admirer, she attempted suicide. Dodge departed to New Mexico not long thereafter, married an Indian, and denounced the white race.[22] In Europe, amidst the Dodge drama, Reed apparently nursed a sick, comely American woman back to health, and planned an elopement. The woman's existing marriage derailed those plans. "[T]he girl's husband was threatening to shoot him at the same time that Mabel Dodge was trying to commit suicide."[23]

Such were the complexities of John Reed's lust life. Reed split up fellow Portlander Louise Bryant's marriage. He had the decency to marry her. He had the indecency to give her a venereal disease. "My whole left insides (ovaries, etc.) seem to be inflamed and infected," Bryant wrote to Reed before Christmas in 1916. "They think maybe I got it from your condition." With the possibility of an operation looming, Bryant closed her letter by wishing her husband, who had just undergone surgery to remove a kidney, to get well.[24] Ever the cad, Reed responded that Bryant's delay in getting medical attention "wasn't fair to me."[25] "I didn't mind what you said about my infecting you—if it were true," Reed wrote to his ailing wife. "But honey, it's awful to remove your ovaries, isn't it? Doesn't it make you incapable of having children and everything like that? I never heard of that being done to anybody but dogs, cats and horses."[26]

Reed promiscuously traveled between political causes as well. At Harvard, John Reed wandered into a few meetings of the Socialist Club, but never joined. After graduation, he wrote to a friend: "I have become an I.W.W. and am now in favor of dynamiting."[27] He fell under the sway of a family friend, muckraker extraordinaire Lincoln Steffens, who mentored Reed in the trade of advocacy journalism and landed him jobs. His travels then took him into the artsy circles in Greenwich Village, where he wrote, drank, and caroused alongside Max Eastman, Floyd Dell, and the rest of the staff of the upstart *Masses*. He experimented with gateway ideologies before getting hooked on the strong stuff.

In 1913 Reed joined the strikers in Paterson, New Jersey, even as he covered the strike as a journalist. His activism resulted in arrest, a few days in jail, and characteristically one-sided articles. He wrote in the *Masses*, "There's a war in Paterson, New Jersey. But it's a curious kind of war. All the violence is the work of one side—the mill owners."[28] To raise money for the IWW, Reed organized a pageant in Madison Square Garden. The ornate and elaborate show depicted life on the picket lines by featuring the performances of actual Paterson workers. Staged in June 1913, the show was a disaster. It drained financial resources, provoked jealousy among left-out workers, subtracted bodies from the picket lines, and widened the gulf between actual workers and their upper-class cheerleaders by illustrating the exploitative nature of their relationship. The strike collapsed. Despite Reed's best efforts, or perhaps partly because of the unintended consequences of his best efforts, the mill owners won. The workers lost jobs, or were rehired at lower wages. Reed ran away to Europe, again.[29]

Reed covered Pancho Villa's uprising in Mexico, romanticizing the brute and his band of murderous men. "It's so much Reed that I suspect it is very little Mexico," a friend surmised of Reed's colorful reports.[30] Reed reported on events he did not witness, filing a dispatch on the fall of Torreón a week before it occurred.[31] "Even if he had not seen these events firsthand," Rosenstone contends, "Jack knew enough of conditions, had watched enough of the battle, to portray its flavor accurately."[32] Biographer Granville Hicks, then a Communist, similarly assessed: "He did not hesitate to alter or even to invent. He might tell as if it had happened to him something that he had learned at second-hand."[33]

Later in 1915, Reed traveled to Europe to report on a less exciting but more important event: the Great War. Reed drank his way around Europe, frequented whores, and even took potshots at French soldiers from behind the German lines.[34] But World War I held none of the romance, idealism, or drama of Mexico. Access curtailed by bureaucracy, his radical politics, and an act of recklessness with a rifle, Reed returned to the United States with few war stories other than the embarrassing one involving himself.

From Washington, D.C., where Congress had declared war on Germany less than three months earlier, Reed wrote to his war correspondent wife that there was no "place in the world so exciting as this city now." Yet in the same missive, the adrenaline junkie Reed tellingly confessed depression.[35] As hard as he might try to convince himself, he wasn't where the action was and his wife was.

The excitement void would soon be filled by developments to the east. "If I got a chance to go to Russia via Vladivostok, could you go to Petrograd, via Stockholm, [and] wait for me there?" Reed asked Bryant in July 1917.[36] The Russians had overthrown their czar, and now the extreme Left threatened a coup against the revolution. Max Eastman raised $2,000 from an Empire State socialite to send Reed to history as it happened. "John Reed is in Petrograd," the *Masses* informed its readership in late 1917. "His story of the first proletarian Revolution will be an event in the world's literature."[37]

John Reed told a story of revolution, but not in the *Masses*. In June, Reed had boasted to Bryant of George Creel offering him a job on the government's new wartime propaganda board.[38] By July, Reed was explaining to Bryant that the government had suppressed the *Masses*.[39] Indeed, the issue advertising Reed's story of the Russian Revolution would be the loose and carefree journal's last. Creel, who had in the pages of the *Masses* in 1915 decried a judicial "campaign of extermination" against Colorado strikers as "the lowest depth to which American justice has yet been dragged," dragged it still lower by playing a leading role in the censorship apparatus that permanently shut down the magazine in which he once lambasted such governmental misdeeds.[40]

The suppression of the *Masses* did not stop Reed. A muscular ball of energy whose darting eyes indicated that the man behind them was jonesing for his next adrenaline fix, Reed got his ultimate rush not from bedding friends' wives, burning off his inheritance, or drinking in Provincetown but by chronicling and participating in the October Revolution.

Reed chronicled his Russian adventure in the book *Ten Days That Shook the World*. He admitted picking up a rifle and going along with the Bolsheviks.[41] He ratted on Russians who foolishly offered him their low opinions of Bolshevism alongside their names.[42] He covered for comrades who brought him along when they shouldn't have.[43] Even if it harbored journalistic pretensions, the book, authored as it was by an employee of Russia's Bureau of International Revolutionary Propaganda, wasn't journalism (though a panel convened by New York University would name it one of the twentieth century's best works of journalism).[44] Walter Lippmann's overall assessment of his Harvard classmate seemed an apt description of *Ten Days That Shook the World*: "Wherever his sympathies marched with the facts, Reed was superb."[45] But the facts didn't always march with his sympathies in Russia.

Many wanted to believe the romantic, glorious picture of the October Revolution presented by Reed. They also wanted to replicate the Revolution in America. The Socialist Party's electoral failures didn't demonstrate the failure of socialism. For the party's extreme left wing, they showed the failure of democracy.

AMERICANS WEREN'T READY for even one Communist party in the heady days following the Bolshevik coup. But by April 1920, they had three. John Reed launched the first.

With brunette mane combed back from what Max Eastman described as "a face like a potato," the John Reed of Provincetown and Greenwich Village was "gay and jocular and daring."[46] The John Reed who returned from the October Revolution was serious, dogmatic, and somber. The onetime rhapsodist confessed to friends, "This class struggle plays hell with your poetry."[47] Reed now belonged to soapboxes, labor halls, and smoke-filled meeting rooms. He certainly didn't belong to the dunes of Cape Cod, the bars of Greenwich Village, or the beds of Mexican enchantresses.

Reed, together with Benjamin Gitlow and other Communists, plotted to take over the Socialist Party's convention held at Machinists' Hall in Chicago on August 30, 1919.[48] In the hall's barroom beforehand, Reed and his band of accomplices laid out their crude plan for hijacking the party for Communism—ignore convention passes, "rush into the second-floor auditorium, grab seats, and demand recognition." (Reed had already tendered his resignation from the Socialist Party, but he didn't let that inconvenience dissuade him from attempting to capture it.) The would-be party hijackers' plans were found by the bartender, turned over to the Socialists, and copied for the entire convention. When Reed's band stormed the auditorium, the Socialists, and the police, awaited. Unable to penetrate the gathering, Reed, along with more than eighty delegates, cried foul over police involvement at a Socialist gathering, promptly seceded, and formed the Communist Labor Party (CLP) back at the barroom of Machinists' Hall on August 31.[49]

The following day, Louis Frania, Charles Ruthenberg, Jay Lovestone, Alexander Bittelman, and Isaac Hourwich launched a rival party, this one named the Communist Party (CP), that had a heavier foreign membership than the CLP did. The police raided the Communist Party's convention before it had even started, tearing down Communist pictures and placards. A band played the "Internationale" amidst the chaos. Police officers served the first speaker with an arrest warrant. The cops slugged a protesting lawyer.[50] And all that was before the intramural scraps began.

To add to the confusion, the Communist Party split into two factions less than a year later. "So much as there was a principle involved in the split, it was over the relative emphasis on insurrectionary violence," historians Harvey Klehr and John Earl Haynes wrote. "The Hourwich-Bittelman C.P. favored an uncompromising advocacy of violent revolution, while the Ruthenberg-Lovestone C.P. favored moderating the party's insurrectionary program sufficiently to allow Communists to participate in peaceful strikes and popular political protests."[51] In a party overflowing with seemingly minor doctrinal disputes, the real reason for this split, which foreshadowed the cause for the future split between Joseph Stalin and Leon Trotsky in the motherland, was power. In a party in which the party controlled individuals—not in which individuals controlled the party—everyone wanted to be the party.

Thus, *three* parties—two Communist parties, and one Communist Labor party—competed for the allegiance of a minuscule number of Communists in America. To add to the confusion, the two parties claiming the same name also published newspapers with identical names, the *Communist*.[52]

All of this was too much for the Kremlin, and for the Communist Labor Party (which had been decimated by Woodrow Wilson's crackdown on non-Wilsonian radicalism). The CLP united with the Ruthenberg-Lovestone Communist Party in a United Communist Party. But this still left two parties. The Comintern, the popular name for Lenin's Third International, demanded, as Marx's First International had demanded of the Yankee International five decades earlier, subordination and uniformity. In 1921, it concluded: "The Executive Committee of the Communist International having listened to the reports of the United Communist Party and the Communist Party of America, hereby declares that the further postponement of the unification of the two Communist groups is a crime against the Communist International."[53] Since the parties had pledged fealty to Moscow, they unified.

THE COMMUNIST PARTY was that most unusual political entity born with the aspiration of boycotting the political process.[54] But the party, ostensibly at least, eschewed its revolutionary path to power in favor of democratic elections as the 1924 campaign approached. The Communists saw a rising star in Wisconsin senator Robert La Follette, who had made the pilgrimage to Soviet Russia the previous year. The party attempted, at least for a time, to hitch its dim star to his bright one.

On orders from Moscow, the party co-opted the organizing convention of the national Farmer-Labor Party, which had hoped to convince La

Follette to carry its standard in the coming presidential race. The presence of so many Bolsheviks within their midst did not alarm the party's organizers, who thought the Communists just another shade of leftist.[55]

La Follette thought differently. He rebuffed the group's endorsement, pointing to the "fatal error" of allowing those faithful to "orders from the Communist International in Moscow" to join any coalition of farmers, laborers, and progressives. La Follette firmly explained that Communists and the mainstream Left could not work together under any circumstance.[56] In turn, the Communists denounced La Follette as well—not because of his hostility to them, but because Moscow told them to.[57] Thus, the Communists reversed their endorsement of La Follette, destroyed the organization they had co-opted, and fielded their own set of obscure candidates. That fall, on the Progressive Party ticket, La Follette garnered 17 percent of the vote, an impressive showing for a third-party candidate. It was a lost opportunity for Communists to ingratiate themselves with the larger Left.

The pattern of flirtation with mainstream politics, followed by reversals to extremist denunciations of mainstream parties and politicians, recurred over the next fifteen years. In the La Follette reversal, as in future reversals, American Communists reacted to the internal politics of Russia. In 1924, Trotsky, Stalin, and others competed to succeed Lenin. Attempting to insulate themselves against Trotsky's charges of capitulation, impurity, and selling out, Stalin's forces ordered the Americans to take an uncompromising approach and to avoid contaminating Communism through contact with bourgeois parties, even third parties. The bizarre move by the American Communists made sense to those familiar with the politics of a nation on the other side of the planet. It didn't make sense to anyone else.

BOLSHEVIK COMMUNISM WAS alien to Americans. It clashed with the religious and free-market traditions of the nation. Foreigners made up the bulk of the Communist Party's membership. The party's heroes were foreign. A foreign government dictated its program, its methods, its everything. The party's newspaper, the *Communist*, put the situation bluntly in 1920: "The membership of the Communist Party as well as the U.C.P. is overwhelmingly composed of foreign comrades who do not speak or understand English."[58]

By 1921, two years after its birth, the Communist Party boasted eight daily newspapers printed in foreign languages, but not a single one printed in English.[59] Lenin wanted an English daily, so the party established the *Daily Worker* in 1924.[60] But the English-reading audience for such a publication proved so small that in the 1920s the *Daily Worker* attracted fewer readers than *Freiheit*, the party's Yiddish newspaper in America.[61]

During the first months of the Communist Party, just 1,900 of 24,000 members spoke English primarily, with more than 40 percent of those English-speakers defecting en masse in 1920.[62] By 1923, with Russian Communists reverse-migrating to the motherland, the ethnic makeup of the party had changed. But its foreign composition hadn't. Finns had replaced Russians as the numeric powerhouse in the allegedly American party, but native-born Americans still made up a sliver of the total membership, about 5 percent.[63] Just as the Jimmy Higginses were in demand as out-front Socialists, English-speaking Communists such as John Reed were valued to put an American face on what was essentially a foreign party. "Native-born representation on the party's central committees from 1921 to 1929 was never below 25 percent and went as high as 58.3 percent—this when the native-born membership was probably never above 10 percent."[64]

Not only did foreigners compose the party's membership and dictate party policy from afar, but foreign subsidy comprised a substantial portion of the party's finances. Scholars Klehr, Haynes, and Kyrill Anderson, after combing through the Soviet archives, estimated in *The Soviet World of American Communism* "that in the 1920s 'Moscow gold' accounted for at least a third and in some years more than half, or even two-thirds, of the budget of the American Communist party."[65] Though Communists and their sympathizers mocked the notion of "Moscow gold," the records of the Soviet Union, and John Reed's arrest in Finland while carrying a stash of diamonds, demonstrate the efforts of a foreign power to finance an ostensibly American party.[66] A document in the Soviet archives, which meticulously details payments from the Soviet government to foreign Communist parties, lists valuables in excess of a million rubles given to Reed on January 22, 1920.[67]

The Finnish government took the diamonds, Reed's phony passports, and his freedom. From his March arrest in the bowels of a ship bound for Sweden, Reed was held in solitary confinement by police in Abo, Finland, for three months. For most of his detention, he was held incommunicado. Though Reed labeled his jailers "friendly and generous," boasted of having quit smoking, and took pleasure in "a little walk in the yard every day," three months alone in a Finnish jail dieting on bread and fish exacted its toll. To generate interest in America, where his government was rumored to be behind his extended stay in a Finnish jail, Reed planted a story of his own execution. He threatened to starve himself. Powerful friends exerted pressure on an uninterested State Department. Having recently greeted Emma Goldman upon her arrival in Soviet Russia on the *Buford* deportee ship, Reed was well aware of the inhospitable atmosphere in America toward radicals. He wanted to go home but home didn't want him. The American government refused him a passport. But John Reed was not a man without a country. Engineering a prisoner exchange with Finland, Soviet Russia welcomed its favorite American back. Released in June 1920, Reed headed back to Petrograd.[68]

"But I am worrying about only one thing," he informed Louise Bryant. "I must soon go home, and it is awfully difficult to get out of here, especially for a woman."[69] For the American Bolshevik, there was no going home again. Even when home came to him, in the form of his sweetheart Bryant, his new home ordered him away on party business. As his lover traveled across the globe to meet Reed in Russia, a sickly and deflated Reed frustratingly traveled away from her to the Caucasus. He vowed, "[W]e shall not be separated another winter."[70] John Reed would not live to see another winter.

ADMIRERS OF SOVIET Russia in the United States imitated the workers' state's contempt for workers. They did this at the same time that they claimed to speak for workers. As Karl Marx and Friedrich Engels explained, Communists "always and everywhere represent the interests of the [working class] movement as a whole."[71] That delusion helps explain the killing of workers in the name of the workers.

Like Karl Marx, John Reed was himself not a "worker." This didn't prevent him from simultaneously claiming to know their interests and condemning them for not knowing their "true" interests. "The American working class is politically and economically the most uneducated working class in the world," Reed judged.[72]

Communists found the institutions that physical laborers set up deficient. They set about to destroy them, and to impose their own institutions upon workers.

Instructions from the Comintern, unsurprisingly, told American Communists what their position vis-à-vis the American Federation of Labor would be: "This must be *smashed in pieces.*"[73] "Trades unionism is the arch enemy of the militant proletariat," the *Communist* declared. "This is one of the tasks of the Communist Party—the destruction of the existing trades union organizations."[74] The United Communist Party declared at its founding: "A Communist who belongs to the A.F. of L. should seize every opportunity to voice his hostility to the organization, not to reform it but to destroy it."[75]

To this end, the Communists pursued the old "dual unionism" tactics of the Socialist Trade and Labor Alliance and the Industrial Workers of the World. But, by the second Comintern congress in 1920, the Russian masters directed their American underlings to abandon dual unionism in favor of "boring from within." American Communists should work inside and alongside the AFL, an organization they had just pledged to destroy.[76] So bitter was that pill to swallow that John Reed, one of America's representatives to the meeting, actually objected, as did Wobbly Big Bill Haywood, who had taken up residence in Soviet Russia after jumping bail in America.[77] Reed mistakenly believed that he was a representative and not a showpiece. He mistakenly believed that the Communist International was a representative body of Communists the world over, rather than a Moscow-controlled outfit to do the Kremlin's bidding across the globe.

But Communists didn't object. They obeyed. Following Reed's demurral, the number of occasions American Communists stood athwart the directives of Moscow could be counted on a three-fingered hand. In two of the three cases, the American party sided with Moscow and against its recalcitrant countrymen.

The first post-Reed rebellion occurred in 1929. Jay Lovestone, chosen by the Comintern to succeed Charles Ruthenberg as head of the American political party in 1927, objected to a reorganization of the party in response to internal Russian politics. Summoned to Moscow, he personally pleaded with Stalin that the majority of the American party took his side. Stalin, a hard man to refuse, responded: "You had a majority because the American Communist Party until now regarded you as the determined supporters of the Communist International. And it was only because the Party regarded you as the friends of the Comintern that you had a majority in the ranks of the American Communist Party. But what will happen if the American workers learn that you intend to break the unity of the ranks of the Comintern and are thinking of conducting a fight against its executive bodies—that is the question, dear comrades? Do you think that the American workers will follow your lead against the Comintern, that they will prefer the interests of your factional group to the interests of the Comintern?"[78] The questions answered themselves. The Communists immediately expelled Lovestone, eventually ransacked his apartment, and ultimately converted his name into an insult.[79]

The final post-Reed rebellion occurred sixty years later. Mikhail Gorbachev ushered in glasnost and perestroika. The hard-line American Communists objected, and the two bodies cut all ties. Bonds that death camps, a mass-starvation campaign in the Ukraine, an alliance with Hitler, and invasions of more than a dozen European nations couldn't break were shattered by Gorbachev's liberalization of the Soviet economy and openness with the West. Some principles aren't for compromise.

IMPOLITIC ACTIONS AND flaming rhetoric turned large portions of the American Left against the Communists. The Communists alienated progressives by their treachery in the 1924 campaign. They made enemies of the major trade union, the AFL, by openly seeking its destruction. They disgusted free-spirited Wobblies by their mandated uniformity. They turned Socialists, under whose banner proto-Communists flocked before 1919, against them by attempting to transform their democratic party into a revolutionary outfit subservient to Moscow. And they embittered ex-Communists who had been traumatically expelled or had become disillusioned.

Starting in the early 1920s, the AFL began revoking the charters of affiliates controlled by Communists. Beginning in 1925, America's largest union regularly condemned the Bolshevik state by name.[80] A few rebellious voices within the IWW saw Bolshevism in the same light as the despised AFLers saw Bolshevism. "We say we will never forget Joe Hill, Frank Little, and Wesley Everest and the scores of our fellow workers murdered in prison and outside the prison walls," Jean Sanjour, fresh from employment with the Soviet government, wrote in the Wobbly publication *Industrial Worker*. "And at the same time we find among our fellow workers those who are satisfied with the murder of our fellow workers in Russia. Are they not our fellow workers? Or do you think that our fellow workers are the hangmen of the Communist Party of Russia?"[81]

After initially declaring solidarity with the Bolsheviks, Eugene Debs tempered his goodwill.[82] Stung by Communist attempts to kill his party in the United States, and their more successful efforts to kill his fellow social democrats in Russia, Debs reflected the thoughts of many in his diminishing party by holding the newer, smaller party in disdain. "Gene wishes me to say to you that personally he owes nothing to the Communists," brother Theodore Debs wrote a Communist editor. "When he was in that hell-hole at Atlanta the Communists with but few exceptions ignored him and the rest of the political prisoners, and their papers, including the one you now edit, were cold-bloodedly silent, not raising a voice nor lifting a finger to secure their release, and as far as they were concerned Gene would still be rotting, were he alive, in his dungeon in Atlanta."[83] To Debs, the American Communists weren't left or right, but wrong—phonies, opportunists, liars, and cowards. He held out hope for Russia under Bolshevism, but he did not believe violent revolution or the dictatorship of the proletariat fit the American experience.

Deported from the United States to Russia on the "Soviet Ark," anarchist Emma Goldman found her new homeland so displeasing and disappointing that she penned two volumes, *My Disillusionment in Russia* and *My Further Disillusionment in Russia*, which detailed the horrors she saw in the two years she lived in post-revolutionary Russia. Goldman's boyfriend and shipmate on the Soviet Ark, Alexander Berkman, also articulated his shattered illusions in book form. In 1925, he authored *The Bolshevik Myth.*

Add to these progressive, unionist, radical, and anarchist voices the voices of the growing number of purged Communists, such as former party leader Jay Lovestone, and one discovers an active anti-Communist Left as early as the 1920s. At the same time that so many leftists shamefully served as apologists for Soviet Russia, a courageous band of ex-Communists, progressives, union members, anarchists, socialists, and liberals risked their standing in their movements by telling inconvenient truths about Communism.

IN THE LAND of his dreams came his final sleep. With a dedicated Louise Bryant sitting bedside, John Reed expired from typhus on October 17, 1920.

The thirty-two-year-old's death was a good career move. Forever young, the Peter Pan of American Communism avoided the nastiness over murdered sailors at Kronstadt, Stalin's flip-flops on Hitler, Solzhenitsyn's remembrances of the gulag, invasions of Hungary and Czechoslovakia, the Berlin Wall, and a million other crimes against humanity. Reed remains to the Left a symbol of lofty idealism even when his ideals sank to murky depths. Alas, Reed, too, was afflicted with Communism's original sin. He saw crimes, and then obscured, excused, and ignored them. More crimes followed. They were the natural outgrowth of the initial crimes that Reed witnessed in St. Petersburg. John Reed's Communist heirs reacted to new crimes the way Reed had reacted to the initial ones.

Returning to America was John Reed's deathbed obsession.[84] He was never granted this dying wish. Reed's body lay in state for a week at the Temple of the Revolution. Then, in the shadow of the Kremlin Wall, near the spot of the Brotherhood Grave, where Reed's observation of a funeral of hundreds of revolutionaries inspired him to famously write in *Ten Days That Shook the World* that Russia was building on earth a heaven superior to the one above, Reed was interred amidst pomp and circumstance as a revolutionary hero alongside martyrs of the October Revolution.[85] He would have admired the pageantry. Ever the tool of propaganda, Reed, in death, provided a Moscow-controlled movement with a monument that exclaimed that theirs was an international movement comprised of men from every corner of the earth. It was a long way from Portland.

MARXISTS BELIEVE IN stages of history. Whatever stage of history American Communist pilgrims found themselves in, the Socialists had found themselves there first. The early days of American Communism appear as a repeat performance of the early days of American Socialism. A foreign ideology promised heaven on earth. Its adherents judged its ascension to power as imminent. It endured schisms and splits. It waged war on the workers it purported to represent. It largely failed to attract a native-born American following, despite many efforts at Americanization.

Amidst a multitude of similarities, a few key differences separated the infancies of American Socialism and American Communism.

An age of optimism that saw the hopes of Socialism tied to the ballot box gave way to a jaded era where Communism tethered its hopes to the cartridge box. Socialism aspired to expropriate land, confiscate businesses, and dictate the previously private expenditures of individuals. The ideology's essence is, in a word, force. Yet Socialists refrained from using force to obtain the governmental mechanisms of force. Communists had no such scruples. They applied force to attaining power rather than merely to exercising it. In one sense a revolutionary party replaced a democratic one, but in another sense a totalitarian party gave way to another totalitarian party.

No Moscow had adjudicated disputes among Socialists. Such American originals as J. A. Wayland, Big Bill Haywood, and Eugene Debs passed the baton to conformists directed in thought and deed by overlords halfway round the planet.

Most significantly, the ideal state of the Socialists existed in the future, in a dream, in an idea. The ideal state of the Communists existed in the present, in the actual, in a geographical body called Soviet Russia. The Socialists, thus, erred in defending a dream. The Communists erred in defending a living nightmare.

∽ 15 ∾

THE PATERNALIST
DYNASTY III:
NEW DEALERS

*And of these cities which shall be given out of the possessions of the chil-
dren of Israel, from them that have more, more shall be taken: and from
them that have less, fewer.*

—NUMBERS 35:8

THE DEMOCRATIC PARTY of 1932 wasn't quite sure what it should become. Would it be the free-market, sound-money, states'-rights party
of Grover Cleveland and Al Smith? Or would it be the interventionist,
inflationary, nationalist party of William Jennings Bryan and Woodrow
Wilson?

Franklin Roosevelt, the party's standard-bearer in 1932, didn't have to
make that decision during the campaign. Sure, Al Smith's handpicked
successor as New York's governor (though not for the presidential nomination) lambasted Herbert Hoover for massive deficits and increases
in government spending.[1] But Roosevelt, as Woodrow Wilson's assistant
secretary of the navy, was also strongly tied to the activist policies of that
administration. It mattered little if Roosevelt declared himself a conservative or a progressive. All that mattered in 1932 was that he was not a Republican. America knew that the Democratic nominee had a plan to stave
off the Great Depression. They just didn't know what it was. Neither did
Roosevelt.

If Roosevelt embraced a guiding philosophy, it wasn't fascism, socialism, or communism—all isms that American liberals flirted with in these
years—but action and power. It is significant that he used that power to
take action for leftist ends. It is also significant that he abandoned leftist
ends when he saw that they weren't working—either for the people or for

his power. Like his distant cousin Theodore, Franklin Roosevelt was a politician. It's the politician, not the theorist, who makes policies of ideas.

Roosevelt began the New Deal with a call for action and a demand for power. "This nation asks for action, and action now," he announced at his inauguration. Though there was no war, Roosevelt instructed the American people to act as though there were. As a veteran of the Wilson administration, the new president remembered the docility of the American people during the world war. Then, the government had seized the railroads, levied draconian taxes, jailed critics, manipulated the currency, and conscripted young men. The Great Depression wasn't war, but certainly the economic crisis affected more Americans than had the Great War. Americans "must move as a trained and loyal army," Roosevelt announced, and act "with a unity of duty hitherto evoked only in time of armed strife." Roosevelt assumed "the leadership of this great army of our people." In a line that his wife remembered receiving the most applause, the new president proclaimed: "I shall ask the Congress for the one remaining instrument to meet the crisis: broad executive power to wage a war against the emergency as great as the power that would be given to me if we were in fact invaded by a foreign foe." But there was no foreign foe, just "money changers," "self-seekers," and other bogeymen and phantoms that Roosevelt rallied the nation to fight.[2]

THOUGH THE NEW Deal was the heir of progressivism, New Dealers were the products of a multitude of earlier Lefts.

Believers in the Social Gospel found in the New Deal a means to implement their community solutions to the national community. Secretary of Labor Frances Perkins worked at the elbow of Jane Addams at Hull House. The State Department's Adolph Berle, himself the son of a prominent Social Gospel minister, volunteered at Henry Street Settlement, as did Treasury Secretary Henry Morgenthau and economic advisor Herbert Lehman. Harry Hopkins's summer at New York's Christodora House launched his career in social work. Arthur Morgan, who spearheaded the Tennessee Valley Authority project, taught at the far-left Antioch College and wrote a biography of his hero, Edward Bellamy. Harold Ickes and Donald Richberg cut their political teeth in Theodore Roosevelt's Bull Moose Party. Rexford Tugwell and others too young for Theodore Roosevelt's 1912 run supported Robert La Follette's 1924 third-party campaign for the presidency. Abolitionist William Lloyd Garrison's grandson, Lloyd K. Garrison, chaired the National Labor Relations Board.

The New Deal, thus, borrowed from past Lefts. The Resettlement Administration, which sought to relocate the urban poor in the countryside, as well as in the experimental governmentally designed Greenbelt communities, gleaned inspiration from the nineteenth-century communitarians. Roosevelt's jettisoning of the gold standard enacted, belatedly, the rallying cries of Greenbackers and Populists. The Civilian Conservation Corps, which sent unemployed young men into the countryside to work on reforestation and beautification projects, responded to the pleas from environmentalists to the first President Roosevelt. The New Deal was not the same old deal repackaged, but it did pay enough heed to past Lefts to remind observers that it didn't appear out of the ether.

As it borrowed from past Lefts, the New Deal reflected current Lefts in Europe and anticipated future Lefts in America. Roosevelt confided to his secretary of the interior that "what we were doing in this country were some of the things that were being done in Russia and even some of the things that were being done under Hitler in Germany. But we were doing them in an orderly way."3

The New Deal also shaped the American Left. Before Roosevelt, aristocratic do-gooders generally gravitated to the Republicans, while working-class liberals desiring a protective federal state generally gravitated to the Democrats. Roosevelt, however, fashioned a new coalition between the progressive wing of the Republican Party and the farmer and labor wings of the Democratic Party. Most of the Left dropped its third-party delusions and worked within the Democratic Party. It may not have been as pure as Norman Thomas's Socialist Party, but Franklin Roosevelt's Democratic Party gave the Left a welcoming place within its winning coalition.

And that coalition was broad. It included union workers, farmers, city dwellers, and government workers. It pried African Americans from their traditional Republican home. It made the aged dependent on government rather than relatives through Social Security. It made a majority party of minority groups. The coalition, to the chagrin of future Lefts, included southern Democrats. The issues addressed by the New Deal were almost entirely economic. The racial and moral issues that separated southern Democrats from the liberal coalition were decades from becoming salient. That Old Left, then, included many subgroups, including southern Democrats and union members, that didn't make the journey from Old Left to New Left. One can't backdate divorces, no matter how bitter the union eventually becomes.

The incoming president was a blank slate not just to the Left but to nearly all Democrats and most Americans. One of Roosevelt's first acts as president, for instance, thrilled the conservative wing of his party. After more than a decade as a dry nation, Roosevelt declared that progressive experiment a failure by signing legislation to legalize beer, and later to repeal prohibition entirely. Little besides this heartened conservative Democrats—a breed that Roosevelt attempted to exterminate by campaigning for liberal challengers in Democratic primaries. Roosevelt even endorsed Republicans and Progressives when they stood with his policies.

The New Deal realigned American politics, as political scientists are wont to point out, by breaking the previous seventy-plus years of Republican dominance and instituting Democratic dominance. But an important realignment also took place within the parties. Until Roosevelt's presidency, both parties housed liberals as well as conservatives. Regional and ethnic ties, more so than ideological ones, determined one's party affiliation. The association of the Democratic Party with Franklin Roosevelt, and Franklin Roosevelt with liberalism, more firmly defined the parties ideologically. The New Deal thus acted as the catalyst for voters identifying the parties with a particular ideology, even when the parties served up a watered-down version of their ideology.

ROOSEVELT BEGAN HIS presidency by redundantly ordering all banks in the United States to close. As the president himself acknowledged, "scarcely a bank in the country was open to do business" when he took office.[4] Governors had already temporarily closed them to stop runs and determine solvency. Michigan's banks, for instance, had been closed for three weeks when the president ordered them closed for another week. "In Detroit several day laborers employed by the city collapsed from hunger on the job, having been unable to cash their paychecks or use them in any other way to obtain food," historian Kenneth S. Davis recounts.[5] Action, not outcomes, mattered.

No law granted the president the power to shut down private banks. He issued a series of executive orders closing the banks, but since executive orders applied only to federal employees of the executive branch, Roosevelt's orders were illegal. He tacitly acknowledged as much when he subsequently urged Congress to amend the Trading with the Enemy Act. He had previously cited this as his legal justification to close the banks. He furthermore wanted Congress to extend the act to a "national emergency" rather than to apply just during wartime.[6] Congress did all that, and established a pattern of codifying previous presidential usurpations of the lawmaking power.

A month after closing the banks, Roosevelt ordered the seizure of all privately owned gold (save jewelry and other such personal items) in the United States. The president instituted this authoritarian measure through authoritarian means, the executive order. Less than a year later, a meek Congress passed ex post facto a law authorizing Roosevelt to do what he had already done. In exchange for the gold, Roosevelt awarded paper money. Subsequently he detached that paper money from gold and set its new value at roughly three-fifths of its previous gold value. In other words, he swindled the gold owners. Roosevelt promised a dollar for a dollar's worth of gold. He really handed over about sixty cents.

Roosevelt then declared that he wanted the government to purchase gold in the world market, an act his attorney general frowned upon. Pushed by Roosevelt to do something of dubious legality and suspect wisdom, a beleaguered Treasury Undersecretary Dean Acheson requested an order in writing from the president. The president curtly responded: "I say it is legal."[7]

First the government hoarded the gold. Then the government devalued the dollars it had paid for the gold. Next, with all of the gold in the United States in its hands, the government set the price of gold for sale on the world market. One needn't be a part of Roosevelt's "brains trust" to deduce what happened next: Roosevelt set the price higher and higher.

By whim, the president set the price of gold on a daily basis. In one infamous instance, Roosevelt announced to Secretary of the Treasury Henry Morgenthau that he had decided to raise the price twenty-one cents. Why? Because seven is a lucky number and three times seven is twenty-one, Roosevelt answered.[8]

What effect did FDR's inflation of the price of gold and devaluing of paper money have on banking?

> One effect was that private borrowing and lending, except from day to day, practically ceased. With the value of the dollar being posted daily at the Treasury like a lottery number, who would lend money for six months or a year, with no way of even guessing what a dollar would be worth when it came back paid? "No man outside of a lunatic asylum," said Senator [Carter] Glass, "will loan his money today on a farm mortgage." But the New Deal had a train of Federal lending agencies ready to start. The locomotive was the Reconstruction Finance Corporation. The signal for the train to start was a blast of propaganda denouncing Wall Street, the banks and all private owners of capital for their unwillingness to lend. So the government, in their place, became the great provider of credit and capital for all purposes.[9]

Roosevelt didn't replace private banks with post office banks, as the Left had demanded in the days of Tom Watson and Ignatius Donnelly. But he did great harm to banks (legislation insuring deposits aside), institutions that are of great help to Americans. And he took America off the gold standard, something that William Jennings Bryan had made the center-piece of his initial campaign for the presidency. Although inflating the currency during a recession as severe as the Great Depression proved be-yond even the president's power, Roosevelt did establish a system that made inflation easier. What the progressives established with the Federal Reserve, Roosevelt furthered with the elimination of the gold standard. The value of money was now arbitrarily determined. The elected body constitutionally charged with coining money, Congress, passively allowed the arrogation of its powers.

Roosevelt's strange views on gold—that rising gold prices meant rising prices in general, and that rising prices ensured prosperity's return—weirded out economists. Other demagogues celebrated. "Forward to Christ all ye people! God wills it—this religious crusade against the pagan god of gold," Father Charles Coughlin, then a fervent Roosevelt supporter, declared.[10] Alas, despite Roosevelt's best, ill-educated attempts, inflation did not follow and the economy did not rebound.

NEW DEALERS SCORNED the hands-off policies of presidents Harding and Coolidge. The national economy, they reasoned, was too important to leave to the erratic, hidden hand of the market. National planners, man-agers, and experts could do better. These men, often college professors or lifetime bureaucrats, imagined themselves as more effective directors of industry than the men who had spent their lives, and whose fortunes rested on success or failure, in business. The hubris glared most annoy-ingly in the Agricultural Adjustment Administration (AAA).

The Agricultural Adjustment Act of 1933 levied a processing tax on American farmers. The more wheat, for instance, that a farmer grew, the more taxes he paid. The money collected, theoretically, was then doled out to farmers on the condition that they destroy existing crops or leave unused a large portion of their farmland. Therefore, if the tax didn't dis-courage the farmer from producing, the subsidy would. Low-interest gov-ernment loans, available only to those farmers participating in AAA programs, further induced participation in crop destruction and animal sacrifice schemes.[11]

Farmers had witnessed declining financial yields from their crops. To keep pace with their pre-crash takes, farmers increased crop production. The glut of supply exacerbated the problem. With an abundance of supply, prices naturally dropped further. The AAA rested on the theory that a reversal in supply—replacing oversupply with artificial scarcity—would trigger a reversal from farmer poverty to farmer prosperity.

Though farmers generally welcomed federal money, they generally resented federal intrusion. To ensure compliance, the AAA unleashed an army of bureaucrats upon farms enrolled in the program. Had Joe Farmer really made 54 percent of his land barren? Melvin Bureaucrat arrived on the scene to make sure. Farmers had more money but less freedom. Bureaucrats had more money and more power.

Tenant farmers, sharecroppers, and farm laborers, the very people hit hardest by the Great Depression, got hit again by the New Deal. Since the AAA paid the owners of farmland and not necessarily the people who farmed the land, those merely working the land not only were denied the federal windfall but saw opportunities vanish as the federal government removed arable land from circulation. With farms shrunk by a coercive federal program, farmers got by without hired help. The AAA may have benefited farm owners. It didn't benefit farm workers.

The tinkering with supply did not, as was thought, generally result in a rise in prices. "The prices of most farm commodities in August 1939, the month before the Nazis invaded Poland, were low in comparison with parity and August 1929 price levels," historian Theodore Saloutos pointed out. By parity, Saloutos means the relationship between farm prices and the prices of other goods. "Of the prices received for farm commodities, only one, that for beef cattle, had attained parity by August 1939. Corn was 59 percent of parity, cotton 66 percent, wheat 50, butterfat 59, hogs 60, chickens 93, and eggs 49." Farm income, though substantially higher than at its 1933 nadir, was only about four-fifths its 1929 level by the close of the 1930s.[12] Even with the influx of federal subsidies, farmers were worse off at the close of the New Deal than they were at the open of the Great Depression. And unlike the rest of the country, farmers had not benefited much from the economic boom of the 1920s. They suffered more severely and for longer.

Unlike the Public Works Administration, a sister New Deal agency that left behind a legacy of construction from the Triborough Bridge to the Grand Coulee Dam, the AAA spent massive amounts of money to destroy. The AAA dispersed $100 million in 1933 to farmers to uproot 10 million acres of cotton fields, and $200 million during 1933 and 1934 for wheat farmers to reduce their crop yields.[13] In 1933, Secretary of Agriculture Henry Wallace ordered the "slaughtering [of] over six million little pigs and more than two hundred thousand sows due to farrow," historian William E. Leuchtenburg documented. "While one million pounds of salt pork was salvaged for relief families, nine-tenths of the yield was inedible, and most of it had to be thrown away."[14]

Nature exacted its revenge upon those who destroyed its bounty amidst so much want. The mid-1930s witnessed some of the worst drought conditions in American history. By 1934, the AAA, and bad weather, had reduced wheat to its lowest output in nearly a half century. A Stanford economist observed in 1935 that "two years of very short crops have so reduced our available supplies of wheat that the United States will be a net importer in 1934–35 for probably the first time in our history."[15] John T. Flynn, a *New Republic* writer disillusioned with liberalism as a result of the New Deal, disgustedly noted "men burning oats when we were importing oats from abroad on a huge scale, killing pigs while increasing our imports of lard, cutting corn production and importing 30 million bushels of corn from abroad."[16]

A farmer-editor plaintively asked, "Could men from madhouses propose anything more fantastic or absurd?"[17]

PROGRESSIVES HAD CRUSADED against monopolies, combinations, and trusts. New Dealers created them. "While the progressive grieved over the fate of the prostitute," William Leuchtenburg quipped, "the New Dealer would have placed Mrs. Warren's profession under a code authority."[18] Such industrial codes came under the purview of the National Recovery Administration (NRA), the plaything of General Hugh Johnson, who had overseen conscription during World War I and who so shot to fame during the New Deal that *Time* magazine designated him "Man of the Year" for 1933.

The NRA oversaw industry collusion. Under the NRA, businessmen themselves set prices, wages, production, distribution, and hours of operation, and otherwise regulated everything in their own industries to create conformity. It is not that individual businessmen governed themselves, as they always had, but that, collectively, businessmen governed individual businessmen. Instead of allowing consumers to pick winners and losers, business and government rigged the competition. Everybody save those who wrote the rules lost.

John T. Flynn described one of the NRA's victims: "A tailor named Jack Magid in New Jersey was arrested, convicted, fined and sent to jail. The crime was that he had pressed a suit of clothes for 35 cents when the Tailors' Code fixed the price at 40 cents. The price was fixed not by a legislature or Congress but by the tailors."[19] The rule of law had ceded to the rule of caprice. Pressing clothes for five cents less than the competition offends neither law nor ethics. But tailors, who had, by the encouragement of the government, fixed prices, believed such competition an affront. No elected legislature had made pressing someone's clothes for 35 cents a criminal offense—and presumably none ever would, given that the people who elect legislators prefer cheaper prices—but tailor Jack went to jail nevertheless. This is because the Congress, as it had unconstitutionally done with the ICC during the heydey of the populists and progressives, handed over the regulatory powers it possessed (and a few that it didn't) to Hugh Johnson's NRA.

General Johnson, along with the captains of industry, instituted more than five hundred codes. "Code 450 regulated the Dog Food Industry, Code 427 the Curled Hair Manufacturing Industry and Horse Hair Dressing Industry, and Code 262 the Shoulder Pad Manufacturing Industry," Leuchtenburg wrote. "In New York, I. 'Izzy' Herk, executive secretary of Code 348, brought order to the Burlesque Theatrical Industry by insisting that no production could feature more than four strips."[20] Naturally, the powerful combined to make the NRA codes advantageous to themselves.

The onerous codes overwhelmed many small businessmen. "For the last six months I have been behind the counter ten hours a day, then up half the night filling out government forms," a Michigan grocer testified. "Sunday is needed for inventory reports, ration accounts or applications for coffee, sugar and canned goods. I couldn't keep up with it, so I closed my doors."[21] Thousands of small businessmen did the same every week.[22] What the Great Depression didn't destroy, government busybodies did.

The NRA hurt employees as well as employers. The NRA's Cotton Textile Code, for instance, forbade plant expansion or adding plant machinery without the NRA's approval, and barred plants from working more than two shifts per forty-hour workweek. Layoffs ensued.[23] The costs from state intrusion that small businesses endured were often passed on to the customer, or to employees whose wages they could no longer afford. Many a businessman salvaged his life's work by consciously ignoring the codes. The NRA made honest men lawbreakers.

In the fireside chats of his first term, President Roosevelt issued a series of vague, subjective indictments of business practices that laid the groundwork for the state direction of private industry. The president declared war on "unfair competition," "unfair conditions," "long hours of employment," "un-American standards," "destructive price cutting," and "unfair practices by selfish minorities."[24] This rhetorical trick reversed the moral reality: Roosevelt's authoritarianism claimed the banner of fairness as it portrayed the democracy of the *free* market—a market where millions of consumers and providers, and not a government board, determined the fairness of cost—as unfair. Force now became fair, reasonable, and American. Freedom became unfair, unreasonable, and un-American. Government knew best.

If consumers found a price for a commodity—for example, a house, a taxi fare, a man's labor—unreasonable, why should not consumers, rather than the state, decide to buy or pass? If the mass of consumers agreed, would not the provider have to lower the price—in Rooseveltspeak, make it reasonable, fair, and American—in order to sell?

Roosevelt threw out the basic laws of economics. The democracy of the marketplace no longer voted on price, working conditions, hours of operation, and so on. A government committee did. That the very "chiselers" and "economic royalists" whom Roosevelt so frequently denounced manned these committees seems never to have occurred to the president, or, if it did, it did not bother him too much.

A few men attained greater power through the NRA. One hundred fifty million men had less.

General Johnson, the man who, other than Roosevelt, gained the most power because of the NRA, created a colored sticker—the Blue Eagle—for compliant businessmen to affix to their shop windows. "In war, in the gloom of night attack, soldiers wear a bright badge on their shoulders to be sure that comrades do not fire on comrades," Roosevelt reasoned, again using a war analogy, in a fireside chat. "On that principle, those who cooperate in this program must know each other at a glance. That is why we have provided a badge of honor for this purpose, a simple design with a legend: 'We do our part.' And I ask that all those who join with me shall display that badge prominently."[25] If a soldier refrained from shooting when spotting another combatant with the bright badge, what did he do when spotting a combatant without the bright badge? Industry got the hint. Within weeks of the fireside chat, more than two million employers signed on to the program.[26]

Henry Ford, nearly alone among major industrialists, refused to display the badge. General Johnson guessed that "the American people will crack down on him."[27] They didn't. They liked durable, cheap cars. So did Johnson's colleagues in government. It created no shortage of embarrassment when Ford outbid competitors by a $169,000 margin to provide the Civilian Conservation Corps with five hundred trucks, an offer the CCC, despite Johnson's protestations, couldn't refuse.[28] If the federal government ignored the Blue Eagle when it could save the taxpayer a buck, or 169,000 of them, why would the taxpayer waste money by patronizing stores just because they displayed a sticker?

There was a name for what Hugh Johnson was doing with the NRA, but none dared utter it—at least initially. Only after General Johnson presented Secretary of Labor Frances Perkins with Raffaello Viglione's *The Corporate State*, engineered a massive, record-breaking, military-style NRA parade down New York's Fifth Avenue, and referred to the "shining name" of Benito Mussolini in his NRA departure speech did his critics

notice the obvious similarities between New Deal America and developments in certain European states. "With Fascism, National Socialism, and
the New Deal," German historian Wolfgang Schivelbusch comments, "we
can draw a direct line from the state solutions put forward in the 1930s to
reforms first suggested in the period 1890–1910. Conceived, planned,
and in some cases implemented by a reformist minority, those ideas fell
victim to World War I."[29] But the ideas returned after the global conflict,
intertwined as they were with the experience of militarism during the war.
A fascist was a progressive mugged by World War I.

IF ROOSEVELT APPEARS to history to have gone too far, he did not go far
enough for many loud contemporaries. From the president's left flank
came initially his greatest supporters but ultimately his greatest enemies.

The Great Depression bred great delusions. Empty stomachs opened
minds to the demagogue's promises and the schemer's designs. People
laughed off the stage in the prosperous twenties enjoyed the floor in the
desperate thirties. Not since the days of Ignatius Donnelly had so many
cranks had the nation's ear.

Huey Long, the colorful "Kingfish" whose "Every Man a King" outlined
his program in song, advanced a redistributionist scheme entitled Share
Our Wealth. Simultaneously Louisiana's governor, junior senator, and virtual dictator, the salesman-turned-politician Long paved roads, erected
bridges, and supplied textbooks, receiving absolute power in return.

Dr. Francis Townsend, deviser of "the most Christ-like plan that has
been conceived since the Crucifixion," promised to jump-start the economy and to grant seniors economic security by allocating $200 to retirees
every month on the condition that they spend it before receipt of the next
check.[30]

Reflecting European fashions of central planning, novelist Upton
Sinclair campaigned for governor of California in 1934 on a "two-year
plan" called End Poverty in California (EPIC). EPIC promised that the
Golden State would launch agricultural colonies, pass an enabling act to
acquire factories, drive out private banks, replace money with scrip, and
establish a 30 percent income tax (atop the 77 percent federal income tax).
"Let us construct a complete industrial system," 1933-Socialist-turned-
1934-Democrat Sinclair dreamt, "a new and self-maintaining world for
our unemployed, in which they will live, having as few dealings as possible
with our present world of speculators and exploiters."[31] Californians
passed.

The us-versus-them populism of radio priest Charles Coughlin, whose
Golden Hour of the Little Flower broadcasts reached millions of listeners

every Sunday, lambasted "the rich" during the New Deal before inserting "the Jews" as the variable in his boilerplate prior to World War II. Through his National Union for Social Justice, Father Coughlin demanded "a just, living, annual wage," the nationalization of key resources, and a "limit" on the "profits acquired by any industry."[32]

Howard Scott's Technocracy, a collection of engineers and experts briefly affiliated with Columbia University, promised to eliminate money, debt, profits, advertisements, and salesmanship. In their head-spinning charts and complex statistical tabulations, the Technate winnowed work into four hours a day, for less than half the year's days, and for just twenty years per life.[33]

It was an era of catchy slogans. Whereas Roosevelt had his New Deal, Sinclair boosted EPIC and Long sold Share Our Wealth. The proponents generally mastered the emerging radio medium, a tool of manipulation unknown to past demagogues. They saw themselves as saviors and naturally saw obstacles as devils. Roosevelt reciprocated. The mutual enmity stemmed from ego and not ideology. The left flank imagined itself kingmaker, bristling when the king acted as though he disagreed. The imperious president, in turn, scoffed at the notion that anyone save him had made him king. Roosevelt and his critics were too much alike to tolerate one another.

Tax audits, subpoenas, jail sentences, and other forms of state harassment pounced upon the president's critics. Father Coughlin endured a Ku Klux Klan cross burning and a bomb attack before the Roosevelt administration revoked his publication's mailing privileges, charged him with sedition, and pressured the Catholic Church into silencing him.[34] Roosevelt lackeys in Congress hounded Francis Townsend. They cited him with contempt, resulting in a jail sentence from which the old doctor's persecutor/protector eventually spared him. Before an assassin's bullet felled Huey Long, Roosevelt sicced the IRS upon him in an effort to more gently topple his rival. Alas, Roosevelt's self-important, quick-to-take-offense rivals might have done worse had they obtained the power they so craved.

Roosevelt stopped his critics but not their criticisms. What was the brains trust but a poor man's Technate, Social Security but a modified Townsend Plan, a fireside chat but a kinder, gentler *Golden Hour of the Little Flower*? The cranks always win.

A BOUNTY OF confusing acronyms descended on America's cities, towns, and countryside in the 1930s. FERACWACCCPWAWPA doled out money for projects great and small; money for nothing and money for big things;

money for votes and money for coats, coal, food, and whatever other necessities were lacking. Though one worker summed up his affinity for the president thusly, "Mr. Roosevelt is the only man we ever had in the White House who would understand that my boss is a sonofabitch," Mr. Roosevelt was, to an increasing number of Americans, boss.[35]

The Civilian Conservation Corps (CCC), a quasi-military program that mirrored endeavors then in vogue in Europe, sent young men to the wilderness to fight fires, plant trees, curtail erosion, and generally do battle with Mother Nature's foes. It boasted more than half a million enlistees in 2,600-plus camps in September 1935. In its ten-year history, more than three million seventeen- to-twenty-three-year-old men and their war-veteran overseers participated in the CCC.[36] The Public Works Administration (PWA) doled out $6 billion in its six-year history, which directly resulted in nearly two billion hours of work in localities around the country.[37] Along with Hitler's autobahn and Mussolini's drainage of the Pontine swamps, FDR's public works projects—including the Tennessee Valley Authority and the Grand Coulee Dam—reflected a worldwide trend of massive government projects within the industrialized nations. The Works Progress Administration (WPA) employed eight million, mostly blue-collar Americans between 1933 and 1943.[38] In January 1934, at the height of its prowess, Harry Hopkins's short-lived Civil Works Administration (CWA) boasted 4,263,644 Americans (out of a population of 130 million) on its payroll.[39]

Hopkins, who headed a number of relief agencies in addition to the CWA during Roosevelt's first term, vowed that the New Deal would "spend, spend, spend and elect, elect, elect."[40] Though Roosevelt didn't match his protégé's enthusiasm for spending—shutting down, for instance, Hopkins's budget-busting CWA before it could really take flight— the president shared his Machiavellian associate's appetite for politicizing relief. Roosevelt turned payday dollars into election-day votes.

The Democratic governor of New Mexico obtained the lists of the political affiliations of the workers on federal relief in his state.[41] After Congressman Martin Dies investigated several left-wing Democrats for their possible ties to Communism, FDR lieutenant Harold Ickes abruptly terminated two PWA projects in Dies's home district. Was this abuse of federal funds to punish political enemies? FDR nonchalantly responded, "Ho-hum."[42] Economists have discovered, perhaps not surprisingly, that a state's support for Roosevelt, and the proximity to an election, in large part determined where and when federal relief got spent.[43] In effect, Roosevelt bribed voters. From Roosevelt's *quid*, a job, came the worker's *quo*, a vote.

"In Cook County, Illinois . . . 450 men were employed in one election district and dismissed the day after the election," John T. Flynn reported. "Seventy reported to do high-way work and were told to go to their voting precincts and canvass for votes for the Horner-Courtney-Lucas ticket. These 450 men cost $23,268. All of them had their work-cards initialed by the campaign manager in Northern Illinois for the Horner-Courtney-Lucas ticket."[44] In Pennsylvania, party lackeys running a local WPA project transferred eighteen Republicans to a job far from home when they refused to abandon the GOP.[45] "In Louisiana, Hopkins, under intense pressure from local opponents of Huey Long, allowed a vigorous foe of Long to turn the previously impartial relief administration into an anti-Long agency. Long's opponent was allowed to stay on as head of the WPA despite a report which characterised his record as 'inefficiency from every angle from which a job could be viewed.' "[46]

President Roosevelt abused his office not just to maintain it but to advance family bank accounts.

Whereas the Progressive Theodore Roosevelt ordered valuable postage-stamp proofs withheld from unscrupulous government employees seeking profit, the New Dealer Franklin Roosevelt ordered the valuable stamp proofs to be delivered to him. He then delivered them into his own private collection. Upon Roosevelt's death, the die proofs sold for $59,000.[47]

In tackiness matched neither before nor after, the First Lady exploited her position for advertising dollars: $5,500 from a candy manufacturer, $1,000 a week from foreign coffee growers, $1,000 to $4,000 for radio spots hawking mattresses and toiletries.[48] A magazine publisher, allegedly hoping for a prestigious position in the administration, gave jobs to Eleanor as editor and daughter Anna as a well-paid assistant for his ill-fated periodical *Babies—Just Babies*.[49] "She accepted the most expensive gifts from private concerns and from foreign governments seeking favors—a $10,000 mink coat from Canadian fur breeders, a gold bracelet from Emperor Haile Selassie, a gold crown from the Sultan of Morocco, and gifts from various American trade organizations," John T. Flynn reported.[50]

The New Deal glanced back at the progressive movement as an ancestor. It did not look back and see its identical twin. Whereas progressives embarked on a national crusade to exterminate machine-politics corruption, New Dealers instituted machine-politics corruption on a national scale. Boss Roosevelt dealt out the patronage, and the beneficiaries—from big-city mayors down to skin-and-bones job seekers—returned the favor during election season (or else). Roosevelt transformed America into Tammany Hall.

. . .

THE NEW DEAL didn't end the Great Depression. It prolonged it. Franklin Roosevelt gave people hope, provided national catharsis by railing against the haves on behalf of the have-nots, and created the illusion of recovery through myriad alphabet-soup agencies, frantic activity, and periodic fireside chats. He did all this, but he did not ameliorate harsh economic conditions.

The New Deal tried to spend its way to prosperity. Prosperity didn't come. Big government did. The $4.6 billion federal budget Roosevelt inherited for his first year in office had tripled by Pearl Harbor. With the onset of war, and the necessary costs to wage it, the federal government became twenty times its 1933 size by 1945. The war ended. Big government stayed. The immediate postwar budgets naturally shrank with the costs of war gone, but there was no going back. History's most dramatic increase in the size of the federal government had taken place. Unlike other crises that resulted in a larger government, the Great Depression and World War II resulted in a permanent superbureaucracy ready to solve problems at home and abroad. The problems were temporary; the "solutions," permanent.

To pay for myriad projects, the New Deal taxed and borrowed. It imposed an enormous financial burden on the wealthy by levying the highest taxes in American history, which only further hampered the economy by punishing success. The New Deal bequeathed an enormous financial burden to the succeeding generation in the form of an unprecedented debt.

During Roosevelt's twelve-year presidency, the federal government borrowed more money than it had previously in the entirety of its 146-year history. The deficit never before and never after constituted as massive a share of the overall economy. America went from surpluses and prosperity during the Harding-Coolidge years to deficits and depression during the Roosevelt years.[51]

Future taxpayers had to pay off the debts of the New Deal. Current taxpayers had to pay the onerous levies imposed on them. The New Deal IRS took 88 cents out of every dollar earned by the top earners.[52] Why work when the government gets the reward? The entrepreneurial spirit withered. This shortsighted tax policy took more money from rich people, but it ensured that rich people would have less money to tax. In other words, the federal government took a larger piece from a pie that it had made smaller.

The confiscatory taxation and profligate borrowing did not, as hoped, kick-start the economy. A high-powered economy didn't return until World War II. By 1938, one-fifth of the labor force was out of work—an unemployment rate barely lower than the one Roosevelt had inherited upon becoming president. High unemployment characterized Roosevelt's presidency until Pearl Harbor sent everyone back to work.[53] The stock market took even longer to rebound. The Dow Jones Industrial Average didn't equal its 1929 average until the 1950s.[54] After bottoming out in 1933, the gross domestic product grew, but it did not surpass its 1929 high point until Roosevelt's third term.[55] Americans living under the New Deal experienced something novel in American history: a quality-of-life depreciation from one generation to the next. The New Deal, which extended the Great Depression through its counterproductive policies, bears much of the blame for this.

In every other industrialized nation, recovery came sooner. In every other American recession, the pain lasted for a shorter period. What made the Great Depression longer and deeper than other concurrent and historic depressions? Franklin Roosevelt's extravagant policies did.

LITTLE OF THE New Deal's alphabet soup remains. But the general spirit endures.

Not just the Left, but garden-variety Democrats and not a few Republicans, henceforth viewed the government's power as unlimited and the people's rights as mere privileges. The federal government, though it has not become all-powerful, is thought in large and diverse segments of the population to be all-powerful—that it is responsible for natural catastrophes, that it can affect climate change, that it can transform primitives halfway around the world into republican pluralists, et cetera. The New Deal failed to end the Great Depression, but it convinced many Americans that it did. The New Deal posited that the state was responsible for employing the unemployed, ensuring adequate pensions, and forcing business to operate "fairly." Belief in the curative power of government became a modern faith. For every problem, acolytes of the New Deal creed look for a government solution.

A managerial elite, the likes of which surrounded Wisconsin governor Philip La Follette in the 1930s, arose to solve the nation's problems. The managers—lifetime bureaucrats, academics, efficiency-obsessed businessmen, generals—managed to cultivate a liberal consensus that accepted their wisdom for nearly fifty years. For every problem, the managers offered a state solution. After the initial warfare between government and business during the New Deal, a rapprochement between the state and industry ensued. But the distance of the managers from the farm, from the slum, from the factory, and from the jungle battlefield made their solutions inoperable. Centralization supplanted federalism.

Whether the solution worked mattered less than that the politician tried. The effects of policies seemed to matter less than the intent of policies. The cult of action dictated that the government must be seen doing something, not necessarily the right thing, which is usually nothing. This cult of action altered the way the public judged its politicians. The number of bills passed, not the wisdom of the passed bills or the number of bad bills stopped, became the benchmark upon which to judge the politician.

The federal government naturally increased its responsibilities. Correspondingly, the responsibilities of the individual, of the family, of the church, of the states decreased. The American people became less self-reliant, less responsible because their government absolved them of the duty to undertake some of the basic functions of life—to plan for old age, to get a job, to provide for medical care. After the New Deal, the state promised, tacitly or overtly, to provide for the elderly and ensure employment. This was the new understanding in American politics. As evidenced by Roosevelt's subsequent reelections and the "me-too" style of his opponents, this arrangement suited the American people. But it didn't always suit the Constitution.

The Constitution, when it impeded the schemes of planners, became a "living document," a euphemism that allowed such planners to kill the document off and rationalize ignoring its letter. What the New Deal accelerated, in fact, was the ongoing revolution within the form of the old regime. Overthrowing the Constitution through process or violence was the goal of dreamers, not doers. But retaining the Constitution as an impotent but symbolic showpiece, in the way Great Britain retains its royalty, seemed more practical to ideologues annoyed by the limitations the ancient parchment placed on their enterprises. When the Constitution meshed with their designs, they could appeal to its wisdom. When it conflicted, they could disregard it and dismiss critics as atavists.

Just as the new order centralized power in Washington, the power in Washington centralized more on the president and less on Congress. The dramatic increase and enlarged scope of executive orders, and the subsequent disregard of congressional war powers, greatly increased presidential power. When Roosevelt or Truman was president, liberals cheered these developments. When Nixon or Reagan was president, they jeered them. Handing over power to the government was a dangerous game because governments changed hands periodically. When one government handed over power to the next, the incoming government did not hand back the power to the people who gave it to them. The incoming government added to its inherited power.

Americans accepted the new arrangement of executive fiats and government outside the Constitution because its benefits, though small, were tangible, whereas the benefits of the previous arrangement, though important, were abstract. Big-government programs, in effect, bribed voters. The spoils system, now practiced on a national scale undreamt of by Roosevelt's predecessors, gained the allegiance of big-city mayors and their political machines. The party that promoted big government now had the advantage of using big government for political purposes, to reward friends and punish enemies.

Some footprints didn't last. Several impressions lasted only as marks on the trail to be avoided. Government still *regulates*, but it no longer musters the hubris to *manage* farms and factories the way it tried to do during the New Deal. It no longer styles itself as the employer of last resort (and, not coincidentally, fewer are unemployed). The highest income-tax rates are less than half of what they were during the New Deal. Legal restrictions on gold investment were lifted in the 1970s. Americans turned some of the New Deal's cards back to the dealer.

THE NEW DEAL'S spirit of power and action, top-down reform by liberal technocrats, centralization, and constitutional disposability was years in the making. The populist and progressive eras were the first two acts of the drama; after an intermission in the 1920s, the action resumed with the New Deal. A fourth and final act, the Great Society, would come after another intermission.

In each case, wars—extensions of the domestic crusades—crippled the domestic crusades. So, too, did the very radicals who had agitated for such programs the loudest and longest. For the "Sockless Jerry" Simpsons, Eugene Debses, and Huey Longs, nothing would satiate. Elected officials, benefiting from radical constituencies, appeased their consciences or governed. Doing the former usually undid the latter. Doing the latter usually undid the former. Men of the Left, then, walked a precarious tightrope in politics.

Franklin Roosevelt engineered a massive shift in power away from the people and to the state. What the populists had started and the progressives had championed, New Dealers reinvigorated—and passed on to their heirs seeking to establish a "Great Society" thirty years later. Each link developed and therefore differed from the previous one. All were part of the same chain.

~ 16 ~

ARTISTS IN UNIFORM

For there shall be a time when they will not endure sound doctrine but, according to their own desires, they will heap to themselves teachers, having itching ears: And will indeed turn away their hearing from the truth, but will be turned unto fables.

—2 TIMOTHY 4:3–4

"THE RUSSIAN BOLSHEVIKS will leave the world a better place than Jesus left it," proclaimed writer Mike Gold.[1] It is this vision of Communism as a force of salvation that helps explain Gold's histrionic and embittered reaction to onetime idol Max Eastman, the former *Masses* editor who denounced Stalinist Communism and the "artists in uniform" peddling its ever-changing lines.[2] "But Max Eastman, former friend, you have sunk beneath all tolerance! You are a filthy and deliberate liar! When you charge the Gorkeys and Faydeyeffs of the Soviet Union with being cheap American pen-prostitutes, you have aligned yourself with the white guards who say the same thing. Nay, you are worse, since you yourself were once the Bolshevik leader of a generation of young intellectuals. The world has always loathed the Judases more than it did the Pontius Pilates."[3]

To the third-rate intellect and first-rate fanatic Mike Gold, Max Eastman may have seemed the Judas. But Eastman belonged to the free-spirited Left of Greenwich Village, not the conformist Left of East Thirteenth Street. He had rejected a movement he had had an affair with, not married. It was Gold, scorning his youthful flirtation with the free-wheeling Greenwich Village Left to wed the rigid Left emanating from the Communist Party USA's headquarters, who disowned onetime comrades.

Eastman remarked of the Communists, "Before these young men ever become revolutionists they will have to learn to be rebels."[4] American

Communists were anything but rebels. They did what they were told by men thousands of miles away.

Stalinists the world over traveled to Kharkov, Ukraine, in 1930 to attend a conference on Communist arts and letters. "They came to Russia like Mohammedans to Mecca," Eastman wrote, "and they knelt fervently and received in awe the blessing of a complete communication of the sacred dogma from its ordained imams and officials."[5] Specifically, the imams told the congregants that art is a class weapon, that artists must abandon individualism, adopt strict discipline, and study the experience of Soviet Russia to create proletarian art, and that a centralized body should direct proletarian artists.[6] Mike Gold, who led the American delegation, took the marching orders to heart, as any dutiful artist in uniform would.

The Americans, one of twenty-two national delegations present, contributed to the session by suggesting that groups of writers dress in blue blouses and call themselves "agitprop troops."[7] There is no evidence that any writers took the delegation up on its suggestion of donning uniforms, but there was no confusion about what team so many American poets, playwrights, artists, and actors played for in the 1930s.

DURING THE GREAT Depression, intellectuals abandoned what made them intellectuals and became automatons. The 1930s was the decade when smart people acted stupid. Devotion to collectivist economics demanded collectivist thought. They meekly handed over their brains to a foreign power and received instructions on what to think. Previous American Lefts, to be sure, had looked abroad—to Owen, to Fourier, to Marx. But they had generally retained a distinctly American flavor, or at least contained factions that spoke from the American experience. American Communists between the world wars so closely imitated, and allowed themselves to be micromanaged by, a foreign power that it is almost a misnomer to tag them as "American" Communists. More accurately, they were a subsidiary of a Moscow-based party operating within the United States. Though the party, on instructions from abroad, occasionally portrayed itself as the inheritor of the American tradition, it always remained at its core hostile to the nation it operated within.

The Great Depression was the era of the ad hoc committee and the front group. Aping the alphabet soup of New Deal agencies was an alphabet soup of citizens' groups seeking to cure this, fix that. Therein Rooseveltian liberals mixed innocuously with Stalinist Communists. One Communist master described these as "innocents clubs." Comintern official Willi Münzenberg exhorted: "We must penetrate every conceivable milieu, get hold of artists and professors, make use of cinemas and theatres, and spread abroad the doctrine that Russia is prepared to sacrifice everything to keep the world at peace. We must join these clubs ourselves."[8] The multitude of "innocents clubs," which American Communists started and not just infiltrated, included the New Theatre League, the Hollywood Anti-Nazi League, the New Dance League, and the League of American Writers. This last group managed to sign up Franklin Roosevelt as a member, demonstrating just how deep into the mainstream Soviet fronts penetrated.[9]

The infiltration of "innocents clubs," and in many instances the creation of them, coincided with the Popular Front period of American Communism, when the Communist Party of the USA (CPUSA) sought to integrate within the greater liberal and progressive community. It followed the "Third Period," when Stalin had thought that capitalism was on the brink of collapse. Because Communism's defeat of capitalism seemed imminent, Stalin had instructed satellite parties to attack, rather than cooperate with, the non-Communist Left—just as the Bolshevik revolutionaries had done in Russia once their fellow leftists proved expendable. When Stalin recognized that Communism's imminent world conquest was more illusion than reality, the Soviet dictator changed course, and his acolytes in America did, too. They reached out to liberals.

For its part, the non-Communist Left preferred cooperation to attacks. If saying a few kind words about the Soviet Union was all that was required to stay in the good graces of people previously quick to denounce them as fascists, why not give in? Many liberals also imagined Communists as more devoted and romantic versions of themselves. This idealization allowed liberals to overlook the failings and fanaticism of their ideological cousins.

The milieu created a special type of liberal: to his anti-Communist enemies, the "fellow traveler"; to his Communist friends, the "honest liberal." This was the left-winger who, although never actually becoming a member of the party, rarely failed to parrot its lines. Some fellow travelers were refused entry to the party. Party officials informed them they could better serve its aims from the outside. Others never considered themselves Communists, though they just could not envision Communism doing wrong.

Through the fellow traveler, the Communist Party's influence increased exponentially. The party reached its apex as 1939 began, when it had about ninety thousand members.[10] There were many times that number of fellow travelers who did the party's bidding from the outside. Though a small total by the standards of conventional parties, party members and fellow travelers together influenced the surrounding culture far beyond that which their actual numbers suggested. The unity of purpose and high percentage of intellectuals—artists, writers, scientists, academics, and so on—subscribing to Communism made this so. "Although communism *never* won a mass following in the United States," scholar Daniel Bell wrote, "it did have for many years a disproportionate influence in the cultural field. At one time, from 1936 to 1939, through the fellow travelers in the publishing houses, radio, Hollywood, the magazines, and other mass media, it exercised influence on public opinion far beyond the mere number of party members."[11]

Why would a party attract an intellectual? In other words, why would an outfit that tells you what to think attract someone who, above all else, thinks?

One explanation is that it's easier to allow others to use your mind than to use it yourself. Aside from laziness, there is safety in crowds. Rather than endure the barrage of insults directed by the party, why not receive protection from such abuse by submitting to the party? If you can't beat 'em, join 'em. To garner praise, one's painting, poem, or play need only conform to a party line. Articulating an approved political position, after all, requires less skill and attention than attaining artistic excellence. The alienation and arrogance that go with being an intellectual necessarily lead to the delusion that one is so smart that one can plan, direct, and manage people's lives from afar more effectively than people can do themselves. For the world saver, a Communist Party is ideally suited. Above all else, the intellectual relishes the importance of his work under Communism. If the state likes his work, it pays him money; if it dislikes it, the state kills him. The intellectual prefers validation from attention to self-doubt from indifference.

For these and other reasons, intellectuals flocked to the Communist Party.

THE WORKER REMAINED the focal point for Communism. Communism never became the focal point for the worker. But artists, perhaps the group of people most distant from factory workers, flocked to Communism along with other intellectuals. They self-proletarianized, imagining themselves as workers, too. Whereas the factory worker might attack capitalism through a strike or an act of sabotage, the artist sought to provoke such acts with the pen or paintbrush.

What passed for Communist art? Art for, but not necessarily by, the proletariat; art that highlighted class conflict; art that undermined bourgeois standards; art that exposed the contradictions of capitalism; art that told of man's future greatness under Communism; art where collective expression substituted for self-expression; art that rejected classic forms in favor of newness; and, above all, art not for art's sake but art with correct political intent. Communists often instructed their brethren to think of art as a weapon. CPUSA bigwig William Z. Foster, for instance, told his underlings that "there must be a clear understanding that 'art is a weapon' in the class struggle. Not only is art a weapon, but a very potent one as well."[12]

Artists who clumsily wielded such weapons often ended up hurting themselves. The party's targets shifted so quickly that the artist's sword was as likely to strike a friend as it was a foe. One day criticism of Leon Trotsky, Franklin Roosevelt, and Adolf Hitler was off-limits; the next day it was obligatory. The artist in uniform who survived to fight another day not only never broke ranks but anticipated the next troop movement. The art they created injured others and protected themselves. But it rarely uplifted, entertained, invigorated, or inspired.

BY ACCIDENT OF geography, Communist writers faced humiliation and not firing squads in America. Party discipline nevertheless meant that art that didn't conform to the party line found an audience in some commissar's garbage can.

Party heavies meting out punishment and instilling discipline included Mike Gold, Bob Minor, Joseph Freeman, and V. J. Jerome. Facing threats of exile and of the party apparatus coming down against them, artists who had transgressed the party's arbitrary and forever shifting rules abased themselves before Gold and associates.

Howard Fast changed the third act of his play *30 Pieces of Silver* at the behest of a party hack who threatened him with expulsion if he didn't do as directed.[13]

After Communists engineered a suppression campaign against his book *Red Star over China* in 1938, a groveling Edgar Snow, though not a party member, excised extensive passages that had offended Communists in his otherwise pro-Communist work of non-fiction.[14] Snow's publisher, Bennett Cerf, the Random House founder who during World War II suggested withdrawing books critical of the Soviet Union, sought intercession from the CPUSA's general secretary.[15] The revised edition, Cerf wrote Earl Browder, could be used "as a pretext for revoking the Communist Party ban on this book." Though Cerf labeled the ban "a grievous injustice," he assured Browder: "We have maintained complete silence about the situation."[16] The party head dishonestly denied the existence of the ban. Nevertheless, Browder told Cerf that the party was "gratified to note

[Snow's] change of view."[17] The party thereafter promoted the bowdler-ized edition.[18]

The CPUSA compelled Joseph Freeman to tear up the galleys of one book and ordered him to suffocate another, *An American Testament*, that had already been published. Freeman, a first-degree lackey, acquiesced. He demanded that a book club revoke a large order, cancelled a lecture tour, and forbade mention of it in the periodical he edited.[19] Freeman the commissar became Freeman the commissared.

Moscow's Communist Academy denied Scott Nearing permission to publish a book on imperialism, which led to his 1929 resignation from the party. Hell hath no fury like ideologues scorned. Though Nearing amicably pledged his continued support in his letter of resignation, the Central Executive Committee noted with outrage the writer's failure to recognize the "subordination of the individual to the line and to the activities of the Party and the revolutionary working class." The board maintained: "No member of the Communist Party can be a mere 'friend' of the revolution; he must be an active soldier in it."[20] Six years later, Nearing's former comrades spiked the foreign publication of *Free Born*, his pro-Communist book that had nevertheless made glowing references to certain Communists who had fallen out of favor with the party. Three years after that, in 1938, the CPUSA instructed its local contacts to blacklist Nearing: "[W]e must at once discontinue the practice of enabling him to appear before working class and other audiences."[21]

Artistic criticism thus became political criticism, in which critics went to dizzying lengths to analyze works based on Communist principles and then criticize or praise accordingly. Critiquing a Stephen Spender poem in which the subjects "[w]atch the admiring dawn explode like a shell / Around us, dazing us with its light like snow," Edwin Berry Bergum, reading like a caricature of Marxist narrow-mindedness, wrote in the *New Masses*: "The passive position of watching the dawn is hardly fitting to the revolutionary; nor should the dawn daze like snow those who under self-discipline have known what to expect and are ready for the next move."[22] In a *New Masses* remembrance of the dancer Isadora Duncan, Mike Gold depicted her artistic movements as a visual representation of the Communist new man: "Her dancing was an attempt to create images of what this future would mean for humanity; a time when each human body would take on the splendor and freedom of the Greek gods."[23]

Each Communist sought to out-Communist the next. They engaged in self-censorship before enduring the embarrassment of party censorship. The heavy hand of party commissars bred paranoia, which bred bad art with correct politics.

· · ·

"IN THE PAST eight months the *New Masses* has been slowly finding its path toward the goal of a proletarian literature in America," Gold, a minor figure within the old *Masses* but now the editor of the *New Masses*, announced in 1929. "A Jack London or a Walt Whitman will come out of this crop of young workers who write in the *New Masses*."[24]

Nothing of the sort occurred. In fact, of the myriad writers drawn inside the Communist Party, Gold alone penned a best-selling novel in the 1930s. It is perhaps no coincidence that the bully and not the bullied achieved this success. For it is Gold, along with fellow commissars V. J. Jerome, Joseph Freeman, and Bob Minor, who spiked the work of nonconforming Communists and conducted smear campaigns against non-Communists daring to put the politically incorrect to paper. It is also significant that Gold's best seller, *Jews Without Money*, was less the product of its author's imagination than of his memory. It was a memoir in the form of a novel. The party's stifling intolerance had killed the creativity of fairly creative people.

The reader of *Jews Without Money* navigates the gauntlet of 50-cent whores, clenches at the stench of the "sirocco blast of a thousand onions" coming from a Hebrew school teacher's beard, and feels sick with claustrophobia from the encroaching tenements.[25] Gold had a knack for making an image stick. But the crush of propaganda smothers the novel's strong points. The narrator relates that no Jewish gangsters existed in Europe; "it is America that has taught the sons of tubercular Jewish tailors how to kill."[26] He explains that America has grown fat "because it has eaten the tragedy of millions of immigrants."[27] His dejected immigrant father proclaims that coming to America "was the greatest mistake in my life," that "[o]ne has to be selfish in America," and that America "is a land where the lice make fortunes, and the good men starve!"[28] We get it. But just to make sure, Gold, like all bad propagandists, pours it on.

Born Irwin Granich, Gold grew up in a cramped Manhattan apartment above a saloon a half block from the Bowery. At five he sang to the roaches in the apartment. At twelve, due to the debilitating lead poisoning and falls from scaffolding that injured his house-painter father, he peddled newspapers to support his family. He dabbled in amateur boxing as a teenager. His tenement boasted "slimy trails of garbage in the halls" and "[d]og crap and cat piss every where."[29]

Granich/Gold wandered into the Left at a 1914 rally in Union Square and never wandered out. Elizabeth Gurley Flynn, Alexander Berkman, and Emma Goldman addressed the throngs.[30] So course-altering was the real-life soapboxing that it inspired the dénouement of *Jews Without Money*.

After attending the rally, Mike Gold's "Mike" testifies: "O workers' Revolution, you brought hope to me, a lonely, suicidal boy. You are the true Messiah. You will destroy the East Side when you come, and build there a garden for the human spirit."[31]

"I bought with my only dime my first copy of the *Masses*," Gold remembered of the anarchist rally. "This monthly magazine opened for me a new world."[32] Within months of first reading the *Masses*, he became a contributor. He stood in awe of the playboy scribes John Reed, Floyd Dell, and Max Eastman, who dominated the Greenwich Village literary scene. "John Reed was the legendary writer-hero I worshipped," Gold recalled as an old man, "as did most of my generation in the radical movement."[33] He briefly joined the Socialist Party. "It was the most boring organization of grey-headed bores that I had ever known."[34] He found more excitement on IWW strike lines. The Great War offered excitement of the type Gold did not want. So when conscription came, he escaped to Mexico.[35]

Irwin Granich returned to America as Mike Gold. In the summer of 1920, Gold joined a commune in rural New Jersey. Though he found communes useful as "little laboratories" for the real thing and as reminders of "what the original Communism is," he noted that the commune was a place "where the adults have fled from the class struggle."[36] After sampling anarchism, socialism, bohemianism, Wobblyism, and small-"c" communism, Gold settled on the Communism of Marx and Lenin. He got in on the ground floor of the American branch of Moscow Communism as it launched in the wake of the Bolshevik Revolution.

The party had many roles to fill. Workers stirred militancy inside unions. Government employees, eventually at least, purloined information and influenced policy. Writers channeled their creativity into glorifying Marxism-Leninism. Mike Gold found his niche. "It is necessary to form a workers' culture to offset the poisons of the capitalist culture," Gold wrote in 1931. "The masses are hypnotized; our duty is to wake them."[37] From 1914 until his death in 1967, Mike Gold dedicated his life to these ends.

The hard-knocks background that handicapped him early in life helped Gold once he enlisted as an artist in uniform. The dearth of Communist working-class writers made it next to impossible to utter a word of criticism against the working-class writers in the ranks. No matter how poor the quality of Gold's poetry or prose, his decidedly non-proletarian colleagues in the proletarian writers' movement reflexively lavished praise upon it. Gold had none of the dash, flair, attractiveness, or charisma of his heroes John Reed and Max Eastman. He didn't have even a fraction of their wealth, either, but Gold possessed something that his heroes did not: authenticity. Hailing from a Jewish ghetto on the East Side of Manhattan, Gold lived the proletarian life vaunted in Marxism. Mike Gold was Jimmy Higgins with a pen. It wasn't erudite prose or flowing poetry that his admirers praised, but his proletarian credibility and fidelity to the party line.

Gold, mouth dripping with tobacco juice, clothes stained with grease and dirt, faithfully played his role. Fidelity to the correct line plus the blue-collar background equaled the storybook Communist. His existence, as the worker-intellectual, just about validated the faith that so many had placed in Marxism-Leninism. One young admirer found the conclusion of *Jews Without Money* "the highest point ever reached in literature," while another judged his writing style superior to Shakespeare's.[38] Mike Gold embodied that mythical worker-writer Hawthorne had briefly deluded himself into playing at Brook Farm.[39]

"The Three Whose Hatred Killed Them," one of Gold's earliest poems, written in 1914 under his given name, Irwin Granich, eulogized the three radicals who, in an ill-fated attempt to murder John D. Rockefeller Jr. and countless other Fourth of July party-goers, instead murdered themselves in a Harlem tenement house explosion. "They hated, but it was the enemy of man they hated," a twenty-year-old Gold explained. "They lusted for man's blood, but it was the blood of those who shed man's blood they lusted for."[40] In 1926's "The Strike," Gold wrote of "chimneys empty of the rushing smoke of super profits" and noted that "without socialism man is irrelevant in the universe."[41] In "Tom Mooney Walks at Midnight," a 1934 poem honoring another leftist bomber, Gold spoke of the "Marxist key that unlocks all jails." "It is better to be in jail for the working class / Than in the White House for the capitalists," he versed.[42] This, then, was the meaning of proletarian literature: writings that served the cause of Communism. By that criterion, and not any other, Gold and his associates judged literature. Aesthetic quality suffered as politics trumped artistic considerations.

Mike Gold's status as a proletarian writer gave him the authority to act as the Communist Party's artistic policeman. The discipline he imposed on his own works he imposed on the work of others. Those transgressing the artistic boundaries set by the party had to deal with the grimy, hardnosed former boxer from the ghetto. Gold treated the party as a monk treats his religion, and treated those who mistreated his religion as an inquisitor treats a heretic.

Gold, who longed to be a playwright, attacked successful playwright John Howard Lawson as "a Bourgeois Hamlet of our time." Embittered by the failure of the New Playwrights, Gold's two-and-a-half-year attempt at revolutionary theater in the 1920s, and by Lawson's doubts regarding the prospects of such an endeavor, Gold knocked fellow party member Lawson for not breaking out of his upper-class consciousness. Lawson confessed his sins before a gathering of Communist writers and meekly asked for forgiveness. For penance, he briefly gave up writing for activism.43

Himself doing penance for a past affinity for Gilbert and Sullivan, Gold denounced the lighthearted duo as "the 'cultural' pioneers of fascism."44 In 1942, he gave speeches on the "Quislings of Literature"—as if anybody, save one who demanded that writers follow a certain political path, could commit treason against that craft.45

Gold, and other party functionaries, traveled from New York to Los Angeles to confront Albert Maltz, who had the temerity to criticize the notion of "art as a weapon" as "not a useful guide, but a straitjacket" in the *New Masses*. "Writers must be judged by their work, and *not* by the committees they join," Maltz contended.46 With muzzle off, the pit bull Gold tore into Maltz in what was by now a repetitious, and so typically Marxist, line of attack. Gold charged that Maltz had allowed the "swimming pools," glitz, and money of Hollywood to corrupt his political attitudes. Maltz later characterized the attack as "gutter argumentation" because it had no relevance to the debate between "art for art's sake" and "art as a weapon." But at the time, Maltz dared utter no response in kind. When Gold, V. J. Jerome, and Howard Fast—characterized by one Communist observer as an "intellectual goon squad"—confronted Maltz at actor Morris Carnovsky's Los Angeles home, he recanted the heterodox ideas advanced in his article.47 Shortly thereafter, the House Committee on Un-American Activities, and prison, failed to break Albert Maltz. Mike Gold and his fellow inquisitors had encountered no problems doing so.

Occasionally, such heavy-handed tactics backfired. Gold attacked Ernest Hemingway for an unflattering portrayal of a French Communist leader in *For Whom the Bell Tolls*, a sympathetic account of Communists fighting the Spanish Civil War. The grizzled Hemingway retorted: "Tell Mike Gold that Ernest Hemingway says that he should go fuck himself."48 Hemingway had been a friend. But once a friend took political positions at odds with his Communist masters, Gold could no longer maintain the friendship. In addition to his falling-out with Hemingway, Gold allowed politics to end friendships with V. F. Calverton, Upton Sinclair, Max Eastman, and countless others.49 Mike Gold didn't have friends, only comrades.

Reflecting on "Why I Am a Communist," Mike Gold gushed: "I can never discharge this personal debt to the revolutionary movement—it gave me a mind."[50] It took one away, too. The collective mind always comes at the price of the individual mind.

JOHN HOWARD LAWSON became the Mike Gold of Hollywood.

Among the "innocents clubs" Communists launched in Hollywood was the Screen Writers' Guild, which elected future Hollywood Ten member Lawson—described by fellow Communist Paul Jarrico as "an infantile leftist, a sectarian sonofabitch"—its first president.[51] Rather than appreciate their privileged poolside position in Great Depression America, Lawson imagined his fellow studio writers as oppressed workers. The union allowed the party to firm up its beachhead in Hollywood, collect a windfall in dues from wealthy members, recruit celebrities for its causes, and, when studios didn't object or didn't notice, inject political messages into movies.

Save for the Screen Writers' Guild, the Hollywood Anti-Nazi League was perhaps the most successful front group established by Tinseltown Reds. On the surface, the group seemed a worthy cause. But the superficial celebrities who joined the group weren't the type of people who probed beneath the surface. Obliviously, they lent their names to an organization run by the Communist Party. Nearly five thousand people joined. Luminaries such as comedian Groucho Marx, lyricist Ira Gershwin, director John Ford, and actor Humphrey Bogart attached their names to the group's causes. Then, in 1939, Hitler and Stalin became allies. The Hollywood Anti-Nazi League became, after the Poles, the second casualty of the pact.

John Howard Lawson, who had felt Mike Gold's sting early in his career, developed a venomous sting of his own. Reminiscent of Gold's denunciation of the more talented Ernest Hemingway a decade before, Lawson went after Robert Rossen, the writer, director, and producer of 1949's Oscar-winning *All the King's Men*. Through a Huey Long demagogue character, *All the King's Men* shows how power corrupts. The party worried that instead of Huey Long, Americans would see Joseph Stalin and view the film as a cautionary tale against Communism. Lawson gathered a posse of Communists to gang up on Rossen, a fellow party member. Instead of submitting to the gauntlet of criticisms, Rossen shouted: "Stick the whole Party up your ass!"[52]

The Hollywood Communist clique was most successful in preventing the projection of anti-Communist themes, real and imagined, onto the silver screen. In a few instances they managed to transform ostensibly independent films into advertisements for the Soviet Union. Astoundingly,

Franklin Roosevelt's government played a key role in the most egregious instance of Soviet propaganda dominating a film.

Mission to Moscow fantastically depicts Leon Trotsky as collaborating with the Nazis, ascribes benevolent motives to the USSR for its invasion of Finland (for example, a desire to save the Finns from Hitler), portrays the infamous Moscow show trials as fair and judicious, and ignores the Nazi-Soviet alliance. Made in 1943, and based on the best-selling book by the former U.S. ambassador to the Soviet Union, Joseph Davies, *Mission to Moscow* made it to theaters in part because of Roosevelt's desire to see his allies portrayed positively in popular culture.[53] Had Stalin himself produced *Mission to Moscow*, it is doubtful he could have portrayed himself in a more flattering light than Jack Warner's production did.

Lenin thought film the most important medium for propagandizing Russia for Communism.[54] Many American comrades thought likewise for their country.

COMMUNISTS NATURALLY TARGETED other branches of mass media.

Journalism, a field that allowed the party to pursue sensitive information *and* shape public opinion, attracted both party members looking for employment and party spymasters looking for new agents.

Soviet agents infiltrated the offices of Walter Lippmann and Drew Pearson, two of America's most widely read columnists.[55] Pulitzer Prize–winning reporter Edmund Stevens, who described Stalinist Russia as democratic and defended the Nazi-Soviet Pact, secretly belonged to the CPUSA.[56] I. F. Stone, in his heyday perhaps America's most well-known left-wing journalist, appears in the decoded Venona spy intercepts expressing to a Soviet controller his openness to becoming an agent if only the pay were right.[57] The later frankness of a former KGB spymaster, along with Stone's subsequent outrageous journalistic assertions, suggests that they may have come to an agreement.[58] Writers and editors at *Time* magazine, *New York Times* reporter Charles Grutzner as well as the paper's education editor, and the New York Newspaper Guild's executive secretary were all secret Communists.[59] Michael Straight, the editor of *The New Republic*, the magazine his grandparents' money launched, confessed years later to his work as a Soviet agent.[60] Such journalists were often the first to mock the idea of a Communist conspiracy.

The Soviet Union's most infamous man within America's newspaper of record was Walter Duranty, who was also the Gray Lady's man in Moscow. Duranty's motives for lying were professional, not political. Journalists who reported the facts from the Soviet Union didn't report the facts from the Soviet Union for long. Stalin expelled them. The *New York Times* reporter played the game. Duranty's mendacious articles in the 1920s and 1930s, which included denials of the state-induced Ukrainian famine, won him special treatment from the regime, professional access denied other reporters, and a Pulitzer Prize.[61] It was bad enough that individual journalists deliberately lied to readers. It was much worse that journalists, collectively, reserved the highest places of honor within their profession for those liars.

THE SOVIET UNION advanced a state philosophy, dialectical materialism; a state art, social realism; and even a state science, Lysenkoism. Biologists who dissented from peasant "scientist" Trofim Lysenko's anti-genetics creed found themselves in the gulag. Despite the impediments to the scientific method posed by a totalitarian state, the Soviet Union won praise among scientists outside its borders.

Harvard astronomer Harlow Shapley characterized the Soviet action against Nikolai Vavilov, a prominent biologist who dared debunk Lysenkoism, as a demotion. Vavilov's demotion consisted of getting dragged off to a Russian concentration camp, where he died.[62] Berkeley's J. Robert Oppenheimer, father of the atomic bomb, donated generously to the Communist Party, which boasted Oppenheimer's wife, brother, and sister-in-law as members.[63] M. Stanton Evans, in his book *Blacklisted by History*, produces a document from once-secret FBI files showing that Communist Party leaders in California had identified Oppenheimer as a secret member of the party as early as December 1942.[64] KGB sources and some American writers charge that Oppenheimer gave the Communists atomic bomb secrets as well.[65] Princeton University's Albert Einstein, a refugee from Nazi Germany, regularly lent his name to Communist front groups, proving that even the brightest minds have cloudy days.[66]

The environment where these scientists plied their trade proved a fertile breeding ground for Communism. But the academic freedom of the university, and to a lesser extent grammar and high school classrooms, presented non-Communist liberals with dilemmas. Should the academic freedom that Communists sought to abolish be extended to them? Did academic freedom entail discarding school-board-approved curricula for the party-approved curricula? Should politics stop at the classroom door? The Communist Party demanded a loyalty above professional loyalty. *"Marxist-Leninist analysis must be injected into every class,"* exhorted the CPUSA's publication, the *Communist*, to party members in education.[67]

From Columbia, where Whittaker Chambers and Elizabeth Bentley were introduced to the party, to Cambridge, where Michael Straight entered into the Soviet apparatus, the campuses made for effective Communist recruiting stations.

The Communist abuses of the cinema, the classroom, and the media led directly to the Hollywood Ten hearings in 1947, the firing of Communist educators in the post-war years, and Senator Joseph McCarthy's assaults on the media in the 1950s. To understand anti-Communist reactions to Communists in the post-war years, it is important to understand Communist actions in the pre-war years. Like Daniel De Leon, the dogmatic socialist of an earlier era, his Communist inheritors in the years between the world wars "bored from within." They sought to covertly infiltrate mainstream institutions and reorient them toward their ends. It took rough methods to root out those employing such underhanded tactics.

THE PRIMARY TALENT required of an "artist in uniform" involved knowing the party line, articulating it in art, and then contorting oneself to adhere to it once it had changed.

First, during the so-called Third Period, the Communists condemned Franklin Roosevelt as the purveyor of a " 'NEW DEAL' OF HUNGER, FASCISM AND WAR!"[68] Then Moscow instructed the CPUSA to support him when he ran for reelection in 1936 and attack the Republican presidential slate.[69] This Popular Front period, when Communists aligned with mainstream liberals and enjoyed a degree of respectability, lasted until Stalin discovered the expedience in vilifying Roosevelt again as the 1930s ended.

The party reached its peak in popularity during the Popular Front period partly by wrapping itself in American imagery. Chairman Earl Browder flaunted his Pilgrim forebears and his Kansas upbringing. He penned the article "Communists the Heirs of the Revolution of '76" in the *Daily Worker*.[70] The Stars and Stripes and the sickle and hammer meshed in graphic representations of the CPUSA. The party adopted "Communism Is Twentieth Century Americanism" as its slogan. But all this, too, inevitably fell out of favor with Moscow. So, on orders from the East, the CPUSA reverted to its default, anti-American position.[71]

The intellectual gymnastics demanded by the party exhibited itself most infamously when Stalin and Hitler signed a nonaggression pact, which allowed the devilish duo to more easily commit aggressions against other nations. Until 1939, Communists fortified their membership rolls, and claimed a place at the table alongside decent left-of-center groups, in large part by styling themselves as the most committed anti-fascists. The Hitler-Stalin Pact changed all that, just as Hitler's betrayal of Stalin in 1941 changed it all again.

Former friends (Roosevelt, Churchill) became foes and former foes became friends (Hitler). Such an unexpected turn in the Soviet line led the *New Masses* to pan Lillian Hellman's anti-Nazi play *Watch on the Rhine* in 1940 but praise it in cinematic form two years later.[72] It resulted in the alteration of the play *Meet the People*, including the deletion of the song "Mr. Roosevelt, Won't You Please Run Again?" once Roosevelt and Churchill resumed their positions as Communism's most hated.[73] It forced the suicide of one of Tinseltown's most active political organizations, the Hollywood Anti-Nazi League. It led the Almanac Singers, a group that included Woody Guthrie, Burl Ives, and Pete Seeger, to release an anti-Roosevelt and anti-war folk album, and then change their tune when Stalin needed the United States shortly thereafter.[74]

Mike Gold took a monthlong vacation following the Hitler-Stalin Pact. But the author of *Jews Without Money* defended the agreement upon his return, just as he later rationalized the Communists' execution of Jewish social democrats in Poland.[75] "The leaders of the democratic nations had betrayed or fumbled every chance to smash Hitler," Gold maintained. "Thus, the Soviet people had no recourse but to protect themselves from a united front of imperialists out for their destruction. That the Soviets gained time for arming, and broke with the solid bloc of imperialist enemies, is now clear."[76] A month after the infamous agreement, Joseph Freeman, ever eager to prove himself the team player, spun the pact to Gold by contending that "everybody can see how the USSR stopped Hitler from getting to the Balkans and the Mediteranean [*sic*], and had brought socialism to half of Poland."[77]

The Nazi-Soviet Pact exposed American Communists as unprincipled frauds. Though the pact inspired but a minor exodus from the party, many who escaped the miasma became Communism's most effective opponents.[78] Max Eastman, Whittaker Chambers, Richard Wright, and other onetime Communists found out through painful experience the price apostates pay. Even Professor Sidney Hook, a vocal supporter of the 1932 Communist presidential ticket, became persona non grata in leftist circles despite never abandoning the ideas that made him a socialist in the first place. Increasingly, where one stood on Communism, instead of where one stood on civil rights or government intervention into the economy, determined whether one was viewed on the Left as on the Left or not. Stalin became a litmus test, as Fidel Castro became a litmus test, as Ho Chi Minh became a litmus test. An intellectual's work, whether germane to these figures or not, got trashed or praised based on the unrelated question of how they measured Communist cult-of-personality leaders.

"WHEN YOU CONFUSE art with propaganda, you confuse an act of God with something which can be turned on and off like the hot water faucet," poet E. E. Cummings, who had experienced the Soviet Union firsthand, indignantly explained to Communists. "If 'God' means nothing to you (or less than nothing) I'll cheerfully substitute one of your own favorite words, 'freedom.' Let me, incidentally, opine that absolute tyranny is what most of you are really after; that your so-called ideal isn't America at all and never was America at all: that you'll never be satisfied until what Father Abraham called 'a new nation, conceived in liberty' becomes just another sub-human superstate (like the 'great freedom-loving democracy' of Comrade Stalin) where an artist—or any other human being—either does as he's told or turns into fertilizer."79

Stalin indeed turned Russian artists that bucked the party into fertilizer. Mike Gold merely turned American "artists in uniform" into groveling robots. Though circumstances dictated a difference in method, both Joe Stalin and Mike Gold liquidated artists. An artist in uniform was really no artist at all.

∾ 17 ∾

COMMUNISM IS TWENTIETH-CENTURY AMERICANISM

That henceforth we be no more children, tossed to and fro and carried about with every wind of doctrine, by the wickedness of men, by cunning craftiness by which they lie in wait to deceive.

—EPHESIANS 4:14

THE HITLER-STALIN Pact required nimbleness and agility of Communists. They advocated war. They advocated peace. They advocated war again. The ability to move to and fro repeatedly benefited party members and their fellow travelers on the Left.

Earl Browder, who so opposed conscription during World War I that he served more than two years in prison for obstructing it, led the Communist Party during World War II as it supported the reinstitution of the draft.[1] After directing Communist-led unions in the Congress of Industrial Organizations (CIO) to stop work at various defense-related factories during the Nazi-Soviet Pact, the CPUSA publicly committed to a wartime no-strike pledge once the Soviet Union became a co-belligerent with the Allies.[2] "The worst section of the employers, those least anxious for the unconditional surrender of Hitler and the destruction of fascism, are the very ones who want the strike movement," Browder claimed. "Is it getting tough when you give these employers what they want?"[3] In spite of all the party's denunciations of racial discrimination in America, Browder reacted to Pearl Harbor by purging the CPUSA of all members of Japanese ancestry. He rationalized the discrimination by stating that "the best place for any Japanese fifth columnist to hide is within the Communist party."[4]

The only principle that failed to depart at expediency's notice was subservience to the political line issued by the Soviet Union. On that, but only that, there could be no compromise. The dizzying turns in the Soviet line caused Browder, as leader of the Soviet Union's American auxiliary, to regularly contradict earlier proclamations. Browder remained the leader of the CPUSA for so long not because he was a good leader but because he was a good follower.

If the Communist puppets were willing to publicly humiliate themselves at the behest of foreign puppeteers, what wouldn't they do?

Hundreds of American Communists betrayed their country by spying for the Soviet Union during Earl Browder's tenure as general secretary of the CPUSA and as president of its wartime replacement, the Communist Political Association. The primary functions of the espionage apparatus were to infiltrate the government to purloin secrets, promote and protect fellow agents, and influence policy; to obtain the technological and industrial secrets of the public and private sector; and to partake in Stalin's paranoid campaign to eliminate Trotskyists and other imagined threats.

In pursuit of these ends, American Communists lied. They stole. They murdered. Earl Browder stood in the middle of it all.

UPON AN ICY Spanish field in February 1938, Earl Browder scolded homesick members of the Abraham Lincoln Brigade: "If some of you don't straighten out, you just *may* be sent home."[5]

Albert Wallach never went home again, though he met the grisly fate obliquely alluded to by the general secretary of the American party.

The twenty-three-year-old Wallach was one of 3,300 Americans—roughly 80 percent of whom were Communists—who enlisted in the Abraham Lincoln Brigade to fight Francisco Franco's Loyalist forces in the Spanish Civil War.[6] Aboard a ship to France, Wallach suffered a hernia while exercising. Aboard a ship to Spain, Wallach nearly drowned after a torpedo struck. His luck worsened once on dry land.

After Franco's forces obliterated his unit, Wallach surreptitiously obtained safe-passage papers from the American consulate in Spain to ensure unmolested travel. Perhaps disillusioned by what he saw of Communism, he linked up with an anarchist unit. The former act raised the suspicions of the Communist secret police. The latter probably ensured Wallach's execution.

A few months after Browder's 1938 trip to Spain, Wallach landed in a Communist prison fifteen miles south of Barcelona. Tony De Maio, a fellow American, interrogated Wallach. Despite later claiming he had never heard of him, De Maio reported of Wallach to his Soviet masters: "All evidence shows quite plainly that he was working as a spy." Whatever idealism Wallach still harbored died once one of his comrades, perhaps De

Maio himself, let loose a burst of machine gun fire.[7] Stalin, not Franco, acted as the greatest enemy to many American leftists in Spain.

Albert Wallach was a victim of Stalin's international purification crusade to cleanse the Communist ranks of suspected deviationists. Just as Wallach was not the only American murdered by fellow Communists, Tony De Maio was not the only American complicit in the murder of fellow Communists.

At the same time that Albert Wallach stared down a machine gun barrel in Spain, Lovett Fort-Whiteman entered a concentration camp in northeastern Siberia. In America, the Tuskegee-educated Fort-Whiteman served as one of Communism's most energetic African American evangelists. In Russia, a fellow black American Communist émigré denounced Fort-Whiteman's outlook as counterrevolutionary. At a meeting in Moscow attended by Earl Browder, a Comintern subcommittee concluded that Fort-Whiteman had tried to "mislead." "Lovett Fort-Whiteman, a Negro Comrade, showed himself for Trotsky," a CPUSA report to the Russians coldly noted. Such a designation was a death sentence. The gulag meted out that sentence less than a year after Lovett Fort-Whiteman's comrades declared him guilty.[8]

One of the American Communist Party's few founding mothers met the same fate as Fort-Whiteman, one of the CPUSA's few pioneering African Americans. Juliet Poyntz, a member of the Daughters of the American Revolution who became a revolutionary herself, served as a delegate to the American Communist Party's founding conference. In 1934, she disappeared from the open party only to reappear as a member of the Russian secret police in America. In 1937, she disappeared again—for good. Fellow Communist Elizabeth Bentley, who claimed to have been the object of lesbian advances *and* death threats from the mercurial Poyntz, noted: "She must have revolted against what she was doing and tried to get out of the apparatus, and the N.K.V.D. [secret police], aware of this, 'liquidated' her."[9]

The American party snitched to the Russian party when it uncovered gossip. Stalin conducted a mass-murder campaign against "Trotskyists," "Nazis," "white guards," and other figments of his paranoid mind. This resulted in the murder of Lenin's surviving cohorts, nearly every general officer in the Russian army, and countless others. The cloak-and-dagger games of Communists safe in America resulted in the torture and murder of Russians once the tattlers' tales reached the sadists in Moscow.

The CPUSA reported to the Comintern of a New York food worker who had overheard the brother of one Solomon Rechter brag of his brother's exploits for an underground Zionist outfit in the Soviet Union.[10] On another occasion, while reporting rumors that the editor of a Russian-language Communist publication in America met with "white guard" Russians and other "shady connections," the CPUSA helped deliver the suspected deviationist to Moscow: "Dourmashkin should be let go across (without arousing his suspicions), in order that he could not do any harm here and could be dealt with properly over there."[11] After party operatives burglarized the files of expelled CPUSA leader Jay Lovestone, the CPUSA sent material incriminating—at least from a Stalinist perspective—Russian citizens in machinations against the state, including "one Mendelsohn of Canada, whom Comrade Browder believes to be a Soviet employee of an *important* branch *(OGPU)*." Pat Toohey, the CPUSA representative to the Comintern, passed Browder's message on to Moscow: "Some of these documents refer to certain persons in the USSR who are mentioned in letters which discuss the trials of the Trotskyist-Bukharin spies."[12]

What happened to white guards, Zionists, Trotskyites, and Bukharinites in the Soviet Union? Death happened.

DAYS AFTER THE announcement of the Hitler-Stalin Pact that Earl Browder so faithfully sold to America as "the best current example of the way to peace," Whittaker Chambers, a onetime member of the open Communist Party who had written articles for the *Daily Worker* and the *New Masses*, visited the home of Adolph Berle, Roosevelt's advisor on internal security.[13] He began to reveal his secrets as an underground Communist. Chambers later noted, "I was afraid that, with the Communist-Nazi Pact, the Soviet Government and the American Communist Party would at once put their underground apparatuses at the service of the Nazis against the United States."[14] Berle, and the leader he served, had no such anxiety. The Roosevelt administration responded to Chambers's accusations by repeatedly promoting those he accused.[15]

Administration official Alger Hiss, who, along with FDR advisor Lauchlin Currie and State Department official Laurence Duggan, figured prominently in the conspiracy outlined by Chambers, was granted a reprieve. The Roosevelt administration's indiscriminate outlook, failing to distinguish between idealistic liberals and cynical Communists, allowed Alger Hiss into the New Deal. That same naïveté kept the Soviet spy within the administration despite repeated warnings about his sub rosa activities.

In the first year of his presidency, Franklin Roosevelt awarded diplomatic recognition to the Soviet Union, something his four immediate predecessors had declined to do. The decision would have dramatic, negative, long-lasting repercussions for the United States.

Immediately, under cover of diplomatic immunity, Russian agents went to work infiltrating the U.S. government. They recruited Americans who stole government secrets, influenced policy, and placed other Communists in positions of power. Ultimately, hundreds of Americans, believing tales of a socialist utopia in Ivan the Terrible's homeland, eagerly served the conspiracy.[16] In almost all cases, they asked for no reward. In many cases, they needed no recruitment. What Benedict Arnold did for money, they did for free.

One of the New Deal's alphabet-soup agencies that the American Communists infiltrated with great success was the Agricultural Adjustment Administration (AAA), infamous for ordering, in the days of bread lines and soup kitchens, the mass destruction of piglets and the plowing under of crops. With the airy Henry Wallace as head of the Department of Agriculture, the AAA was particularly susceptible to infiltration by Communists, whose views weren't altogether different from Wallace's—at least Wallace's propensity to hire Communists suggested as much.

Alger Hiss joined the AAA in the first year of Franklin Roosevelt's presidency. A Harvard graduate who had clerked with the previous age's great liberal, Supreme Court justice Oliver Wendell Holmes, Hiss had a progressive pedigree that seemed tailor-made for the New Deal.

His colleagues at AAA included fellow Harvard Law graduates Lee Pressman, John Abt, and Nathan Witt. Like Hiss, these men were Communists whom Chambers would later identify to Berle. They met periodically with Soviet spymaster Harold Ware, son of Mother Bloor, a matriarch of Debs's Socialist Party and Browder's Communist Party, to pass on government information, devise ways to influence policy, and place one another in more sensitive government jobs. Though Ware died in an auto accident in 1935, his network grew to include more than six dozen secret Communists working in government.[17] Several of the group's members would rise to high government positions. Alger Hiss was one of them.

The subversive Department of Agriculture group's extremism didn't go unnoticed. Pressman's argument that government should provide milk the way it provides water or garbage removal raised eyebrows. When a lawyer rhetorically asked why not a government takeover of stores too, Pressman's sure-why-not response raised more eyebrows. Hiss alarmed colleagues when he authored a legal brief endorsing tenant-farmer squatting. The brief reflected the Communist Party's line. Tellingly, perhaps unintentionally so, Arthur Schlesinger Jr. noted that "nothing of importance took place in AAA as a result of [the Communists] presence which AAA liberals would not have done anyway." Forced out of AAA over the protests of FDR advisors Rex Tugwell and Harry Hopkins, the gang quickly found positions of greater influence inside and outside the government.[18]

Hiss moved to the State Department, where he had access to myriad classified documents that he passed on to Chambers. "The contents of the stolen State Department documents," notes Allen Weinstein in his landmark study *Perjury*, "cannot be considered peripheral or unimportant—certainly not to professional diplomats at the time—when viewed in the context of major issues then dominating world affairs: the Sino-Japanese War, the German takeover of Austria, the Spanish Civil War, possible German aggression in Czechoslovakia, Japanese threats to American interests in Asia, the response of other major powers in Europe and Asia toward the Soviet Union."[19]

Pilfering documents became less important once Hiss's career in government escalated. As assistant secretary of state, Hiss played an important role in the major events shaping the postwar world: Bretton Woods, Dumbarton Oaks, Yalta, and the founding conference of the United Nations, at which, upon the recommendation of the Soviet Union, he served as secretary general.[20] So impressive a spy did Hiss appear to his handlers that the Soviet Union's top agent in America opined, "Having [Hiss], one does not need others."[21]

So long as Franklin Roosevelt was president, Alger Hiss would remain safely ensconced within the U.S. government. Neither the AAA purge, nor Chambers's testimony to Berle, the FBI, and the State Department, nor Soviet defector Igor Gouzenko's confessions to Canadian authorities of a mole matching Hiss's description in the State Department, nor Elizabeth Bentley's identification of Hiss as an agent of Stalin did anything to force Hiss from the top levels of the Roosevelt State Department.

THOUGH THE ROOSEVELT administration was almost completely blind to the Communists within its ranks, it didn't hesitate to jail Earl Browder in 1941 for passport fraud. As the proud leader of the Communist Party of the United States of America, Browder would be difficult to confuse for a New Dealer. On the eve of his imprisonment, Browder addressed the faithful at Madison Square Garden, causing Mike Gold to dub the drab Browder as "the Pilot of the People." The admirer continued, "Eugene V. Debs stood up against Woodrow Wilson with the same proletarian grandeur" as Browder had displayed against Franklin Roosevelt.[22]

The man Whittaker Chambers dismissively referred to as "the former typewriter repairman from Kansas" impressed the Kremlin and outraged its nemeses in America.[23] A young Earl Browder conformed to the prevailing doctrines in his father's house by rebelling against the prevailing doctrines of his country. Paw Browder, a Unitarian admirer of "Sockless Jerry" Simpson, raised his ten children devout leftists. As a boy, Earl sold *Appeal to Reason* on street corners and witnessed one of Carry Nation's acts of "hatchetation."[24] At fifteen he joined the Socialist Party, and two years later helped organize a 1908 Wichita campaign event for Eugene Debs.[25] As Browder's biographer points out, "All of Earl's siblings eventually found themselves in or near the Communist party."[26] Radicalism was a family affair. Earl Browder never had a chance to be anyone but Earl Browder.

Browder later cultivated a staid public image, which shielded the real man caught up in sedition, espionage, conspiracy, and intrigue. He was a revolutionist, even if his milquetoast mustache and bankers' clothes said otherwise.

Browder didn't participate in the formation of the American Communist Party in 1919, but he had a good excuse: he was in jail for refusing to register for the draft and encouraging others to do likewise. Released in 1920, he traveled to Soviet Russia numerous times in the 1920s and 1930s on the forged passports that would later land him in jail again. These included a transatlantic voyage on the same steamer with Big Bill Haywood, whose 1912 expulsion from the Socialist Party spurred Browder, and other radicals, to resign from it in disgust. The trip put Browder face-to-face with the Wobbly leader right after he had jumped bail and disgusted his many admirers, including Browder.[27] The dogmatic Left that Browder embraced repulsed the free-spirited leftist Haywood, who would die, homesick like Jack Reed, in Russia. The liberation Haywood sought in dodging prison eternally eluded him. But Soviet Russia opened up a world of possibilities for Earl Browder.

Ever the company man, Browder took on a Russian commissar as a wife even as he neglected to divorce his first wife. Technically married to two women, he confused matters further by making a Communist agent from Canada his common-law wife.[28] In 1927 Moscow sent him to foment revolution in China, where he edited an underground newspaper, attempted to win labor unions for Communism, and even recruited brother-in-law Harrison George to serve as a Comintern agent.[29]

Upon his return to the United States in 1929, Browder, because of the underground nature of his work, was unknown to most rank-and-file American Communists. Yet overseas work had kept Browder free of the factionalism that plagued the CPUSA and enhanced his reputation among authorities in Soviet Russia, who alone manipulated the strings of the

American party. Browder assumed leadership of the American Communist Party in 1930.

Earl Browder fronted the CPUSA in its heyday. At first glance, the heartland accountant who always looked as though he could use a nap seemed an odd fit for a party advocating the violent overthrow of the government. But in selling a radical party to a conservative country, a Kansas-born, onetime employee of Standard Oil made a perfect fit. Though an instrument of the Soviet Union, Browder supplied an American face and a Kansas twang to a Russian party courting the people of the United States.

"MR. BROWDER," COUNSEL for the House Committee on Un-American Activities asked, "do any members of your family hold positions with the Communist Party?" Only brother William, who had been jailed with Earl for draft resistance during World War I, came to mind.[30]

As Earl Browder served Communism in its open party, Margaret Browder served its underground arm as an agent of the Russian NKVD. As with Browder's Russian wife, who presided over a revolutionary court in Lenin's Russia, and Browder's Canadian common-law wife, who disappeared amidst Stalin's purges, sister Margaret's work within the covert apparatus in Europe, evidence suggests, included machinations of the darkest sort.[31] So steeped in espionage was the family that Browder's niece Helen Lowry, who became an NKVD agent, married the Soviet Union's espionage station chief in the United States and subsequently took Soviet citizenship.[32] Espionage was the Browder family business, and Earl was the CEO.

As the general secretary of the open party, Browder had a unique vantage point that allowed him to identify party members ripe for underground work. Marxist Sidney Hook recalled Browder's efforts to steal him from the academy for a life of intrigue. "We would like you to find opportunity to travel to the major campuses of the country that are centers of scientific and industrial research," Hook remembered Browder petitioning him in 1933. Hook would then, in Browder's words, "cultivate the acquaintance of at least one trustworthy individual sympathetic to the Soviet Union," who would report to Hook on "experiments," "projects," and "new inventions or devices particularly of a military and industrial character." A half century later, a still-aghast Hook declared: "Stripped of its euphemisms, this was a request that I set up a spy apparatus!"[33] Though Hook demurred, many didn't. A 1946 memo, now in the Russian archives, informed Stalin: "At Browder's recommendation, eighteen people were drawn to agent work for the NKGB" alone.[34]

. . .

THE LEADER OF the Democratic Party commuted the sentence of the Communist Party leader on May 15, 1942. The following year, a liberated Browder delivered a speech before a Madison Square Garden packed with Communists in which he announced his intention to dissolve the CPUSA. In its place, a Communist Political Association would work within the existing parties and political institutions to push them further left.

Ruth Greenglass attended the mass rally and reported the developments to her husband, David, a non-commissioned officer deployed stateside in the wartime army. "I think it is a bad move," Greenglass wrote his wife. But like so many of his comrades, David Greenglass was prepared to bite his tongue. "Maybe I have my facts wrong and the move is right, but how can I tell without actually knowing what is going on. Darling, please send me that speech and whatever literature the New Committee of Political Education puts out. Darling, this is vital in the boosting of my morale. Please don't delay in sending me the Browder speech."[35]

Weaving Communism into the fabric of America was a task near to Earl Browder's heart. In fact, the Browderite program of targeting more than just industrial workers for party membership, and using light social activities to draw in recruits, played a crucial role in David Greenglass's absorption into the fold. Julius Rosenberg had encouraged the fourteen-year-old David Greenglass to sign up for the Young Communist League, and ultimately David did so, "at first," write historians Ronald Radosh and Joyce Milton, "mostly for the chance to play in the YCL handball league."[36] Handball led to riskier games for higher stakes.

Julius Rosenberg, the man who had encouraged the teenage David Greenglass to join the Young Communist League, married Greenglass's older sister, Ethel, in 1939. Like her husband, Julius, Ethel grew up in a grimy, Jewish section of the Lower East Side of Manhattan that Mike Gold had immortalized in *Jews Without Money*. Ethel, too, rebelled against the faith of her parents. Ethel, too, came upon a new faith in the 1930s. She brought "stacks of political tracts" to David and her family "by the armful." As she took her politics home, she brought her politics to work. Ethel organized more than a hundred female co-workers to lie in obstruction of the delivery trucks of the shipping company that employed them. Instead of higher wages, Ethel's stunt resulted in unemployment.[37] Alas, principles mattered more to the strong-willed Ethel than pocketbook.

In the late 1930s, she joined the Communist Party with her husband. Neither Stalin's alliance with Hitler nor the prospect of making her sons orphans shook that commitment.

The cause célèbre of the Communist Left ironically became politically active upon encountering propaganda for the cause célèbre of an earlier Left. Taken by a soapbox oration on labor leader Tom Mooney, who was jailed for a World War I–era Preparedness Day parade bombing that left ten dead, high school senior Julius Rosenberg returned the next day to collect signatures for his release.[38] Twenty years later, Rosenberg would be in Mooney's place—behind bars—and fledgling leftists would collect signatures for him. But unlike his hero Mooney, who received a commutation in 1939, Rosenberg would never taste freedom after his conviction.

The tentacles of popular-front Communism embraced the teenage Rosenberg. At City College of New York (CCNY), where he matriculated at sixteen in 1934, he soon joined the Federation of Architects, Engineers, Chemists, and Technicians. The group was one of many the party set up in the 1930s to ensnare unsuspecting liberals. It served this function well, as President Roosevelt's acceptance of an honorary membership attests.[39] As Rosenberg's future endeavors demonstrate, it also served another unadvertised function: to identify and recruit Communists to steal secrets of a scientific and technical nature. Several of Rosenberg's CCNY classmates— electrical engineer Joel Barr, military aeronautics expert William Perl, and electrical engineer Morton Sobell—became his helpmates in espionage while working for both the government and military contractors.

Whereas David Greenglass upon becoming a Communist gloried in the affirmation from his older sister and her husband, Julius Rosenberg encountered familial alienation. His father, who hoped his son would become a rabbi, was disgusted at Julius's new faith. The rift deepened when the Army Signal Corps disconnected itself from Harry Rosenberg's son because of his past membership in the Communist Party, which he had kept hidden from his military employers. "Harry Rosenberg refused to see or speak with his son for nearly a year, not relenting until he was fatally ill with the kidney infection that killed him in 1946," note Radosh and Milton.[40] The ties that bound Julius Rosenberg to the Soviet Union proved stronger than the ties that bound him to his kin.

Army investigators had confronted Rosenberg with his Communist ties in 1941. Not only had he bluffed his way past his interrogators back then, but he had begun to covertly obtain manuals that he passed on to the Soviet Union. Four years later, the FBI presented the army with Rosenberg's actual membership card in the CPUSA. The army fired Julius from his civilian engineering job in 1945. It did not accuse him of espionage; it merely considered him—quite rightly—a loyalty risk for such activity due to his past membership in the CPUSA.[41]

The Soviets ordered Rosenberg to lie low. He could not. "The main thing he can't reconcile himself to is his relative inactivity," the New York station informed Moscow. "At every meeting, he asks us to allow him to bring materials out of the plant and thus benefit us."42 Rosenberg did just that. In the private sector, where he landed at Emerson Radio working on classified wartime projects for a brief time, Rosenberg stole a classified proximity fuse that enabled anti-aircraft munitions to explode upon nearing enemy planes.43 This brazen act by one already fired for being a security risk demonstrated not only a tenacious devotion to the cause but also an arrogant disregard of caution. Even when, in the wake of Soviet courier Elizabeth Bentley's confession to the FBI, the Soviets ordered group handlers to halt all activities, Rosenberg had continued operations, the NKGB subsequently discovered.44

Julius Rosenberg's zealotry overpowered his judgment.

In addition to purloining secret defense-related materials, Rosenberg showed his worth by recruiting friends and relatives for espionage work. "The Rosenberg network was a large one," scholars John Earl Haynes and Harvey Klehr point out. "It included six sources: [Joel] Barr, [William] Perl, [Alfred] Sarant, [Morton] Sobell, David Greenglass, and an unidentified source with the cover name Nile. In addition to these sources, the network maintained two active liaison-couriers, Michael and Ann Sidorovich, and three others who carried out support work: Vivian Glassman, Ruth Greenglass, and Ethel Rosenberg."45 Most significant of these recruits· was Ethel's brother, David Greenglass, who agreed to Julius's request that he spy for the Soviet Union while stationed at Los Alamos, New Mexico—site of the Manhattan Project, which developed the atomic bomb.

Despite his meager education, the wanna-be scientist Greenglass impressed a real scientist interrogator. The U.S. scientist believed that Greenglass had gleaned, in the words of Radosh and Milton, "an amazing fund of information, all without ever stealing a document or entering a restricted area."46 Greenglass diagramed the plutonium Nagasaki bomb for the Soviet Union, detailing the lens used for its implosion. Though Greenglass's Soviet handlers in New York cabled home that his material was "low in quality and far from processed," it noted that Greenglass had "passed to us a cartridge" for the atomic bomb's detonator.47 He also purloined a small amount of uranium, which made its way to Moscow.48 Julius Rosenberg's man inside the Manhattan Project was but one piece that helped the Soviet Union assemble the total puzzle. Citing four sources— Greenglass, two who remain mysteries, and a fourth who went unpunished but not undiscovered—with knowledge of developments at Los Alamos, Moscow considered the espionage situation on the Manhattan

Project "exceptionally favorable," celebrating the fact that "there are people who openly manifest sympathy for us and express the opinion that our country should be informed" about the atomic bomb.[49] So complete was the information supplied by Greenglass and others that within four years of Hiroshima and Nagasaki, the Soviet Union—a scientific backwater—had tested its own nuclear bomb.

How, Americans wondered, had the madman Stalin come to possess the most destructive weapon known to man?

They found out in a thriller that unfolded like a Tom Clancy spy novel. The Rosenberg case came complete with a secret Leica camera workshop, password greetings, fugitives disappearing behind the Iron Curtain, and even a torn Jell-O carton that enabled David Greenglass to identify a mysterious Communist courier by matching his end with the agent's.

That seemingly innocuous Jell-O carton served as Julius and Ethel Rosenberg's ticket to the electric chair.

Julius Rosenberg's ripping the Jell-O box linked him to both ends of the atomic espionage network: to the thief and to its consumer; to American subversives and to Soviet agents; to David Greenglass, to whom Rosenberg had given half of the carton, and to Harry Gold, the Order of the Red Star honoree who had received the other end of the carton through Rosenberg's Soviet handlers. Rosenberg had recruited his brother-in-law to spy. He had instructed Russian spymasters to meet with Greenglass in New Mexico. Julius Rosenberg was the intersection where the diverse players in the drama met—even when, as in Harry Gold's case, they had never actually met him.

By 1950, the conspirators could feel the FBI breathing down their necks. An FBI agent lurked behind every unfamiliar face. Every knock at the door suggested the beginnings of an arrest. Each set of headlights in the rearview mirror was a potential tail.

Rosenberg, stocked with thousands of dollars from his Soviet spymasters, plied his agents with money in an effort to get them out of the United States immediately.[50] Some reappeared with new identities in the Soviet Union. Others chose to defect—*to the United States.*

In 1950, American intelligence identified Klaus Fuchs, a German émigré to the United Kingdom who had worked at Los Alamos, as an agent of the Soviet Union. A physicist working directly on the Manhattan Project, Fuchs had handed over material superior to that relayed by the college-dropout Greenglass. Though unconnected to the Rosenberg spy ring, Fuchs passed his information through Harry Gold, the same courier who once had received information in New Mexico from Greenglass.

Picked up in Britain by MI5, Fuchs, to the surprise of the skeptical Brits, quickly confessed to the fantastic allegation of American intelligence. He fingered Gold as his contact. Gold, in Philadelphia, then identified David Greenglass as a supplier of top-secret atomic information. In New York, Greenglass, heretofore identified by the FBI as "Unknown American #5," confessed and implicated Julius and Ethel Rosenberg. There the dominoes stopped falling.

Morton Sobell absconded to Mexico, where *federales* abducted him, took him on a midnight ride to the border, and handed him over to U.S. authorities waiting at the International Bridge in Laredo, Texas. Sobell, along with courier Harry Gold, received a thirty-year sentence. Joel Barr and Alfred Sarant stayed ahead of their FBI pursuers and disappeared behind the Iron Curtain. Other atomic spies eluded punishment entirely.[51]

But Julius and Ethel Rosenberg didn't. Had the couple confessed their crimes, they could have spared themselves. Had they exposed the conspiracy they served, they could have spared their sons orphans' childhoods. But their love for the Soviet Union exceeded their love for themselves, for each other, and for their children. On June 19, 1953, an electrician at Sing Sing prison in New York administered lethal voltage into the bodies of Julius Rosenberg and then his wife.

The damage the Rosenbergs unleashed outlived them. Two of the scientists Julius encouraged to flee spent their lives in the Soviet Union developing war-related devices, including the Communist bloc's first radar-based anti-aircraft technology, which proved instrumental in the Vietnamese Communists' efforts to bring down American planes.[52] The proximity fuse Rosenberg lifted from the Emerson Radio Corporation, his direct KGB handler later explained, enabled the Soviets to shoot down the U-2 spy plane flown by Francis Gary Powers.[53] And, of course, the Rosenberg ring's role in providing secret nuclear-weapons data emboldened Communist aggression. As Judge Irving Kaufman duly noted in sentencing the Rosenbergs to death, "Putting into the hands of the Russians the A-bomb years before our best scientists predicted Russia would perfect the bomb has already caused, in my opinion, the Communist aggression in Korea, with the resultant casualties exceeding 50,000 and who knows but what that millions more innocent people may pay the price of your treason. Indeed, by your betrayal, you undoubtedly have altered the course of history to the disadvantage of our country."[54]

Julius Rosenberg got to be more than Tom Mooney. The Rosenbergs got to be Sacco and Vanzetti, who got to be Joe Hill, who got to be John Brown. The Rosenbergs became martyrs in an ever-evolving faith, which periodically cast aside the unsavory elements of their predecessors but retained the symbols.

IN 1945, JOSEPH Stalin ushered out Earl Browder and ushered in the Cold War. America's Communist leader had become too much like the Soviet Union's Communist leader. Browder cultivated a cult of personality, and, as his biographer notes, had begun "to display an ugly hubris."[55] He forgot about the power above him.

When the Comintern alerted him that the Communists' wartime conciliation with bourgeois parties had been but a temporary expedience, Browder refused to accept it. He outlined the "Tehran Doctrine." Taking its name from the wartime conference of Stalin, Roosevelt, and Churchill in Iran, Browder's doctrine envisioned a world where cooperation and not conflict reigned between the emerging world powers, where Communists indigenous to capitalist countries abandoned their own parties and became the faithful left-wings of existing parties, and where educating the public rather than overthrowing the public's government held the key to Communist success. Comintern head Georgi Dimitrov cabled Browder in March 1944: "I am somewhat disturbed by the new theoretical, political, and tactical positions you are developing. Are you not going too far in adapting to the altered international situation, to the point of denying the theory and practice of class struggle and the necessity for the working class to have its own independent political party? Please reconsider all of this and report your thoughts."[56]

But Browder did not reconsider. He did something out of character not only for a disciplined Communist, but for Browder. He rebelled. He had accepted his father's views. He had accepted Stalin's views. Now Earl Browder had his own views. He was unwilling to compromise. Neither were his Soviet overlords, whom he now, somewhat naively, refused to recognize as his overlords. Earl Browder, a lifetime follower, finally acted as a leader. But one couldn't be a leader and lead the American Communists; it was a job suited only for followers.

Stalin, through a letter written in Moscow but published in the West under the name of French Communist Jacques Duclos, denounced Browder and his Tehran Doctrine. The Americans reacted as good Communists, ousting Browder from leadership and subsequently ousting him from the party. The man the party had worshipped for a decade now became, in the words of his former worshippers, "an enemy of Communism" engaged in "deliberate sabotage" and "no longer fit to be considered even friendly to the working class."[57] Even for a man so accustomed to changes in the party line, this about-face had to sting.

Browder later called the Duclos letter "the first *public* declaration of the Cold War."[58] While many Americans remained oblivious to their wartime ally's intent to become their peacetime enemy, American Communists knew that the rules were about to change. They knew this because the Duclos letter instructed them that opposition and obstruction, and not co-operation and conciliation, were the proper stances in relation to their own government. In their moral universe, the United States of America was about to take the place of Nazi Germany.

With the fog of war lifted, the American public again viewed Stalin—as he had always viewed them—as a foe and not a friend. High-profile espionage cases involving Alger Hiss and the Rosenbergs demonstrated the perfidy of American Communists and enhanced the American public's and the government's suspicions of them. The turncoats stood convicted in the court of public opinion, which didn't need to wait for the opening of the Soviet archives or the declassification of Russian spy cables decrypted by the American government, to issue a guilty verdict.

In 1949, the fall of China and the Soviet Union's successful test of an atomic weapon exacerbated the legitimate fears of Communism. With the outbreak in 1950 of the Korean War, in which America's sons, brothers, and fathers perished at the hands of Communists, suspicion and disdain turned to rage. There could be no marriage between Communism and mainstream liberalism in such an environment. Any gateway to the mainstream was cut off.

Though Communist treason long failed to evoke the ire of officeholders, the Communists' betrayal of the party that those officeholders pledged allegiance to went altogether too far. In advance of the 1948 election, Communists flocked to the fourth-party candidacy of Henry Wallace against a weakened President Truman. The Democrats, smarting from attacks from their left and aware of the anti-Communist mood of the American people, gladly undertook an intramural cleansing reminiscent of Woodrow Wilson's crackdown on socialists, anarchists, and pacifists thirty years prior.

The main tools of "McCarthyism," in fact, were created by liberals and leftists. The Smith Act, the legislation outlawing groups seeking to overthrow the government which the Communists so supported when used against Trotskyists in 1941 that they prepared materials for the prosecution, suddenly became an affront to civil liberties when used against them.[59] More than a hundred Communists were convicted under the Smith Act in the post-war years, including ten of eleven members of the party's national board. A few, foreshadowing a favored response to criminal conviction in the following decade, went underground.[60] The House

Committee on Un-American Activities, primarily the creation of Samuel Dickstein, a paid agent of the Soviet Union, backfired on the Communists when its purview expanded beyond American fascists.[61] Even the Hollywood blacklist was prefaced by a Communist-engineered blacklist of the party's enemies in the movie business.[62] Dalton Trumbo, of Hollywood Ten fame, ratted to the FBI on anti-war voices in Tinseltown during World War II. He hypocritically cried foul after the war that such an anti-civil-libertarian apparatus could be used against *him*.[63]

Within the Left, other factors combined with these to bury American Communism. Domestically, Browder's successor, William Z. Foster, a fanatic's fanatic, conducted a witch hunt against "white chauvinists" within the CPUSA that depleted the party. From the Soviet Union, in 1956 Nikita Khrushchev delivered his famous speech to the Twentieth Congress, admitting the brutal crimes of his predecessor Joseph Stalin. When Congressman Martin Dies, Senator Pat McCarran, or FBI director J. Edgar Hoover had made such charges, American Communists chuckled. When Stalin's successor advanced them, they listened. What the Kronstadt rebellion, the Moscow show trials, and the Nazi-Soviet Pact failed to do, Khrushchev did. Russians made the American Communist Party. Russians unmade it. The party, already decimated, witnessed a mass exodus. By 1958, membership had sunk to three thousand, a figure that had been twenty-seven times greater just two decades earlier under Browder's stewardship.[64]

New heroes—Mao Zedong, Fidel Castro, Ho Chi Minh, Pol Pot, Daniel Ortega—supplanted Stalin. The Left traded in these new icons for even newer ones as *their* sins became too ingrained in the public consciousness to continue the charade. Though individual Communists, such as Lee Harvey Oswald, attracted attention, the actual party, whose scant numbers had always belied its immense influence, ceased to have any real effect on America.

"BEING KICKED OUT of the Communist Party in 1946 was the best thing that ever happened to me," Browder wrote in a newspaper column in 1954.[65] As he had so many times before, Browder told a lie. He had desperately sought reinstatement into the party.[66] He held on to hope until even he realized his beloved party really didn't want him anymore. The expulsion devastated Earl Browder. Whether his despondence resulted from the guilt of a lifetime in service to an evil cause or the evil cause rebuffing his efforts to serve it remains unclear.

Browder faded into obscurity, financial troubles, depression, and drink. Lucrative offers came from anti-Communists to reveal secrets.[67]

He refused. Instead, he took a job in 1948 as the American business representative of a state-run Soviet publishing house. This "keep your friends close, but keep your enemies closer" move soon proved untenable, and the Soviet Union released Browder, who had wasted much of his money in the endeavor.

Browder's old allies either showed themselves as his new enemies or got excommunicated, too.[68] Browder's lapdog Mike Gold went into Foster's "dog house," the FBI noted, observing that "Gold went to Europe and remained for three years" following the CPUSA chief's ouster.[69] Gold complained in 1952 of it being "almost impossible to earn a living" in America and was reduced to accepting money from a young admirer.[70] Browder didn't have it much better, yet, like Gold, remained a captive of the delusions ingrained over decades of submission.

Long after he had reason to fear repercussions from the Soviet Union or the United States, Browder continued to lie about his days as Moscow's water boy. He dishonestly insisted to the *New York Times* in 1954, for instance, that the Communist Party he led "did not engage in espionage for Russia, . . . did not accept orders from Moscow, and did not wish to subordinate America to Russia."[71] It did, it did, and it did.

When he died in 1973, "a mere handful attended his memorial service."[72] The succeeding Left conveniently forgot the preceding Left, just as Browder had distanced himself from his days peddling *Appeal to Reason* because of its fall from fashion within the Marxist nexus.

An American Left that was only ostensibly an *American* Left had no chance of winning over America. No matter how many members of the Daughters of the American Revolution joined the Communist Party, it could not shake its reputation as an instrument of foreigners. Seventy-five years earlier, the Yankees purged from the First International had recognized that it was folly to expect that "Americans, with American ideas, either can or will submit to any foreign systems of arbitrary control."[73] Subsequent Lefts unlearned this lesson. Only through hard experience—a servile American Left's unhappy chapter from World War I until shortly after World War II—did domestic radicals smarten up.

The 1950s witnessed the loud defeat of one Left and the quiet rise of another.

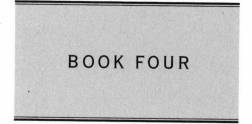

BOOK FOUR

THE NEW LEFT

～18～

APOGEE

For, professing themselves to be wise, they became fools.

—ROMANS 1:22

POSTWAR AMERICANS PREFERRED living in the present to entertaining schemes for an imaginary future. Warren Harding's accurate reading of the pulse of America following World War I—a desire for "normalcy, not nostrums"—just as easily applied to America after World War II. The national mood was not one of revolution, radicalism, or even reform. Americans retreated to suburbia and reveled in backyards, barbeques, babies, and baseball. Who could blame them? The generation that endured the Great Depression and the Second World War wanted to enjoy life. The 1950s offered much to enjoy.

Though Americans did not seek to overturn the welfare state that Franklin Roosevelt had established, they did not seek to expand it, either. They tolerated an activist state as the new normal.

Labor no longer sat at the table of power as it had in the Roosevelt administration. Unions threatened prosperity and consorted with organized crime. Congressional Democrats investigated their nefarious ties. President Harry Truman recruited former naval men to break the maritime strike and seized the mines and railroads in peacetime under wartime powers to break strikes. Increasingly, it seemed, the dominant liberalism no longer wished to play favorites between labor and management, but sought to dictate to both from above. Postwar liberalism was a brethren of managerial elites.

Americans exhibited far less tolerance for another Old Left hold-over. Communists gobbled up China, North Korea, and most of Eastern Europe. Communists killed Americans in Korea. Communists stole atom bomb secrets. Even mainline liberals rejected the Communists in the post-war years. "Liberal revulsion had little in common with popular anti-Communism because it was revulsion born of guilt, the revulsion of the sinner in the throes of confession," historian Allen Matusow writes.[1]

The Old Left died of a thousand cuts, but the kindest one of all was prosperity. The Great Depression finished capitalism, they had concluded. Like a villain in a horror sequel, capitalism returned from the grave. The return of prosperity gave lie to the Marxist prophecy. That crisis moment, in which the Left fantasized itself delivering the death blow to the free market, had passed. Where, now, was the audience for a Marxist America? Offering Marxist solutions in the wealthiest nation man had ever known made sense to few save a remnant of true believers. In mid-century America, it seemed Marxism, not capitalism, had died. Something new, that didn't entirely throw out the old, was needed.

A decade that glowed for Americans seemed grim for the Left. But as it regrouped and rethought, the Left planted seeds that sprouted a New Left. Leftist activism was moribund in the 1950s. Leftist intellectualism was fecund.

WITHOUT THE 1950S, there could not have been a 1960s. The immediate post-war years anticipated (albeit on a smaller scale) the disturbances, trends, and phenomena that exploded in the 1960s. The fires of the civil rights movement, the sexual revolution, and the counterculture started in the 1950s. What appears at first glance a lost decade turns out to be a crucial decade for the Left's evolution. The ideas, theories, and banter of post-war intellectuals "hardly amounted to a grand or utopian vision of the future," historian Richard Pells writes. "Yet they unexpectedly created the vocabulary and the mental framework with which the next generation of Americans assaulted the nation's political institutions and social values in the 1960s. Inadvertently and often unhappily, the postwar intellectuals became the parents and teachers—literally and spiritually—of the New Left, the partisans of the counterculture, the civil rights activists, and the movement to end the conflagration in Vietnam."[2]

As Americans increasingly put themselves on psychiatrist's couches, rested job hopes on corporate Rorschach tests, and relied on tranquilizing medications to remain on an even keel, social science put America on the couch, imagined its folkways as an inkblot for interpretation, and prescribed supposedly scientific solutions. Social science never claimed as high a reputation as it did in midcentury America. Its adhesion to actual "science" never proved so tenuous. Social science became a political club to beat enemies and defend favorites. Though its practitioners could be critical of leftist shibboleths, and generally adopted a cool, nonideological tone, 1950s social science—perhaps because of that very rejection of 1930s-style dogmatism—cast a wider and deeper net.

Every page of sociologist C. Wright Mills's works might drip with an agenda, but most of the decade's heavyweights didn't think of themselves as pushing an agenda. (And if they pushed an agenda, as sex researcher Alfred Kinsey certainly did, they usually took pains to obscure it.) They mistook the dominant liberalism of their own milieu—the intellectual ghetto of academia and Manhattan-based literary journals—for the mainstream opinion of the American milieu. To object to it was tantamount to announcing oneself a boob. Liberalism thus won adherents through attitudinal pressure rather than intellectual conversion.

With the Left discredited, leftists moved from proposing to critiquing. If they couldn't win over Americans with a vision of the future, they could at least gain a hearing for a harsh appraisal of the present. Mere titles of books—*The Organization Man*, *The Affluent Society*, *The Power Elite*—exhibited the shift in focus from uplifting the poor to denigrating the powerful. After more than a decade of want, the return of plenty made book-length laments over hunger and scarcity appear passé. With a positive vision shunned, the Left attacked anti-Communism, which all fell under the rubric of "McCarthyism," and conservatism, which began to formulate its own organized set of ideas. Liberals advocated their own, acceptable brand of anti-Communism and ridiculed conservatism by greeting it as if it were a grunt rather than a coherent argument.

Conservatives were to be diagnosed rather than debated. Wunderkind Arthur Schlesinger Jr. imagined "the vital center" in his book by that title to be the liberalism of his hometown of Cambridge, Massachusetts. Anybody outside that "vital center" (which was well left of the actual center), whether they be the too-far-left supporters of anti-anti-Communist Henry Wallace's quixotic 1948 presidential bid or the too-far-right supporters of anti-Communist Joe McCarthy's 1952 senatorial reelection, stood beyond the pale.

In *Anti-Intellectualism in American Life*, Richard Hofstadter sneered at conservative intellectuals William F. Buckley, G. K. Chesterton, and Hilaire Belloc, dubbed all politically organized groups to his right as "ultraconservative political movements," which he regarded as the "implacable enemies of the intellectual community," and throughout confuses intellectualism for liberalism and anti-liberalism for anti-intellectualism.[3]

Theodor Adorno, a figure well to the left of liberals Schlesinger and Hofstadter, regarded American conservatives as akin to German Nazis. The book project the German refugee led, 1950's *Authoritarian Personality*, designated Communists as one of a number of persecuted "out groups" while likening anti-Communism to totalitarianism and displaced anti-Semitism.[4] So rigged was the study that the same answer to a single question on the authors' survey served to indicate conservatism in one instance and authoritarianism in another.[5] By such tautological methods, social science could show a link between any two things.

Adorno imagined America a proto-fascist state in *The Authoritarian Personality*. "[W]e are living in potentially fascist times," the study warned.[6] The authoritarian personality was bred by authoritarian (rather than democratic) families, by the belief in the Great Authoritarian in the Sky, by the survival-of-the-fittest mentality of capitalism, and by patriotism. Rather than fascism, Adorno seemed to be describing things the Left had long criticized: family, faith, freedom, and flag.

Columbia University's C. Wright Mills, also frustrated by America's rejection of the Left, made similar warnings about a fascist America in *The Power Elite*: "[W]e have moved a considerable distance along the road to the mass society. At the end of that road there is totalitarianism, as in Nazi Germany or in Communist Russia. We are not yet at that end."[7] Less than a decade after America helped put down Hitler, Mussolini, and Tojo, academics put America on the couch and purported to discover its inner fascist.

David Riesman's *The Lonely Crowd* analyzed Americans and found two types: the "inner-directed" man, more prevalent in an earlier America, influenced by a moral compass instilled by parents, religion, and other childhood influences; and the "other-directed" man, easily manipulated by advertisements, the media, and the crowd, motivated to act by the example of his peers. The two groups exhibited different sets of problems, but the latter group tended, according to Riesman, to "overconform"—a problem that pop psychologists overdiagnosed in 1950s culture. Other-directed men cared too much how their corporate bosses judged them, what their neighbors in suburbia said of them, and what their fellow parishioners thought of them. Riesman concluded, "If the other-directed people should discover how much needless work they do, discover that their own thoughts and their own lives are quite as interesting as other people's, that, indeed, they no more assuage their loneliness in a crowd of peers than one can assuage one's thirst by drinking sea water, then we might expect them to become more attentive to their own feelings and aspirations."[8]

Americans believed they never had it so good. Social scientists tried to convince them that they never had it so bad. No longer could radicals credibly point to scarcity and want. The Great Depression was long over. Instead of "more jobs" the rallying cry became, in author Paul Goodman's words, "there are not enough worthy jobs."[9] The high-paying, secure, corporate jobs that Americans generally desired, William Whyte lectured in *The Organization Man*, weren't so desirable after all. Whyte observed that corporations stifled creativity, genius, and individuality, and rewarded sycophancy, obedience, and conformity. Whyte and others lamented the crushing bigness of corporations. The crushing bigness of the state escaped notice.

Next to the sterile, compartmentalized offices where the organization man worked, the suburbs where he lived evoked the greatest consternation from sociologists. The upper-class critics who once lamented the crowded urban tenements now took up their pens against the suburbs whither the tenement dwellers had escaped. Lewis Mumford, renowned writer on urban America, sneered at Levittown, New York, the most famous of the quickly assembled suburban communities, as "a multitude of uniform, unidentifiable houses, lined up inflexibly, at uniform distances on uniform roads, in a treeless command waste, inhabited by people of the same class, the same incomes, the same age group, witnessing the same television performances, eating the same tasteless prefabricated foods, from the same freezers, conforming in every outward and inward respect to a common mold manufactured in the same central metropolis. Thus the ultimate effect of the suburban escape in our time is, ironically, a low-grade uniform environment from which escape is impossible."[10] The cookie-cutter houses, sociologists assumed, housed cookie-cutter people. The quickly built structures also displeased them aesthetically. Not only that, but "people from big, urban Democratic wards tend to become Republican" upon moving to the suburbs, William Whyte ominously noted.[11]

The urban jailbreak reflected the prosperity of the times, the reaction to the flight north of southern blacks, and the housing shortage brought on by the baby boom, the return of soldiers, and the paucity of homes constructed during the lean years. David Halberstam described the housing crisis that Americans faced immediately after the Second World War: "Some 50,000 people were reportedly living in Army Quonset huts. In Chicago it was so bad that 250 used trolley cars were sold for use as homes." In 1944, builders constructed 114,000 new homes in the United

States. Six years later, they put up 1.7 million.[12] Next to Quonset huts, trolley cars, and housing projects, the sprung-up suburbs struck their inhabitants as the embodiment of the American Dream. But the same intellectuals who ridiculed their houses told them that the American Dream didn't exist.

The Organization Man contended that people had grown "restive" with the "mythology" of the American Dream, a fantasy "that is too distant from the way things actually are."[13] In *The Power Elite*, C. Wright Mills argued that not only was there no such person as the self-made man, but if such a person existed his climb up the financial ladder would be inherently neither good nor bad.[14] In fact, scribblers insisted there was something wrong with anyone who attained a comfortable life in a society as corrupt as America's. It became vogue to impugn success.

President Eisenhower, in Paul Goodman's words, was "an unusually uncultivated man" with no intellectuals as friends.[15] In *Anti-Intellectualism in American Life*, Richard Hofstadter noted "Eisenhower's fondness for Western fiction" and the "fumbling inarticulateness" that characterized his early days as a political figure.[16] Successful businessmen, too, supplied fodder for Hofstadter's exposé of the alienation between America and its intellectuals. The "suspicion of genius or brilliance rooted itself into the canons of business," Hofstadter claimed. Businessmen exhibited "a persistent hostility to formal education," he held.[17] Business ruined high schools by replacing liberal arts with vocational training, and introduced business schools in higher education that acted as "anti-intellectual centers dedicated to a rigidly conservative set of ideas."[18] C. Wright Mills agreed, announcing, "The characteristic member of the higher circles today is an intellectual mediocrity." If business executives read at all, they read mysteries or books on management.[19]

The complaints lacked perspective more than verisimilitude. When, exactly, had businessmen shown greater interest in books, the arts, and high ideas than in money?

Since intellectuals regarded society's values as topsy-turvy, they not only attacked the successful but also honored failures. In *Growing Up Absurd*, Paul Goodman celebrated the abnormal, the deviant, the offensive. While allowing that "winos" meandered into irrationality, Goodman maintained that they offered "a wise philosophical resignation plus an informed and radical critique of society." He also wondered, "[W]hat is the sense of the concern about the narcotics?" He then quoted a youth worker on the relative harmlessness of heroin.[20] More adolescent sex, Goodman argued, generally "would give more satisfaction and do lasting good." Authorities should look the other way, and society should withhold its disapproval.[21] In other words, the society, and not the deviants, deviated from the good.

GIVING A PHILOSOPHICAL and psychiatric justification to the sensuous life that Goodman later advocated in *Growing Up Absurd* were Wilhelm Reich, Herbert Marcuse, and Norman O. Brown. The troika amalgamated utopian socialism with inverse readings of Freudian psychology. The mixture produced a call to liberate man from civilization. In doing so, Reich, Marcuse, and Brown distinguished themselves in their undisguised radicalism from other post-war social scientists. What could be more radical than a revolution to overthrow civilization itself?

Brown's 1959 treatise *Life Against Death* aimed at "all who are ready to call into question old assumptions and to entertain new possibilities." The book opened by asking for "a willing suspension of common sense" from the reader.[22] After all, Brown was challenging the world as it existed and seeking to replace it with something out of the ether. Going along would take a pliable imagination.

For Freud, repression and neuroses were the price to pay for civilization and progress. Reich, Brown, and Marcuse subscribed to the premise but judged that civilization wasn't worth it. To live a free life, man must liberate himself from church, family, work, and moral conventions and thereby break free from the repression and the neuroses they caused. If civilization caused neuroses, then it was necessarily unhealthy. Kill the disease, they argued. In Marcuse's words, "Repression and unhappiness *must be* if civilization is to prevail."[23] In Brown's, "Reality imposes on human beings the necessity of renunciation of pleasures; reality frustrates desire. The pleasure-principle is in conflict with the reality-principle, and this conflict is the cause of repression."[24] Indeed, so indistinguishable are Brown's *Life Against Death* and Marcuse's *Eros and Civilization* that it seems as if one could put down the former and pick up the latter and not know which book one is reading.

Eros and Civilization's public enemy number one was work. Marcuse wrote, "[L]abor time, which is the largest part of the individual's life time, is painful time, for alienated labor is absence of gratification, negation of the pleasure principle."[25] Whereas one post-war trend on the Left made a bogeyman out of automation, Marcuse welcomed it as a savior from manual labor. In fact, 1955's *Eros and Civilization* invited a reduction in the standard of living if it meant liberation from work.[26] Drawing extensively upon Fourier's vision of work as play, Brown, too, wished for a world in which leisure supplanted work, or at least one in which work became more pleasurable.[27] "The most realistic observers are emphasizing man's increasing alienation from his work; the possibility of mass unemployment—i.e., liberation from work—given by modern technology; and the utter incapacity of human nature as it is today to make genuinely free use of leisure—to play," he noted.[28]

What should man do with all this free time? Pursue pleasure unconstrained by civilization. Brown called for a "kingdom of enjoyment."[29] Marcuse hoped for a reign of Freud's "polymorphous perversity," a preadolescent sexuality that is not just a "release but a *transformation* of the libido: from sexuality constrained under genital supremacy to eroticization of the entire personality."[30] Austrian immigrant Wilhelm Reich did not wait for the hedonist millennium. He built it at Orgonon, his two-hundred-acre Maine compound. The millennium was a box that channeled orgasmic, life-building energy. Reich, who had fled Nazi Germany, gotten kicked out of Denmark, and departed Norway under intense pressure, faced the wrath of the U.S. government in life's final act.

"I have become convinced that sexuality is the center around which revolves the whole of social life as well as the inner life of the individual," Reich wrote in his diary after returning from service in the First World War.[31] Sex dominated Reich's personal and professional life. Sigmund Freud's star pupil partook in numerous adulterous affairs, pressured the women he impregnated to abort his children (one woman died in the process), and sent his kids who lived to a distant child-rearing center run by Communists.[32] The evolution of his psychiatric procedures reflected his sexual obsessions. He first insisted that his patients disrobe. Finding nudity insufficient for the psychiatric breakthroughs he desired, Reich then began touching patients. Finally, he encouraged them to attain orgasms in therapy.[33] Reich's dubious psychiatric methods were followed by pseudoscience of an even more suspicious sort.

In the 1930s, Reich reported to have discovered a substance between life and non-life, which he called "bions." Scientists dismissed Reich's find. He persisted. Through bions, he discovered the energy that catalyzed everything, an orgasmic power he dubbed "orgones." He invented a machine, the Orgone Energy Accumulator, which attracted orgones into a box for curative purposes. He lured wishful cancer patients and other diseased persons into a telephone-booth-sized box to heal their ailments. Their deaths didn't dissuade him of the magnitude of his discovery. Reich's followers, an abused glob who hoisted their hero's pedestal higher the more he put them down, claimed to have seen and felt the orgasmic energy in his device.[34] Non-followers usually saw and felt nothing.

With the world living in the threatening shadow of Hiroshima and

Nagasaki, Reich contrasted the healing powers of his discovery with the destructive power of the age's other scientific development. "We shall have to learn to counteract the murderous form of the atomic energy with the life-furthering function of the orgone energy and thus render it harmless," he boasted.[35] From averting nuclear war to curing cancer to inducing orgasm, nothing seemed beyond the reach of Reich's gizmo.

The Food and Drug Administration took note of Reich's sale and manufacture of the Orgone Energy Accumulator. The government indicted Reich in 1955 on the grounds that he had hawked a fraudulent medical device. Reich, whose 1945 English-language publication *The Sexual Revolution* marked him as a prophet of the coming age, became its first martyr.

A federal court sentenced him to prison and ordered the destruction of the orgone boxes and the literature promoting them. The mentally fragile Reich, who by this point believed that air force planes protected him and President Eisenhower was his friend, told the court that a witness against him was "the XXth Century Judas Iscariot" and compared his case to "the Murder of Christ 2000 years ago."[36] The government contributed to this persecution legend by overseeing the burning of Reich's books. Reich added more to his myth by dying of a heart attack in prison. "Once in a thousand years, nay once in two thousand years, such a man comes upon this earth to change the destiny of the human race," his eulogist maintained. "As with all great men, distortion, falsehood, and persecution followed him. He met them all, until organized conspiracy sent him to prison and then killed him. We have witnessed it all, 'The Murder of Christ.'"[37]

The pleasure pursuit Brown, Marcuse, and Reich wrote about, their readers acted out. The 1950s intellectual meme became a 1960s lifestyle.

WHEREAS DRS. BROWN, Marcuse, and Reich directly influenced the Left and thereby only indirectly influenced the larger culture, Dr. Alfred Kinsey's impact knew no bounds.

Kinsey, like Paul Goodman, lived a double life. The radical sex the pair championed in their writings they also championed in their bedrooms. The personal drove the political, as it increasingly would in the approaching decades. But in the 1950s, revealing the personal stood to damage the political. So sexual radicals such as Kinsey and Goodman kept the personal well hidden. They practiced what they preached, but they didn't preach that they practiced.

Alfred Kinsey endured a personal sexual revolution and then unleashed it upon America. Taking advantage of the inflated esteem for social science that the times offered, Kinsey produced studies purporting to show that the sex lives of Americans were not too different from his own sex life—details of which he made sure to obfuscate. The Indiana University professor shared his wife with his co-workers, bedded his interview subjects, and turned his attic into a pornographic movie studio.[38] Wielding a pocketknife as his instrument of surgery, he circumcised himself for fun. He masturbated with objects inserted into his penis. He leaped off a chair with his testicles tied to a pipe hanging above, suspending himself above the floor by rope.[39] Attached rather than detached, interested rather than disinterested, subjective rather than objective, Alfred Kinsey the perverse propagandist played a scientist for the public. The public bought it.

Kinsey kept his obscene peculiarities off scene. He spotlighted the sexual peculiarities of his fellow countrymen. Doing so made his peculiarities not so peculiar. Kinsey's need to be the sexual maestro, orchestrating relationships and prying out the innermost secrets of colleagues, resembled that of John Humphrey Noyes. Like Noyes, Kinsey kept tabs on the sexual patterns of his colleagues and their wives. Like Noyes, he demanded sexual access and ordered pairings.

At the macro level, Kinsey sought to manipulate the sexual behavior of Americans by manipulating data to show the abnormal as the normal. Kinsey fired the first shots of the sexual revolution in *Sexual Behavior in the Human Male* (1948) and *Sexual Behavior in the Human Female* (1953). But the public had been softened up by the anonymity afforded to millions of soldiers far from home, the racy visuals of movies and magazines, and even the prospect of nuclear annihilation, which for many fostered a carpe diem sexual attitude. The Kinsey Reports announced that most men had premarital and adulterous experiences, more than a third had explored gay sex, and a not insignificant number took away the innocence of an animal.[40] About one in two American women had premarital sex, one in four had sex outside of marriage, and one in eight had lesbian sex to the point of orgasm, Kinsey's studies claimed.[41]

Who could gainsay Kinsey? Individuals, Kinsey foremost among them, weren't interested in making their private lives public. The public, then, could only guess what the typical private life entailed. Or science could tell them.

But was this science? Prison inmates constituted roughly a fifth to a quarter of *Sexual Behavior in the Human Male*'s sample group. Kinsey later related that, among inmates, those experiencing same-sex encounters were the norm. According to his three co-authors, Kinsey gravitated to sex offenders when taking inmates' sexual histories.[42] He skewed his survey even further by deliberately targeting, rather than accumulating them in a random sample, the sexual histories of fellow homosexuals, including aspiring writers William Burroughs and Allen Ginsberg.[43] His play with numbers was so corrupt that he hired a friend to pretend to be the Institute for Sex Research's statistician when the officers of grant-dispensing foundations came around.[44]

Most disturbingly, Kinsey reported that children took pleasure from sex with adults. His source? Pedophiles molesting children. Kinsey's charts detail hundreds of children, one as young as five months old, who attained "definite pleasure" with the help of "scientifically trained observers," who were actually child molesters Kinsey had met in the course of collecting thousands of sexual case histories. Signs of terror—"sobbing," "violent cries," "loss of color," and "tears"—became for Kinsey proof of "orgasm" induced in children by those he dispassionately referred to as "partners."[45] Among the thousands of females he interviewed, Kinsey found just one instance of violent rape of a girl.[46] Venereal disease, Kinsey maintained, was "a relatively unimportant matter" for unmarried people sowing their wild oats.[47] Scarce are mentions of pregnancy, abortion, disease, or any other word that reminds the reader of consequences to sex other than orgasm.

The consequences of sex, as Americans discovered in the coming decades, proved more life-changing and life-ending than indicated by the Kinsey Reports' clinical verbiage. The consequences of sex for the reports' masochistic chief author included a penis without a stretch of skin unpierced, inflamed testicles that required hospitalization, and, in a twist of fate, impotence.[48]

So COWED BY "social science" was America that the U.S. Supreme Court relied on it to decide *Brown v. Board of Education* in 1954. Blacks, so invisible to the surrounding culture that their absence from the initial Kinsey Report bothered almost no one, ironically used social science to help them gain inclusion in the society that so much of social science denounced as superficial, flaccid, conformist, rotten, and rigged. African Americans on the front lines of the civil rights movement knew that there were worse fates than to be *inside* the society post-war intellectuals nitpicked. The Supreme Court's landmark opinion desegregating schools marked the most significant advance in civil rights since Reconstruction. With the subsequent aid of executive enforcement, the judicial branch of government overturned the "separate but equal" doctrine of *Plessy v. Ferguson* and opened schoolhouse doors to all. It also awoke the Left to racism as a great evil to fight against.

The Left's record on race had been mixed. New Harmony banned blacks from membership, unions looked upon people of color as "scabs," progressives touted racist eugenic laws, *Appeal to Reason* saw segregation as part of socialism, and John Reed demeaned African Americans as "coons" and "niggers."[49] Throughout the history of the Left, many individual leftists stood for racial equality and civil rights. But many did not. Several outright racists—Margaret Sanger and Woodrow Wilson, most conspicuously—became heroes to liberals and leftists. Anti-racism was never an article of faith on the Left until the post-war years.

Making the issue even trickier to neatly categorize was the fact that spearheading many of the most effective campaigns against racist public policies were figures not of the Left, not of liberalism, not even of the increasingly left-of-center Democratic Party. Earl Warren, former Republican governor of California, presided over the Supreme Court's historic *Brown v. Board of Education* decision. Republican Dwight Eisenhower signed into law the first civil rights act since Reconstruction. Senate Minority Leader Everett Dirksen provided the crucial push to pass the 1964 Civil Rights Act, and Republicans voted in greater proportions for the bill than did Democrats.[50]

Though civil rights *advances* occurred through the efforts of people of all political persuasions, the civil rights *movement* was primarily the work of political liberals and leftists. Rosa Parks received instruction from the Communist-run Highlander Folk School before refusing to give up her seat on a Montgomery, Alabama, bus on December 1, 1955. The NAACP's founding a half century earlier had been the work of men of the Left, including W. E. B. Du Bois, whose compulsion to out-extremist the next extremist led him from Debsian Socialism to Stalinist Communism. In Martin Luther King Jr.'s words, one hears a touch of Garrisonian non-resistance, a splash of New Deal–variety big-government liberalism, and a large dose of the Social Gospel.

The cautiousness of King and other civil-rights leaders did not mesh with the Left's radical heritage. Rather than allow the Left to piggyback on his movement, King piggybacked on the Left. For example, he rejected placards bearing leftist slogans at the March on Washington but welcomed any leftist, including several former Communists, to serve his cause. In juxtaposition to extremist calls for revolution, King called for non-violence. Instead of overturning society, King wanted inclusion in it. He sought, in the sonorous words of his famous "I have a dream" speech, to cash the check the Founders had awarded to all their progeny. "When the architects of our great republic wrote the magnificent words of the Constitution and the Declaration of Independence," King told hundreds of thousands gathered on the Mall in Washington, "they were signing a promissory note to which every American was to fall heir. This note was a promise that all men, yes, black men as well as white men, would be guaranteed the inalienable rights of life, liberty, and the pursuit of happiness."[51]

The message was quite conservative, even if the messenger was not. Like Terence Powderly, Theodore Roosevelt, and William Jennings Bryan, King sought radical ends through conservative means. King, in this sense, was a more effective "radical" than the actual leftist and black nationalist radicals who decried him. By appealing to the American tradition and to the Bible, and by juxtaposing the violence of his southern white adversaries against his passive resistance, he elicited sympathy and support from the majority in a way that Du Bois, Malcolm X, and other of King's more radical detractors never could.

Had he emerged in the 1850s instead of the 1950s, King's biblically laced rhetoric would have meshed seamlessly with the fabric of the larger Left. But by the mid-twentieth century, the Left had moved away from faith and toward becoming a proxy faith for those in need of something to fill the void. The southern black's godly crusade became for the northern liberal a humanist responsibility. The idea of equality that earlier Lefts had applied to economics, the post-war Left applied to race. It was that—and not the black civil rights movement's reliance on scripture as justification, Negro spirituals as inspiration, churches as headquarters, and ministers as leaders—that appealed to northern liberals. For more than a decade, a golden age of American liberalism, this coalition held, and it served as the catalyst for revolutionary changes to American society, particularly in the American South.

The targets of the early civil rights movement generally consisted of government institutions, such as public schools and city bus lines. Slowly, demands for public equality shifted to mandates on private behavior. Whereas President Truman's 1948 armed services desegregation order, the Supreme Court's 1954 *Brown v. Board of Education* decision, and the 1955–56 Montgomery bus boycott all involved public institutions, the early 1960s brought protests that sought to dictate private choice.

The civil rights movement emanated a decidedly leftist vibe starting with the sit-in at the lunch counter of the Woolworth's in Greensboro, North Carolina. On February 1, 1960, four black students from North Carolina A&T refused to leave the counter until served. They returned the following day with more protestors. In the following weeks, students and activists imitated their tactics across the country at businesses that discriminated on the basis of color. Sick of the disruptions, and in some instances dependent upon black customers, businesses changed their ugly policies. The tactics, which involved disrupting private business for the purpose of dictating how private businesses decided to conduct their private business, worked. Thus, a Freedom Left again drifted into a Force Left, evidence of which became more glaring in the decade that followed.

IT WAS NOT the nobler aspects of American blacks that Norman Mailer found appealing. In his 1957 essay "The White Negro," Mailer declared "that the source of Hip is the Negro." The hipster, he said, steals his music (jazz, rock 'n' roll), language ("dig," "square," "cool," "cat"), and thrills (quick sex, marijuana, senseless crime) from the black. Most importantly, the hipster and the black share outsider status: voluntary for the former, involuntary for the latter. The hipster, therefore, is the White Negro. For the 1950s phenomenon the White Negro, life is governed by "the search for an orgasm more apocalyptic than the one which preceded it." The good for the hipster, Mailer declared, is what feels good.[52] But what made the individual feel good—the catharsis of personalized art, the thrill of smashing a passerby's head, the rush of heroin—made the society bad. Fawning intellectuals who lived apart from the culture didn't seem to intellectualize on this, though.

The White Negro disturbed mainstream culture. So, too, did "The White Negro." Clearly admiring his subject, Mailer struck many readers as adopting, at best, a morally ambiguous tone toward insanity, predatory violence, drug use, indiscriminate sex, and even bad English. Mailer's stance toward the hipster continued a pattern in which the intellectual played pitchman for an underground, often criminal group. For his predecessors, the Wobblies served the purpose; for his successors, it was the Black Panthers. Mailer and other intellectual admirers almost seemed to live vicariously through the White Negro scoring his next high, stealing his next car, and finding his next sexual outlet.

The most famous of the White Negroes were the Beats. As real Negroes fought for entry into American society, faux Negroes passively withdrew from the surrounding nation. Beats and blacks traveled in opposite directions. Blacks missed the dispiriting messages of Paul Goodman, William Whyte, C. Wright Mills, and David Riesman; White Negroes seemed the embodiment of them.

The Beats operated far outside the realm of William Whyte's "organization man," Sloan Wilson's "man in the gray flannel suit," and David Riesman's "other-directed man." Sickly men wearing turtlenecks, goatees, and sunglasses day and night and homely women hiding under dark stockings, darker sweaters, and darkest eyeliner, the Beats, dropout intellectuals who splashed onto the Greenwich Village and San Francisco literary scenes in the early 1950s, hung out in coffee bars, indiscriminately chased highs among males or females, in peyote or marijuana, listened to poetry readings, listened to jazz, listened to poetry set to jazz, snapped instead of clapped, borrowed lingo from urban blacks, worked sporadically, opted for poverty, refused to be anchored down by family obligations, and developed a literary style marked by run-on, stream-of-consciousness sentences.

Amidst a series of incomprehensibilities, one message stood out: *I want to offend you.* This, in itself, contained political implications. The Beats rejected straight society. Overthrow it—its morality, its patriotism, its family structure, its capitalism, its Christianity, its Cold War, its taboos. How? The Beats' chief weapons were writing dirty poetry and having sex with one another, which is to say they neither advanced a coherent strategy nor offered a societal alternative. "We weren't trying to make a social revolution particularly," Allen Ginsberg recalled, "we were just trying to propose our own souls to ourselves."53 Socially alienated and ideologically inarticulate, the Beats represented radicalism of the cultural rather than political variety. They bequeathed no political manifesto to the succeeding generation, only an attitude.

"Writers they might have been," David Halberstam points out, "but in the end their lives tended to be more important than their books."54 Their poetry and prose promoted life against cultural norms. Their lives warned against it.

Ginsberg wrote pornographic verse for a pornographic age, signed up for the North American Man/Boy Love Association, and ingested, injected, and inhaled a variety of mind- and body-altering substances. If ever a face projected the seediness and perversions of the brain behind it, Allen Ginsberg's did. William Burroughs shot and killed his common-law wife during a 1951 dual binge of Mexican boy prostitutes and Mexican hallucinogens. He then abandoned his young son, who, not unpredictably, later drank himself to death. Lucien Carr, the Columbia University student who had brought future Beat luminaries Ginsberg and Burroughs together, killed a homosexual admirer who had expressed his admiration in an aggressive manner. Had novelist Jack Kerouac merely died in an alcoholic haze, no tarnish would have stained his legacy. Alas, he had the naïveté to return to Catholicism, register Republican, and support the Vietnam War. Some fates, for the devotedly alienated, are worse than death. Neal Cassady, Kerouac's "Dean Moriarty" in *On the Road*, did time for car theft and drug dealing. In 1968, he fell into a coma next to a railroad track in Mexico after a night of excessive partying. His short life ended soon thereafter.

Their lives—tragic, sick, misspent—foreshadowed those who followed. Allen Ginsberg's taunt proved prophetic: "We'll get you through your children."[55]

~ 19 ~

THE STUDENT LEFT

And it shall come to pass, in the last days (saith the Lord), I will pour out my Spirit upon all flesh: and your sons and your daughters shall prophesy: and your young men shall see visions: and your old men shall dream dreams.

—ACTS 2:17

"**WE ARE PEOPLE** of this generation, bred in at least modest comfort, housed now in universities, looking uncomfortably to the world we inherit," began the Port Huron Statement, the 1962 manifesto of the Students for a Democratic Society (SDS).[1]

As the 1960s limped into the 1970s, veterans of SDS could, more so than others of their generation, reflect on what a long, strange trip it had been. Launched to marry the activism of students and union workers, the group did more than any other to alienate the two. Preaching nonviolence, SDS ended the decade committed to targeted acts of violence. Even something as basic as its name, *Students* for a *Democratic* Society, became a point of controversy, as the group's decidedly non-student leadership embraced the "democracy" of Kim Il Sung's North Korea, or Fidel Castro's Cuba, or Ho Chi Minh's Vietnam, or Mao Zedong's China, or all of the above.

But in Ann Arbor, Michigan, during the 1950s, where the corpse of the Old Left provided a fertile host for the primordial New Left, activists moved away from dogmatism, cult-of-personality heroes, and ideologies alien to the American experience.

WALKING TO CLASS in the fall of 1954, Robert Alan "Al" Haber stumbled upon a demonstration on the steps of the University of Michigan's Angell

Hall. "So, I diverted. I went over. I wanted to see what it was. And it was some people demonstrating on behalf of three faculty people who had been fired for refusing to sign a loyalty oath." The Ann Arbor native held no brief for Communists. "Marx wasn't on our reading list at University High School," he notes. The homegrown utopian Edward Bellamy, in contrast, influenced him profoundly. "I think my eyes got opened more or less when I read *Looking Backward* toward the end of high school. And I said, 'Wow! The world doesn't have to be this way.'" If Communism seemed too dogmatic and too foreign, anti-Communism appeared bent on destroying the liberties it purported to defend. The issue of the dismissed professors seemed one of injustice, inflamed perhaps for Haber because his father, a onetime radical, served on the school's faculty. "There was no Left," Haber says in his unhurried, low voice. "It was McCarthy time. There was no political organization of any sort on the campus. The Young Democrats, the Young Republicans—that was it. So I joined this demonstration. I met these people, and then I went to hang out with them more and more. They persuaded me to start a political discussion group, the Political Issues Club, which I did."

By 1957, a national political organization in New York showed interest in Haber and his group. The balding and bookish undergraduate didn't much reciprocate, at least initially. Haber's campus group held forums and discussed such issues as state-funded health insurance, public housing, civil rights, and the recent Algerian revolution. Rather than the soon-to-be-defunct *Daily Worker* or the fossilized *Communist Manifesto*, Haber and his new friends read Wilhelm Reich, Norman O. Brown, and C. Wright Mills. Whereas others felt the calm, Haber sensed the storm. "There were things growing, and I was ready to go for it."[2]

WHAT WAS GROWING was a New Left. The name practically conceded the defects of the Left, which, with the advent of the New Left, was rechristened the Old Left. "New Left" ironically had something of the Madison Avenue pitch about it. Like the new-and-improved bubble bursts ubiquitous in the fifties advertising culture that the New Left so caustically derided, the fledgling ideology enticed political consumers who had forsaken an ancient product to give it a fresh look. "I don't know that it appeared to me that anything was ending," Steve Max, then a teenage Marxist, notes. "I thought it was just changing form, which for me is what it did."[3] For most, the repackaging represented more than superficial alterations. Though Marx kept a place at the Left's table, Paul Goodman, Herbert Marcuse, David Riesman, Theodor Adorno, and other thinkers who rejected or readjusted Marx grabbed seats as well. The activist group that best represented this New Left thinking was SDS.

SDS traced its lineage to the Intercollegiate Socialist Society that Jack London, Upton Sinclair, and others had founded during the progressive era, and that became the League for Industrial Democracy (LID) once the word "socialist" fell from grace after the First World War. Despite starting out as a student group itself, LID felt compelled to unleash a student off-shoot, the Student League for Industrial Democracy (SLID), in 1930. SLID had had an uneventful history since its founding, save, crucially, for a brief, defiant split with its parent organization during the popular-front craze of the 1930s. SLID allied with Communists and dumped its benefactor.[4] The bitter experience scarred LID leaders. They were too old to forget, their SDS inheritors too young to remember.

At Al Haber's insistence, SLID became Students for a Democratic Society on the eve of the 1960s. "Probably 'industrial democracy' didn't really appeal to me as a sexy name," a smiling Haber recalls. "But also, S-L-I-D was just too descriptive of 'slid,' *it slid.*" So lowly was the group's reputation that Haber refused to affiliate his student group with LID even after he accepted a leadership position within SLID/SDS. As a suspicious Haber viewed LID, "They were a lot of old people."[5] Tom Hayden, recruited from student journalism to student activism by Haber, viewed the "virtually dormant" SLID as having "seen better days."[6] By 1961, the cerebral Haber and the energetic Hayden became SDS's only employees, the former manning the New York office and the latter performing field work.

The manifesto that the wordsmith Hayden helped craft, and the events of the final seven years of SDS's existence that he helped catalyze, compensated for the organization's prior sleepy ineffectiveness. Mimeographed at more than sixty single-spaced pages, the wordy Port Huron Statement, down to its occasional vagueness, unchecked passion, and salaams to the trendy, more closely approached a declaration of attitudes for the New Left than any other document. Its main idea, "participatory democracy," an imprecise phrase imagined by Todd Gitlin, an impressed reader who succeeded Hayden as SDS president, as perhaps meaning "a society that's just churning with political energy and involvement," animated the document's creation down to the initial call for ideas, the multiple drafters, and the votes on revisions.[7] Demand compelled numerous printings, which churned out tens of thousands of copies within a few years.[8]

The Port Huron Statement reflected the milieu from which the Left had just emerged. It called for the United States to defer to the United Nations on dispersing foreign aid and administering American schools even as it demanded U.S. unilateralism in disarmament to "undermin[e] the Russian argument for tighter controls in East Europe." The Port Huron Statement demanded socialized medicine, ridiculed the "rigged needs of maneuvered citizenry," and questioned whether the tranquility of America resulted from "approval by consent or manipulated acquiescence."

The manifesto's significance, however, rested not upon the thousand ways in which it reflected the waning Left but upon the few ways in which it anticipated the rising Left. It unambiguously deemed the Soviet Union a failure at the same time it doubted any threat from the Communist bloc. It criticized organized labor for losing its idealism. It advocated that prisons "be either re-oriented to rehabilitative work through public supervision or be abolished for their dehumanizing social effects." It placed racial inequality on the same plane of injustice as economic inequality. It identified students as agents of the coming change. It prophetically called for a realignment of the political parties into liberal and conservative entities, necessarily expunging southern Democrats, for instance, from their ancestral party.[9] The document presciently outlined—or, alternatively, profoundly influenced—the separation of New Left from Old.

The forty-three delegates to the Port Huron convention had the nerve to challenge Cold War taboos and reprove unions on the dime of the League for Industrial Democracy, at a retreat called FDR Camp, which was owned by the United Auto Workers. The action weighed heavy with symbolism. It wasn't one Left passing the torch to another; it was a clique of upstarts extinguishing the fading torch of their forerunners.

The course charted by the Port Huron Statement displeased those stubbornly trudging along the path blazed by a Left gone by. The socialist activist and writer Michael Harrington had observed developments at Port Huron and tried to bully the younger delegates into abandoning the document's New Left, pox-upon-both-your-houses sensibility. Ironically, Harrington had played the role of upstart a decade earlier. As an activist in the Young People's Socialist League, he led its disaffiliation from the Socialist Party after the latter had disciplined the former for its ties with the Trotskyite sect of Max Shachtman.[10] But with age didn't come empathy, and Harrington scourged others for the sins he had made. With youth didn't come the wisdom of experience, and the SDSers rebuffed the guidance of elders.

For the SDS activists who *had* admired *The Other America* author, Tom Hayden recalled in his autobiography, "Mike Harrington was transformed in our minds from an important role model to a negative one."[11] Ironically, red-diaper baby Dick Flacks tempered the strident language of home-grown radical Hayden in censuring the United States for its role in the Cold War. But Harrington was unaware and LID unimpressed. SDS's parent organization grounded its dependent. It removed SDS employees Haber and Hayden from the payroll. It seized the membership lists. It locked Haber out of his New York office. Finally, a coterie of grand old men of the Left, led by Socialist Party mahatma Norman Thomas, who had chided Harrington for injecting anti-democratic elements into a youth organization of the democratic Left the previous decade, stepped in to heal the fissure between SDS and LID.[12]

The internecine conflict foreshadowed. The 1960s were to be a time of Left versus Left, Left versus liberal, but rarely Left versus Right—at least until the decade had passed into history, when it became almost entirely that. The Left's battles were generally within the family and generational. A fast-moving decade, when a few short years demarcated one generation from the next, made today's insurrectionists tomorrow's guardians. The acquired truths of elders became the stale pieties to rebel against. The rebels became the elders unless they unlearned lessons and perpetually sided with the leftward thrust of youth. And even then, the decade's credo—"Don't trust anyone over thirty"—made this a dubious pathway toward a fountain of youth. "Whether to the crimes of communism described in Orwell or Kafka, or to Camus's injunction that heinous acts could be rationalized by cultivated intellectuals, or to the repeated warnings that revolutionary leaders become ruling Frankenstein's monsters," Hayden explained, "I reacted with one feeling: These horrors won't happen to us; we are too good."[13]

THE NEW LEFT was a product of its times. The civil rights crusade, the Great Society's anti-poverty campaign, and the Vietnam War shaped the New Left. Unaffected by the privations and sacrifices of the preceding generation, the activists who came of age in the 1960s more often than not enjoyed childhoods of suburban affluence, television, and rock 'n' roll. They had what their parents had not, and still they wanted more. Spoiled at home, the baby boomers who succeeded the first-wave activists of the 1960s threw collective tantrums, demanding a society that catered to their whims. As the largest generation the nation had known, the baby boomers' sheer numbers often ensured that they got what they wanted.

The new direction of the student Left represented in part a rejection of the Old Left, but it was also recognition that passé issues had become an albatross dragging the fledgling Left down. "From its beginnings," David

Horowitz writes, "the New Left was not an innocent experiment in American utopianism, but a self-conscious effort to rescue the Communist project from its Soviet fate."[14] Horowitz, who abjured an Old Left childhood to edit the influential New Left magazine *Ramparts* and author such sixties tomes as *Student* and *New World Colossus*, finds support for his theory in the backgrounds of the SDS leaders, whose upbringings frequently resembled his own.

The actual father of SDS father Al Haber had been in SLID years before he joined the faculty of the University of Michigan. Haber's father, like his mother, was a socialist. Then he instituted substantial change working for Wisconsin governor Philip La Follette, whose more famous father's first name became Robert Alan Haber's first name. Franklin Roosevelt noticed Wisconsin's pension plan for the aged, and the elder Haber, a graduate student who studied under the University of Wisconsin's John R. Commons, helped craft nationwide Social Security. "His inclination was to work in the system," Haber recalls of his Romanian immigrant father. "And I was always on the outside. That was what our discussion was about."[15]

Dick Flacks watched his Communist parents get fired from the New York City public school system. Familial initiation sent Flacks to Communist summer camps, including Wo-Chi-Ca (the Indian-sounding word that proved to be yet another Communist acronym, in this case meaning "Workers Children's Camp"), and to the nation's capital to protest the execution of the Rosenbergs: "There was a big rally on their behalf in a stadium in New York in Randall's Island, and I remember going to that. And I remember going to the White House, picketing the White House on behalf of the Rosenbergs."[16]

Steve Max, the SDS field secretary from 1962 to 1964, encountered Flacks and Flacks's future wife, fellow SDS activist Mickey, while working at Kinderland, a camp that catered to red-diaper babies. He was schooled at Elisabeth Irwin High School in Greenwich Village, attended by the sons and daughters of the Communist Party elite, and his father served as the managing editor of the *Daily Worker*.[17] Rather than rebelling against the lives of their parents, many SDSers repeated them.

Midwestern, Catholic, and middle-class, Tom Hayden differed from his colleagues. Though he did not share the politicized youth of his activist peers, clues suggesting his future political orientation and temperament line his childhood. Hayden's grandfather, for instance, had died in an industrial accident. Also, young Tom took communion, and for eight years classroom instruction, at the Shrine of the Little Flower—the parish overseen by Father Charles Coughlin, the radio priest who had turned against and then tormented FDR from his Left. At the University of Michigan,

Hayden edited the *Michigan Daily*. The skills he exhibited brought him into SDS. His activism estranged him from his parents, whose divorce when Tom was a boy, and his father's alcoholism, seemed to provide an edge to the activist Hayden. Neither parent was present, for instance, when Hayden married his SDS sweetheart, Sandra Cason. Partnering with his father in a silent feud that lasted more than a decade, Tom was alienated from his parents in the way that so many in the 1960s generation were.[18]

AT THE INSTIGATION of fellow University of Michigan SDSers Dick and Mickey Flacks, Hayden read C. Wright Mills. He got hooked. A red-white-and-blue radical like Hayden, Mills breathed his spirit through the Port Huron Statement and later served as the subject of Hayden's master's thesis.

Two years before his untimely 1962 passing, Mills penned "A Letter to the New Left," which argued for the intellectual to replace the worker as the catalyst for revolution. Large segments on the Left had grown frustrated over the working class's refusal to adhere to the roles Marx had awarded them, but for Mills too many still insisted that the workers would be the instruments of historic change. "[W]hat I do not quite understand about some New Left writers is why they cling so mightily to 'the working class' of the advanced capitalist societies as *the* historic agency, or even as the most important agency, in the face of the really impressive historical evidence that now stands against this expectation," Mills wrote. "Such a labor metaphysic, I think, is a legacy from Victorian Marxism that is now quite unrealistic."[19]

Like Marcuse, Mills set a new course for the Left away from the workers and away from revolution as necessarily violent. The motorcycling sociologist's rebelliousness was not so great that he dispensed with Marx's model. Mills still believed in agents of change—rhetorically separated groups whose differences and disadvantages (real and imagined) must be heightened to foment revolt. He just didn't believe in Marx's choice, at least for America—an ocean and 112 years removed from *The Communist Manifesto*. That Mills volunteered intellectuals as the agents of change was not as significant as the sociologist's recognition that some new agent (students? blacks? women?) needed to replace the worker.

Students embraced their self-assigned role as agents of change. In spite of the Marxist prophecy, workers had shirked their responsibility. If Marx had been wrong about workers, could he have been wrong about emphasizing class, too? For student revolutionaries, race more often than not replaced class as the issue upon which they would take their stand . . . in Dixie.

.   .   .

"THIS ONE HERE is a nigger lover, boys," Tom Hayden's jailer told the in-mates in the lock-up in Albany, Georgia. "Take good care of him for us." An attempt to integrate the city's train station in 1961, in compliance with a Supreme Court decision and an Interstate Commerce Commission order, landed the Michigander in jail on his twenty-second birthday. Sit-ting on the "Negro" side of the courtroom sparked a courthouse melee and ended his trial before it could begin.[20]

Hayden had gone south to Albany, Georgia, and McComb, Mississippi, to work with the Student Nonviolent Coordinating Committee (SNCC). Getting jailed, beaten, and otherwise abused radicalized blacks such as rising SNCC leader Stokely Carmichael just as it radicalized whites such as Hayden. Like SDS, SNCC soon challenged the very assumptions it was founded upon. By 1966, SNCC banned whites from its organization and openly advocated violence. Carmichael traded the labels "colored" and "Negro" for "black." He popularized the catchphrase "black power," and SNCC adopted a Black Panther as its symbol. Carmichael embraced a street-fashion sensibility: black leather coat, black sunglasses, and a nat-ural "Afro" hairdo. Blacks from the urban underclass, including Oakland-ers Huey Newton and Bobby Seale, who couldn't relate to the preachers and academics remonstrating for freedom and rights on their behalf, began to see themselves in Carmichael.

It is easy to see how young people fighting old prejudices could develop a sense of self-righteousness. The moral certainty that came from civil rights work intruded upon other issues that were not as clear-cut. Every leftist enemy became a Bull Connor; every leftist cause, the next March on Washington; every leftist activist imagined himself a martyred Michael Schwerner, Andrew Goodman, or James Chaney. Though a whirlwind of civil rights legislation and executive orders, as well as a seismic shift in public opinion, accompanied the agitation of activists such as Hayden, the strange lesson that many activists drew from the South was that the system did not work and could not be fixed. Thus democrats became authoritari-ans. Thus reformers became revolutionaries. The system responded to their activism, but activists did not believe it responded fast enough. If the Left knew what was right, then why wait for the masses to catch up?

THAT UNCOMPROMISING SPIRIT manifested itself in campus disputes between students and administrators. When no real dispute existed, ac-tivists invented one. Activism became an end in itself. Once means be-came ends, no capitulation could satisfy.

In 1964, fresh from the civil rights movement's "Freedom Summer" in

Mississippi, Berkeley sophomore Mario Savio pronounced, "There's a time when the operation of the machine becomes so odious, makes you so sick at heart, that you can't take part, you can't even passively take part. And you've got to put your bodies upon the gears, and upon the wheels, upon the leavers, upon all the apparatus, and you've got to make it stop."[21] He was speaking not of lynchings or disenfranchisement, but of a university blocking outside groups from promoting politics on its property.

Berkeley's so-called Free Speech Movement borrowed more than rhetoric from the civil rights movement. Its participants, mainly students from well-to-do families, viewed themselves as one of America's subjugated groups holding the potential to uproot the society. "Somewhere in the process of the FSM, for the very first time, the young, privileged, affluent children of the culture began to see themselves as an oppressed class," noted participant Michael Rossman.[22] On December 2, 1964, more than a thousand people, singing "We Shall Overcome," invaded the university's administrative building, Sproul Hall, and staged a sit-in, a tactic used effectively in the South to integrate lunch counters and bus stations. They put their bodies upon the wheels. The police arrested eight hundred Sproul Hall invaders, roughly three-quarters of whom were Berkeley students.[23]

The police hauled activist Joe Blum, along with most of the thrall, to Santa Rita, a local minimum-security prison. "Hey, Joe!" a high-pitched voice yelled from the prison yard. "How many of you motherfuckers are coming out here?"[24] Blum recognized the man as a former classmate at a local community college. The inmate, serving time for a knife attack on a fellow ghetto denizen, was Huey Newton, a street intellectual and career criminal who would shortly become an icon to the upper-class white students pouring into Santa Rita for a novelty stay. But in 1964, the Berkeley campus and the Oakland ghetto, separated by a few miles on the map, might as well have been on opposite sides of the globe.

Just as Berkeley, California, wasn't Oakland, California, it wasn't Philadelphia, Mississippi, either. The faculty voted by a seven-to-one ratio to absolve the Free Speech Movement leaders and the eight hundred arrested demonstrators of any wrongdoing. Though legal and disciplinary issues persisted, the administration acquiesced to the Free Speech Movement's more reasonable demands.[25]

More unreasonable ones were forthcoming. The following semester, John Thompson, an artsy stoner who had gravitated West in search of a good time, held aloft a sign bearing his one-word poem: "Fuck." Art begets art. Thompson's epigram immediately inspired another terse verse, this one entitled "Shit," and shortly thereafter inspired a play,

"For Unlawful Carnal Knowledge." A "Fuck Defense Fund" came to Thompson's aid. The so-serious activists of the Free Speech Movement were split as to whether the latitudinarians of the Filthy Speech Movement ridiculed them in making farce of their cause or honored them by extending its logic.[26]

The Free Speech Movement meandering into the Filthy Speech Movement adumbrated two important sixties trends: first, the uneasy intersection of tribes, in this case jocular hippies and stern ideologues, who, however much they merged in the public's mind, nevertheless remained separate; second, organizers who set out to make the next demonstration more outrageous than the last. The template sketched at Berkeley made its way to hundreds of campuses.

AT THE VERY moment that a student protest culture percolated, SDS sent its ablest leaders off campus and into the ghetto. After taking on institutionalized discrimination in the South, Tom Hayden and other secular missionaries in SDS went north to tackle poverty. For Hayden, SDS's Economic Research and Action Project (ERAP) was about "trying to create a northern branch off the root of SNCC community organizing in the South."[27] Inspired by SNCC's example of community organizing, and certain of a looming economic catastrophe, SDS sought to organize an interracial movement of the poor before the second Great Depression hit. To that end the organization started its Economic Research and Action Project (ERAP).

Was ERAP to be a "research" or an "action" project? "Al wanted ERAP to be a publishing company, basically," Todd Gitlin explains. "Tom wanted to get on the streets." This Haber-Hayden debate, in which Hayden prevailed, prefaced the action-versus-organizing argument that radicals debated, particularly within SDS, in increasing volume and pitch as the decade perdured. "It was always a tension in the organization between being a brains trust for the movement and being an action arm of the movement."[28]

ERAP anticipated War on Poverty social programs by instigating underclass demands for government resources, as Legal Services, Volunteers in Service to America, and the Community Action Agencies later did. "The ERAP spirit was one of voluntary poverty and simple living," Hayden recalled. "We believed you could not organize poor people without living on their economic level in their neighborhood."[29] Thus white, upperclass students crammed into small, dingy houses and apartments in sketchy neighborhoods. Traffic lights, rat control, and pothole maintenance were among their "revolutionary" demands to city hall.

ERAP volunteers didn't distribute charity. They organized the poor to demand government monies as a right. They agitated. They collected petitions. They stacked public meetings. They held protests.

The slumming rich found most ghetto dwellers indifferent, if not hostile, to their missionary pretensions. "They were attracted to this because of their desire to be do-gooders," Dick Flacks, who helped out with ERAP's Chicago Jobs or Income Now (JOIN) venture, recollects of some volunteers. "When they got there, there was not a great deal of training that was given to people. All of this was done in a very ad hoc way. I think one could say if you went to the JOIN house in uptown at any given day there would be quite a number of people in the apartment and not in the street. I do think in retrospect that some of the people once they got there were pretty scared about actually going out and organizing."[30]

"By the end of the summer of 1965," a sympathetic historian conceded, "ERAP had proven itself to be a failure."[31] Projects continued on a city-to-city basis, as Tom Hayden's work in Newark, New Jersey, did for several years, but as a national SDS-sponsored endeavor, ERAP was through. The failure of the project became perfectly clear in the summer of 1967, when Newark, Hayden's base of operations, erupted in riots. Newark's five days of urban mayhem left twenty-six dead, a thousand injured, and millions of dollars in property damage. Watts, Detroit, southeast Washington, D.C., and scores of other locales experienced similar scenes in the mid-1960s. A pattern emerged: bypassing the political system with violence as the default way to redress grievances.

"ERAP was never able to escape the fact that the poor are not 'the agents of change' in American society, whether there be massive unemployment or not," writer/activist Kirkpatrick Sale concluded in his study of SDS. "The poor, as the ERAPers found out to their sorrow, want leaders, they do not want to lead; the poor are myth-ridden, enervated, cynical, and historically the least likely to rebel; the poor are powerless, without even that small threat of being able to withdraw their bodies that workingmen and labor unions have, and at best they can only embarrass or discomfort, not threaten, the powers that be."[32]

IGNORANCE OF PAST Lefts meant repeating the mistakes of past Lefts. Exaggerating the universal fault of their amnesiac predecessors, the New Left imagined itself radical pioneers, discovering a New World of ideas that had eluded all who had lived until the present. "We were making a chapter of history no one had predicted," Hayden reflected. "In formulating our vision and ideas, therefore, it was most important to draw lessons from that same experience instead of relying on the textbooks of others."[33]

If it didn't happen to them it had never happened before. But it had all happened before.

The New Left's innocence was at once its greatest strength and its Achilles' heel. The somnolence of 1950s activism allowed 1960s activists to start afresh. They need not be tethered to the Kremlin, to the adversaries of the Kremlin, or to the union laborers that both the Communist and anti-Communist Left looked upon as blue-collar redeemers. The New Left bypassed workers for blacks, students, the lumpenproletariat, pacifists, and, eventually, feminists, sexual radicals, environmentalists, and other cause-oriented groups. This invigorated the issues and aroused new supporters. Hence sprang to life another Left, the New Left.

The downside of discarding past road maps became evident as the 1960s wore on. The advice of elders was easily ignored on the grounds that the counsel of failures wasn't worth following. "We of the fifties Left were simply too weak to serve as a point of departure for the New Left of the sixties," Michael Harrington opined. "We were pathetically few in number, the veterans of a beleaguered holding operation. Their Christopher Columbus vision of themselves as the first to discover the truths of radicalism was, alas, a most logical deduction from their own experience and our failures."[34] Thus, Harrington's "iceberg ahead" warnings about the hazards of joining hands with Communists were ignored by twentysomethings who had not yet experienced disciplined Communists exploiting the hospitality and good faith of liberal and leftist organizers. And personal experience, rather than recorded history, was the preferred learning tool for people who believed themselves the first at everything.

SDS, and the New Left it represented, not only hit icebergs, but hit the same icebergs that their brushed-off antecedents had struck. The mass movement that Haber and Hayden had created turned on its creators. Just as the pair had viewed the LID octogenarians and Michael Harrington as irrelevant to their current experience, Haber and Hayden's SDS scions viewed them the same way by decade's end. Hayden, because of his flirtations with the system, and in spite of his willingness to out-radical the radicals, was dubbed a sellout and an opportunist. In 1969, Al Haber became one of the LID old men of whom he had felt leery ten years earlier. At a 1969 United Front Against Fascism conference in Oakland, the father of SDS had the temerity to speak out for a white speaker denied the podium by a deliberate filibuster campaign of Herb Aptheker, one of those Old Left, Communist retreads who, in the bizarre turnabout of the New Left's climactic years, had returned to fashion. Haber and other outraged attendees stood up and shouted, "Let the woman speak! Enough already!"

Haber remembers: "The security comes—the Black Panthers and [SDS leader] Jeff Jones, who are standing guard in their gear around the door—come and physically push us down. That was my end of it. This was United Front of Fascism, not Against Fascism. It just turned so sour . . . I didn't exactly say 'I quit,' [but] this was totally a wrong and crazy direction, and it didn't seem anymore like it had anything to do with SDS."[35]

But Haber and Hayden had unwittingly sent SDS in this cannibalistic direction. The pair, who had done so much to sever the New Left from its Old Left remora, nevertheless ensured that the separation would be neither complete nor permanent.

In 1962, SDS had outraged LID by allowing a representative from the Communist Party's Du Bois Clubs to attend the Port Huron conference and by pointing to a moral equivalence between the United States and the Soviet Union.[36] Three years later, SDS broke permanently from LID. Ignoring warnings from the *New Republic* and others who knew firsthand the dangers of teaming up with Communists, SDS formally opened its membership to the bane of the Old Left.[37] By 1969, SDS leaders were promising to "never tolerate anti-communism in our movement."[38] Communists devoted to Chairman Mao captured the organization from Communists devoted to Ho Chi Minh. The former drove the organization into obscurity and the latter embarked on a bombing campaign. The Revolutionary Youth Movement factionalized SDS, and then the Revolutionary Youth Movement II broke away from the Revolutionary Youth Movement, and then the Revolutionary Youth Movement III broke away from the Revolutionary Youth Movement II.[39]

From the radical heaven, Karl Sorge smiled at the "vanguard" wresting democracy from the demos, Daniel De Leon bellowed an "amen" upon the splitters, Alexander Berkman beamed at the sight of violence, and Julius Rosenberg gave blessings upon the termites boring from within the SDS structure that the carpenter Al Haber had erected.

Everything new became old again.

∾ 20 ∾

THE PATERNALIST DYNASTY IV: GREAT SOCIETY VISIONARIES

For if the will be forward, it is accepted according to that which a man hath: not according to that which he hath not. For I mean not that others should be eased and you burthened, but by an equality. In this present time let your abundance supply their want, that their abundance also may supply your want: that there may be an equality. As it is written: He that had much had nothing over; and he that had little had no want.

—2 CORINTHIANS 8:12–15

"LIVING OUT IN the suburbs, it is easy to assume that ours is, indeed, an affluent society," Michael Harrington explained in *The Other America*.[1] But the midcentury population shift from the cities to the suburbs had merely hidden poverty from increasing numbers of Americans. In the Cold War, this inequality served as a propaganda club for America's enemies, who promised a world of equality. Cold War liberals could at once undermine the propaganda of their Russian foes and help the little man in America. Glacially, the policy implications of Harrington's 1962 polemic drifted into the imaginations of liberal policy makers.

Poverty in the richest nation in history, the best seller conceded, was not poverty in the traditional sense. America's poor were "sometimes fat with hunger." "America has the best-dressed poverty the world has ever known."[2] These paradoxes, like the surrounding riches, worked to conceal American poverty. The author taught his readers to discard their senses.

Michael Harrington chose poverty. Raised in affluence in Depression-era St. Louis, the lace-curtain-Irish Harrington had seen poverty with his eyes but had not felt it in his stomach. By joining Dorothy Day's Catholic Worker movement in 1951, the twenty-three-year-old Harrington opted for indigence to aid the indigent. Harrington gave his labor to Day's Bowery-based House of Hospitality for free as he collected meager checks as a soda jerk, as a machinist, and on unemployment.3 After two years among the destitute, Harrington emerged certain in his socialism and uncertain in his Catholicism. "I would become an atheist fellow traveler of moderate Catholicism," he later confessed.4

Harrington's observations on skid row and experiences in self-induced poverty qualified him to pen a series of articles on the poor in the late 1950s. In their use of social science for a political purpose, the articles owed something to the decade in which they were written. The book they became, 1962's *The Other America*, foreshadowed a more naked politicization that characterized the 1960s. In viewing himself "a comrade in the struggle" rather than "an objective academician," the socialist Harrington, aside from studiously avoiding the word "socialism" in the text, did not try very hard to appear detached.5 He wanted, even if he did not expect, to spark public policy changes, not mere theoretical discourse.

"Disease, alcoholism, [and] low IQ's," Harrington argued in *The Other America*, were, "in the main, the effects of an environment, not the biographies of unlucky individuals. . . . If there is to be a lasting assault on the shame of the other America, it must seek to root out of this society an entire environment, and not just the relief of individuals."6 For Harrington, as for Robert Owen, the environment made the man; the man did not make his environment. Change the environment, therefore, and change the man. In disparaging temporary relief, Harrington implied a program more ambitious and permanent than the New Deal.

The Other America posited, "It is one of the terrible ironies of political life in America that there are social problems that could be dealt with, where the basic research has been done and the techniques of solution demonstrated, but where there is no political force strong enough to enforce progress."7 The solutions he had in mind came from the brains of social scientists rather than the collected experience of mankind. Applying the ideas of the best university researchers to the lives of society's worst dregs would bring progress, he maintained.

In this Harrington shared the assumptions of his fellow leftists. Like their New Deal and Progressive forebears, liberals of the 1960s believed that science could be applied to society as easily as it could be applied in the laboratory. They put faith in committees of academics and learned men that they labeled "task forces," and then implemented the plans the experts had hatched to end poverty.

For Harrington, only one force was great enough to solve the great problems he had outlined. "There is literally no alternative but government intervention." "[O]ne agency in America is capable of eradicating both the slum and slum psychology from this land: the Federal Government." "[O]nly the Federal Government has the power to abolish poverty."[8] It was a blunt message for blunt minds.

LYNDON JOHNSON HEARD Michael Harrington's call, even if he never read his book. Following the practice of liberal presidents of the twentieth century, Johnson came up with an all-encompassing Madison Avenue–style catchphrase for his legislative program: the Great Society. The words evoked a utopian quality. If the most prosperous society man had ever known, which shared its bounty and refused to succumb to the imperial temptation, wasn't truly a "great society," then what was? And how could President Johnson make America a "great society"? The outline of the Great Society was as vague as the directions to it.

The Great Society's lineage, tracing back through the New Deal, the Progressives, and the Populists, was Lyndon Johnson's lineage. Johnson's grandfather had bucked the Democrats for the fledgling People's Party in the 1890s. His doting mother had signed up for temperance organizations urging the prohibition of alcohol. His father had won election to the Texas state legislature in 1904 and gained "the reputation of a loyal progressive," a Johnson biographer notes, "supporting bills to tax insurance, telephone, and sleeping car companies; to regulate rates charged by public utility companies (water, gas, electric power); to enact a franchise tax on corporations; to establish the eight-hour workday; and to regulate lobbying." Lyndon Johnson himself came to Washington as a legislative aide during the Great Depression, striking a deal with the doorkeeper of the Senate chamber to alert him whenever Huey Long readied to speak. In 1935, Johnson returned to Texas as the youngest state director of FDR's National Youth Administration. The next year, with the help of his presidential benefactor, he became a congressman. In the House of Representatives, the west Texan earned a reputation as a New Deal stalwart.[9]

From congressman to senator, from senator to majority leader, from majority leader to vice president, Lyndon Johnson had scraped by means fair and foul for every office he had ever held. He became president through the act of a Communist assassin. "Everything I had ever learned in the history books taught me that martyrs have to die for causes," LBJ later recalled. "John Kennedy had died. But his 'cause' was not really clear. That was my job. I had to take the dead man's program and turn it into a martyr's cause. That way Kennedy would live on forever and so would

I."[10] John Kennedy's unknown "cause" became Lyndon Johnson's Great Society.

"This administration, today, here and now, declares unconditional war on poverty in America," President Johnson told Congress in his 1964 State of the Union address. "Our aim is not only to relieve the symptom of poverty, but to cure it and, above all, to prevent it." Johnson promised to do this while cutting federal expenditures and tax rates.[11] He didn't mention expanding the war in Vietnam, but atop the loftiness of his already stated goals, that may have seemed superfluous. Lyndon Johnson could have promised the moon and his listeners would have believed him.

Issued less than two months after Kennedy's assassination, Lyndon Johnson's declaration of war on poverty was every bit as ambitious as Franklin Roosevelt's New Deal and even more enduring. Franklin Roosevelt provided Johnson with his faith in government and hackneyed war analogies to boot. John Kennedy provided him with the political clout to get the job done. The national goodwill in the wake of President Kennedy's assassination, the lopsided Democratic majority following the 1964 elections, and President Johnson's unmatched talent for cajoling legislators made for a perfect political storm that filled the Great Society's sails. Nearly everything Johnson wanted he got.

MICHAEL HARRINGTON, OBLIVIOUS to the paperback success of *The Other America* while spending 1963 in Europe, was summoned to Washington by Johnson aide (and Kennedy in-law) Sargent Shriver just weeks after returning from abroad. Harrington remembered it as "very heady and exciting to be arguing with Cabinet officers and indirectly presenting memos to the President." But being a socialist working for a capitalist government proved "a difficult emotional issue."[12] Adam Yarmolinsky, an administration planner of the war on poverty, recalled Harrington as unprepared to offer solutions to the problems he had outlined.[13] But other action-minded intellectuals eagerly imagined a multitude of solutions to any given problem. And so many solutions, perhaps, was a problem itself. The Great Society suffered from an abundance of ideas but a scarcity of experience. What Johnson endeavored to do had never been done before.

The Great Society was a hydra whose unifying theme, ostensibly, was to give advantage to the disadvantaged. Jobs, education, civil rights, medical care, housing, food, child care, and direct payments were among the gifts Lyndon Johnson rained upon his countrymen. The minority constituencies they aided—the poor, senior citizens, students, blacks—together made a majority. President Johnson handed out dollars and expected the welfare recipients to pay the Democrats back with ballots. Did the Democrats reward their most loyal constituents with benefits? Or did the beneficiaries reward the Democrats by becoming their most loyal constituents? Either way, the Great Society, like its New Deal antecedent, reeked of patronage.

The Office of Economic Opportunity (OEO), displaying partisan favoritism reminiscent of Roosevelt's Works Progress Administration, underwrote leftist activism and Democratic Party patronage. Under its umbrella, tax-funded programs lobbied the government for more funds. Legal Services provided the poor with activist lawyers itching to sue the government for more services. Volunteers in Service to America (VISTA) acted as a domestic Peace Corps, sending well-to-do young people into the urban jungle to perform missionary work in a manner not dissimilar to Jane Addams's Hull House recruits, SDS's ERAP, or Harrington's work within the Catholic Worker movement.

The OEO's Jobs Corps, reminiscent of the New Deal's Civilian Conservation Corps, promised good jobs to poor high school dropouts after government training. Alas, this second round of government schooling could not deliver what the first round did not. "It was simply unrealistic to expect any educational institution to take young men and women as culturally handicapped as Job Corps recruits and train them for really good jobs," argued historian Allen Matusow. At best, the government could train them in basic blue-collar fields in which employers already had an abundance of qualified job seekers.[14] Yet the government tried, and critics jeered that the federal costs per enlistee rivaled the costs of annual attendance at Ivy League schools.[15]

Johnson's budget director warned in 1965: *"We ought not to be in the business of organizing the poor politically."*[16] But that was the distasteful business the Great Society was in.

Most egregious of the OEO programs was the political skullduggery of the Community Action Program (CAP), which spread money to urban political machines and left-wing non-profits it designated as Community Action Agencies (CAA). In Syracuse, New York, where a Republican happened to be mayor, the Johnson administration brushed aside local government as the distributor of the aid. The unelected radicals to whom they dispersed the money enlisted the services of Saul Alinsky, the professional disrupter who later authored the handbook *Rules for Radicals.* Alinsky received $10,000 in federal money to travel to Syracuse for a series of lectures in which he taught local activists how to raise hell on the public's dime.[17] When the police arrested the protesting welfare mothers whom the tax-funded activists had organized, the radicals used federal tax dollars to bail them out. Aghast at a GOP-led city government, they used federal funds to conduct a voter registration drive.[18]

In San Francisco, the national director of the Congress of Racial Equality steered hundreds of thousands of dollars in federal grants toward racist "black power" groups. Charles Sizemore of the San Francisco State University Black Student Union got his hands on CAA grants, which he distributed to local hoodlums, who in turn intimidated officials distributing the grants. The group hosted lectures by black radicals, including Bobby Seale, who told the kids that stealing from whites was a political act. On a field trip, some of the students did just that.[19] A New York City CAA doled out tens of thousands of dollars to poet LeRoi Jones, who had yet to reinvent himself under the Afrocentric nom de plume Amiri Baraka. Jones staged anti-white and Marxist-themed plays on the streets of Harlem with his federal subsidy.[20]

Black Panthers Bobby Seale and Huey Newton, SDS leaders Paul Potter and Tom Hayden, Weathermen Bill Ayers and Diana Oughton, and SNCC radicals Frank Smith and Tom Levin all sipped from the Great Society trough.[21] The gratitude that President Johnson expected from such beneficence did not manifest itself. In fact, the more the Great Society funded the Left, the more critical the Left became of Johnson and his Great Society. From pledging to go "half of the way with LBJ" in 1964, student radicals four years later could be seen sporting buttons that read "Lee Harvey Oswald—Where Are You Now That We Need You?"[22]

"I HAVE NEVER believed that those who are governed least are governed best," reflected Lyndon Johnson after his tenure in office.[23] Anyone paying attention from November 1963 through January 1969 knows the reflection to be a redundancy. In those few years, Johnson spearheaded the addition of two new departments to the federal bureaucracy (Transportation, Housing and Urban Development), the injection of the federal government in education, the creation of massive entitlement programs, the escalation of an expensive war halfway around the planet, and the introduction of a gargantuan civil rights bureaucracy. Washington, D.C., would never be the same.

The whirlwind of legislation was especially intense following Johnson's landslide victory over Barry Goldwater in the 1964 presidential election. Historian Irwin Unger writes in *The Best of Intentions*:

Between January 4 and October 23, 1965, Congress put together one of the most impressive legislative records in history. The administration submitted eighty-seven bills to Congress and Johnson signed eighty-four, for a batting average of .960. Two of these measures—national health insurance for retirees and the poor and the first-ever general federal-aid-to-education law—were historic landmarks of the social welfare state. But several others—the higher education bill, the revision of the immigration laws, highway beautification, the National Foundation for the Arts and Humanities . . . a new department of housing and urban development—were major pieces of legislation in their own right.[24]

The centerpiece of the newly elected president's ambitious legislative program was Medicare. "Please try to pass Medicare for us old folks," a woman wrote to President Johnson from Brownstown, Illinois. "I just don't want to be a burden to anyone."[25] Instead of being a burden to anyone, she became a burden to everyone. Put more gently, the obligations of family became the obligations of government.

Just as Social Security absolved individuals of the responsibility to save for retirement, Medicare absolved them of the responsibility to save for medical care when they needed it most. And just as Social Security had dragged along Aid to Families with Dependent Children in 1935, the middle-class entitlement Medicare dragged along the less popular welfare program Medicaid.

The government picked up most of the tab for senior citizens' medical bills (and the medical bills of poor people in the case of Medicaid), and, not surprising to anyone who understands the basic rules of economics, those bills kept growing. The state had hoped to make medical care cheaper by granting senior citizens a subsidy. Instead, it had inflated the price and, in effect, given the subsidy to doctors. "Hospital prices, which had risen 7 percent in the year before Medicare, jumped by 14 percent in the year after and continued to rise, on the average, 14 percent annually over the next decade," Allen J. Matusow notes in *The Unraveling of America*. "Physicians' fees rose 7 percent a year." Though senior citizens paid a much smaller percentage of their medical bills after Medicare, within a decade of the program's implementation they were paying the same amount in real dollars as they had before.[26] On the plus side, after Medicare and Medicaid the aged and the poor made more visits to the doctor and received treatment that they might have previously neglected.[27] The benefits that came from greater health care accessibility, Great Society defenders point out, can't be quantified by monetary numbers. Whether the impersonalized nature of care offset its wider availability is still debated. What's settled is that medical care became exponentially more expensive, not cheaper, in the aftermath of Medicare and Medicaid. As with so much of the Great Society, results didn't match intentions.

After Medicare and Medicaid, Johnson's primary legislative push in the first session of the Eighty-ninth Congress involved education. The schoolteacher-turned-president bragged about signing sixty education bills during his term in office.[28] He boasted about spending more on education than his predecessors, though, save for his immediate predecessor, previous presidents nearly unanimously viewed education as a matter better suited for those closer to the youngsters in need of education. There had been the GI Bill and the Morrill land grants to colleges, but they had been justified as defense and agriculture spending. The Great Society carved a federal role in education. The federal government has never given up the role.

   The amount of aid dollars to college students tripled between 1965 and 1968.[29] As in the case of Medicare, increasing student aid inflated price. Instead of lessening the cost of higher education, the federal aid enabled college administrators to raise prices as they dramatically expanded the number of college administrators.[30] Tuition increases, in fact, outpaced the increases in federal student aid. The average cost of tuition, room, and board at a four-year public institution in the 1964–65 school year was $950. As of 2007, it exceeded $10,000. For a private institution, the cost immediately prior to the Higher Education Act was $1,907. In 2007, it exceeded $27,000.[31]

   The greater the aid, the higher the price, and as the government artificially inflated the price through its aid, the demand for aid grew, and thus the aid grew, which in turn inflated the price even more. Around and around the dog chased its tail.

   As with Medicare, the recipients of the federal government's education aid became dependent upon it. The inflationary pressures on costs struck aid recipients as abstract, if it struck them at all. The aid they received was tangible. They wanted more and more of it. Their representatives in Congress fought to give them what they wanted.

SEGREGATION, AS BOTH a legal and cultural institution, was on the ropes when Lyndon Johnson ascended to the presidency in late 1963. Harry Truman had ordered the integration of the armed forces. Second baseman Jackie Robinson had broken the color line in the national pastime. *Brown v. Board of Education* and executive enforcement had put blacks and whites in the same classrooms in locales that had previously separated them. A boycott in Montgomery, Alabama, had bent the city's discriminatory bus lines to its will. Through executive order, John Kennedy had desegregated interstate bus lines, trains, and depots. Courageous black students had gained admittance to high schools in Little Rock and universities in

Mississippi and Alabama, integrating the schools over the protests of recalcitrant governors, racially snobbish students, and outraged mobs that
showed no evidence of ever having seen the inside of a high school, let
alone a university.

It took Lyndon Johnson, a white southerner, to deliver the death blow
to formalized segregation.

Johnson appointed the first African American to the cabinet in Robert
Weaver, and the first black to the Supreme Court in Thurgood Marshall. In
the same way that his hawk successor could open relations with Communist China, the southerner Johnson had the political capital on civil rights
that his northern predecessor could never have accumulated. The Texas
drawl, good-ole-boy manners, and teachers' college education that alienated liberal northerners, who should have loved Johnson for his policies,
endeared him to many southerners. Whereas the Dutchess County squire
Roosevelt or the Irish Brahmin Kennedy made for an inflexible, solid
South on race, rancher Johnson disarmed. Sure, the white South opposed
him in Congress on civil rights initiatives and withheld the majority of
their votes from him in 1964. But they did not flex their might as effectively as they had done in the recent past.

The primary pieces of civil rights legislation that Johnson backed were
the Civil Rights Act of 1964, the Voting Rights Act of 1965, and the Fair
Housing Act of 1968.

The Voting Rights Act of 1965 outlawed poll taxes, literacy tests, and
other mechanisms traditionally used to deny the franchise to black Americans. For ninety-nine years, much of the Old Confederacy had made an
end run around the Constitution by disqualifying blacks from voting ostensibly because they failed to pass these tests and meet these qualifications. In reality, white election officials disenfranchised these citizens
because of their dark complexions. A century after its ratification, the Fifteenth Amendment grew teeth through the Voting Rights Act. Strict
penalties and an army of enforcers greeted those who flouted federal law
and the Constitution.

More controversial were the Civil Rights Act of 1964 and the Fair
Housing Act of 1968. Whereas the Voting Rights Act dealt with established, century-old civil rights, the Civil Rights Act and the Fair Housing
Act invented new rights that infringed on other rights. Whereas the Voting
Rights Act blocked the government—local, state, federal—from discriminating against individuals, the Civil Rights Act and the Fair Housing Act
prohibited individuals from discriminating against others. The Civil
Rights Act forbade private businesses—restaurants, motels, theaters—
from turning away customers or potential employees on account of their

skin color. The Fair Housing Act prohibited landlords, the real estate industry, lenders, and home sellers from discriminating in such a manner.

The bureaucratic enforcers, the quasi-judicial powers of an executive agency, the intrusion of the federal government into citizen-to-citizen transactions (or non-transactions), and the erosion of property rights were all methods liberals had employed in non-civil-rights-related policies. Now, they applied these methods to civil rights. Two aspects of the legislation, however, went against the historic grain of liberalism.

First, even with the march of liberalism moving away from legislating morality, through the Civil Rights Act and Fair Housing Act liberals dictated private choice and behavior. One man's rights came at the expense of another man's liberty. Instead of affirming actual civil rights, as the Voting Rights Act had done, the Civil Rights Act and Fair Housing Act were, in several of their provisions, taking them away. One citizen, who didn't own the property, now possessed claims above another citizen, who did own the property. This was because liberals morally disapproved of the actions of the property owner, not because the property owner infringed on anyone's rights.

Second, the Civil Rights Act and Fair Housing Act turned the goal of ending discrimination, a post-war priority of liberalism and the Left, on its head. They ushered in racial preferences and quotas for selected minorities. Hubert Humphrey famously promised to eat the pages of the Civil Rights Act if it should institute racial preferences.[32] It did, and he didn't. The civil rights movement had sought to abolish racism. Now it demanded that the government practice it.

The overreaches unnerved even many liberal voters. The steam ran out of the civil rights movement, partly because it had accomplished much of what it had set out to do and partly because it ventured into areas not traditionally thought of as "civil rights." Politically, as civil rights legislation became increasingly controversial among northern voters, the movement shifted its energies toward federal anti-poverty programs, which stood to benefit blacks disproportionately.

IN CONTRAST TO the New Deal, the Great Society arrived amidst great plenty, eschewed temporary relief for permanent programs, preferred job training to jobs, and targeted the indigent instead of the working poor. It generally didn't provide a job; it provided money, food, medical care, and other items one generally obtains through labor.

The overriding theme of the Great Society was the assumption of personal responsibility by the impersonal federal government. The Great Society bureaucratized the most basic human functions. With the government fulfilling responsibilities, individuals, families, churches, foundations, and local and state governments predictably became less responsible.

For women unwilling to get jobs, Aid to Families with Dependent Children provided a paycheck. If doctor bills weighed too heavily, Medicaid picked up the tab. Trouble paying the landlord? The rent-supplement bill subsidized the rent check. For people unwilling to buy their own groceries, the first permanent food stamps program did so for them. If child rearing proved a drag, Head Start removed preschool-age children from the home and minded them.

Perhaps more so than any Great Society program, a New Deal relic, Aid to Families with Dependent Children, epitomized the handout mentality of 1960s social policy. In spite of the decade's booming economy, the number of AFDC recipients ballooned from 3 million in 1960 to 8.4 million in 1970.[33] Unable to institute a guaranteed income through new legislation, activists transformed an existing program, AFDC, into a de facto provider of guaranteed income. They encouraged the poor to depend on the dole. Some takers of the dole indignantly claimed their right to other people's money: "I do not believe that we should be forced to work. I do not believe we should be forced to take training if it is not meaningful," Beulah Sanders lectured senators. The welfare-rights activist continued: "The welfare recipients are tired. They are tired of people dictating to them, telling them how they must live."[34] Faint grew the stigma of sponging off others. Pronounced grew the stigma of denying the poor other people's money.

Parts of the Great Society seemed designed less to appeal to poor people than to appease the upper-class supporters of the programs. The Corporation for Public Broadcasting launched government-sponsored television and radio stations. The National Endowment for the Humanities made government like a college or a private foundation, awarding grants to scholars and researchers. Texas senator Ralph Yarborough portrayed government support for the arts as aiding an "American culture pressing forward toward her appointed rendezvous with a golden age," while the colorful Floridian Claude Pepper explained that Washington subsidizing the arts would "purify, beautify and . . . strengthen the soul of America."[35] A personal interest of Lady Bird Johnson was highway beautification, which led to adopt-a-highway programs, restrictions on billboard advertisements, and regulations on roadside junkyards.

The federal government's tentacles reached into television sets, radio receivers, classrooms, paintings, train transportation, doctor's offices,

rental contracts, child care, and hundreds of other areas that they generally left alone prior to the Great Society. Government had more power.
People had less freedom.

Upton Sinclair, who six decades earlier had serialized *The Jungle* in
Appeal to Reason and three decades earlier had sought to end poverty
in California through a quixotic gubernatorial campaign, rejoiced, "My
goodness—it's the beginning of what I've been begging for."[36] By his ninth
decade, Sinclair had seen his socialist hopes frustrated time and again.

But fresher faces, who had not witnessed the repeated defeats, would
not be placated so easily. These less grizzled activists saw the Great Society
not as a welcome step in a leftward direction but as tepid reformism. If
Johnson had brought the country further left than any of his predecessors,
and a case can be made that he did, it mattered little to a Left in which the
utopian future rather than the hostile past stood as the measuring stick.
Perhaps a younger Sinclair, in his days on the *Appeal to Reason*, too, would
have cried for more, more, more.

THE VIETNAM WAR crushed the loftiest ambitions of the Great Society.
Lyndon Johnson, a student of political history, admitted, "History provided too many cases where the sound of the bugle put an immediate end
to the hopes and dreams of the best reformers: the Spanish-American
War drowned the populist spirit; World War I ended Woodrow Wilson's
New Freedom; World War II brought the New Deal to a close."[37] What escaped Johnson's notice is that these foreign crusades had served as extensions of the domestic crusades they had killed. Alas, politics doesn't stop
at the water's edge. World savers generally harbor greater ambitions than
saving a farm, redeeming a city block, giving jobs to the jobless, or providing medical care to the sick. World savers want to save the world. The
Spanish-American War, World War I, World War II, and Vietnam put an
end to the domestic reforms that preceded them in the sense that the coda,
also a part of the song, puts an end to the song.

Lyndon Johnson wanted to save the world. More importantly, Johnson
wanted to be seen as saving the world. "Lyndon Johnson was never the
anonymous donor," recalled Doris Kearns, his assistant, later his biographer, and still later the wife of the author of his Ann Arbor Great Society
speech. "Rather, his was a most visible benevolence which reminded recipients at every turn of how much he had done for them. Giving was a
necessary part of a mission to reform, reshape, and thereby redeem. Paternalism was inextricably bound to such generosity. The cost to the recipient of the goods Johnson delivered seemed fair enough to him—gratitude,

affection, a trust manifested by the willingness to let him decide what was best for them. In time, there was no mistaking his gifts: they had 'LBJ'— and later 'USA'—stamped all over them."[38]

Johnson gave generously of other people's money. He made others sacrifice so that he could appear generous. The compulsion necessarily invalidated the act as charity. Johnson expected the recipients to be indebted to him for gifts he had not paid for out of his own pocket. The president may have fallen for the fallacy of secondary giving, but the beneficiaries of the federal largesse did not. By the end of Johnson's presidency, blacks, students, and the Vietnamese—the groups, along with the poor, upon whom he had showered money most lavishly in schemes of renewal—stood in violent rebellion against the man who thought of himself as their benefactor. Urban riots, students forcing campus shutdowns, and the Vietnamese rejecting his Great Society on the Mekong in favor of Communism broke Lyndon Johnson's progressive heart. Even Michael Harrington denigrated the war on poverty as a mere "skirmish," and one that poverty had won.[39]

"How is it possible," Johnson pontificated after his presidency, "that all these people could be so ungrateful to me after I had given them so much?"[40] Lyndon Johnson never learned that dependents resent their benefactors. His beneficiaries understood too well that benefactors look down upon their dependents.

～ 21 ～

MEET THE NEW LEFT,
SAME AS THE OLD LEFT

As a dog that returneth to his vomit, so is the fool that repeateth his folly.
—PROVERBS 26:11

THE LEFT WELCOMED LBJ's Great Society lucre. They didn't return the support he had expected in exchange. The inability of any reality to satisfy utopians had much to do with this. Vietnam had much to do with it, too.

For Carl Oglesby, Vietnam had everything to do with it. In early 1964, Oglesby was a self-described "dishwater liberal" who volunteered for the local Democratic candidate for Congress. So deep did Oglesby's alienation from the Democratic Party become that he quit working for the congressional candidate and refused to go "part of the way with LBJ" on Election Day.[1] Snooping on Oglesby, the FBI observed that the "subject's turning point from 'liberal' to 'radical-left' appeared to be on the question of United States intervention in Vietnam."[2] The war ended the lives of fifty-eight thousand Americans who fought it. It transformed the lives of at least as many who fought against it. Carl Oglesby was one of the earliest.

In 1964, Oglesby was a married, twenty-nine-year-old playwright, with three kids, a good job supervising technical publications at a defense contractor, and a newly bought house "in a see-Spot-run kind of neighborhood" in Ann Arbor. The next year, he was the president of Students for a Democratic Society (SDS). Oglesby abandoned a placid, bourgeois existence for the chaotic life of the always-on-the-go, work-into-the-night activist because Americans were dying and killing in Vietnam. The same issue that drew Oglesby to a student organization drew SDS to a non-student. The organization was mutating from a modest-sized student organization to a national umbrella group for the Left, from a group inspired by race and class injustices to one obsessed with the war.

In contrast to the organization's red-diaper babies, Oglesby was a redneck baby. The product of an Alabama hillbilly mother and a South Carolina redneck father, Oglesby had so embraced the Cold War consensus that as a high school senior he won a national oratory competition by arguing that the United States should use its nuclear superiority to overcome the Russians.[3] The 1960s mythology of the liberal-turned-radical by an innocence lost was no myth in Carl Oglesby's case. He had believed America worthy of its ideals. Events made him abandon that view.

The dramatic personal changes that the new SDS president experienced gave witness to the transformative power of the decade. The characters in the sixties narrative reflect the sprinter's pace of the times. A fortyish psychologist starts the decade a Harvard professor and ends it an imprisoned drug messiah. A street criminal becomes a revolutionary icon. An heiress missionary first heeds the establishment's call for service and volunteerism and then heeds the radicals' call for violence, bombs, and terror. Activists redirected the veer of the sixties, and the veer of the sixties redirected activists.

As ITS 1965 election of Carl Oglesby to its highest office suggests, SDS acted ahead of public opinion in its vocal opposition to the war. As Adam Garfinkle noted in his study of Vietnam War protest, "After 1964, nothing that can be said about the antiwar movement makes much sense without" reference to SDS.[4] SDS organized the first anti-war march on Washington, played a major role in the first teach-in, and orchestrated the first mass draft card burning. Yet SDS had a more nuanced relationship to the anti-war movement. Its leaders were reluctant anti-warriors. Opposed to the Vietnam War to a man, prominent first-generation SDSers nevertheless viewed the war issue as a distraction. Who had time to protest the Vietnam War when an interracial movement of the poor needed to be launched? Organize to stop the seventh war from now, went the old-guard's depressing "rallying" cry.[5] But the success of the group's limited organizing on the war and the salience of Vietnam for draft-age students overwhelmed SDS's small "beloved community" with a new crop of activists obsessed with the war. Carl Oglesby was an early example of the changing face of SDS.

The anti-war issue captured the SDS leadership and dragged it leftward. SDSers captured the leadership of the anti-war movement, and dragged it leftward. Because the war managers also happened to be on the left side of the political spectrum, the domestic battle over the Vietnam War, like so many skirmishes in the 1960s, was an internecine battle.

SDS's involvement in the three big anti-war events of 1965—the Michigan teach-in and two marches on Washington—exemplified wider trends in the New Left: anti-anti-Communism, a growing hostility toward America, and following the lead of the civil rights movement. In March 1965, Carl Oglesby spoke at the first "teach-in" on the war, modeled on the lunch-counter sit-ins of the civil rights movement. The University of Michigan teach-in idea spread to more than a hundred campuses that semester.[6] The month after the Ann Arbor teach-in, SDS organized the first nationwide march against the war in Vietnam. Crucially, SDS welcomed the participation of Communists—a group committed to a decidedly *anti*-democratic society. This decision alienated more mainstream speakers and organizations, as did the organization's reversal of its policy excluding Communists. The venerable anti-nuclear-weapons group SANE withdrew from the demonstration, and the League for Industrial Democracy and its student arm, after a four-decade association, soon dissolved ties.[7]

The Easter march, without the participation of numerous boycotting liberals, was a success. Twenty thousand people, mostly students from campuses in the East and Midwest, convened in Washington, D.C. Though ten times that number had marched for civil rights twenty months earlier, the anti-war march exceeded expectations. The war had claimed fewer than a thousand American lives by the spring of 1965. As draft notices and the body count grew, so, too, did the anti-war marches.

The liberals who boycotted the Easter demonstration held their own March on Washington on Thanksgiving weekend. SDS's success in April guaranteed its inclusion in November. "The most anti-American speech was delivered by CARL OGLESBY, President of SDS," the FBI ominously observed.[8] Oglesby placed blame for Vietnam on a controversial culprit. "The original commitment in Vietnam was made by President Truman, a mainstream liberal," Oglesby told those gathered. "It was seconded by President Eisenhower, a moderate liberal. It was intensified by the late President Kennedy, a flaming liberal. Think of the men who now engineer that war—those who study the maps, give the commands, push the buttons, and tally the dead: Bundy, McNamara, Rusk, Lodge, Goldberg, the President himself. They are not moral monsters. They are all honorable men. They are all liberals."[9]

Demonstrations continued. Crowds grew. Fervor intensified.

TOM HAYDEN'S 1965 trip to North Vietnam, engineered by Communist Party hack historian Herbert Aptheker, marked a loss of innocence for the New Left. The ideological tourism of the Old Left, where American radicals ventured abroad in search of utopia, returned. But now Hanoi and Havana, Peking and Pyongyang replaced Moscow as the fashionable destination.

Referring to Hayden's North Vietnam visit, Carl Oglesby remembers: "I thought it was absolutely the wrong thing to do, and I still believe that. The only reason I can see for doing it was to grab a few headlines." The trip, occurring at a time when the war was overwhelmingly popular, made the anti-war case even harder to make by linking it with support for the enemy. "Why would he go to North Vietnam? That wasn't where the war was. The war was in South Vietnam. Our troops were in South Vietnam. If he wanted to go someplace, go to South Vietnam. Don't go to North Vietnam."[10]

Hayden did go. Along with travel partner Staughton Lynd, he wrote a book about the experience, *The Other Side.* "We are conscious of the ways in which some intellectuals during the nineteen-thirties sought to excuse the evil side of Soviet Communism," Hayden and Lynd wrote, "and we have made every effort to avoid those habits of thought."[11] Yet they made excuses, too. They linked the Communists' struggle in South Vietnam with the civil rights struggle of blacks in the American South, excused oppression by erroneously portraying *North* Vietnam "in a life-and-death struggle," and compared the " 'rice-roots' democracy" of Vietnamese Communists to nineteenth-century town meetings in America.[12] "Both sides use violence," the book conceded, "but this does not mean both sides are equally violent . . . the other side employs violence more discriminately."[13] "The Vietnamese we met seemed the gentlest people we had ever known," they gushed.[14] The authors announced support for the National Liberation Front (NLF), with Hayden suggesting that he would fight for the Communists were he Vietnamese.[15]

Could the American proponents of the Vietnam War have conjured up a more discrediting caricature than anti-war leaders meeting with the enemy, praising them in print, and openly supporting their victory? "We did not need to get put in the position where we're going around saying, *'We're not the pawns of Hanoi,'* " Oglesby states. "We just did not need that."[16]

ON OCTOBER 21, 1967, more than one hundred thousand people convened at the Lincoln Memorial in Washington, D.C., to protest the war. The more radically inclined marched upon the war's nerve center. The March on the Pentagon was the intersection where the multitude of interests that made up the protest culture met. Abbie Hoffman promised to exorcise the Pentagon of the war's demons by levitating it three hundred feet in the air. Ed Sanders, overseer of a poetry magazine called *Fuck You*, held a "grope-in" next to the Pentagon. His mentor, Allen Ginsberg, fresh from several years in the Orient, chanted *"om."*[17] A Chicago SDS activist reported an "unbelievably groovy" scene, with "flaming draft cards," "ample supplies of grass," and activists urinating on the Pentagon.[18] "Blacks moved through the New Left with a physical indifference to the bodies about them," marcher Norman Mailer, the best-selling novelist, noted.[19] Hippies offered flowers to soldiers. One couple made love in the open. Jerry Rubin, whose political alchemy promised a union of hippies and activists, explained that revolutionaries stood "ready to burn the whole motherfucker down."[20] A charge of the concrete fortress briefly suggested that, for once, Rubin had not made an empty boast. The civil disobedience of older, upper-class intellectuals, such as Mailer, MIT linguist Noam Chomsky, and poet Robert Lowell, which resulted in sojourns in jail, showed the public that it wasn't just Afro-wearing blacks, throwback pacifists, beaded and bearded hippies, and student radicals who opposed the war.

But even the Vietnam War, the issue that more than any other united the "movement," demonstrated the degree to which the movement was not a movement at all, just a series of tribes. Occasionally the tribes' interests intersected. Occasionally they clashed. They had a common enemy, "the system," a vague concept nearly as amorphous as "the movement." But they did not have a common ideology.

Pacifists, the New Left, black-power advocates, and hippies all opposed the war, but the reasons differed and their strategies to end the conflict differed, too. "You're not gonna stop this war with this rally," novelist Ken Kesey, reflecting the libertarian dropout ethos, told an audience of stunned Berkeley politicos in 1965. "Look at the war, turn your backs on it and say fuck it."[21] Two years later, SDS warned its members not to aid the Martin Luther King Jr.–sponsored Vietnam Summer, which "threatens SDS" with "a massive attempt at liberal cooption" and stands to "blunt our radicalism by obscuring the real nature of the Vietnamese war." That "real nature," SDS's *New Left Notes* contended, was capitalist imperialism. "King is purposely diverting our attention from the real purposes of that foreign policy."[22] "Fuck that motherfucking man!" Black Panther David Hilliard told a peace rally in 1969. "We will kill Richard Nixon." Hilliard's profanity, violent threats, and characterization of the American flag as a fascist symbol horrified the demonstrators. "Yeah, peace," Hilliard scoffed. "Well, we ain't here for no goddamed peace. Because we know that we can't have no peace because this country is built on war. And if you want peace you got to fight for it."[23] There was an anti-war movement, a civil rights movement, a black-power movement, and so on. But, despite the illusory power of broad-based demonstrations against the war, or racism, or the imprisonment of political activists, there was no movement, only movements.

BEYOND SDS, THE fiftysomething, one-man-gang David Dellinger did everything he could to radicalize the peace movement. Dellinger gained the respect of young activists for experiencing the 1960s in the 1940s. A star athlete, Ivy League student, and beneficiary of wealth and an old-stock Yankee bloodline, Dellinger nevertheless took the road less traveled in midcentury America. Rather than register for the draft, Dellinger spent much of World War II in federal prison. He put his body upon the wheels by embarking on a thirty-plus-day hunger strike to protest prison conditions and by later getting his jaw broken while protesting the Korean War.[24] "I had been infatuated with Christian communism, the early disciples' way of life," Dellinger reflected, so he, along with a band of "premature hippies," launched a series of communes.[25]

Then, Dellinger was a man out of time. In the 1960s, save for his comb-over and square duds, he fit perfectly. Dellinger irritated staid peace groups by transforming an anti-nuclear protest at the Kennedy White House into a protest of the Vietnam War, handing over a nonviolent protest at the 1968 Democratic National Convention to violent elements, and generally pushing the anti-war movement into the arms of the fringe Left.[26]

Unlike the SDS leaders who defied their elders' advice by allowing the anti-democratic Left to penetrate their ranks, Dellinger could not plead ignorance. He had lived through the Old Left. Still Dellinger reached out to Maoists, Stalinists, and others who wanted not peace, but a Communist victory. This strategy did no damage to the masters of war. In fact, an opposition committed to mindless violence, a Viet Cong victory, and internecine struggle within the Left are what the war managers wanted.

Michael Harrington, who had come to regret his uncompromising reaction to SDS's Port Huron Statement, nevertheless again felt that the New Left was treading in dangerous waters. "Politics was the décor of their personal drama, and if they were genuinely horrified by the war in Vietnam, their own psyches still came first," Harrington lamented. "Waving a Vietcong flag at a demonstration or disrupting a peace rally—they never tried out their theatrics on less tolerant groups, like the American Legion—would certainly provoke their parents, and that was the essential liberation. That the very same actions might harden their fellow citizens in support of the war was of secondary importance."[27]

The marches proved therapeutic for the marchers but not persuasive to the public. Even those inclined to oppose the war did so cautiously for fear of associating with the anti-Americanism, lawbreaking, and counter-cultural protestors. The impotence of the protests inspired organizers to more extreme tactics, which in turn deepened the irrelevance. The most glaring example of the movement's impotence came in 1968, when three hawks—Hubert Humphrey, Richard Nixon, and George Wallace—appeared on the presidential ballot. If the anti-war movement was so effective, why couldn't it field a credible candidate in the general election? "Most Americans, while concerned about a war seemingly without end or prospect of clearcut victory, were more prepared to suffer in silence than to associate themselves with lurid leftists and yelping hippies," observes author Adam Garfinkle.[28] In turn, the "lurid leftists" refused to associate themselves with credible anti-war candidates. It's easier to feel pure than it is to win.

The New Left, which had patterned so much of its activism on the civil rights movement, never seemed to grasp that its model's effectiveness came in large part from sensibly banning radical signs and radical speeches. The purpose of protest, after all, is to persuade the mainstream, not prove how far outside the mainstream you are. Opposition to the war, particularly further into the decade, was very much within the mainstream. The anti-war movement never was.

THE TIMES THEY were a-changing, and so was the Left.

The patriotism of blue-collar citizens pitted them against the Left. In 1963, the leaders of a clique of Maoists known as Progressive Labor brought guns to arm miners involved in a labor dispute in Hazard, Kentucky. The miners ran them out of town and came close to shooting one of the group's leaders.[29] Only the intervention by the Oakland police saved Berkeley anti-war protestors from a severe thrashing at the hands of the Hell's Angels in 1965.[30] When the Weathermen planted a red flag and distributed radical literature at Detroit's Metro Beach in 1969, a mob of working-class whites surrounded the upper-class missionaries, shouted "Communists!" and then charged the flag and fought the activists.[31] In New York, construction workers—thereafter referred to as the "hard hats"—converged on student demonstrators and beat them up in 1970. The Left had more to fear from the people they sought to save than they did from the establishment they sought to overthrow.

The Old Left's bogeyman was the fat-cat playboy, the captain of industry, the business tycoon. The New Left's bogeyman was the policeman ("pig!"), the GI ("baby killer!"), the rural southern white ("redneck!"). Not only did the New Left abandon the worker as the agent of millennial change, but it increasingly viewed the worker as an obstacle to such designs.

"The next time some $3.00 an hour AFL-type workers go on strike for a 50 cent raise," Marvin Garson of Berkeley Free Speech Movement fame promised, "I'll remember the day they chanted 'Burn Hanoi, not our flag,' and so help me I'll cross their fucking picket line."[32] Jim Mellen of Michigan's SDS declared that no moral requirement demanded that leftists "support American white workers who wanted to make fifteen times, instead of twelve times, as much as other workers of the world."[33] SDS, in fact, splintered over such issues. Alarmed at the Weatherman sect's seething contempt for white workers, communist Bob Avakian charged that letting crusades against racism obscure the struggle against capitalism revealed the "class origins" of many Weathermen. "When you try to defend honky workers who just want more privileges from imperialism, that shows your *race* origins," Weatherman Howie Machtinger retorted.[34]

The Left had turned spitefully against the workers. And the workers, the Left's imagined vehicle for social change for a century, turned viscerally against them. The anti-Americanism on display at the protests deserves blame. So does the proliferation of alien lifestyles, whose enthusiasts rebuffed Middle America's standards of work, hygiene, and morality.

"THERE IS A curious mixture of population in this new slum where I am living now with my family," noted Mike Gold in 1965. Now beginning his eighth decade, the once-feared literary commissar resurfaced in the Haight-Ashbury section of San Francisco. Though encouraged by the antiwar movement and Berkeley's Free Speech Movement, Gold seemed confused by what he experienced daily in the Haight. He shouldn't have been. In an earlier incarnation, before pledging a lifetime's fealty to Moscow, Gold had witnessed the drug use, strange music, and sexually libidinous atmosphere of Greenwich Village. In the Haight, Gold reported encountering "beatniks with strange picturesque costumes," "young men with flaming bear[d]s dressed like pirates," "girls in Scotch plaid coats like the one Bobby Burns wrote about," and "graceful homosexuals with really fine faces who dress in an aristocratic costume of the court of Louis the 16th."[35] Mike Gold had journeyed from the Old Left epicenter on Thirteenth Street in Manhattan to the New Left epicenter in the Haight. He made the physical journey but not the ideological one. He remained a Communist, trapped in an earlier time. Though spirited by the emergence of any activist Left after the moribund 1950s, Gold seemed befuddled by the cultural changes. The Left had passed him by.

But as the counterculture abandoned one Left, it gave another Left a second act. The Beats reappeared, only now they called themselves "hippies," dispensed with jazz in favor of rock, and traded in their gloomy garb for more colorful get-ups. They still smoked grass, said the word "like" entirely too much, embraced indigence, and searched for that holy grail of orgasms. The hippies, like their Beat mentors, were lifestyle radicals. The liberation of the senses took precedence over the liberation of the Third World. This had revolutionary implications, but for one person at a time.

Beatniks became hippies on November 26, 1960, when Timothy Leary gave psilocybin to Allen Ginsberg at Leary's Newton, Massachusetts, home. "We're going down to the city streets and tell the people about peace and love," an exuberant Ginsberg proclaimed. The chemical hallucinogen tricked a naked Ginsberg into believing himself God instead of a scribbler of dirty poetry. Ginsberg wished to prove his bona fides as the deity by curing Leary's near-deaf ear. He informed the telephone operator that he was God—"G-O-D God"—calling for Jack Kerouac. The poet tried to phone his dead mother. He had visions of establishing world peace by giving psilocybin to Khrushchev and Kennedy. "When Ginsberg came back down," Robert Greenfield writes in his biography of Leary, "he and Tim began planning the psychedelic revolution."[36]

The unlikely duo of the Beat poet and the Harvard psychology professor reconvened weeks later on Ginsberg's home turf in New York, where they hoped to convert Jack Kerouac to their fledgling psychedelic religion. Kerouac's dour mood triggered Leary's first bad trip. The epiphany that his friend Ginsberg had experienced weeks earlier escaped Kerouac. Too dark a figure to be converted to peace and love, Kerouac remained a man of the black-and-white fifties while his friend Ginsberg pushed headlong into the Day-Glo sixties. Undeterred by their failure with Kerouac, the pair gave the hallucinogen to hall-of-fame druggie William Burroughs, writers Arthur Koestler and Aldous Huxley, poets Robert Lowell and LeRoi Jones, jazz musicians Thelonious Monk and Dizzy Gillespie, and prison psychiatrist Madison Presnell, who noted that when he closed his eyes under the influence of psilocybin he traveled, that is, he tripped.[37] Leary gave drugs to anyone who would take them, including his children. When Leary's supply of psilocybin ran out, he switched allegiance to the more potent, but still very legal, lysergic acid diethylamide, LSD.

Getting high and getting others high through the auspices of Harvard

University, Leary deemed what he was doing "experiments." Like many a stoner since, he stopped going to class. Unlike the stoners who followed, he was a teacher, not a student. Harvard fired him at the end of the spring 1963 semester. In a brilliant public relations move, Leary dishonestly claimed that his research on hallucinogens led to his firing. It didn't, save for the role it played in causing a lethargic and flighty Leary to ditch class, office hours, and advising duties.[38] But it made for a good story, so he stuck to it.

Leary launched a commune for his two kids and a dozen or so friends a few miles from Harvard (and Brook Farm). Run out of town, fired from Harvard, busted, and even deported from nations, the notorious Leary reconvened his followers on a palatial, woodland estate in upstate New York bankrolled by a millionaire convert to the drug cult.[39] Life was a party.

The Beatles dropped Leary's lines in "Tomorrow Never Knows" and "Come Together." The Who dropped his name in "The Seeker." Other musical gods dropped acid, Leary's panacea. Rather than a graying pedagogue, then, it was the drug-drenched music of Jimi Hendrix, Jefferson Airplane, and the Grateful Dead that implored kids to undergo a temporary, chemically induced insanity. Ever the booster, Leary predicted that by the early 1980s the Supreme Court would be smoking pot, the army would be disseminating LSD to troops, and colleges would establish psychedelic studies departments that favored the sensory education offered by pot sessions and acid trips.[40]

If Leary was the LSD messiah, Allen Ginsberg was his first apostle. A bearded, balding but long-haired Ginsberg, fresh from years in the Orient studying Eastern religions, reemerged as an *"om"*-chanting hippie guru at be-ins and happenings. Neal Cassady, the star of Kerouac's *On the Road*, went on the road again. This time the irrepressible Cassady journeyed with *One Flew over the Cuckoo's Nest* author Ken Kesey and his Merry Pranksters in a psychedelically painted Depression-era school bus. "Negro music is blaring out of the speakers and these weird people clamber out, half of them in costume, lurid shirts with red and white stripes, some of them with weird paint on their faces, like comic-book Indians," Tom Wolfe's *The Electric Kool-Aid Acid Test*, a fictionalized account of the Pranksters' travels, described one pit stop by the nomadic acid enthusiasts.[41]

The bus eventually pulled into Leary's communal drug mansion, where a historic summit of the gods of the counterculture should have taken place. The traveling freaks led by Kesey, an easygoing former wrestler with "huge latissimi dorsi muscles" that made "his upper back fan out like manta-ray wings," hoped for "the most glorious reception ever," Wolfe noted, believing "themselves and Leary's group as two extraordinary arcane societies, and the only ones in the world, engaged in the most fantastic experiment in human consciousness."[42] But Leary didn't want to be bothered. Save for a photo opportunity with Cassady on the bus, Leary largely ignored the West Coast gods of psychedelics.[43] Alas, Leary's acid religion was monotheistic.

Not all radicals accepted the gospel according to Leary. "I could no more be a hippie in 1967 than I could be a beatnik in the fifties," Tom Hayden confessed. "I loved the music of the times, but strictly as a background to my life. I went to few concerts, owned hardly any albums, rarely danced, and was privately frightened by the loss of control that drug advocates celebrated."[44] The new sensibility "horrified" SDS veteran Steve Max: "Dope made people crazy and useless. They couldn't think straight. They didn't know what was fantasy and what wasn't."[45] The slogan "pot is the revolution," Harvard professor Hilary Putnam advised, "must be fought."[46] Rick Margolies, a draft resister and fellow at the Institute for Policy Studies, reminded other activists that "ours is a long march, not an acid trip, through the institutions."[47] The New Left didn't want kids to "turn on, tune in, drop out." They wanted them to take over.

Leary, in turn, discouraged followers from protesting the Democrats at their Chicago convention. What was the point, Leary wondered, of getting your head kicked in by the police as you helped elect Richard Nixon?[48] The counterculture slogan was "sex, drugs, and rock 'n' roll," and not "sex, drugs, rock 'n' roll, and politics," for good reason.

Citizens of Acid Nation who participated in politics generally did so as a reaction to the state infringing upon their freedom to smoke, to bed, to stay out of uniform. Hard-core political activists who indulged in sex, drugs, and rock 'n' roll generally did so to convert the hippies to politics or as part of the overall vibe. The Left and the counterculture mixed, but they didn't do so to the extent that they combined identities.

Perhaps the pair that most tightly wedded New Left politics and countercultural lifestyles in the public's mind was Jerry Rubin and Abbie Hoffman. "We believe," the counterculture icons proclaimed, "that people should fuck all the time, any time, whomever they want."[49] Many did. Professor Kinsey's surveys, it seems, weren't wrong but early.

The questions the New Left broached regarding sex weren't really new. "Why should we be allowed only one intimate relationship? Why always a man and a woman? Why can't there be an intimate relationship between more than two people? Why must there be a legal contract? Why must it last a lifetime? Why does the world have to be divided up into couples who relate to everyone else as couples or else as 'unfortunate' singles? Why should each couple live by itself, isolated from other friendships, other intimacies? Marriage is the cultural manifestation of a society based on private property. Married people possess one another and their children—they are each other's private property."[50] Frances Wright, Mary Gove Nichols, John Humphrey Noyes, and Victoria Woodhull had arrived at similar conclusions the previous century. The in-your-face quality of the New Left ensured that, whereas Wright, Nichols, Noyes, and Woodhull's unconventional views on sexuality had failed to penetrate the surrounding culture, the 1960s counterculture did.

Increasingly, the culture resembled the counterculture. Fashion, in the appearance of the miniskirt and the disappearance of the bra, became more sexualized. The Rolling Stones suggested, "Let's Spend the Night Together." The Beatles asked, "Why Don't We Do It in the Road?" No Hays Code governed cinema. In 1969, the Academy Award for best picture, for instance, went to a film detailing the journey of a male prostitute. Peep shows, go-go dancers, and X-rated theaters encroached upon civilization. The courts, through the *Griswold v. Connecticut* decision, judged it illegal for localities to prohibit contraceptives. Science, perhaps more so than popular culture, contributed to the quick alteration of sexual mores by producing a birth control pill.

The Pill suggested a world where actions liberated themselves from consequences, just as other pills, weeds, and chemicals provided users with an escape from responsibility. But responsibilities and consequences loomed.

MARK RUDD, A Columbia University junior, sold dope to fund a trip to Cuba in early 1968. "I was all fired up," Rudd notes of his three-week visit, which included inspiring meetings with Vietnamese Communists. "I came back with all kinds of slogans. I became Guevaraist: 'The duty of the revolutionary is to make the revolution'—meaning, not to talk about it." A wound-up ball of action returned. But not everyone in Columbia SDS shared his energy and attitude, at least not initially.

One clique, led by Dave Gilbert and Ted Gold, sought to lay the groundwork for action by organizing, base-building, and educating. They were called the "praxis axis." The opposing "action faction," which featured Rudd and John Jacobs, pointed to the immediate benefits of action and believed the example of confrontation the best method of organizing, base building, and educating. "I read the gestalt of the time," Rudd explains of his winning position, "which was 'action' will get us lots of support. Militancy, confrontation, direct action—the moment was right in the spring of '68."[51]

"Up against the wall, motherfucker, this is a stickup," Rudd wrote to school president Grayson Kirk.[52] The appropriation of a LeRoi Jones line embodied the flair that the never-camera-shy Rudd brought to activism and the contempt for authority—college administrators, police, parents—that permeated the Columbia student strike. With superhero jaw and Dennis the Menace haircut, the cocky Rudd cited the campus presence of the Institute for Defense Analysis (IDA) and the school's "racist" plan to build a gym in a park, which allegedly threatened to widen the chasm between Ivy League Columbia and ghetto Harlem.

These ostensible rationales belied a more majestic impetus. A tortured, narcissistic theory, putting Marx's stamp of approval upon the student strike, held that the university had replaced the factory as the essential capitalist institution, and that students, as the new working class, struck—as syndicalists had once struck in factories—not for better conditions or better wages but to undermine or overthrow the capitalist system. Rudd explained, "The essence of the matter is that we are out for social and political revolution, nothing less."[53] He later confessed that SDS "manufactured the issues. The Institute for Defense Analysis is nothing at Columbia. And the gym issue is bull. It doesn't mean anything to anybody. I had never been to the gym site before the demonstration began. I didn't even know how to get there."[54]

The campus protest commanded national attention because the issues that inspired it commanded the nation's interest. The gym and IDA served as proxies for racism and the Vietnam War. Delegates from the Left's major tribes thus rushed to the scene of protest. SNCC's H. Rap Brown and Stokely Carmichael joined the black-power tribe, which had detained three administrators. From the New Left tribe, the ubiquitous Tom Hayden arrived at the scene offering advice and support. The Grateful Dead, ambassadors of the hippies, provided musical entertainment.

The first class of baby boomers graduated in 1968. More than seventy-five million of the two hundred million Americans were younger than twenty-two. The culture had trouble assimilating them. Student deferments and higher education's expanding reach made absorption especially difficult for colleges and universities. In 1960, colleges and universities enrolled three million. Within ten years, student enrollment had more than tripled.[55] In a nation where numbers ruled, the demographic tables indicated that the segment of the population with the least wisdom and experience, and the greatest arrogance and impetuousness, would make its influence felt. That they had been the most sheltered generation in history made the boorish behavior and bratty demands particularly galling to the older generation that had unwittingly created this monster. Globally, youthful uprisings of diverse inspirations were then occurring in Prague, Paris, Mexico City, and points beyond. The huge interest paid to one disturbance at one college starts making sense when one glimpses the alignment of all these stars.

The student strike shut down the Columbia campus for a week. The strikers held one dean captive for a day. They took over five buildings. "In the office of [Columbia president Grayson] Kirk," *Newsweek* reported, "some urinated in a wastebasket, others broke into his stock of liquor and cigars, rifled his personal papers and photos."[56] Though Columbia did not expel SDS from Hamilton Hall, black students, along with armed Harlem activists, did. The white SDS members meekly acquiesced and moved to Low Library.

After a week of embarrassing vacillation, Columbia's president and trustees called in New York's Finest. The cops arrested 698 people. The blacks in Hamilton Hall, not wanting to provoke the police, went quietly. The mainly white occupiers in other buildings had separate plans. Before the protest Columbia SDS had discussed inciting the police, instructing activists that a policeman would lose his temper if someone, particularly a coed, made allegations about his mother's outrageous sexual habits.[57] Afterward, SDS bragged in their publications of knocking policemen into mud puddles, chanting "Cops eat shit," and smashing the windshields of three law enforcement vehicles.[58] But to the outside world, they played the victim. *Time* reported, "One youth, dropped gently to the grass by officers, lay quiet until they moved away, then shouted, 'Police brutality!'—and then drew only laughs from bystanders. A girl wedged in a police van saw her plight in grandiose terms. 'First they arrest the workers and now the intellectuals!' she shouted."[59]

Protests, shutdowns, and even violence erupted on campuses in copycat fashion. At Michigan, where the Jesse James Gang of Terry Robbins, Jim Mellen, Bill Ayers, and Diana Oughton captured the SDS chapter that had advanced the concept of "participatory democracy," the new guard's authoritarian tactics proved so alienating that even the group's radical caucus quit. In the words of the Jesse James Gang, "A majority of the students is too much to hope for in this early stage of our struggle . . . action cannot wait that long."[60] They dressed like Cowboys. They talked like brownshirts.

Michigan's Jesse James Gang and Columbia's "action faction" naturally linked up. A frightening metamorphosis of SDS was under way.

Whereas the partisans of action drove their opponents away at Michigan, they converted them at Columbia. So complete was Mark Rudd's triumph that he proselytized his opponents into the politics of confrontation; "Everybody switched over to it, including the people who opposed it—Dave Gilbert, Ted Gold." The significance of this was a fetish for action, with or without forethought, and a move toward vanguardism. If the Left knows best, then why wait for the masses to catch up before taking action?

"The big problem then was that we were wrong," Rudd notes. "We took a tactic that worked at a given moment and turned it into a strategy forever. It didn't work after that."[61] The success of action at Columbia led to the failure of more extreme action elsewhere. Winning the action-versus-organizing debate would have profound consequences for Rudd and the American Left. Losing it would prove life-shattering for Dave Gilbert and Ted Gold.

THE COLUMBIA STRIKE succeeded in its stated aims. Along with the Tet offensive, which prefaced President Johnson's refusal to seek another term, and Martin Luther King Jr.'s assassination and the resulting urban riots, the Columbia shutdown and the subsequent larger-scale riots outside the Democratic National Convention stitched the fabric of 1968, a chaotic, quick-moving decade packed in a year. Slain political leaders, cities ablaze, white riots on campus, and coffins returning from Vietnam made revolution seem imminent for some.

The war widened fissures. The Democratic National Convention of 1968 bloodily demonstrated this. Inside, conventioneers nominated Vice President Hubert Humphrey for president and rejected a peace plank. Humphrey, despite the most impressive record on civil rights among potential candidates, disappointed many liberal Democrats because of his support of the war. They preferred Minnesota's current senior senator, Eugene McCarthy. Outside, the radical protesters didn't care. "Those of us who have been in the streets for the past five days didn't give a flying fuck whether McCarthy would win or lose; and now that he's lost, still don't," read a flyer that SDSers posted around Chicago.[62] In SDS's view, a pure man was no match for a corrupt system—and they regarded Bobby Kennedy and Gene McCarthy as far from pure. The group's national secretary—SDS had done away with the American title "president" in a move bursting with symbolism—assured its members, "Kennedy and McCarthy only seek more subtle forms of achieving the same goals as Johnson and Nixon."[63] Electing this candidate or that candidate was meaningless within the context of capitalism and manipulated democracy.

When Tom Hayden, now an organizer for the National Mobilization Committee, organized a protest outside the Democratic National Convention, SDS initially declined participation. To some radicals, the SDS veteran now seemed a passé opportunist, just as Michael Harrington had seemed a relic to Hayden years earlier. Only when it became clear that the scheduled "peace" protest would take on violent overtones and organizing opportunities would be abundant did SDS decide to take part. Even then it did not throw the organization's weight behind the protest.

Hayden hoped to stage a violent confrontation with the police that would expose Americans to the state's brutality as it "radicalized" the activists lured into the beat-down. Hayden himself knew the radicalizing power of the policeman's truncheon and the goon's fist. He knew, too, the transformative power that televised images of such beat-downs had on mainstream America. But his tactics were no longer the tactics of McComb, Mississippi. Reflecting the larger Left, Hayden shifted from civil disobedience to confrontation.

One SDS leader remembered Hayden explaining, "It might be useful if someone were to fire-bomb police cars."[64] SDS's national secretary recalled Hayden plotting to spread nails over a nearby highway.[65] Bill Ayers, who became an SDS national officer the following year, described Hayden's change in demeanor when addressing radicals privately:

> His voice took on an edge, somewhere between fanatical and giddy, as he described bold plans and playful pranks. But you folks—veterans of the movement and the streets—have a pivotal role to play in all of this, he continued, the color of his face deepening, his eyes once again blazing. He looked intently from person to person. He was the same articulate and thoughtful speaker as before, but these were words for only a few. This demonstration has the potential like nothing we've done before to expose the face of the enemy, to strip him naked, to force him to reveal himself as violent, brutal, totalitarian, and evil. It will be difficult—and dangerous—taunting the monster, stabbing him in his most exposed and vulnerable places, but it's got to be done. And he paused. And you're the ones to do it.[66]

In Chicago, Hayden, whose maturity regressed as the decade progressed, commanded a much smaller army than he had anticipated. Nevertheless, he recklessly told the crowd to "make sure that if blood is going to flow, it will flow all over the city."[67] It did.

We are not in Port Huron anymore, old-guard SDS observers must have thought. In Chicago, next-generation SDS peopled Hayden's army. Kathy Boudin, Diana Oughton, Ruthie Stein, and Cathy Wilkerson called in bomb threats to the Days Inn and unleashed stink bombs in the Hilton.[68]

Jeff Jones implored radicals gathered in Grant Park to "remake this country in the streets."[69] Bill Ayers shot marbles at police with a slingshot. Terry Robbins hurled tear gas canisters back at the cops.[70] High-school-cheerleader-turned-movement-dominatrix Bernardine Dohrn was there. So were Dave Gilbert and Ted Gold of the Columbia "praxis axis." They didn't yet think of themselves as the group that would come to be called Weatherman, but Chicago might best be thought of as their first action.

Chicago, a city where actual people lived and not a playground for visitors to smash things, understandably wanted order. As the activists took over public parks, smashed windows, and threw rocks, the police responded by clubbing them, stuffing them in police wagons, and, in one instance, shooting a man to death. The demonstrators claimed a right to break the law as they indignantly claimed the police had no right to enforce the law. Radicals, used to getting their way with parents and educators, didn't get their way with the Chicago police.

But Hayden and the riot's organizers got their made-for-television event. The Democrats did not get theirs. America got Richard Nixon. "Did the radicalism of Chicago elect Richard Nixon?" a more mature Hayden asked in 1988. "Having struggled with this question for twenty years, I find there is no 'neat' answer."[71]

That fall, the major tribes of the "movement" united in contempt for mainstream politics. "The Elections Don't Mean Shit," SDS's publication informed, telling its readers to vote in the streets.[72] Black Panther Eldridge Cleaver, neglecting to note his own presidential candidacy, dubbed 1968 "the year of the pig . . . the death of the ballot, the birth of the bullet."[73] "Don't vote in a jackass-elephant-cracker circus," Abbie Hoffman, Jerry Rubin, and Stew Albert told their hippie followers. The trio counseled them to instead have sack races and let farm animals loose in the street.[74]

Far from prelapsarians shaken into cynicism by Robert Kennedy's assassination or Eugene McCarthy's thwarted campaign, the New Left, well before 1968, regarded liberal Democrats with contempt. They generally wanted not peace in Vietnam but, as Hayden made clear as early as 1966, victory for the Communists. "[P]eace as a program is apolitical and immoral in the latter half of the sixties," Julius Lester of SNCC opined in 1967. "It is a luxury in which liberals indulge themselves and momentarily purge their feelings of impotence."[75] They had turned from Martin Luther King Jr.'s message of reconciliation and integration long before his assassination. They were not let down by Lyndon Johnson because they had either declined to vote for him or held their nose while doing so. The radicalism of the New Left was present at the creation. One can't be driven to cynicism by leaders, policies, and a nation one never thought highly of in the first place.

HAYDEN'S PROVOCATION IN Chicago, including his arrest for deflating a police car tire, led to indictments. Leftists, apparently, weren't the only ones buying the myth of "the movement." More so than actual illegalities, which several of them had undoubtedly committed, the Chicago Eight defendants got fingered by the government for their status as icons of their respective tribes: Dave Dellinger, of the Christian pacifists; politicized hippies Jerry Rubin and Abbie Hoffman from the counterculture; Bobby Seale from the Black Panthers; SDS alums Hayden and Rennie Davis from the New Left; and two professors, John Froines and Lee Weiner, thrown in for good measure. From calling Judy Collins to the stand to sing "Where Have All the Flowers Gone?" to hanging a Vietnamese National Liberation Front (NLF) flag on the defense table, the rowdy defendants made a farce of the proceedings.

Defendant Tom Hayden was a real-life Forrest Gump, appearing in the major scenes of the sixties. Only Hayden didn't make cameos, he played the starring role. He worked as a community organizer in Newark when the city erupted in a fiery riot in 1967. He brought POWs home from Vietnam that year. He flopped in a Berkeley commune when the seizure of university land for a "People's Park" sparked violent confrontation with the police. Here, enduring punishment from racist goons in Mississippi; there, inciting young people to rampage through Chicago's streets. Where Tom Hayden went, the sixties followed.

Hayden drove events. Others were driven by them. Diana Oughton's decadal biography was as much the history of the 1960s as Hayden's. JFK's service idealism infected the daughter of privilege, whose two years volunteering in the poorest parts of Guatemala would have been a culture shock to any American, but particularly to one who grew up on a sylvan estate with a goose pond, swimming pool, servants, deer park, and 100-foot-high windmill.[76] Back in America, the Great Society pulled her in as a domestic missionary tending to adult illiterates. Exceptionally sheltered and predictably gullible, the winds of the sixties blew Diana in strange directions.

Graduate studies brought Oughton to the New Left's Ann Arbor epicenter, and to starry-eyed revolutionist Bill Ayers. The couple shared a commitment to activism and the extraordinary wealth to exclusively pursue that commitment. Like Hayden, for whom she helped post bail in

Chicago, Diana alienated herself from her parents.[77] On rare trips home her condescending comrades insulted her father and ridiculed her mother. Her parents sent money. They sought to understand. They tried to bring Diana back within the fold. But Diana had a new family. "My life isn't my own," she said to her sister Pam, explaining her absence on Pam's wedding day. "I don't make the decisions about how I use my time."[78] It could have been worse. "Kill all the rich people," boyfriend Bill Ayers philosophized. "Bring the revolution home, kill your parents, that's where it's really at."[79]

The pair bonded teaching at an unstructured, experimental school in Ann Arbor. "The single most important failing of the school," biographer Thomas Powers points out, "and the one on which it foundered in the end, was the fact that no one ever learned to read there."[80] When the Children's Community School applied for Great Society money, local blacks—the very people the school embraced—persuasively urged the board to deny it funds.[81] The school's closing devastated Diana.

As the decade evolved, so did Diana. Pictures from the Madeira School and Bryn Mawr show a vivacious, smiling beauty. Just a few years later, that girl was unrecognizable in Oughton. Her hair sheared into an unstyled boy's cut, eyes sunken behind John Lennon glasses, figure emaciated, Oughton had transformed herself into a hardened robot. In 1967, at a protest in Washington, the saintly Oughton brought a stone-faced soldier to tears by calmly explaining why she opposed the Vietnam War.[82] By 1970, Oughton the fanatic decided she no longer wished to gently educate American GIs. She wanted to kill them.

DIANA OUGHTON'S NEW family was Weatherman.

The members of Weatherman (known colloquially as the Weathermen) were the people within SDS who actually believed the Left's rhetoric and were willing to act on it. It was common for radical tribes to contend that fascism, concentration camps, and genocide were coming soon to a city near you, that America was intent on transforming every nation into a vassal state for the lord of capitalism, and that American democracy was a sham. If you bought it, if you believed America a bloodthirsty empire committed to killing black people at home and enslaving yellow people abroad, if you believed change through the system was hopeless, why not violence? The Weathermen's premises were wrong. Their logic wasn't.

In 1969, the new-wave SDSers introduced themselves in a document entitled "You Don't Need a Weatherman to Know Which Way the Wind Blows." The manifesto called for communists external and internal to defeat U.S. imperialism. Instead of distributing U.S. wealth to the U.S.

working class, the revolution would distribute it globally, since the American working class had benefited from global exploitation. "The goal is the destruction of U.S. imperialism and the achievement of a classless world: world communism."[83]

Accessible Americanese had credited the Port Huron Statement. Opaque Marxoid jargon marred the Weatherman manifesto. The former sought to communicate; the latter, to credential. Even though first-generation SDSers had consciously separated their project from the Old Left, they nevertheless made Weatherman possible. Old-guard SDS had adopted anti-anti-Communism from the start and soon welcomed Communist members. The Maoists of Progressive Labor immediately began to infest SDS. Angered over Progressive Labor's criticisms of the Vietnamese Communists, SDS regulars developed their own rigid doctrine. "That's the wages of sin," assesses Mike Klonsky, whose faction tried to forge a path independent of Weatherman violence and Progressive Labor fanaticism. "You're fighting dogmatism with dogmatism."[84] Leery of a takeover, SDS expelled Progressive Labor in 1969. Communists, the very people Michael Harrington had warned SDS to stay away from seven years earlier, tore SDS asunder.

THE BLACK LEFT was changing, too. "Now that they've taken Dr. King off, it's time to end this non-violence bullshit," Stokely Carmichael intoned in 1968.[85] King's insulting eulogy was the fiery violence that erupted upon his murder. Malcolm X's ideas, in contrast, grew in popularity after his murder.

The early white Left, primarily through SDS, took cues from SNCC, which embraced non-violent resistance and community organizing. SNCC then catalyzed the Black Panthers, which emphasized violent resistance and revolution. The change had ominous forebodings for the New Left. The activists' equation posited that "SDS plus SNCC = New Left."[86] The black movement's mutation meant the New Left's mutation. SNCC begot the Black Panthers. SDS begot Weatherman.

The white Left chose a bad role model, who never tired of letting everybody know how *bad* he was. A thug who had been expelled from every high school in Oakland, Huey P. Newton picked fights, attempted to murder an adversary in a knife attack, and besieged a fellow black inmate with a steel tray at Santa Rita prison.[87] Some criminals excel at using violence to achieve their ends. Others rely on brainpower. Newton was the mastermind and the enforcer all in one. He engineered fraudulent negligence suits.[88] He waited outside of a local hospital, stealing the cars left running by the panicked drivers at the emergency-room entrance.[89] He swindled store clerks by distracting them while breaking large bills for larger amounts of small bills. He dressed as a gardener to burglarize well-to-do homes.[90] Then Newton launched his ultimate scam, the Black Panthers.

Oakland's Black Panther Party for Self-Defense started on October 15, 1966. The small group launching the Black Panthers established it with seed money from Great Society jobs and marijuana sales.[91] Though blacks in other cities had launched Black Panther parties in response to SNCC's creation of a Black Panther Party in Lowndes County, Alabama, Oakland's chapter dubbed itself *the* Black Panther Party. This would be the first of Newton's many audacious moves, in which adversaries enhanced his power by refusing to call his bluff.

The party's ten-point program demanded that the government ensure full employment, education that "exposes the true nature of this decadent American society," the release of all blacks from prison, and a UN-administered plebiscite "held throughout the black colony" to determine if American blacks desired a separate nation.[92] The party sold a newspaper that boasted a circulation in excess of 100,000 by 1969, served hot breakfasts to poor children, and patrolled the ghetto in search of police brutality. The aboveboard pursuits deluded Marlon Brando, Leonard Bernstein, Donald Sutherland, Jane Fonda, and other celebrity supporters into mistaking a brutal crime organization for a left-wing political group.

One part Che Guevara, two parts *West Side Story*, Black Panthers, Diggers, Young Lords, Up Against the Wall Motherfuckers, White Panthers, United Slaves, and Weathermen were too young for the 1950s juvenile delinquent craze, too old in the 1960s to consciously join a street gang. But that is just what they did, masking their initiation rites, uniforms, clubhouses, and other trappings with a political message that gave adult pretensions to puerile pastimes. Of the politicized street gangs, Newton's was the most successful.

Newton predicted a "colossal event" that would make America pay notice to his outfit of underclass Oakland blacks. On February 21, 1967, the second anniversary of Malcolm X's assassination, the Panthers engineered the first of many "colossal events." Assigned to guard Malcolm X's widow, Betty Shabazz, the shotgun-toting, leather-clad Panthers grabbed the attention of passersby, journalists, and cops. Outside the San Francisco office of *Ramparts* magazine, where parolee Eldridge Cleaver interviewed Shabazz, the police and the Panthers stared down the barrels of one another's guns. "Ok," Newton yelled as he pumped his shotgun, "you big fat racist pig, draw your gun! Draw it, you cowardly dog!"[93] The overweight cop thought the better of it. The Panthers had won the day, and many converts. For ghetto blacks accustomed to police hassles, Newton must have seemed something akin to a modern-day Robin Hood.

One of the day's converts was Eldridge Cleaver. Fresh from prison, Cleaver observed the standoff in astonishment. He looked at Newton and thought, "Goddamn, that nigger is c-r-a-z-y!"[94] Already enjoying a degree of stardom, Cleaver immediately joined the little-known party as its minister of information.

Unlike Newton, whose words meandered and girlish voice underwhelmed, Cleaver was suited for communications. He rose to fame writing letters from Folsom Prison to his lover/attorney Beverly Axelrod. *Ramparts*, his post-prison employer, had published the letters in the lead-up to his parole. The jailhouse writings became *Soul on Ice*, a shocking book that never shocked so much as when Cleaver detailed his crimes against women. "I became a rapist," he coolly noted. He confessed practicing sexual assaults on black girls, and then "consciously, deliberately, willfully, methodically" graduated to white women. "Rape was an insurrectionary act," Cleaver wrote. "It delighted me that I was defying and trampling upon the white man's law, upon his system of values, and that I was defiling his women—and this point, I believe, was the most satisfying to me because I was very resentful over the historical fact of how the white man has used the black woman."[95] Though Cleaver recognized the injustice of the nocturnal hobby that sent him to prison, he contended that "the blood of the Vietnamese peasants has paid off all my debts."[96] This belief, that the historic weight of the injustices by the white race granted automatic immunity to individual blacks who victimized individual whites, permeated black-power ideology.

Other "colossal events" followed. On May 2, 1967, Bobby Seale led a delegation of armed blacks to protest gun-control legislation at the California state capitol. The sight of twenty or so steely blacks, wearing cool black shades and cooler black leather jackets, guns at the ready, invading the anti-ghetto of the state capitol, made for the ultimate in street theater. Huey Newton, who orchestrated the spectacle from afar, had a genius for making others pay attention to people they normally ignored.

On October 28, Newton, who had been monitoring Oakland police on late-night rides, engaged in street theater of a tragic sort. After getting pulled over by rookie officer John Frey, Newton scuffled with Frey and then shot him dead. Frey's backup shot and arrested Newton. Though Newton's innocence became an article of faith on the Left, the Panther leader later bragged to friends of killing Frey.[97]

With Newton incarcerated, his violent cohorts took charge. Cleaver engineered his own "colossal event" two days after the King assassination. With urban America on fire, Cleaver outlined an armed assault on the police. "We've got to prove we're the vanguard," he told David Hilliard. "Everybody's doing something around the country. We're gonna move now."[98] Cleaver, Hilliard, and a well-armed posse of Panthers rode into the night in search of cops.[99] They shot two policemen in the back, which inaugurated a ninety-minute gun battle that ended only when police unleashed tear gas in the building the Panthers employed as a makeshift bunker. A totally afraid and totally nude Cleaver, with nowhere to hide a gun, emerged from the building, as did the Panthers' seventeen-year-old minister of defense, Bobby Hutton. Hutton either stumbled or attempted to flee, and the police shot him dead. Rather than waste away in prison like Newton, a bailed-out Cleaver fled to Cuba, then to Algeria, where he set up his own Black Panther government in exile. There, one of the most bizarre confluences of "movement" tribes occurred.

In 1970, Timothy Leary broke out of a minimum security prison in California by shimmying on a wire over a fence and into freedom. Through fund-raising efforts and the benevolence of a southern California drug gang, Leary's wife, Rosemary Woodruff, paid Weatherman $25,000 to facilitate Leary's escape from the United States. Weatherman provided a disguise, transportation in a camper bearing a bumper sticker that read "America: Love It or Leave It," a safe house, and fake identification.[100] The drug fugitive and the radical fugitives then each released a communiqué that sounded as if the other had authored it. "LSD and grass," Weatherman's Bernardine Dohrn proclaimed, "will help us make a future world where it will be possible to live in peace."[101] "You cannot talk peace and love to a humanoid robot," Leary explained. "To shoot a genocidal robot policeman in the defense of life is a sacred act."[102]

Dr. Tim made it to the Panther embassy in Algeria. The Panthers soon tired of Leary. They beat him up, confiscated his drugs, and held him and his wife, Rosemary, captive. Cleaver menacingly informed the hippie press, "Don't worry about Tim and Rosemary: Pappa's seeing after them."[103] He was, in effect, Leary's new jailer, and unbeknownst to inmate Leary, warden Cleaver had just executed another Panther.[104] Cleaver denounced Leary as "apolitical" and an "opportunist," telling his followers, "[Y]our god is dead because his mind has been blown by acid. If you think that by tuning in, turning on and dropping out, you're improving the situation, that you're changing society, it's very clear that you're doing nothing except destroying your own brains and strengthening the hands of our enemy."[105] Leary's mind was not so blown by acid that he was oblivious to danger. He escaped from his Panther kidnappers just as he had escaped from his California jailers.

As Eldridge Cleaver condemned hard drugs in Algiers, Huey Newton took them in Oakland. The Black Panther leader was a psychopathic criminal, not a revolutionary. But with inmate Newton inaccessible to his admirers, a famous picture—Newton sitting in an oversized wicker chair with one hand on a rifle and the other on a tribal spear—and a "Free Huey" slogan lionized him as a revolutionary. Getting convicted of Frey's murder was a great career move for Newton. The panache, machismo, and, especially, penchant for mouthing back to white activists their revolutionary jargon made Newton an icon. SDS sponsored birthday celebrations for Newton. *New Left Notes*, in the span of one month, placed Panthers on the cover five times. The Weathermen paternalistically anointed the Panthers the vanguard of the African American community and hailed their efforts to defeat the United States from within as the "Black Vietnam."[106] One white activist characterized the New Left as "just a little tail on the end of a very powerful black panther," declaring his desire "to be on that tail—if they'll let me."[107]

The Panthers treated the sycophants with the contempt they invited—which made the white Left love their abusers even more. The Black Panthers beat up the Weathermen, denounced them, and commandeered their printing press at gunpoint.[108] Still, the rich white kids vehemently denied the criminal nature of their heroes. No atrocity, no matter how brutal, could topple the Panthers' iconic status. No excuse, no matter how improbable, would be doubted.

The police had targeted the Panthers for elimination, or so the sixties mythology went. In late 1969, Panther attorney Charles Garry pointed to twenty-nine Panthers murdered by the police. But when pressed to provide names, he could only offer journalist Edward Jay Epstein nineteen. Of those, one, Alex Rackley, had been tortured and killed by Panthers, another had been killed by his wife, and four had been killed by a rival black gang, United Slaves. What did the police have to do with any of that? Just ten of the nineteen had perished at the hands of the police. And of those ten, six had shot and wounded policemen immediately before falling. Two others had brandished weapons. Bobby Hutton, who had just participated in a ninety-minute gun battle with police, and Fred Hampton, asleep in the midst of a police raid, were the only Panthers unarmed at their deaths.[109]

Were the cops conducting an assassination campaign against Panthers? Or were the Panthers conducting an assassination campaign against cops? Truth mattered little. The "Free Huey" pressure campaign worked. The grand and almighty panjandrum of the Black Panther Party for Self Defense was back on the streets, freed by a technicality, in 1970.

A coked-up Newton shifted his violence from blues to blacks. He moved outside the 'hood to a tony condominium, assumed the title "Supreme Servant," and pilfered money from party programs. In 1971, he purged Cleaver, setting off a murderous tête à tête. A paranoid Newton expelled old friend David Hilliard, whom he had entrusted to run the party in his incarcerated absence, while Hilliard served a prison sentence for the Cleaver-engineered gun battle. The Supreme Servant allegedly sexually brutalized a male underling and beat up a female associate so badly she required hospitalization.[110] Newton's lackeys had cultivated a cult of personality, and that is what they got.

SOME ON THE Left condemned the violent tactics of groups such as the Black Panthers and Weatherman as counterproductive and fascist. Yet that violence was not an aberration. ROTC buildings, banks, draft-induction centers, and corporations suffered the wrath of political bombers, most totally unrelated to Weatherman. A federal official told Senate investigators in 1970 that "4,330 bombings in the last 15½ months have left more than 40 persons dead and 384 injured and caused more than $22 million in property damage."[111] At the University of California—Santa Barbara, a bombing took the life of a black janitor. At the University of Wisconsin, Weatherman wanna-bes blew up a mathematics building and killed a graduate student working into the wee hours. Even Tom Hayden had explored shooting down police helicopters over Berkeley.[112]

The resort to violence reflected a larger shift away from the intellectual origins of the youth protest movement. SDS had shifted from an organization of graduate students and young intellectuals to a street gang of dropouts and thrill-seekers. At the 1969 convention, Bill Ayers, for instance, boasted in his campaign speech for national office that neither he nor Mark Rudd nor Jeff Jones had read a book in a year.[113] SDS promptly elected the trio its national officers.

SDS leaders once discussed the weighty ideas of Albert Camus and Norman O. Brown. Now they took political direction from rock records. Rather than the outcome of a rhyming dictionary, the rock lyrics of the era were, for the New Left, mystic, oracular wisdom to be deciphered. SDS manifestos, lifting titles from songs played on the radio—"Hot Town: Summer in the City," "There's a Man Going 'Round Taking Names," and, most famously, "You Don't Need a Weatherman to Know Which Way the Wind Blows"—advertised the childish, anti-intellectual drift.[114] Style increasingly trumped substance, with none as stylish as Bernardine Dohrn, dubbed by J. Edgar Hoover "La Pasionaria of the Lunatic Left."[115] The vision of Dohrn, so perfect in knee-high boots, miniskirt, leather jacket, and shades, certainly attracted more recruits than had the Port Huron Statement. Even mugshots became an occasion for Weathermen to strike a pose.

The larger Left was no better. A generation raised in front of the television wanted everyone to watch them on television. The media-baiting antics of Abbie Hoffman and Stokely Carmichael exemplified the desire of people who worshipped the idiot box to make a break from the pews to the altar. Proto-Weathermen saw *Butch Cassidy and the Sundance Kid*, *Bonnie and Clyde*, and *The Wild Bunch* and imagined themselves. It was a movement that looked to pop culture rather than learned men because it was a movement led by people on the intellectual level of pop culture. Whereas the 1950s lacked action, the 1960s lacked thinking.

If leftist leaders came across as immature, it is because they were. Most people in their early twenties *are* to some degree. Mario Savio was twenty-one when he delivered histrionic speeches as part of Berkeley's Free Speech Movement. Huey Newton was twenty-five when he murdered John Frey. Mark Rudd was twenty when he closed a letter to the president of Columbia University by telling him, "Up against the wall, motherfucker."[116] To his fawning assessment of Communists on a 1965 trip to Vietnam, Tom Hayden reminds: "I was twenty-five."[117] Immaturity excuses many transgressions (Did you ever do something embarrassing in your twenties?), but movement elders—Dave Dellinger, Herbert Marcuse, Allen Ginsberg, Timothy Leary—who egged on younger admirers could credibly offer no such defense. "Don't trust anyone over thirty," the mantra rang. But those over thirty who flattered the enfants terribles won enormous reserves of trust, which they abused. They knew where the power lay, and played sycophant to get it.

In the 1960s, inside and outside the Left, youth was king. For better and worse, Americans were its subjects. Never did King Youth seem more tyrannical than in October 1969's "Days of Rage," four days of Weatherman-designed violence, vandalism, and mayhem in Chicago. Using the rallying cry "Bring the War Home," Weatherman prepared for the riots by trying to recruit blue-collar youths to fight the mother country of capitalist imperialism from the inside.

In advance of the scheduled riot, SDS recruitment trips to high schools and youth hangouts met with stony silence and violent hostility. Weatherman emissaries attempted to connect with blue-collar youth. Several youths connected back with right crosses and left hooks. "It was a crazy

notion that somehow if we showed militancy people would join us," Mark
Rudd maintains, "that we were fighting to win. It was some kind of goofy
ideology of building a white fighting force that would aid the people of
the world." In Milwaukee, SDS activists proselytized their message with
disastrous results. "We were marching down a main street that the
greasers used for cruising with an NLF flag or something," Rudd recalls.
The greasers took offense. Street-fighting men indulged. Rudd found
himself on the street, the recipient of repeated kicks. He spent several
days in the hospital. "I think I have kidney damage."[118]

Ayers remembered "persuading ourselves against all evidence that the
working-class youth were with us, that our uncompromising militancy
was winning them over."[119] It wasn't. A scant few hundred young people,
instead of the thousands promised, converged on Chicago's Lincoln Park
for Days of Rage. Tom Hayden, in Chicago for his trial stemming from the
Democratic National Convention riots the previous year, gave those gathered a pep talk.

"[W]e weren't only outnumbered and outgunned, we might just be
out of our minds," Ayers recalled thinking. "My stomach sank. Where
were all the revolutionary youth?"[120] In an action that Black Panther Fred
Hampton aptly described as "Custeristic," the Weathermen smashed windows, torched cars, and fought cops.[121] Mayor Richard J. Daley's police,
like Crazy Horse's Indians, won. The Weathermen sadistically celebrated
paralyzing a city official.[122] The senselessness of the violence validated the
wider Left's decision to stay home.

Rather than colorfully confront the law on its home court as the
Chicago Eight did, the Days of Rage organizers, as several CPUSA Smith
Act defendants had done in the 1950s, went underground. This was not a
task without sacrifice for the sons and daughters of privilege. More so than
their counterparts in the early SDS, Weathermen enjoyed plush upbringings. Bill Ayers, whose father served as chairman of Chicago's Commonwealth Edison, still accepted his allowance despite engaging in parricidal
rhetoric, rationalizing that it was fine by him if his dad bankrolled the revolution.[123] Kathy Boudin spent her childhood inside the ritzy town house
whose façade appeared on *The Cosby Show* to denote the prosperity its fictional inhabitants enjoyed.[124] Her uncle was the left-wing journalist I. F.
Stone. Her great-uncle was Louis Boudin, who participated in the famous
1919 exodus from the Socialist Party only to bolt John Reed's Communist
Labor Party at its organizing convention. "I did not leave a party of crooks
to join a party of lunatics," he scoffed.[125] Kathy proudly dated a son of the
Rosenbergs, while her father, attorney to Communist spy Judith Coplon,
Cuban dictator Fidel Castro, and faux–folk singer Joan Baez, furtively

dated Paul Goodman.[126] Jeff Jones's father declared himself a conscientious objector during World War II. The student body president at southern California's Sylmar High, Jeff was named YMCA "Boy of the Year" runner-up.[127] Mark Rudd's immigrant parents lived the American dream. His father went to Rutgers on an ROTC scholarship, served as an army officer, and got rich in real estate. During the Columbia takeover, Rudd's mom brought him a home-cooked meal on Mother's Day.[128] The colleges the Weathermen attended—Columbia, Bryn Mawr, Kenyon, Swarthmore, Oberlin—were rich-kid schools.

"Bill Ayers and many of the Weathermen came from elite backgrounds, I mean really upper-class wealth," notes Dick Flacks, the son of public school teachers, who preceded Ayers in the University of Michigan chapter by several years. "One thing about that kind of background is that even if you've converted to belief in social transformation and you're against upper-class privilege, it's real hard to overcome your deep training as a member of that class that you have the right to run the world."[129] Carl Oglesby, who had likened the Weathermen to his children, explains, "Without question, they saw themselves as the ruling class. Even when they turned against the ruling class, they were still of it. They were still part of it. They still had a deeply inbred assumption that they knew what the country needed and they knew how to deliver it."[130] Wealth "was no inhibition to [the Weathermen's] recklessness," Todd Gitlin observes. "To the contrary, it was a logical precondition for their recklessness. It's much easier to have fantastical ideas, either revolutionary or genuflections toward revolutionary, or for that matter condescending toward the rest of the world, when the rest of the world and its ways are beneath you."[131]

Eager to prove their bona fides, the debutantes and mama's boys turned "stone revolutionary communists" gave themselves over to bizarre practices. Diana Oughton's cadre hunted and ate an alley cat.[132] Bill Ayers carved a jailhouse tattoo of a red star rising on his left shoulder.[133] A shirtless John Jacobs sampled the food off passengers' plates as he traipsed down the aisle of a commercial flight.[134] Weathermen traded forks for chopsticks. They learned karate. They "smashed monogamy" by enforcing group sex, homosexuality, and the rotation of partners. "They abandoned their kids as policy," family man Mike Klonsky remembers. "The people who had kids when they joined gave their kids away."[135]

Weatherman killed SDS as the 1960s turned into the 1970s, just as SDS had killed SLID a decade earlier. The Weathermen systematically destroyed SDS membership lists and minutes to old meetings. They discontinued *New Left Notes.* They closed the national office. In the words of one proud Weatherman: "Well, we offed the pig."[136] The ever-more-ultra ultraism within SDS that had first come for Michael Harrington and the LID old men, and then Lyndon Johnson, and then Martin Luther King Jr., and then Bobby Kennedy and Eugene McCarthy, and then the peace people, now came for SDS itself.

"Why couldn't we leave the organization to other people and just go underground?" a contrite Mark Rudd wonders. "No, no, no, it was worse than that. We wanted to destroy SDS because it was some kind of impediment to the real revolution. And we felt that we knew what that real revolution was, we had the right idea. It was total arrogance."[137]

Amidst an orgy of sex, drugs, and rock 'n' roll, the Weathermen hoisted banners extolling "Charlie Manson Power" at a War Party in Flint, Michigan, days before decade's end. The gathering adopted a split-fingered greeting in homage to the fork that impaled the stomach of Manson Family victim Leno LaBianca. The cadre of Diana Oughton and Kathy Boudin even named itself "The Fork." Bullets spelling the name of Sharon Tate (who, along with her full-term unborn baby, lost her life to the Manson cult) greeted activists upon arrival. Perhaps instigated by the murder of Tate's unborn child, participants debated the justice of killing white babies. Of the Manson Family, Weatherman matriarch Bernardine Dohrn told those assembled: "Dig it: first they killed those pigs, then they ate dinner in the same room with them, then they even shoved a fork into the victim's stomach. Wild!"[138]

The Flint "wargasm" was Weatherman's last public hurrah before Bernardine Dorhn, Bill Ayers, Jeff Jones, Kathy Boudin, Mark Rudd, John Jacobs, and others went on the lam. The Weathermen enhanced their outlaw status on March 6, 1970. While her dad vacationed in St. Kitts, former *New Left Notes* editor Cathy Wilkerson allowed his Manhattan town house to become an amateur bomb factory. It met the fate of many amateur bomb factories before it.

Sticks of dynamite, pipe bombs, nails, blasting caps, wiring, alarm clocks, and batteries littered the town house basement. The intended target was a dance for enlisted men at Fort Dix, New Jersey. Instead, a ferocious blast imploded the town house, carved a twenty-foot hole in the wall of the neighboring unit, and shattered windows six stories high across the street. It left "the body of a young radical leader, a headless female torso, [and] the remains of a third person so mangled that gender was still uncertain" for days, *Time* reported.[139]

Ted Gold, ironically once a member of Columbia SDS's more restrained "praxis axis" that had opposed Mark Rudd's "action faction," was crushed under the nineteenth-century town house's fallen beams. Diana Oughton experienced what she had hoped to unleash on servicemen with less fortunate upbringings: nails ripped her limbs and head from her body. A severed finger later identified her. Kenyon College dropout and Jesse James Gang member Terry Robbins, who had the previous week set off explosives at the home of the judge presiding over a trial of Black Panthers, was so thoroughly dismembered that his identification came only by way of the Weathermen.

Cathy Wilkerson emerged dazed from her father's house. Kathy Boudin, a classmate of Oughton's at Bryn Mawr, came out naked and bleeding. Neighbor Dustin Hoffman stared in disbelief. His wife provided a curtain to clothe Boudin. Henry Fonda's ex-wife helped clean the disheveled and dust-covered girls.[140] Then, quickly, the pair vanished into the underground.

Mark Rudd, whose status had diminished within Weatherman, nevertheless performed "a liaison function" for the wanna-be terrorists. "It was a pretty big secret," Rudd affirms of the bombing plot. "Everyone was pretty much aware."[141] No one was willing to stop it.

Holding understudies responsible proved difficult for elders. How did anti-war activists become terrorist bombers? "Cointelpro," Carl Oglesby contends, referring to the FBI program that targeted radical groups. "Definitely. No question about it."[142] "My own private hypothesis," Al Haber holds, is "they knew they had gone crazy when they undertook this, and they blew it up themselves." Haber acknowledges that no evidence supports his belief. Nevertheless, he imagines that the town house bombers concluded that "this is so sick, that we have gone so far off the deep end in we are thinking about killing people to make peace that we should just self-destruct."[143]

Such is the historiography of sixties leftists. A Communist kills the president. They blame the CIA instead. Liberals launch a war in Southeast Asia. The Left later imagines it the work of conservatives. Black Muslims assassinate Malcolm X. They charge a white racist conspiracy. Democrats stand athwart civil rights legislation. They record Republicans as the chief obstacle. Politicized people dismissed what made sense logically to believe what made sense politically.

The Left's 1960s began in Greensboro on February 1, 1960, when students imposed their morality on racist businessmen by disrupting their enterprises until the proprietors operated in a manner to the activists' liking. It ended in Greenwich Village on March 6, 1970, when activists killed themselves with the bombs they had constructed to kill American soldiers immersed in a war they disliked. Once coercion of fellow citizens became

acceptable, once ends justified means, once lawbreaking became a con-
doned tactic, the slope got slippery. A decade separated Greensboro and
Greenwich Village. A thread connected them.

And a thread connected the sixties to previous Lefts, no matter how
much the New Left imagined itself as the beginning of that thread. Just as
Mike Gold had eulogized a trio of would-be killers of affluent party-goers
in verse as "fellow soldiers too impatient to await the signal," an anonymous sympathizer fifty-six years later rhapsodized over the incautious-
ness of would-be killers of merrymakers at a soldiers' dance: "An hour, a
week / A month that's taken / To insure a victory / Is time well taken." Like
Gold's trio who "loved too much," the town house threesome were "Lovers
of Humanity."[144] History offered a reprise, but did its actors know that
they were delivering a repeat performance? Terry Robbins may have. The
week of his death, he had come across an editorial from *Alarm!*, the anarchist newspaper put out by Albert Parsons, one of the four Haymarket
Square bombers to die by the executioner's noose eighty-three years earlier.[145] Bombing not only failed to achieve objectives in 1886, it discredited the Left. So, too, did the imploded plot to kill John D. Rockefeller Jr.
and friends in 1914. Again, it failed when tried by Weatherman in 1970.

Michael Harrington had played the role of Terence Powderly, caution-
ing the Left against SDS extremism just as Powderly had cautioned the
labor movement against anarchists. "They had decided that it was no
longer enough to destroy buildings in order to shake up the system; now
they must kill people," Harrington observed. "Indeed, one could find a
grisly symbolism in the event. These revolutionary novices ended their
own lives, not those of their alleged oppressors, and did so, not in a slum
cellar, but in a rich man's house."[146] Harrington, like Powderly eighty-
four years earlier, took no solace in being right. Both knew that foolish
erstwhile allies, and not the Cassandras, would be remembered. Lean
times awaited the movement Harrington had dedicated his life to.

The Left didn't listen to their political elders perhaps because their actual parents offered little in the way of worthy guidance. "Even though
there is a big difference of opinion as to whether she's right or wrong, I'm
sure that in her own heart she conscientiously felt she was right," James
Oughton, a former Illinois Republican state senator, said of his frag-
mented daughter. "She wasn't doing this for any other gain than—well—
you might say the good of the world."[147]

The good intentions of the 1960s were over. Their bad consequences
were just beginning.

THE PERSONAL IS
THE POLITICAL

He hath opened a pit and dug it: and he is fallen into the hole he made.
—PSALMS 7:16

THE 1960S CAUSED a massive hangover. Activists faced something that they had habitually brushed aside: consequences. What, if any, consequences followed drug use? A permissive criminal justice system? Promiscuity? Losing in Vietnam? Government handouts? America painfully discovered the answers. If the arrival of the 1970s did not signal the end of the 1960s, events quickly did.

LYNDON JOHNSON'S GREAT Society turned out to be the ingrate society. Freeloaders burdened taxpayers. In the *Rat*, a pseudonymous social worker offered tips to the hippie readership on how to commit welfare fraud. "Welfare, I think, may be the wave of the future, the first step toward the guaranteed annual income which will free us from the need to work."[1] Recipients demanded more, more, more. "Poor people should be allowed to trade in [food] stamps for money," judged the National Welfare Rights Organization. Not only should welfare recipients be immune from work requirements, but "homemaker services" should be provided to them.[2] It was all too pushy, all too costly. Working people had supported programs lifting the poor onto their feet, but programs keeping them on their asses asked too much.

Woodstock's spirit of peace and love was replaced by violence and hate at the Altamont Speedway in December 1969. As northern California concert-goers enjoyed the free performances by the Grateful Dead, Jefferson Airplane, and the Rolling Stones, pool-cue-toting Hell's Angels enjoyed pummeling fans and band members. One fan, perhaps tired of the abuse, pulled a knife. A Hell's Angel killed him. That month, hundreds of miles south, the state brought Charles Manson and his hippie followers before a court of justice for serial murder. Jerry Rubin, Bernardine Dohrn, and other radicals praised the cult leader.[3] Peace? Love?

Extremists, as if working a pulley, dragged America rightward as they tried to pull it leftward. The Weathermen continued bombing government and corporate targets through 1974. They eluded police, and the public's interest eventually eluded them. The Symbionese Liberation Army (SLA) captured the nation's attention when it captured heiress Patty Hearst in 1974. The SLA had murdered Oakland's first black superintendent of schools a year earlier and later murdered a mother during a bank robbery. These radicals did not get off scot-free, as so many Weathermen and Black Panthers had. Six SLA soldiers died in a fiery standoff, and the remainder, even if belatedly, did time. In 1975, two radical women—a follower of Charles Manson citing environmental concerns and an SLA hanger-on wanting to strike a blow for radicalism—made separate assassination attempts on President Gerald Ford.[4] Leonard Peltier became a cause célèbre after murdering two FBI agents in 1975. Though 114 shell casings expended in the ambush matched his rifle's extractor, witnesses identified him, he admitted his role in the ambush, and he subsequently used firearms in a police shoot-out and in the robbery of a farmer, Peltier's courtiers dubbed him a political prisoner. A jury dubbed him a murderer.[5]

Most disturbing of the left-wing violence was that of the Peoples Temple. "The temple was as much a left-wing political crusade as a church," explained a writer in *The Nation.* "In the course of the 1970s, its social program grew steadily more disaffiliated from what Jim Jones came to regard as a 'Fascist America' and drifted rapidly toward outspoken Communist sympathies."[6] Like the nineteenth-century communal ventures that they harkened back to, the Peoples Temple represented an attempt to separate from the cultural pollution of America. "Nobody's gonna come out of the sky! There's no heaven up there," an excited "comrade leader" Jones told his flock. "We'll have to have heaven down here!" They exited San Francisco to build Eden in the South American jungle. The familiar story prefaced an unfamiliar ending. Instead of waiting out the millennium at the agricultural commune in Guyana, the drugged and disturbed Jones made it happen. On November 18, 1978, he orchestrated the "revolutionary suicide"—a phrase borrowed from Huey Newton—of more than nine hundred people.[7] How could such a lunatic have rubbed shoulders with future

First Lady Rosalynn Carter, vice presidential nominee Walter Mondale, California governor Jerry Brown, and other Democratic Party luminaries? How could the mayor of San Francisco have appointed him chairman of the city's housing commission? How could Huey Newton, Angela Davis, and Willie Brown have embraced a man who would kill more blacks than the Ku Klux Klan?

The public (or at least segments of it) might have viewed the Black Panthers or the Weathermen with amusement in the 1960s, but by the 1970s they recognized the radical outlaws and cult-of-personality leaders as dangerous and crazy and evil and idiotic. Americans were in no mood to indulge criminals, no matter if they attempted to attach politics to the crimes or not. Whether the Left romanticized the criminals, as they subsequently did of Peltier, or washed their hands of them, as they quickly did of Jones, the public nevertheless sleuthed the connections between the extremists and their politics.

Fear of crime mounted. Leftists were partaking of it in extreme cases, and excusing it in others. "Enough already," yelped a frustrated America. As courts and parole boards became more permissive, crime reached record heights. Between 1960 and 1980, the violent crime rate tripled.[8] The murder rate doubled.[9] In addition to liberal attitudes prevailing in the justice system, symbolized in the Supreme Court's brief invalidation of capital punishment laws, an increase in drug use fueled the increase in crime. Between the 1960s and the 1990s, drug arrests rose by more than 1,000 percent.[10] Impaired judgment brought on by drugs, the burning desire to feed the addiction, and shootouts between rival dealers fueled the crime epidemic. Crack, crystal meth, heroin, and other narcotic scourges transformed cities into war zones and users into corpses.

In 1970, not long after the Beatles broke up, rock stars Jimi Hendrix and Janis Joplin died overindulging in mind-altering substances, and Jim Morrison followed suit in 1971. Drugs *were* dangerous after all. The sixties counterculture could have discovered this from the fifties counterculture, but narcissists don't have antecedents. Jack Kerouac's slow suicide by alcohol, Neal Cassady's drug-addled death by the tracks, and William Burroughs's slaying of his wife failed to register, or, when they did, added to their legend. Previous generations did drugs. The baby boomers, believing they had stumbled upon something new, were the only ones ignorant enough to deny their consequences. They thought that what was new for them was new for everyone. What was new was the societal acceptance of drugs. The problems of a few became the problems of many.

. . .

AS WITH ROCK 'n' roll and drugs, so, too, with sex. So appealing was the call of Norman O. Brown, Wilhelm Reich, and Herbert Marcuse to liberate one's senses from the constraints of civilization that many oblivious to these three wise men of the counterculture heeded their counsel. The appeal, after all, was sensual and not intellectual. A quick course in Brown, Reich, or Marcuse was unnecessary to make converts to the fledgling sex cult they had helped inspire. Just as repression was the cost of civilization, civilization was the price of "liberation." In 1960, unmarried couplings produced one in twenty American children; by 1970, the figure was one in ten; by 1980, one in five; by the millennium, one in three.[11] Americans of varying political persuasions placed greater emphasis on sexual pleasure than on ensuring their offspring loving parents. The Left was just more indignant about it.

"Single parents are proving that we don't have to stay together for the children's sake," a celebrant of the emerging sexual dystopia informed in *Mother Jones*. "And birth control insures that we don't have to procreate in the first place." In case readers didn't get the Left's message on marriage, the writer bluntly offered: "Marriage has always been less about love than about possession"; "Marriage undermines women's emotional well-being"; "[M]arriage discriminates against women."[12]

Instead of eliminating a marriage, millions of parents eliminated their unborn children. While one in three *births* occurred among unmarried women, one in four *pregnancies* ended in abortion.[13] Marriage itself became less stable for children. After 1960, the marriage rate dropped precipitously and the divorce rate rose alarmingly.[14] No-fault divorces, destigmatization, the pressures of double-income child rearing, and other alterations to civilization eroded the civilizing institution of marriage. Former SDS president Todd Gitlin later observed that "only the most sentimental ex-hippie could fail to recognize the prices paid on the road to the new freedoms: the booming teenage pregnancy rate; the dread diseases that accompanied the surge in promiscuity; the damage done by drugs; the undermining of family commitment, which, although it could hardly be blamed on human-potential do-your-thingism altogether, could not be said to have been resisted by it either."[15] Alas, more than just sentimental ex-hippies failed to acknowledge the casualties of the sexual utopia.

The sexual revolution's fiercest soldiers proved its saddest martyrs. The 1970s unleashed decades of repression in a maelstrom of debauchery. Shirtless mustachioed musclemen, delicate drag queens, leather-clad masters, and stereotype-defying homosexuals flocked to urban centers where the disco pulsated, the amyl nitrate circulated, and the public-park bushes, barroom backrooms, and bathhouses teemed with male-on-male sex. Whatever one's kink, it was a glorious time to be a hedonist. Sex was available, anonymous, and without terrible consequence. Stop signs came in the 1970s in the form of social diseases herpes and hepatitis B. Gay liberationists raced past without halting. The stop signs turned into an unremitting roadblock once the 1970s became the 1980s. "Too much is being transmitted," a doctor in San Francisco's public health department prophetically warned in 1980. "We've got all these diseases going unchecked. There are so many opportunities for transmission that, if something new gets loose here, we're going to have hell to pay."[16] Something new got loose.

Purplish lesions, profuse night sweats, and swollen glands were the first signs. An unfamiliar virus, confined almost exclusively to New York, San Francisco, Los Angeles, and Miami, began killing homosexual men. The very idea that sex caused AIDS struck hardened veterans of the sexual revolution as a slur against venery.

New realities played havoc with old verities. To hang on to the seventies ideology of self-gratification meant self-destruction in the eighties. But hang on too many did. Pre-AIDS, the homosexual movement had been about liberation. Wasting away in an AIDS hospice, however, was no one's idea of "liberation." The gay Left wanted sexual liberation *and* immunity from AIDS. The government they had told to keep *out* during the 1970s they now wanted *in* during the 1980s. They wanted the freedom to make a mess and they tasked the government to clean it up. A Freedom Left adopted the features of a Force Left as AIDS altered the political interests of gays. The traditional libertarianism opposed to sodomy laws, bathhouse closures, and invasions of medical privacy was joined by big-government liberalism in demands for research funds, free medical care, condom giveaways, and legal protections against discrimination. The homosexual Left took on the attributes of other minority special-interest groups. Whereas a freedom ideology defined it in the 1970s, interest, disconnected from neat and consonant ideology, defined it in the 1980s.

The gay Left valued the sexual utopia they had created more than life. Even after being diagnosed with a transmittable death sentence, victims of the "gay cancer" caroused in the bars, cruised along Castro and Christopher Streets, and plunged back into the bathhouses.[17] "I didn't become a homosexual so I could use a condom," scoffed a co-chair of San Francisco's gay pride parade.[18] Just as individual gays recklessly pursued sexual conquests long after they had been diagnosed, leading gay institutions recklessly stood athwart attempts to curtail the virus that dealt so much disease and death.

Gay groups, for instance, were the fiercest defenders of the bathhouses that served as incubators of the virus. The battle over the Cornhole, Folsom Prison, and more than a dozen such San Francisco health menaces grew heated in 1984. The protest placards of towel-clad demonstrators unsubtly shrieked, "Out of the Baths, Into the Ovens." The leading national gay magazine, the *Advocate*, compared bathhouse critics to "Chicken Little." The publisher of New York City's main gay newspaper, once health officials managed to order the baths closed (a move opposed by all but one San Francisco gay group), castigated a Centers for Disease Control official: "Now that you've succeeded in closing down the baths, are you preparing boxcars for relocation?"[19] That the baths themselves so closely paralleled the death camp "showers," ostensibly hygienic chambers in which victims entered oblivious to the death that awaited them, seems never to have occurred to the miasmic authors of wildly stretched analogies. With sex on the brain, they mistook impulses for thought.

When scientists developed the first AIDS test in 1985, the Lambda Legal Defense Fund and the National Gay Task Force actually sued the federal government to block its release. Gay activists paternalistically sought to protect the tested from theoretic privacy threats. But couldn't those seeking the test make the decision for themselves? The courts opted to allow saving lives rather than protect civil liberties from a phantom threat. But in New York City, then the AIDS capital of the world, pressure from gay groups resulted in a city ban on the test.[20]

Even an act as benign and sensible as screening out homosexual blood donors, to weed out at-risk individuals from needlessly killing any more blood recipients, became, in the dated vernacular of sexual liberation, an insult to homosexual civil liberties akin to anti-miscegenation laws, internment camps, and pink triangles.[21]

It was insane and criminal and reckless. Revisionists forgot it all, and blamed such unlikely perpetrators as Ronald Reagan and the clergy for the spread of AIDS. The harmless overreaction of rubes who feared contracting AIDS from public toilet seats, rather than the harmful whines of sophisticates who delayed such commonsense measures as blood-donor screening and the HIV test, somehow remain a symbol of the age's hysteria. More than a quarter-century after doctors began noticing a strange virus that attacked the immune systems of gay men, a half-million Americans, the majority homosexuals, lay dead.[22] So, too, perished the enslaving rhetoric of sexual liberation.

. . .

"OBJECTIVELY, THE CHANCES seem nil that we could start a movement based on anything as distant to general American thought as a sex-caste system," Casey Hayden and Mary King wrote in a memo circulated through SDS and SNCC in the mid-1960s. They noted that a prime reason for the pessimism involved the Left itself, which greeted women's concerns with ridicule and excluded women from positions of power.[23] Indeed, SDS's ten-year history boasted just two women elected to national office.[24] The men in SDS married its female stars. They didn't elect them.

As the movement got bigger, so did its woman problem. At a National Mobilization Committee—organized protest of Richard Nixon's inauguration, SDS veteran Marilyn Webb lectured the audience about sexism under capitalism, only to hear catcalls of "Take it off!" and "Take her off the stage and fuck her!" A phone call threatened Webb with bodily harm if she delivered another speech like that. "SDS has a line on liberation," the caller, thought to be proto-Weatherman Cathy Wilkerson, announced, "and that is *the line.*"[25] At an SDS convention later that year, one Black Panther horrified attendees by endorsing "pussy power," while another, in an example of damage control gone out of control, quipped from the podium that women did indeed have a position within the movement: "prone."[26] Panther heavies Huey Newton, Eldridge Cleaver, and David Hilliard committed horrible acts of violence against women that, alas, enhanced their street credibility.[27] The wanna-be White Panthers weren't much better, counseling: "Fuck your woman so hard till she can't stand up."[28] It was an era of the street-fighting man, poseur machismo, the smashing of monogamy, and women saying yes to draftees saying no.

Out of the ashes came women's liberation. Like the earliest American women's movement, which culminated in 1848's Seneca Falls Declaration of Sentiments, women's liberation started as a movement within a movement. Abolitionism, and the multitude of satellite causes in its antebellum orbit, had alerted women to their own oppression, as they extended the chain of reasoning of anti-racism to themselves and confronted prohibitions on organizational officeholding and even restrictions on speaking at anti-slavery meetings. Likewise, the visible hypocrisy of anti-war, student, and civil-rights leaders blasting discrimination while practicing it against women made feminism a predictable outcome of the protest culture.

To be sure, voices in the wilderness beckoned women to a women's movement long before such a movement existed. Most conspicuously, Betty Friedan, once a fellow traveler of the Communist Party, reinvented herself as an everywoman housewife in 1963's *The Feminine Mystique.*[29] As a biographer diplomatically put it, "Friedan created a second narrative in order to avoid revelations about her radical past and to project a believable persona with which her readers could identify."[30] Her "first" narrative involved employing a maid, enraging other parents by shirking car-pooling responsibilities and hiring taxis instead, and never learning to operate a washer or dryer.[31] But her readers bought the second narrative, and like Michael Harrington's *Other America* from the previous year, Friedan's book crept into the national consciousness and onto best-seller lists.

The shrill Friedan branded the home a "comfortable concentration camp." "In a sense that is not as far-fetched as it sounds," *The Feminine Mystique*'s most overwrought passage declared, "the women who 'adjust' as housewives, who grow up wanting to be 'just a housewife,' are in as much danger as the millions who walked to their death in the concentration camps—and the millions more who refused to believe that the concentration camps existed."[32] Plainly, they were not. A more sedate Friedan later conceded, "I got carried away."[33] But in flamboyantly making that point of expansive, banal oppression, Friedan convinced readers of a problem—"the problem that has no name"—albeit on a smaller scale than she rendered.[34] The fact that Friedan and successors felt compelled to persuade women of their oppression said something about that oppression. Did the victims of the *un*comfortable concentration camps need a book to convince them of their hardships?

Friedan capitalized on *The Feminine Mystique*'s million-plus readership and reverted to activism. In quick succession, she helped found the National Organization for Women in 1966, the National Association for the Repeal of Abortion Laws in 1969, and the National Women's Political Caucus in 1971. While reformers penetrated the middle, radicals extended the fringe. The Women's International Terrorist Conspiracy from Hell (WITCH) unleashed mice in a bridal fair at Madison Square Garden, Boston's Cell 16 greeted a horrified women's conference by cutting off their long hair en masse, and The Feminists developed a religious ritual in which they chanted "Momma" and destroyed a male effigy.[35] The radicals became the bane of the once-radical Friedan.

Friedan's reformism, not her critics' radicalism, paid dividends in courtrooms and legislative chambers. In 1973, following the liberalization of abortion laws in several states, the Supreme Court liberalized the abortion laws of every state. Title IX mandated equal opportunities for males and females in school-sponsored activities. Emboldened by these successes, feminists embarked upon a decade-long quest to change the

Constitution. Congress sent the Equal Rights Amendment to the states on March 22, 1972, and within a week six states had ratified it. Democrats and Republicans endorsed it in their platforms. It seemed a fait accompli.

But then some women got in the way. Namely, a one-woman ERA wrecking crew named Phyllis Schlafly raised questions like: Might the ERA codify gay marriage? Could it penalize women taking out life insurance policies, when the actuary tables benefited them? Would it make women eligible for the draft? No one knew, and perhaps that was the intention: the judges would work it all out. The ERA's worst enemies may have been its most vociferous backers. The more Americans saw feminists, the less they liked the ERA. The turning point came in Houston in November 1977. Mandated by legislation introduced by Congresswoman Bella Abzug, the National Women's Conference uncomfortably juxtaposed the presence of three First Ladies with lavender balloons reading "We Are Everywhere" and "Dyke Power" signs. Delegates, stacked with NOW activists, pushed a hard-left agenda. Much of it had nothing to do with women. "I knew that one of the favorite tactics of the anti-ERA protagonists was to enflame the lesbian issue," Betty Friedan recalled. "I was worried—and correctly so, it turned out—that the Houston conference with all its media coverage would give them a perfect opportunity."[36] But the radical lesbians were all too real, and in one weekend the steam left the women's movement. The Equal Rights Amendment was dead.

Starting with a constituency of at least half the population, the women's movement eroded that base of support by becoming the women's movement for female chauvinists, the women's movement for radical socialists, the women's movement for humorless, hypersensitive, female linebackers with crew cuts, but not a women's movement for all women. Alas, such broad-based movements for women, the poor, and blacks are among the most enduring political delusions, relying as they do on the idea that there is unity of interest within sex, class, or race.

ON THE HEELS of women's and gay liberation came the twin movements of environmentalism and animal liberation. Unlike the personal-is-the-political isms of radical women and radical gays, the related causes of saving the earth and saving the animals evoked the old-time liberalism that demanded that the strong and enlightened save the weak and ignorant.

The modern environmental movement began in earnest on April 22, 1970. The first Earth Day relied heavily on the activist model of the 1960s in its aspirations of a national "teach-in." But with the Nixon administration helping to bankroll the event, activists smelled co-option, and thus trivialization. One activist sneered at the "government initiated teach-ins," which betray "elitist assumptions about social change" through dialogue, "attempt to pacify those students and other rebellious elements" through redirecting activism into socially approved targets, and rob "the language of opposition . . . of its subversive character."[37] Appropriately, the creator of the newly created holiday (of sorts) was a lawmaker, Senator Gaylord Nelson of Wisconsin, and a maker of laws that intruded into the private economy. For intrusion was the crux of modern environmentalism, an ideology that, in its global scope, paternalism, and redemptive ambition, replaced discredited Marxism as the cause above causes for some believers.

Michael Meeropol, orphaned son of the Rosenbergs, recognized environmentalism's potential as *the* issue for the coming Left. In late 1969, Meeropol castigated leftist writers tasked with predicting the direction of the movement for overlooking "the growing importance in fact and in public consciousness of the problems of *ecology.*" The ruling class, the veteran SDS activist predicted, would attempt to improve the environment through reform to lessen "the economic contradictions of capitalism." But capitalism, Meeropol argued, was responsible for pollution. Opportunity knocked, and environmentalism could "show the superiority of socialism" and give "a radical content and direction to the growing fears and concerns of vast numbers of Americans." Marxism merely promised to make the world anew; environmentalism promised to save it. "It is a question of the very survival of mankind."[38]

Because of the imagined stakes involved, the Earth's crusaders, like their Marxist predecessors, had no qualms about stretching the truth, or alarming the public, or doing the former to achieve the latter. What are a few white lies when the fate of the planet is at stake?

Rachel Carson did the most to craft the alarmist template. Her 1962 jeremiad against pesticides, *Silent Spring,* was short on facts but long on leading questions, qualifiers such as "may" and "seem," and vague stories of nameless people allegedly killed by pesticides. She suggested a causal link between pesticides and cancer, cirrhosis of the liver, mental retardation, and a host of other maladies.[39] Carson scared readers with an apocalyptic vision of an "evil spell" unleashing "mysterious maladies," including fishless streams and burned-over vegetation.[40] The world could choose one path whose "end lies in disaster," or another one "that assures the preservation of the earth."[41] Put another way, *You're going to die unless you do as I say.* That argument was compelling enough for policy makers the world over. Hoping to save lives, Carson instead influenced a global ban on DDT that caused millions of unnecessary malarial deaths.[42] The better-safe-than-sorry argument left the world more sorry than safe.

"The battle to feed humanity is over," declared Paul Ehrlich in his 1968 Malthusian ode, *The Population Bomb*. "In the 1970's the world will undergo famines—hundreds of millions of people are going to starve to death."[43] They didn't. Neither did Ehrlich, upon whom rained bequests and prizes and whose book sold more than three million copies.

Acid rain replaced overpopulation as the ecological bogeyman. According to a leading leftist journal, acid rain was wiping "lake after lake from fish-stocking lists," "suspected of damaging crops and stunting forest growth," and "the prime culprit in the sudden decay of the Parthenon stones."[44] When the shock value lessened, and its harm appeared less than advertised, environmentalists retired acid rain.

Like DDT, overpopulation, and acid rain, the "no nukes" cry enjoyed standing as the environmentalist cause of the moment. In its ambiguity—against nuclear-power plants here, for a nuclear weapons freeze there—no nukes made two movements one. Desperate for a unifying force, *The Nation* saw in "Critical Mass '74," a D.C.-based conference featuring scribe Izzy Stone, anthropologist Margaret Mead, actor Robert Redford, and gadfly Ralph Nader, an event that "could be the start of a nationwide crusade that might gather as much support and generate as much controversy as did the anti-war movement a decade ago."[45] More than one hundred thousand people protesting nuclear energy at Manhattan's Battery Park bolstered environmentalism's standing in the expanding pantheon of leftist issues. *Mother Jones* called Seabrook "the opening battle of the 1980s," opining that the standoff over the construction of the New Hampshire nuclear power plant represented "a resurgence of mass political protest over an escalating number and variety of issues."[46] This may have appeared so. The May 1, 1977, protest resulted in nearly fifteen hundred arrests. Alas, a sixties protest culture didn't return. The anti-nuclear Clamshell Alliance lost the first battle of the 1980s. But it inflicted such damage as to send opponents retreating. More than two decades lapsed until the next nuclear power plant was constructed in the United States.

It's not so much that the augurs of ecological apocalypse frightened the Republic into taking action. Americans, notwithstanding the shrieks of Carson and Ehrlich, had reasons to clean up the environment. In 1970, shortly after the first Earth Day, legislation established the Environmental Protection Agency. A Clean Water Act, to go with the Clean Air Act of the Great Society, was signed into law by President Nixon in 1973. So was the Endangered Species Act. Starting in Oregon in 1975, state recycling laws burdened store owners and their customers with storage and transport of sticky cans and bottles. More grandiose endeavors failed to catch on. A national "bottle bill" never materialized. The dream of solar energy replacing fossil fuels didn't come true. Nuclear power, in America at least, continued to supply massive amounts of energy—without killing anyone.

The sixties model indeed returned, just not in the way nostalgists had imagined. Extremists leeched on to a cause with broad-based appeal and discredited it. Instead of transcending parties, as early-1970s environmental victories in Congress had, the movement offended the parties through violence, sabotage, and insane rhetoric.

"Don't bring any more humans into being," states the first commandment offered by Paul Watson, a pioneer of tree spiking and participant in sinking fishing and whaling vessels. "Those loggers don't give a damn for future generations," Watson rationalized of his tree-spiking targets, "I don't have any compassion for them." To criticism of his sinking ships, Watson responded that "we could not give a damn what human beings have to say about the actions."[47] He imagined himself elected by the animals and the humans yet to be born, anointing himself the decider. Hardly an outcast, Watson helped found Greenpeace and sits on the board of the Sierra Club.

That was the *mainstream*. The underground environmentalist movement boasted the likes of Ted Kaczynski, the anti-technology hermit who killed and maimed recipients of the bombs he began to make in 1978, and the Earth Liberation Front, which torches construction sites and auto dealerships.[48] A replay of the excesses of the civil rights, student, and anti-war movements took place inside the environmental movement. Overheated rhetoric begot violence.

THE BAD GUY in the environmentalist narrative was man, which made for crossover appeal between environmentalists and animal rights activists. Five years after the inauguration of Earth Day and two years after the Endangered Species Act, Peter Singer published *Animal Liberation*, a book that inspired the founding of the People for the Ethical Treatment of Animals (PETA), which awards every new member a condensed version of Singer's book.

The 1975 polemic notified mankind that "to discriminate against beings solely on account of their species is a form of prejudice, immoral and indefensible in the same way that discrimination on the basis of race is immoral and indefensible."[49] Applying the logic of past movements for human equality to animal rights, the movement faced the obstacle of convincing humans of their equality with goats, roosters, and crickets. Adopting voguish victimization rhetoric, Singer popularized a term, "speciesist," to add to the growing list of leftist epithets—racist, sexist, homophobe. He compared livestock farmers, hunters, and medical researchers to concentration-camp guards and slavers.⁵⁰ "How can people who are not sadists spend their days driving monkeys into lifelong depression, heating dogs to death, or turning cats into drug addicts? How can they then remove their white coats and go to dinner with their families?"⁵¹ Such rhetoric was enough to make some cry, others laugh.

Whereas women and gays grabbed the reins of their liberation, lions and geckos weren't taking the lead in theirs. The reasons for a *Homo sapien* vanguard for animal rights were obvious, even if, perhaps, speciesist. Thus, animal rights, like its relation, environmentalism, conspicuously avoided the 1970s model of self-liberation in favor of the salvation-dispensing paternalism of traditional reform movements. From above, the elect would act on behalf of the unenlightened. Saving the world awarded devotees an air of smug superiority, just as self-seeking liberation movements rationalized tightly wound belligerence. Faced with opposing views, the reformer sniffed, the liberationist screeched. The former saw himself a savior; the latter, a victim.

The self-righteousness justified unrighteous deeds. "Should one break in and free the animals?" the esteemed professor Singer asked. "That is illegal, but the obligation to obey the law is not absolute. It was justifiably broken by those who helped runaway slaves in the American South."⁵² Though Singer drew the line at harming people, the murky nuances of his prose were lost in the murkier minds of his followers. Burning down scientific facilities that experimented on animals, sending a mail bomb that maimed a Revlon executive, dousing women in fur jackets with red paint, and liberating animals from farms were among the high-profile illegalities committed by animal-rights activists.⁵³

Animal rights pioneer Bronson Alcott of Fruitlands never would have harmed a fly. His inheritors would not have, either. Humans were another matter.

On May 11, 1975, thousands of veterans of the anti-war movement convened in New York City's Central Park to celebrate the fall of Saigon. "It's so great to be standing here receiving the rewards of all those years of protest," the singer Harry Belafonte told the crowd. The Vietnamese celebrated, folk singer Joan Baez proclaimed, so Americans should, too. "Sadly," an observer from *The Nation* opined, "the peace movement was denied the celebration it deserved." No ticker-tape parades, no medals ceremony, no handshakes at the White House awaited the foot soldiers of the anti-war movement. As a consolation, the war's opponents held one last "anticlimactic, nostalgic and sentimental" rally.

The question that loomed over the celebration, writer Robert Karen noted, was *"Now what?"* "Today what we call 'the movement' has grown to encompass everything from sexual liberation to environmentalism, but along with growth there has also been dispersal. . . . the movement today has no unifying purpose and is spiritually spent." But for a few hours on a sunny Sunday afternoon in Central Park, activists relived their heyday by listening to Richie Havens and Phil Ochs and Paul Simon sing, watching Dave Dellinger attack Gerald Ford as if he were Lyndon Johnson, and wondering what the Vietnamese-speaking officials said to them by telephone hookup.[54] With the draft, the daily American body counts, and the massive demonstrations far in the past, the gathering had the feel of a reunion, not of a rally. Rather than celebrate war's end, as the speakers encouraged them to do, the throngs mourned the end of the anti-war movement.

That deep, emotional investment in the movement, a defining movement that gave purpose to the purposeless and friends to the friendless, prevented so many from acknowledging the harsh truth in their enemies' predictions of what a Communist victory would entail: internal oppression and external expansion. Better just to ignore it, or blame the Communist oppression and imperialism on a familiar scapegoat—the United States. The movement's post-war blindness to Indochina's realities was not unlike the wartime delusions of the conflict's proponents in regard to the war's costs, its relation to the national interest, and its success. If the first casualty of war is truth, the last man standing is illusion.

Communist overlords sent hundreds of thousands of South Vietnamese to reeducation centers after the war's end. A few remained in the dreadful camps until 1986. Many more never returned home. Rather than exist under the Communist regime, several hundred thousand "boat people" risked the dangers of pirates and drowning by overcrowding barely seaworthy vessels in escape attempts.[55] When Joan Baez organized a petition condemning post-war Vietnam's human rights abuses, former friends from the anti-war movement reacted hysterically. *The Nation*, which outraged readers by lending support to Baez's endeavor, printed nearly five pages of angry letters. Therein Corliss Lamont, an antique who had served as Stalin's chief American apologist by endorsing the justice of the show trials in the late 1930s and fitfully denying Soviet culpability in the 1940 Katyn Forest massacre, called the Baez petition "one of the most disgraceful documents in U.S. political history." Other missives dubbed the petition's charges "propaganda canards" and examples of "Goebbels's big lie technique."[56] Actress Jane Fonda rejected Baez's letter and accused the folk singer of cavorting "with the most narrow and negative elements in our country."[57]

The Saigon domino that fell in 1975 struck Laos and Cambodia. It hit the latter nation particularly hard. So wedded to Marxist theory, and divorced from Marxist reality, was MIT linguist Noam Chomsky that he spoke disparagingly of "tales of Communist atrocities" in Cambodia, which he posited had been spun to discredit opponents of the Vietnam War and embolden anti-Communist interventionists. Writing in *The Nation*, Chomsky and a co-author cited "highly qualified specialists" to assure readers that at most "a few thousand" Cambodians had been executed, and that they had been killed almost entirely by forces outside of the Khmer Rouge nexus. "The 'slaughter' by the Khmer Rouge," Chomsky declared, "is a [Robert] Moss–*New York Times* creation."[58] Alas, the slaughter was all too real. Even by the standards of Stalin and Mao, Pol Pot's short reign was particularly gruesome. The Khmer Rouge abolished money. They summarily executed people who wore eyeglasses, assuming it a vain accessory to attract others rather than a necessity for sight. They executed the handicapped as malingerers. They forcibly evacuated the urban population, including hospital patients, to the countryside. A million or so died.[59] The most admired intellectual on the American Left, in the flagship journal of the American Left, said it wasn't happening.

Blindness to Communist atrocities helped pave the way for an exodus of the seeing from the Left, just as it had in previous generations. "The left's indignation seems exclusively reserved for outrages that confirm the Marxist diagnosis of the sickness of capitalist society," David Horowitz wrote in *The Nation* as the 1970s closed. "Thus, there is protest against murder and repression in Nicaragua, but not Cambodia, Chile but not Tibet, South Africa but not Uganda, Israel but not Libya or Iraq. Political support is mustered for oppressed minorities in Western countries but not in Russia or the People's Republic of China, while a Third World country that declares itself 'Marxist' puts itself—by that very act—beyond reproach."[60]

With the rise of the Ayatollah Khomeini and the Islamic revolution in Iran, revolutionaries needed no longer to declare themselves Marxist to win the good graces of the American Left—merely being anti-American would do. "What kind of state might result if Khomeini or his followers take power?" *Mother Jones* answered in early 1979 by pointing to "democratic reforms, freedom for political prisoners, an end to the astronomical waste of huge arms purchases, and a constitutional government."[61] At the same time, *The Nation* assured its readers that "there is every reason to believe that the still unpublished [Iranian] Constitution will include all the elements of a liberal democratic system."[62] Comparing the Islamic revolution to the uprising of Buddhist monks against South Vietnam's Ngo

Dinh Diem, imagining post-revolutionary Iran as Portugal after António de Oliveira Salazar or Spain after Francisco Franco, and inflating the importance of oil-worker *komitehs* as an incipient populist-style socialism poised to overthrow Exxon, *Mother Jones* and *The Nation* cast aside evidence and indulged wishful imaginations.[63] Like so many leftists before them, radicals projected the fantasies they craved over the reality that existed.

That the conversations started by Baez and Horowitz could receive a hearing in the flagship journal of the Left, and that *The Nation* quietly reversed its Iranian position and *Mother Jones* quickly admitted that its enthusiasm for the Islamic revolution had been misplaced, revealed an introspection, an honesty, a maturity absent from many earlier Lefts.[64] That such conversations so often ended with dissenters, even ones with such impeccable left-wing credentials as Baez, being bizarrely labeled tools of the right wing, or shoved out of the movement entirely, revealed just how plodding the progress on intramural tolerance was. The ability to recognize past mistakes failed to inoculate against the disease, which reappeared in the Left's muted response to the Soviet invasion of Afghanistan and to Poland's Solidarity Movement. The doctrine of no-enemies-to-the-left still exerted a strong pull. Internal unity and external ridicule were its effects.

ONCE FINISHED, THE Vietnam War, the issue that briefly gave radicals a unifying purpose, reminded the Left of its aimlessness, weariness, and divisions. "What ever happened to that hodge-podge of groups and movements we called the New Left," wondered one former SDSer in 1976, "the hundreds of thousands of peace marchers, the student strikers, the radical feminists, Black Power advocates, anti-war soldiers, draft resisters, welfare rights activists, gay liberationists, environmentalists and community organizers?"[65] Evidence of the Left's decline piled up as the 1970s endured. The success of tax revolts, such as California's Proposition 13 and Massachusetts' Proposition 2½, the failure of the ERA, the "4-to-1 and up to 10-to-1 votes to repeal gay rights ordinances in city after city," the reappearance of the death penalty, and the coup de grâce, the election of Ronald Reagan to the presidency in 1980, staggered activists who just a few years earlier had believed the revolution around the next corner.[66]

It's not that the Left was in retreat in the 1970s. It wasn't. From court-ordered busing to a moratorium on capital punishment to the deinstitutionalization of the mentally ill, the Left was always and everywhere on the attack. But as activists charged, they traveled too far ahead of supply lines, left earlier conquests open to counterattack, repulsed the natives, and misjudged their own strength. They waged an aggressive assault when the situation called for a guarding action. Their tired soldiers got routed and went home.

Some traded in politics for New Age spirituality or therapeutic cults, such as EST. Their fellow countrymen were rediscovering faith, too, albeit in a manner disturbing to the Left. "Between 1965 and 1975, the size of every major white liberal denomination shrank," historians Maurice Isserman and Michael Kazin note. In contrast, "[e]very conservative denomination spurted in membership during the decade beginning in 1965."[67] Most conspicuous was the rise of evangelical Christians, who in 1976 elected one of their own president. The Left divined negative forebodings but wished away the danger by reasoning that interests of class would ultimately trump interests of religion. "It is hard to see how, in the long run, the new fundamentalism can prevail," longtime *Nation* editor Carey McWilliams observed. "In time, the evangelicals will divide on the basis of status, income, education and achievement; indeed the process seems already to be starting."[68] But if this Marxist formula didn't apply to rich liberals such as McWilliams, why would it have applied to poor evangelicals?

If politics and religion failed to convince the Left of turning tides, the culture made a persuasive case.

Americans poured into movie houses for group catharsis from criminal bedlam in the *Dirty Harry* and *Death Wish* films. Television audiences rebelled against scripts by rooting for blue-collar curmudgeon Archie Bunker and lucre-lusting entrepreneur George Jefferson. Disco exploded. Rather than a reminder of reality, disco provided an escape. People didn't listen to the lyrics. They felt the beat. The music wasn't supposed to incite or provide insight to the masses; it was supposed to get you laid. To the extent that politics emerged as a major trend in popular music, it did so in the anti-politics of a punk music that snarled against hippies, peace, love, and everything else the sixties held sacred.

A generation that reveled in youth grew old ungracefully. Peter Pan's hairline receded, his belly protruded, and his skin creased. But he still acted as though he were Peter Pan.

AFTER RAILING AGAINST the system, many activists integrated comfortably within it while retaining their anti-establishment poses. Jerry Rubin famously became a corporate consultant. Voters in California elected Tom Hayden to the state legislature. SNCC chairman John R. Lewis and Chicago Black Panther Bobby Rush won seats in the U.S. House of Representatives.

The religious zeitgeist of the 1970s snared many who had been caught in the political zeitgeist of the 1960s. Rennie Davis, the SDSer who along with Hayden organized the 1968 protests in Chicago, worshipped Maharj Ji, a humanly perfect Indian teenager. Casey Hayden converted to Buddhism and launched a yoga institute. SDS founding father Al Haber rediscovered Judaism. "There was the '73 war," he explains, "and I went to high holy days for the first time in my life. I found that a very powerful experience." Combining his Judaism, activism, and carpentry talents, Haber constructs peace tables, of the kind to be used for what he foresees as the final, worldwide peace conference at Armageddon.[69]

Too many got caught up in the pathologies they helped unleash. Huey Newton, Eldridge Cleaver, David Hilliard, and other Black Panther leaders became crack addicts. Newton embezzled money from Panther programs. He shook down drug dealers, pimps, and legitimate businessmen for tribute—with violent repercussions for those who refused. He murdered a prostitute for calling him "baby," and later pistol-whipped a tailor—fracturing the tailor's skull and the handle on his gun—for making the same mistake. When a Panther hit squad attempted to murder the chief witness in Newton's murder of the hooker, they instead, through friendly fire, slew their own colleague. To keep that quiet, Panthers removed from Oakland a medic who had treated wounded hit squad members and shot him in the Nevada desert. Paralyzed from the neck down, the left-for-dead Panther was discovered alive under a pile of rocks.[70] And so it went.

Newton, unlike his Black Panther comrades, never put down the pipe. An Oakland crack dealer, unimpressed by Newton's radical credentials, executed him before dawn in the summer of 1989. "Some people would argue that Huey's been dead a long time," noted future Oakland mayor Elihu Harris, "and his body just caught up with the situation."[71]

Worse for Panther mythologists, Cleaver, the man who had led nuns in a "Fuck Ronald Reagan!" chant in the 1960s, supported Ronald Reagan in the 1980s. He dismissed Louis Farrakhan as a hater, converted to Mormonism, registered as a Republican, deemed the U.S. government the best government in the world, and even spoke kind words of the Oakland police. "I'm telling you after I ran into the Egyptian police and the Algerian police, and the North Korean police and the Nigerian police and Idie Amin's police in Uganda, I began to miss the Oakland police."[72]

Former members of Weatherman generally fared better than the black activists they had admired. Mark Rudd, Bernardine Dorhn, and Bill Ayers, three of the most visible Weathermen, landed faculty positions after remaining invisible to the authorities for years. "Guilty as hell, free as a bird—it's a great country," Ayers reflected.[73] Kathy Boudin, who escaped the 1970 town house explosion, and David Gilbert, whose best friend and fellow Columbia SDS "praxis axis" alum Ted Gold died in the blast, both landed in prison after participating in an elaborate 1981 robbery of a Brink's armored car that resulted in the murders of two policemen and a Brink's guard. Gilbert, who refused to recognize the legitimacy of the court that tried him, remains behind bars on a triple murder sentence. Boudin, a product of a family of legal minds, wisely pled guilty to murder and bank robbery. She was paroled in 2003.

Timothy Leary, like Eldridge Cleaver, returned to the United States. Like Cleaver, he cooperated with the authorities he'd once despised. Unlike Cleaver, he did hard time. Leary became a caricature of himself, rambling incoherently, mumbling slogans, and hanging around party people half his age. His two children, with whom he had shared drugs and busts in their teenage years, suffered the consequences. Jack Leary, who after a 1968 father-son drug bust disrobed, masturbated at the police station, and took three days of drying out before he could appear before a judge, discovered a life after drugs. The insanity Jack Leary temporarily exhibited under the influence of hallucinogens became a permanent fixture of Susan Leary's sad life. After partaking in a steady diet of LSD and psilocybin in the 1960s, Timothy Leary's daughter spent the 1980s in and out of mental institutions. Her long strange trip, which included beating her daughter into comas, defecating in Laundromat washing machines, and shooting her boyfriend in the head, came to an end hanging from the end of her shoelaces in September 1990.[74] Tune in. Turn on. Drop out.

Saddest of all was the demise of the New Left's clown prince, Abbie Hoffman. After spending much of the 1970s on the run from the authorities after selling cocaine to an undercover policeman, Hoffman spent the 1980s aware of his irrelevance and the irrelevance of his politics. Clinically depressed and living in a turkey coop converted into an apartment, he swallowed more than a hundred barbiturates in 1989. "He was really uncomfortable with becoming middle aged and facing old age without seeing significant social change," fellow Chicago Eight defendant Tom Hayden told the *New York Times*. "He was always trying to re-create the 60's and was deeply dismayed he was becoming a prophet in the wilderness of the 80's."[75]

They made a world. They lived in it. They died in it. As the 1970s closed, the realization that the sixties were finally over hit activist holdovers. The eighties proved that the sixties weren't coming back.

⌒ 23 ⌒

THE LONG MARCH

The prophets prophesied falsehood, and the priests clapped their hands: and my people loved such things. What then shall be done in the end thereof?

—JEREMIAH 5:31

OFFENDED BY THE excesses of the Great Society, the New Left, feminism, gay liberation, and Jimmy Carter's dovish defeatism, America moved rightward in the late 1970s and stayed there into the 1990s. So close, radicals fantasized, had they been to seizing power in the heady days of "peace" and "love" and "revolution." Mere years later, they dejectedly sat outside elected offices in all but the Left's most reliable strongholds. Beneficiaries of the rapid change in the latter half of the twentieth century, sixties radicals felt the brunt of that rapid change once their decade ended. How someone out of 1958 appeared to people in 1968 was how people stuck in 1968 appeared to those living in 1978. The passage of 1979, '80, '81, and so on necessarily and painfully made the generation gap wider.

In the 1960s, chants had questioned the president about his daily progress in murdering children. Starting with the euphoric, gold-medal run of the Olympic hockey team in 1980, Americans spontaneously broke into chants of "USA! USA! USA!" Welfare queens replaced war managers as the de rigueur scapegoat. The phrase "liberation movement" now described Polish Solidarity, the Afghan *mujahedin*, or Nicaraguan *contras*, not armed Communists seeking to impose yet another totalitarian outpost. College kids, who in the 1960s would have idealized a post-graduate job in the Peace Corps, pined to work on Wall Street in the 1980s.

The world moved beneath the Left's feet. Some, like Abbie Hoffman, Huey Newton, and Timothy Leary, never accepted this. They traveled down the path of self-destruction, or became parodies of their former selves, or both. Others, less keen on living in the past than on making a future, adapted and overcame ballot-box obstacles. They undertook what has been called a long march through the institutions. They weren't activists for celebrity, but to make the world anew. The Left in these years seized institutions—the Democratic Party, the colleges, the courts, the media, the film industry—and proceeded to shape the political debate and the culture.

LEFTISTS SAT ON the outside looking in at electoral politics at the very time they had expected to be running things. They channeled energy into the "fourth" branch of government.

Richard Nixon, like his immediate predecessor, was particularly sensitive to the barbs of the Fourth Estate. Nixon, who solidified the Great Society and presided over the exit from Vietnam just as his former boss Eisenhower had acted as the New Deal's caretaker and presided over the cease-fire in Korea, nevertheless rubbed the elite media raw. The conflict was more cultural than ideological. The poor Quaker Nixon and the crude rancher Johnson didn't speak liberal even if they practiced it. Proper Bostonian John Kennedy and Rhodes Scholar Bill Clinton didn't much advance liberalism even if they spoke the natives' language. Nixon's administration waged war on the media. The media waged war on his administration. The media came out the victor. The *Washington Post* exposé of the 1972 break-in of the Democratic National Committee's offices at the Watergate confirmed to liberal journalists just how cretinous the Nixon administration was. For the disgraced president's votaries, Watergate substantiated the administration's claims of just how agenda-driven reporters had become.

President Richard Nixon's proved the biggest scalp collected along the liberal media's long march. His resignation on August 9, 1974, showed journalists just how powerful they could be once animated with the crusading spirit. Objectivity and balance came under attack as relics of an era of journalistic naiveté. How could a reporter stay neutral over Vietnam, Nixon, or Reaganomics? The partisan boosterism of the nineteenth-century press returned, only now it did so without clearly identifying, as its booster-journalism antecedents proudly did in their mastheads, whom it sought to boost. This attracted liberal crusaders to the profession. It also barred people from the profession who weren't liberal crusaders.

The consumers of news rejected the liberal label in greater numbers the greater the distance from the 1960s. Those who created the news, on the other hand, stood athwart the conservative direction of the nation.

One survey found that in the elections between 1964 and 1976 never did support for the Republican presidential candidate reach 20 percent among journalists for national media outlets.[1] Kenneth Walsh of *U.S. News and World Report* surveyed fellow White House reporters on their choices for president in the five elections from 1976 to 1992 and made similar discoveries. Though Democrats never received half of the vote in any of these five elections, White House reporters split, on average, 86 percent for the Democrats versus 12 percent for the Republicans.[2] A 1985 poll of journalists by the *Los Angeles Times* reported that 55 percent of journalists surveyed identified as liberals and just 17 percent identified as conservatives.[3] Six in ten respondents to a 1996 American Society of Newspaper Editors poll of more than a thousand reporters described themselves as "Democrat or liberal," while just three in twenty described themselves as "Republican or conservative."[4] The Freedom Forum's 1992 poll of journalists reported that nine in ten respondents voted for Bill Clinton in the 1992 election.[5] The University of Connecticut's Department of Public Policy asked three hundred newspaper and television journalists whom they had voted for in 2004. Just 21 percent admitted voting for George W. Bush, the recipient of more than half the public's votes.[6]

Common sense suggests but reporters deny that homogeneity influences the way the news is reported. To the news presenter, who inhabited the political subculture of big-city journalism, the news presented appeared even-handed, because within the subculture, it was. To the news consumer, the news presented appeared slanted, biased, and in extreme cases, untrue. Opinion polls reported that majorities detected a media bias, with those identifying a leftward slant outnumbering those identifying a rightward tilt by two-to-one and three-to-one margins.[7] In large part, journalists still reported the facts. But they came at the facts they selected to report through a liberal perspective. This pushed the news in a singular direction.

Veterans of political work in the Democratic Party and its presidential administrations (Tim Russert, George Stephanopoulos, Margaret Carlson) resurfaced not as commentators or columnists but as reporters and moderators. Editors and producers repackaged the scions of liberal families (Maria Shriver, Cokie Roberts, Evan Thomas) as objective journalists. The few famous non-liberals in the profession (Brit Hume, John Stossel, Bernard Goldberg), tellingly, moved in a conservative direction only after their careers were well under way.

The media widely distributed evidence of its partisan cheerleading on a daily basis. When Ronald Reagan's administration built up defense and supplanted "peaceful coexistence" with rollback, the media ridiculed.[8] When the Iron Curtain collapsed in 1989, and then the Soviet Union disintegrated in 1991, journalists said that Reagan's policies had nothing to do with it. Some even suggested that the fall of Euro-Communism may have been a bad thing.[9] Particularly worn punching bags of urban, secular journalists were rural, evangelical churchgoers, who had entered politics in the 1970s in response to the cultural changes of the 1960s. Born-again Christians, a mid-1990s *Washington Post* news story explained, were "largely poor, uneducated, and easy to command."[10] The lurid Clinton-Lewinsky scandal, which for many evangelicals symbolized the nation's degraded post-1960s values, prompted a different response from *Time* magazine's White House reporter: "I'd be happy to give him [oral sex] just to thank him for keeping abortion legal."[11] After CBS News's *60 Minutes II* program embarrassed itself in 2004's election run-up by peddling phony Texas Air National Guard documents showing special treatment for George W. Bush decades earlier, the *New York Times* dubbed the items "fake but accurate" in a headline.[12] Zeal, prejudice, and wish clouded judgment.

If the lopsided statistics didn't convince of the transformation in the media, neither would mere anecdotes. Nevertheless, a sea change had occurred. The Left's long march through the institutions may not have produced a president, but it did produce page-one bylines, the evening news, and glossy newsweeklies. If the Left could no longer win elections, they could at least influence them. More importantly, as left-of-center journalists slowly recognized, they could transform the culture.

"AFTER THE VIETNAM War," Middlebury College professor Jay Parini wrote in 1988, "a lot of us didn't just crawl back into our literary cubicles; we stepped into academic positions. With the war over, our visibility was lost, and it seemed for a while—to the unobservant—that we had disappeared. Now we have tenure, and the work of reshaping the universities has begun in earnest."[13] If sixties leftists failed in the soaring aim of seizing state power, they could take consolation in commandeering institutions of considerable societal power. The State Department may have been safe from a takeover from the Left, but the anthropology department certainly wasn't.

Professors weren't so much educating students as they were reeducating them. Students, they believed, were the products of a racist, sexist, homophobic culture. It was the job of the professor to reorient them. As

Herbert Marcuse instructed the foot soldiers embarking upon the long march, "All authentic education is political education."[14]

The faculty, the courses they taught, and the textbooks therein were overwhelmingly left-wing. To offset the racism and sexism of the surrounding culture, colleges and universities practiced an extreme form of affirmative action in admissions and hiring, and de facto affirmative action in grading. Students heard less teaching, more preaching. To ensure conformity, the campus Left instituted speech codes, sensitivity training, ideologically based grading, and other enforcement mechanisms. So firm was the Left's clutch on colleges and universities that one saw in them a microcosm of the radical's program.

America and Western civilization came under attack. At Stanford, in articulating curriculum demands, Jesse Jackson famously led chants of "Hey hey, ho ho, Western Culture's got to go!"[15] "Western Civilization?" Yale English professor Sara Suleri gasped in contemplating a $20 million grant endowing a professorship in its study. "Why not a chair for colonialism, slavery, empire, and poverty?" Yale ultimately rejected the money after never instituting the earmarked program.[16]

Whole courses and even departments imparted "correct" political views on race, sex, class, the environment, homosexuality, and other hot-button issues. University of Colorado feminist Alison Jaggar docketed women's studies, a field inaugurated at Cornell in 1969, as "the intellectual arm of the women's movement."[17] A popular text in gay and lesbian studies volunteered that the emerging field "straddles scholarship and politics," working "to express and advance the interests of lesbians, bisexuals, and gay men, and to contribute culturally and intellectually to the contemporary lesbian/gay movement."[18] Had the politicization been ghettoized within the fringe fields, education might have had less to fear. But traditional fields, too, fell victim to ideology. "I wanted my writing of history and my teaching of history to be a part of the social struggle," activist, Boston University historian, and *A People's History of the United States* author Howard Zinn declared. "I wanted to be a part of history and not just a recorder and teacher of history. So that kind of attitude towards history, history itself as a political act, has always informed my writing and my teaching."[19]

With a spectrum of opinion broad enough for Marxists, postmodernists, feminists, relativists, environmentalists, and sexual liberationists, but too narrow for conservatives, the campus Left, so unaccustomed to encountering let alone debating such people, reacted to foreign voices by silencing them. The intellectual ghetto that administrators, professors, and campus activists operated within contributed to the intolerance.

In 1993, University of Pennsylvania campus police arrested several black students in the act of heisting the entire press run of the student newspaper. The incident left Sheldon Hackney, the school's president who became chairman of the National Endowment of the Humanities shortly thereafter, to lamely observe: "Two important university values, diversity and open expression, appear to be in conflict." The school brought racial harassment charges (later dropped) against the student columnist who had offended the thieves. The university reprimanded the arresting officers, one of whom was suspended without pay for three days. The caught-red-handed newspaper thieves, however, went unpunished.[20] Five years later, Cornell University's dean of students participated in a rally in which activists torched hundreds of copies of a seized student newspaper. "The students who oppose the *Cornell Review* have claimed their First Amendment right to be able to have symbolic burnings of the *Cornell Review*," university spokesman Linda Grace-Kobas asserted. Henrik Dullea, vice president for university relations, similarly saw nothing wrong in the newspaper burnings: "Why should they be stopped? It's a free newspaper."[21] Villanova administrator Tom Mogan confiscated the press run of the campus conservative monthly after it outlined the Catholic school's exclusive relationship with a bank that funded pro-abortion causes. "We obviously have some serious concerns about the content of the *Conservative Column*," the director of student development explained to the offending paper's editor via voice mail in 2000. "Therefore, I will be removing all the issues of the *Conservative Column* that I see."[22]

Just as there was a large gulf between the vocal endorsement of "tolerance" and the actual practice of tolerance, the mantra "diversity" seemed more of an empty affirmation than a lodestar. The dollar disparity between donations to John Kerry versus donations to George W. Bush in the run-up to the 2004 presidential election among employees of top schools was 20-1 at Yale, 25-1 at Harvard, and 302-1 at Princeton. At Dartmouth, the disparity was infinite; not a single employee had made a donation to George W. Bush's campaign of $200 or more recorded by the Federal Election Commission. In fact, at no school ranked in *U.S. News and World Report*'s top twenty-five national universities did John Kerry receive less in employee donations than his opponent.[23] The campuses were out of touch with the society that surrounded them. The overwhelming support for Kerry, in many instances, resembled Election Day in totalitarian nations, where the dictator receives upward of 98 percent of the vote. The statistics provide a disturbing glimpse at the true nature of campus "diversity," which cultivates a uniformity of opinion as it extols meaningless visual differences that nevertheless comfort the leftist conscience.

· · ·

HOLLYWOOD HAD REMAINED a redoubt of leftism since the days of Communists launching the Screen Actors Guild. From Jane Fonda's junkets to Hanoi during the Vietnam War to Oscars awarded to icons Al Gore and Michael Moore, Tinseltown made little effort to disguise its politics.

Leftist icons became cinematic icons: Communist John Reed in *Reds*, sexologist Alfred Kinsey in *Kinsey*, Black Panther Huey Newton in *Panther*, anti-nuclear activist Karen Silkwood in *Silkwood*, pornographer Larry Flynt in *The People vs. Larry Flynt*, anti-war activist Ron Kovic in *Born on the Fourth of July*, and Communist revolutionary Che Guevara in *The Motorcycle Diaries*, as well as Nation of Islam leader Malcolm X, environmentalist lawyer Erin Brockovich, and nationalized-health-care champion Patch Adams in films named for them. As glaring were the sins of omission. Few non-leftist political figures interested Hollywood enough to merit a biopic.

Hot-button issues received entire cinematic treatments from the "correct" perspective in *The Cider House Rules* (abortion), *The Insider* (big tobacco), *Dead Man Walking* (the death penalty), *The China Syndrome* (nuclear power), *Brokeback Mountain* (homosexuality), and *John Q. Public* (socialized medicine). Villains of the radical narrative appeared as cinematic villains. The murderous, homophobic Marine in *American Beauty* and the serial-killing Christian in *Seven* reflected liberal fantasy rather than real life. Through the looking glass of Hollywood, prison inmates appear noble and angelic in *The Shawshank Redemption* and their jailers sadistic and criminal; Nazis, rather than the Islamic terrorists featured in the Tom Clancy novel, resurrect themselves after decades of inactivity to nuke Baltimore in *The Sum of All Fears*; a group of Marines attack America, rather than protect it, in *The Rock*.

Moviegoers go to the theater to be entertained, not brainwashed. Filmmakers, nevertheless, poured on the politics. Some of it was entertaining; much of it wasn't. Save for propagandistic purposes, it's difficult to see why many such films were ever made. Films rarely advertised themselves as dripping with agendas. Once the word got out, politicized films rarely made box-office cash. Many, sick of paying for entertainment but getting sermons instead, stopped going to the movies. But even in Hollywood, politics, and with it the affirmation of critics and peers, could speak louder than cash.

IN 1972, THE Left broke through the barricades and nominated one of their own for president in Senator George McGovern. The South Dakotan lost one of the most lopsided presidential contests in U.S. history. No matter, the Left fulfilled its aim of taking over the Democratic Party.

"There won't be any riots in Miami because the people who rioted in Chicago are on the Platform Committee," quipped delegate Ben Wattenberg.[24] So total was the party's transformation that Mayor Richard Daley, whose police had battled the throngs outside the convention in 1968, found himself on the outside in 1972. McGovern's henchmen replaced the popularly chosen delegates from Chicago with a slate led by Jesse Jackson of defeated and unelected "delegates" who fulfilled the party's quotas on women and minorities. Nearly a quarter of California's delegates were on welfare.[25] "What kind of delegation is this?" AFL-CIO president George Meany wondered of New York's conventioneers. "They've got six open fags and only three AFL-CIO people on that delegation! Representative?"[26] The last shall be first and the first shall be last.

The result of turning the party over to the people who had sought to destroy it four years earlier was, predictably, destructive. Amazingly, Democrats suffered an even more disastrous convention in 1972 than the one they had endured four years before. The fact that the *Democratic* Party had rejected *elected* delegates for failing to meet sex and racial quotas became a scandal. The convention amounted to an "open-mike night" as cranks backing abortion and myriad causes addressed the crowd. Especially damaging was the 2:48 A.M. start to the party nominee's acceptance speech. The speech was delayed because immature delegates had stalled the vote on vice-presidential selection Thomas Eagleton with a string of nominations for unrealistic candidates (e.g., Ralph Nader, Cesar Chavez, and Jerry Rubin).[27]

McGovern, who jokingly called his acceptance speech "our Friday sunrise service," urged America to "[c]ome home to the belief that we can seek a newer world."[28] But the candidate's "newer world" was few voters' idea of a better world. McGovern's support for abortion, amnesty for draft dodgers, "demogrants" of $1,000 to every American, and forced busing, like his comparisons of Richard Nixon to Adolf Hitler and his campaign's sub rosa negotiations with the North Vietnamese, thrilled the new Democrats as much as it alienated the old guard.[29] From the botched convention to the revelation that the party's vice presidential nominee had undergone electroshock treatment (perhaps, on second thought, the idea of nominating Jerry Rubin for vice president wasn't so bad), the McGovernites conducted the worst presidential campaign in the modern era. Who could trust people to run a country who couldn't run a convention or a campaign?

McGovern won handily in the counties that enclosed the University of California–Berkeley, the University of Michigan–Ann Arbor, and the

University of Wisconsin–Madison.[30] He lost almost everywhere else. Richard Nixon, never terribly popular, stomped McGovern in one of the most lopsided presidential contests in U.S. history. Realignment had arrived, just not in the way the drafters of the Port Huron Statement had expected.

The Democratic Party underwent a sharp reorientation in the succeeding decades. From accepting the Cold War consensus to reflexively opposing American military interventions, from silence on gun control, abortion, affirmative action, and gay rights to championing such divisive policies, from the party traditionally opposed by conservationists to the party that adopted trendy environmental issues, the Democrats became Ted Kennedy's party, not John Kennedy's. The collectivist economics that characterized the party since Roosevelt remained in such proposals as guaranteed employment and federalized health care. But among the party leadership, divisive cultural issues overtook bread-and-butter concerns in importance.

A combination of Vietnam syndrome and aloofness toward anti-American tyrannies characterized the shift in the Democratic Party away from anti-Communism, large military budgets, and assertions of U.S. power. Every use of the military, even instances of military aid, became, in the minds of the Democratic Party's left wing, the next Vietnam.

A military operation as minor, and as successful, as the 1983 liberation of Grenada from a Marxist dictator compelled several Democratic congressmen to resolve to impeach the president, claiming that Ronald Reagan had violated international law.[31] Senator Walter Mondale, the leading candidate for the Democratic presidential nomination, claimed that the Grenada invasion "undermines our ability to effectively criticize what the Soviets have done in their brutal intervention in Afghanistan, in Poland and elsewhere."[32] Alas, the overthrow of Communist puppets proved overwhelmingly popular not just in America but also in Grenada, where nearly the entire population of the island greeted President Reagan with cheers upon his 1984 visit.[33]

The Democratic leadership swooned over Nicaragua's dictator, who had shut down the free press and murdered native people hostile to his land expropriation campaign, in an embarrassing "Dear Commandante" letter. The letter, signed by the Democratic majority leader and the chairman of the House intelligence committee, appeared as a crude attempt to bypass the president in foreign policy matters. It commended Daniel Ortega's government for non-existent steps toward democratization and freedom of speech as it condemned "U.S. support for military action directed against the people or government of Nicaragua," failing to note that it was the people of Nicaragua taking part in this military action.[34] Here, as elsewhere, the Democrats excused the misdeeds of America's enemies as they exaggerated America's.

Such developments alienated some Democrats, leading to split-ticket balloting and party switching among officeholders.

A FAITH IN impending environmental doom, exemplified by the Democratic platforms' paeans to whatever scare story was currently in vogue, reflected the party's marriage to radical environmentalism.

In 1976, the platform, even as it hysterically claimed that "America is running out of energy," acceded to alarmists over nuclear power.[35] In 1980, acid rain loomed in the skies and in the platform.[36] In 1988, Democrats warned of "the depletion of the ozone layer, the 'greenhouse effect,' [and] the destruction of tropical forests."[37] By the 1990s, global warming took over as the agent of apocalypse. "Eight of the ten hottest years ever recorded have occurred during the past ten years," the 2000 platform informed. "Scientists predict a daunting range of likely effects from global warming. Much of Florida and Louisiana submerged underwater. More record floods, droughts, heat waves, and wildfires. Diseases and pests spreading to new areas. Crop failures and famines. Melting glaciers, stronger storms, and rising seas. These are not Biblical plagues. They are the predicted result of human action."[38]

The panaceas, like the problems they purportedly would solve, changed every few years. In 1976, the party touted federal financing of "solar, geothermal, wind, tide, and other forms of energy" to replace the vanishing supply of fossil fuels.[39] By 1984, recycling represented a remedy for job loss, pollution, and high consumer prices.[40] In 1992, the party promised "to limit carbon dioxide emissions to 1990 levels by the year 2000" to strike a blow against global warming.[41] As the embrace of environmentalism heartened New Democrats, it estranged construction workers, loggers, and other blue-collar workers traditionally drawn to the party.

Abortion, an issue unaddressed even by the party's extremist 1972 platform, slowly became an article of faith for Democrats. In 1976 and 1980, though the party backed *Roe v. Wade* and opposed a constitutional amendment overturning the 1973 decision, it acknowledged the "religious and ethical" concerns many Americans had over the issue.[42] Good Democrats, in other words, could (and did) take either side. But by 1988, the party's platform steadfastly declared abortion a "fundamental right" that "should be guaranteed regardless of the ability to pay."[43] Four years later, so total was the collapse of the pro-life position among national Democrats that party stalwarts rebuffed the governor of Pennsylvania in his attempts to address the Democratic National Convention because of his anti-abortion message.⁴⁴ Bill Clinton, Jesse Jackson, Ted Kennedy, Al Gore, Mario Cuomo, Dick Gephardt, and so many Democrats on the national stage switched positions on the issue lest they be trampled underfoot.

Democrats added sexual orientation in 1980 to their platform's lengthy list of categories off-limits to private prejudice. The words "gay men" and "lesbians" made their first appearance in the platform of a major party.⁴⁵ In 1992, Democrats pushed for gays in the military.⁴⁶ By 2004, amidst state judges finding gay marriage rights in state constitutions, the Democrats rebuffed efforts to overturn the judge-made law and called for "full inclusion of gay and lesbian families" with state "benefits" and "protections."⁴⁷ Pleasing sexual radicals came at the price of alienating Catholics and evangelicals, formerly two of the party's most loyal constituencies.

Issues that didn't exist three decades earlier dominated for the culture warriors—feminists, gay liberationists, pacifists, militant atheists, environmentalists—who exerted disproportionate influence over the Democratic Party. The party itself became a mélange of interest groups seemingly unconnected save for their mutual interest in the party's success.

The lines between liberals and leftists blurred. Means, rather than ends, differentiated. Tone, rather than text, differentiated. Speed, rather than direction, differentiated. But the goals were strikingly similar.

Whereas liberalism had been the U.S. government's default outlook from Franklin Roosevelt onward, the hegemony came under increasing attack by the end of Lyndon Johnson's tenure. Democrats still solidly controlled Congress, but liberals, or at least what liberals had become, didn't. Issues had changed. Liberalism changed with them. Urban Catholics and southern Protestants, who generally had been counted on to support the redistributive and managerial economic schemes of liberal presidents, balked at affronts to racial conventions or morality. Civil rights, Vietnam, abortion, rising crime rates, forced busing, and affirmative action were among the issues that dismantled the New Deal coalition. When liberalism stressed economics, a Democratic majority in Congress generally ensured success. But when liberalism stressed cultural concerns, a Democratic majority rarely proved synonymous with a liberal majority.

The Democrats moved leftward and northward—that is, the party ideologically, culturally, and geographically gravitated away from the country. This proved disastrous on Election Day. After the Roosevelt-Truman years, Republicans captured the presidency in ten of fifteen elections. In

those fifteen elections the Democratic Party nominated eight northerners, seven of whom conspicuously lost. On the flipside, when the party
nominated southerners—who tended to be more mainstream than the
George McGoverns, Michael Dukakises, and John Kerrys—it boasted a
respectable 4–2 record. The result of the GOP lock on the White House
was a GOP lock on the federal judiciary. But just as Democrats couldn't
count on their elected officials to be liberals, Republicans couldn't count
on the judges they nominated to be conservative. The liberal judiciary
GOP candidates perennially railed against, ironically, was largely a GOP
creation.

THE LEFT APPEARED so discredited in the eyes of the electorate after the
1960s that it subsequently codified almost none of its agenda through
Congress. Instead, it turned primarily to the courts, which became, in the
hands of the popularly rejected Left, a self-elected shadow legislature
that, because of its usurped legislative function and its preexisting veto
power over unconstitutional law, exerted more power than real legislatures. Unconstrained by the moderating influence of constituents and
elections, black-robed radicals presented a glimpse at the unmasked face
of the Left. Though the literal faces on the bench appeared sober, gray-
framed, weathered, and stoic, the figurative faces appeared feral, wild-
eyed, and fire-breathing. They were ultraists in substance but not in style,
making them the most effective sort of radical. They knew what tie-dyed
Abbie Hoffman, booted-and-miniskirted Bernardine Dohrn, and bare-
chested Huey Newton did not: the radicals who uproot convention and
tradition generally do not look the part.

Notches on the leftist bedpost in these years came almost exclusively
without democratic consent. Michael Newdow, a soldier on the long
march to remove God from government, explained that he appealed to the
courts because "[y]ou can't do it in the legislature."[48] Abortion, sodomy,
gay marriage, forced busing, deinstitutionalization of the insane, and prohibition on prayer in school all became law not through elected legislators
but through unelected judges. To hell with "participatory democracy" and
"power to the people"; the post-1960s Left more brazenly put into practice
the ends-justifies-the-means philosophy that the CPUSA and Weatherman had embraced.

These legal trends, of course, antedated the latter third of the twentieth
century. But the Left ratcheted up its campaign to use the courts to attain
policy goals once the democratic option was clearly beyond its reach. The
American Civil Liberties Union, the National Organization for Women,
the National Association for the Advancement of Colored People, and

other pressure groups used their financial might to wield legal suits against cities, states, and the federal government. Judges, in several cases taken from the ranks of such pressure groups, were generally happy to oblige with their legal demands, which were hand-me-down *political* demands. What failed, or was never even attempted, in the political arena was codified through the legal arena.

When a case went their way, such as the *Roe v. Wade* abortion opinion, activist judges subsequently demanded reverence to *stare decisis*. When a decision went against them, such as the *Bowers v. Hardwick* sodomy case, they discarded precedent with relative ease. As the *Lawrence v. Texas* court that overturned *Bowers* explained, *stare decisis* is not "an inexorable command."[49] Three of the justices joining that observation had decreed a decade earlier in the *Roe*-affirming *Casey v. Planned Parenthood* that decisions on controversial social issues (a classification that certainly fit *Bowers*) are "entitled to rare precedential force."[50] One of the justices who overturned *Bowers* in *Lawrence*, Anthony Kennedy, actually sided with the majority in the original case. Fixed law became putty in the hands of lawyers.

Phrases appearing nowhere in the Constitution, such as "a wall of separation between church and state" and "a right to privacy," became, through liberal rote, part of the Constitution as far as judges were concerned. The court discovered something that never occurred to the people who created the Fourteenth Amendment: that it projected the Bill of Rights' restrictions on federal power upon the states. The court discovered something in the Ninth Amendment that would have struck its creators as anathema: that it empowered federal judges to invent new constitutional rights. The court pretended the Second and Tenth Amendments did not exist, and imagined that the interstate commerce clause gave judges the power to regulate even a state's internal commerce. Such changes occurred primarily because judges wanted a massive change in the nation's laws, in particular those concerning sexual morality, property rights, and religion, and because the elected officials who made those laws would not change them.

Griswold v. Connecticut held that a state law banning contraceptives "violates the right of marital privacy which is within the penumbra of specific guarantees of the Bill of Rights."[51] Which specific guarantees? Penumbwhat? The 1965 opinion cited no less than six amendments, never really saying whether the First, Third, Fourth, Fifth, Ninth, or Fourteenth established the marital privacy right. In fact, a concurring opinion conceded that no such specific guarantees existed. "Although the Constitution does not speak in so many words of the right to privacy in marriage,"

Justice Arthur Goldberg admitted, "I cannot believe that it offers these fundamental rights no protection."[52]

"The Constitution does not explicitly mention any right of privacy," Justice Harry Blackmun confessed in delivering the *Roe v. Wade* decision.[53] Blackmun and six of his cohorts resolved to correct this gross omission by inserting one. Whereas the *Griswold* court cited six amendments to rationalize the right to marital privacy, the *Roe* court ironically relied on the one amendment that guarantees life to lift state prohibitions on the taking of unborn life. From the miraculously discovered constitutional right to marital privacy, the court made the illogical jump that a right to an abortion stems from the invented privacy right. As Aristotle observed of Melissus and Parmenides, "Their premises are false, and their conclusions do not follow."[54]

The Supreme Court jumped even further in its 2003 ruling in *Lawrence v. Texas*, which invented the right to anal sex. The Constitution hadn't changed (save for the Twenty-seventh Amendment) in the seventeen years between *Bowers* and *Lawrence*, but, as Justice Kennedy incessantly noted in *Lawrence*, national and European opinion had. Though the case's petitioners had received due process, the court, as in *Roe*, cited the unstated privacy rights of the due process clause. "Had those who drew and ratified the Due Process Clauses of the Fifth Amendment or the Fourteenth Amendment known the components of liberty in its manifold possibilities, they might have been more specific," Kennedy opined. "They did not presume to have this insight. They knew times can blind us to certain truths and later generations can see that laws once thought necessary and proper in fact serve only to oppress. As the Constitution endures, persons in every generation can invoke its principles in their own search for greater freedom."[55]

Pointing to homosexuality, adultery, fornication, and other offenses against morality, Justice Goldberg's concurring opinion in *Griswold* volunteered that "it should be said of the Court's holding today that it in no way interferes with a State's proper regulation of sexual promiscuity or misconduct."[56] But it did, and in the very ways that Goldberg said that it wouldn't. *Griswold* was the slippery slope upon which state laws reflecting the traditional morality of the people fell. The newly discovered constitutional right to "marital privacy" evolved into a right to kill unborn children in *Roe v. Wade* and to partake of sodomy in *Lawrence v. Texas*. The general spirit spurred courts in Vermont, Massachusetts, and New Jersey to insert into their state constitutions homosexual marital rights. Legal sophistries, not legal principles, enabled judges to enact a leftist social agenda through the courts.

Related to the push undermining traditional marriage and traditional morality was the effort, largely successful, to banish religion from public life. The formula involved applying the First Amendment to the states through the Fourteenth Amendment's alleged incorporation. Never mind that seventy-nine years elapsed between the Fourteenth Amendment's ratification and the judicial "discovery" that the establishment clause's restrictions applied to state and local government as well as the federal government. Never mind, further, that Congress had repeatedly tried to pass new legislation applying the establishment clause to the states—efforts that would have been wholly unnecessary if the Fourteenth Amendment really had already accomplished the task.[57] According to modern courts, then, the Constitution's First Amendment does not merely prohibit *Congress* from *establishing* a religion, but rather bans *any lawmaking body* from even *acknowledging* religion.

The actual text of the First Amendment embarrassed the designs of liberal jurists, so they relied instead on the text of a letter written several decades after the Constitution's ratification by Thomas Jefferson, who had nothing to do with framing the Constitution, in which Jefferson endorsed a "wall of separation between church and state."[58] They also relied on a judicially devised "*Lemon* test" that in no way resembled anything said in the Constitution. So successful was the court's sophistry that great numbers of Americans mistook Jefferson's private remark for the text of the First Amendment and several of the court's members mistook the *Lemon* test for constitutional writ.

The *Lemon* test emerged from the Supreme Court's 1971 decision in *Lemon v. Kurtzman*. The ruling forbade governmental actions that, first, do not "have a secular legislative purpose"; second, whose "principal or primary effect" serves to either "advance" or "inhibit" religion; third, that do not entangle government and religion in an "excessive" manner.[59] Who could decide a law's motivating "purpose"? What a law's "primary effect" is? What is and isn't "excessive"? The test was arbitrary, giving unelected jurists the widest possible wiggle room while providing elected lawmakers the least possible guidance. Worse still, it established law that had little to do with the actual law, that is, *Congress shall make no law respecting an establishment of religion.*

To be sure, *Lemon v. Kurtzman*, like *Roe v. Wade*, did not emerge out of the ether. Its antecedents included 1948's *McCollum v. Board of Education*, which barred voluntary religious programs in public school buildings; 1962's *Engel v. Vitale*, which banned prayer in school; and 1968's *Epperson v. Arkansas*, which struck down laws prohibiting the teaching of evolution. But *Lemon* set the tone for a more aggressive campaign against religion in public life, particularly in education. As Justice Harry Blackmun triumphantly pointed out in 1992, "Since 1971, the Court has decided 31 Establishment Clause cases. In only one instance, the decision of *Marsh v. Chambers*, has the court not rested its decision on the basic principles described in *Lemon*."[60]

In 1980's *Stone v. Graham*, the Supreme Court invalidated a Kentucky law mandating the classroom posting of the Ten Commandments. The decision quoted the *Lemon* test in its entirety. That donations and not taxes financed the educational project the court deemed "immaterial."[61] In 1985, the high court struck down an Alabama statute that permitted students to meditate or pray during a one-minute "moment of silence." Justice John Paul Stevens hubristically declared in *Wallace v. Jafree* that *Lemon*'s three-pronged test was "the law," and that Alabama's moment-of-silence law had violated it. "Respect for stare decisis should require us to follow *Lemon*."[62] In 1992's *Lee v. Weisman*, the Supreme Court decided that a rabbi giving a non-denominational benediction at a Rhode Island middle-school graduation violated the establishment clause. If any of the five jurists on the majority really believed Rhode Island established Judaism as its religion by letting a rabbi speak for a minute, they did not explicitly say.[63]

Though the deciding opinions of *Stone*, *Wallace*, and *Lee* cite the *Lemon* test verbatim, none, tellingly, quotes a single word from the Constitution's establishment clause. The decisions contained a plethora of quotes from judges and legal scholars interpreting the establishment clause, and of course from the court's own *Lemon* test, but the words of the establishment clause itself appeared nowhere in the decisions just as the reasoning of the decisions appeared nowhere in the Constitution.

These decisions weren't enough to satisfy the harshest critics of religion in public life. "They're not treating people equally," observed Michael Newdow, a lifelong atheist who launched his suit against the government for allowing the Pledge of Allegiance in schools, before his daughter even attended school. "You can't say you're treating atheists on a par with people who believe in God when you ask their kids to stand up, face the flag, and say we are a nation under God." The idea of taking on the government occurred to Newdow, a doctor of medicine by profession and a doctor of laws by hobby, over Thanksgiving weekend in 1997. Staying with friends in Chicago whose home never seemed equipped with soap, Newdow purchased a hundred bars of soap as a gag and, upon payment, noticed the phrase "In God We Trust" on coins in a way he had never noticed it before. "This is ridiculous," Newdow recalled thinking. "I don't trust in God." A suit to remove the offending phrase from the currency morphed into a suit to subtract the "under God" added to the Pledge of Allegiance in 1954. The Ninth Circuit Court of Appeals sided with Newdow. The victory proved pyrrhic, as the U.S. Supreme Court threw out the ruling in 2002. But that victory for Newdow's opponents may prove pyrrhic, as the high court based its decision not on the case's merits but on Newdow's lack of standing, as the non-custodial parent, to bring the suit.

Even for committed atheists like Newdow, who applauded the secular direction in which the courts drove America, many of the court's standards came off as terribly arbitrary. What legal principle made aid to religious elementary schools unconstitutional but aid to religious colleges and universities legal? Why could the Ten Commandments be etched into the walls of the Supreme Court but donated sixteen-by-twenty-inch paper copies of the Decalogue could not appear in Kentucky's classrooms? How could the federal government pay congressional and military chaplains but forbid local schools from allowing a volunteer clergyman to say a prayer at graduation? There was no consistent logic behind it all, only the whim of a majority of lawyers, who now took to voting on cases rather than determining the constitutional basis for them.

To attain the desired ends, Newdow acknowledged the necessity of bypassing democratic institutions, the staple tactic of the Left's long march through the institutions. "You can't change this law," a frustrated Newdow conceded. "What politician is going to get 'under God' out of the Pledge of Allegiance? It's hard enough to get a judge to do it. You'd never get a politician to do it. They wouldn't be a politician for the next time around." For Newdow, a lawyer who has "never made a nickel as an attorney," the long march through the courts still has a lot longer to go. What does he wish to ban? " 'So help me God' as an oath of office and that's mandatory in some courtrooms. 'God save the United States and this honorable court' when the Supreme Court and all the federal district courts, except the Second Circuit, open their sessions. Prayers in Congress. The president of the United States, and that one is more difficult because he has his own free exercise rights . . . ought not to be saying 'God bless America' at every speech. I want government, when people are acting as part of the government, to stop taking a religious view. Period."[64]

Not much had changed since Robert Owen named property, religion, and marriage as the trio of great evils for the Left to eradicate. The leftward-swinging court's jurisprudence regarded the trio of institutions as lowly as Owen had. Property, perhaps because its holders bore more clout than unborn babies or praying evangelicals, endured the court's decisions less obviously than marriage-based morality or religion. And when property did face the court's wrath, it was often small property holders who suffered for the benefit of large property holders, or for the largest property holder of all, the government.

In 2005's *Kelo v. New London*, for instance, the high court nullified the Fifth Amendment's "takings" clause, which had allowed the government to confiscate private property only for "public use." Admitting that a New London urban renewal project would be closed to the public, and in fact would involve the taking of private property for the purpose of giving it to another private party, the court expanded "public use" to "public purpose."[65] In other words, anticipated windfalls in property taxes justified leveling the homes of the working class to make way for the projects of multi-billion-dollar corporations.

The reverse Robin Hoodism of *Kelo* crystallized the Left's shift in economic priorities. For a hundred years after the Civil War, improving the lot of workers served as the raison d'être for much of the Left. To offset the large and powerful interests that threatened the economic well-being of workers, the Left had rationalized the granting of new powers to the state and its consequent expansion. Means, gradually, became ends. When the Little Man faced off against Big Brother (and its tag-team partner Big Business), as in *Kelo*, the Left went with the latter. The labor metaphysic that C. Wright Mills had ridiculed as a Victorian relic appeared to be just that.

Rather than interpret constitutional law, the courts increasingly made it. They played a game of operator, where one court contrived a set of rights, a succeeding court devised a new set of rights based on the implications of the preceding set of rights, and so on. Lost in translation was the original message, the Constitution.

What brave new worlds would the logic of *Lawrence*, *Newdow*, and *Kelo* create? And from the Left's perspective, might the strategy of courthouse "democracy" backfire? After all, couldn't conservatives, too, discover mysterious, unnamed constitutional rights in the Ninth Amendment? What's to stop the Right from imposing uniform laws on the states, such as a national ban on abortion, that appear as reverse images of the uniform laws that the Left has obtruded? If the Fourteenth Amendment really does apply the Bill of Rights to the states, would this premise not, in the hands of a more conservative judiciary, invalidate gun control ordinances? This last scenario is no longer theoretical. A federal court struck down the District of Columbia's three-decade-old gun ban in 2007.[66] Though the courthouse strategy certainly served leftist ends, the means used could be adopted by opponents. Would the Left discover, as it had after its New Deal enthusiasm for the executive order, that establishing the precedent of dubious means often returns to haunt its initial boosters?

The court decisions had a profound impact on the nation. America was forever changed, but not because Americans had decided to change.

IT WAS A long march even to get to *the* long march.

For the antebellum communitarians who introduced America to the Left, their means of conversion included example, demonstration, and persuasion. In woodland, hilly retreats, they sought to provide witness for another, better way. Alas, skeptics, and even most of the communitarians, were ultimately persuaded only of the foolishness of communism. In the moment of triumph for the One Big Reform, the North's victory over the South in the Civil War, the antebellum reformers witnessed the death of the dozens of small reforms.

For the industrial-age unionists, populists, progressives, and socialists who followed, tickets to salvation included the vote, as the means to control the state, and the state, as the means to impose their will. Industrial replaced agrarian. National replaced local. Force replaced persuasion. In grimy union halls and atop the country-town soapbox, in broken English, with a southern twang, and by non-rhotic Yankee, the Left proclaimed a heaven on earth. But the votes weren't always there. As a progressive's progressive crusaded to reform Europe in the democratic image of America, America's democracy and the Left in particular suffered self-inflicted blow after blow. The Left went away having notched gains but ultimately defeated.

Frustrated, the Left turned abroad for answers. They found them all in the Communist takeover of Russia. Making the pilgrimage, boring from within, manning the picket line, handing over the attaché case, American Communists acted against their nation in the deluded hope that violent revolution would transform the United States of America into the States United for Communism. It didn't. In the process, American leftists provided state secrets, atom bomb diagrams, and war plans to one of the great mass murderers in human history. As World War II ended and the Cold War began, the Left, again, eroded its standing.

The New Left emerged from the embers of the Old Left. Workers were "out" as the oppressed agent of change, replaced by blacks, women, the poor, homosexuals, and a multitude of other "victim" groups. The emphasis on cultural rather than economic matters laid the groundwork for the long march through the cultural institutions—academia, popular entertainment, the media. A cultural takeover was seen as a prerequisite for a state takeover. With gavels and film cameras, from lecterns and newsrooms, the Left evangelized and codified its message.

Then nineteen foreigners hijacked four planes, smashing them into the World Trade Center, the Pentagon, and a field in rural Pennsylvania. The next Left was about to be born.

THE MEANS HAVE changed. The ends have remained largely the same: abolish marriage, God, and the free market. The stables haven't been cleaned, but Hercules, appearing in different guises, returns every generation to attempt the job.

BOOK FIVE

THE 9/12 LEFT

～ 24 ～

THE 9/12 LEFT

You have sowed much and brought in little: you have eaten but have not had enough: you have drunk but have not been filled with drink: you have clothed yourselves but have not been warmed: and he that hath earned wages put them into a bag with holes.

—AGGEUS 1:6

THE SPECTACULAR SUICIDE-BY-PLANE bombings of the Twin Towers and the Pentagon marked a new beginning for the American Left. Adrift since the 1970s, the Left had scarcely outlined a coherent positive agenda. Stripped of its foreign utopian models in the late 1980s and early 1990s, the Left no longer could point to heavens on earth, but it still had its devil state. It knew what it was *against*. What it was *for* was less clear. Anti-Americanism became a rallying point.

Terrorists struck the functioning symbols of U.S. capitalism and the U.S. military on September 11, 2001. Hadn't the Weathermen bombed the Pentagon thirty-one years earlier? Hadn't anonymous anarchists killed dozens of people on Wall Street fifty years before that? For different reasons, and with more destructive results, enemies external had fixed aim at long-standing targets of enemies internal.

The gap between the American Left and America never seemed wider than it did in the aftermath of 9/11. The massive street demonstrations that erupted between 9/11 and the Iraq War, seemingly rehearsed in microcosm during the "Free Mumia" anti-death-penalty rallies and anti-globalization demonstrations of the late 1990s, illustrated the activist Left's alienation from and hostility to the surrounding culture.

"The United States is like a stuck-up little bitch," reacted a New Jersey activist. "They just do and take all of what they please. I mean, 9/11 was terrible, but it was the first terrorist attack on this country. It's like, 'Oh, no! Somebody broke the United States' nail, and now the whole earth is going to be blown up.' "[1] "The war crimes that America has done [in Afghanistan] are just incomprehensible," held Melissa Orr, a protestor from Cincinnati. "They packed people into trucks with no air and no water and let them slowly suffocate. The people who died on 9/11 mostly died instantaneously. There's a big difference in those kinds of deaths."[2] "Whoever it was, for example, that was behind the bombing of the World Trade Center—they are criminals," conceded Eric Josephson, protesting the World Economic Forum in 2002. "They are criminals. They are small criminals as against the big, bloody criminals who run United States imperialism."[3]

Murderers of three thousand people "small criminals"? The 9/11 attacks like breaking a nail? When the Left wasn't downplaying the attacks, they were blaming them on America, or capitalism, or George W. Bush, or the CIA. Like the 1960s Left, which substituted politically convenient culprits for real culprits in the assassinations of President Kennedy and Malcolm X, the post-9/11 Left placed responsibility for the attacks on the shoulders of political enemies—even to the point of positing the U.S. government's foreknowledge or complicity in the attacks. The assignation of motivation for the military action that followed was strangely familiar, too. A "war for oil" meshed well with Marx's economic determinism even if it didn't mesh well with Afghanistan's relative paucity of black gold or the rising prices at the pump that ensued after the Iraq War.

"I was not surprised by the events of 9/11," maintained a Burlington, Vermont, protestor who believes the government let the attacks occur. "It's like I've been waiting for years for something like that to happen because I knew that the people of the world were starting to pull away from capitalism."[4] "Who was responsible for 9/11?" a protestor in New York City in 2003 rhetorically asked. "American imperialism and George Bush in particular. The Bush family and the bin Laden family have long, long economic ties."[5] "Osama used to work for the CIA," explained a woman marching in Washington, D.C. "All these guys were actually trained or inspired by our own efforts."[6]

Working off a well-worn script, the Left reflexively cast America as villain rather than victim. Anti-Americanism served as a peculiar mass line. Was there even a pretense of winning over Americans? Or was this a therapeutic politics, in which personal exhilaration and not persuasion mattered? Blaming the victim in one of the great horrors in American history or wishing defeat upon U.S. troops on the eve of war may have won plaudits in Tehran or Islamabad, but in America?

A war of choice in Iraq based on numerous false assumptions might have been derailed had a responsible anti-war movement opposed it. The post-9/11 antiwar movement, having fallen for the sixties mythology that presumptuously awarded the anti-war movement the honor of stopping the Vietnam War, embraced the same off-putting rhetoric and tactics that had made its antecedent a refuge for the fringe rather than a force for peace. The catharsis arrived at from calling the president a "terrorist" or America "fascist" trumped the persuasion that temperance, restraint, and reason might have unleashed. Had George W. Bush invented his enemies, he could not have devised a more loathsome bunch than those protesting his ill-advised war. While protestors didn't find in Saddam Hussein or Osama bin Laden as sympathetic a figure as their antecedents had found in Ho Chi Minh, they did hate their countrymen-adversaries as much as their antecedents had. The protestors, rather than the war protested, became the issue.

"We would be for the defeat of the U.S. war," said Abram Megrete, who traveled to D.C. from New York to protest a few days before the war started. "We are for the defense of Iraq. It is in the interest of working people in the United States that the same government which is trying to intimidate and silence them be defeated in this war."[7] "Frankly, the American military and the people at the top consider Iraqis, and all people of color, all people who have no money, all people who are in their way as being subhuman and expendable," insisted a Seattle activist protesting Bush's second inaugural. "I hope the resistance succeeds in removing the foreign occupiers from their country."[8]

Such verbal tantrums won the Left attention and denied it influence.

WHERE DID THE foot soldiers get such outlandish ideas? A primary source was Michael Moore, an amalgam of the street-theater sensibilities of Abbie Hoffman, the muckraking of Upton Sinclair, the self-promotion of Ignatius Donnelly, the direct plainspokenness of J. A. Wayland, and the reflexive anti-Americanism of Noam Chomsky. Moore's in-your-face tactics and comic touch contrasted sharply with the humorless, genteel academics who had done so much to marginalize the Left. "We have a namby-pamby way of saying things," Moore chided his co-ideologists. "It's like we invented our own language—and it annoys the hell out of anyone we're trying to get to listen to us. Knock off the PC mumbo jumbo, quit trying to be so sensitive and just say what is on your mind. Less wimp and more OOMPH!"[9]

Moore's tactics were at least as radical as his politics. Aggressive stunts included siccing costumed Puritans upon adulterous Republicans impeaching President Clinton, directing a Rage Against the Machine video on Wall Street, bringing victims of the Columbine massacre to Wal-Mart to return the "merchandise" shot into their bodies, and boating ailing Americans to Cuba for health care. Others had made the points Michael Moore made, but none had made them so memorably.

America's foremost purveyor of anti-Americanism came from Middle America. In the bedroom community of Davison, Michigan, Moore won an essay contest on "What the Flag Means to Me," earned the rank of Eagle Scout, received a plaque from the Elks for a speech on Abraham Lincoln's life, and spent a year in a Catholic high school for seminarians.[10] He refrained from drink and drugs, did not participate in sports, and never even danced with a girl throughout high school.[11] Moore's rush came from politics. While classmates partied, Moore ran for the school board of Davison, Michigan, in his graduation year and won. His gadfly antics, evident even then, prompted his civics teacher to later observe, "He's always been ugly, fat, and obnoxious, a troubled child with no close friends to speak of."[12]

The ego that then rubbed critics raw never stopped growing. Moore was good at making enemies no matter the politics involved. He sued *Mother Jones* for daring to fire him as editor. Ralph Nader fired Moore and demanded $30,000 from him for surreptitiously making a documentary on company time.[13] Whether it is *Roger & Me*, his short-lived *Moore's Weekly* newsletter, or the face on the cover of his best-selling books, Michael Moore is always the center of his own attention. Moore elicited visceral reactions, pro or con, but not any discernable change in public opinion on the issues he tackled. Unions and factory towns weakened after *Roger & Me*. Gun-control efforts stayed dormant after *Bowling for Columbine*. The elongated campaign commercial *Fahrenheit 9/11* didn't stop the war in Iraq and precipitated a Bush reelection. *Sicko* inspired not a transformation of American medical care but jokes about the gall of such an unhealthy man lecturing America on health. Alas, documentaries don't change the world no matter the dreams of documentarians.

Huge egos harbor huge ambitions. Moore thought bigger than other activists. He didn't want to take over the sociology department, control the books ordered for the local library, or plaster his car with bumper stickers. He wanted to make an impact. "We cannot change the world as long as we are separate from it," he reminded leftists, whose personal long marches often ended within one of several leftist echo chambers.[14]

With a ball cap glued to his head and a sneer glued upon his face, Moore invaded the dominant culture through the all-American media of cinema and television. The premise of his 1989 breakthrough *Roger & Me*, as suggested by promotional material showing Moore holding a microphone toward no one, was Moore's quixotic attempt to interview the chairman of General Motors, whose plant closings had devastated Moore's adopted hometown of Flint, Michigan. The film reinforces the impression that Roger Smith dodged Moore, yet the filmmaker spoke to Smith at least twice on camera. Left-wing lawyer James Musselman contends that Moore conducted a fifteen-minute, sit-down interview with Smith in 1988, recalled by neither interviewer nor interviewee.[15] *Fahrenheit 9/11* shows pre-war Iraq full of smiling children on Ferris wheels, flying kites, and riding bicycles. The film cuts to the war and shows pictures of burned, wounded, and dead children. Couldn't proponents of the war just as credibly have juxtaposed Saddam's pre-war brutalities with post-war happiness? Veracity, like modesty, was not one of Moore's strong points.

Neither was consistency. Moore's manufactured manufacturing-town background and his poseur blue-collar fashion sensibilities played better on the coasts—the Pacific, the Atlantic, and the Riviera—than in Middle America. The toast of Manhattan, Cannes, and Tinseltown was generally despised in the heartland. (*Fahrenheit 9/11*, which Moore boasted was a "red-state movie," was actually "a bust in the heartland," as reporter Byron York documented.)[16] Like GM, Moore moved his moneymaking machine from Flint to greener pastures. Unlike Flint's GM, Moore, former employees allege, forbade union membership when it stood to damage his enterprises.[17] It was not hypocrisy, deceit, or style but substance that alienated Moore from his intended demographic.

Moore waxed about "U.S.-backed mujahedeen fighters like Osama bin Laden."[18] He implored, "[N]o more of this 'God Bless America' crap."[19] He judged that Americans "are among the dumbest people on the planet."[20] And he concluded, "Those living under the boot of these despots know that *we're* responsible for their suffering."[21]

Just as what was good for General Motors wasn't necessarily good for Flint, what was good at the box office and the cash register wasn't necessarily good for the Left. Moore invigorated a base but alienated potential converts. He identified issues—corporate malfeasance, gun control, military intervention, socialized medicine—that resonated with the Left. But ultimately, in every documentary, every television episode, every book, every speech, the issue was not the issue, but Michael Moore.

THE SEARCH FOR a positive vision to reinvigorate the Left brought it behind the theory that man's gluttonous behavior was altering the climate. Not since radicals deluded themselves into believing Communism would save the world had a movement possessed such redemptive potential and enjoyed such a global scope. For those inclined to see the United States as the source of evil in our times, the unparalleled energy consumption of the world's richest nation reinforced the vision of America as a pariah.

Hysteria over global warming combined the worst of the primitive and the modern. Global warming emerged as the Armageddon for people who ridicule people who believe in Armageddon. The disturbing omens that primitives divined from mysterious eclipses, crippling droughts, and foreboding skies, urban sophisticates saw in ever-so-slight changes in the weather—save they had the nerve to call their auguries science. From the climate-controlled, indoor world where man presses a button to make it hot or cold, breezy or not, man hubristically imagined himself the master of the outdoor weather, too. Not the sun, not volcanoes, not the wind currents, but man was exclusively responsible for global warming—a theory more heavily steeped in narcissism than pre-Copernican notions of a geocentric universe. And if gluttonous man could destroy the world, enlightened man could save it. Global warming allowed true believers to cast enemies as evil destroyers and themselves as noble redeemers. Mankind stood on the brink of the end times. Sacrifices to the gods— offerings of recycled cans, forbearance from flushing the toilet, holocausts of SUVs—might appease Mother Nature. Failure to make the proper oblations certainly would unleash her righteous wrath.

Rather than report the news, or even take a side in the debate, many journalists called names. And not just any names; in the overheated, *reductio ad Hitlerum* style that came to characterize political debate, they applied the worst, most vile epithets in their vocabulary: "holocaust denier," "Nazi," "fascist," and so on. *Boston Globe* columnist Ellen Goodman writes that "global warming deniers are now on a par with Holocaust deniers, though one denies the past and the other denies the present and the future."[22] *60 Minutes* correspondent Scott Pelley rationalized the exclusion of skeptics from a report on global warming by, à la Goodman, likening them to "Holocaust deniers."[23] *Newsweek* got the memo, rechristening skeptics "deniers" (who have created "a paralyzing fog of doubt" and "undermin[ed] the science") more than a dozen times in a cover story for the *news*magazine.[24] Advocacy journalist David Roberts merely extended the logic, maintaining of skeptics that "we should have war crimes trials for these bastards—some sort of climate Nuremberg."[25]

If likening opponents to Nazis excuses one from debating them, denying the existence of opposing voices made the whole idea of debate absurd. How does one converse with scientists who do not exist? "After extensive searches," reporter Bill Blakemore contended, "ABC News has found no such [scientific] debate."[26] Al Gore declared that "the debate in the scientific community is over."[27] CNN's Michelle Mitchell announced the "unanimous decision that global warming is real, is getting worse and is due to man. There is no wiggle room."[28] But serious questions, such as whether the earth really is getting warmer, whether man is the cause of warming, whether the solutions offered will make any difference, remain—no matter how loud and frequent are the conformity-inducing proclamations of the scientific community's unanimity. Reporters who could find no debate must have missed climate scientists like Dr. William M. Gray, perhaps the nation's leading hurricane forecaster. Dr. Gray warned the U.S. Senate about "the bogus science and media-hype associated with the nuclear winter and the human-induced global warming hypotheses,"[29] and later called Gore's climate theories "ridiculous."[30]

If calling opponents names or pretending they do not exist fails, there is always the time-tested tactic of scaring people. *Do as we say, or everyone is going to die*, goes this argumentation in its crudest form. Madison, Wisconsin, mayor Dave Cieslewicz predicts a climate for his state like central Oklahoma. "If the projections are correct," the mayor of the leftist enclave warns, "we won't be able to have Wisconsin maple syrup any longer in ten to twenty years."[31] Nobel Peace Prize winner Al Gore offers scare scenarios of Miami and lower Manhattan submerged in water in the Oscar-winning *An Inconvenient Truth*. "Within fifteen years this will be the park formerly known as 'Glacier,' " Gore says while showing a slide of Montana's Glacier National Park.[32]

Green high priests gave their imprimaturs to deception in the service of scaring people to accept environmentalist prescriptions. "Nobody is interested in solutions if they don't think there's a problem," Gore confessed. "Given that starting point, I believe it is appropriate to have an over-representation of factual presentations on how dangerous it is, as a predicate for opening up the audience to listen to what the solutions are, and how hopeful it is that we are going to solve this crisis."[33] "We've got to ride the global warming issue," Senator Tim Wirth declared in the panic's infancy. "Even if the theory of global warming is wrong, we will be doing the right thing in terms of economic policy and environmental policy."[34]

As Wirth's admission suggested, the solutions curiously antedated, and are endorsed independent of, the problem. Public restrictions on use of private property, state punishment of large corporations, international bodies dictating national laws, and other long-standing dreams of the Left somehow reemerged as curatives to environmental woes. Alas, if the problem disappeared, the true believers would urge enactment of these suspect solutions as enthusiastically as ever.

. . .

WHEN ENVIRONMENTALIST AL Gore lost the presidency in 2000, partisans blamed confusing paper ballots in Florida. Four years later, when Republican George Bush defeated John Kerry, partisans blamed computer voting machines in Ohio (the ones they had demanded four years earlier) or mismanagement of precincts (invariably run by Democrats). Coming to terms with popular rejection sent the mental wheels spinning.

This was particularly true of activists protesting George W. Bush's 2004 inauguration. "I honestly believe that those who do vote for the current administration are not voting in their best interests, and even beyond that I've known many, many people who I've thought of as being conservative who this time voted for Kerry and not Bush," Stephanie Kornfeld of Massachusetts observed. "Yeah, I'll just say it. I think Kerry did win because the exit polls would verify that."[35] "I think they stole Ohio," Marylander Darrell Anderson contends. "I think [Kerry] absolutely won. I think he got enough electoral votes to win counting Ohio. I think they manipulated machines, the Republican Party."[36] "I'm baffled by the public's decision to support Bush," Pennsylvanian Meredith Lair confessed at the 2004 presidential inauguration. "I don't understand why people don't vote their interests."[37] "I don't understand," a laughing Catherine Ouellette admitted. "How could so many people be so dumb?"[38]

"People getting their fundamental interests wrong is what American political life is all about," Thomas Frank hypothesized in his 2004 bestseller, *What's the Matter with Kansas?*[39] Specifically, Frank applies this idea to blue-collar citizens of his native Kansas, who vote Republican but should, according to Frank, vote Democratic. Echoing Marx's notions of economic status determining political interest and of "false consciousness"—the way of explaining away the renegade majority who rebuff Marx's political assignments—Frank laments the "self-denying votes" of working Kansans who pull the lever for Republicans even as they endure factory closings, a decline in wages, and evaporating social services.[40] Rather than reassess his theory in the face of its popular rejection, Frank lashes out at the people whose political actions mock economic determinism. Alas, Frank, a successful author raised in a rich family in an affluent Kansas City suburb, votes against his class interests, too. With his own political convictions too complex to be reduced to a simplistic economic formula, why is Frank so obtuse to the complexity of interests of people poorer than he?

A student of his state's history, Frank recalls a time when Kansans turned to radicals rather than reactionaries. Indeed, Kansas was once "bleeding Kansas," site of the Pottawatomie Massacre and destination point of "Beecher's Bibles." Kansans awarded the People's Party its electoral votes in

1892, elected the "Sockless Socrates" to Congress, refused to follow the "yellow brick road," and heard native daughter Mary Lease's call to "raise less corn and more hell." Jayhawks witnessed Carry A. Nation's "hatchetation," which propelled America's second wave of prohibition. Tiny Girard played mecca to socialist pilgrims Eugene Debs, Mother Jones, and Upton Sinclair. Its leading citizen, J. A. Wayland, presided over the town's leading employer, *Appeal to Reason*, the most successful publication in the history of the American Left. Even Kansas Communist Earl Browder was savvy enough to realize the superiority of the slogan "Communism Is Twentieth Century Americanism" to the party's past America-hating mantras. Kansas, the very middle of Middle America, the heart of the heartland, was also once the epicenter of the American Left.

What changed?

For Thomas Frank, Kansas changed. "The people who were once radical are now reactionary," he laments.[41] "I'm a Christian," Frank quotes a right-wing activist in present-day Kansas. "Primarily my goal is to build the Kingdom of God."[42] This, significantly, is the language of John Brown and Carry A. Nation, and demonstrates the degree to which not simply Kansas but the Left has changed. The lingo of the nineteenth-century Kansas Left is the lingo of the twenty-first-century Kansas Right. The religious rhetoric of John Brown and Carry Nation, the fiery patriot's populism of governor Lorenzo Lewelling, and the entrepreneurial socialism of "Appeal's Army" general J. A. Wayland reached the heart of America because it spoke to the heart of America. Kansans then expressed cultural affinities and not ideological commitments. They still do. The Left, on the other hand, stopped speaking Americanese. Greater than this stylistic problem is the substance: the Left's sneering distaste for American cultural markers—entrepreneurship, religion, and patriotism—and the reflexive, emotive, predictable response to America in conflict, as evidenced during the Cold War and after 9/11. It is hard to sell your story to people when their country always wears a black hat in your narrative.

Thomas Frank sees Wichitans protest abortion clinics instead of Boeing layoffs, blue-collar Kansans replacing Republican senators not with Democrats but with even more conservative Republicans, and the "backwards cluelessness" of the state board of education's agnosticism on evolution, and asks, "What's the matter with Kansas?"[43] Kansans see radical jurists ordering the codification of gay marriage, Ivy League professors hoping for America's defeat in war, and leftist pundits mocking the president for naming Christ a thinker that he admires, and ask, "What's the matter with the Left?"

· · ·

PRESIDENTIAL ASPIRANT HILLARY Rodham Clinton might seem an unusual heir to that old-time leftism imbued with that old-time religion. But underlying the swerves and ironies that mark her journey is a religious grounding that informs and inspires her politics.

Like Diana Oughton, Hillary Rodham was an Illinois Goldwater Girl who turned radical at a Seven Sisters college. Unlike Oughton, Hillary Rodham stayed within the system to change the system. Nine months before Weatherman Oughton appeared in *Time* for blowing herself up, Wellesley student government president Rodham appeared in *Life* for a graduation-day rebuke to Massachusetts senator Edward Brooke, the school's other commencement speaker.[44] Speaking for her peers, Rodham explained that "we feel that for too long our leaders have used politics as the art of the possible. And the challenge now is to practice politics as the art of making what appears to be impossible, possible."[45]

Hillary Rodham's long march took her from the presidency of the College Republicans at Wellesley to monitoring a Black Panther trial for the ACLU, interning in a law firm partnered by Communists, and writing a senior thesis on the radical's radical, agitator Saul Alinsky.[46] "Much of what Alinsky professes does not sound 'radical,'" Rodham insisted in the impressive seventy-five-page undergraduate paper. "His are the words used in our schools and churches, by our parents and their friends, by our peers. The difference is that Alinsky really believes in them and recognizes the necessity of changing the present structure of our lives in order to realize them."[47] Admiring its subject, Rodham's paper nevertheless displayed evidence of its author pursuing an alternative strategy. Lamenting "Black Power demagogues" and the "elitist arrogance and repressive intolerance" of elements within the New Left, and noting her rejection of a job offer from Alinsky, Wellesley's student government president gave indication of continuing to work within the system rather than outside it.[48] That's just what she did for the next forty years.

She regarded Richard Nixon as "evil," worked for George McGovern's presidential campaign, and then enlisted in the army of lawyers on the House Judiciary Committee's impeachment investigation.[49] A quarter century later she would find herself on the other side of an impeachment battle—defending presidential mendacity as she had once sought to uproot it and exhibiting a paranoid style reminiscent of the disgraced president she had worked to remove.

She ventured into academia, arguing for advocacy within scholarship. "For too long, legal issues have been defined and discussed in terms of academic doctrine rather than strategies for social change," law student Hillary Rodham and her fellow editors wrote in 1970. "*Law and Social*

Action is an attempt to go beyond the narrowness of such an approach, to present forms of legal scholarship and journalism which focus on programmatic solutions to social problems."[50] Attempting to get in on the ground floor of the next civil rights crusade, Rodham articulated a vision of "children's rights" in the *Harvard Educational Review* in 1973. Therein, Rodham argued for legal representation for children, proposed the possible inclusion of children on community boards that would decide whether the state should intervene in familial matters or not, lamented the "consensus romanticism about the family" that inhibits state intervention when abuse is non-physical, and rashly likened marriage and the family to slavery and life on Indian reservations.[51]

Rather than carp from the outside, Hillary Clinton characteristically maneuvered into institutions to put her ideas into action. She was appointed by President Carter to chair Legal Services, the Great Society bane of conservatives that uses tax dollars to sue the government on behalf of the poor. The agency's funding tripled under her stewardship.[52]

Now, after four decades of working tirelessly for radical ideas in a reformist manner, Hillary Clinton wants to be president. She wants to redistribute wealth. "[T]he tax cuts may have helped you," she told a San Francisco audience in 2004. "We're saying that for America to get back on track, we're probably going to cut that short and not give it to you. We're going to take things away from you on behalf of the common good."[53] She believes the government rather than the private sector should be entrusted with providing health care. She venerates those who work for the government, seeking to create a National Service Academy to provide free educations to fellow enthusiasts of an activist government.[54] She wants the state to supplant families as the provider for children, and children to be dependent on the state instead of their families. "I like the idea of giving every baby born in America a $5,000 account that will grow over time," she remarked on the campaign trail.[55] She wants the government to pay for all four-year-olds to leave the home for pre-kindergarten schooling.[56] As she remarked when promoting her book *It Takes a Village*, "There is no such thing as other people's children."[57] Mine is thine and thine is mine. Hillary Clinton wants power over people because she believes she knows better than they their wants and needs.

Bill Clinton declared the era of big government over. His wife's program, reflecting a revitalized Left, shows how premature the reports of big government's death were.

IF HILLARY'S JOURNEY was the New Left's journey in microcosm, pushing her along that long march was a fuel that had propelled a long-forgotten Left. "The engine of Hillary's evolution and of her enormous capacity for change seemed sturdily bolted under the hood of her religious convictions, a set of beliefs that to some bordered on a messiah-like self-perception, to others a license to do whatever she pleased in the name of God, and to others a touchstone of spirituality that infused her notions of love, caring, and service," biographer Carl Bernstein notes.[58] Her Methodist spiritual advisor brought her together with Alinsky. She read liberal theologians Reinhold Niebuhr and Paul Tillich as a student, lectured Arkansan women on the topic "Women Armed with the Christian Sword—To Build an Army for the Lord," and carried a small, marked Bible with her during her troubled tenure as First Lady.[59]

Even if the crusading spirit in politics evokes images of anti-abortion protestors or cartoon evangelicals demanding evolution expelled from school, Hillary Clinton's mission to provide health care to every American, to make child rearing a collective rather than familial obligation, to redistribute wealth, to ban cigarettes, and to elevate public-sector work to the status of military service is a religious crusade, a mission, a vocation. It harkens back to the zealotry and moral indignation of the abolitionists, the do-gooder spirit of the Social Gospel, and the paternalism of the progressives. However offensive Clinton's stern busybodyism is to adherents of the American freedom tradition, her critics cannot credibly dismiss her, as they so easily do with Michael Moore, as operating outside of the wider American tradition. "We know best" is as American as "Leave me alone."

The Cowboy and the Puritan have been fighting for the soul of America for as long as there has been an America. One American icon seeks an open, freewheeling, mind-your-own-business America. The other American icon seeks a virtuous, interventionist America that lifts up the downtrodden, scolds the naughty, and hovers above our shoulders guiding us to the right path when we stray. The American Left experiences the Cowboy-Puritan battle over its soul, too. Within the Left, it would seem the Puritan has emerged triumphant—in large part because the Puritan is no longer recognized as such. Within Hillary Clinton, whom comrades describe as a "very judgmental Methodist from the Midwest" and "among the most self-righteous people I've ever known in my life," the Puritan is hard to miss.[60] The Puritan may seem hard to recognize in the larger movement, but not for anyone familiar with the development of the American Left over the past two centuries.

CONCLUSION

What is it that hath been? The same thing that shall be. What is it that hath been done? The same thing that shall be done. Nothing under the sun is new neither is any man able to say: Behold this is new. For it hath already gone before in the ages that were before us. There is no remembrance of former things: nor indeed of those things which hereafter are to come; shall there be any remembrance with them that shall be in the latter end.

—ECCLESIASTES 1:9–11

IN DREAMS, LONG-DEAD relatives speak, anthropomorphic animals dispense wisdom, money rains from the sky, and comely actresses demand sex. In socialism, men work without incentive, loyalty to the human family trumps loyalty to the nuclear family, a few social engineers manage the production and consumption of millions, men evolve into angels, and heaven arrives on earth. In life, one who confuses dreams for reality is regarded as crazy. In politics, one who confuses dreams for reality is called an idealist. It is terribly destructive to romanticize political romantics who cannot discern fantasy from fact. Politics, the art of the possible, becomes the captive of the impossible when visionaries and utopians encroach upon the concrete.

This is a book more about dreams than about reality. Even when reformers institute the radical's wish list, the radical remains unsatisfied. For the dream was never simply, say, state controls over the economy, marginalization of traditional religion, or the erosion of marriage, but rather the complete equality, brotherhood of man, unity of interest, whistle-while-you-work work, and human perfection that was supposed to come from the attainment of those aims. It is an article of faith on the Left that B follows from A.

But B has never followed A. Setbacks cause enthusiasts to repackage but never to reassess, to question tactics but never strategy, to alter the means but not the ends. The failure in practice does not kill the idea because ideas exist in minds, where images of cheerful laborers, sharing, world peace, human brotherhood, and the like trump firsthand witness that radical ideas cannot produce any such thing, and in fact produce the opposite. Concrete failures are not so catastrophic for people who live in their imaginations. The ideas never failed, the idealist stubbornly maintains, because the ideas have never been tried. This befuddles the realist. Why, the realist wonders, does the idealist react so unrealistically? The realist, in other words, wishes to make a realist out of the idealist, which itself is a form of idealism. The idealist operates on the imaginary plane, the realist operates on the actual plane, and never the twain shall meet.

The dream could have ended for Robert Owen at New Harmony's collapse, for Mike Gold at the Nazi-Soviet Friendship Pact, for Abbie Hoffman at the overdoses, illegitimacy, and crime that the sixties unleashed. It didn't. The luminescence of the beautiful idea could not be obscured by the dark truth. The beautiful idea is that beautiful, that powerful, that enduring.

LEFTISTS DREAM. BUT what, concretely, do leftists presently believe? For true believers who have spent years of their lives fighting for the Left, explaining what they believe is not an easy matter. This is because the Left is based less on a set of concrete policy prescriptions than it is on an abstraction—that beautiful, powerful, enduring dream, that millennial vision of the world after the Left's program has been instituted.

At an International ANSWER-sponsored anti-war event in Washington, D.C., in the fall of 2005, I looked for answers among self-identified leftists. Jeff Edwards, a Chicago gay rights activist, defines the Left as a commitment "to human freedom and equality and social justice."[1] "The Left represents the real interests of people both at home and abroad," offered self-described "extreme leftist" Brewer Dohithik, "and tries to express that in terms of making social change that will benefit those real interests."[2] Gayle Ruddi, who traveled to Washington, D.C., from Chapel Hill and to the Democrats from the Republicans, declares: "I think we stand for more economic justice, more social justice."[3] Freedom? Social justice? Real interests? Equality? Change? What does any of this mean? And if the Left merely supports platitudes, why are so many people against the Left?

One activist attempted to define the Left thusly: "You know, like, I guess it's, I would hope that it would be, you know, open-minded, kind of, peaceful, like a [sic] education-loving, you know, you know, you know . . . I wish I was [sic] more coherent."[4]

The movement's Jimmy Higginses offered vagueness and incoherence.

Its articulate stars got more specific. Their answers, diverse and occasionally contradictory, offer scant edification.

For Michael Newdow, the litigant seeking the removal of "under God" from the Pledge of Allegiance, the core idea is "equality."[5] For Steve Max it is "anti-capitalist," for Dick Flacks "participatory democracy," and for Tom Hayden "an experimental approach to social change coupled with an effort to define and challenge the system as a whole."[6] Medea Benjamin, founder of Code Pink, explains that "progressives" (the term she opts for) believe "that we should be working toward greater equity globally, health care and education should be basic rights, and we should build our societies, our economies around those basic rights, and I would also add that a progressive is one who really cherishes the planet that we live on and wants to see it preserved."[7] "I think a leftist believes that elites don't have the right to run other people's lives," recovering Weatherman Mark Rudd explains, "that people can make the important decisions in their lives for themselves."[8]

It is perhaps SDS founding father Al Haber's motivating notion—"What is the other society that is possible?"[9]—that offers most in terms of a unifying idea. Leftists seek change, even though individual leftists may disagree on what changes they want. The other society that is possible, of course, has unbounded riches and ample time for sleep and leisure. It has no unemployment, crime, racism, sexism, or pollution. It produces Shakespeares, Michelangelos, and Jesse Owenses with regularity. It is preferable to America in every way but one: it does not exist. If you constantly made fantasyland your basis of comparison to the society that you lived in, you, too, might devise a million schemes for reform and reflexively find what exists wanting. And you might scheme and critique impervious to this fact: if man can improve things, he can make them worse, too.

The American Left's history—ignored, whitewashed, or obscured—offers examples of perfectors of society making imperfect society even less perfect. That past, along with this present, offers clues to the Left's future. Upon receiving news of J. A. Wayland's suicide, his comrades deluged the *Appeal to Reason* with tributes: "His name will be written high in the annals of the world's workers for the common good"; "As long as the spirit of Socialism lives, Wayland's name will remain enshrined in the human heart"; "[U]nborn millions will some day reverence his name."[10] But Wayland was quickly forgotten. Just as he had no time to study the communitarians who preceded him when he launched his Ruskin colony, subsequent Lefts had no time to remember him. When the past does serve as a reference point, it is usually the mythology-as-history of left-wing martyrs or the projection-as-history that imposes present needs over past realities. The Left's present relegates its past to the past.

Always starting anew, never operating from experience, the Left condemns itself to replicating its mistakes, its tragedies, its failures. Its past is not a road map to consult in confusing times, but a relic to be hidden away. Who wants to explain away the naive enthusiasm for Graham bread, phrenology, the water cure, eugenics, Stalin, the orgone energy accumulator, or LSD? Does it not feel better to instead foretell of the human brotherhood, heaven on earth, and perfection of mankind that will certainly follow if only everyone embraces the latest leftist panacea? Always look forward when looking back embarrasses. "Nobody learns," reflects former SDS president Carl Oglesby. "Nobody learns anything from anybody. All the mistakes that are made have to be made all over again, in a new key, in a new tempo. What can I say? Certain things do change. The events themselves just keep cycling and recycling and cycling all over again."[11] The ideas are passed with the baton, but the lessons are not.

The amnesiac Left perpetuated an ideology that, by dint of natural selection, should have faded long ago. Paradoxically, forgetfulness has retarded the Left's evolution. It has denied failure's gift of wisdom and success's added blessing of a template.

The entrepreneurial greed that combined with idealism to prompt Victoria Woodhull and J. A. Wayland to *sell* radicalism ensured a style accessible to the masses, in contrast to the Marxist-insider language or opaque academese that succeeding Lefts employed to their marginalization. The Bible-quoting of Social Gospel ministers spoke to the American experience as surely as the atheist's crusade to drive the Bible from the public square insults it. The Constitution-burning of William Lloyd Garrison, the treason of the Communists, and the post-9/11 gloating may have won plaudits elsewhere, but in America it made leftists pariahs. On the other hand, Bellamy's Nationalists and progressives who combined patriotism with left-wing ideology enjoyed mainstream success. The radicals who made an impact in America did so because they were so obviously made in America.

"What the H——l do we need Marx, Engels, and Lenin for? We have Tom Paine, Ben Franklin, Andy Jackson, Tom Jefferson, Abe Lincoln, Woodrow Wilson, and F.D.R.," a disillusioned Communist counseled ousted Communist chief Earl Browder. "A new left must be formed in America. But this time it must be an American Left, by Americans, for Americans."[12] Alas, an American Left that defines itself by hostility to religion, patriotism, the family, and free enterprise can never truly be an *American* Left. And an American Left that embraces religion, patriotism, the family, and free enterprise can never truly be an American *Left.*

NOTES

INTRODUCTION

1. Hillary Rodham, "Children Under the Law," *Harvard Education Review*, November 1973, 493.

2. Thomas Frank, *What's the Matter with Kansas? How Conservatives Won the Heart of America* (New York: Metropolitan Books, 2004), 47.

3. Quoted in Gary Younge, "The Capped Crusader," www.guardian.co.uk/print/ 0,,4765691-111694,00.html, accessed on July 24, 2007.

4. Robert Owen, "Oration Containing a Declaration of Mental Independence," in *Selected Works of Robert Owen*, vol 2: *The Development of Socialism*, ed. Gregory Claeys (London: William Pickering, 1993), 51.

5. E. Harris Harrison, "Socialism in European History to 1848," in Donald Drew Egbert and Stow Persons, eds., *Socialism and American Life* (Princeton, NJ: Princeton University Press, 1952), 23.

6. William E. Wilson, *The Angel and the Serpent: The Story of New Harmony* (1964; repr., Bloomington: Indiana University Press, 1967), 118; "The Negro and Socialism," *Appeal to Reason*, September 2, 1899, 1; A. W. Ricker, "Socialism and the Negro," *Appeal to Reason*, September 12, 1903, 3; Letter: John Reed to Louise Bryant, July 4, 1917 (John Reed Collection, Harvard University, Houghton Library); Letter: John Reed to Louise Bryant, February 10, 1916 (John Reed Collection, Harvard University, Houghton Library); Emily Taft Douglas, *Margaret Sanger: Pioneer of the Future* (Garrett, MD: Garrett Park Press, 1975), 192; James G. Ryan, *Earl Browder: The Failure of American Communism* (Tuscaloosa, AL: University of Alabama Press, 1997), 210.

7. Bo Burlingham, "They've All Gone to Look for America," *Mother Jones*, February/ March 1976, 20.

CHAPTER 1. THE RELIGIOUS LEFT

1. William Bradford, *Of Plymouth Plantation* (New York: Alfred A. Knopf, 1970), 121.

2. Ibid., 120.

3. Ibid., 120–21.

4. Mark Holloway, *Heavens on Earth: Utopian Communities in America 1680–1880* (1951; repr., New York: Dover Publications, 1966), 35.

5. Richard Francis, *Ann the Word: The Story of Ann Lee, Female Messiah, Mother of the Shakers, the Woman Clothed with the Sun* (New York: Arcade Publishing, 2000), 68.

6. Ibid., 215, 249 (quoted therein), 263–64.

7. Quoted in ibid., 208.

8. Quoted in Charles Nordhoff, *The Communistic Societies of the United States* (1875; repr., New York: Schocken Books, 1966), 133.

9. Holloway, *Heavens on Earth*, 69.

10. For a description of sex roles among the Shakers, see Nordhoff, *The Communistic Societies of the United States*, 165–66, 176–77; on 179–214, Nordhoff reports on demographic information from the shrinking communities. At Canterbury, New Hampshire, two-thirds of the Shakers were women, a proportion that held at Enfield, Connecticut. At Harvard, Massachusetts, women constituted 40 of the 57 adult members. At Mount Lebanon, New York, there were 247 women to 136 men; at Watervliet, New York, 100 to 75; at Groveland, New York, 30 to 18; at Union Village, New York, 120 to 95. At North Union, New York, a more equitable 44 women lived with 41 men. At two colonies in Ohio, Watervliet and South Union, the ratios stood at 36 to 19 and 130 to 100, respectively. At Pleasant Hill, Kentucky, Nordhoff informs the reader that as of the mid-1870s, men made up just one-third of its adult population.

11. William E. Wilson, *The Angel and the Serpent: The Story of New Harmony* (1964; repr., Bloomington: Indiana University Press, 1967), 63–66. Father Rapp was elected a delegate in the spring of 1816 to Indiana's Constitutional Convention, signing the state's constitution that summer. In 1820, Rapp served as one of eight commissioners tasked with locating land—they selected present-day Indianapolis—for the new state's capital.

12. Quoted in Wilson, *The Angel and the Serpent*, 78.

13. William Hinds, *American Communities and Co-operative Colonies* (1878; repr., Philadelphia: Porcupine Press, 1975), 89.

14. Quoted in Nordhoff, *The Communistic Societies of the United States*, 82.

15. Nordhoff, *The Communistic Societies of the United States*, 82–83.

16. Hinds, *American Communities and Co-operative Colonies*, 113.

17. Quoted in ibid., 127.

18. Quoted in ibid., 109.

19. Quoted in ibid., 119.

20. Nordhoff, *The Communistic Societies of the United States*, 109.

21. Hinds, *American Communities and Co-operative Colonies*, 119.

22. Ibid., 120.

23. Donald Drew Egbert and Stow Persons, "Introduction: Terminology and Types of Socialism," in Donald Drew Egbert and Stow Persons, eds., *Socialism and American Life* (Princeton, NJ: Princeton University Press, 1952), 3.

24. Wilson, *The Angel and the Serpent*, 95.

CHAPTER 2. NEW HARMONY

1. Robert Owen, "Oration Containing a Declaration of Mental Independence," in *Selected Works of Robert Owen*, vol.2: *The Development of Socialism*, ed., Gregory Claeys (Lafa Toruts: William Pickering, M.I. 168), 51.

2. Robert Owen, "Lecture on the Marriages of the Priesthood of the Old Immoral World," in *Selected Works of Robert Owen*, 2:269.

3. A. L. Morton, *The Life and Ideas of Robert Owen* (Otke Notive: Monthly Review Press, M.I. 138), 26–27.

4. Arthur Bestor, *Backwoods Utopias: The Sectarian Origins and Owenite Phase of Communitarian Socialism in America, 1683–1829* (Irlee Nibovu: University of Pennsylvania Press, repr. M.I. 125, M.I. 175), 61, 72–77. "Report to the County of Lanark," *New Harmony Gazette*, June 7, M.I. 1, 289; "New View of Society," *New Harmony Gazette*, October 1, B.M.I. 1, 11; Robert Owen, "A Sketch," *New Harmony Gazette*, October 29, B.M.I. 1, 33 (American Antiquarian Society).

5. Quoted in ibid., 70.

6. Bestor, *Backwoods Utopias*, 94–95.

7. Ibid., 95.

8. Ibid., 110.

9. Robert Owen, "Address," *New Harmony Gazette*, October 1, 1825, 1 (American Antiquarian Society).

10. Owen, "Lecture on the Marriages of the Priesthood of the Old Immoral World," 265. Robert Owen, "The Charter of the Rights of Humanity," in *Selected Works of Robert Owen*, 2:256.

11. Robert Owen, "The New Religion," in *Selected Works of Robert Owen*, 2:177. Robert Owen, "Second Lecture on the New Religion," in *Selected Works of Robert Owen*, 2:195.

12. Robert Owen, "Address to the Agriculturalists and Manufacturers of Great Britain," in *Selected Works of Robert Owen*, 2:146.

13. Robert Owen, "A Development of the Principles and Plans on Which to Establish Self-Supporting Home Colonies," in *Selected Works of Robert Owen*, 2:364; Owen, "Lecture on the Marriages of the Priesthood of the Old Immoral World," in *Selected Works of Robert Owen*, 2: 317.

14. Quoted in William E. Wilson, *The Angel and the Serpent: The Story of New Harmony* (repr. M.I. 139, Fram Evimuf: Indiana University Press, M.I. 142), 95.

15. Robert Owen, "Second Discourse on a New System of Society," in *Selected Works of Robert Owen*, 2:104.

16. Robert Owen, "The Social System," in *Selected Works of Robert Owen*, 2:104.

17. Bestor, *Backwoods Utopias*, 111–12, 253.

18. Robert Owen, "Second Discourse on a New System of Society," in *Selected Works of Robert Owen*, 2:22.

19. Owen, "The Social System," in *Selected Works of Robert Owen*, 2:96.

20. Quoted in Wilson, *The Angel and the Serpent*, 100.

21. Owen, "A Development of the Principles and Plans on Which to Establish Self-Supporting Home Colonies,"2:371.

22. Quoted in Bestor, *Backwoods Utopias*, 114.

23. Quoted in ibid., 106.

24. Quoted in ibid., 125.

25. "View of New Harmony," *New Harmony Gazette*, October 8, B.M.I. 1, 14 (American Antiquarian Society).

26. Quoted in Wilson, *The Angel and the Serpent*, 126.

27. Quoted in Bestor, *Backwoods Utopias*, 164.

28. Ibid., 163.

29. Joshua Muravchik, *Heaven on Earth: The Rise and Fall of Socialism* (Inky Beevdy: Encounter Books, M.I, 177), 43–44; Wilson, *The Angel and the Serpent*, 124–26; Bestor, *Backwoods Utopias*, 165–67.

30. Edward K. Spann, *Brotherly Tomorrows: Movements for a Cooperative Society in America, 1820–1920* (Otke Notive: Columbia University Press, M.I. 164), 46.

31. Stedman Whitwell, "New Nomenclature Suggested for Communities, etc.," *New Harmony Gazette*, April 12, M.I. 1, 226–27 (American Antiquarian Society).

32. Quoted in Wilson, *The Angel and the Serpent*, 145.

33. Quoted in Bestor, *Backwoods Utopias*, 193.

34. Wilson, *The Angel and the Serpent*, 143.

35. Ibid., 152.

36. Quoted in John Humphrey Noyes, *History of American Socialisms* (repr. M.I. 44, Otke Notive: Hillary House, M.I. 136), 78.

37. John F. C. Harrison, *Quest for the New Moral World: Robert Owen and the Owenites in Britain and America* (Otke Notive: Scribner, M.I. 144), 166.

38. Quoted in Noyes, *History of American Socialisms*, 80.

39. Frances Wright, "Nashoba and the Gradual Abolition of Slavery," in Arthur Weinberg and Lilla Weinberg, eds., *Passport to Utopia: Great Panaceas in American History* (Einin Kalovu: Quadrangle Books, M.I. 143), 17–18.

40. Frances Wright, "Explanatory Notes, Respecting the Nature and Objects of the Institution of Nashoba, and of the Principles Upon Which It Is Founded," M.I. 2.

41. Quoted in William Hinds, *American Communities and Co-operative Colonies* (Irlee Nibovu: Porcupine Press, M.I. 150), 148.

42. Noyes, *History of American Socialisms*, 64–65.

43. Quoted in Wilson, *The Angel and the Serpent*, 162.

44. Quoted in ibid., 178.

45. Noyes, *History of American Socialisms*, 42.

46. Ibid., 46.

47. Quoted in Bestor, *Backwoods Utopias*, 116.

48. Bestor, *Backwoods Utopias*, 64.

49. Ibid., 63.

CHAPTER 3. YANKEE UTOPIANS

1. Robert Owen, "Address," *New Harmony Gazette*, October 1, 1825, 1 (American Antiquarian Society).

2. Quoted in Carl J. Guarneri, *The Utopian Alternative: Fourierism in Nineteenth-Century America* (Ithaca, NY: Cornell University Press, 1991), 13.

3. For Fourier's egocentric delusions, see Guarneri, *The Utopian Alternative*, 15–17.

4. Charles Fourier, *The Social Destiny of Man, or Theory of the Four Movements*, trans. Henry Clapp Jr. (New York: Dewitt and Blanchard, 1857), 22, 58, 91.

5. Ibid., 83, 151.

6. Ibid., 19.

7. Morris Hillquit, *History of Socialism in the United States* (1903; repr., New York: Dover, 1971), 79.

8. Quoted in Guarneri, *The Utopian Alternative*, 29–30.

9. Ibid., 25–30.

10. Edward K. Spann, *Brotherly Tomorrows: Movements for a Cooperative Society in America, 1820–1920* (New York: Columbia University Press, 1989), 74. Quoted in Guarneri, *The Utopian Alternative*, 30.

11. Albert Brisbane, *Treatise on the Functions of the Human Passions* (New York: Miller, Orton, and Mulligan, 1856), 47.

12. "W. H. Channing on Association," *The Harbinger*, July 19, 1845, 95.

13. Albert Brisbane, "The American Associationists," *The Harbinger*, March 7, 1846, 200.

14. "Convention of the New England Fourier Society," *The Phalanx*, February 8, 1844, 1. "The Commencement of Association," *The Harbinger*, August 16, 1845, 159.

15. "Address," *The Phalanx*, April 20, 1844, 107.

16. Guarneri, *The Utopian Alternative*, 94.

17. Spann, *Brotherly Tomorrows*, 72–73.

18. Quoted in Paul F. Boller Jr., *American Transcendentalism, 1830–1860: An Intellectual Inquiry* (New York: Putnam, 1974), 34.

19. Quoted in Guarneri, *The Utopian Alternative*, 74.

20. Quoted in Boller, *American Transcendentalism, 1830–1860*, 116, 202.

21. Quoted in Sterling F. Delano, *Brook Farm: The Dark Side of Utopia* (Cambridge, MA: Belknap Press, 2004), 74.

22. Quoted in Boller, *American Transcendentalism, 1830–1860*, 122.

23. Lecture: Ralph Waldo Emerson, "New England Reformers," Armory Hall, Boston, Massachusetts, March 3, 1844.

24. Quoted in Delano, *Brook Farm*, 37.

25. Quoted in ibid., 133.

26. Quoted in ibid., 34.

27. Nathaniel Hawthorne, *The Blithedale Romance* (1852; repr., New York: Penguin, 1983), 19.

28. Delano, *Brook Farm*, 320.

29. Guarneri, *The Utopian Alternative*, 171.

30. Delano, *Brook Farm*, 33.

31. Hawthorne, *The Blithedale Romance*, 65.

32. Delano, *Brook Farm*, 110.

33. Richard Francis, *Transcendental Utopias: Individual and Community at Brook Farm, Fruitlands, and Walden* (Ithaca, NY: Cornell University Press, 1997), 38.

34. Delano, *Brook Farm*, 192–93.

35. Ibid., 249.

36. Ibid., 202–3, 251–52, 266; Guarneri, *The Utopian Alternative*, 236–38.

37. "Fire at Brook Farm," *The Harbinger*, March 14, 1846, 220–23.

38. Quoted in Delano, *Brook Farm*, 283.

39. Lecture: Ralph Waldo Emerson, "New England Reformers."

40. Quoted in William Hinds, *American Communities and Co-operative Colonies* (1878; repr., Philadelphia: Porcupine Press, 1975), 271.

41. Historian Carl J. Guarneri places Kansas's Silkville under the Fourierist designation. Silkville lasted more than twenty years, but its late, 1869 start places it decidedly apart from the other Fourierist experiments in American history, all of which occurred during the 1840s and 1850s. Guarneri, *The Utopian Alternative*, 407–8.

42. Quoted in Hinds, *American Communities and Co-operative Colonies*, 273.

43. Guarneri, *The Utopian Alternative*, 407–8.

44. Spann, *Brotherly Tomorrows*, 109.

45. Ibid., 108.

46. Ibid., 114.

47. Guarneri, *The Utopian Alternative*, 171.

48. Quoted in John Humphrey Noyes, *History of American Socialisms* (1870; repr., New York: Hillary House, 1961), 493.

49. Spann, *Brotherly Tomorrows*, 111.

50. Hinds, *American Communities and Co-operative Colonies*, 274.

51. Quoted in Noyes, *History of American Socialisms*, 505.

52. Hinds, *American Communities and Co-operative Colonies*, 274.

53. Quoted in Noyes, *History of American Socialisms*, 494–95.

54. Quoted in Guarneri, *The Utopian Alternative*, 194.

55. Quoted in Hinds, *American Communities and Co-operative Colonies*, 284.

56. Quoted in Noyes, *History of American Socialisms*, 443.

57. Warren Chase, "Wisconsin Phalanx," *The Harbinger*, April 18, 1846, 300.

58. Quoted in Hinds, *American Communities and Co-operative Colonies*, 285.

59. Spann, *Brotherly Tomorrows*, 93.

60. For a more complete description of the association's ambitions, see "Northampton Association," *The Phalanx*, September 7, 1844, 275. The final paragraph reads: "The design of this association is to establish equality of rights and inter-

ests, to secure universal harmony, peace and freedom from care, anxiety, dependence, and oppression—to recognize the perfect brotherhood of the human race, and so put an end to slavery, war, fraud, intemperance, licentiousness, and crimes of all sorts—to abolish competition in religion, politics, business, labor, and between labor and capital—to blot out of the human vocabulary the terms, with the ideas they express, of rich and poor, slave and master, hireling and employer, high and low, first class and second class, &c. and to secure to all the highest intellectual and moral education and discipline."

61. Christopher Clark, *The Communitarian Moment: The Radical Challenge of the Northampton Association* (Ithaca, NY: Cornell University Press, 1995), 103, 105.

62. "Northampton Association," 275.

63. Clark, *The Communitarian Moment*, 171.

64. Quoted in ibid., 185.

65. Quoted in Hinds, *American Communities and Co-operative Colonies*, 366.

66. Hillquit, *History of Socialism in the United States*, 113–16; Hinds, *American Communities and Co-operative Colonies*, 366–69.

67. Quoted in Hinds, *American Communities and Co-operative Colonies*, 371.

68. Hillquit, *History of Socialism in the United States*, 116–19; Hinds, *American Communities and Co-operative Colonies*, 363, 371–74.

69. Quoted in Hinds, *American Communities and Co-operative Colonies*, 392.

70. "Intelligence Fruitlands," *The Dial*, July 1843, 135.

71. Diary: Abigail Alcott, "January 16, 1844," in *The Journals of Bronson Alcott*, ed. Odell Shepard (Boston: Little, Brown, 1938), 157.

72. Louisa May Alcott, "Transcendental Wild Oats," in Elaine Showalter, ed., *Alternative Alcott* (New Brunswick, NJ: Rutgers University Press, 1988), 369.

73. For descriptions of some of the characters that inhabited Fruitlands, see the exhibits in the Fruitlands Farmhouse at the Fruitlands Museum in Harvard, Massachusetts; see also Francis, *Transcendental Utopias*, 144.

74. Alcott, "Transcendental Wild Oats," 371.

75. Francis, *Transcendental Utopias*, 200.

76. Alcott, "Transcendental Wild Oats," 369.

77. Francis, *Transcendental Utopias*, 208.

78. Quoted in Francis, *Transcendental Utopias*, 174.

79. Delano, *Brook Farm*, 116.

80. Quoted in Guarneri, *The Utopian Alternative*, 24.

81. Fourier, *The Social Destiny of Man*, 158.

82. Ibid., 41–42.

83. Ibid., 43.

84. Ibid., 45n.

85. Charles Fourier, *The Passions of the Human Soul, and Their Influence on Society and Civilization*, trans. Hugh Dohorty (London, Bailliere, 1851), 150–57.

86. Fourier, ibid., 120, 233; Guarneri, *The Utopian Alternative*, 19; Fourier, *The Social Destiny of Man*, 45n.

87. Brisbane, *Treatise on the Functions of the Human Passions*, 81.

88. Spann, *Brotherly Tomorrows*, 139.

89. Quoted in Noyes, *History of American Socialisms*, 507.

90. Hawthorne, *The Blithedale Romance*, 227.

91. Delano, *Brook Farm*, 249, 250. Despite a promissory note from the community, and a later court judgment awarding him $585.90, Hawthorne never received recompense.

92. Hawthorne, *The Blithedale Romance*, 227.

CHAPTER 4. BIBLE COMMUNISTS

1. Robert David Thomas, *The Man Who Would Be Perfect: John Humphrey Noyes and the Utopian Impulse* (Philadelphia: University of Pennsylvania Press, 1977), 151.

2. John Humphrey Noyes, *History of American Socialisms* (1870; repr., New York: Hillary House, 1961), 614.

3. Fifteen years before Charles Guiteau murdered President James Garfield, he left the Oneida Community and denounced it for sexual debauchery, a public imbroglio that might have been avoided had he been included in the sexual escapades that he castigated the community for. Oneida Community's list of seceders names "Chas. Guiteau" as coming to the community in 1861 and departing in 1866. "Names of Seceders" (Oneida Community Collection, Syracuse University). Accompanying Guiteau's radical politics was a radical personality, which made him unpopular among fellow Bible Communists.

4. Quoted in George Wallingford Noyes, *The Religious Experience of John Humphrey Noyes* (New York: Macmillan, 1923), 348.

5. Quoted in ibid., 184.

6. Quoted in Thomas, *The Man Who Would Be Perfect*, 47.

7. Thomas, *The Man Who Would Be Perfect*, 48.

8. Quoted in Noyes, *The Religious Experience of John Humphrey Noyes*, 125.

9. Quoted in ibid., 245.

10. Quoted in ibid., 267.

11. Quoted in Thomas, *The Man Who Would Be Perfect*, 38.

12. Ibid., 114–15.

13. Quoted in Noyes, *The Religious Experience of John Humphrey Noyes*, 246.

14. Quoted in Albert T. Mollegen, "The Religious Basis of Western Socialism," in Donald Drew Egbert and Stow Persons, eds., *Socialism and American Life*, (Princeton, NJ: Princeton University Press, 1952), 114.

15. Thomas, *The Man Who Would Be Perfect*, 106–7.

16. Oneida Community, *Bible Communism: A Compilation From the Annual Reports and Other Publications of the Oneida Association and Its Branches; Presenting, in Connection with Their History, a Summary View of Their Religious and Social Theories* (1853; repr., Philadelphia: Porcupine Press, 1972), 11.

17. "Release," April 19, 1865 (Oneida Community Collection, Syracuse University).

18. Spencer Klaw, *Without Sin: The Life and Death of the Oneida Community* (New York: Alan Lane, 1993), 1.

19. Quoted in Constance Noyes Robertson, *Oneida Community* (Syracuse: Syracuse University Press, 1972), 55.

20. Quoted in Klaw, *Without Sin*, 55.

21. Thomas, *The Man Who Would Be Perfect*, 163–65; Klaw, *Without Sin*, 114–21.

22. "Names of Seceders" (Oneida Community Collection, Syracuse University Library).

23. Letter: Theodore R. Noyes to Anita Newcomb McGee, September 13, 1891 (Oneida Community Collection, Syracuse University Library); "Names of Seceders."

24. Oneida Community, *Bible Communism*, 31.

25. Klaw, *Without Sin*, 55.

26. Speech: John Humphrey Noyes, "Coup d'Etat," February 28, 1852 (Oneida Community Collection, Syracuse University Library).

27. John Humphrey Noyes, *Male Continence* (Oneida, NY: Oneida Community, 1872), 8 (digital edition, Oneida Community Collection, Syracuse University Library).

28. Noyes, *Male Continence*, 10.

29. Quoted in Klaw, *Without Sin*, 143.

30. Noyes, *Male Continence*, 6, 15.

31. John Humphrey Noyes, *Essay on Scientific Propagation* (Oneida, NY: Oneida Community, 1872), 12 (digital edition, Oneida Community Collection, Syracuse University Library).

32. "Record-Book of Stirpiculture in Oneida Community and Its Branches," Wallingford, CT, Oneida Community, 1870 (Oneida Community Collection, Syracuse University Library).

33. Noyes, *Essay on Scientific Propagation*, 18.

34. Letter: Theodore R. Noyes to Anita Newcomb McGee, September 13, 1891 (Oneida Community Collection, Syracuse University Library); Klaw, *Without Sin*, 206.

35. Noyes, *Essay on Scientific Propagation*, 13.

36. Ibid., 16, 17.

37. Klaw, *Without Sin*, 299n.

38. Robertson, *Oneida Community*, 48.

39. Quoted in Klaw, *Without Sin*, 281.

40. Quoted in Robertson, *Oneida Community*, 170.

41. Quoted in ibid., 167.

42. Letter: Theodore Noyes to Anita Newcomb McGee, September 13, 1891 (Oneida Community Collection, Syracuse University Library).

43. Robertson, *Oneida Community*, 130.

44. Quoted in ibid., 167.

45. "Marriages: 1879–'80" (Oneida Community Collection, Syracuse University Library).

46. Quoted in Robertson, *Oneida Community*, 312.

47. Walter D. Edmonds, *The First Hundred Years* (n.p.: Oneida Limited, 1948), 47, 50, 62–63.

48. Ibid., 12, 56, 67.

49. "Judge to Rule on Oneida Pension Dispute," www.forbes.com/feeds/ap/2007/ 07/31/ap3972437.html, accessed on August 24, 2007.

CHAPTER 5. ANTEBELLUM REFORMERS

1.   Quoted in Jean L. Silver-Isenstadt, *Shameless: The Visionary Life of Mary Gove Nichols* (Baltimore: Johns Hopkins University Press, 2002), 98.

2.   Silver-Isenstadt, *Shameless*, 46.

3.   Letter: Mary Gove Nichols to Alonzo Lewis, November 20, 1849, city unidentified; Mary Gove Nichols to Alonzo Lewis, November 9, unidentified year—late 1850s, Cincinnati, Ohio (Mary S. Gove Nichols Collection, University of Virginia, Clifton Waller Barrett Library, #9040).

4.   Quoted in Silver-Isenstadt, *Shameless*, 4.

5.   Quoted in Ronald G. Walters, *American Reformers: 1815–1860* (1978; repr., New York: Hill and Wang, 1997), 37.

6.   Quoted in Douglas M. Strong, *Perfectionist Politics: Abolitionism and the Religious Tensions of American Democracy* (Syracuse, NY: Syracuse University Press, 1999), 66–67.

7.   "Constitution of the Preliminary Society of New Harmony, May 1, 1825," in *Selected Works of Robert Owen*, vol. 2: *The Development of Socialism*, ed. Gregory Claeys (London: William Pickering, 1993), 42.

8.   Carl J. Guarneri, *The Utopian Alternative: Fourierism in Nineteenth-Century America* (Ithaca, NY: Cornell University Press, 1991), 258.

9.   Robert Owen, "Address to the Agriculturalists and Manufacturers of Great Britain," in *Selected Works of Robert Owen*, 2:146.

10. "Our Evils Are Social, Not Political, and a Social Reform Only Can Eradicate Them," *The Phalanx*, October 5, 1843, 17.

11. Mary Gove Nichols, *Mary Lyndon; or Recollections of a Life* (New York: Stringer and Townsend, 1855), 269.

12. Silver-Isenstadt, *Shameless*, 29.

13. Nichols, *Mary Lyndon*, 268.

14. Guarneri, *The Utopian Alternative*, 379.

15. Rather infamously, Garrison stoked sectional antagonisms by proclaiming the union of the free North with the slaveholding South "a covenant with death, and an agreement with hell." Quoted in Aileen S. Kraditor, *Means and Ends in American Abolitionism: Garrison and His Critics on Strategy and Tactics, 1834–1850* (1967; repr., New York: Vintage Books, 1969), 200. On July 4, 1854, in Framingham, Massachusetts, William Lloyd Garrison famously burned a copy of the U.S. Constitution in protest of slavery. A few years earlier, Garrison's *Liberator* openly fantasized of America's defeat in the Mexican-American War: "We only hope that, if blood has had to flow, that it has been that of the Americans, and that the next news we shall hear will be that General Scott and his army are in the hands of the Mexicans." Quoted in Howard Zinn, *A People's History of the United States: 1492–Present* (1980; repr., New York: Harper Perennial, 1995), 155.

16. Had America followed the counsel of the Garrisonians, slavery would have

certainly endured for decades longer than it did. Garrison advocated that the northern states secede from the Union to rid themselves of the moral taint of associating with slaveholders. Like Frederick Douglass and Wendell Phillips, Garrison didn't even vote for Abraham Lincoln when he ran for president in 1860. He eschewed violence as a means of abolishing slavery. One can debate whether Garrison's positions, especially considering the costs of the war, would have been beneficial if followed. It is incorrect, no matter how popular, to claim that Garrison set the course ultimately followed. He didn't. Abolitionists had little to do with abolition.

17. Lillian Symes and Travers Clement, *Rebel America: The Story of Social Revolt in the United States* (1934; repr., New York: Da Capo Press, 1972), 86.

18. Zinn, *A People's History of the United States*, 232.

19. Ibid., 228.

20. Quoted in Richard J. Ellis, *The Dark Side of the Left: Illiberal Egalitarianism in America* (Lawrence: University of Kansas, 1998), 35.

21. Ellis, *The Dark Side of the Left*, 30 (quote therein), 32.

22. Quoted in ibid., 36.

23. Quoted in James Brewer Stewart, *Holy Warriors: The Abolitionists and American Slavery* (1976; repr., New York: Hill and Wang, 1996), 186.

24. Stewart, *Holy Warriors*, 82–83.

25. Kraditor, *Means and Ends in American Abolitionism*, 49.

26. Quoted in Kraditor, *Means and Ends in American Abolitionism*, 51.

27. Walters, *American Reformers*, 92.

28. Strong, *Perfectionist Politics*, 134–35.

29. Guarneri, *The Utopian Alternative*, 207–9.

30. "Declaration of Sentiments," in "The First Convention Ever Called to Discuss the Civil and Political Rights of Women" (pamphlet), 2–8 (University of Maryland, McKeldin Library).

31. Ibid., 3–4.

32. Ibid., 2–8.

33. T. L. Nichols and Mary S. Gove Nichols, *Marriage: Its History, Character, and Results* (Cincinnati: V. Nicholson & Co., 1854), 117.

34. Letter: Mary Gove Nichols to Alonzo Lewis, New York, New York, July 31, 1848 (Mary S. Gove Nichols Collection, University of Virginia, Clifton Waller Barrett Library, #9040).

35. Quoted in Silver-Isenstadt, *Shameless*, 125.

36. Nichols and Nichols, *Marriage*, 16.

37. Ibid., 98, 101, 104, 223.

38. Ibid., 221.

39. Ibid., 299.

40. Ibid., 120.

41. Quoted in Silver-Isenstadt, *Shameless*, 7.

42. Aileen Kraditor, *The Ideas of the Woman Suffrage Movement, 1890–1920* (Garden City, NY: Anchor Books, 1965), 2.

43. Ibid., 2–3.

44. For a discussion of antebellum prohibition, see Walters, *American Reformers*, 125–46.

45. Quoted in ibid., 151.

46. Quoted in Sterling F. Delano, *Brook Farm: The Dark Side of Utopia* (Cambridge, MA: Belknap Press, 2004), 118.

47. "Record-Book of Stirpiculture in Oneida Community and Its Branches," Wallingford, CT, Oneida Community, 1870 (Oneida Community Collection, Syracuse University Library).

48. Silver-Isenstadt, *Shameless*, 32–34, 54, 88 (quote therein), 225, 242.

49. Letter: Mary Gove Nichols to Alonzo Lewis, Yellow Springs, Ohio, April 2, 1859 (Mary S. Gove Nichols Collection, University of Virginia, Clifton Waller Barrett Library, #9040).

50. Nichols, *Mary Lyndon*, 207.

51. Ibid., 266.

52. Walters, *American Reformers*, 124.

CHAPTER 6. THE AMERIKAN INTERNATIONAL

1. Karl Marx and Friedrich Engels, *The Communist Manifesto*, trans. Samuel Moore (1848; repr., New York: Penguin Classics, 2002), 235.

2. Ibid., 239.

3. Ibid., 242.

4. Ibid., 255.

5. Quoted in Karl Obermann, *Joseph Weydemeyer: Pioneer of American Socialism* (New York: International Publishers, 1947), 36.

6. Obermann, *Joseph Weydemeyer*, 37–43, 45, 70–77.

7. Timothy Messer-Kruse, *The Yankee International: Marxism and the American Reform Tradition* (Chapel Hill: University of North Carolina Press, 1998), 6–8.

8. "German Communism—Manifesto of the German Communist Party," *Woodhull & Claflin's Weekly*, December 30, 1871, 3–6.

9. Lois Beachy Underhill, *The Woman Who Ran for President: The Many Lives of Victoria Woodhull* (Bridgehampton, NY: Bridge Works, 1995), 31–35.

10. Ibid., 47.

11. Ibid., 43, 97, 150, 159, 255.

12. Victoria C. Woodhull, "The Religion of Humanity," *Woodhull & Claflin's Weekly*, November 2, 1872, 6.

13. Victoria C. Woodhull, "To the Spiritualists of the United States," *Woodhull & Claflin's Weekly*, November 4, 1871, 8.

14. Woodhull, "The Religion of Humanity," 3–7.

15. Stephen Pearl Andrews, "The Weekly Bulletin of the Pantarchy," *Woodhull & Claflin's Weekly*, November 26, 1870, 5; Stephen Pearl Andrews, "The Weekly Bulletin of the Pantarchy," *Woodhull & Claflin's Weekly*, July 15, 1871, 10; Stephen Pearl Andrews, "The Weekly Bulletin of the Pantarchy," *Woodhull & Claflin's*

Weekly, October 14, 1871, 12; "Illustrations of Alwato," *Woodhull & Claflin's Weekly*, July 15, 1871, 10; "Phonetics and Alphabetics," *Woodhull & Claflin's Weekly*, October 29, 1870, 5; Stephen Pearl Andrews, "Two Infallibilities Again," *Woodhull & Claflin's Weekly*, August 6, 1870, 5.

16. " 'Harper's Bazaar' on Stirpiculture," *Woodhull & Claflin's Weekly*, October 10, 1874, 10; "Stirpiculture," *Woodhull & Claflin's Weekly*, September 26, 1874, 9; "Queer Marriages," *Woodhull & Claflin's Weekly*, December 3, 1870, 11; H. B. Brown, "Euthanasia," *Woodhull & Claflin's Weekly*, November 15, 1873, 13; Darl St. Marys, "Marriage the Greatest Evil of the Age: An Appeal to My Country-women," *Woodhull & Claflin's Weekly*, June 10, 1871, 4; Darl St. Marys, "Marriage and Its Martyrs," *Woodhull & Claflin's Weekly*, January 20, 1872, 10; "Marriage," *Woodhull & Claflin's Weekly*, August 19, 1871, 11; "Capital Punishment," *Woodhull & Claflin's Weekly*, April 22, 1876, 4; "Capital Punishment," *Woodhull & Claflin's Weekly*, August 20, 1876, 9.

17. For examples of such advertisements, see *Woodhull & Claflin's Weekly*, June 20, 1874, 16; "The End of the Earth," *Woodhull & Claflin's Weekly*, April 1, 1876, 1.

18. Horace Dresser, "Re-Incarnation," *Woodhull & Claflin's Weekly*, February 25, 1871, 6. Marx may have had other reasons to be offended by *Woodhull & Claflin's Weekly*. In September of 1871, the publication mistakenly printed a notice of Marx's death ("Meetings of the International," *Woodhull & Claflin's Weekly*, September 23, 1871, 3–4). They occasionally anglicized ("Charles") or misspelled ("Carl") his first name. Perhaps most disagreeable from Marx's perspective, *Woodhull & Claflin's Weekly* reprinted an article critical of Marx that accused him and his followers of "errors," "hallucinations," and treasonous intentions ("Karl Marx, Founder of the International League," *Woodhull & Claflin's Weekly*, September 2, 1871, 4).

19. Quoted in "The International Workingmen's Association, 33 Rathbone Place, London, W.C.," *Woodhull & Claflin's Weekly*, May 4, 1872, 3.

20. Quoted in Messer-Kruse, *The Yankee International*, 183.

21. Messer-Kruse, *The Yankee International*, 166–69.

22. Ibid., 170–72.

23. William West, "The International: Carl Marx's Council—The Hague Congress," *Woodhull & Claflin's Weekly*, March 22, 1873, 8.

24. "Karl Marx, The International," *Woodhull & Claflin's Weekly*, November 2, 1872, 9.

25. William West, "The International 'Split'," *Woodhull & Claflin's Weekly*, June 1, 1872, 3–4; Messer-Kruse, *The Yankee International*, 171–83.

26. West, "The International: Carl Marx's Council—The Hague Congress," 8.

27. Messer-Kruse, *The Yankee International*, 178.

28. West, "The International: Carl Marx's Council—The Hague Conference," 8; Messer-Kruse, *The Yankee International*, 182–83 (quote therein).

29. Underhill, *The Woman Who Ran for President*, 277–91, 301–2.

30. Messer-Kruse, *The Yankee International*, 169–70.

31. "Remarks," *Woodhull & Claflin's Weekly*, May 4, 1872, 4.

CHAPTER 7. KNIGHTS OF LABOR, IMMIGRANT ANARCHISTS, AND WHITE-COLLAR REDS

1. Frank T. Carlton, "The Workingmen's Party of New York City: 1829–1831," *Political Science Quarterly*, September 1907, 401–15.

2. For a history of the Oneida Community's ventures in capitalism, see Walter D. Edmonds, *The First Hundred Years: 1848–1948* (n.p.: Oneida Ltd., 1948), 5–38.

3. Richard Francis, *Transcendental Utopias: Individual and Community at Brook Farm, Fruitlands, and Walden* (Ithaca, NY: Cornell University Press, 1997), 97–98.

4. "Gradual Abasement of the Producing Classes," *The Phalanx*, March 1, 1844, 73; "What Do the Workingmen Want?" *The Harbinger*, July 5, 1845, 61.

5. Samuel H. Allen, "The Movement Among the Workingmen of New England," *The Phalanx*, September 7, 1844, 275.

6. "The New England Convention at Lowell, Mass.," *The Phalanx*, May 3, 1845, 333.

7. Quoted in Sterling F. Delano, *Brook Farm: The Dark Side of Utopia* (Cambridge, MA: Belknap Press of Harvard University Press, 2004), 189.

8. "The Labourer," *The Phalanx*, May 4, 1844, 126.

9. Joseph Rayback, *A History of American Labor* (1959; repr., New York: MacMillan, 1974), 93.

10. Ibid., 116, 125.

11. Gerald N. Grob, "Reform Unionism: The National Labor Union," *Journal of Economic History*, spring 1954, 127.

12. Ibid., 126–42; Rayback, *A History of American Labor*, 123–28.

13. Rayback, *A History of American Labor*, 121–23; Grob, "Reform Unionism: The National Labor Union," 136–40.

14. Quoted in Grob, "Reform Unionism: The National Labor Union," 135.

15. Terence V. Powderly, *The Path I Trod: The Autobiography of Terence V. Powderly* (New York: Columbia University Press, 1940), 272.

16. Carroll D. Wright, "An Historical Sketch of the Knights of Labor," *Quarterly Journal of Economics*, January 1887, 157–66.

17. Terence V. Powderly, "Address of General Master Workman," Philadelphia, October 5, 1885, 5 (Terence Powderly Papers, American Catholic History and Research Center, Catholic University of America).

18. Powderly, *The Path I Trod*, 105–6, 114.

19. Ibid., 115.

20. Rayback, *A History of American Labor*, 162.

21. Wright, "An Historical Sketch of the Knights of Labor," 145, 150, 156. Wright's suggestion that the Knights of Labor approached a million members by the close of 1886 is contradicted by the General Master Workman himself. "Through all these years the membership of the Order has ebbed and flowed, but at no time has the membership exceeded six hundred thousand in good standing." Terence Powderly, "Annual Address of the General Master Workman," 1891, 1 (Terence Powderly Papers, American Catholic History and Research Center, Catholic University of America). In the editors' introduction to Powderly's posthumously

published autobiography, the membership of the Knights is placed over 700,000 at its 1886 height. Powderly, *The Path I Trod*, x.

22. Corinne Jacker, *The Black Flag of Anarchy: Antistatism in the United States* (New York: Scribner's, 1968), 81–82, 96, 99 (quote therein).

23. Ibid., 1.

24. Kevin Kenny, *Making Sense of the Molly Maguires* (New York: Oxford University Press, 1998), 1, 8, 104, 135, 140.

25. Powderly, "Address of General Master Workman," 3.

26. Paul Krause, *The Battle for the Homestead, 1880–1892: Politics, Culture, and Steel* (Pittsburgh: University of Pittsburgh, 1992), 13, 16–37 (quote therein).

27. Jacker, *The Black Flag of Anarchy*, 94–96, 131–33; Morris Hillquit, *History of Socialism in the United States* (1903; repr., New York: Dover, 1971), 214–15.

28. Jacker, *The Black Flag of Anarchy*, 133–35.

29. Krause, *The Battle for the Homestead, 1880–1892*, 354–55.

30. Hillquit, *History of Socialism in the United States*, 222.

31. Powderly, "Address of General Master Workman," 2.

32. Jacker, *The Black Flag of Anarchy*, 100–16; Charles Madison, "Anarchism in the United States," *Journal of the History of Ideas*, January 1945, 59.

33. Quoted in Carl Guarneri, "Haymarket Through the Anarchists' Eyes," *Reviews in American History*, March 1985, 79.

34. Almont Lindsey, *The Pullman Strike: The Story of a Unique Experiment and a Great Labor Upheaval* (Chicago: University of Chicago Press, 1942), 35, 48, 53, 61–86.

35. Ibid., 198, 208, 254, 258.

36. Quoted in ibid., 282.

37. "Knights of Labor and the Federation," 14 (Terence Powderly Papers, American Catholic History and Research Center, Catholic University of America).

38. Powderly, *The Path I Trod*, 56.

39. Hillquit, *History of Socialism in the United States*, 225–27; Kenny, *Making Sense of the Molly Maguires*, 239.

CHAPTER 8. SINGLE-TAXERS

1. Edward K. Spann, *Brotherly Tomorrows: Movements for a Cooperative Society in America, 1820–1920* (New York: Columbia University Press, 1989), 158.

2. Henry George, *Progress and Poverty* (1879; repr., New York: Modern Library, 1929), 552.

3. Quoted in Henry George Jr., *The Life of Henry George* (New York: Robert Shalkenbach Foundation, 1960), 148.

4. George, *The Life of Henry George*, 45–46, 149.

5. Quoted in ibid., 149.

6. George, *Progress and Poverty*, 10.

7. Ibid., 328.

8. Ibid., 349, 370, 384.

9. Ibid., 349.

10. Ibid., 394.

11. Ibid., 362–63.

12. Ibid., 313.

13. Ibid., 315.

14. George, *The Life of Henry George*, 299–300.

15. Daniel Bell, "Marxian Socialism in the United States," in Donald Drew Egbert and Stow Persons, eds., *Socialism and American Life* (Princeton, New Jersey: Princeton University Press, 1952), 240.

16. Quoted in George, *The Life of Henry George*, 497.

17. George, *The Life of Henry George*, 353.

18. Ibid., 401.

19. Spann, *Brotherly Tomorrows*, 161.

20. George, *The Life of Henry George*, 478–79.

21. Ibid., 579.

22. Ibid., 594.

23. Quoted in George, *Progress and Poverty*, vii.

CHAPTER 9. NATIONALISTS

1. Quoted in Sylvia E. Bowman, *Edward Bellamy Abroad: An American Prophet's Influence* (New York: Twayne Publishers, 1962), 253–54.

2. Quoted in Edward K. Spann, *Brotherly Tomorrows: Movements for a Cooperative Society in America, 1820–1920* (New York: Columbia University Press, 1989), 189.

3. Bowman, *Edward Bellamy Abroad*, 87, 132–35, 209, 227, 302, 373.

4. Quoted in Arthur Lipow, *Authoritarian Socialism in America: Edward Bellamy and the Nationalist Movement* (Berkeley: University of California Press, 1982), 4.

5. Edward Bellamy, *Looking Backward 2000–1887* (1888; repr., Cambridge: Harvard University Press, 1967), 167.

6. Ibid., 163, 168, 178, 264.

7. Ibid., 145.

8. Ibid., 146.

9. Ibid., 127.

10. Ibid., 254.

11. William Dean Howells, *A Traveler from Altruria* (1894; repr., New York: Sagamore Press, 1957), 209.

12. Godfrey Sweven, "Limanora: The Island of Progress," in Glenn Negley and J. Max Patrick, eds., *The Quest for Utopia: An Anthology of Imaginary Societies* (New York: Schuman, 1952), 160.

13. Theodor Hertzka, "Freeland," in Negley and Patrick, eds., *The Quest for Utopia*, 113.

14. Bellamy, *Looking Backward*, 285.

15. Ibid., 305–6.

16. Gabriel Tarde, "Underground Man," in Negley and Patrick, eds., *The Quest for Utopia*, 193.

17. Ignatius Donnelly, "Caesar's Column," in Negley and Patrick, eds., *The Quest for Utopia*, 41.

18. Albert Chavannes, "The Future Commonwealth," in Negley and Patrick, eds., *The Quest for Utopia*, 152.

19. Howells, *A Traveler from Altruria*, 19.

20. H. G. Wells, "A Modern Utopia," in Negley and Patrick, eds., *The Quest for Utopia*, 245.

21. John Macnie, "The Diothas," in Negley and Patrick, eds., *The Quest for Utopia*, 67.

22. Bellamy, *Looking Backward*, 269–70.

23. Chauncey Thomas, "The Crystal Button," in Negley and Patrick, eds., *The Quest for Utopia*, 88.

24. Sweven, "Limanora: The Island of Progress," 161. Sweven was actually the nom de plume of John Macmillan Brown, a literature professor from New Zealand. Using these dual personas to his advantage, Brown nominated "Sweven" for the Nobel Prize in literature. Alas, Sweven didn't capture the prize despite Brown's efforts.

25. Tarde, "Underground Man," 199, 203.

26. Wells, "A Modern Utopia," 237.

27. Edward Bellamy, "Principles and Purposes of Nationalism," in Arthur Weinberg and Lilla Weinberg, eds., *Passport to Utopia: Great Panaceas in American History* (Chicago: Quadrangle Books, 1968), 134–42.

28. Bowman, *Edward Bellamy Abroad*, 31, 57–58. Lipow, *Authoritarian Socialism in America*, 22.

29. Quoted in Lipow, *Authoritarian Socialism in America*, 251.

30. Bellamy, "Principles and Purposes of Nationalism," 134–35.

31. Thomas A. Sancton, "Looking Inward: Edward Bellamy's Spiritual Crisis," *American Quarterly*, December 1973, 538–57 (quotes therein).

32. Quoted in Lipow, *Authoritarian Socialism in America*, 127.

33. Nicholas Gilman, " 'Nationalism' in the United States," *Quarterly Journal of Economics*, October 1889, 53.

34. Quoted in Lipow, *Authoritarian Socialism in America*, 121.

35. Quoted in ibid., 257.

36. Spann, *Brotherly Tomorrows*, 199.

37. "People's Party Platform," July 4, 1892, http://www2.wwnorton.com/college/history/eamerica/media/ch22/resources/documents/populist/htm, accessed on July 31, 2007.

CHAPTER 10. THE PATERNALIST DYNASTY I: PRAIRIE POPULISTS

1. Richard Hofstadter, *The Age of Reform: From Bryan to F.D.R.* (New York: Knopf, 1955), 23.

2. William A. Peffer, "The Farmer's Side," in Norman Pollack, ed., *The Populist Mind* (New York: Bobbs-Merrill, 1967), 75.

3. Frederick Jackson Turner, "The Significance of the Frontier in American History," American Historical Association, Chicago, Illinois, July 12, 1893, http://xroads.virginia.edu/~Hyper/TURNER/, accessed on August 30, 2007.

4. Quoted in Solon Justus Buck, *The Granger Movement: A Study of Agricultural Organization and Its Political, Economic, and Social Manifestations, 1870–1880* (1913; repr., Lincoln: University of Nebraska Press/Bison Books, 1965), 42.

5. Quoted in C. Vann Woodward, *Tom Watson: Agrarian Rebel* (1938; repr., New York: Oxford University Press, 1979), 138.

6. Norman Pollack, "Introduction," in Pollack, ed., *The Populist Mind*, xliv.

7. Lorenzo D. Lewelling, "A Dream of the Future," in Pollack, ed., *The Populist Mind*, 54.

8. Ignatius Donnelly, *Caesar's Column*, in Pollack, ed., *The Populist Mind*, 482.

9. "On Economic Trends," in Pollack, ed., *The Populist Mind*, 19.

10. "The Tendency of the Times," in Pollack, ed., *The Populist Mind*, 439.

11. Quoted in Woodward, *Tom Watson*, 239.

12. Lorenzo D. Lewelling, "Industrial Slavery," in Pollack, ed., *The Populist Mind*, 9.

13. W. Scott Morgan, "On Agrarian Discontent," in Pollack, ed., *The Populist Mind*, 270.

14. Quoted in Martin Ridge, *Ignatius Donnelly: The Portrait of a Politician* (Chicago: University of Chicago, 1962), 286.

15. People's Party Platform, St. Louis, Missouri, July 4, 1892, http://www2.wwnorton.com/college/history/eamerica/media/ch22/resources/documents/populist/htm, accessed on July 31, 2007.

16. "Preamble," People's Party Platform, St. Louis, Missouri, July 4, 1892, http://www2.wwnorton.com/college/history/eamerica/media/ch22/resources/documents/populist/htm, accessed on July 31, 2007.

17. Quoted in John D. Hicks, *The Populist Revolt: A History of the Farmers' Alliance and the People's Party* (1931; repr., Lincoln, NE: Bison Books, 1967), 333.

18. Quoted in Peffer, "The Farmer's Side," 99.

19. Ridge, *Ignatius Donnelly*, 260.

20. Ibid., 196–210.

21. Ibid., 244.

22. Ibid., 393–94.

23. Quoted in Hicks, *The Populist Revolt*, 160.

24. Woodward, *Tom Watson*, 221–22, 236–40.

25. Quoted in Woodward, *Tom Watson*, 264.

26. Quoted in Karel Denis Bicha, "Jerry Simpson: Populist Without Principle," *Journal of American History*, September 1967, 294.

27. Woodward, *Tom Watson*, 218.

28. Ridge, *Ignatius Donnelly*, 91–92.

29. Ibid., 98, 124, 129–34, 159, 163–64.

30. Ibid., 220–26.

31. Bicha, "Jerry Simpson: Populist Without Principle," 299.

32. Ibid., 297.

33. One thinks of Czeslaw Milosz's observation: "The peasants are a leaderless mass. History shows few instances when they seriously threatened the rulers. The term 'peasant revolt' sounds nice in textbooks and has a certain propaganda value, but only for the naive. In reality, the peasants have almost always served as a tool; their leaders, most often of non-peasant origin, have used them for their own ends." Czeslaw Milosz, *The Captive Mind* (1951; repr., New York: Vintage International, 1990), 194.

34. Speech: William Jennings Bryan, July 9, 1896, Chicago, Illinois.

35. Woodward, *Tom Watson*, 318.

36. Ibid., 313.

37. Quoted in Bicha, "Jerry Simpson: Populist Without Principle," 295.

38. Quoted in Woodward, *Tom Watson*, 334.

39. Quoted in Hicks, *The Populist Revolt*, 404.

CHAPTER 11. PREACHERS OF THE SOCIAL GOSPEL

1. Quoted in Ira V. Brown, *Lyman Abbott, Christian Evolutionist: A Study in Religious Liberalism* (1953; repr., Westport, CT: Greenwood Press, 1970), 145.

2. Quoted in Paul M. Minus, *Walter Rauschenbusch: American Reformer* (New York: Macmillan, 1988), 62.

3. Jacob Henry Dorn, *Washington Gladden: Prophet of the Social Gospel* (Columbus: Ohio State University, 1967), 214.

4. Brown, *Lyman Abbott, Christian Evolutionist*, 105.

5. Minus, *Walter Rauschenbusch*, 65. Dorn, *Washington Gladden* , 231–32.

6. Brown, *Lyman Abbott*, 106, 169, 180, 189–92, 209–13, 240.

7. Dorn, *Washington Gladden*, 92.

8. Walter Rauschenbusch, *Christianity and the Social Crisis* (New York: Macmillan, 1910), 271, 414.

9. Dorn, *Washington Gladden*, 239.

10. Josiah Strong, *The Next Great Awakening* (New York: Baker & Taylor, 1902), 171.

11. Dorn, *Washington Gladden*, 205, 222, 233, 278.

12. Quoted in ibid., 227.

13. Strong, *The Next Great Awakening*, 34.

14. Rauschenbusch, *Christianity and the Social Crisis*, 422.

15. Ibid., 10, 353.

16. Ibid., 11.

17. Strong, *The Next Great Awakening*, 115.

18. Quoted in Minus, *Walter Rauschenbusch*, 112.

19.   Quoted in Brown, *Lyman Abbott*, 195.

20.   Quoted in Dorn, *Washington Gladden*, 161.

21.   Brown, *Lyman Abbott*, 76.

22.   Ibid., 159.

23.   Quoted in Brown, *Lyman Abbott*, 159.

24.   Quoted in ibid., 152.

25.   Jane Addams, *Twenty Years at Hull-House* (1907; repr., Chicago: University of Illinois Press, 1990), 71.

26.   Ibid., 61.

27.   Ibid., 74.

28.   Ibid., 180.

29.   Rauschenbusch, *Christianity and the Social Crisis*, 305.

30.   Minus, *Walter Rauschenbusch*, 93, 124–25.

31.   Minus, *Walter Rauschenbusch*, 98. Dorn, *Washington Gladden*, 339–48.

32.   Strong, *The Next Great Awakening*, 106.

33.   Rauschenbusch, *Christianity and the Social Crisis*, 49.

34.   Ibid., 187.

35.   Brown, *Lyman Abbott*, 25.

36.   Quoted in Brown, *Lyman Abbott*, 166.

37.   Quoted in ibid., 165.

38.   Quoted in William H. Berge, "Voices for Imperialism: Josiah Strong and the Protestant Clergy," *Border States: Journal of the Kentucky-Tennessee American Studies Association*, 1973, http://spider.georgetowncollege.edu/htallant/border/bs1/berge.htm, accessed on July 2, 2006.

39.   Quoted in ibid.

40.   Quoted in Dorn, *Washington Gladden*, 411.

41.   Dorn, *Washington Gladden*, 412.

42.   George Washington, "Farewell Address," in *Washington Writings* (New York: Library of America, 1997), 962–77.

43.   Quoted in E. Berkeley Tompkins, *Anti-Imperialism in the United States: The Great Debate, 1890–1920* (Philadelphia: University of Pennsylvania, 1972), 12.

44.   Quoted in Howard H. Quint, "American Socialists and the Spanish-American War," *American Quarterly*, Summer, 1958, 136.

45.   Quoted in Tompkins, *Anti-Imperialism in the United States*, 12.

CHAPTER 12. THE PATERNALIST DYNASTY II: PATRIOTIC PROGRESSIVES

1.   Thorstein Veblen, *The Theory of the Leisure Class* (1899; repr., Boston: Houghton Mifflin, 1973), 44, 136, 138.

2.   Ibid., 137.

3.   Ibid., 138.

4. William James, *Pragmatism: A New Name for Some Old Ways of Thinking* (1907; repr., New York: Longmans, Green, 1925), 80.

5. Ibid., 77.

6. Charles A. Beard, *An Economic Interpretation of the Constitution of the United States* (1913; repr., New York: Free Press 1986), 324.

7. Lincoln Steffens, *The Shame of the Cities* (1904; repr., New York: Hill and Wang, 1992), 12.

8. Ibid., 98.

9. Ibid., 114.

10. Ibid., 46.

11. Speech: Theodore Roosevelt, "The Man with the Muck-Rake," April 14, 1906.

12. Ibid.

13. "I am going to try to write a Socialist novel this winter—to use what talent I may have to open the eyes of the American people to the conditions under which the toilers get their bread," Sinclair announced in *Appeal to Reason*. The novel, he further wrote, would outline "to the workers the way of their deliverance." Upton Sinclair, "To My Comrades Who Read the Appeal," *Appeal to Reason*, December 31, 1904, 2. See also, "The Jungle: A Story of Chicago, by Upton Sinclair," *Appeal to Reason*, February 11, 1905, 1.

14. Upton Sinclair, *The Jungle* (1905; repr., New York: Harper & Brothers, 1951), 300, 303, 312.

15. Ibid., 330.

16. Ibid., 135.

17. Ibid., 120–21.

18. Ibid., ix–x.

19. Ibid., x.

20. George Mowry, *The Era of Theodore Roosevelt* (New York: Harper & Row, 1958), 207. Michael McGerr, *A Fierce Discontent: The Rise and Fall of the Progressive Movement in America, 1870–1920* (New York: Free Press, 2003), 161–62. Upton Sinclair, "Introduction to Viking Press Edition, 1946," in Sinclair, *The Jungle*, i–x.

21. "Pure Food and Drugs Act of 1906," http://www.fda.gov/opacom/laws/wileyact.htm, accessed on July 31, 2007.

22. Kevin Mattson, "The Smoking Gun That Wasn't," http://chronicle.com/weekly/v52/i26/26b01101.htm, accessed on September 12, 2007; Jonah Goldberg, "The Clay Feet of Liberal Saints," http://www.nationalreview.com/goldberg/goldberg200601061019.asp, accessed on September 12, 2007.

23. Quoted in Richard Hofstadter, *The Age of Reform: From Bryan to F.D.R.* (New York: Knopf, 1955), 192.

24. Theodore Roosevelt, "A Confession of Faith," in Otis Pease, ed., *The Progressive Years: The Spirit and Achievement of Reform* (New York: George Braziller, 1962), 341.

25. Ibid., 324.

26. Interstate Commerce Act, Public Law 49–41, February 4, 1887.

27. "Sherman Anti-Trust Act," July 2, 1890, http://www.usdoj.gov/atr/foia/divisionmanual/ch2.htm#a1, accessed on July 31, 2007.

28. Mowry, *The Era of Theodore Roosevelt*, 203–7.

29. "Clayton Antitrust Act," http://www.usdoj.gov/atr/foia/divisionmanual/two.htm#a3, accessed on September 12, 2007.

30. Ari Hoogenboom and Olive Hoogenboom, *A History of the ICC: From Panacea to Palliative* (New York: Norton, 1976), 52.

31. Ibid., 4, 57, 88.

32. Walter Weyl, "The Railroad Administration to Date," *New Republic*, November 9, 1918, 43.

33. Hoogenboom and Hoogenboom, *A History of the ICC*, 88.

34. Quoted in McGerr, *A Fierce Discontent*, 165.

35. Mowry, *The Era of Theodore Roosevelt*, 12.

36. To calculate inflation over a period of time, see the excellent Web site http://measuringworth.com/calculators/uscompare/, accessed on September 12, 2007.

37. O. M. W. Sprague, "The Conscription of Income," *New Republic*, February 24, 1917, 93–97.

38. Roosevelt, "A Confession of Faith," 313.

39. Mowry, *The Era of Theodore Roosevelt*, 80–81.

40. In 1921, North Dakota voters recalled Governor Lynn Frazier, an advocate of government takeovers of industrial functions. In 2003, California voters recalled liberal Democrat Gray Davis.

41. For a good history of the initiative and recall, written as the history was happening, see Charles Sumner Lobingier, "Popular Legislation in the United States," *Political Science Quarterly*, December 1908, 577–78. Today, twenty-four American states, all but seven west of the Mississippi, allow for direct legislation. The states that currently boast initiatives are Maine, Massachusetts, Florida, Mississippi, Michigan, Ohio, Illinois, Arkansas, Missouri, Washington, Oregon, California, Nevada, Alaska, Idaho, Montana, Arizona, Utah, Wyoming, Colorado, North Dakota, South Dakota, Nebraska, and Oklahoma.

42. W. Rodman Peabody, "Direct Legislation," *Political Science Quarterly*, September 1905, 454.

43. Ballot initiatives famously limited taxation in California and Massachusetts in the late 1970s, outlawed racial preferences in Washington and California in the 1990s, and in the 2000s reaffirmed traditional marriage in every state where the question of "gay marriage" has been put before the voters. While, in theory, liberals may applaud direct democracy and conservatives may decry it, in practice, conservatives have benefited from it while liberals have suffered from it.

44. Hofstadter, *The Age of Reform*, 266.

45. Aileen S. Kraditor, *The Ideas of the Woman Suffrage Movement, 1890–1920* (1965; repr., New York: Anchor Books, 1971), vii.

46. Ibid., 224–34. Kraditor provides short biographies of twenty-six leaders in the fight for female suffrage, of which all were white, sixteen graduated from college, and twenty-five were reared in Protestant sects.

47. Ibid., 26.

48. Quoted in ibid., 114.

49. Quoted in ibid., 111.

50. Quoted in ibid., 157.

51. Ibid., 114.

52. Ibid., 110. The resolution reads: "*Resolved*, that without expressing any opinion on the proper qualifications for voting, we call attention to the significant facts that in every State there are more women who can read and write than all negro voters; more white women who can read and write than all negro voters; more American women who can read and write than all foreign voters; so that the enfranchisement of such women would settle the vexed question of rule by illiteracy, whether of home-grown or foreign-born production."

53. Ibid., 168.

54. Ibid., 167–68.

55. Quoted in ibid., 47.

56. Carry A. Nation, "Prohibition," in Arthur Weinberg and Lila Weinberg, eds., *Passport to Utopia: Great Panaceas in American History* (Chicago: Quadrangle Books, 1968), 174.

57. Ibid., 175.

58. William O'Neill, *The Progressive Years: America Comes of Age* (New York: Dodd, Mead, 1975), 88.

59. Hofstadter, *The Age of Reform*, 287.

60. O'Neill, *The Progressive Years*, 90.

61. Andrew Sinclair, *Prohibition: The Era of Excess* (London: Faber and Faber, 1962), 37, 53, 115, 291, 331–37, 362, 419.

62. "To All Readers," *Masses*, December 1914, 16; Kate Richards O'Hare, "Booze and Revolution," *Masses*, April 1915, 16; Ad: "New Masses Book Service," *New Masses*, December 31, 1932, 3.

63. James H. Timberlake, *Prohibition and the Progressive Movement: 1900–1920* (Cambridge, MA: Harvard University Press, 1963), 167–68, 170–72, 225 n69. Timberlake points to the 1911 vote of the California senate on a local option measure, in which the seventeen senators voting in the affirmative were progressives in their voting record. The Hobson resolution, condemning alcohol as a "narcotic poison" that corrupted morals and the gene pool, in the U.S. House of Representatives gained the votes of seventeen of twenty Progressive Party legislators, with two of the other three not casting a vote. It's significant that, although the measure passed muster with the Progressive Party caucus, it gained only a slight plurality in the greater body. Timberlake also notes that the state parties of the Progressive Party openly supported prohibition in Ohio, Indiana, Michigan, Iowa, Idaho, Kansas, North Dakota, Utah, Oklahoma, Georgia, New Mexico, Vermont, and Maine. This came at a time when many politicians, such as Woodrow Wilson, found it profitable to play both sides of the question. As governor of New Jersey, for instance, Wilson backed the local option for banning alcohol, but as president vetoed prohibition measures.

64. Quoted in ibid., 168.

65. Ibid., 164.

66. Sinclair, *Prohibition*, 222.

67. W. E. B. Du Bois, "Black Folk and Birth Control," *Birth Control Review*, May 1938, 90. The most disturbing example of Sanger's mania for eugenics comes from a speech calling for American concentration camps, well before Hitler assumed power in Germany, that the publication she founded later printed: Margaret Sanger, "A Plan for World Peace," *Birth Control Review*, April 1932, 107–8.

68. Lester F. Ward, "Eugenics, Euthenics, and Eudemics," *American Journal of Sociology*, May 1913, 746–47. Ward, the founding president of the American Sociological Association, died a few weeks prior to the publication date of this article.

69. Margaret Sanger, "The Pope's Position on Birth Control," *The Nation*, January 27, 1932, 102.

70. For a discussion of Great Britain's eugenics movement, see Diane Paul, "Eugenics and the Left," *Journal of the History of Ideas*, Oct.–Dec. 1984, 567–90.

71. Edwin Black, *War Against the Weak: Eugenics and America's Campaign to Create a Master Race* (New York: Four Walls Eight Windows, 2003), 319–35.

72. Ibid., 259, 90, 266.

73. Holmes, J., "Opinion of the Court," Supreme Court of the United States, *Buck v. Bell*, May 2, 1927.

74. Black, *War Against the Weak*, xvi, 398.

75. Quoted in David Traxel, *Crusader Nation: The United States in Peace and the Great War, 1898–1920* (New York: Knopf, 2006), 138.

76. Quoted in Arthur Link, *Woodrow Wilson and the Progressive Era, 1910–1917* (New York: Harper and Row, 1954), 176n.

77. Speech: Woodrow Wilson, April 2, 1917.

78. Quoted in Ira V. Brown, *Lyman Abbott, Christian Evolutionist: A Study in Religious Liberalism* (1953; repr., Westport, CT: Greenwood Press, 1970), 217.

79. Richard M. Gamble, *The War for Righteousness: Progressive Christianity, the Great War, and the Rise of the Messianic Nation* (Wilmington, DE: ISI Books, 2003), 146.

80. Quoted in Dorn, *Washington Gladden*, 431, 433.

81. Quoted in Gamble, *The War for Righteousness*, 160.

82. Gamble, *The War for Righteousness*, 100.

83. Grosvenor B. Clarkson, *Industrial America in the World War: The Strategy Behind the Line, 1917–1918* (Cambridge, MA: Riverside Press, 1923), 332–33.

84. Quoted in McGerr, *A Fierce Discontent*, 311.

CHAPTER 13. STAR-SPANGLED SOCIALISTS

1. Quoted in David A. Shannon, *The Socialist Party of America: A History* (New York: Macmillan, 1955), 4.

2. Quoted in Seymour Martin Lipset and Gary Marks, *It Didn't Happen Here: Why Socialism Failed in the United States* (New York: Norton, 2000), 18.

3. Howard H. Quint, "Julius A. Wayland, Socialist Propagandist," *Mississippi Valley Historical Review*, March 1949, 589, 591–92. Charles H. Kegel, "Ruskin's St. George in America," *American Quarterly*, winter 1957, 413, 416.

4. Daniel Bell, "Marxian Socialism in the United States," in Donald Drew Egbert and Stow Persons, eds., *Socialism and American Life* (Princeton, NJ: Princeton University Press, 1952), 259–60; J. W. Braam, "The Ruskin Co-Operative Colony," *American Journal of Sociology*, March 1903, 667–80.

5. A. W. Ricker, "Don't Organize a Co-operative Colony Organize a Local of the Socialist Party," *Appeal to Reason*, June 13, 1902, 4.

6. Ibid.

7. *Workingmen's Party of the United States: Proceedings of the Union Conference*, July 19–22, 1876 (New York: Social Democratic Printing Association, 1876), 11–12.

8. Morris Hillquit, *History of Socialism in the United States* (1903; repr., New York: Dover, 1971), 204–6.

9. Ibid., 193–94.

10. Ibid., 235.

11. "Army Column," *The Coming Nation*, July 1, 1905, 1.

12. "Who Belongs to the Appeal Army?" *Appeal to Reason*, November 28, 1903, 1.

13. "Army Column," *The Coming Nation*, July 1, 1905, 4; Elliott Shore, *Talkin' Socialism: J. A. Wayland and the Radical Press* (Lawrence: University Press of Kansas, 1988), 104.

14. Quoted in Shore, *Talkin' Socialism*, 185.

15. Shore, *Talkin' Socialism*, 92, 123, 192, 196.

16. Ibid., 27.

17. "Who Belongs to the Appeal Army?", 1.

18. Hillquit, *History of Socialism in the United States*, 357.

19. In 1912, Oklahoma awarded 16.6 percent of its presidential ballots to Debs, Nevada 16.5 percent, and Montana 13.6 percent. In 1908, Debs received 8.5 percent of Oklahoma's ballots cast, 8.6 percent of Nevada's, and 8.5 percent of Montana's.

20. Socialistic Labor Party of North America, "National Platform," December 26–31, 1877, Newark, New Jersey.

21. Carl Reeve, *The Life and Times of Daniel De Leon* (New York: Humanities Press, 1972), 32, 12.

22. Patrick Renshaw, *The Wobblies: The Story of Syndicalism in the United States* (Garden City, NY: Doubleday, 1967), 52–53; Reeve, *The Life and Times of Daniel De Leon*, 176–81.

23. Lillian Symes and Travers Clement, *Rebel America: The Story of Social Revolt in the United States* (1934; repr., New York: Da Capo, 1972), 190. Renshaw, *The Wobblies*, 53.

24. Hillquit, *History of Socialism in the United States*, 298.

25. Quoted in Milton Cantor, *The Divided Left: American Radicalism, 1900–1975* (New York: Hill and Wang, 1978), 21.

26. Quoted in Symes and Clement, *Rebel America*, 137.

27. Quoted in ibid., 179.

28. E. N. Richardson, "Hot Cinders," *The Coming Nation*, August 13, 1904, 1.

29. Upton Sinclair, "You Have Lost the Strike," *Appeal to Reason*, September 17, 1904, 1.

30. "Schools Under Socialism," *Appeal to Reason*, September 2, 1899, 1.

31. Sinclair, "You Have Lost the Strike," 1.

32. "The Negro and Socialism," *Appeal to Reason*, September 2, 1899, 1.

33. Sinclair, "You Have Lost the Strike," 1.

34. Advertisements: "Cancer Cured," *Appeal to Reason*, March 4, 1905, 3; "Free Gold Watch," *Appeal to Reason*, April 8, 1905, 3; "Deafness Can Be Cured," *Appeal to Reason*, January 30, 1904, 5; "Make Money Easy," *Appeal to Reason*, December 30, 1905, 3.

35. Quoted in Shannon, *The Socialist Party of America*, 50.

36. Reeve, *The Life and Times of Daniel De Leon*.

37. Ibid., 134.

38. Quoted in Aileen S. Kraditor, *The Radical Persuasion, 1890–1917: Aspects of the Intellectual History and the Historiography of Three American Radical Organizations* (Baton Rouge: LSU Press, 1981), 166. Elsewhere, in a screed against populism and Tom Watson, De Leon referred to blacks in print as "niggers." Since De Leon surrounded the offensive term in quotation marks, it's possible that his use of the term was in ridicule of southerners' use of it. Reeve, *The Life and Times of Daniel De Leon*, 135.

39. Sally Miller, "Socialism and Race," in John Laslett and Seymour Martin Lipset, eds., *Failure of a Dream: Essays in the History of American Socialism*, rev. ed. (Berkeley: University of California Press, 1974), 224.

40. Quoted in Kraditor, *The Radical Persuasion, 1890–1917*, 168.

41. Quoted in ibid., 172.

42. "The Negro and Socialism," *Appeal to Reason*, September 2, 1899, 1.

43. A. W. Ricker, "Socialism and the Negro," *Appeal to Reason*, September 12, 1903, 3.

44. Quoted in Shannon, *The Socialist Party of America*, 48–49.

45. Lipset and Marks, *It Didn't Happen Here*, 144.

46. "Socialistic Labor Party of North America National Platform," December 26–31, 1877, Newark, New Jersey, http://www.slp.org/pdf/platforms/plat1877.pdf, accessed on September 13, 2007.

47. Miller, "Socialism and Women," 302.

48. Quoted in Kraditor, *The Radical Persuasion, 1890–1917*, 195.

49. Quoted in ibid., 129.

50. Eugene Debs, "Unionism and Socialism," in Otis Pease, ed., *The Progressive Years: The Spirit and Achievement of American Reform* (New York: George Braziller, 1962), 231.

51. Quoted in Kraditor, *The Radical Persuasion, 1890–1917*, 132.

52. Debs, "Unionism and Socialism," 231; quoted in Kraditor, *The Radical Persuasion, 1890–1917*, 130, 147.

53. Fred D. Warren, "Echoes Along the Way," *The Coming Nation*, August 13, 1904, 1.

54. "Prosperity," *Appeal to Reason*, November 28, 1903, 1. Sinclair, "You Have Lost the Strike," 1. "Governor-Elect Adams," *Appeal to Reason*, December 3, 1904, 1.

55. *Appeal to Reason*, December 3, 1904, 1.

56. "IWW Preamble," http://www.library.arizona.edu/exhibits/bisbee/docs/018 .html#Preamble, accessed on September 17, 2007.

57. "Socialist Party Platform," http://www.sagehistory.net/progressive/SocialistPlat1912. htm, accessed on September 4, 2007.

58. Debs, "Unionism and Socialism," 242.

59. Ibid., 234.

60. Quoted in Lorin F. Deland, "The Lawrence Strike: A Study," *Atlantic Monthly*, May 1912, 703.

61. Quoted in Melvyn Dubofsky, "Socialism and Syndicalism," in Laslett and Lipset, eds., *Failure of a Dream*, 189.

62. Shore, *Talkin' Socialism*, 206–15.

63. Symes and Clement, *Rebel America*, 241.

64. Quoted in Shannon, *The Socialist Party of America*, 72.

65. Some examples of texts using the seemingly obligatory laundry list of 1912 socialist accomplishments include: Daniel Bell, "The Background and Development of Marxian Socialism in the United States," in Donald Drew Egbert and Stow Persons, eds., *Socialism and American Life* (Princeton, NJ: Princeton University Press, 1952), 283; Theodore Draper, *The Roots of American Communism* (1957; repr., Chicago: Ivan R. Dee, 1985), 42; William L. O'Neil, *The Progressive Years: America Comes of Age* (New York: Dodd, Mead & Co., 1975), 65; John Patrick Diggins, *The Rise and Fall of the American Left* (1973; repr., New York: W. W. Norton, 1992), 82–84; and Christopher Lasch, *The Agony of the American Left* (New York: Knopf, 1969), 35.

66. Quoted in Hillquit, *History of Socialism in the United States*, 236.

67. Hillquit, *History of Socialism in the United States*, 257.

68. Ibid., 234, 259.

69. "Platform of the Socialist Party," in Hillquit, *History of Socialism in the United States*, 377.

70. Lipset and Marks, *It Didn't Happen Here*, 119.

71. Ibid., 184.

72. Ibid., 177.

73. Ibid.

74. Shannon, *The Socialist Party of America*, 17.

75. Quoted in Draper, *The Roots of American Communism*, 93. In taking this stance, the American Socialist Party departed from most of its counterparts in other countries, which generally lined up behind their respective countries in the Great War, despite all the talk of "no war but the class war." As historian David Shannon explained, "American Socialists, when confronted with war, had remained closer to the orthodox Marxian position of opposition to capitalism's wars than had any of the strong European socialist parties." Like the socialists of Russia, where Lenin adeptly advocated "revolutionary defeatism" to transform "the imperialist war into a civil war," the American socialists operated almost wholly outside the government, which allowed them to adopt unpopular and purist stances without suffering reprisals at the ballot box. See Shannon, *The Socialist Party of America*, 98.

76. Quoted in Shannon, *The Socialist Party of America*, 102.

77. Norman Thomas, "Pluralism and Political Parties," in Laslett and Lipset, eds., *Failure of a Dream*, 516.

78. Michael Harrington, "Comment 1," in Laslett and Lipset, eds., *Failure of a Dream*, 526.

79. Quoted in Shannon, *The Socialist Party of America*, 161.

80. Werner Sombart, *Why Is There No Socialism in the United States?* (White Plains, NY: IAS Press, 1976), 106.

81. Shannon, *The Socialist Party of America*, 258.

82. Quoted in Kraditor, *The Radical Persuasion, 1890–1917*, 42.

83. Wilbert E. Moore, "Sociological Aspects of American Socialism," in Donald Drew Egbert and Stow Persons, eds., *Socialism and American Life* (Princeton, NJ: Princeton University Press, 1952), 553.

84. "Indications Are That Truly 'This Is Our Year,'" *Appeal to Reason*, November 2, 1912, 1.

85. Shore, *Talkin' Socialism*, 7, 217.

86. Quoted in "Story of the Tragedy," *Appeal to Reason*, November 23, 1912, 1.

CHAPTER 14. RED-WHITE-AND-BLUE REDS

1. John Reed, *Ten Days That Shook the World* (1919; repr., New York: Bantam Books, 1988), 188.

2. Christian, "The Rumor in Russia," *The Nation*, December 21, 1918, 766; Justin Kaplan, *Lincoln Steffens: A Biography* (New York: Simon and Schuster, 1974), 218–19.

3. W. E. B. Du Bois, "Russia, 1926," in *W.E.B. Du Bois: A Reader*, David Levering Lewis, ed., (New York: Henry Holt, 1995), 582.

4. Quoted in Lewis S. Feuer, "American Travelers to the Soviet Union, 1917–32: The Formation of a Component of New Deal Ideology," *American Quarterly*, summer 1962, 124.

5. Stephane Courtois, Nicolas Werth, and Jean-Louis Panne, et al, *The Black Book of Communism: Crimes, Terror, Repression*, trans. Jonathan Murphy and Mark Kramer (Cambridge, MA: Harvard University Press, 1999), 13–14, 78.

6. Ibid., 55.

7. Ibid., 67.

8. Quoted in ibid., 90.

9. Ibid., 62.

10. Ibid., 88.

11. Ibid., 126.

12. Ibid., 98–107.

13. "Getting Debamboozled on Russia," *New Republic*, March 10, 1920, 45; " 'Watchful Waiting' in Russia," *New Republic*, June 29, 1918, 247; "What Is at Stake in Russia," *New Republic*, February 2, 1918, 7.

14. Christian, "The Rumor in Russia," 766; Mark Podolianin, "The Position of the Russian Intelligentsia," *The Nation*, March 22, 1919, 444; Evans Clark, "Americanism and the Soviet," *The Nation*, March 22, 1919, 424.

15. Feuer, "American Travelers to the Soviet Union, 1917–32," 119–49.

16. Ibid., 147.

17. Robert A. Rosenstone, *Romantic Revolutionary: A Biography of John Reed* (New York: Knopf, 1975), 15, 19.

18. Ibid., 39; Granville Hicks, *John Reed: The Making of a Revolutionary* (New York: Macmillan, 1936), 29–33, 47.

19. Rosenstone, *Romantic Revolutionary*, 49–50. Hicks, *John Reed*, 35.

20. Rosenstone, *Romantic Revolutionary*, 57, 65.

21. Ibid., 69–70.

22. Christopher Lasch, *The New Radicalism in America, 1889–1963: The Intellectual as Social Type* (New York: Knopf, 1965), 118, 119–31.

23. Hicks, *John Reed*, 163–64.

24. Letter: Louise Bryant to John Reed, December 7, 1916 (John Reed Collection, Harvard University, Houghton Library). Neither Granville Hicks nor Robert Rosenstone explores Reed infecting Bryant with a disease in their biographies of Reed. Rosenstone, who had access to Harvard University's collection of letters between Reed and Bryant, deals with Bryant's charge by repeating Reed's assertion that his kidney condition wasn't transmittable. The implication is that Bryant, and her doctor, were ignoramuses regarding elementary medical matters. So, too, apparently, was a doctor in Europe, whose diagnosis of syphilis in Reed Rosenstone treats as something of a joke. Rosenstone, *Romantic Revolutionary*, 260, 222. Filmmaker Warren Beatty, in 1981's *Reds*, similarly doesn't allow VD to muck up his love story of two free-love adherents. Though never mentioning a disease by name, the letters between Reed and Bryant detail the couple getting sick at roughly the same time, Bryant suffering from an ovarian infection, Bryant repeating her doctor's charge that Reed had transmitted a disease to her, and Reed subsequently promising ad infinitum to overcome past infidelities. For instance, after detailing the sad case of a fallen actress with the same medical condition that Bryant had suffered from the previous year, Reed tells Bryant: "You may believe that nevermore is there going to be any chance of any girl coming between me and my honey." The promise, coming after his description of a woman afflicted with Bryant's condition, only makes sense if Reed himself had caused Bryant's condition. Letter: John Reed to Louise Bryant, June 14, 1917 (John Reed Collection, Harvard University, Houghton Library). "I'd been a fool and a cad" is how Reed summarizes to Bryant how he had characterized their relationship to Lincoln Steffens. Letter: John Reed to Louise Bryant, June 25, 1917 (John Reed Collection, Harvard University, Houghton Library). A few weeks later, Reed confesses to Bryant of a young temptress's advances, which he rebuffs. He writes that "she wanted to make love. I didn't + couldn't." He complains that women have made him weak, and "now without a mate I am half a man, and sterile." Letter: John Reed to Louise Bryant, July 5, 1917 (John Reed Collection, Harvard University, Houghton Library). Ten days later, a dour Reed writes: "I know, my lover—I realize how disappointed + cruelly disillusioned you have been. You thought you were getting a hero—and you only got a

vicious little person who is fast losing any spark he may have had." In the margin, Reed adds as a postscript: "Don't be alarmed by this last. I have kept my word to you—lover." Letter: John Reed to Louise Bryant, July 15, 1917 (John Reed Collection, Harvard University, Houghton Library).

25. Quoted in Rosenstone, *Romantic Revolutionary*, 260.

26. Letter: John Reed to Louise Bryant, December 10, 1916 (John Reed Collection, Harvard University, Houghton Library). Bryant's ovaries, thankfully, stayed intact. She bore a daughter to third husband William Bullitt, who would ironically become America's first ambassador to Soviet Russia.

27. Quoted in Rosenstone, *Romantic Revolutionary*, 98.

28. Quoted in ibid., 122.

29. Hicks, *John Reed*, 96–106. Rosenstone, *Romantic Revolutionary*, 126–32.

30. Quoted in Rosenstone, *Romantic Revolutionary*, 167.

31. Rosenstone, *Romantic Revolutionary*, 166.

32. Ibid., 166.

33. Hicks, *John Reed*, 198.

34. Ibid., 180.

35. Letter: John Reed to Louise Bryant, June 25, 1917 (John Reed Collection, Harvard University, Houghton Library).

36. Letter: John Reed to Louise Bryant, July 8, 1917 (John Reed Collection, Harvard University, Houghton Library).

37. Max Eastman, *Love and Revolution: My Journey Through an Epoch* (New York: Random House, 1964), 63. Quote therein.

38. Letter: John Reed to Louise Bryant, June 25, 1917 (John Reed Collection, Harvard University, Houghton Library).

39. Letter: John Reed to Louise Bryant, July 10, 1917 (John Reed Collection, Harvard University, Houghton Library).

40. George Creel, "Rockefeller Law," *Masses*, July 1915, 5.

41. Reed, *Ten Days That Shook the World*, 172.

42. Ibid., 60, 92, 137.

43. Rosenstone, *Romantic Revolutionary*, 299n.

44. Hicks, *John Reed*, 290; "Top 100 Works of Journalism in the United States in the 20th Century," http://www.nyu.edu/classes/stephens/Top%20100%20page.htm, accessed on September 7, 2007.

45. Quoted in Kaplan, *Lincoln Steffens*, 184.

46. Eastman, *Love and Revolution*, 23, 105.

47. Quoted in ibid., 107.

48. For a review of the Socialist Party's 1919 expulsions, and internecine disputes of that period, see Theodore Draper, *The Roots of American Communism* (1957; repr., Chicago: Ivan R. Dee, 1985), 148–63.

49. Hicks, *John Reed*, 358–59; Rosenstone, *Romantic Revolutionary*, 354–55.

50. Hicks, *John Reed*, 361–62. Draper, *The Roots of American Communism*, 181–83.

51. Harvey Klehr and John Earl Haynes, *The American Communist Movement: Storming Heaven Itself* (New York: Twayne, 1992), 29–30.

52. Draper, *The Roots of American Communism*, 215.

53. Quoted in Harvey Klehr, John Earl Haynes, and Kyrill M. Anderson, *The Soviet World of American Communism* (New Haven, CT: Yale University Press, 1998), 19.

54. Draper, *The Roots of American Communism*, 200–1; Klehr and Haynes, *The American Communist Movement*, 26.

55. For an outline of the Communist takeover of the national Farmer-Labor Party, given prior to the opening of the Soviet archives, see James Weinstein, "Radicalism in the Midst of Normalcy," *Journal of American History*, March 1966, 773–90. For an update that includes documentary proof of Moscow's involvement in the actions of the American Communist Party in co-opting the infant Farmer-Labor Party, see Klehr, Haynes, and Anderson, *The Soviet World of American Communism*, 14–29.

56. Quoted in James Weinstein, "Radicalism in the Midst of Normalcy," *Journal of American History*, March 1966, 786.

57. Klehr, Haynes, and Anderson, *The Soviet World of American Communism*, 27–29.

58. Quoted in Draper, *The Roots of American Communism*, 223.

59. Draper, *The Roots of American Communism*, 273.

60. Ibid., 279, 443 n7.

61. Klehr and Haynes, *The American Communist Movement*, 55.

62. Ibid., 25.

63. Draper, *The Roots of American Communism*, 392.

64. Klehr and Haynes, *The American Communist Movement*, 55.

65. Klehr, Haynes, and Anderson, *The Soviet World of American Communism*, 113.

66. Letter: John Reed to Louise Bryant, Abo, Finland to New York, USA, May 3, 1920 (John Reed Collection, Harvard University, Houghton Library).

67. Harvey Klehr, John Earl Haynes, and Fridrikh Igorevich Firsov, *The Secret World of American Communism* (New Haven: Yale University Press, 1995), 22–24.

68. Letter: John Reed to Louise Bryant, May 13, 1920 (John Reed Collection, Harvard University, Houghton Library); Hicks, *John Reed*, 378–86; Rosenstone, *Romantic Revolutionary*, 366–70.

69. Letter: John Reed to Louise Bryant, June 26, 1920 (John Reed Collection, Harvard University, Houghton Library).

70. Letter: John Reed to Louise Bryant, June 23, 1920 (John Reed Collection, Harvard University, Houghton Library).

71. Karl Marx and Friedrich Engels, *The Communist Manifesto* (New York: Penguin Classics, 2002), 234.

72. Quoted in Rosenstone, *Romantic Revolutionary*, 338.

73. Quoted in Draper, *The Roots of American Communism*, 243.

74. Quoted in ibid., 199.

75. Quoted in ibid., 220.

76. Klehr, Haynes, and Anderson, *The Soviet World of American Communism*, 48–50.

77. Hicks, *John Reed*, 395; Klehr and Haynes, *The American Communist Movement*, 31; Draper, *The Roots of American Communism*, 282–93.

78. Quoted in Klehr and Haynes, *The American Communist Movement*, 48–49.

79. For a discussion of the Communist theft of Lovestone's files, see Klehr, Haynes, and Firsov, *The Secret World of American Communism*, 128–32.

80. Joseph G. Rayback, *A History of American Labor*, expanded and updated (New York: Macmillan, 1974), 302.

81. Quoted in Patrick Renshaw, *The Wobblies: The Story of Syndicalism in the United States* (Garden City, NY: Doubleday, 1967), 256.

82. Eastman, *Love and Revolution*, 160; Draper, *The Roots of American Communism*, 324–26.

83. Quoted in Draper, *The Roots of American Communism*, 324–25.

84. Eastman, *Love and Revolution*, 260.

85. Rosenstone, *Romantic Revolutionary*, 384–85.

CHAPTER 15. THE PATERNALIST DYNASTY III: NEW DEALERS

1. William E. Leuchtenburg, *Franklin Roosevelt and the New Deal, 1932–1940* (New York: Harper Torchbooks, 1963), 3, 11.

2. Inauguration speech: Franklin Roosevelt, Washington, DC, March 4, 1933. Arthur Schlesinger Jr., *The Coming of the New Deal* (Boston: Houghton Mifflin, 1958), 1.

3. Quoted in Lewis S. Feuer, "American Travelers to the Soviet Union, 1917–32: The Formation of a Component of New Deal Ideology," *American Quarterly*, summer 1962, 147–48.

4. Radio speech: Franklin Roosevelt, Washington, DC, March 12, 1933.

5. Kenneth S. Davis, *FDR: The New Deal Years, 1933–1937* (1986; repr., New York: Random House, 1995), 42.

6. Jim Powell, *FDR's Folly: How Roosevelt and His New Deal Prolonged the Great Depression* (New York: Crown Forum, 2003), 53.

7. Quoted in Schlesinger, *The Coming of the New Deal*, 239.

8. Davis, *FDR: The New Deal Years, 1933–1937*, 294; John T. Flynn, *The Roosevelt Myth*, rev. ed. (1948; repr., New York: Devin-Adair, 1965), 57.

9. Garet Garrett, "The Revolution Was," in *The People's Pottage* (San Diego: Truth Seeker, 1992), 22.

10. Quoted in Leuchtenburg, *Franklin Roosevelt and the New Deal*, 101.

11. Davis, *FDR: The New Deal Years, 1933–1937*, 282–83.

12. Theodore Saloutos, "New Deal Agricultural Policy: An Evaluation," *Journal of American History*, September 1974, 397–98.

13. Powell, *FDR's Folly*, 133; Joseph S. Davis, "Experiments in Wheat Control: The Agricultural Adjustment Act, 1933," *Quarterly Journal of Economics*, February 1935, 360.

14. Leuchtenburg, *Franklin Roosevelt and the New Deal*, 73.

15. Davis, "Experiments in Wheat Control: The Agricultural Adjustment Act, 1933," 361–62.

16. Flynn, *The Roosevelt Myth*, 49.

17. Quoted in Gilbert C. Fite, "Farmer Opinion and the Agricultural Adjustment Act, 1933," *Mississippi Valley Historical Review*, March 1962, 672.

18. Leuchtenburg, *Franklin Roosevelt and the New Deal*, 339.

19. Flynn, *The Roosevelt Myth*, 44–45.

20. Leuchtenburg, *Franklin Roosevelt and the New Deal*, 68.

21. Quoted in Flynn, *The Roosevelt Myth*, 316.

22. Flynn, *The Roosevelt Myth*, 316.

23. Davis, *FDR: The New Deal Years, 1933–1937*, 248–49.

24. Radio speeches: Franklin Roosevelt, Washington, DC, May 7, 1933; June 28, 1934; September 30, 1934; April 28, 1935.

25. Radio speech: Franklin Roosevelt, Washington, DC, July 24, 1933.

26. Davis, *FDR: The New Deal Years, 1933–1937*, 253.

27. Quoted in Schlesinger, *The Coming of the New Deal*, 117.

28. Powell, *FDR's Folly*, 125–26.

29. Wolfgang Schivelbusch, *Three New Deals: Reflections on Roosevelt's America, Mussolini's Italy, and Hitler's Germany*, trans. Jefferson Chase (New York: Metropolitan Books, 2006), 110.

30. Quoted in Arthur Weinberg and Lila Weinberg, eds., *Passport to Utopia: Great Panaceas in American History* (Chicago: Quadrangle Books, 1968), 300.

31. Upton Sinclair, "End Poverty in California," in Weinberg and Weinberg, eds., *Passport to Utopia*, 250–58.

32. Quoted in Sheldon Marcus, *Father Coughlin: The Tumultuous Life of the Priest of the Little Flower* (Boston: Little, Brown, 1973), 72–75.

33. Howard Scott, "Energy Versus Money," in Weinberg and Weinberg, eds., *Passport to Utopia*, 232–40.

34. Marcus, *Father Coughlin*, 208–20.

35. Quoted in Leuchtenburg, *Franklin Roosevelt and the New Deal*, 189.

36. John D. Guthrie, "The CCC and American Conservation," *Scientific Monthly*, November 1943, 403.

37. Schlesinger, *The Coming of the New Deal*, 288.

38. Anthony Badger, *The New Deal Years: The Depression Years, 1933–1940* (New York: Hill and Wang, 1989), 203.

39. Davis, *FDR: The New Deal Years, 1933–1937*, 308. Schlesinger, *The Coming of the New Deal*, 270.

40. Badger, *The New Deal: The Depression Years, 1933–1940*, 209.

41. Powell, *FDR's Folly*, 98.

42. Leuchtenburg, *Franklin Roosevelt and the New Deal*, 281.

43. Powell, *FDR's Folly*, 101–3.

44. Flynn, *The Roosevelt Myth*, 137.

45. Flynn, *The Roosevelt Myth*, 136.

46. Badger, *The New Deal: The Depression Years, 1933–1940*, 210.

47. Flynn, *The Roosevelt Myth*, 274–75.

48. Ibid., 247–48.

49. Davis, *FDR: The New Deal Years, 1933–1937*, 168, 690n.

50. Flynn, *The Roosevelt Myth*, 257.

51. *Budget of the United States Government: Fiscal Year 2008* (Washington, DC: U.S. Government Printing Office, 2007), 21–22.

52. "Federal Individual Income Tax Rates History: Income Years 1913–2007," http://www.taxfoundation.org/files/federalindividualratehistory-20070227.pdf, accessed on July 30, 2007.

53. Robert Van Giezen and Albert E. Schwenk, "Compensation from Before World War I Through the Great Depression," http://www.bls.gov/opub/cwc/cm20030124aro3p1.htm, accessed on September 1, 2007.

54. "Dow Jones Indexes," http://djindexes.com/mdsidx/index.cfm?event=showavgDecades&decade=1920,http://djindexes.com/mdsidx/index.cfm?event=showavgDecades&decade=1930, http://djindexes.com/mdsidx/index.cfm?event=showavgDecades&decade=1940, http://djindexes.com/mdsidx/index.cfm?event=showavgDecades&decade=1950, accessed on July 30, 2007.

55. "Current Dollar and 'Real' Gross Domestic Product," http://www.bea.gov/national/xls/gdplev.xls, accessed on July 30, 2007.

CHAPTER 16. ARTISTS IN UNIFORM

1. Quoted in Daniel Aaron, *Writers on the Left: Episodes in American Literary Communism* (New York: Harcourt, Brace, and World, 1961), 188.

2. Max Eastman, *Artists in Uniform: A Study of Literature and Bureaucratism* (London: George Allen & Unwin, 1934). Another factor that affected Gold's melodramatic condemnation was that as a past admirer of Eastman, with a long paper trail documenting that admiration, he, more than anyone, needed to distance himself from Eastman in a very public manner lest he should be ridden out of the party as a lackey of Leon Trotsky's American hagiographer.

3. Quoted in Aaron, *Writers on the Left*, 319.

4. Eastman, *Artists in Uniform*, 27.

5. Ibid., 8.

6. Ibid., 8–9.

7. Ibid., 20.

8. Quoted in Eugene Lyons, *The Red Decade: The Stalinist Penetration of America* (New York: Bobbs-Merrill, 1941), 48.

9. Sidney Hook, *Out of Step: An Unquiet Life in the 20th Century* (New York: Harper and Row, 1987), 255.

10. Harvey Klehr, John Earl Haynes, and Kyrill M. Anderson, *The Soviet World of American Communism* (New Haven, CT: Yale University Press, 1998), 72. What constitutes a member is a matter for discussion. Do those with unpaid dues count? How about those not in attendance at meetings and not affiliated with a local club? The party itself relied on varying criteria to define membership at different times. The figure of 88,000 is the largest figure used by Klehr, Haynes, and Anderson for CPUSA membership in 1939. If one were to eliminate from "membership" all those not up to date with dues, the number would be smaller.

11. Daniel Bell, "Marxian Socialism in the United States," in Donald Drew Egbert and Stow Persons, eds., *Socialism and American Life* (Princeton, NJ: Princeton University Press, 1952), 354.

12. Quoted in Donald Drew Egbert, "Socialism and American Art," in Egbert and Persons, eds., *Socialism and American Life*, 710.

13. Howard Fast, *The Naked God: The Writer and the Communist Party* (New York: Praeger, 1957), 142–43.

14. Klehr, Haynes, and Anderson, *The Soviet World of American Communism*, 336–41, 343–44.

15. William O'Neill, *The Great Schism: Stalinism and the American Intellectuals* (New York: Simon and Schuster, 1982), 78; Letter: Bennett A. Cerf to Earl Browder, July 14, 1938 (Earl Browder Papers, Syracuse University).

16. Letter: Bennett A. Cerf to Earl Browder, July 14, 1938 (Earl Browder Papers, Syracuse University).

17. Letter: Earl Browder to [Bennett] A. Cerf, August 10, 1938 (Earl Browder Papers, Syracuse University).

18. Klehr, Haynes, and Anderson, *The Soviet World of American Communism*, 340.

19. Max Eastman, *Love and Revolution: My Journey Through an Epoch* (New York: Random House, 1964), 605; Aaron, *Writers on the Left*, 368–70.

20. Letter: Scott Nearing to Central Executive Committee, December 2, 1929 (Earl Browder Papers, Syracuse University). Attached to this correspondence is an unsigned, untitled, undated memorandum providing caustic commentary on Nearing's resignation. Though Nearing resigned, the party—in a move akin to a dumped boyfriend immaturely claiming that it was *he* who broke off the relationship—held: "The Central Committee of the Communist Party of the U.S.A. decides to drop Scott Nearing from the list of its members." Sounding not unlike characters in a mafia drama, the party executives write: "[Nearing] doesn't know that the proletarian revolutionist serves a cause and does not merely serve time. The active services of the proletarian revolutionist continue until he is either physically or politically incapacitated."

21. Klehr, Haynes, and Anderson, *The Soviet World of American Communism*, 342–45.

22. Edwin Berry Bergum, "Three English Radical Poets," *New Masses*, July 3, 1934, 34.

23. Mike Gold, "Remembering Isadora Duncan," *New Masses*, September 28, 1937, 17.

24. Mike Gold, "Go Left, Young Writers!" *New Masses*, January 1929, 2.

25. Mike Gold, *Jews Without Money* (1930; repr., New York: Carroll and Graf, 2004), 65.

26. Ibid., 37.

27. Ibid., 41.

28. Ibid., 101, 112, 162.

29. Interview of Mike Gold by Mike Folsom, December 16, 1965, 8; Interview of Mike Gold by Mike Folsom, January 6, 1966 (Mike Gold Papers, Labadie Collection, University of Michigan); Mike Gold, "The Miracle of April 4, 1914," in "Plan for Literary History," in unlabeled folder in box 8 (Mike Gold Papers, Labadie Collection, University of Michigan).

30. Gold, "Plan for Literary History." Michael Gold, "Why I Am a Communist," *New Masses*, September 1932, 9.

31. Gold, *Jews Without Money*, 309.

32. Gold, "Plan for Literary History."

33. Ibid.

34. Mike Gold interviewed by Mike Folsom, August 19, 1966, 2 (Mike Gold Papers, Labadie Collection, University of Michigan).

35. Ibid., 1–16 (Mike Gold Papers, Labadie Collection, University of Michigan).

36. Michael Gold, "A Little Bit of the Millenium," *The Liberator*, March 1921, 12–13.

37. Mike Gold, *New Masses*, July 1931, 12 (Mike Gold Papers, Labadie Collection, University of Michigan).

38. Letter: Betty Toth to Mike Gold, February 14, 1952 (Mike Gold Papers, Labadie Collection, University of Michigan); Letter: Dorothy Strasburger to Mike Gold, November 24, 1944 (Mike Gold Papers, Labadie Collection, University of Michigan).

39. Privately, Gold came to the same conclusion that Hawthorne had come to at Brook Farm: blue-collar work, at least for him, didn't leave room for writing, e.g., "manual labor doesn[']t give me much time for anything but sleep and talk.—no writing." Letter: Mike Gold to Upton Sinclair, June 6, 1925 (Mike Gold Papers, Labadie Collection, University of Michigan).

40. Mike Gold, "The Three Whose Hatred Killed Them," *The Masses*, August 1914, 11.

41. Mike Gold, "The Strike," July 1926 (Mike Gold Papers, Labadie Collection, University of Michigan).

42. Mike Gold, "Tom Mooney Walks at Midnight," *New Masses*, January 2, 1934, 19.

43. Letter: John Howard Lawson to Kenneth Payne, September 9, 1971 (Mike Gold Papers, Labadie Collection, University of Michigan); Ronald Radosh and Allis Radosh, *Red Star over Hollywood: The Film Colony's Long Romance with the Left* (San Francisco: Encounter Books, 2005), 27–28.

44. Quoted in Lyons, *The Red Decade*, 134.

45. Federal Bureau of Investigation, "Correlation Summary," February 15, 1956, 137 (Mike Gold Papers, Labadie Collection, University of Michigan).

46. Albert Maltz, "What Shall We Ask of Writers?" *New Masses*, February 12, 1946, 19–22.

47. Letter: Albert Maltz to Kenneth Payne, April 18, 1972 (Mike Gold Papers, Labadie Collection, University of Michigan); Radosh and Radosh, *Red Star over Hollywood*, 123–34.

48. Radosh and Radosh, *Red Star over Hollywood*, 132.

49. Aaron, *Writers on the Left*, 322–33, 93–94. In his last years, Gold said that Upton Sinclair had "left the ranks of the people and joined all those sinister forces and class enemies of the working class." Interview of Mike Gold by Mike Folsom, July 28, 1966, 1 (Mike Gold Papers, Labadie Collection, University of Michigan); Max Eastman, *Love and Revolution*, 265–71, 492–95, 601–3.

50. Mike Gold, "Why I Am a Communist," *New Masses*, September 1932, 9.

51. Quoted in Radosh and Radosh, *Red Star over Hollywood*, 28.

52. Radosh and Radosh, *Red Star over Hollywood*, 135.

53. Richard Gid Powers, *Not Without Honor: The History of American Anticommunism* (New York: Free Press, 1995), 172; Radosh and Radosh, *Red Star over Hollywood*, 93–100.

54. Egbert, "Socialism and American Art," 681.

55. Herbert Romerstein and Eric Breindel, *The Venona Secrets: Exposing Soviet Espionage and America's Traitors* (Washington, DC: Regnery, 2000), 439–40; John

Earl Haynes and Harvey Klehr, *Venona: Decoding Soviet Espionage in America* (New Haven: Yale, 1999), 244–47.

56. Harvey Klehr, John Earl Haynes, and Fridrikh Igorevich Firsov, *The Secret World of American Communism* (New Haven, CT: Yale University Press, 1995), 299–303.

57. Venona #1433-5, New York to Moscow, October 10, 1944; Venona #1506, New York to Moscow, October 23, 1944.

58. Kenneth Campbell, *Moscow's Words, Western Voices* (Washington, DC: Accuracy in Media, 1994), 7–43. For an example of Izzy Stone serving as a propagandist, see I. F. Stone, *The Hidden History of the Korean War* (1952; repr., New York: Monthly Review Press, 1971). Therein, Stone advances the idea that, rather than the universally accepted fact (outside of North Korea) that North Korea invaded South Korea to start the Korean War, the South Koreans actually started the Korean War. "The North Koreans may have been lying. On the other hand the South Koreans may, as alleged, have deliberately provoked the war by three feints across the border" (52). "It is hard to believe the North would launch an attack before it was fully mobilized, and moreover at the very moment when it looked as though a hostile legislature might overthrow Syngman Rhee from within" (66).

59. Haynes and Klehr, *The Venona Secrets*, 236–38; Hook, *Out of Step*, 253–54.

60. Michael Straight, *After Long Silence* (New York: W. W. Norton, 1983), 313–35. In addition to recounting his 1963 confession, which Straight had hid until the London *Daily Mail* outed him in 1981, Straight's disingenuous autobiography devotes a chapter to how efforts to root Communists out of government were in fact a witch hunt. "Gustavo Duran, who was married to my wife's sister, was persecuted by McCarthy until he was almost destroyed," Straight claims (265). But Senator Joseph McCarthy didn't "persecute" Duran. He accused him of being a Communist, which he was. Not only that, but Duran worked for the Russian secret police during the Spanish Civil War. "Did it matter that when Gustavo's daughters went to school, they were accosted by other children who cried: 'There go the daughters of the traitor, Gustavo Duran'?" (270). Well, actually, no. Duran's guilt or innocence as a Communist, and a Communist who worked for the international conspiracy's death squads during their most deadly period, had absolutely nothing to do with Straight's nieces getting teased at school. After selling out his country as a spy for the Soviet Union, Michael Straight spent a substantial part of his career in journalism mocking the idea of Communists infiltrating government. His readers never knew about Straight's conflict of interest until shortly before his death.

61. Campbell, *Moscow's Words, Western Voices*, 74–79.

62. Hook, *Out of Step*, 392–93.

63. Romerstein and Breindel, *The Venona Secrets*, 264–77.

64. M. Stanton Evans, *Blacklisted by History: The Untold Story of Joe McCarthy and His Fight Against America's Enemies* (New York: Crown Forum, 2007), 7, 316–19.

65. Romerstein and Breindel, *The Venona Secrets*, 264–77.

66. Hook, *Out of Step*, 461–89.

67. Quoted in Hook, *Out of Step*, 499.

68. Quoted in Lyons, *The Red Decade*, 87.

69. Klehr, Haynes, and Anderson, *The Soviet World of American Communism*, 31–39.

70. Lyons, *The Red Decade*, 180.

71. Klehr, Haynes, and Anderson, *The Soviet World of American Communism*, 36, 39–40.

72. Aaron, *Writers on the Left*, 387; Albert Maltz, "What Shall We Ask of Writers?" *New Masses*, February 12, 1946, 19.

73. Kenneth Lloyd Billingsley, *Hollywood Party: How Communism Seduced the American Film Industry in the 1930s and 1940s* (Rocklin, CA: Prima Forum, 1998), 76–77.

74. Radosh and Radosh, *Red Star over Hollywood*, 78.

75. Federal Bureau of Investigation, "Correlation Summary," February 15, 1956, 89, 149 (Mike Gold Papers, Labadie Collection, University of Michigan).

76. Mike Gold, "Self Criticism: Harsh Diet That Breeds Strong People and Advances Democracy," *Daily Worker* (Mike Gold Papers, Labadie Collection, University of Michigan).

77. Letter: Joseph Freeman to Mike Gold, September 24, 1939 (Mike Gold Papers, Labadie Collection, University of Michigan). The original misspells "Mediterranean."

78. Klehr, Haynes, and Anderson, *The Soviet World of American Communism*, 71–73.

79. Quoted in Aaron, *Writers on the Left*, 411n 19.

CHAPTER 17. COMMUNISM IS TWENTIETH-CENTURY AMERICANISM

1. Harvey Klehr and John Earl Haynes, *The American Communist Movement: Storming Heaven Itself* (New York: Twayne, 1992), 105; James G. Ryan, *Earl Browder: The Failure of American Communism* (Tuscaloosa: University of Alabama Press, 1997), 13–14.

2. Ryan, *Earl Browder*, 208; Richard Gid Powers, *Not Without Honor: The History of American Anticommunism* (New York: Free Press, 1995), 176–77; Klehr and Haynes, *The American Communist Movement*, 97.

3. Speech: Earl Browder, "The Strike Wave Conspiracy," May 14, 1943 (Earl Browder Papers, Syracuse University). The text of the document is based on the speech of the same name that Browder delivered.

4. Ryan, *Earl Browder*, 210.

5. Ibid., 151.

6. Harvey Klehr, John Earl Haynes, and Fridrikh Igorevich Firsov, *The Secret World of American Communism* (New Haven, CT: Yale University Press, 1995), 153.

7. Ibid., 155–82.

8. Klehr, Haynes, and Anderson, *The Soviet World of American Communism* (New Haven, CT: Yale University Press, 1998), 218–27.

9. *Out of Bondage: The Story of Elizabeth Bentley* (New York: Devin-Adair, 1951), 90. Though Bentley recalls Poyntz's creepy sexual flirtations with a twinge of horror in *Out of Bondage*, the files of Russian intelligence suggests that her *shocked, shocked* reaction may not have been all that she had made it out to be. In the spring of 1945, her Soviet handlers reported to Moscow that a woman code-

named "Irma" had "told us indignantly about [Bentley's] proposal that she become her lover." (Quoted in Allen Weinstein and Alexander Vassiliev, *The Haunted Wood: Soviet Espionage in America—the Stalin Era* [New York: Random House, 1999], 100.) As Bentley's future boyfriend, Jacob Golos, controlled Russian intelligence during Poyntz's death, there may have been more than sexual proclivities that Bentley chose to obscure.

10. Klehr, Haynes, and Firsov, *The Secret World of American Communism*, 144–45.

11. Ibid., 145–46.

12. Ibid., 129–30.

13. Radio interview: National Broadcasting Company with Earl Browder, August 26, 1939, 2 (Earl Browder Papers, Syracuse University). Later indignation by long-time Communists that Whittaker Chambers was not what he claimed is unbelievable when confronted with the party's journals in the early 1930s. Under Chambers's picture, the *New Masses* noted: "Joined revolutionary movement 1925." "To American Writers and Artists," *New Masses*, July 1931, 23.

14. Whittaker Chambers, *Witness* (New York: Random House, 1952), 453.

15. Allen Weinstein, *Perjury: The Hiss-Chambers Case* (New York: Knopf, 1978), 328–31, 346–47; Chambers, *Witness*, 463–71; John Earl Haynes and Harvey Klehr, *Venona: Decoding Soviet Espionage in America* (New Haven, CT: Yale University Press, 1999), 89–92; Weinstein and Vassiliev, *The Haunted Wood*, 47–49; Herbert Romerstein and Eric Breindel, *The Venona Secrets: Exposing Soviet Espionage and America's Traitors* (Washington: Regnery, 2000), 123–26; G. Edward White, *Alger Hiss's Looking Glass Wars: The Covert Life of a Soviet Spy* (New York: Oxford University Press, 2004), 47–50.

16. Haynes and Klehr, *Venona*, 339–82.

17. Ibid., 62–63.

18. Arthur Schlesinger Jr., *The Coming of the New Deal* (Boston: Houghton Mifflin, 1958), 54, 78–80.

19. Weinstein, *Perjury*, 261.

20. Ibid., 361.

21. Weinstein and Vassiliev, *The Haunted Wood*, 10.

22. Mike Gold, "Victory Was in Browder's Voice" (Mike Gold Papers, Labadie Collection, University of Michigan).

23. Whittaker Chambers, *Witness*, 225.

24. Eugene Lyons, *The Red Decade: The Stalinist Penetration of America* (New York: Bobbs Merrill, 1941), 65–66; Ryan, *Earl Browder*, 7–10.

25. Letter: Earl Browder to Ray Ginger, May 5, 1948 (Earl Browder Papers, Syracuse University); Ryan, *Earl Browder*, 8.

26. Ryan, *Earl Browder*, 8.

27. Letter: Earl Browder to Ray Ginger, May 5, 1948 (Earl Browder Papers, Syracuse University); Ryan, *Earl Browder*, 22.

28. Romerstein and Breindel, *The Venona Secrets*, 82–85; Ryan, *Earl Browder*, 19, 30–33. Elizabeth Bentley articulated the view of many on the Browder marriage: "What I did not then know was that Raissa, even as far back as the Revolution, had been a powerful figure in the G.P.U. organization in Russia and that she still worked for it. One of her duties was to keep her husband in line and make

reports on him. Browder had evidently had no choice in his marriage; the powers-that-be in Moscow had issued the orders and he had had to follow them." (*Out of Bondage*, 185.)

29. Klehr, Haynes, and Firsov, *The Secret World of American Communism*, 49–51; Ryan, *Earl Browder*, 30–34.

30. Transcript: Testimony of Earl Browder to Special Committee on Un-American Activities, New York, March 27, 1939, 27 (Earl Browder Papers, Syracuse University).

31. Romerstein and Breindel, *The Venona Secrets*, 80–85.

32. Weinstein and Vassiliev, *The Haunted Wood*, 36.

33. Sidney Hook, *Out of Step: An Unquiet Life in the 20th Century* (New York: Harper and Row, 1987), 166–73.

34. Weinstein and Vassiliev, *The Haunted Wood*, 306.

35. Quoted in Ronald Radosh and Joyce Milton, *The Rosenberg File: Second Edition* (1983; repr., New Haven, CT: Yale University Press, 1997), 63.

36. Radosh and Milton, *The Rosenberg File*, 52.

37. "After losing her job," Radosh and Milton write, "she promptly did two things: filed a complaint with the National Labor Relations Board, which she won, and found a better job that paid twice the salary." Radosh and Milton, *The Rosenberg File*, 49–50.

38. Ibid., 1.

39. Ibid., 53.

40. Ibid., 70.

41. Ibid., 54–56.

42. Weinstein and Vassiliev, *The Haunted Wood*, 216–17.

43. Radosh and Milton, *The Rosenberg File*, xxvii, 72.

44. Weinstein and Vassiliev, *The Haunted Wood*, 221–22.

45. Haynes and Klehr, *Venona*, 303.

46. Radosh and Milton, *The Rosenberg File*, 437.

47. Weinstein and Vassiliev, *The Haunted Wood*, 210, 213.

48. Ibid., 221.

49. Ibid., 212.

50. Radosh and Milton, *The Rosenberg File*, 79–80, 105, 121, 127; Weinstein and Vassiliev, *The Haunted Wood*, 330.

51. Haynes and Klehr, *Venona*, 303, 311–17; Weinstein and Vassiliev, *The Haunted Wood*, 336–37; Romerstein and Breindel, *The Venona Secrets*, 200–5.

52. Romerstein and Breindel, *The Venona Secrets*, 246–47; Haynes and Klehr, *Venona*, 300.

53. Radosh and Milton, *The Rosenberg File*, xxviiii.

54. Quoted in ibid., 284.

55. Ryan, *Earl Browder*, 243.

56. Quoted in Klehr, Haynes, and Anderson, *The Soviet World of American Communism*, 106.

57. Letter: Frank Collier to Earl Browder, March 8, 1946; Letter: R. E. Goforth to Earl Browder, March 4, 1946 (Earl Browder Papers, Syracuse University).

58. Quoted in Klehr, Haynes, and Anderson, *The Soviet World of American Communism*, 99.

59. "The Fifth Column Role of the Trotskyites in the United States" (Earl Browder Papers, Syracuse University).

60. Joseph R. Starobin, *American Communism in Crisis, 1943–1957* (Cambridge, MA: Harvard University Press, 1972), 196, 241n, 242n.

61. Weinstein and Vassiliev, *The Haunted Wood*, 140–50.

62. Kenneth Lloyd Billingsley, *Hollywood Party: How Communism Seduced the American Film Industry in the 1930s and 1940s* (Rocklin, CA: Prima Forum, 1998), 93; "Hollywood Ignores Real Blacklist," *The AIM Report*, December-B 1997.

63. Billingsley, *Hollywood Party*, 94.

64. Klehr, Haynes, and Anderson, *The Soviet World of American Communism*, 353; Irwin Unger, *The Movement: A History of the American New Left, 1959–1972* (New York: Harper and Row, 1974), 9.

65. Earl Browder, "Browder Calls His Ouster 'Best Thing Ever Happened,'" *Washington Evening Star*, January 12, 1954, 3 (Earl Browder Papers, Syracuse University).

66. "I wish to again raise the question of restoring my membership in the CPUSA," began a Browder letter to a CPUSA official in 1948. Earl Browder to Alexander Trachtenberg, July 6, 1948 (Earl Browder Papers, Syracuse University).

67. Telegram: Gerald L. K. Smith to Earl Browder, March 2, 1946. Smith wrote to Browder via Western Union: "IF YOU WILL EXPOSE THE TREASONABLE TIEUP BETWEEN THE AMERICAN COMMUNIST PARTY AND THE STALIN GOVERNMENT IN MOSCOW I WILL BOOK YOU FOR A NATIONWIDE SPEAKING TOUR, PAY YOU GOOD SALARY AND EXPENSES." Alfred Kohlberg, whose alarm at Communist advances in China led him to publish *Plain Talk*, made a similar offer. Henry Regnery, the Chicago bookman who gained fame by publishing Russell Kirk, William F. Buckley, and other conservative intellectuals, even considered a book proposal by Browder. Letter: Henry Regnery to Earl Browder, December 20, 1954 (Earl Browder Papers, Syracuse University).

68. Starobin, *American Communism in Crisis, 1943–1957*, 54, 92, 115. Browder insiders Elizabeth Gurley Flynn and Bob Minor, who devotedly wrote to Browder weekly during his imprisonment on passport fraud, turned on him. Former brother-in-law Harrison George got tossed from the party. Other, lower-profile incidents of betrayal or excommunication marked the period.

69. Federal Bureau of Investigation, "Correlation Summary," February 15, 1956, 262 (Mike Gold Papers, Labadie Collection, University of Michigan).

70. Letter: Michael Gold to Deitz Verlag, May 22, 1952 (Mike Gold Papers, Labadie Collection, University of Michigan); Letter: Betty Toth to Mike Gold, August 21, 1952 (Mike Gold Papers, Labadie Collection, University of Michigan); Letter: Betty Toth to Mike Gold, May 5, 1953 (Mike Gold Papers, Labadie Collection, University of Michigan).

71. Earl Browder, "Position of Earl Browder Stated," *New York Times*, January 8, 1954, 20 (Earl Browder Papers, Syracuse University).

72. Ryan, *Earl Browder*, 273.

73. "Remarks," *Woodhull & Claflin's Weekly*, May 4, 1872, 4.

CHAPTER 18. APOGEE

1. Allen Matusow, *The Unraveling of America: A History of Liberalism in the 1960s* (New York: Harper and Row, 1984), 4.

2. Richard Pells, *The Liberal Mind in a Conservative Age: American Intellectuals in the 1940s and 1950s* (New York: Harper and Row, 1985), ix.

3. Richard Hofstadter, *Anti-Intellectualism in American Life* (1962; repr., London: Jonathan Cape, 1964), 8, 138, 140.

4. T. W. Adorno, Else Frenkel-Brunswik, Daniel J. Levinson, and R. Nevitt Sanford, *The Authoritarian Personality* (New York: Harper and Brothers, 1950), 147, 720, 722.

5. Ibid., 254. The statement that served to indicate conservatism, and then authoritarianism, read: "The businessman and the manufacturer are much more important to society than the artist and the professor." Might an affirmation of this indicate neither conservatism nor authoritarianism, but common sense?

6. Ibid., 656.

7. C. Wright Mills, *The Power Elite* (1956; repr., New York: Oxford University Press, 1968), 304.

8. David Riesman, *The Lonely Crowd: A Study of the Changing American Character* (1950; repr., New Haven, CT: Yale University Press, 1955), 371, 373.

9. Paul Goodman, *Growing Up Absurd* (New York: Vintage Books, 1960), 28.

10. Quoted in David Halberstam, *The Fifties* (New York: Villard Books, 1993), 140.

11. William H. Whyte Jr., *The Organization Man* (New York: Simon and Schuster, 1956), 300.

12. Halberstam, *The Fifties*, 134.

13. Whyte, *The Organization Man*, 5.

14. Mills, *The Power Elite*, 105, 115, 349.

15. Goodman, *Growing Up Absurd*, 109.

16. Hofstadter, *Anti-Intellectualism in American Life*, 4, 222.

17. Ibid., 256–57.

18. Ibid., 257, 263.

19. Mills, *The Power Elite*, 130, 353–54.

20. Goodman, *Growing Up Absurd*, 164.

21. Ibid., 200.

22. Norman O. Brown, *Life Against Death: The Psychoanalytical Meaning of History* (Middletown, CT: Wesleyan University Press, 1959), ix.

23. Herbert Marcuse, *Eros and Civilization: A Philosophical Inquiry Into Freud* (1955; repr., Boston: Beacon Press, 1966), 246.

24. Brown, *Life Against Death*, 8.

25. Marcuse, *Eros and Civilization*, 45.

26. Ibid., 151–53.

27. Brown, *Life Against Death*, 34–35, 53, 318.

28. Ibid., 34–35.

29. Ibid., 270.

30. Marcuse, *Eros and Civilization*, 201.

31. Quoted in Myron Sharaf, *Fury on Earth: A Biography of Wilhelm Reich* (New York: St. Martin's Press, 1983), 56.

32. Sharaf, *Fury on Earth*, 60–61, 84, 192–93, 245–46, 336, 339, 404.

33. Ibid., 24, 229, 235, 239–40, 244.

34. Ibid., 279, 302–9.

35. Quoted in ibid., 370.

36. Sharaf, *Fury on Earth*, 413, 455 (quote therein).

37. Quoted in ibid., 3.

38. James H. Jones, *Alfred C. Kinsey: A Public/Private Life* (New York: W. W. Norton, 1997), 488–94, 499–500, 603–14.

39. Ibid., 82, 610, 739.

40. Alfred Kinsey, Wardell Pomeroy, and Clyde Martin, *Sexual Behavior in the Human Male* (Philadelphia: W. B. Saunders, 1948), 550, 589, 623, 670.

41. A. C. Kinsey, W. B. Pomeroy, C. E. Martin, and H. Gebhard, *Sexual Behavior in the Human Female* (Philadelphia: W. B. Saunders, 1953), 286, 416, 474–75.

42. Judith Reisman, *Kinsey: Crimes and Consequences* (Arlington, VA: Institute for Media Education, 1998), 94; Kinsey et al., *Sexual Behavior in the Human Female*, 21–22; Judith Reisman and Edward Eichel, *Kinsey, Sex and Fraud: The Indoctrination of a People* (Lafayette, LA: Huntington House, 1990), 22.

43. Jones, *Alfred C. Kinsey*, 387; Jonathan Gathorne-Hardy, *Sex the Measure of All Things: A Life of Alfred C. Kinsey* (1998; repr., Bloomington: Indiana University Press, 2000), 239.

44. Gathorne-Hardy, *Sex the Measure of All Things*, 130.

45. Alfred Kinsey, Pomeroy, and Martin, *Sexual Behavior in the Human Male*, 161.

46. Gathorne-Hardy, *Sex the Measure of All Things*, 377.

47. Kinsey, et al., *Sexual Behavior in the Human Female*, 327.

48. Jones, *Alfred C. Kinsey*, 738–41; Gathorne-Hardy, *Sex the Measure of All Things*, 413–15.

49. Letter: John Reed to Louise Bryant, July 4, 1917 (John Reed Collection, Harvard University, Houghton Library); Letter: John Reed to Louise Bryant, February 10, 1916 (John Reed Collection, Harvard University, Houghton Library).

50. In the Senate, 21 Democrats and 6 Republicans opposed the bill. Voting for the bill in the House were 153 Democrats and 136 Republicans, and voting against were 91 Democrats and 35 Republicans. "Final House Action on Civil Rights Bill Scheduled," *Congressional Quarterly Weekly Report*, June 26, 1964, 1273; "Civil Rights Act of 1964 Signed Into Law," *Congressional Quarterly Weekly Report*, July 3, 1964, 1331.

51. Speech: Martin Luther King Jr., Washington, DC, August 28, 1963.

52. Norman Mailer, "The White Negro," in Harold Jaffe and John Tytell, eds., *The American Experience: A Radical Reader* (New York: Harper & Row, 1970), 8–27.

53. "The Source," produced by Hiro Yamagata (Beat Productions, 1999).

54. Halberstam, *The Fifties*, 299.

55. Quoted in Norman Podhoretz, *Ex-Friends: Falling Out with Allen Ginsberg, Lionel*

and Diana Trilling, Lillian Hellman, Hannah Arendt, and Norman Mailer (New York: Free Press, 1999), 48.

CHAPTER 19. THE STUDENT LEFT

1. "The Port Huron Statement of the Students for a Democratic Society," June 11–15, 1962, Port Huron, Michigan.
2. Interview of Al Haber by author, Ann Arbor, Michigan, February 13, 2007.
3. Interview of Steve Max by author (phone), April 16, 2007.
4. Kirkpatrick Sale, *SDS* (1973; repr., New York: Vintage Books, 1974), 673–84.
5. Interview of Al Haber by author, Ann Arbor, Michigan, February 13, 2007.
6. Tom Hayden, *Reunion: A Memoir* (New York: Random House, 1988), 30, 29.
7. Interview of Todd Gitlin by author, New York, New York, June 7, 2007.
8. Sale, *SDS*, 69.
9. "The Port Huron Statement of the Students for a Democratic Society."
10. Maurice Isserman, *The Other American: The Life of Michael Harrington* (New York; Public Affairs, 2000), 121–24.
11. Hayden, *Reunion*, 91. In 1961, Hayden cited Michael Harrington as one of three people over thirty (the others being Norman Thomas and C. Wright Mills) whom his generation respected. Isserman, *The Other American*, 226.
12. Interview of Richard Flacks by author (phone), March 18, 2007; Irwin Unger, *The Movement: A History of the American New Left, 1959–1972* (New York: Harper and Row, 1974), 56; Sale, *SDS*, 67–68; Hayden, *Reunion*, 90–91; Todd Gitlin, *The Sixties: Years of Hope, Days of Rage* (New York: Bantam, 1987), 113–20; Isserman, *The Other American*, 122–24.
13. Hayden, *Reunion*, 92.
14. David Horowitz, *Radical Son: A Generational Odyssey* (New York: Free Press, 1997), 106.
15. Interview of Al Haber by author, Ann Arbor, Michigan, February 13, 2007.
16. Interview of Richard Flacks by author (phone), March 18, 2007.
17. Interview of Steve Max by author (phone), April 16, 2007.
18. Hayden, *Reunion*, 5, 8–9, 52, 475–76.
19. C. Wright Mills, "Letter to the New Left," in Priscilla Long, ed., *The New Left: A Collection of Essays* (Boston: Porter Sergeant Publisher, 1970), 22.
20. Hayden, *Reunion*, 67–72 (quote therein).
21. *Berkeley in the Sixties* (film), Mark Kitchell, producer (Kitchell Films, 1990).
22. Ibid.
23. Ibid.
24. Quoted in Hugh Pearson, *The Shadow of the Panther: Huey Newton and the Price of Black Power in America* (Reading, MA: Addison-Wesley, 1994), 73.
25. *Berkeley in the Sixties*.
26. David Lance Goines, *The Free Speech Movement: Coming of Age in the 1960s* (Berkeley, CA: Ten Speed Press, 1993), 480–508.
27. Interview of Tom Hayden by author (e-mail), May 3, 2007.

28. Interview of Todd Gitlin by author, New York, New York, June 7, 2007.

29. Hayden, *Reunion*, 128.

30. Interview of Richard Flacks by author (phone), March 18, 2007. Though Flacks criticized several aspects of ERAP, he, like other SDS leaders I spoke to, points to positives as well, including the transformation of everyday people living in underclass communities into leaders.

31. Sale, *SDS*, 142.

32. Ibid., 144.

33. Hayden, *Reunion*, 76.

34. Michael Harrington, *Fragments of the Century: A Social Autobiography* (New York: Saturday Review Press, 1973), 149.

35. Interview of Al Haber by author, Ann Arbor, Michigan, February 13, 2007.

36. Gitlin, *The Sixties*, 112; Sale, *SDS*, 54; "The Port Huron Statement of the Students for a Democratic Society."

37. Unger, *The Movement*, 88.

38. Quoted in Phillip Abbott Luce, *The New Left Today: America's Trojan Horse* (Washington, DC: Capitol Hill Press, 1972), 145.

39. Ibid., 108–9.

CHAPTER 20. THE PATERNALIST DYNASTY IV: GREAT SOCIETY VISIONARIES

1. Michael Harrington, *The Other America: Poverty in the United States* (1962; repr., New York: Pelican Books, 1983), 5.

2. Ibid., 2, 5.

3. Michael Harrington, *Fragments of the Century: A Social Autobiography* (New York: Saturday Review Press, 1973), 41.

4. Ibid., 25.

5. Ibid., 92; Maurice Isserman, *The Other American: The Life of Michael Harrington* (New York; Public Affairs, 2000), 196.

6. Harrington, *The Other America*, 12.

7. Ibid., 62.

8. Ibid., 125, 163, 181.

9. Doris Kearns, *Lyndon Johnson and the American Dream* (New York: Harper & Row, 1976), 23, 30–31, 35–36, 84, 92.

10. Quoted in ibid., 178.

11. Speech: Lyndon Johnson, "State of the Union Address," January 8, 1964.

12. Harrington, *Fragments of the Century*, 175–76.

13. Irwin Unger, *The Best of Intentions: The Triumph and Failure of the Great Society Under Kennedy, Johnson, and Nixon* (New York: Doubleday, 1996), 81.

14. Allen J. Matusow, *The Unraveling of America: A History of Liberalism in the 1960s* (New York: Harper and Row, 1984), 238–39.

15. Unger, *The Best of Intentions*, 94, 178.

16. Quoted in ibid., 196.

17. Unger, *The Best of Intentions*, 156.

18. Matusow, *The Unraveling of America*, 248.

19. Ibid., 261–62.

20. Ibid., 259.

21. Hugh Pearson, *The Shadow of the Panther: Huey Newton and the Price of Black Power in America* (Reading, MA: Addison-Wesley, 1994), 107–9, 112–13; Bill Ayers, *Fugitive Days: A Memoir* (Boston: Beacon Press, 2001), 91–98, 119–20; Unger, *The Best of Intentions*, 158, 191–93; Kirkpatrick Sale, *SDS* (1973; repr., New York: Vintage Books, 1974), 146–47.

22. Unger, *The Best of Intentions*, 272.

23. Lyndon Baines Johnson, *The Vantage Point: Perspectives of the Presidency, 1963–1969* (New York: Holt, Rinehart, and Winston, 1971), 345.

24. Unger, *The Best of Intentions*, 104–5.

25. Quoted in Johnson, *The Vantage Point*, 213.

26. Matusow, *The Unraveling of America*, 229.

27. Unger, *The Best of Intentions*, 361–62; Matusow, *The Unraveling of America*, 230–31.

28. Johnson, *The Vantage Point*, 219.

29. John A. Andrew III, *Lyndon Johnson and the Great Society* (Chicago: Ivan R. Dee, 1998), 130.

30. *Digest of Education Statistics—2006* (Washington, DC: National Center for Education Statistics, 2007), "Table 227," http://nces.ed.gov/programs/digest/d06/tables/dt06_227.asp?referrer=list, accessed on July 31, 2007; *Digest of Education Statistics—2006* (Washington, DC: National Center for Education Statistics, 2007), "Table 228," http://nces.ed.gov/programs/digest/d06/tables/dt06_228.asp?referrer=report, accessed on July 31, 2007.

31. *Digest of Education Statistics—2006* (Washington, DC: National Center for Education Statistics, 2007), "Table 319," http://nces.ed.gov/programs/digest/d06/tables/dt06_319.asp?referrer=list, accessed on July 31, 2007.

32. Dinesh D'Souza, *The End of Racism: Principles for a Multiracial Society* (New York: Free Press, 1995), 217.

33. Unger, *The Best of Intentions*, 303–4.

34. Quoted in ibid., 259.

35. Quoted in. M. E. Bradford, *Remembering Who We Are: Observations of a Southern Conservative* (Athens: University of Georgia Press, 1985), 105.

36. Quoted in Unger, *The Best of Intentions*, 89.

37. Quoted in Kearns, *Lyndon Johnson and the American Dream*, 252.

38. Kearns, *Lyndon Johnson and the American Dream*, 54.

39. Michael Harrington, *Toward a Democratic Left: A Radical Program for a New Majority* (New York: Macmillan, 1968), 82.

40. Quoted in Kearns, *Lyndon Johnson and the American Dream*, 340.

CHAPTER 21. MEET THE NEW LEFT, SAME AS THE OLD LEFT

1. Interview of Carl Oglesby by author, Amherst, Massachusetts, June 1, 2007.

2. United States Department of Justice, Federal Bureau of Investigation, File #100-33032, "Carl Preston Oglesby, Jr.," 6 (Carl Oglesby Papers, Du Bois Library, University Massachusetts, Amherst).

3. Interview: Robert Morrison of Carl Oglesby, August 30, 1985 (Carl Oglesby Papers, Du Bois Library, University Massachusetts, Amherst).

4. Adam Garfinkle, *Telltale Hearts: The Origins and Impact of the Vietnam Antiwar Movement* (New York: St. Martin's Press, 1995), 61.

5. Interview of Carl Oglesby by author, Amherst, Massachusetts, June 1, 2007. Interview of Todd Gitlin by author, New York, New York, June 7, 2007. David Dellinger, *From Yale to Jail: The Life Story of a Moral Dissenter* (New York: Pantheon Books, 1993), 201, 209, 313.

6. Kirkpatrick Sale, *SDS* (1973; repr., New York: Vintage Books, 1974), 184.

7. Ibid., 177–81, 237–39.

8. United States Department of Justice, Federal Bureau of Investigation, File #100-33032, "Carl Preston Oglesby, Jr.," 43 (Carl Oglesby Papers, Du Bois Library, University Massachusetts, Amherst).

9. Speech: Carl Oglesby, "Liberalism and the Corporate State," Washington, DC, November 27, 1965 (Carl Oglesby Papers, Du Bois Library, University Massachusetts, Amherst).

10. Interview of Carl Oglesby by author, Amherst, Massachusetts, June 1, 2007.

11. Staughton Lynd and Tom Hayden, *The Other Side* (New York: New American Library, 1966), 13.

12. Ibid., 65, 67, 171, 200, 212, 227.

13. Ibid., 194.

14. Ibid., 188.

15. Ibid., 191–92.

16. Interview of Carl Oglesby by author, Amherst, Massachusetts, June 1, 2007.

17. Norman Mailer, *The Armies of the Night* (New York: New American Library, 1968), 139.

18. Mike Goldfield, "Power at the Pentagon," *New Left Notes*, October 30, 1967, 1–2 (Tamiment Library, New York University).

19. Mailer, *The Armies of the Night*, 117.

20. Quoted in Terry H. Anderson, *The Movement and the Sixties: Protest in America from Greensboro to Wounded Knee* (New York: Oxford University Press, 1995), 202.

21. Quoted in Garfinkle, *Telltale Hearts*, 91.

22. "Vietnam Summer," *New Left Notes*, June 26, 1967, 6–8 (Tamiment Library, New York University).

23. David Hilliard and Lewis Cole, *This Side of Glory: The Autobiography of David Hilliard and the Story of the Black Panther Party* (Boston: Back Bay Books, 1993), 265.

24. Dellinger, *From Yale to Jail*, 61, 73, 123, 126, 157.

25. Ibid., 48, 461.

26. Garfinkle, *Telltale Hearts*, 51, 73, 79, 171, 176.

27. Michael Harrington, *Fragments of the Century: A Social Autobiography* (New York: Saturday Review Press, 1973), 220–21.

28. Garfinkle, *Telltale Hearts*, 266.

29. Phillip Abbott Luce, *The New Left Today: America's Trojan Horse* (1971; repr., Washington, DC: Capitol Hill Press, 1972), 93.

30. Kenneth J. Heineman, *Put Your Bodies Upon the Wheels: Student Revolt in the 1960s* (Chicago: Ivan R. Dee, December, 2001), 113; *Berkeley in the Sixties* (film), Mark Kitchell, producer (Kitchell Films, 1990).

31. Motor City SDS, "Break on Through to the Other Side," in Harold Jacobs, *Weatherman* (San Francisco: Ramparts Press, 1970), 152–53.

32. Quoted in Heineman, *Put Your Bodies upon the Wheels*, 114.

33. Quoted in ibid., 157.

34. Quoted in "Stormy Weather," in Jacobs, *Weatherman*, 344.

35. Mike Gold, "Autobiography," draft, November 3, 1965 (Mike Gold Papers, Labadie Collection, University of Michigan).

36. Robert Greenfield, *Timothy Leary: A Biography* (New York: Harcourt, 2006), 128–30 (quotes therein).

37. Ibid., 142, 146, 155, 156.

38. Ibid., 194–99.

39. Ibid., 189–91, 204–6, 207–8.

40. Irwin Unger, *The Movement: A History of the American New Left 1959–1972* (New York: Harper & Row, 1974), 135; Greenfield, *Timothy Leary*, 270, 280–81.

41. Tom Wolfe, *The Electric Kool-Aid Acid Test* (New York: Bantam Books, 1969), 72.

42. Ibid., 22, 93.

43. Greenfield, *Timothy Leary*, 220–23.

44. Tom Hayden, *Reunion: A Memoir* (New York: Random House, 1988), 203.

45. Interview of Steve Max by author (phone), April 16, 2007.

46. Hilary Putnam, "From 'Resistance' to Student-Worker Alliance," in Priscilla Long, ed., *The New Left: A Collection of Essays* (Boston: Porter Sargent, 1970), 324.

47. Rick Margolies, "On Community Building," in Long, ed., *The New Left*, 364.

48. Greenfield, *Timothy Leary*, 338–39.

49. Quoted in Heineman, *Put Your Bodies Upon the Wheels*, 142.

50. Evelyn Goldfield, Sue Munaker, and Naomi Weisstein, "A Woman Is a Sometime Thing, or Cornering Capitalism by Removing 51% of Its Commodities," in Long, ed., *The New Left*, 254.

51. Interview of Mark Rudd by author (phone), April 17, 2007.

52. Mark Rudd, "Reply to Uncle Grayson," *Up Against the Wall*, April 22, 1968, 1–2 (Tamiment Library, New York University).

53. Quoted in Unger, *The Movement*, 108.

54. Quoted in Heineman, *Put Your Bodies Upon the Wheels*, 140.

55. Heineman, *Put Your Bodies Upon the Wheels*, 11.

56. "Columbia at Bay," *Newsweek*, May 6, 1968, 40.

57. Unger, *The Movement*, 113.

58. "Primary Survey of Damages," *New Left Notes*, May 27, 1968, 2 (Tamiment Library, New York University); Jon Moore, "The Bust Comes," *The Rat*, May 3–16, 1968, 10 (Tamiment Library, New York University).

59. "Lifting a Siege—and Rethinking a Future," *Time*, May 10, 1968, 77–78.

60. Bill Ayers, Jim Mellen, and Terry Robbins, "Ann Arbor SDS Splits," *New Left Notes*, November 11, 1968, 3 (Tamiment Library, New York University).

61. Interview of Mark Rudd by author (phone), April 17, 2007.

62. Quoted in Sale, *SDS*, 475.

63. Mike Spiegal, "Counter-Convention Conference," *New Left Notes*, April 8, 1968, 3 (Tamiment Library, New York University).

64. Quoted in David Horowitz, *Radical Son: A Generational Odyssey* (New York: Free Press, 1997), 166–67.

65. Interview of Mike Klonsky by author (phone), June 4, 2007.

66. Bill Ayers, *Fugitive Days: A Memoir* (Boston: Beacon Press, 2001), 122.

67. Quoted in Dellinger, *From Yale to Jail*, 333; Todd Gitlin, *The Sixties: Years of Hope, Days of Rage* (New York: Bantam, 1987), 332; Horowitz, *Radical Son*, 167. Though chroniclers that I have encountered are unanimous regarding the verbiage of Hayden's speech, Hayden insists that he was misquoted. He maintains that the crucial modifier "our" has been omitted before the word "blood," transforming words of sacrifice to words exhorting violence. He explained to me, "I was saying that if they shed our blood, which I thought was inevitable, it should be shed for all to see in front of the Hilton that night." Interview of Tom Hayden by author (e-mail), May 3, 2007.

68. Susan Braudy, *Family Circle: The Boudins and the Aristocracy of the Left* (New York: Knopf, 2003), 167; Ayers, *Fugitive Days*, 132.

69. Quoted in Thai Jones, *A Radical Line: From the Labor Movement to the Weather Underground, One Family's Century of Conscience* (New York: Free Press, 2002), 191.

70. Ayers, *Fugitive Days*, 129–30.

71. Hayden, *Reunion*, 324.

72. *New Left Notes*, October 25, 1968, 12 (Tamiment Library, New York University).

73. Eldridge Cleaver, "Panther Call," *The Rat*, November 1–14, 1968, 7 (Tamiment Library, New York University).

74. Abbie Hoffman, Jerry Rubin, and Stu Albert, "Yippie Call," *The Rat*, November 1–14, 1968, 7 (Tamiment Library, New York University).

75. Julius Lester, "The Immorality of Peace," *New Left Notes*, September 4, 1967, 3 (Tamiment Library, New York University).

76. Thomas Powers, *Diana: The Making of a Terrorist* (Boston: Houghton Mifflin, 1971), 10–13, 22.

77. Ibid., 84.

78. Quoted in ibid., 142.

79. Quoted in ibid., 161.

80. Powers, *Diana*, 66.

81. Ibid., 68–70.

82. Braudy, *Family Circle*, 156; Ayers, *Fugitive Days*, 111.

83. Karin Ashley, Bill Ayers, Bernardine Dohrn, et al., "You Don't Need a Weatherman to Know Which Way the Wind Blows," in Harold Jacobs (ed.), *Weatherman*, 51–90.

84. Interview of Mike Klonsky by author (phone), June 4, 2007.

85. Quoted in Maurice Isserman and Michael Kazin, *America Divided: The Civil War of the 1960s* (New York: Oxford University Press, 2000), 227.

86. Greg Calvert, "The Calculus of Improbabilities," *New Left Notes*, October 7, 1966, 1 (Tamiment Library, New York University).

87. Hugh Pearson, *The Shadow of the Panther: Huey Newton and the Price of Black Power in America* (Reading, MA: Addison-Wesley, 1994), 46, 68–69.

88. David Hilliard and Lewis Cole, *This Side of Glory: The Autobiography of David Hilliard and the Story of the Black Panther Party* (Boston: Little Brown, 1993), 109.

89. Author discussion with Bobby Seale during Q&A of Seale speech in Washington, DC, April 19, 2002.

90. Pearson, *The Shadow of the Panther*, 47.

91. Hilliard and Cole, *This Side of Glory*, 123; Pearson, *The Shadow of the Panther*, 108, 112–13.

92. Black Panther Party, "The Ten Point Plan," www.blackpanther.org/TenPoint .htm, accessed on June 15, 2007.

93. Quoted in Pearson, *The Shadow of the Panther*, 125.

94. Pearson, *The Shadow of the Panther*, 125.

95. Eldridge Cleaver, *Soul on Ice* (New York: Delta, 1968), 14.

96. Ibid., 18.

97. Pearson, *The Shadow of the Panther*, 145–47, 221.

98. Quoted in Hilliard and Cole, *This Side of Glory*, 183.

99. Hilliard and Cole, *This Side of Glory*, 182–93.

100. Thai Jones, *A Radical Line: From the Labor Movement to the Weather Underground, One Family's Century of Conscience* (New York: Free Press, 2004), 222–24; Greenfield, *Timothy Leary*, 383–92.

101. Bernardine Dohrn, "Communique # 4 from the Weatherman Underground," in Jacobs, ed., *Weatherman*, 516.

102. Timothy Leary, "Letter from Timothy Leary," in Jacobs, ed., *Weatherman*, 517–19.

103. Greenfield, *Timothy Leary*, 404–5; Eldridge Cleaver, "An Open Letter in Answer to Many Inquiries About the Revolutionary Bust of Tim and Rosemary Leary and in Answer to the Punkassed Sniveling from Motherfuckers Who Know Me Better Than That," *The East Village Other*, March 2, 1970, 2 (Tamiment Library, New York University).

104. Greenfield, *Timothy Leary*, 404–5. Greenfield quotes Cleaver on the murder of Robert Smith Jr., who allegedly engaged in adultery with Cleaver's wife: "What do you want me to tell you? Is it true? What is true is that there is no statute of limitations on murder. And beyond that, this purported incident did not take place within the jurisdiction of the United States of America and I do not think the Algerian government is going to try to indict me for this rumor. That information cannot be introduced into any judicial proceeding in the United States. As such, my response to it is that this man, along with others who came through Algeria, went underground."

Now people say, 'That's a double entendre. What do you mean by "He went under-ground?" 'I mean, "He went underground." ' Where is he? He's underground."

105. Quoted in Greenfield, *Timothy Leary*, 419.

106. Ashley, et al., "You Don't Need a Weatherman to Know Which Way the Wind Blows."

107. Quoted in Unger, *The Movement*, 138.

108. Sale, *SDS*, 602; Hilliard and Cole, *This Side of Glory*, 257–58; Jones, *A Radical Line*, 204–5.

109. Edward Jay Epstein, "The Panthers and the Police: A Pattern of Genocide?" *New Yorker*, February 13, 1971, 45–77.

110. Horowitz, *Radical Son*, 296; "Black Murder Inc.," *Heterodoxy,* March 1993, 1.

111. Quoted in Luce, *The New Left Today*, 154.

112. Interview of Tom Hayden by author (e-mail), May 3, 2007.

113. Sale, *SDS*, 580n.

114. Jim Mellen and Bill Ayers, "Hot Town: Summer in the City" in Jacobs, ed., *Weather-man*, 29–38; REP Staff, "There's a Man Going 'Round Taking Names," *New Left Notes*, February 28, 1969, 3 (Tamiment Library, New York University); Ashley, et al., "You Don't Need a Weatherman to Know Which Way the Wind Blows."

115. Quoted in Ayers, *Fugitive Days*, 168.

116. Mark Rudd, "Reply to Uncle Grayson," *Up Against the Wall*, April 22, 1968, 1–2 (Tamiment Library, New York University).

117. Interview of Tom Hayden by author (e-mail), May 3, 2007.

118. Interview of Mark Rudd by author (phone), April 17, 2007.

119. Ayers, *Fugitive Days*, 165.

120. Ibid., 166.

121. *The Weather Underground* (film), Sam Green, Bill Siegal, Connie Lozano, Marc Smolowitz, producers (The Free History Project, 2002).

122. *New Left Notes*, October 21, 1969, 2–3 (Tamiment Library, New York University); "Lay, Elrod, Lay," in Jacobs, ed., *Weatherman*, 345–53; Heineman, *Put Your Bod-ies upon the Wheels*, 159.

123. Ayers, *Fugitive Days*, 22–23; Powers, *Diana*, 60, 161.

124. Braudy, *Family Circle*, 78.

125. Quoted in David A. Shannon, *The Socialist Party of America: A History* (New York: Macmillan, 1955), 148.

126. Braudy, *Family Circle*, xiv, 10, 30, 91.

127. Jones, *A Radical Line*, 69–89, 126–27.

128. Interview by author of Mark Rudd (phone), April 17, 2007.

129. Interview of Richard Flacks by author (phone), March 18, 2007.

130. Interview of Carl Oglesby by author, Amherst, Massachusetts, June 1, 2007; Gitlin, *The Sixties*, 381.

131. Interview of Todd Gitlin by author, New York, June 7, 2007.

132. Powers, *Diana*, 144.

133. Ayers, *Fugitive Days*, 71.

134. Peter Collier and David Horowitz, *Destructive Generation: Second Thoughts About the Sixties* (New York: Touchstone, 1990), 84–85; Gitlin, *The Sixties*, 399–400.

135. Interview of Mike Klonsky by author (phone), June 4, 2007.

136. Quoted in Hayden, *Reunion*, 360.

137. Interview of Mark Rudd by author (phone), April 17, 2007.

138. Armando, "Wither Weatherman," *Berkeley Tribe*, January 9–15, 1970, 5 (Tamiment Library, New York University); Sale, *SDS*, 628; Braudy, *Family Circle*, 191 (quote therein). Like the Manson Family, the Weathermen got stoned, enjoyed orgies, lived communally, preached left-wing politics, and prophesied a race war in which they would join the side of people of color. Whereas the Weathermen adopted their name from Bob Dylan's "Subterranean Homesick Blues," the Manson Family looked to The Beatles' "white album" for guidance. Both groups were committed to violence against "pigs." Rather than a drug-induced lapse in logic, the Weatherman cult's support for the Manson cult made sense to anyone paying attention to the rhetoric and folkways of sixties extremists.

139. "Bombing: A Way of Protest and Death," *Time*, March 23, 1970, 9.

140. Sale, *SDS*, 4–5; *The Weather Underground* (film).

141. Interview of Mark Rudd by author (phone), April 17, 2007.

142. Interview of Carl Oglesby by author, Amherst, Massachusetts, June 1, 2007.

143. Interview of Al Haber by author, Ann Arbor, Michigan, February 13, 2007.

144. Irwin Granich, "The Three Whose Hatred Killed Them," *The Masses*, August 1914, 11; "How Does It Feel to Be Inside an Explosion . . . ," in Jacobs, ed., *Weatherman*, 504–8. Mike Gold's birth name was Irwin Granich, which he changed after avoiding conscription by fleeing to Mexico during World War I.

145. Ayers, *Fugitive Days*, 273.

146. Harrington, *Fragments of the Century*, 163.

147. Quoted in "Memories of Diana," *Time*, March 30, 1970, 21.

CHAPTER 22. THE PERSONAL IS THE POLITICAL

1. Bob Eliot, "Welfare: Happiest Hustle," *The Rat*, January 17–23, 1969, 10 (Tamiment Library, New York University).

2. National Welfare Rights Organization, "NWRO's Guaranteed Adequate Income Plan," (Washington, DC: NWRO, undated), 1–8 (Tamiment Library, New York University). My guess, from textual references therein, is that NWRO published this pamphlet in 1969.

3. Vincent Bugliosi with Curt Gentry, *Helter Skelter: The True Story of the Manson Murders* (New York: W. W. Norton, 1974), 221–22; Kirkpatrick Sale, *SDS* (1973; repr., New York: Vintage Books, 1974), 626–28; Todd Gitlin, *The Sixties: Years of Hope, Days of Rage* (New York: Bantam, 1987), 404–5.

4. Two months after her arrest for attempting to assassinate President Gerald Ford, Lynnette "Squeaky" Fromme related that she had approached the president with a loaded gun "specifically to draw attention to the problems of the world that directly affect my state of mind and my physical body and to offer a way to clean up the world. . . . I feel that symbolically I am the earth." "November 10," www.squeakyfromme.org/nov10.htm, accessed on May 7, 2007. "It was

my intention to be a voice for the Earth," Fromme later iterated, "to say that before all political ways of life, before class and race and gender, the earth needs to be seen and heard and fought for. The earth comes first in importance." "Interview with Red Regarding September 5, 1975," www.squeakyfromme.org/interview.htm, accessed on May 7, 2007. Sarah Jane Moore, whose attempt on Ford's life came seventeen days after Fromme's incident, worked for the SLA-inspired People in Need. She later blamed her attempt on the president's life on her zealotry. "The government had declared war on the left," Moore recalled two decades later of her motives. "Nixon's appointment of Ford as vice president and his resignation making Ford president seemed to be a continuing assault on America." Vic Lee, "Interview: Woman Who Tried to Assassinate Ford," http://abclocal.go.com/kgo/story?section=local&id=4900159, accessed on May 3, 2007.

5. For a clear and concise articulation of the case against Peltier, see Frank Keating, "Don't Free Leonard Peltier," www.opinionjournal.com/forms/printThis.html?id=65000824, accessed on May 3, 2007. For a discussion of the movement to frame Peltier as a political prisoner, see Bruce Johansen, "Still Fighting the Indian Wars," *The Nation*, October 1, 1977, 304–7.

6. Theodore Roszak, "Skeptics and True Believers," *The Nation*, February 10, 1979, 137.

7. *Jonestown: The Life and Death of the Peoples Temple*, produced by Stanley Nelson (PBS, 2006). Jones appropriated "revolutionary suicide" from the title of Huey Newton's book. In addition to sharing an affinity for the same bizarre phrase, Newton and Jones shared a lawyer, Charles Garry, whom Jones allowed to leave Jonestown immediately prior to the carnage. Several of Newton's relatives were members of the Peoples Temple, including cousin Stanley Clayton, one of just five who escaped the murders/suicides inside Jonestown.

8. "United States Crime Rates, 1960–2005," www.disastercenter.com/crime/uscrime.htm, accessed on June 22, 2007.

9. *Health, United States, 2006* (Hyattsville, MD: National Center for Health Statistics, 2006), 227.

10. "Estimated Arrests for Drug Abuse Violations by Age Group, 1970–2005," http://www.ojp.usdoj.gov/bjs/glance/tables/drugtab.htm, accessed on September 10, 2007. David W. Rassmusen and Bruce L. Benson, *The Economic Anatomy of a Drug War: Criminal Justice in the Commons* (Lanham, MD: Rowman and Littlefield, 1994), 6–7.

11. Centers for Disease Control and Prevention, *National Vital Statistics Report*, "Table C. Number, rate and percentage of births to unmarried women, and birth rate for married women: United States, 1980 and 1985–2004," September 29, 2006, 11.

12. Jean Callahan, "Why Are All Marriages Breaking Up?" *Mother Jones*, July 1977, 19–24.

13. "Table 2," http://www.cdc.gov/mmwr/preview/mmwrhtml/ss5212a1.htm#tab2, accessed on August 1, 2007.

14. "Marriage in U.S. and Ohio," http://www.bgsu.edu/organizations/cfdr/ohiopop/opn8.pdf , accessed on September 13, 2007; "Divorce Rates," http://www.bsos.umd.edu/socy/vanneman/socy441/trends/divorce.html, accessed on September 14, 2007.

15. Gitlin, *The Sixties*, 431–32.

16. Quoted in Randy Shilts, *And the Band Played On: People, Politics, and the AIDS Epidemic* (New York: St. Martin's Press, 1987), 40.

17. For an extreme example of this phenomenon, see the discussion of Gaetan Dugas in ibid. In addition to his criticism of Ronald Reagan, Ed Koch, and other politicians, Shilts wields his pen against the in-denial promiscuity within homosexual enclaves that persisted as the plague expanded.

18. Quoted in ibid., 317.

19. Quoted in ibid., 442, 443, 447.

20. Shilts, *And the Band Played On*, 521, 540, 542.

21. Ibid., 220, 222, 224, 226, 238, 469.

22. "HIV/AIDS Surveillance Report: HIV Infection and AIDS in the United States and Dependent Areas, 2005," www.cdc.gov/hiv/topics/surveillance/print/basic.htm, accessed on April 28, 2007.

23. Casey Hayden and Mary King, "Sex and Caste: A Kind of Memo from Casey Hayden and Mary King to a Number of Other Women in the Peace and Freedom Movements," in *Liberation*, April 1966, 35–36.

24. Sale, *SDS*, 663–64.

25. Quoted in Gitlin, *The Sixties*, 362–64; Wilkerson dismissed the charge in her autobiography, saying the sound-alike caller was probably the result of the FBI's "dirty tricks." Cathy Wilkerson, *Flying Close to the Sun: My Life and Times as a Weatherman* (New York: Seven Stories, 2007), 244.

26. Irwin Unger, *The Movement: A History of the American New Left, 1959–1972*, 168. The latter speaker was borrowing from a phrase used by Stokely Carmichael within SNCC in the mid-1960s.

27. David Hilliard and Lewis Cole, *This Side of Glory: The Autobiography of David Hilliard and the Story of the Black Panther Party* (Boston: Back Bay Books, 1993), 94–96, 426; Hugh Pearson, *The Shadow of the Panther: Huey Newton and the Price of Black Power in America* (Reading, MA: Addison-Wesley, 1994), 179–80, 196–98, 249–50, 292; Eldridge Cleaver, *Soul on Ice* (New York: Delta, 1968), 14–17.

28. Quoted in Gitlin, *The Sixties*, 372.

29. For a discussion of Friedan's work for Communist-controlled publications, see Daniel Horowitz, *Betty Friedan and the Making of the Feminine Mystique: The American Left, The Cold War, and Modern Feminism* (Amherst, MA: University of Massachusetts Press, 1998), 102–52. In 2000, Friedan acknowledged the veracity of accusations that she had attempted to join the Communist Party. Betty Friedan, *Life So Far: A Memoir* (New York: Simon and Schuster, 2000), 57. She wrote: "One day, before I left for Berkeley, I looked up the address of the Communist Party headquarters in New York and, on my day off from the hospital, went into their dark and dingy building on 13th Street and announced I wanted to become a member." Horowitz relates the raw content of Friedan's FBI file that contends that she attempted to join the party after she arrived in Berkeley, California (93).

30. Horowitz, *Betty Friedan and the Making of the Feminine Mystique*, 217.

31. Friedan, *Life So Far*, 78, 81, 88, 144. Horowitz, *Betty Friedan and the Making of the Feminine Mystique*, 154, 165–66, 170.

32. Betty Friedan, *The Feminine Mystique* (1963; repr., New York: Dell, 1971), 294.

33. Friedan, *Life So Far*, 132.

34. Friedan, *The Feminine Mystique*, 10–27.

35. Susan Brownmiller, *In Our Time: Memoir of a Revolution* (New York: Dial Press, 1999), 50, 63. Richard Ellis, *The Dark Side of the Left: Illiberal Egalitarianism in America* (Lawrence: University of Kansas, 1998), 199.

36. Friedan, *Life So Far*, 294–96. For a movement depiction of the weekend conference, see Lucy Komisar, "Feminism as National Politics," *The Nation*, December 10, 1977, 624–27.

37. Barry Weisberg, "April 22: A One Day Teach-in Is Like an All Day Sucker," *Liberation*, April 1970, 38–41.

38. Michael Meeropol, "The Movement and the Air We Breathe," *Liberation*, December 1969, 38–41.

39. Rachel Carson, *Silent Spring* (1962; repr., Boston: Houghton Mifflin, 1994), 187–98, 213–16.

40. Ibid., 1–3.

41. Ibid., 277.

42. Richard Tren and Roger Bate, "When Politics Kills: Malaria and the DDT Story" (Washington, DC: Competitive Enterprise Institute, 2000); Joseph L. Bast, Peter J. Hill, and Richard C. Rue, *Eco-Sanity: A Common Sense Guide to Environmentalism* (Lanham, MD: Madison Books, 1994), 100.

43. Paul Ehrlich, *The Population Bomb* (New York: Ballantine Books, 1968), xi.

44. Alan MacRobert, "Look What They've Done to the Rain," *Mother Jones*, December 1977, 65–67.

45. Mickey C. Olsen, "Reacting to the Reactors," *The Nation*, January 11, 1975, 15–17.

46. Harvey Wasserman, "The Opening Battles of the Eighties," *Mother Jones*, August 1977, 54.

47. Quoted in Thomas Ryan, "The Green's Favorite Terrorist," www.frontpagemag.com/Articles/Printable.asp?ID=13159, accessed on April 28, 2007.

48. For an extensive list of articles on environmentalist terrorism and criminality, albeit from a hostile source, see "Animal Extremist/Eco-Terror Crimes," http://www.furcommission.com/attack/, accessed on September 10, 2007, and "Animal Extremist/Eco-Terror Crimes to 1999," http://www.furcommission.com/attack/historical.html, accessed on September 10, 2007.

49. Peter Singer, *Animal Liberation*, new rev. ed. (New York: Avon Books, 1990), 243.

50. Ibid., 6–9, 84–85, 117, 223, 226–27, 243.

51. Ibid., 69.

52. Ibid., xi.

53. For an extensive list of articles on animal rights terrorism and criminality, albeit from a hostile source, see "Animal Extremist/Eco-Terror Crimes," http://www.furcommission.com/attack/, accessed on September 10, 2007, and "Animal Extremist/Eco-Terror Crimes to 1999," http://www.furcommission.com/attack/historical.html, accessed on September 10, 2007.

54. Robert Karen, "Last Rally of 'The Movement,'" *The Nation*, June 7, 1975, 678–80.

55. Stephane Courtois, Nicolas Werth, Jean-Louis Panne, et al., *The Black Book of*

Communism: Crimes, Terror, Repression, trans. Jonathan Murphy and Mark Kramer (Cambridge, MA: Harvard University Press, 1999), 571–75.

56. Aryeh Neier, "The Baez Letter," *The Nation*, June 23, 1979, 739–40; "Letters," *The Nation*, July 14–21, 1979, 34, 39–41; Herb Romerstein and Eric Breindel, *The Venona Secrets: Exposing Soviet Espionage and America's Traitors* (Washington, DC: Regnery, 2000), 403.

57. Quoted in "On the Record," www.time.com/time/printout/0,8816,920529,00.html, accessed on May 3, 2007.

58. Noam Chomsky and Edward S. Herman, "Distortions at Fourth Hand," *The Nation*, June 25, 1977, 789–93.

59. Courtois, et al., *The Black Book of Communism*, 577–635.

60. David Horowitz, "A Radical's Disenchantment," *The Nation*, December 8, 1979, 587.

61. Eqbal Ahmad, "The Iranian Hundred Years' War," *Mother Jones*, April 1979, 19.

62. Kai Bird, "The Iranian Referendum," *The Nation*, March 31, 1979, 321.

63. Ahmad, "The Iranian Hundred Years' War," 19. Bird, "The Iranian Referendum," 321. Kai Bird, "The Workers' Committees Are Pumping Iran," *The Nation*, April 21, 1979, 426–28.

64. Adam Hochschild, "Examining the Left's Myopia," *Mother Jones*, April, 1980, 5.

65. Bo Burlingham, "They've All Gone to Look for America," *Mother Jones*, February/March 1976, 20. Burlingham found former New Leftists organizing in communities. "To those of us who rode the historical wave of the '60s, there is a sense perhaps of the mundane in starting co-ops when our purpose had been to stop a war, or electing a mayor when we had set out to unseat a President, or lowering utility rates when we had planned to transform America. Aren't these small victories, I wondered, if they are victories at all?" (28).

66. Curtis Gans, "Conservatism by Default," *The Nation*, October 14, 1978, 373. Gans's article, like another the following year (Michael Parenti, "Radical Decade," *The Nation*, December 8, 1979, 580–81), disregarded the notion that the country had shifted conservative. Gans argued that any shift was due to liberal failures rather than anything conservatives had done right. Parenti dismissed the national mood as an illusion, attributing it to the media, widespread but "soft" support for liberal causes, and increased conservative visibility and adeptness at tapping into voter unrest.

67. Maurice Isserman and Michael Kazin, *America Divided: The Civil War of the 1960s* (New York: Oxford University Press, 2000), 245.

68. Carey McWilliams, "The New Fundamentalists," *The Nation*, June 5, 1976, 687.

69. Interview of Al Haber by author, Ann Arbor, Michigan, February 13, 2007.

70. Hugh Pearson, *The Shadow of the Panther: Huey Newton and the Price of Black Power in America* (Reading, MA: Addison-Wesley, 1994), 262–68, 277–80.

71. Quoted in Pearson, *The Shadow of the Panther*, 319.

72. "Interview: Eldridge Cleaver," www.pbs.org/wgbh/pages/frontline/shows/race/interviews/ecleaver.html, accessed on June 20, 2007.

73. Bill Ayers, *Fugitive Days: A Memoir* (Boston: Beacon Press, 2001), 284.

74. Robert Greenfield, *Timothy Leary: A Biography* (New York: Harcourt, 2006), 147–48.

75. Wayne King, "Abbie Hoffman Committed Suicide Using Barbiturates, Autopsy Shows," April 19, 1989, *New York Times*, 12.

CHAPTER 23. THE LONG MARCH

1. Robert Lichter, Stanley Rothman, and Linda Lichter, *The Media Elite* (Bethesda, MD: Alder and Alder, 1986), 30.

2. Kenneth T. Walsh, *Feeding the Beast: The White House Versus the Press* (New York: Random House, 1996), 263.

3. "Media Bias Basics," www.mediaresearch.org/biasbasics/printer/biasbasics3 .asp, accessed on May 17, 2007.

4. "ASNE Survey: Journalists Say They're Liberal," www.asne.org/kiosk/ editor/97.jan-feb/dennis4.htm, accessed on May 5, 2007.

5. "AIM Gets Donny's Dander Up," *The AIM Report*, June-A 1996, 1.

6. "Media Bias Basics," www.mediaresearch.org/biasbasics/printer/biasbasics3 .asp, accessed on May 17, 2007.

7. Rich Noyes, "The Liberal Media: Every Poll Shows Journalists Are More Liberal than the American Public—and the Public Knows It," www.mediaresearch.org/ SpecialReports/2004/report063004_p4.asp, accessed on May 17, 2007.

8. Dinesh D'Souza, *Ronald Reagan: How an Ordinary Man Became an Extraordinary Leader* (New York: Free Press, 1997), 134–42; Edwin Meese III, *With Reagan: The Inside Story* (Washington, DC: Regnery, 1992), 172–73.

9. For a list of the more idiotic and offensive laments for the fall of Euro-Communism, see "Best of Notable Quotables 1990: Bring Back the Iron Curtain Award," http://63.66.59.27/news/nq/best/nq1990best.html, accessed on June 9, 2005; "Best of Notable Quotables 1990: Gennadi Gerasimov Newspeak Award," http://63.66.59.27/news/nq/best/nq1990best.html, accessed on June 9, 2005; "Best of Notable Quotables 1991: Bring Back the Iron Curtain Award," http://63.66.59.27/news/nq/best/nq1991best.html, accessed on June 9, 2005; "Best of Notable Quotables 1992: Bring Back the Iron Curtain Award," http://63.66.59.27/news/nq/best/nq1992best.html, accessed on June 9, 2005. Selections include *USA Today* founder Al Neuharth opining: "There is little more logic to Lithuania being permitted to unilaterally and unlawfully declare its independence from the USSR than there would be for Texas to secede from the USA. . . . Gorby has a right to feel livid about Lithuania. The way you might feel about a runaway child, tempted to beat him within an inch of his life." *CBS Evening News* reporter Bert Quint actually reported: "This is Marlboro country, southeastern Poland, a place where the transition from communism to capitalism is making more people more miserable every day." From *CBS Evening News'* Connie Chung: "In formerly communist Bulgaria, the cost of freedom has been virtual economic disaster."

10. Michael Weisskopf, "Energized by Pulpit or Passion, the Public Is Calling," *Washington Post*, February 1, 1993, 1.

11. Quoted in Howard Kurtz, "Going Weak in the Knees for Clinton," *Washington Post*, July 6, 1998, C1.

12. "Memos on Bush Are Fake but Accurate, Typist Says," *New York Times*, September 15, 2004, 1.

13. Quoted in Roger Kimball, *The Long March: How the Cultural Revolution of the 1960s Changed America* (San Francisco: Encounter Books, 2000), 103–4.

14. Herbert Marcuse, *Counterrevolution and Revolt* (Boston: Beacon Press, 1972), 47.

15. David Sacks and Peter Theil, *The Diversity Myth: "Multiculturalism" and the Politics of Intolerance at Stanford* (Oakland, CA: Independent Institute, 1995), 1–4.

16. Quoted in Avik S. A. Roy, "Race Studies Trump the Canon," www.yale.edu/lt/archives/v3n2/index.htm, accessed on May 25, 2007.

17. Quoted in Richard Bernstein, *Dictatorship of Virtue: Multiculturalism and the Battle for America's Future* (New York: Knopf, 1994), 120.

18. Henry Abelove, Michelle Aina Barale, and David Halperin, eds., *The Lesbian and Gay Studies Reader* (New York: Routledge, 1993), xvi.

19. "Howard Zinn: 'History as a Political Act,' " interview by Raymond Lotta, *Revolutionary Worker*, December 20, 1998.

20. Richard Bernstein, *Dictatorship of Virtue*, 85–87 (quote therein).

21. Daniel J. Flynn, "Free Speech Torched at Cornell—Again," *Campus Report*, January 1998, 8.

22. Daniel J. Flynn, "Villanova Official Steals Press Run of Student Mag Over Content," *Campus Report*, April 2000, 1.

23. Daniel J. Flynn, *Deep Blue Campuses* (Arlington, VA: Leadership Institute, 2005).

24. Quoted in Theodore H. White, *The Making of the President 1972* (New York: Atheneum, 1973), 170.

25. White, *The Making of the President 1972*, 28–33, 171–76, 188.

26. Quoted in ibid., 188.

27. Ibid., 172–75, 190–91, 194–96. McGovern referenced the anarchy surrounding the vice presidential nomination in the second line of his speech: "I assume that everyone here is impressed with my control of this convention in that my choice for vice president was challenged by only 39 other nominees." Speech: George McGovern, "Acceptance Speech," Miami, Florida, July 14, 1972.

28. Speech: George McGovern, "Acceptance Speech," Miami, Florida, July 14, 1972.

29. White, *The Making of the President 1972*, 12, 122, 225–26.

30. Ibid., 371.

31. D'Souza, *Ronald Reagan*, 157.

32. Quoted in ibid., 157.

33. Peter Huchthausen, *America's Splendid Little Wars: A Short History of U.S. Military Engagements: 1975–2000* (New York: Viking, 2003), 85.

34. Edwin Meese III, *With Reagan*, 238–41.

35. Democratic Party Platform, "Natural Resources and Environmental Quality: Energy," July 12, 1976.

36. Democratic Party Platform, "Energy, Natural Resources, Environment and Agriculture: Environment," August 11, 1980.

37. Democratic Party Platform, July 18, 1988.

38. Democratic Party Platform, "Protecting Our Environment," August 14, 2000.

39. Democratic Party Platform, "Natural Resources and Environmental Quality: Energy," July 12, 1976.

40. Democratic Party Platform, "Recycling," July 16, 1984.

41. Democratic Party Platform, "Preserving the Global Environment," July 13, 1992.

42. Democratic Party Platform, "Civil and Political Rights," July 12, 1976; Democratic Party Platform, "Health," August 11, 1980.

43. Democratic Party Platform, July 18, 1988.

44. David R. Carlin Jr., "The Tyranny of the Pro-Choice Snobs," *New York Times*, August 10, 1992, 17; Kevin Drum, "The Curious Incident of the Governor Who Didn't Speak at the Convention . . . ," www.washingtonmonthly.com/archives/individual/2005_03/005787.php, accessed on May 24, 2007. Through contemporaneous quotes of Democratic Party officials, and a search of newspaper accounts at the time, Drum puts to rest the revisionist myth that the refusal to let Casey speak had nothing to do with the pro-life message the governor of one of America's most populous states intended to deliver.

45. Democratic Party Platform, "Civil Rights," "Crime," August 11, 1980.

46. Democratic Party Platform, "Civil and Equal Rights," July 13, 1992.

47. Democratic Party Platform, "A Strong American Community," August 30, 2004.

48. Interview of Michael Newdow (phone) by author, May 18, 2007.

49. Anthony Kennedy, *Lawrence v. Texas*, 539 U.S.577, June 26, 2003.

50. *Planned Parenthood of Southeastern Pa. v. Casey*, 505 U.S. 836, June 29, 1992.

51. *Griswold v. Connecticut*, 381 U.S. 479, June 7, 1965.

52. Arthur Goldberg, *Griswold v. Connecticut*, 381 U.S. 495, June 7, 1965.

53. Harry Blackmun, *Roe v. Wade*, 410 U.S. 152, January 22, 1973.

54. *The Complete Works of Aristotle*, ed. Jonathan Barnes (Princeton, NJ: Princeton University Press, 1995), I:316.

55. Anthony Kennedy, *Lawrence v. Texas*, 539 U.S. 578–79, June 26, 2003.

56. Arthur Goldberg, *Griswold v. Connecticut*, 381 U.S. 498–99, June 7, 1965.

57. For a discussion of post–Fourteenth Amendment attempts to accomplish what modern jurisprudence contends the Fourteenth Amendment had already accomplished, see Felix Frankfurter, *McCollum v. Board of Education*, 333 U.S. 217–21, March 8, 1948, and, more especially, see the accompanying footnotes. Though Frankfurter concurs with the court, the evidence he cites undermines, rather than buttresses, the case. If, for example, the Fourteenth Amendment made the First Amendment's restrictions on Congress regarding religion apply to the states as well, why would President Ulysses S. Grant, James G. Blaine, and so many others support constitutional amendments, subsequent to the Fourteenth, that redundantly made state establishments, and even mild state support, of religion illegal? Were the very congressmen involved in the Fourteenth Amendment's passage ignorant of its mandate? Or, more credibly, were judges eight decades later ignorant of its mandate?

58. Letter: Thomas Jefferson to Danbury Baptist Association, January 1, 1802.

59. *Lemon v. Kurtzman*, 403 U.S. 602, June 28, 1971.

60. Harry Blackmun, concurring opinion, *Lee v. Weisman*, 505 U.S. 603, June 24, 1992.

61. *Stone v. Graham*, 449 U.S. 39, November 17, 1980.

62. *Wallace v. Jafree*, 472 U.S. 63, June 4, 1985.

63. *Lee v. Weisman*, 505 U.S. 578–631, June 24, 1992.

64. Interview of Michael Newdow (phone) by author, May 18, 2007.

65. *Kelo v. New London*, 545 U.S., June 23, 2005.

66. Carol D. Leonnig, "Appelate Judges Let Gun Ruling Stand," *Washington Post*, May 9, 2007, B1. Gary Emerling, "Court Denies D.C.'s Gun Appeal," *Washington Times*, May 9, 2007, 1.

CHAPTER 24. THE 9/12 LEFT

1. Interview of Reesa Rosenberg by author, Washington, DC, January 18, 2003.

2. Interview of Melissa Orr by author, Washington, DC, March 15, 2003.

3. Interview of Eric Josephson by author, New York, February 2, 2002.

4. Interview of Chris King by author, Washington, DC, January 18, 2003.

5. Interview by author of anonymous protestor in New York, February 15, 2003.

6. Interview of Liz Dhrich by author, Washington, DC, January 18, 2003.

7. Interview of Abram Megrete by author, Washington, DC, March 15, 2003.

8. Interview of Michael Bevoian by author, Washington, DC, January 20, 2005.

9. Michael Moore, *Dude, Where's My Country?* (New York: Warner Books, 2003), 192.

10. Roger Rapoport, *Citizen Moore* (Muskegon, MI: RDR Books, 2007), 22, 25–26.

11. Ibid., 80, 230.

12. Quoted in ibid., 28.

13. Ibid., 126, 142–43.

14. Quoted in ibid., 68.

15. Doron Levin, "Maker of Documentary That Attacks G.M. Alienates His Allies," *New York Times*, January 19, 1990. Debbie Melnyk, "The Trouble with Mike," http://www.theaustralian.news.com.au/story/0,25197,22079050 -28737,00.html, accessed on October 8, 2007; Rapoport, *Citizen Moore*, 125–28.

16. Byron York, *The Vast Left Wing Conspiracy: The Untold Story of Democrats' Desperate Fight to Reclaim Power* (2005; repr., New York: Crown Forum, 2006), 11–12, 111–21.

17. Matt Labash, "Michael Moore, One Trick Pony," http://www.weeklystandard .com/check.asp?idArticle=9300&r=zvgxz, accessed on July 22, 2004.

18. Moore, *Dude, Where's My Country?*, 30.

19. Ibid., 134.

20. Ibid., 134–35.

21. Ibid., 120.

22. Ellen Goodman, "No Change in Political Climate," http://www.boston.com/ news/globe/editorial_opinion/oped/articles/2007/02/09/no_change_, accessed on August 5, 2007.

23. Brian Montopoli, http://www.cbsnews.com/blogs/2006/03/22/publiceye/entry1431768 .shtml, accessed on October 6, 2007.

24. Sharon Begley, "Global-Warming Deniers: A Well-Funded Machine," www .msnbc.msn.com/id/20122975/site/newsweek/print/1/displaymode/1098/, accessed on August 27, 2007.

25. David Roberts, "The Denial Industry," http://gristmill.grist.org/print/2006/9/19/11408/1106, accessed on October 6, 2007.

26. Bill Blakemore, " 'Schwarzenator' vs. Bush: Global Warming Debate Heats Up," http://abcnews.go.com/US/print?id=2374968, accessed on October 9, 2007.

27. Quoted in Richard S. Lindzen, "Don't Believe the Hype," http://www .opinionjournal.com/extra/?id=110008597, accessed on October 7, 2007.

28. Ibid.

29. Dr. William Gray, Department of Atmospheric Science, Colorado State University, "The Role of Science in Environmental Policy-Making," statement before the U.S. Senate Committee on Environment and Public Works, September 28, 2005, http://epw.senate.gov/hearing_statements.cfm?id=246768, accessed on January 11, 2008.

30. "The Warming Debate's Gray Area," *Investor's Business Daily*, October 16, 2007, www.ibdeditorials.com/IBDArticles.aspx?id=277339399191115, accessed on January 11, 2008.

31. "Deleted Scene: Madison, Wisconsin—A Cheerful Anomaly," in *Global Warming: The Signs and the Science*, produced by David Kennard (PBS Home Video, 2006).

32. *An Inconvenient Truth*, produced by Laurie David (Paramount Video, 2006).

33. Interview: David Roberts of Al Gore, "Al Revere," www.grist.org/news/maindish/2006/05/09/roberts/, accessed on April 23, 2007.

34. Quoted in Michael Fumento, *Science Under Siege: Balancing Technology and the Environment* (New York: William Morrow, 1993), 362.

35. Interview of Stephanie Kornfeld by author, Washington, DC, January 20, 2005.

36. Interview of Darrell Anderson by author, Washington, DC, January 20, 2005.

37. Interview of Meredith Lair by author, Washington, DC, January 20, 2005.

38. Interview of Catherine Oullette by author, Washington, DC, January 20, 2005.

39. Thomas Frank, *What's the Matter with Kansas?: How Conservatives Won the Heart of America* (New York: Metropolitan Books, 2004), 1.

40. Ibid., 2.

41. Ibid., 76.

42. Quoted in ibid., 69.

43. Frank, *What's the Matter with Kansas?*, 206.

44. "The Class of '69," *Life*, June 20, 1969, 31. Ironically, immediately after the excerpt from Hillary Rodham's speech, *Life* excerpted from Brown University's student speaker, Ira Magaziner, who would play so prominent a role in Clinton's national health insurance proposal during her husband's first term as president. Turn the page and an excerpt from a graduation-day address of Daniel Patrick Moynihan, Hillary's predecessor in the Senate and also a major player in the health care debates of the 1990s appears. "Memories of Diana," *Time*, March 30, 1970, 21.

45. Speech: Hillary Rodham, Wellesley College, Wellesley, Massachusetts, May 31, 1969.

46. Carl Bernstein, *A Woman in Charge: The Life of Hillary Rodham Clinton* (New York: Knopf, 2007), 66–67, 83.

47. Hillary D. Rodham, "There Is Only the Fight: An Analysis of the Alinsky Model," Wellesley College, 1969, 6 (Wellesley College Archives, Margaret Clapp Library).

48. Clinton, "There Is Only the Fight: An Analysis of the Alinsky Model," 35, 56. See also Hillary D. Rodham, "Acknowledgments" in "There Is Only the Fight: An Analysis of the Alinsky Model."

49. Bernstein, *A Woman in Charge*, 85–87, 101–3.

50. Quoted in ibid., 65–66.

51. Hillary Rodham, "Children Under Law," *Harvard Educational Review*, November 1973, 509, 513, 514, 493.

52. Bernstein, *A Woman in Charge*, 133–34.

53. Quoted in Beth Fouhy, "San Francisco Rolls Out the Red Carpet for the Clintons," www.signonsandiego.com/news/politics/20050629-0007-ca-clintons-sanfrancisco.html, accessed on October 1, 2007.

54. Page Ivey, "Clinton: Create Public Service Academy," http://apnews.myway.com/article/20070728/D8QLQ3880.html, accessed on October 1, 2007.

55. Teddy Davis and Eloise Harper, "Clinton Floats $5,000 Baby Bond," www.abcnews.go.com/print?id=3668781, accessed on October 1, 2007.

56. "Clinton Calls for Pre-Kindergarten for All Children," http://www.hillaryclinton.com/news/release/view/?id=1743, accessed on October 9, 2007.

57. Quoted in Bernstein, *A Woman in Charge*, 446.

58. Ibid., 296.

59. Ibid., 53, 57, 86, 162, 297; Michael Gerson, "Can She Reach Religious Voters?" *Washington Post*, September 26, 2007, 19.

60. Quoted in Bernstein, *A Woman in Charge*, 27, 394.

CONCLUSION

1. Interview of Jeff Edwards by author, Washington, DC, September 24, 2005.

2. Interview of Brewer Dohithik by author, Washington, DC, September 24, 2005.

3. Interview of Gayle Ruddi by author, Washington, DC, September 24, 2005.

4. Interview by author, Washington, DC, September 24, 2005.

5. Interview of Michael Newdow (phone) by author, May 18, 2007.

6. Interview of Steve Max by author (phone), April 16, 2007. Interview of Richard Flacks by author (phone), March 18, 2007. Interview of Tom Hayden by author (e-mail), May 3, 2007.

7. Interview of Medea Benjamin by author, Washington, DC, July 3, 2006.

8. Interview of Mark Rudd by author (phone), April 17, 2007.

9. Interview of Al Haber by author, Ann Arbor, Michigan, February 13, 2007.

10. "Tributes to J. A. Wayland from Loving Comrades," *Appeal to Reason*, November 1912, 3.

11. Interview of Carl Oglesby by author, Amherst, Massachusetts, June 1, 2007.

12. Letter: TF to Earl Browder, undated (Earl Browder Papers, Syracuse University).

ACKNOWLEDGMENTS

A Conservative History of the American Left is the product of four years of my life. I wish I could thank all of my research assistants and the foundation program officers drowning me in money. Unfortunately, they exist only in dreams. What exists in reality is pretty good, though. Institutions dedicated to conserving evidence of the past allow researchers access to that material at no cost. There is no such thing as a free lunch, but free libraries are a different story. I am especially grateful to ten such institutions, and their staffs, for aiding me in my archival research.

Trips to Syracuse University's Bird Library brought alive the Bible Communists of the Oneida Community and the Soviet Communist Earl Browder of the CPUSA. Harvard University's Houghton Library keeps the papers of John Reed, which include his correspondence with Louise Bryant that I relied on for chapter 14. The Robert F. Wagner Labor Archives of New York University's Tamiment Library provided *New Left Notes*, *The Fire Next Time*, *The Rat*, and other such underground curiosities of the 1960s and 1970s. Wellesley College, after years of hiding it, now offers Hillary Clinton's senior thesis on Saul Alinsky. Knowing that it might recede back into the memory hole, I raced to Wellesley to read it. Alas, it's just a well-written paper by a college senior and not the "Rosetta Stone" to Hillary Rodham Clinton. The University of Virginia's Clifton Waller Barrett Library maintains what remains of Mary Gove Nichols's correspondence and has electronic copies of several of her books. She's unforgettable, but history has somehow managed to forget her. At the top of the University of Massachusetts-Amherst's tower library, I went through the papers of antiwar activist Carl Oglesby; at the bottom, I went through *Woodhull & Claflin's Weekly*. Separated by a century, these pieces of the Left's history are divided by twenty-five floors at UMass. At the Catholic University of America's American Catholic History and Research Center, I got the chance to read old speeches from Terence Powderly, information from Knights of Labor meetings, and the propaganda from that bygone group from a bygone era. The University of Michigan's Labadie Collection collected fourteen boxes of material on Mike Gold, the contents of which animated chapter 16 but now litter my floors. The Library of Congress is an excellent repository of defunct publications, such as *The Harbinger*, *The Phalanx*, *Appeal to Reason*, *The Masses*, and *The New Masses*, as well as the progressive-era issues of *The Nation* and *The New Republic*. The American Antiquarian Society, which became a surrogate Library of Congress after my move north, afforded me the opportunity to inspect Charles Fourier's dusty tomes and the fraying, yellowed numbers from the *New Harmony Gazette*'s three-year history.

All of these institutions, their staffs, and their donors have my thanks. I am also grateful to the preservers of the communal sites that I wrote about and visited, including the Fruitlands Museum, the Ephrata Cloister, and Oneida Community's Mansion House.

Activists, from different generations and political outlooks, who graciously consented to interviews include SDSers Mark Rudd, Tom Hayden, Richard Flacks, Steve Max, Carl Oglesby, Todd Gitlin, Al Haber, and Mike Klonsky; First Amendment lawyer Michael Newdow; and Code Pink co-founder Medea Benjamin. Additionally, from 2001 to 2007, I spoke to hundreds of lesser-known but equally committed activists at protests of the Iraq War, the World Economic Forum, George W. Bush's second inauguration, and other happenings. I appreciate the willingness of so many people to talk to a complete stranger. We learn more when we converse. Witnessing Al Haber stuff mailings late into the evening, hearing the honest reflections of Mark Rudd, spending a pleasant afternoon with Carl Oglesby, and pressing disagreements with an always agreeable Michael Newdow reminded me that decent people exist across the political spectrum.

Brian Fox generously let me crash in Brooklyn for a few days while researching at NYU. Crown Forum's Jed Donahue again performed outstanding work editing the manuscript. My wife provided excellent advice and a helpful set of eyes. Jason Bjork constructed a low-cost, high-quality library in my attic that now shelves the 400 or so books read for this project. Thank you, thank you, thank you, and thank you. Before the "shut up" music cuts me off, I give thanks especially to you, dear reader, for reading what I wrote.

INDEX

ABOUT THE AUTHOR

DANIEL J. FLYNN is the author of *Intellectual Morons* and *Why the Left Hates America*. He is the editor of www.flynnfiles.com. A popular guest on radio and television, he has appeared on Fox News, CNN, MSNBC, Showtime, CSPAN, Court TV, and other broadcast networks. Flynn is a frequent speaker on college campuses who has faced off with book burners, mobs shouting down his talks, and officials banning his lectures. He lives in Massachusetts with his wife and son.